Identity, Gender, and Status in Japan

Takie Lebra

The Collected Papers of
Twentieth-Century Japanese Writers
on Japan

VOLUME 2

Collected Papers

of

TAKIE LEBRA

Identity, Gender, and Status in Japan

GLOBAL
ORIENTAL

Series: COLLECTED PAPERS OF TWENTIETH-CENTURY JAPANESE WRITERS ON JAPAN

Volume 2
Takie Lebra: Identity, Gender, and Status in Japan

First published in 2007 by
GLOBAL ORIENTAL LTD
PO Box 219
Folkestone
Kent CT20 2WP
UK

www.globaloriental.co.uk

ISBN 978-1-905246-17-5

British Library Cataloguing in Publication Data
A CIP catalogue entry for this book is available from the British Library

Set in Plantin 10.5 on 11.5 point by Mark Heslington, Scarborough, North Yorkshire
Printed and Bound in England by Antony Rowe Ltd, Chippenham, Wilts

Contents

Introduction

Why do we study any culture or society other than our own? We come to know what is X by finding what is not X. We develop insight to our own culture by finding the difference between ourselves and 'Other,' between the North American and another culture, between X and Y. Why Japan, then? In my discipline of anthropology, it used to be that the more alien the other culture is, the more worthwhile to study. Since anthropology was centered in Western Europe, the ideal alien culture was an isolated community in Africa or in Oceania – ideally the places yet untouched by the West. For this reason Japan was not a legitimate or attractive area since it was neither isolated nor untouched.

This colonial viewpoint no longer holds, because the world does not contain totally isolated tribal societies. Accordingly, Japan has risen to an anthropologically, let alone politically, more respectable 'other.' More visitors, including many non-professionals, not just diplomats, from the West began to study and report on Japan. No doubt, certain similarities have been observed. It might be argued that since we are all human beings there is no real difference between societies, particularly between the West and the more or less Westernized Japan. Basically, I agree with this claim on human universals, without which it would be impossible to reach 'cross-cultural' understanding to begin with. With a sociology degree I am all the more sympathetic with a universalistic viewpoint. Furthermore, our post-internet revolution makes us aware of the ever-expanding cyber-space tempting us to speculate on the eventual erasure of cultural or national boundaries, assuming that the so-called cultural differences will be reduced to remnants of the past which would vanish as all societies catch up. The enormous speed of change, taking place every moment in Japan today like everywhere else, inclines us to give up on speculating on the survival of national cultures.

This simple and perhaps optimistic conclusion does not measure up at least as observed today. One visitor after another to Japan, equipped with sophisticated, instantaneous recorders, keeps releasing 'astonishing' revelations from Japan – often in ambivalence with disapproval and praise. I suspect that both claims to similarities and to differences are selective and thus exaggerated, whereas in reality there is a wide range of variation between similarity and difference. It would be audacious, therefore, to make a simple either-or judgment over 'whether' Japan is similar to 'or' different from the US-centered West. I think the significance of studying Japan derives precisely from the two-sided relationship: similarity *and* difference, closeness *and* distance.

The present volume is meant to reveal those aspects of Japanese feeling, thinking, and acting which I have singled out possibly as significant messages for Western *and* Japanese readers. I will be making cross-cultural comparisons often in reference to the US or Western culture, only concerning the particular issues raised in particular contexts of given articles. Occasionally, I may speculate on universalistic, intercultural similarities or differences, but the main point of these writings leans more modestly towards empirical observations.

The above statement reflects my academic background with a sociology doctorate and the post-doctoral anthropology career. As will be revealed toward the end of this essay, I was hired as an anthropology instructor to teach Japan to American students, which eventually turned me into a full-time faculty member at the Anthropology Department, University of Hawaii. The present collection is primarily of academic articles and essays which I have published throughout my postgraduate career and which could have been buried without this wonderful opportunity to bring them back to light. Articles revived here reflect a variety of my research topics, mostly presented first at academic meetings and later published in professional journals and occasionally as book chapters over the years. These reproduced articles constitute the bulk of the present book.

The subject matters reflect my obsessions ever since 1958 when I landed on this alien continent of North America – obsessions over who and what I was. Some mini-evolution has also taken place over the years as I have engaged in teaching, researching, presenting, and writing since 1969.

My purpose is to characterize the Japanese as I have observed and understood them, while refraining from value judgments either positively or negatively. It was this principle of objectivity that I came to absorb through graduate training in the United States, which made me renounce my earlier naïve 'mission to save the world (!).' Max Weber, with his difficult and sober writing, awakened me to my spiritual or intellectual backbone for adherence to value neutrality. I am aware that Weberian objectivity may be out of date in the contemporary, more impatient academic climate which urges us to take sides over controversial issues. But I adhere as much as possible to the old-fashioned scholarly standard of objectivity and value-neutrality instead of joining the crowd demanding for or against one urgent political agenda or another. This commitment to value-neutrality is necessary because we tend to change value standards from time to time, often in opposite directions, without knowing it.

This work stems from my enduring interest in what has become professionally known as 'Psychological Anthropology,' a subfield of cultural anthropology, which has turned out to be the area of my specialization.

ARTICLES SELECTED FOR THIS VOLUME

The present volume consists of a set of printed articles selected from my entire publications list, which is to be found in the Bibliography. More than forty articles have been published over time, and twenty-four of them have been selected for this collection. The selection was determined partly because of space limitations, and partly because not all the articles fit into the threefold categories of subject, namely, 'Self,' 'Gender,' and 'Status' for the present volume, as will be clarified below. This Introduction summarizes, rationalizes, and illustrates some of these articles, covering a wide range of interests and approaches: Part 1 (Self, Identity, and Interaction), Part 2 (Gender), and Part 3 (Status). These three parts will be illustrated in this Introduction with reference to four or more articles arbitrarily selected for each part. (This threefold classification will be followed in the Bibliography as well, to appear at the end of the book. The Bibliography consists of two kinds of referential information: (A) titles of original articles to be reproduced – the articles that fill a greatest portion of the present volume; (B) only references to articles cited by year of publication in the text, which will appear fully in the Bibliography.

Part 1: Self, Identity, and Interaction

The eleven articles in Part 1 deal with self, identity and interpersonal connections – the theme that has followed me from the beginning of my career. Themes include a variety of directions and manifestations of self: religious conversion, self-other exchange, communication modes, silence, guilt and shame, interpersonal conflict management, moral values, ancestor-descendant interchange, and the like. This initial but enduring focus of interest was signaled by my first book (Lebra 1976, *Japanese Patterns of Behavior*), based on years of accumulated lecture notes. This book marks my primary preoccupations which have been reactivated in a more theoretical version in my latest book (Lebra 2004, *Japanese Self in Cultural Logic*).

Some articles on the list reveal my early preoccupations with religious faith and conversion, including the Dancing Religion, transplanted from Japan to Hawaii and followed by local Japanese Americans (see 1969–70, 1972c). For illustration, a few articles of Part 1 are examined below.

(1–2: 1971) *The Social Mechanism of 'Guilt and Shame': The Japanese Case*

In this article, I rely on an abstract, sociological reasoning *and* on anthropological inspirations derived from a sense of reality. Guilt, defined in terms of the universal rule of reciprocity, is generated when that rule is violated by the actor self. Shame results from the failure in performing the role expected of the status occupant.

While the reciprocity-based guilt is more simple and clear-cut, the status-bound shame is much more complicated, taking more space for elaboration. A West-Japan contrast will be noticed regarding these two concepts, guilt and status. Guilt is extensive and generalized in the West whereas it is specific and concrete in Japan. The reverse is true with status: status is specifically defined for Westerners, while it is widely extended over and beyond the Japanese individual.

Guilt and shame persisted in my research. The present article (1971) actually sensitized me to the fact that the Japanese sense of shame intensifies guilt, because 'exposure avoidance embedded in the shame complex orients one inward,' to build up the guilt complex. The 1983 study on guilt and shame (see Bibliography) involved a cross-cultural comparison of TAT (Thematic Apperception Test) stories given by Chinese, Korean, and Japanese respondents. The Japanese sample stood out in expressing self-blame, which is equated here with guilt.

(1–4: 1972b) ***Religious Conversion and Elimination of the Sick Role***
My first research on a Japanese cult – Tenshô Kôtai Jingû*u*-kyô, a popularly known as a dancing religion – imported to Hawaii, resulted in my doctoral dissertation and has produced a number of articles, including this one. The 'divine' message from Japan's 'Great Goddess' prompted a group of men and women – mostly first-generation Japanese immigrants – to start '*muga no mai*' (ego-less dance) – whom I witnessed dancing in a Waikiki park in front of curious or snickering tourists.

Interested in religion, I involved myself in observing and interviewing Tensho converts in Hawaii for two years. Sickness turned out to be the initial motive for conversion in many cases, and was explained either as God's benevolent message to straighten out the sick, or caused by evil spirits loaded with hate, grudge, and revenge attacking the convert. Among the post-conversion commitments were a renunciation of external affiliations, symbols, and paraphernalia; minimization of medicine and indulgence. Sickness, now deprived of its justification, ceased to be an occasion for indulgence under a caretaker, which meant the convert to make investment in his well-being.

Eventually, the Hawaii division was institutionalized into its local 'church' rendering prestige to the sect and its members.

(1–10: 1987) ***The Cultural Significance of Silence in Japanese Communication***
Attention is drawn to the meaning of silence in Japanese conversation, in contrast to Western (including Judaic) culture that puts a premium on the ability or tendency of articulating one's thoughts in spoken words or utterances. Japanese culture by comparison tends to approve of or even endorse silence as part of conversation. Silence for one thing is to maintain sociability in avoidance of offending the listener through open verbal utterance – a common social phenomenon among Japanese. Conversely, silence could convey anger and hostility, while verbal utterances of these emotions could be disastrous. A woman in particular reveals her fury and open protest by displaying a firmly closed mouth.

Most important in cultural meaning is the moral message of silence which outweighs speech communication with word utterance: silence conveys modesty or truthfulness more than does articulated speech. The more serious the matter, the more silence may predominate. Exactly an opposite communicational mode may be observed in the United States where earnest communication takes the form of verbal articulation to express seriousness exactly through word utterance. Compare the noise level of two televised dramas in serious scenes: the Japanese drama often resorts to dead silence exactly where heated argument predominates in the American scene.

But we know that silence can inhibit or preclude satisfactory communication in Japan as well. One familiar way of opening up the communication channel is to resort to special occasions, set apart, now and then, to disclose and release the built-up frustrations. I have known such married couples, periodically breaking rigid silence with spontaneous loquaciousness, often facilitated by alcohol. Other, perhaps more common forms of solution are to shift from *dialogue* to other modes of communication. One is *monologue* in writing, as we know many Japanese (women in particular) keep notes or diaries, which could be read by others including the addressee of the message. Indeed, writing essays or letters to imaginary addressees is a popular engagement, and internet messages to anonymous readers may possibly serve similar purposes to substitute for dyadic communication. The other more common alternative is *trialogue,* that is, communication or negotiation through a third party's mediation, a widespread practice among Japanese indeed. In a word, silence is a subtle key that carries multiple levels of messages, instead of a simple lack of communication.

(1–11: 1994c) *Migawari (Surrogacy): The Cultural Idiom of Self-Other Exchange in Japan*

Migawari refers to identity-surrogacy in which one person takes over another person's identity to carry social conduct in a smooth and acceptable fashion. The frequency of the migawari surrogacy is indicated paradoxically by the Japanese insistence in certain circumstances that calls for a warning that something X must be done by the *honnin,* the person himself, not by a surrogate – a warning necessary in a society where surrogacy is so common. The term honnin is difficult to translate because it is meaningful only where surrogacy is taken for granted (I cannot find an English equivalent for honnin). It is nice to have an option to depend upon someone in your place, but the price could be high as illustrated below.

The honnin as a status holder, such as the master of a household, tends to rely upon a surrogate like his wife for discharging his responsibility as the house-head. As I recall, the neighborhood assembly in a town decades ago, supposedly composed of male house-heads, turned out to be a gathering entirely of housewives as 'proxies' whose names did not appear on the formal list of assembly members. Occasionally 'signatures' of the supposedly participating house-heads were called for, but, the male heads' names were given in writing on the attendance record by the female 'delegates.' I should add 'signature' does not mean in Japan a legally implicated display of personal identity, but usually a commercially available, and often artistically elaborated seal with a name on it which is personal but can be carried and used by family members. In my past experience in Japan, I found such commercially ordered seals more acceptable than personally unique signatures. Today, the meaning of 'signature' as a unique display of personal identity is accepted by Japanese, although I still carry a commercially made seal to simplify bank transactions in Japan.

The higher the status of the honnin, the more such surrogacy is necessary. In my aristocratic sample, to appear in Part III below, a large-scale surrogacy by upper-level servants was taken for granted, so much so that it ended up in just a few cases with the lord of the house who was left deaf and blind to realize much too late that the bulk of wealth had been stolen by these surrogates to leave him bankrupt.

In the imperial court, the emperor simply could not afford to do away with surrogates. His periodical visit to imperial shrines that existed across the Japanese archipelago was made in practice by his surrogates ranging from imperial kin to chamberlains. Further, every morning, the Showa emperor (Hirohito, re. 1926–1989) was supposed to visit the shrine complex standing right on the Tokyo imperial palace ground to pay respect to gods and, above all, to the Sun goddess (*Amaterasu*), to whom the origin of the imperial line was traced. It was his surrogate, usually, one of the chamberlains, who visited the palace shrine-complex 'as a real emperor' clad in proper imperial attire, and treated as such respectfully by shrine staff. When the reigning Showa emperor died in 1989 which resulted in polluting the entire group of imperial kin and personal chamberlains as well, imperial ritual was relegated to the only unpolluted personnel, namely, palace-shrine staff (*shôten*) – relatively low-level palace priests – to emerge as a temporary 'emperor.' A picturesque instance of *migawari!*

Part 2: Gender

The second layer looks at womanhood, marriage and motherhood, sexuality, and feminism, as stimulated by the sudden emergence in the 1970s of the gender issue involving power imbalance, as voiced by M. Z. Rosaldo (1974), Reiter (1975), Kanter (1977) and many others. It was under this movement of 'gender' politicization that I began to be involved later as shown in my bibliography. Stereotypes are both confirmed and challenged with new directions added. Gender is tied to career because of the employer's traditional preference for male workers with prospect for future promotion to managerial and administrative positions from which women were excluded. It is as if the career vs. non-career issue is a major criterion for gender distinction.

Working women were predominantly tenure-less part-timers. Full-time housewives and mothers were a typical subject for women, but new types of women have entered the so-far male-monopolized careers, like regular full-time staff or company presidency – nothing unusual these days but a newsworthy topic at the time of my research drawing special attention from media. Articles trace how a full-time career evolved out of an ordinary woman's life. Women and men are seen primarily as status-holders and role-players rather than as genetic, biological beings. This focus on women and gender materialized into another book *Japanese Women: Constraint and Fulfillment* (Lebra 1984)). Eight articles in total are reproduced on gender.

Again a few examples of summaries are given below.

(2–12:1976a) *Sex Equality for Japanese Women*

This article encounters the complexity of what is meant by 'equality' by presenting three 'morphs' of gender equality: Dimorphism, Bimorphism, and Amorphism. *Dimorphism* intensifies the traditional division of roles and labor between the two sexes, and by so doing a man and woman become totally interdependent. The housewife dominates the domestic realm including the household budget, becomes the center of attention from the point of view of both the children and husband. The price she has to pay is her dependency on her husband for external income and an overall household prestige in public, while she can be a powerful queen in a private sphere. Dimorphism conforms to the traditional gender distinction to an extreme degree.

Bimorphism refers to a thoroughly new type of gender equality in which the two sexes duplicate the same role – domestic and occupational combined. This type reflects the phenomenal change in recent years to push women into the so-far male-monopolized labor market on the one hand, and on the other to bring men into the domestic sphere, including child-care. While dimorphism maximizes genderized role specialization, bimorphism promotes role sharing. It is self-evident that both dimorphism and bimorphism entail stress and tension.

The third type, *amorphism,* is a way of restoring the freedom of choice, away from the role constraint embedded in both dimorphism and bimorphism. This offers an alternative to the other two by preserving, restoring, and expanding one's role options regardless of gender. Ultimately, amorphism would result in a random distribution of roles or behavior patterns between men and women, eventually in role-free, or asexual individuation. None of the three types of 'equality' offers a solution to the contemporary gender dilemma, but in combination, hopefully, they may suggest a way of minimizing gender-role stress and conflict.

(2–15:1981a) ***Japanese Women in Male Dominant Careers: Cultural Barriers and Accommodations for Sex-Role Transcendence***

Special attention is called to those women who emerged as successful career achievers in male-dominant professions at the time when the majority of Japanese were still bound by the idea of role dichotomy with women tied to domestic specialization or to part-time, temporary jobs. The sample of ten women included professionals in higher education, law, government, business, and journalism. The article explores what social mechanisms were available to produce such exceptional women. Surprisingly, it was those mechanisms which operated to the advantage of men that came to support these women as well as to overcome gender-biased discrimination. First, the male-headed household and succession ruled out a daughter taking up an occupation, even in a nursing career. But for my sample women, it was the father, the head of the house, who would be considered the most conservative, who came out as a strong supporter for his daughter's career. In one case the father practically dragged his reluctant daughter into a pharmaceutical profession. Even though the daughter was precluded from a house-head-successor status if the family had a son, these fathers apparently expected their daughters to be a sort of his career successor apart from the legal androcentricity. The mother, more conservative, tended to veto the daughter's risky adventure, with some exceptions.

Other general conditions which bolstered male supremacy also came paradoxically to reinforce these women's career commitment and success. One was a series of examinations that men and women have to go through for career entry as well as career promotion: my successful career women accepted the examinations as the very insurance of gender equality. Bureaucratic universalism was another bolster against arbitrary gender discrimination; even internal patronage under a male boss benefited women by making their career path smooth. But behind all this, one must remember, there was another woman who supported the career woman's success, and that was the woman's mother (or hired women) who did all the domestic chore and child-rearing.

This last point signals the direction I was further to take in gender studies – the field was to occupy my interest as a focus of speeches as well as writing. What remained unchanged was my position against a dichotomization or 'opposition' between women and men. Rather I was interested in forms of alliance between women and men, the female subordinate and male boss, fully aware of the disapproval of militant feminists. Looking back, I realize that my way of understanding the gender issues was by taking a 'Japanese' viewpoint as an alternative to the Western feminism. I should add that I did personally encounter Japanese men's unconcealed despise of their female colleagues, which infuriated me. But such experience did not entice me to join the feminist movement 'against men' as led by Western colleagues, while I was quite sensitized to gender conflict.

(2–18: 1999a) ***Non-Western Reactions to Western Feminism: The Case of Japanese Career Women***

Women continued to enter the sacred male-only domains of professions, which partially reflects the tendency in the Western world toward feminism. The twenty-four sampled Japanese women had gained national and international reputations for their extraordinary accomplishments. They were all in contact with West, especially in the United States and Europe. The article reveals how these women suffered discrimination and harassment before their eventual status attainment, largely because their career expectation was unprecedented. A fully-licensed architect could not get more than a clerical job; a Juliard graduate, wanting to be a composer, realized composition was 'the most androcentric profession.' Another woman, who started a film-making career, the only woman in a whole male staff, was frightened at night on location when one male staff after another tried to sneak into her bedroom which had a basically paper-covered door with no lock.

Unlike these solitary professionals, women in bureaucratic structures were better off and secure. In fact, a male executive nominated himself as a trainer for the new, often naïve female subordinate. It turns out that the female boss had no trouble in controlling male subordinates because men were used to structured, hierarchical constraint, more than female subordinates who assumed shared equality as 'women.' Even a specially trained and competent professional woman thus encountered rejection and discrimination at the beginning of a career, but eventually she would find a career road opened up without fighting openly.

(2–13: 1979b) ***The Dilemma and Strategies of Aging Among Contemporary Japanese Women***

Apart from feminist agenda and career issues, we might note other human relations involving women. This article considers the aging issues involving women in intergenerational relations between old mother and her children. By the time of writing this article, it was no longer taken for granted that two generations of the family 'reciprocally' interdependent so that the parents, especially the mother here, after dedicating her time and labor for her child, could expect to be cared for by her child when she becomes aged. This cultural rule of intergenerational , long-cycled reciprocity was no longer at work at the time of this research. The paper delves into how the aged mother was trying to remain autonomous from dependency as long as possible, after having dedicated her entire life to her children, toward a life-long self-sufficiency under a new type of life plan. Ultimately, they sought security from ancestors – dependency on earlier generations instead of later generations.

The mother-child dyad is sometimes held as a model and extended as a cultural trope into other relationships: husband and wife, man and mistress, or even female boss and male subordinate (Lebra 1978). Further, I delineate two types of marriage: 'structured' and 'unstructured. The structured type is characterized by a relative distance between husband and wife, beginning with meeting a prospect through a formal introduction by a go-between, and more or less remaining under the mediator's inspection and protection. The unstructured type is a straightforward 'union' of man and woman with no third party mediation or intervention. Both types of marriage were strained but for opposite reasons: one because of too much structure creating distance between spouses in the presence of the husband's relatives in co-residence as the most oppressive element, and the other because there was no structural protection of the bride from the husband's unreasonable self-centered waywardness, alcoholism, and violence. Overall, the latter turned out to be more stressful, disastrous and destructive of marriage.

Part 3: Status

Part 3 focuses on status and takes the reader to a special category of people, namely, aristocracy, the subject that calls for a greater historical detail for introduction. The initial stimulus came as early as 1976 when I happened to meet and listen to a famous actress of aristocratic origin, an eye-opening experience. I had to wait eight years before I was able to engage in ten months of full-time fieldwork exclusively on aristocracy in 1984–85. The new project continued into years of transcribing interviews and writing afterward, all of which was made possible by a number of supportive agencies, Japanese and American, who took risks in investing in the proposed research. These years of endeavor at great cost culminated in a book, Lebra 1993, *Above the Clouds: Status Culture of the Modern Japanese Nobility,* which earned an Association of University Presses Hiromi Arisawa Award. Reviewers credited the publication with a new vista opened up with regard to the status-bound, hierarchically-ordered life style and fate, and nostalgia of the Japanese. The Japanese partial translation was published in 2000 (trans. Takeuchi, Kaifu, and Inoue 2000).

The 'modern aristocracy' was formally institutionalized in 1884, after the European model, with five ranks – (non-royal) prince, marquis, count, viscount, and baron – to replace the older aristocracy, the primitive origin of which goes back to the fourth-to-seventh century Yamato state under the imperial suzerainty. Several centuries afterwards, it developed into a double system of elite – one was the older court nobility around the emperor in Kyoto, the other consisted of upstart upper-ranking warrior class loyal to the *shogun* whose capital was first established in Kamakura by Minamoto Yoritomo, who began to undermine the Kyoto-based imperial supremacy. By the formation of the Tokugawa *shōgunal* regime in Edo (Tokyo) at the very beginning of the seventeenth century, the warrior aristocracy, economically to be enriched by their land-based dominion imposing rice-tax on laboring commoners – in fact the power of a warrior lord was indicated, simply put, by the amount of rice tax he was entitled to collect from producing commoners and peasants. The result was an eventual impoverishment of Kyoto-centered and land-alienated imperial court and its aristocracy now reduced to a nominal status dependent on the all powerful warrior lords.

Meiji Japan (1868–1912), created after a civil war, under the newly-energized leadership of low-ranking or rankless warriors (*samurai*) who had been deprived under the Tokugawa regime, gave birth to a modern aristocracy in 1884, under the rehabilitated emperor, compromising with the past to a large extent. But a significant change was introduced by an aristocratization of low-ranking samurai, especially of southwestern domains (Chôshû and Satsuma), who were credited with contributions to the reinstallation of the imperial dynasty of Meiji by defeating the warrior rulers under shōgunal suzerainty. Eventually, commoners were also recruited into the new aristocracy depending on their meritorious performances. About 1000 families, specifically family heads, were entitled by the last stage of its existence.

In 1947, two years after Japan's defeat in World War II, this Meiji aristocracy of Japan was abolished to conform to the principle of the already constitutionally declared universal equality, thus ending the sixty-three year-short history of Japan's modern aristocracy. My study was done almost four decades afterward – the period short enough for my informants to remember and long enough to be relatively free from hang-ups.

It is my intention to call attention not only to these members of the old elite but to Japanese in general surrounding them and expecting them to behave like elite more than resenting and rejecting them. Without a conservative bias, I expect aristocracy or emperorship as sources of 'data' to suggest a key to the Japanese sense of self-identity. What is remarkable is the Japanese fascination with aristocratic names and life style observed in a country that is firmly committed to democracy.

(3–19: 1989) ***Adoption among the Hereditary Elite of Japan: Status Preservation through Mobility***

Adoption for the 'hereditary' elite sounds contradictory, but it turns out that Japan's aristocracy, while adhering to the principle of uni-genitural patrilineal succession, adopted sons as freely as imaginable, sometimes one generation after another continuously. Behind the pressure for adoption was the necessity, for one thing, of securing a successor before the incumbent's unexpected death, to avoid losing the title and privilege as a titled aristocrat. And candidates for adoption were abundant as many as non-successor sons for whom being adopted was the best deal for his otherwise gloomy future. But this need for successor assurance turned out merely to be a minor reason explaining the astonishing frequency of adoption. And even at the highest level of the national hierarchy such as the five top noble houses called *sekke,* traceable to the Fujiwara ancestry and the shogunal house, a surprising number of adoptions did occur – the reasons to be clarified by this article.

Historically, adoption was also enforced on a family as a punishment. The present article refers to cases of politically compelled punitive adoptions, as exemplified by the Meiji government mandating the Tokugawa shogunal main house to be taken over by one of its branch houses (the Tayasu) – notice Japanese rulers having avoided a total punitive termination of the line for good. In this particular case, while the main line of the Tokugawa, as embodied by the last Shogun Yoshinobu was terminated (but in fact has continued in blood to this day), its collateral Tayasu-Tokugawa descendants thereafter attained the identity of the main house of the Tokugawa in modern Japan (when and where, in fact, there was no shogunate, no daimyo, no warrior class any longer). Despite the enormous frequency of adoption for various reasons from political to expediential, once adoption took place there were efforts to 'naturalize' the blood to contribute to an image of 'a single unbroken line' of succession.

Adoption was often an expediency for altering one's birth status to fit into a given role or a spousal entitlement. A daughter from a modest-ranking nobility acquired a high aristocratic birth rank such as marquis through such expediential adoption to come out with a full title to the chief royal priestess, called *monzeki* – of an established royal temple. History is loaded with such cases of expediential adoption, even at the very top of national hierarchy, to ease the way to remove status discrepancy. The five top court-noble sekke families of Fujiwara origin – Konoe, Kujo, Ichijo, Nijo and Takatsukasa – had historically supplied highest-level royal consorts to emperors. They became expediential adopters of girls of modest origin as their daughters just to raise these women's status to qualify as imperial consorts, as 'Fujiwara daughters.'

This status-elevating adoption was inherited and accepted by the Tokugawa rulers as well so that the shogun secured 'Fujiwara women' as their number-one wives. What is remarkable is that Japanese in general accepted this kind of rearrangement of birth in order to fit a given role. (The prestige of the Fujiwara name persisted into the modern age. The Meiji emperor had an Ichijo daughter, and the Taisho emperor a Kujo daughter, as empresses. There were objections, thus, when the Showa emperor (Hirohito) married an imperial princess, Nagako, instead of a Fujiwara woman.)

Adoption thus turned into a common, expediential way of what I regard as a culturally managed 'blood transfusion.' Furthermore, the adopted status came to surpass the natural kinship so much so that the initial de-naturalization (through adoption) of a natural son was institutionalized. A natural son was ousted in name first, to come back as a full-fledged adopted son in order to be promoted into a formally qualified imperial son (*shinnô*) through *shinnô senge,* a declaration of a prince as a legitimate son of an emperor. This amounted to the need of adopting one's own son before re-legitimizing a natural son as a true son of an emperor.

In other words, the natural filiarity became established only after being denaturalized, that is, adopted. Adoption was thus a way of culturalizing and regulating kinship which, in natural condition, apparently was out of control. Behind the 'persistence' of a tradition was such an institutionalized flexibility in adjusting to actual, situational variations and unpredictability. The 'cultural' control of child birth, namely adoption, seemed necessary to minimize the chaos of natural birth! The anthropologically popular issue of 'culture vs. nature' thus takes a subtle and complicated twist when it applies to adoption as historically practiced by the ruling class of Japan.

Japan's examples of interchange between natural birth and matter-of-fact adoption serve as a warning against an over-exaggeration of the anthropological 'nature-culture' opposition. This recalls another article of mine (Lebra 1995) in connection with the famous anthropological controversy, started by Derek Freeman's challenge against Margaret Mead in her report on Samoan adolescents. Freeman came out as a biological naturalist, refuting Mead who represented Boasian culturalism against naturalism. This anthropological basic opposition between 'culture and nature, ' notwithstanding, I warn that cultural rules and regulations could be so deeply internalized that they were often taken for granted as 'natural' rather than 'against nature.' It was only after World War II that aristocratic Japanese women came to realize the 'repressive' influence of cultural rules and some of them began to openly violate them, including women running away from their 'titled' husbands to be with their loved commoners – at my interview time several such 'scandals' of high-ranking aristocratic women were circulating. It was only then that culture and nature began to appear in a sharp 'opposition.'

This warning against the tempting oppositional model applies to the other categories – 1 and 2 – as well. Recall the above illustration of 'self' (1) where we have seen how self interchanges with other in several ways as against the oppositional model of self vs. other. Likewise, I have described 'gender' (2) more in light of female-male contingency than in a more familiar Western feminist model of the female-vs.-male oppositional confrontation.

(3–20: 1990) ***The Socialization of Aristocratic Children by Commoners: Recalled Experiences of the Hereditary Elite in Modern Japan***

This article attempts to answer the question, How did aristocratic children internalize their status identity? The childhood recollection of former aristocrats typically excluded the father as involved in child-rearing. This is nothing unique to this class, fathers having little to do with child-rearing across classes. It was in the mother's role that class difference showed up. Unlike the middle-class mothers, most aristocratic mothers stood away from direct child-rearing responsibility. In my informants' narratives, the mother typically appeared absent when the child was in body contact with a caretaker. It was the ubiquitous personal servants (*otsuki*) coming from the commoner class who raised the aristocratic children as surrogate mothers. But there was a distinct difference in treatment of daughters and sons.

Some households, particularly of warrior origin, removed sons from the comfort of home life to live in a boys' dormitory or even to move to a commoner's home in their young age, in order to teach a son the bare facts of tough life. Some of the commoner households in charge, according to these poor aristocratic 'trainees,' exploited them practically as their servants! One such informant ended up mentally deranged. None of my informants who had gone through this kind of tough dislocation appreciated it positively. There were some incredible signs that the deliberate dislocation of a son, if he was not a successor to house-headship, was intended possibly to abandon him.

Daughters were much better off, continuing to live in their own comfortable homes with their parents. What distinguished aristocratic households from middle-class ones was that here the mother was not available as a main caretaker for the child. She was, foremost, the lady of the house, socially available as the wife to the house-head, leaving childcare and other domestic chores to the abundantly available maids. A co-living, full-time nanny, each assigned to one child, all day and all year around, for many years until perhaps the caretaker's marriage, often became a full-time surrogate for the mother. Sibling rivalry was taken over by rivalry between these personal maids assigned to their respective master-children. Not only did the maid indulge the child but maintained linguistic distance by using deferential expressions in talking to her charge whereas the natural mother would have been in no such position – this is one thing mentioned by my informants to credit their nursemaid as a perfect teacher of respect words (*keigo*), which was to turn out extremely valuable when they began to have their own social lives. This suggests that aristocratic culture was refurbished and reinforced not so much by members of the elite but by class outsiders. Indeed, it was these commoner maids who were most concerned with and did teach them the status-proper behavior of their masters.

(3–21: 1991) *Resurrecting Ancestral Charisma: Aristocratic Descendants in Contemporary Japan*

Ancestors enter descendants' lives in two contrasting ways: on the one hand ancestors are beyond descendants' control like genes, but on the other, ancestors as a symbolic creation are inventible and manipulable as resources for a descendant's identity. Descendants – my informants – all had a ready and clear answer as to how many generations had passed since 'the first ancestor.' They would say with no uncertainty, 'I am the seventeenth-generation descendant.' In some cases the informants did not bother to elaborate on their ancestors because it was all in 'public knowledge.'

The descendant-informants described their careers as ancestor-resurrectors in a number of ways:

(a) Reorganizing symbols of the dead such as tombs, studying records to trace 'true ancestors' and to eliminate the unfit.
(b) Documenting ancestral history, often helped by professional historians and archaeologists, which typically resulted in reaching the historical (even prehistoric or mythological) depth to surprise the investigator: 'We were with Emperor Jimmu (the mythological first emperor) and came down as occupation troops.'
(c) Preserving and displaying the heritage, which involved in the case of feudal-lord descendants the duty to visit the castle towns, interfering with their regular job.
(d) Reenacting the ancestor roles in community festivals, in which descendants would appear in full costume of a daimyo ancestor – somewhat comical and embarrassing. Revivalism of local towns often centered on a reconstruction of castles, and for annual festivals the contemporary 'lord' was mobilized to play the central role in full costume 'because nobody else would dare to play this role.' Not only daimyo descendants but those of court nobles on some occasions play a conspicuous role at festivals in Kyoto.
(e) Ancestral identity as a credential for post-retirement employment: the head of a top court noble (*sekke*) derived from the Fujiwara ancestry, upon retirement from a long career as an electronic engineer, accepted the position of grand head priest of the most sacred imperial Shrine at Ise.
(f) Professionalization of household tradition of arts among some court-nobles to open 'classes' with fees to general public in court tradition of tea ceremony, flower arrangement, poetry, incense art, calligraphy, and the like.

Involvement in the ancestor career ranged from 'obligatory' role-play to 'living it up,' from collusive clowning to serious role embracement. Most aristocratic descendants led a double life – mundane and other-worldly, contemporary and ancestral – more noticeably than other Japanese.

(3–24: 1999b) ***Fractionated Motherhood: Gender and the Elite Status in Japan***

This article refers to a particular aspect of motherhood exhibiting a special attribute of the aristocratic status. The complexity of gender issues is maximized in this layer of society – hereditary elite. Different kinds of motherhood are recognized. At one level, the woman who actually gave birth to the child did not engage in child-rearing, which task was taken over by another woman, the resident maid as a full-time caretaker. The child tended to develop a deeper and life-long attachment to the latter, while contact with mother remained distant.

Another dichotomy occurred between the formal, genealogical mother and the 'uterine' mother who did give birth to the aristocratic offspring. This refers to cases of concubinage, in which the child had two mothers – one was the formal mother carrying the elite status of the house, and the other was the 'belly mother' who was the biological mother to remain in a servile, shadowy existence until, possibly, a stroke of fortune could strike to integrate her into the main household toward a full-fledged mistress of the house. Many of my informants had grandmothers who were 'belly mothers.' Mother fractionation in this sense was very common down to the generation of my informants' grandmothers, and was justified by the need of preserving the 'hereditary' or genealogical status. I recall an old lady discussing the Meiji emperor's two daughters: when they visited with Empress Shôken, Meiji's formal wife under this full-fledged name as an imperial widow, the latter tried to concede higher seats for them because they carried Meiji's sacred 'blood.' The daughters were astonished and insisted that Empress was their true mother (*Otâsan*). Implied here was their view of their natural mother (belly mother) as if she were their servant.

These differences in motherhood are tabulated, along the scale of nature and culture (from natural to cultural motherhood), to come up with six types of motherhood variation, ranging between two extremes: purely cultural and purely natural. The purely cultural mother was described as 'mere ornament,' whereas the purely natural mother, with no cultural sanction, emerged as a pitiful being, confined to a clandestine, shameful existence.

Could we derive any lessons from this old aristocratic sample for the 1970's feminism? The feminist movement, as I understood, was oriented toward a removal of the cultural constraint on gender relations. Hence the general trend has been toward a liberation of the 'natural' gender. But the present article does suggest that there can be an optimal balance between nature and culture.

THE CONTEMPORARY CONTROVERSY OVER THE ROYAL LINEAGE CONTINUITY

Before I switch to my final conclusion, and while I am at the status issues, especially those of royal status, I interject a word on one of the most controversial debates going on in today's Japan, and that is, over the continuity of the royal lineage. While I was writing the introduction to the last section on status, Japan was witnessed being involved in controversy and debate over Japan's royal lineage – the issue that deserves an additional commentary here before shifting to another subject. Many concerned Japanese leaders were trying to manage the very problem that Japan might come to see the day when the world longest surviving imperial throne would soon be left vacant, because the present crown prince and princess, both middle-aged, gave birth only to a daughter. Under the 1947 imperial house law (*Kôshitsu tempan*), which has retained the basic character of its Meiji-era precedent, daughters were excluded from succession rights and must leave their natal imperial house eventually in marriage just as most recently did Princess Sayako, the daughter of the imperial couple: Emperor Akihito and Empress Michiko. Other historical destinies for imperial daughters were to marry into branch royal families (see below), to enter the royal nunnery, or to marry priests of the special Buddhist sects that legitimized the priest's marriage (but this last option being limited to priests of the Honganji-temple group, which was originated by Japan's Luther , Shinran, unlike other Buddhist sects still adhering, at least in principle if not in practice, to the proclaimed celibacy of priests).

What if no male successors were available? Meiji leaders prepared for this possible constitutional crisis by creating a number of new male-headed collateral royal houses to add to the surviving but disappearing old such princely houses, which were to provide their sons as emperors when necessary. This would mean the imperial succession line shifting from the older main line to a collateral one. The collateral royal houses also had served as a market for marriage or adoption for royal sons and daughters as well. This was the rationale of re-creating and expanding the number of new collateral imperial houses of Meiji Japan. Thus far, each imperial generation of modern Japan – the eras of Meiji, Taisho, and Showa – happened to have male successors on the direct line (including the mentally-deranged Taisho who was in fact taken over by his son Hirohito as 'regent,' an historically-established practice when the emperor himself proved incapable or otherwise unavailable). But now, it is quite likely that Crown Prince and Princess, with only their daughter Princess Aiko, will have no son. This leads to the following speculations, signaling the critical importance of the succession issue from the point of view of concerned Japanese.

Voices from ultra-conservatism have proposed a return to the old succession system that would revitalize the now almost extinct princely collateral houses as suppliers of successors in case the main line terminates – to revive imperial satellite branch houses – the obsolete idea that most contemporary Japanese dismiss simply as silly. But a totally innovative alternative has also been proposed in 2005: (http://www.yomiuri.co.jp/dy/national/20051108TDY01005.htm (Daily Yomiuri, November 8, 2005); Asahi.com, November 25, 2005 (The Asahi Shimbun).

It was reported that the Japanese government, headed at the time by Prime Minister Koizumi Jun'ichiro, came up with a bold proposal: to revise the *Kôshitsu tempan* drastically so that the male-centered succession rule shall be replaced by a gender-blind one so that Princess Aiko, as an example, could be the next full-fledged emperor. This novel proposal would mean the abolition of the so-far decidedly androcentric principle of succession by removing gender for successor qualification.

This proposal may not be so astonishing after all. Some would argue that there have been precedents of female emperors in Japan's imperial history. But we know this is not a proof of Japan's gender-blind tradition – only nine female emperors (actually seven only, because two of these are counted as four in the formal imperial history because each of these ladies was enthroned twice) in the history of one hundred male emperors since Emperor Keitai (re. 507–531). What we do know is that the Meiji imperial constitution had finalized the rigidly male-only principle for imperial succession, ousting all daughters.

The new proposal, which might amount to a brand new 'Heisei constitution,' expanded the recruitment field for successors by neutralizing their gender criterion, and thereby terminating the old practice of de-royalizing daughters upon their marriage to commoners. In the new proposal, the emperor's daughters and other female relatives, like male counterparts, were to retain their royal title, even after their marriage to commoners – thus preserving their rights as successors, if necessary, to the throne, according to given priority ranks, thereby to preserve a pool of imperial genes. Many issues and solutions still remain to be worked out, but one thing is clear and definite, and that is, Princess Aiko, the daughter of the Crown Prince and Princess, appeared to be most likely to be the emperor upon her father Naruhito's death, if the present government proposal was to be accepted. The final decision was expected to be reached sometime in 2006.

However, the succession crisis turned into a media blitz for blessing when Princess Akishino, the wife of the younger brother of Crown Prince Naruhito had given birth to a boy. As a result, the budding idea of gender-blind succession seems to have suddenly disappeared. The gender issue in succession was temporarily quieted down, without reaching a permanent, institutionalized solution, leaving the succession issue, instead, to a precarious condition for securing a male successor in each generation.

The whole question will involve our discussion above on the two subjects: status and gender. Ultimately, the Japanese self, also, may become a point of reconsideration. The imperial succession issue may thus come to touch the tissue of Japanese selves. In the meantime, strong voices from conservative camps were heard as surmised from internet campaigns and announcements, which insisted on adherence to the male-only principle. See, for example, Japan Policy Institute Official Website, Shukan News: November 25, 2005.

The final question is whether the proposal of gender-blind succession was really so revolutionary after all as it was claimed? Away from the imperial house to commoners, I want to draw the reader's attention to the article by Brown (1966), and another article by Suenari (1972) who reminded us decades ago of the *cognatic* tradition of succession – succession either by son or daughter, whichever is eldest – amongst commoners in the northeastern regions (but probably to wider regions) of Japan. Known somewhat misleadingly under the name *Ane-Katoku* (literally elder-sister house-headship), commoners in pre-Meiji Japan followed the gender-neutral principle of the eldest-child – daughter was as likely as son to be successor. This is an appropriate time to remind ourselves that the 'astonishing' proposal in favor of gender-blind succession by Prime Minister Koizumi is not exactly new but was part of Japan's age-old tradition that prevailed among commoners in rural Japan. It was the Meiji 'reform' that turned the whole of Japan around toward the androcentric, upper-class model, as historically practiced by the pre-Meiji dominant warrior class. By the late-Meiji period, commoners had become also wrapped up into the imperial model of androcentric succession.

A REVERIE ON MY OWN SELF AS A 'NATIVE OUTSIDER'

To complete this Introduction, may I indulge, briefly, in a sentimental reverie of my personal life and identity? My nostalgia goes back to 1958 when I was offered, out of the blue, an opportunity to enroll at an American university, which proved to be a sharp turning-point of my life and identity. Born in a rural town of Japan, and fully exposed to the fifteen-year war (1930–45) since day one of my life, I grew up without knowing anything but the militarily regimented way of life. Education served as little more than an agency to brainwash the supple mind for a readiness to die for the sake of the empire and emperor of Japan. In the last years of the war – World War II (1944–45) – we were mobilized away from home and school to be full-time navy-factory workers. All this time, I was too naïve to have any critical view of the war. Instead, I only complied with whatever the authorities – as embodied by schoolteachers, town leaders, government representatives – expected us to do.

On August 15, 1945, Emperor Hirohito, now known posthumously as the Showa emperor, announced 'the end of the war' with the voice we had heard for the first time. We could not make head or tail what he said in his high-pitched voice. In the factory dorm, we were retold the emperor's message – Japan's defeat in the 'divine war'! We were simply stunned, stupefied. And we cried. There was a rumor circulating that the victorious enemy would land and attack us, women to be raped, as we had been warned by our 'leaders.' But despair lasted only two days. After the end-of-the war crisis was over, the whirlwind of the times overwhelmed my life and transformed it into a balloon.

At age fifteen, the former factory worker returned to the high school campus. From then on through college graduation, I remained internally empty, susceptible to one ideology after another, ranging from pro-American to anti-American, from pragmatism to Marxism all in an embarrassingly naïve fashion. A former honor student thus turned into an unpredictable balloon. It was when I was totally lost and depressed in hopelessness that an unexpected chance to study at an American university flew into my life. With nothing to lose, I grabbed what I thought the last opportunity to do something for my otherwise doomed life. In 1958, already at age twenty-eight, I left Yokohama harbor onboard a freighter.

For the first time in my life I became a 'foreigner' studying at the graduate school of the University of Pittsburgh. After an MA in political science which is a very sign of my political involvement until then, I switched to sociology because the department had just imported European scholars to teach in theory, primarily derived from the Weberian-Parsonian general theory. Although the 3000-page reading assignment for a week was beyond belief, I continued to feel blessed with this new exposure, challenge, and above all freedom. Everyday I encountered something new which shook up my Japan-rooted old identity. Even the dormitory life was full of daily excitement, teaching me the American girls' overwhelming preoccupation with their boy friends. Occasionally, they displayed their nude bodies to one another for mutual inspection!

In time, I developed the habit of turning around to look at myself and Japan through the lens of others and non-Japanese. The campus life in my early thirties, both in classrooms and campus dormitory, was more blissful than expected, although tough examinations for core courses, and later doctoral comprehensive examinations brought me restless days and sleepless nights. A major difference between myself and fellow-American graduate students was that I had made an irreversible commitment of 'having burned my bridges,' whereas American peers remained free to take off for other career options any time.

My doctoral dissertation research on a religious sect in Hawaii imported from Japan was theoretically guided by Max Weber. Why Hawaii? This brings me into a private sector. My husband-to-be, William P. Lebra, was a grandson of immigrants of Czechoslovakian and German descent. My mother-in-law, though a smart lady, was prejudiced against Jews, but Bill was convinced he had inherited Jewish genes through his Prussian grandmother as a point of his pride. Bill had been invited as an East-West Center scholar, and further at the invitation of the University of Hawaii, which was innovating itself under new energetic administration (of President Hamilton and Vice-President Hyatt), he was launching directorship for the newly established Social Science Research Institute when I joined him.

Our marriage was an occasion for less than open celebration: for both of us it was second marriage, ridden with the guilt of betraying the reluctant spouse of the first marriage. After marriage registration at the local government office, just the two of us toasted the start of a new joint life in a living room of Bill's Waikiki apartment. We were determined to make this second try successful with faith in each other.

I received a PhD, but no job, stuck in Hawaii where the job market was horribly limited. The so-called 'double career' family was no more than a nice-sounding word, even on the mainland USA. Rumors of the suicide of professional wives reached me from there. When the chair of the University of Hawaii anthropology department suggested that I teach just one course on Japan as a temporary lecturer, I jumped for it as my last chance, without regard for my ignorance of anthropology. My husband was a Harvard PhD in anthropology specializing in Okinawa and we had often argued on the difference between sociology and anthropology, each insisting on the superiority of his/her own discipline. But everything had changed now. I was eager to re-educate myself by reading anthropological classics, which began to open up my eyes to the depth and charm of anthropological scholarship. Sensitive attention by anthropologists to perceived detail captivated me.

To add a related anecdote, about this time, I started to submit manuscripts to academic journals. To my surprise, the major official journal of anthropology accepted my papers in the 1970s: the reason was that my 'non-anthropological' approach appealed to reviewers – so I had two articles published in a row in the official journal, *American Anthropologist,* before my career was really started.

With a fearful enthusiasm, I launched teaching an anthropology undergraduate class on Japan, with only five enrollees. From the second year on, enrollment spiraled necessitating a closure within a few days after it was opened – for which I could only credit my desperate zeal and the then spreading popularity of the Japan field. After three years of temporary lectureship, I was accepted into the faculty of the anthropology department under the unanimous endorsement of the department faculty, solely because of the speedy and full course enrollment. While preparing for my lecture notes, I devoted all remaining time to writing for publication.

Bill, my husband, was faithful to our marriage and supportive of my career, up until New Year's Day 1986 when, without a warning sign, while in bed in the daytime from a flu, he was found not breathing and already cold – the shock that I still re-live. My screaming reached my neighborhood, prompting several neighbors to come over. Bill passed away in silence from cardiac arrest at the young age of sixty-three!

Not just sorrow but guilt overwhelmed me because I was working in another room on a paper due in a few days, instead of being by his bedside, without, of course, knowing the seriousness of his illness. On the bedside table, I found a pencil-scratched note on what he was going to do the next day. He was ready to retire to engage in full-time research and writing. Instead, Bill is finally and permanently resettled in the beautiful national cemetery at Punchbowl, Honolulu, as a World War II veteran.

This shocking tragedy coincided with the very first day of my second sabbatical. Changing my original plan to do fieldwork in Japan, I traveled in search of an alternative way of life with no confidence in continuing my teaching career. Before long, I began to receive many telephone calls and letters not only in condolence, but also inviting me to academic, and professional meetings. Self-pity of a mourning widow gradually transformed into a new resolution to rededicate her solitary life to full-time professional activities.

I accepted an increasing number of academic invitations for symposia and special conferences. In 1983–84, I was nominated 'Distinguished Lecturer' by the Northeast Asian Council of the Association for Asian Studies, to deliver lectures at four universities, to promote Japan studies. Teaching, which had consumed most of my energy until then, became a second to professional participation, involving trips to Mainland American cities, Canada, Japan, Asia and Europe. This turn of events led to my early retirement in 1996 at age sixty-six, primarily to devote more time to writing. As time availability of a retiree became known, I received more invitations to present speeches at several campuses. In the 1990s, I delivered a series of guest lectures at American campuses, including Pittsburgh, Austin, Minneapolis, Urbana, Chicago, Berkeley, Stanford, and New York. The Program on US-Japan Relations at Harvard University invited me to deliver distinguished lectures twice in 1998. It was in my post-retirement years that I was most active as a visiting speaker.

Also memorable is a series of European trips, all arranged by Professor Joy Hendry at Oxford Brookes University – the initial host for my visiting lectureship there. I made a hasty series of tours to several other campuses and lecture halls in the United Kingdom, including Scotland. Travel further extended to continental Europe, to Leiden, to Munich, to Vienna, Ascona (Switzerland), and to Paris. It was an exhilarating series of momentary exposures to campuses, lecture halls, scholars, and cities of Western Europe! Even the challenge of bathing in a European bathtab is recalled with nostalgia.

Today, such a breathlessly active period of life being over, my mind is more contemplative, inclined to indulge in self-centered reverie. With an American PhD, married to an American scholar, naturalized as an American citizen with permanent residency in the United States, I may have appeared as more American than Japanese. But, while being grateful to the American host, I have never left Japan at heart. Yes, I was once alienated from Japan, but I knew I wouldn't be able to cease being a Japanese, if only because I left Japan at a fully mature age. But more than anything else, my professional specialization in the Japan field has intensified my Japan identity. Yes, Japan stood not just as a birthplace, but as a site for my professional commitment. I came to learn how to observe and represent Japan from a cultural-outsider standpoint, adhering to the principle of value neutrality. Japan has continued to offer not only field-sites but an ultimate source of intellectual stimulus. Nevertheless, there was something else that came to occupy me and my identity.

For me, there was no way of reproducing the striking gap, as experienced by non-native anthropologist, between the 'native' and the observer's own culture – the gap which is a crucial source of knowledge for an anthropological fieldworker. There is some advantage for a native observer with an easy understanding of what goes on, particularly at subtle levels. But 'easy understanding' itself amounts to an anthropological blindness. While alien anthropologists are full of why questions, native observers take too many things too much for granted.

In the meantime, to overcome this problem of mine or rather my enduring complex, I attempted to create my alien self by choosing a new direction of research. In the 1980s, I set up a project which would simulate myself as a sort of foreign anthropologist by choosing a subject, remote from myself, and that was the aristocracy in Japan. This project was generously funded by several foundations – American and Japanese.

The class gap between the new subject and myself allowed me to replicate something that resembles a foreign anthropologist's experience. I met a warm reception and cooperation, which made me realize why foreign anthropologists dearly love their 'natives.' My being a class-outsider did help me indeed. I was told by an insider friend that someone like herself would never be able to be helped as much as I was. Indeed, she as an insider would have been spurned. But , of course, I could never really simulate a foreign researcher. I must confess that at times I went as far as to pretend ignorance about their way of life as if I were a naïve foreigner. The following is just one piece of information for illustration, taken from my studies of the aristocracy, of insider-outsider issues.

We are now observing a tiny group of the Japanese aristocracy, and yet I find a great heterogeneity therein. Here is a microcosm of a cosmic level of differentiation between insider and outsider, between native and alien, between core and peripheral members. Internal, central, core members were ultimately embodied by the head of the house who personified the titled status, prestige, and the name of the house, and who carried the house glory handed down over generations. The rest of the personnel encircled this head at various distances in various degrees of outsided-ness.

On the other hand, aristocratic culture was taught the children, not by insiders but by status outsiders – daughters by nannies, and sons more severely by outside male commoner trainers. Cross-status exposure and training thus turned out to be maximized in the aristocratic childhood, to be taught by status-outsiders. The above point on commoners as the main preservers and teachers on aristocratic culture seems to carry a significant message for anthropologists.

Today, the so-called 'native anthropology' is becoming a legitimate option, a trend regarded as a promising alternative to the so-far West-centered anthropology. I am for non-Western anthropology, but not sure if 'native anthropology' in the strict sense of the word is really an answer. I may be wrong but it seems that nativity and anthropological work do not match. Why is it necessary to retain the label 'anthropology,' which I think is based on intercultural, or cross-cultural contact, stimuli, and comparisons in which a cultural outsider's angle is crucial. The anthropologist, as a cultural outsider, like a servant who, as a class outsider to the upper-class household, could train the child in her charge in aristocratic culture better than insider parents.

In the meantime, Western or American anthropologists were also shifting from the earlier adherence to studying non-Western societies as a basic principle, now going back to restudying their own culture and societies, but this time, with a purpose of self-criticism. This drive for the so-called 'Repatriation of Anthropology' (Marcus and Fischer 1986: Chapter 5) as a self-critique of Western anthropology, is not necessarily new because earlier anthropology had done the same but self-criticism there was only implied, not openly declared. This new trend further alienated me from the academic culture of Western anthropology, putting me totally out of place in the nativized Western anthropology as an alternative. I felt even more alien than ever before.

After many years of self-questioning, I came to realize that my field is not just in Japan or amongst Japanese but perhaps more significantly in lecture halls, audiences, readers in and out of Japan. I realize how, when I did fieldwork, I had in mind whom to convey my message as my ultimate objective. I thus have come to visualize my professional identity, not comfortably settled within Japan nor outside Japan, but rather unsettled and hanging over the bridge between Japan and the outside world of English readership. Japan may remain my primary field, but a more important field for me is the classroom, auditorium, or readership in and out of Japan. At this late stage of life, I confess that it is my audience and my readers who constitute the major anthropological informants for me.

It should be obvious that this reverie does not reflect our unavoidable and universal exposures to the internet flow of information. I have been long engaging in e-mail exchange with my colleagues, American and international. Otherwise internet connection has been limited, I confess, for myself only as a passive receiver and beneficiary of whatever information is generated and circulated by its creators, as testified by this brief essay. I cannot do without a computer, but only as a consumer, I confess, of whatever information generated by others on the internet.

Back to the present volume, I acknowledge my debt to countless unnamed colleagues and friends. Unable to list all the names, I first want to mention two individuals: Alan Howard and Matthew Carlson for helping me with their expertise with the computer whenever I got stuck or lost on the computer maze-way. Michel Cooper, the historian who most recently published *The Japanese Mission to Europe, 1582–1590* (Global Oriental, 2005), kindly offered to go over the proofs with his compulsive perfectionism. Finally, I acknowledge Paul Norbury, the Publisher, for his proposal of the present volume, patience with my tardy progress as well as for his editorial savoir faire. It was Paul who started to scrounge around for my articles published between 1970 and 1999, and worked on the assembled set. Soon, I received a volume of galleys to my surprise. This book could not have been thought out or completed without Paul's commitment, wisdom and skill in preparing and producing it. Thank you, Paul Norbury.

January 2007
Takie Sugiyama Lebra

REFERENCES

Armstrong, Karen. 1993. A History of God: The 4,000-Year Quest of Judaism, Christianity, and Islam. New York: Ballantine Books.

Brown, Keith. 1966. Dozoku and the Ideology of Descent in Rural Japan, *American Anthropologist* 68:1129–1151.

Kanter, Rosabeth Moss. 1977. 'Some Effects of Proportions on Group Life: Skewed Sex Ratios and Responses to token Women'. *American Journal of Sociology* 82 (5): 965–990.

Lebra, Takie Sugiyama. 1976. *Japanese Patterns of Behavior*. Honolulu, University of Hawaii Press.

——. 1984. *Japanese Women: Constraint and Fulfillment*. Honoululu, University of Hawaii Press.

——. 1993. *Above the Clouds: Status Culture of the Modern Japanese Nobility*. Berkeley, University of California Press. Partly translated into Japanese by Takeuchi, Kaifu, and Inoue, *Kindai nihon no jôryu kaikyu* (2000 Kyoto: Sekai Shisosha)

——. 2004. *The Japanese Self in Cultural Logic*. Honolulu: Univesity of Hawaii Press.

Marcus, George E. and Michael M. J. Fischer, 1986. *Anthropology as Cultural Critique:* An Experimental Moment in the Human Sciences. Chicago, The University of Chicago Press.

Reiter, Rayna. 1975. 'Men and Women in the South of France: Public and Private Domains'. In *Toward an Anthropology of Women*, ed. R. Reiter. New York: Monthly Review Press.

Rosaldo, Mchelle Zimbalist. 1974. 'Woman, Culture and Society: A Theoretical Overview'. In *Woman, Culture, and Society*, ed. M. Z. Rosaldo and L. Lamphere. Stanford, Stanford University Press.

Suenari, Michio. 1972. First Child Inheritance in Japan. *Ethnology* 11:122–126.

PART 1

SELF, IDENTITY, AND INTERACTION

First published in *The International Journal of Social Psychiatry*, Vol. XVI, No. 1, 1970

1 The Logic of Salvation: The Case of a Japanese Sect in Hawaii[1]

INTRODUCTION

This paper attempts to explore what is involved in religious commitment with focus on the idea of salvation. My objective is to delineate a set of symbolic mechanisms for maintaining faith in salvation. Faith refers to a high degree of autonomy of the internalized belief system maintained in confrontation with external events which an uninvolved observer would consider to contradict and undermine the system. Faith in salvation refers to such autonomy of the conviction either that one is going to attain the state of salvation in the foreseeable future or that one has attained that state irreversibly. If a religion promises salvation to its believer in spite of unpredictable miseries and misfortunes as likely to befall him as anyone else, then there must be some mechanism whereby such disturbing 'errors' can be immediately dismissed or integrated with the promised salvation. The mechanism for maintaining faith in salvation may be labeled variously: system-boundary maintenance or equilibrium maintenance in functionalist terms; negative feedback, negative entropy, or uncertainty reduction, in the cybernetic or information-theory language; defense mechanisms in the psychoanalytic sense; cognitive dissonance reduction in Festinger's (1957) theory. All these theoretical propositions, though derived from different perspectives, seem to overlap one another and together to throw light upon the problem set forth in this paper.

The following analysis is based on the data collected in 1964 from the Hawaii division of a post-war Japanese sect commonly known as the Dancing Religion (for a comprehensive report, see Lebra, 1967). Fifty-five informants were selected from among the most committed converts of Japanese ancestry, first and second generations, over thirty years of age, and Honolulu-branch members. The local members of the sect as a group were found lower in education and occupational status than members of the largest Buddhist church in Hawaii. Its active membership, scattered over four Hawaiian islands, was estimated at 500.

Most converts had had one or more favorable experiences, often described as miracles, which only strengthened their faith in salvation. Among such experiences were curing and rejuvenation, economic success, finding a job, improvement in marital relationship, overcoming alcoholism, etc. However, there were converts whose life conditions were not improved at all or even deteriorated after conversion. Those who had experienced 'miraculous' healing also often found themselves under attack from another disease. Nor were 'errors' distributed at random only, but in some cases conversion itself generated tragedies as when the conversion of one member of a family against the rest resulted in family dissolution. To meet these contingencies, the sectarian culture seemed to provide a number of symbolic mechanisms so that faith in salvation might be kept intact or possibly reinforced. These mechanisms may be conceptualized in the following categories,[2] although the informants were using them without awareness of such differentiation and variety.

ANALYSIS

1. Functional Relevance of Suffering

The misery left unabated or generated after conversion was most often accounted for in terms of its functional relevance to salvation. Suffering was interpreted as a preparatory step toward final salvation or incorporated into salvation schema in terms of means-end rationality. Suffering thus assumed positive significance as either a necessary phase or a useful means for ultimate salvation. It was further contended that suffering was allocated by the *Kami* (the sect's equivalent to God) as a part of his 'strategy' to attain his purpose, or that the sufferer was under the Kami's test for screening those who would qualify to be his protégés.

Such logic was made more convincing by religious euphemism: converts used the vague term *gyo* (which might be equated with discipline or ordeal) to designate suffering. In his view *gyo* seemed to imply a diffuse combination of suffering, preparation for salvation, and the Kami's intent.

Convinced of such a dignified function of suffering, the convert would be ready to admit that his post conversion life was not necessarily a continuous series of 'miraculous' successes. 'In fact it is more common to receive all sorts of *gyo* after you enter this religion.' 'The more *gyo*,' the informant would add, 'the better, because that's the sign that the Kami has not forsaken you yet. If you were hopeless, the Kami would let you have your way.'

The Kami's favoritism was sometimes thus measured by the amount of misery one had received. The extreme result of this was promotion of suffering to the status of an end itself which had to be served by some means. In explaining her frustrating married life, a woman said. 'I am convinced the Kami used my husband [as a means] to give me *gyo*.'

Suffering as a necessary preparation for salvation seemed supported by the idea of purification, particularly when *gyo* took the form of illness. Certain diseases were considered good 'because all filthy things must come out before you can make a fresh start.' The conception of illness or other forms of *gyo* as instrumental to eradicating pollution seemed to go well with the sectarian doctrine that the convert should have his body (especially his *hara*, stomach) ready for the Kami to enter. This meant that salvation could be anticipated only after the body had been emptied and cleansed. Skin disease and other externally visible disorders thus should be gratefully accepted since they signaled internal purification being completed.

2. Comparative Salvation

Comparative salvation refers to the realization of an unfavorable experience as a salvation in comparison with a worse alternative which one might have encountered. Salvation here is stated in the subjunctive mood to justify a lesser evil. A relatively small disturbance was interpreted as salvation since the other only alternative would have been a disaster: choice of one alternative excluded and thus prevented the occurrence of the other. A temporary eye disease was believed to have saved its victim from the otherwise inevitable course of events: namely, permanent blindness; a finger injury was welcomed as that which had protected one from the fate of death. Even a healthy convert who did not need healing miracles would be made convinced that he had been saved, for example, from palsy which would have struck him unless he had joined this sect.

The reference for comparison was not only the alternative course of events ego might have undergone but another person's suffering. If an unqualified fellow-member received heavy *gyo* as 'punishment', that would serve as a measure for one's own comparatively negligible suffering. Conversely, an ideal believer, or even the foundress of the sect[3] herself, became a reference point for comparison as when the informant dismissed his own *gyo* as 'nothing compared with what *Ogamisama* [the name used for the foundress, meaning a great deity] has gone through'. Furthermore, comparative salvation was repeatedly confirmed and reassured among converts every time they looked outside and pitied the godless people in the 'maggot' world.

Comparative salvation was sometimes attained through substitution of one individual for another to be saved – this might be called substitutive salvation as a subtype of comparative salvation. Ego might have been destined to die at a specified date but this fate was avoided by the substitutive death of someone else. Such exchange of fate seemed to occur most often within a family, especially between husband and wife or parent and child. A convert was told that her little granddaughter's death ought to be thanked for because it was substitutive death for her son, the breadwinner.

The logic of substitutive salvation, it may be noted, seems based on the assumption that salvation is attained only by a limited number of people; salvation, in other words, has scarcity value so that one person's salvation is gained at the expense of another person's chance. It was the Kami's will, the convert believed, to sacrifice some individuals in order to save others. According to an informant, only one percent of the human population would be saved.

The belief in such discriminatory salvation was further supported by the idea that malevolent spirits do not perish but simply move from one person to another as the object of possession. A local leader complained that the members were saved at the expense of his children: 'They come to my house and unload a lot of evil spirits by the power of prayer. These free-floating spirits are now attacking my children.'

3. Time Coordination

In the convert's career there were two important turning points: one was the time of conversion, the other the time of salvation, although they often overlapped. It was found that adjustment of these temporal turning-points served as a major logical resource for maintaining faith in salvation.

Coordination of the conversion time involves memory adjustment as to what one's life condition was like before conversion and what has happened since conversion. Needless to say, coordination was made in such a way as to maximize the credit attributable to conversion for beneficial experiences. The easiest thing in an interview was to elicit one or more episodes involving a striking contrast between the pre-conversion predicament and the post-conversion felicity. Scrutiny of some cases, including checking with other witnesses, however, disclosed no change or reverse change after conversion. A businessman declared that he would dedicate his life to the foundress, because he owed his life to her since she saved him from bankruptcy by her advice on business management. Other sources disclosed that bankruptcy actually had occurred after conversion and that it was due to conversion since he followed the sect's austerity rule so rigidly as to neglect all 'secular' obligations such as gift-giving. (Informants implied that success in business depended upon the fulfillment of extra-business obligations to its clients.) It was only long after conversion that he recovered from being destitute. Another convert who claimed that his physical and mental illness had miraculously disappeared on entry into this religion was described differently by another informant: 'His depression lingered on after his conversion.' Time coordination was made the more easy, the more remote one's conversion memory became and the fewer fellow-members remembered it.

The other reference for time coordination was salvation. Time coordination here involves transferring the turning point from the past to the future. When heavy *gyo* fell upon the convert he realized that his salvation had not yet come true but was a future-projected goal. The functional relevance of suffering as discussed in (1) above includes this futuristic re-orientation. How far in the future? Some converts specified dates for their final salvation: 'I must wait for two more years.' To many others such dates were unknown and speculations on them were considered as sacrilege. Extension of salvation time into such indefinite future made the whole belief system extremely flexible.

The 'time-lag' theory was a convenient device for time coordination. One was not supposed to expect a miracle instantly on conversion 'as many uninformed people tend to,' because a time-lag must be allowed for conversion to take visible effects. This was explained either in terms of sins the convert had committed in the past which must be expiated first, or in terms of the foundress' favorite phrase: 'Don't fool yourself by asking for a salary without working to earn it.' In other words, one must either pay his debt or build his credit before deserving salvation.

4. Collective Salvation

Reference has so far been made only to individual salvation. Conversion to the sect, however, entailed intensive participation in collective activities, and the sect's doctrine included the idea of collective salvation in a typically millenarian (Cohn, 1962) fashion. The micro-salvation episode of an individual believer was linked up with the macro-salvation drama, characterized by its magnitude and drastic quality, involving the catastrophic end of the universe and the simultaneous creation of the Kami's kingdom. While the individual found his career a miserable failure, he could still be convinced of his salvation by being a member of the sect and thereby participating in the grandiose construction of a new universe. The shift of focus from an individual to a collectivity thus served as a faith-maintaining mechanism.

The collectivity as the unit of salvation ranged from the local branch to the sect as a whole with its center in Japan, and to a more imaginary community of the Kami's children irrespective of membership in the sect. Whatever unit was chosen, Japan seemed to play a crucial role in its creation and leadership. Japan's post-war re-emergence as a power was considered to verify the millenarian prophecy of the sect.

The functional relevance of suffering may be reinterpreted in the light of collective salvation. The individual's suffering was tolerated or even welcomed as a means to the Kami's end, namely to build a paradise for his children. Individuals were said to exist only as tools for this collective goal. The foundress would instruct her followers: 'If you are useful, be ready to be used by the Kami. If useless, be ready to die any time.'

Similarly, the mechanism of comparative salvation may be mobilized in favor of the priority of collective salvation. When one faced the choice between one's own goal and the sect's collective goal which was formulated by the foundress or other lesser leaders, the former had to be sacrificed much in accordance with the logic of comparative salvation.

The mechanism of time coordination was fully activated for collective salvation. Initially, the Kami's kingdom was announced to have been created at the end of World War II, and a newly instituted calendar marked 1946 as the first year of the millennium; later the last day of judgment was moved into the future and the present day was described as the time for preparation or struggle between the Kami's children and his enemy. Once in a while the foundress' prophecy included a specific date for the coming of the millennium, but it was never clearly confirmed. (At the time of my fieldwork some local converts hinted that 1965 would be the year.) The predicted catastrophe was synchronized with the anticipation of a third world war.

5. Inner Salvation

Salvation in this religion, as in most post-war religions in Japan, involved external 'evidence' such as healing, making money, etc. The dominant themes of salvation stories thus referred to organic and environmental changes. However, informants also referred to inner salvation attainable independently of the physical condition. When external salvation appeared beyond reach, salvation seemed to be equated with the 'happy', 'unspeakably joyful' state of mind which one could acquire in the midst of an apparently hopeless situation. Furthermore, this state of mind was associated with the idea of *muga*, the egoless or desireless state much like the Buddhist ideal.

At one extreme, inner salvation was manifested in the form of a trance, or as informants would say, 'a feeling like floating in the sky.' Concentrated prayer was said to lead one into such a state. The dancing ritual taking place once a month seemed a public, formalized expression of inner salvation; the dance was called *muga-no-mai*, ego-less dance.

Another extreme was found in other-worldly salvation. If salvation was entirely of an internal state of mind, it was perfectly compatible with physical death. There was no single exception among the converts in the conviction that one's dead kin had been saved; even the husband who the informant believed had died because he was 'useless' in the Kami's kingdom was supposedly saved with death. Other-worldly salvation occurred around the moment of death – just before death (the convert would say that his mother was completely cured just before she died), at the very moment of death, or right after death. Evidence of other-worldly salvation was variable: excretion of all 'filthy things' (or poison); the painless, 'Buddha-like' countenance of the dying person; the sectarian prayer involuntarily uttered by the dying; the corpse remaining soft and pink without odor; the joyful-looking image of the dead appearing in a dream or hallucination of the bereaved; the dead person not being missed at all by the bereaved; and the 'telepathic' foundress' announcement of the dead person's salvation as *fait accompli.*

Death-anchored salvation was labeled 'jobutsu', attainment of Buddhahood, indicative of the sect's cultural debt to folk Buddhism. *Jobutsu* was such an important aspect of salvation that some informants referred to salvation as synonymous with death. A convert, told by the foundress that his ailing father would be all right in three months, became convinced of her omniscience when his father did die at the predicted date. This reasoning, of course, implied comparative salvation in that the father might have been bedridden for years and years.

6. Conspiracy by Jealous Spirits

For the convert the supernatural played a crucial role in causing and determining his daily experiences. While various types of spirits were identified, in addition to the central deity, the Kami, the role played by jealous spirits particularly deserves attention in light of faith-maintaining mechanisms. Jealousy was a characteristic of a certain hostile spirit called *ikiryo*, a live spirit. Ikiryo was charged with jealousy, as well as grudge, from a living person who generated and sent it out against the person he was jealous of.

Ikiryo was an often-mentioned causal agent of sudden illness and other unfortunate events that took place after conversion. To think of oneself as the object of jealousy seemed self-elevating and reconfirming of one's achieved salvation. Indeed no convert found it impossible to understand why someone was jealous of him. It was even more flattering if conspiracy by a jealous spirit against ego was identified by someone else, since that indicated the public recognition of ego's enviable quality or performance.

Jealousy seemed generated due to the victim's success in economic and other activities which was often attributed to conversion. The ikiryo originator was not always identified but, when identified, was usually found among the victim's peers: colleagues, the people in the same trade, fellow-members of a home-villagers' association, members of a church he had once belonged to, former schoolmates, etc. It was often the case that an outsider was suspected of releasing an ikiryo against a convert. However, as the most significant peers were now found within the sect, the convert sometimes claimed to have been attacked by a fellow-believer. The latter was jealous, he would explain, of his exalted status in the local congregation or of the special favor he had received from the foundress.

7. Explanatory and Prescriptive Certainty
This last mechanism refers to the informational armament that provides a ready, unequivocal answer to why one is suffering and what ought to be done to correct the situation. All the six mechanisms above imply such explanatory and prescriptive certainty, and therefore can be considered as subsets of this seventh category. Salvation here is identified with the maintenance of certainty as to the meaning of an experience and the norm of action to be taken accordingly, regardless of whether that experience is good or bad from the point of view of salvation chance. By this mechanism one is protected from meaninglessness and anomie.

The convert readily found an explanation for any serious or trivial experience in the activation of supernatural agents including the Kami, ikiryo, dead spirits, evil spirits, animal spirits. Especially important was the concept of *innen*, translated as karma-relation, fate or destiny, referring to a chain of events which is beyond human control. This Buddhistic notion of predestination was fully used as an explanatory panacea. Relief came from resignation to the irresistible force of the universe rather than expectancy of future salvation.

Prescriptive certainty was attained by the conviction of the omnipotence of the sectarian prayer. The convert believed that there was no problem in this world that could not be solved by the prayer. For him, thus, the intensive, repeated prayer was the answer to any trouble he came up against. An informant stressed as the most gratifying benefit from this religion that 'you know exactly what must be done whenever in trouble.'

Explanatory and prescriptive certainty made the convert self-assured with the sense of superiority over outsiders. It was by no means unusual that a convert with low status, such as a janitor, expressed pity for a member of the elite – a state governor, a president, or a university professor – for his ignorance of the cause of evil as well as of the proper measure to overcome evil.

CONCLUDING REMARKS

Seven mechanisms have been delineated as operating to maintain and reinforce one's faith in salvation. They could be combined in a mutually supportive or contradictory way. The way the informants combined them tended to be emotionally reassuring and logically contradictory. The death of an informant's granddaughter, for instance, was first explained by the foundress as retribution for the informant's disobedience (the Kami's punishment); when the informant, crushed by the sense of guilt, hastened to apologize in a letter to the foundress, she was told that all this had been predestined for 3,000 years (explanatory certainty, particularly the *innen*-predestination) and that the little girl had died in place of her father (comparative, substitutive salvation); the child then was announced to have attained *jobutsu* (inner, other-worldly salvation). Such superimposition of one mechanism upon another was accepted by the convert without objection. Generally, it seems that the multiplicity of interpretations served as an insurance against skepticism for any single interpretation. It is also probable that, when there was a lengthy time interval between two interpretations, the earlier interpretation was replaced (forgotten, that is) by the later one.

To conclude, it seems necessary now to touch upon the question of how the logic of salvation analyzed in this paper was fed and reinforced in the convert. This question has sociological and psychological aspects. Sociologically, the salvation logic was learned, sustained, and elaborated through the continuous transmission of information between the following pairs of interactors: leaders and followers; proselytizers (members) and potential converts (outsiders); voluntary speakers and listening fellow-members at the weekly local meeting as well as in private interaction. Most important among the leaders was the foundress of the sect who claimed that she carried the shrine of the Kami in her abdomen. She visited Hawaii several times between 1952 and the time of my research, and her utterances were regularly heard through her taped sermons mailed from Japan. While she was alive (she died in 1967), the convert's learning of the sectarian belief system depended heavily upon her personal guidance because of her charismatic role which was officially established and which suppressed open emergence of lesser leaders.

Information on salvation was solicited and supplied in one-to-one or one-to-many interaction. Its transmission was through face-to-face communication or correspondence. Literate members could find another source of information in the monthly organ published by the sect's 'headquarters' in Japan which contained the members' reports of 'experiences' as well as instructive essays by the better educated members. As the belief system was thus learned by the individual convert and socially supported by fellow-members sharing the same information, the point was reached where he no longer required an interpreter for his experiences but found himself sufficiently equipped to understand them.

Psychologically, the receptivity to the logic of salvation may be explained in terms of guilt and shame derived from the sense of responsibility or 'complicity' (the latter was suggested to me by Raymond Firth, personal comment, 1969) for whatever has happened to ego. It appeared that the convert, guilty or ashamed of what he was or of what had occurred to him, became suddenly freed from such guilt or shame, either by exposure to one or more of the above identified logical mechanisms or by overcoming the *gyo* thus interpreted. One's self-blame for a kinsman's death may be alleviated by the conviction of the latter's other-worldly salvation. The guilt-feelings would cease to trouble the convert once he became aware of the functional significance of suffering for future salvation. The idea of *innen* would relieve the convert of the tension of shame for his negative self-image. The initial guilt or shame thus seemed to serve as a leverage for internalization of the symbolic mechanisms. There is enough evidence that the foundress successfully manipulated her followers' guilt and shame as if she were aware of the dialectic interdependence between self-blame and faith in salvation. She inflated and deflated the followers' feelings of shame or guilt in such a way that drastic relief from self-blame could be attained. There was no scarcity of guilt to manipulate. Conversion itself engendered guilt toward ancestors and dead kin by the prescribed abandonment of the household religion (Buddhism and/or Shinto) with all its symbolic objects including the ashes. Moreover there was guilt toward one's former 'secular' associates who had been abandoned in terms of social interaction and obligations on conversion.

What has been presented in this paper is based on a single case study, and yet is meant to be a step toward a cross-cultural generalization on the faith-maintaining mechanisms. These findings are presumed to be relevant not only to other religions but to political ideologies as well in so far as extreme belief systems are concerned.

REFERENCES

Bateson, G. 'Cybernetic explanation.' *American Behavioral Scientist*, 1967, **10**, 8. 29–32.

Buckley, W. (ed.) *Modern Systems Research for the Behavioral Scientist.* Chicago: Aldine, 1968.

Cohn, N. 'Medieval millenarism: Its bearing on the comparative study of millenarian movements.' *Comparative Studies in Society and History*, 1962. Supplement II (Millennial Dreams in Action, edited by S. L. Thrupp), 31–43.

Deutsch, K. W. *The Nerves of Government.* New York: The Free Press, 1963.

Festingor, L. *A Theory of Cognitive Dissonance.* Stanford: Stanford University Press, 1957.

Firth, R. 'Gods and God: An anthropologist's standpoint.' Reprinted from *The Humanist Outlook.* London: Pemberton, 1968.

Lebra, T. S. *An Interpretation of Religious Conversion: A Millenial Movement among Japanese-Americans in Hawaii.* Ph.D. Thesis. University of Pittsburgh, 1967.

Lifton, R. J. *Thought Reform and the Psychology of Totalism.* New York: Norton, 1963.

Lofland, J. *Doomsday Cult.* Englewood Cliffs, N.J.: Prentice-Hall, 1966.

Miller, G. A. *et al. Plans and Structures of Behavior.* New York: Holt, Rinehard & Winston, 1960.

Morris, C. W. *Signification and Significance.* Cambridge: MIT Press, 1964.

Selznick, P. *The Organizational Weapon: A Study of Bolshevik Strategy and Tactics.* New York: McGraw-Hill, 1952.

Simmons, J. L. 'On maintaining deviant belief systems.' *Social Problems*, 1964, **11**, 250–56.

NOTES

1. For the revision of the original draft of this paper, I am indebted to Professor Raymond Firth and participants in his seminar at the Department of Anthropology, University of Hawaii, 1969. Support

in preparing this paper was provided by NIMH Grant Number MH-09243 which is gratefully acknowledged.
2. The maintenance of deviant belief systems has been studied by Simmons (1964) with reference to a mystic cult in Georgia. While he delineated a set of general psychological mechanisms, I specifically focus on symbolic mechanisms.
3. On the leadership role of the foundress, see Concluding Remarks.

First published in *Anthropological Quarterly*, Vol. 44, No. 4, October 1971

2 The Social Mechanism of Guilt and Shame: The Japanese Case[1]

A social mechanism is delineated which is considered as useful for distinguishing guilt and shame. Guilt is defined on the basis of the rule of reciprocity, and shame is characterized in conjunction with status occupancy. It is suggested in conclusion that in a monotheistic culture guilt is generalized and shame is specific whereas in a 'sociocultic' culture the reverse is true. Japan is considered to represent a sociocult.

INTRODUCTION

Among many dichotomous typologies which have been anthropologically stigmatized as ethnocentric is the typology of guilt and shame. Ausubel (1955), among others, refutes the dichotomous characterizations of guilt and shame as proposed by Benedict (1946), Leighton and Kluckhohn (1947), and Mead (1949, 1950). Specifically, he invalidates the popularized association of guilt with such factors as superego, parental authority, hierarchical control, and internal sanction, and the association of shame with either the lack of these factors or the opposite of them. These associations can be exactly reversed, he claims. De Vos (1960) presents the Japanese case to show that striving toward goal achievement is motivated by guilt rather than shame, and thus brings into question Piers' and Singer's (1953: 11) point of view that shame corresponds with living up to ego-ideal while guilt corresponds with submission to superego. Most critics agree as to the untenability of the guilt-shame distinction in terms of internal vs. external sanction, and argue that internalization of norms is necessary for both (Isenberg 1949; Lynd 1961; Moriguchi 1965; Piers and Singer 1953; Sakuda 1967; Spiro 1961). Lynd (1961: 49-56), especially, emphasizes the deeply inner experience of shame involving 'the whole self.' It has become tabooed to characterize a total culture as either a shame or a guilt culture. We are, instead, advised to pay more attention to the overlap or mutual substitution between shame and guilt within a single culture, or to look at them as different phases of the individual's psycho-social development.

These critics did shed light upon the naiveté of some postulates underlying the guilt-shame typology. Nevertheless, it seems that confusion has reached such a point that we would rather dismiss the concepts of guilt and shame as either useless or dangerous.

While accepting the critics' contention that no culture can be characterized exclusively in terms of guilt or shame, I want to argue that these terms are conceptually distinguishable, and that there is cultural variation in the usage of them. In this paper I shall attempt to delineate a mechanism which conceptually differentiates guilt from shame. The mechanism I am suggesting is strictly 'social,' unlike past studies which have approached this subject primarily with a psychoanalytic or culture-personality frame of reference.

In order to illustrate the social mechanism to be presented below, reference will be made to the Japanese case. In addition to information from literature, I shall use, where relevant, a part of the TAT material obtained from 130 Japanese respondents, residents of a provincial city in central Japan, ranging from high school children to adults of between thirty and sixty.

The TAT was meant to be a pre-test to elicit a variety of responses with regard to shame and guilt rather than to yield frequency distributions.

The subjects who were organized in five separate groups – three classrooms, a PTA meeting, and a women's association meeting – were requested to write three stories in response to three pictures arbitrarily selected from a Japanese version of TAT (Togawa 1953). They were given instructions to use three expressions equivalent to guilt, shame, and pride respectively in making up these stories. The guilt-eliciting stimulus consisted of a picture depicting an old man and a young person (Togawa TAT 10), plus the instruction to use one of the three commonly used expressions which I considered closest to 'guilty,' *sumanai*, *moshiwakenai*, and *kigatogameru*. The noun *tsumi* was avoided because it is closer to 'sin' or 'crime' than 'guilt.' The shame-eliciting stimulus was a combination of a picture of a man and a woman, the latter placing her arm over the man's shoulder (Togawa TAT 6), with one of the words, *haji*, *hajiru*, *hazukashii*, which stand for the noun, verb, and adjective forms of 'shame.' Finally, pride-responses were elicited to supplement the information on the shame complex. The subjects were presented with a picture of a man standing alone downcast (Togawa TAT 16) and told to use *menboku*, *meiyo*, or *taimen*, which roughly correspond with 'pride,' 'honor,' and 'face.' Some examples taken from the result of this pre-test are expected, first, to clarify the social mechanism to be proposed below, as a general tool, and secondly, to elucidate a cultural bias involved in differentiating guilt and shame.

This paper will examine shame more closely than guilt because shame is a more 'socially' complex phenomenon, the reason for which will be understood from the text.

RECIPROCITY AND GUILT

The following analysis is derived from the distinction of two types of social structure in both of which we get involved in every society. One is identified as 'reciprocal' and the other as 'asymmetric.' I postulate that this distinction offers a social mechanism to distinguish shame from guilt. Guilt relates to reciprocity, I argue, while shame involves asymmetry.

By reciprocity I mean the rule by which two actors in interaction, Ego and Alter, expect of each other to maintain a balance between mutual rights and duties, social assets and liabilities, debt and payment, give and take. The rule of reciprocity urges the debtor to pay to the creditor, the benefit-receiver to make return to the donor. Guilt emerges, I contend, when such a balance collapses, that is, when Ego has over-exercised his rights vis-à-vis Alter without fulfilling corresponding obligations, when he is in debt over and beyond his capacity for payment, or when he has received a benefit which he has no means to reciprocate or does not deserve. Guilt, then, is accompanied by the sense of social injury unjustifiably inflicted by Ego upon Alter. Alter, conversely, can generate guilt in Ego by doing an unrepayable favor or by sacrificing himself for the benefit of Ego. If the debtor feels guilty, the creditor may appear, at least in the debtor's eyes, as punitive, self-righteous, expectant for future pay-off, or generously forgiving.

In applying this reciprocity model to culturally variable situations, I suggest that there is cultural variation in the degree of specificity of the Alter who appears injured by Ego and thus makes Ego feel guilty. At one extreme, Alter may be a specific person with whom Ego happens to be interacting here and now. At the other extreme, guilt may be stabilized by substitution of all specific 'social' Alters by the universally generalized 'symbolic' Alter, namely, the omnipotent single God. Between these extremes, one may find variously specific or general Alters such as an internalized parental figure which may or may not resemble the transcendental God, a master to whom Ego owes an unforgettable benefit, the ancestors without whom Ego would not have existed, or the Messiah crucified for the sake of sinful men.

Generalization of Alter distorts the ideal form of reciprocity in that the involved partners are not equal in bargaining power at the outset of reciprocal engagement. An extreme cultural example is found in the original sin man owes to God. Moreover, the symbolic projection of Alter in the form of a supernatural being, or a scripture itself, obscures the reciprocal aspect of guilt in terms of what and how much Ego owes to whom.

As far as the Japanese case is concerned, guilt feelings tend to be expressed vis-à-vis a relatively specific Alter. In response to the guilt-eliciting stimulus most respondents described guilt as felt vis-à-vis a specific Alter such as a father or grandfather whose wish was ignored, Ego's husband while Ego engages in an extramarital affair, a stranger run over by Ego's automobile, the victim of murder, etc. In a few cases the father or grandfather, widowed, feels guilty toward the child either for not providing the maternal care which the child deserves, or conversely, for letting the child take a maternal role. The latter happens when the child is perceived as a daughter. We find 75 percent of our respondents relating guilt to one or another sort of harm done to someone by the guilty partner. Furthermore, 17.2 percent explicitly refer to the unbalanced state of reciprocity in terms of under-giving and over-taking by the guilty partner vis-à-vis Alter. Such a relationship occurs typically between a parent who has taken pains in bringing up a child, and the latter who has run away from home in spite of such indebtedness and now is remorseful. In a more romantic situation, an old man falls in love with a beautiful young woman and feels guilty due to discrepancy in terms of exchanged values as a romantic partner. Sixteen percent of the cases find the young person guilty vis-à-vis a deceased Alter. Guilt is triggered, it seems, when Alter's death deprives Ego of the last chance of repayment, thus leaving Ego permanently indebted.

The Japanese guilt behavior seems closely connected with the idea of *on*. *On* is a favor or benevolence which makes its receiver morally indebted to its donor (for analysis of *on*, see Lebra 1969). Guilt will be maximized when Ego finds the received *on* unrepayable and yet the *on*-donor identifies himself with Ego so much that he not only makes no demand for pay-off but blames himself for Ego's fault. Such a benefactor tends to be represented by the mother. It is not surprising, therefore, that, as De Vos (1960) discovered, the Japanese feel guilty primarily toward the mother as the generalized creditor and sufferer. This may be evidenced if a wrongdoer feels guilty vis-à-vis his mother more than the direct victim of his wrongdoing, although our TAT results cannot substantiate this simply because the parental figure in the guilt-eliciting picture looks distinctly male.

Specificity of Alter as well as the connection between guilt and *on* can be further demonstrated by the Naikan method developed and practiced by Yoshimoto originally for correction of prison inmates and, later, for psychotherapy in general (Ishida 1968; Kitsuse 1962; Yoshimoto 1965). The Naikan-ho, the method of self-reflection, is a semi-religious discipline which mobilizes the client's guilt and, if successful, is climaxed by an acute conversion experience involving dramatic confession. The client is systematically made aware of the *on* he owes to a series of specific individuals, alive and dead, of whom he is reminded one by one – mother, father, grandmother, grandfather, sibling, school teacher, employer, etc. According to Takao Murase (personal communication), a Japanese psychologist who is undertaking an intensive research on the Naikan, the client is told to calculate the sum total of the received *on* and translate it into the amount of monetary debt. This may be considered as an extreme representation of the relationship between guilt and reciprocity.

Despite cultural variation in terms of specificity and generality of Alter, my general argument is that guilt hinges upon tension between the lost balance of reciprocity and the pressure to restore it.

STATUS OCCUPANCY AND SHAME

Unlike guilt, shame relates to the asymmetric dimension of social structure where the norm of reciprocity is not directly relevant. Specifically, I refer to social status as a unit of an asymmetric social structure. If guilt involves reciprocal 'role' obligation, shame is generated or triggered, I argue, in conjunction with 'status' occupancy. It is assumed here that an actor is vulnerable to shame when and where he poses as a status occupant. Shame results from whatever happens to undermine or denigrate the claimed status by revealing something, however 'trivial' (Lyrid 1961: 40), of the claimer which is inconsistent with the status. The drastic expression for this situation is 'losing face,' or as Japanese say, 'crushing,' 'injuring,' or 'soiling' face. What kind of undesirable state brings about such a status-incongruent situation is not essential to our delineation of shame, since the same state is likely to generate guilt as well. We are not concerned with whether shame is generated by incompetence and inferiority (Alexander 1938; Isenberg 1949; Piers and Singer 1953; Moriguchi 1965), or by behavioral errors in propriety or appropriateness (Benedict 1946; Lynd 1961; Riesman 1954), or whether or not shame has anything to do with the violation of a moral standard. What makes shame distinct from guilt in our definition is whether a wrong or undesirable state of affairs or conduct, whatever it may be, induces status incongruency and thus makes status occupancy awkward. The same state or conduct may bring about guilt if the actor interprets it as a hindrance to fulfillment of reciprocal obligations or an unjustified harm done to Alter.

The following social characteristics of shame are derived from this basic assumption that shame is contingent upon status occupancy:

(1) Status identification

Recognition of a certain situation as status-incongruent requires the observer's knowledge of the status occupied. Incompetence, for example, induces shame only if the status in question is known together with certain competence, discipline, style, or any other attributes required of the status occupancy. The ideal situation where mutual status identification among actors is maximized, then, is found in a Gemeinschaft where everyone knows everyone else. This may have led some authors on the subject of guilt and shame to associate shame with an earlier stage of socio-evolutionary development than guilt.

Mutual familiarity among members of society based upon a Gemeinschaft structure, however, is neither a sufficient nor a necessary condition. Every society provides a cultural classificatory system whereby its members can identify the status of a stranger on the basis of physically observable characteristics. Among such characteristics may be mentioned age, sex, skin color, dress style, speech, demeanor, etc. Furthermore, the stranger's status may be known through social devices like formal introductions.

From the standpoint of status identifiability, we can say that the higher the status, the more vulnerable the person tends to be to shame. This formula immediately reminds us of the need for social protection of prestigious persons – a point to be considered later.

Our sample contains a number of statuses identified as affected in shame situations. Among the most frequently mentioned in response to the shame-eliciting and the pride-eliciting stimulus are occupational status (a company president, a section chief, a detective, etc.); familial status (head of household, breadwinner, husband); and sexual status. The female status, for example, comes into focus when its occupant takes initiative in expressing love and thus feels embarrassed vis-à-vis the male partner.

(2) Exposure

If status identification is a latent basis for shame-sensitivity, shame is further contingent upon a manifest display of status performance. Thus a second social condition of shame is exposure, actual or anticipated, to observers of an action or a state which is incongruous with the claimed and socially identified status. Lynd (1961: 27–34) stresses the 'unexpected exposure' of self as essential to shame.

Exposure as a necessary condition for shame derives from the fact that status maintenance requires that only the ritual, theatrical aspect of the actor consistent with his status be socially visible, while his other aspects are supposed to be hidden or ignored. The unexpected and salient intrusion of the 'back stage' into the 'front stage' induces shame, the situation which Goffman (1959) described with such expertise. If socially protected privacy is necessary, as we contend, for sensitization to shame, a perfect Gemeinschaft would be shame-free at least within itself. One must be on guard, therefore, against the temptation to correlate shame, as Leighton and Kluckholn (1947: 106) did, with the lack of privacy characteristic of a Gemeinschaft such as Navaho society.

Exposure takes a dramatic form in a situational conflict where a double-status occupant is exposed simultaneously to two groups of audiences whose expectations are mutually incompatible. Sakuda (1967) finds the essence of shame in the simultaneous exposure to a private group and a public audience. Double exposure may also occur in the form of double expectation from the same audience. Among the shame-responses, we find shame felt by the man and woman in the picture toward each other or spectators when they are exposed to sexual intimacy either as a sender or a receiver of a love message. While expecting each other to be intimate physically or emotionally, a man and woman, married or in love, are constrained, in my interpretation, by the norm of heterosexual distance which seems to have been internalized by our respondents. Thirty-seven percent of the shame-respondents referred to the awkwardness of the situation created by such double expectation. A few respondents ruled out status-incongruity by identifying the couple as father and daughter and stating that they are acting intimately without embarrassment 'because they are father and daughter.' The implications are that the subjects saw no room for sexuality in parent-child relationship, but they would find such intimacy embarrassing if the couple were recognized as married or as lovers.

As far as exposure is necessary for shame, shame is far apart from guilt. In our sample, the majority (76 per cent) of shame responses explicitly involve actual or anticipated exposure, whereas guilt responses either exclude the necessity of exposure for guilt or imply it to be totally irrelevant. In some cases guilt derives its tension precisely from non-exposure, since voluntary exposure such as confession will lessen or redeem guilt.

To the extent that status is sanctified and thus needs protection from unexpected exposure, social interaction tends to be ritualized, spontaneity to be suppressed. Japanese culture is among those which endorse ritual politeness, humility, and reserve, which recommend indirect, mediated communication (through a go-between), and which foster anticipatory responsiveness to untold wishes of others, as well as inclination for understatement and subtlety. Shyness is also recommended as a defensive shame in the situation where one's status identity relative to the audience is uncertain. That face-sensitivity is encouraged for both defensive and protective purposes – saving Ego's face and saving Alter's face (Goffman 1967: 14) – may be well illustrated by a psychiatric sample. According to Kasahara (1969), the fear of eye-to-eye confrontation found among Japanese neurotic patients refers not only to anxiety of being looked at by others but to anxiety of embarrassing others by unintentionally staring at them. It is open to investigation whether this sort of eye-sensitivity is really pathological or socially grounded in that there does exist a group of nosey, curious neighbors trying to 'peep in' in spite of cultural disapproval of such behavior.

While exposure avoidance is an indispensable part of culture for the society where status is sanctified, the same society is likely to instruct the individuals to take shaming by exposure as the most undesirable and thus most effective punishment. In the same vein, the retaliation against unwarranted ridicule in public may be considered a virtue.

Exposure varies in scope. It would be minimal if Ego is exposed to one person only. A shame situation, however, typically involves not only a dyad consisting of Ego and Alter but a 'triad' including a third actor as an audience. That is why shame is maximized when experienced 'in front of everybody.' Here, shame behavior involves, rather than eye-to-eye confrontation, side-glancing at the third person. Forty-six percent of our shame responses were found to have actors shame-faced toward a third party, and 41 percent toward Alter. This is another point clearly distinguishing shame from guilt. Guilt in our definition is a product of 'dyadic' interdependence involving reciprocal obligations. This difference has been suggested in anthropological literature on socialization, specifically with reference to the role of the socializing agent in feeding guilt and shame. Spiro (1961: 119–120), for example, proposes that shame orientation is produced where the socializing agents train the child by claiming that other people will sanction him. Hence, the norm, but not the person, of the significant other is internalized. Guilt, conversely, Spiro says, presupposes that the socializing agent himself is introjected by the child.

The triadic nature of the shame situation accounts for the unlimited extensibility of the scope of exposure. The third party to which Ego is subject to be exposed can thus be extended to a diffuse, anonymous collectivity of fellow-members of society. This is the reason why the social object toward whom one feels ashamed tends to remain undefined and implicit.

What has been said above is subject to cultural variation. The Japanese seem to stress a third party's role in downgrading or upholding Ego's status, and that third party tends to be unlimitedly extended to a diffuse, anonymous whole. The social object 'in front of' whom shame is felt thus tends to be implicit whereas guilt-feeling is addressed to an explicitly-defined social object. This was corroborated by our sample: the social object was made explicit by 27.7 percent of shame-respondents, 30.8 percent of pride-respondents, and 68.7 percent of guilt-respondents. Such extensibility of the scope of exposure implies that Ego's status can be identified by a large collectivity, and that information on Ego's performance is likely to flow extensively far beyond the circle of eyewitnesses.

(3) Social sharing of shame

The third point I want to make in characterizing shame as status-contingent is the social sharing of shame. This is a consequence rather than a condition of shame relative to status. Since shame in our definition hinges upon status occupancy, shame feelings are not confined to the particular individual who has committed a shameful action or who is the target of ridicule. His shame is vicariously experienced by others who share the same status, because what is shamed is not an individual person but the status itself. Status is derived from two sources, i.e. from membership in a group and from the state of belonging in a social category. Shame is therefore shared by Ego either when the shamed person is looked upon as a representative of the group of which Ego is a member, or when the shamed person belongs to the same social category as Ego does. Some examples are taken from our sample. A man is ashamed that his wife revealed her ignorance of etiquette at a social gathering (shame on the family membership status); a section chief of a company loses face for the errors made by his subordinate (shame on the section membership status); a woman blushes and hides behind her lover at the sight of a wall picture showing a semi-nude woman (shame on the social category status, 'woman'). Ego, on the other hand, can cause others to share shame as in the case of a soldier who is determined to fight bravely 'lest the country should be ashamed.'

Where collective sharing of shame is institutionalized, members of the collectivity are likely to take caution not to cause vicarious shame for others; or conversely to make efforts to achieve honor to be shared by others. We can understand in the light of collective sharing of shame why, in literature, shame is often associated with identification with peers, and pressure for conventional conformity, while guilt is treated as an individualistic trait.[3]

Social sharing of shame may also vary from culture to culture in terms of scope and intensity. It may also be variable in terms of what status arouses sharing more than others. Our sample reveals a relatively high discrepancy (25.9 percent of shame-respondents) between the person who feels ashamed and the person who has made the shame-causing error. In contrast, guilt responses are characteristically more 'centripetal' in that the person who feels guilty is more frequently identical with the person who committed a guilt action.[4] The Japanese as a whole may be said to be susceptible to shame sharing once the status as a 'Japanese' is at stake. Thus they tend to assume a collective face vis-à-vis foreigners, and to become readily shame-faced or pride-faced by the performance of a fellow Japanese.

CONCLUSION

In this paper I have attempted to delineate a social mechanism which may be useful for distinguishing guilt and shame. Guilt was defined on the basis of the reciprocity model, and shame was related to social asymmetry, particularly, status occupancy. Cultural variations for each were suggested. I shall conclude this paper by speculating on two extreme cultural types regarding shame and guilt. While agreeing with many authors that a culture cannot be described as 'a shame culture' or 'a guilt culture,' I suggest that there is cultural choice in terms of which of the two, guilt or shame, is more generalized and which is more specific. It is proposed that in a 'monotheistic' culture guilt, on the one hand, is more generalized in terms of ubiquitous and unlimited debt to the single, universal creditor. Shame, on the other hand, tends to be more specifically confined in terms of status identification, exposure, as well as social sharing of shame. The reverse would be true in a non-monotheistic culture, especially where the place of God is taken by 'society' itself. I shall label the culture which deifies society 'sociocultic.' In a sociocultic culture it is shame that is generalized, and guilt that is specific in defining Alter.

It is further proposed that Japan represents a sociocult. Here shame is generalized in the following sense. First, status identification is facilitated by the general inclination for exhibiting status-indicators such as uniforms and calling cards. This reflects the awareness of the fact that the individual is not trusted until his status, group membership, or origin becomes clearly known. Moreover, Japanese culture is articulate in recommending status-fitted conduct. Second, shame is generalized with reference to exposure in terms of the cultural equipment for status-protection from exposure, as well as a widely-shared anticipation of exposure to an unlimited extensive aggregate of direct and indirect witnesses. Third, social sharing of shame is also extensive in that every Japanese assumes the status of being Japanese, which is made easy by the physical and cultural uniformity of the Japanese. The generalized sharing of a member's shame makes the Japanese intolerant of deviance by fellow-members, which, in turn, warns them to conform to fellow-members' expectations.

I speculate that monotheism and guilt are mutually hooked up in that the transcendental God tolerates or even encourages 'social' aggressivenes which results in feeding guilt, as if guilt were constantly generated within the system. A similar self-generating mechanism is found for shame in a sociocult. Here the actor is not only inhibited by his status but wishes to display it for social recognition. The ritually prescribed exposure avoidance is, thus, counteracted by the voluntary exposure of self as the object of expected deference. Furthermore, inasmuch as striving for higher status on a competitive basis prevails, as in Japan, together with the actually available opportunity for mobility, vulnerability to shame is constantly reproduced and amplified.

Needless to say, the above remarks are widely open to empirical investigation. Also it should be noted that monotheism and sociocult imply differential distributions of guilt and shame on the generality-specificity scale only, not the intensity scale. We cannot say a priori that guilt is more intense than shame where guilt is more generalized than shame, or vice versa. It is possible that the generally shame-sensitive Japanese may be even more intensely guilt-oriented vis-à-vis specific Alters.

Nothing has been said about the dynamic interchange between guilt and shame. One example may be sufficient to illustrate such interchange. Guilt and shame may be exchanged on a social market as when the guilty person makes public apology so that the price of shame is paid to buy freedom from guilt. Such an occasion may reveal the degree of generality of shame. Where shame is generalized, the amount of guilt may be matched by the amount of shame measured by the extension of exposure (the size of the audience in front of which apology is made); by the degree of involvement of the group to which the culprit belongs (such that an apology is felt necessary); by the status of the group leader who makes a representative apology on behalf of the culprit (the higher the status, the more severe the shame). This and other types of 'bargaining' between shame and guilt will be delineated elsewhere.

REFERENCES

Alexander, F. 1938. Remarks about the relations of inferiority feelings to guilt feelings. *International Journal of Psychoanalysis* 19: 41–49.

Ausubel, D. P. 1955. Relationships between shame and guilt in the socialization process. *Psychological Review* 62: 378–390.

Benedict, R. 1946. *The chrysanthemum and the sword*. Boston: Houghton Muffin.

De Vos, G. 1960. The relation of guilt toward parents to achievement and arranged marriage among the Japanese. *Psychiatry* 23: 287–301.

Goffman, E. 1959. *The presentation of self in everyday life*. Garden City, New York: Doubleday.

—— 1967. *Interaction ritual*. Garden City, New York: Doubleday.

Isenbero, A. 1949. Natural pride and natural shame. *Philosophy and Phenomenological Research* 10: 1–24.

Ishida, R. 1968. Naikan bunseki ryoho (Naikan analysis). *Seishin Igaku* 10: 478–484.

Kasahara, Y. 1969. Hitomishiri – Seishi (shisen) kyofusho ni tsuite no rinsho-teki kosatsu (Hitomishiri – On fear of eye-ball to eye-ball confrontation). *The Japanese Journal of Psychoanalysis* 15, 2: 30–33.

Kitsuse, I. J. 1962. A method of reform in Japanese prisons. *Orient/West* 7, 11: 17–22.

Lebra, T. S. 1969. Reciprocity and the asymmetric principle: an analytical reappraisal of the Japanese concept of *on*. *Psychologia* 12: 129–138.

Leighton, D. and C. Kluckhohn 1947. *Children of the people*. Cambridge: Harvard University Press.

Lynd, H. M. 1961. *On shame and the search for identity*. New York: Science Editions.

Mead, M. 1949. Social change and cultural surrogates. In *Personality in nature, society and culture*. C. Kluckhohn and H. A. Murray, eds. New York: Knopf.

—— 1950. Some anthropological considerations concerning guilt. In *Feelings and emotions*. M. L. Reynert, ed. New York: McGraw-Hill.

Moriguchi, K. 1965. Guilt and shame in connection with the developmental stages of self-respect. *Psychologia* 7: 153–158.

Piers, G. and M. B. Singer 1953. *Shame and guilt*. Garden City, New York: Doubleday.

Riesman, D. 1954. *The lonely crowd*. Garden City, New York: Doubleday.

Sakuda, K. 1967. *Haji no bunka saikō* (Reconsideration of shame culture). Tokyo, Chikuma Shobō.

Spiro, M. E. 1961. Social systems, personality, and functional analysis. In *Studying personality cross-culturally*. B. Kaplan, ed. New York: Harper & Row.

Togawa, Y. et al., eds. 1953. *TAT Nihon-ban shian 1, kaiga tokaku kensa zuhan* (The Japanese tentative version of the Thematic Apperception Test, No. 1). Tokyo: Kaneko Shobō.

Yoshimoto, I. 1965. *Naikan yonjunen* (Forty years of Naikan). Tokyo: Shunjusha.

NOTES

1. An earlier version of this paper was read at the 1969 annual meetings of the American Anthropological Association in New Orleans. I wish to acknowledge the criticisms expressed by the participants in the program on Culture and Mental Health in Asia and the Pacific (NIMH grant MH 09243) at the Social Science Research Institute, University of Hawaii. Special gratitude is due to Dr. Richard Jung for his stimulating and helpful comments, which in part have been integrated within my scheme. However, responsibility for ideas expressed in this paper rests exclusively with myself.

2. I am aware that such specificity of Alter in guilt responses resulted in part from the guilt-terms the respondents were instructed to use. *Sumanai* and *mōshiwakenai* are more than 'guilty' in that they also can mean 'sorry' or 'unpardonable.' These terms may make their users more 'socially' conscious than the users of 'guilty.' However, the difficulty of translating 'guilt' or 'guilty' into Japanese equivalents may be the very indication of cultural difference in guilt feelings. In any event the reported TAT material should not be taken as more than a pre-test.

3. It is true that guilt also can be socially shared as when the mother shares guilt with the guilty son. It seems that guilt-sharing is derived from the sense of complicity: if many a Japanese felt guilty for Japan's aggressive role in World War II, he did so since he found himself to be an accomplice in the act of aggression if only because he had not tried to prevent fellow-Japanese from committing such an act. No complicity is involved in shame-sharing because, here, Ego is a victim of the shameful state of someone else, by virtue of a shared status.

4. The following abstract from our sample shows variability in discrepancy and identity between the primary actor who commits the action of shame, pride, or guilt and the person who feels ashamed, proud, or guilty:

	Discrepant	*Identical*
Shame	25.9%	51.8%
Pride	19.7	64.1
Guilt	6.9	74.1

Added Note: The subject of 'Shame and Guilt' continued to occupy me, having resulted in another article 'Shame and Guilt: A Psychocultural View of the Japanese Self', *Ethos* 11:3, Fall 1983. This later article shows a greater 'intensity' of guilt than shame among Japanese.

First published in *American Anthropologist*, Vol. 74, No. 3, June 1972

3 Acculturation Dilemma: The Function of Japanese Moral Values for Americanization[1]

THEORETICAL CONSIDERATIONS

The recent anthropological literature on the subject of acculturation tends to discredit the linear model for describing acculturative processes. Gluckman (cited in Mayer 1962), for example, refutes the validity of the 'de-tribalization' postulate which is based upon the idea of linear change from tribal to non-tribal culture. He offers, instead, the 'alternation model' in which the native switches freely back and forth between the two cultures – tribal and urban – depending upon whether he finds himself in the hinterland or in an urban setting.

This alternation model, based on the principle of situational selection, is further extended by Mayer with reference to social roles. For him the urban-tribal antithesis is that of 'sets of relations' and, therefore, whether an individual exhibits an urban or tribal pattern of behavior depends on which set of social relations he happens to be in. 'In this model, the question of what one means by an 'urban African' does not arise at all. The adjective is not applicable to persons: it applies only to roles, relations, systems, and the like' (Mayer 1962; 585).

Along the same line of argument, McFee (1968) replaces the 'continuum model' with what he calls the 'matrix model' in analyzing the acculturation of Blackfeet Indians. While the continuum model assumes the linear change from the more Indian to the more white culture, the matrix model suggests all four possible combinations of the two cultures in terms of two degrees, high and low–high in white orientation and low in Indian; low in white and high in Indian; low in both; and high in both. Among all the four possibilities, the author singles out the last one, namely, 'high in both White and Indian culture,' as the main point of argument. The Indian of this type is 'more than a culture container (McFee 1968:1101), and scores more than 100 percent – the very point of the title of the article, 'The 150% Man, A Product of Blackfeet Acculturation.' Here McFee refutes 'the container error' which he claims is implied in the continuum model.

Summing up these theoretical contributions, I have come up with the following typology of the non-linear and the linear model of acculturation.

Non-Linear	*Linear*
(1) Bi-culturality	Replacement
(2) Selectivity	Conflict
(3) Social contingency	Cultural embracement

First, the non-linear model assumes that acculturation generates biculturality, that is the addition of a new culture to the old one, whereas the linear model involves replacement of the old culture by a new one. Second, biculturality in the non-linear model gives freedom of choice or bicultural repertoire in action; whereas the linear model, bound by the idea of replacement, implies the opposite of freedom, namely, conflict. The latter is underscored by dramatic, often destructive action associated with nativistic movements among those undergoing acculturation. (See, for Instance, O'Brien and Ploeg 1964.) Third, the nonlinear model stresses that acculturation processes are contingent upon social environment and therefore should be seen as a function of social relationship, roles, audiences; or as Berreman (1964) perceives, of reference groups. The linear model, on the other hand, seems to take for granted the direct and entire embracement of the individual by a culture.

To my mind the non-linear model seems much more sophisticated and acceptable. This paper thus attempts to reinforce the three points of the non-linear model – biculturality, selectivity, and social contingency. At the same time, however, it is undeniable that the linear model does contain a certain degree of validity. We know that natives do undergo replacement of their own culture by another culture however slow the process may be. We also know that many, if not all, natives under acculturation experience strain and conflict, or 'double bind,' in varying degrees of acuteness. Finally, crucial as social contingency may be to acculturation, social interaction, in turn, is determined by a set of culturally defined norms: some cultures may provide norms of interaction more favorable to acculturation than other cultures do.

I would like to take into account these relevant implications of the linear model as well. In sum, my paper purports to integrate the two models of acculturation: linear and non-linear.

AN ALTERNATIVE HYPOTHESIS ON ACCULTURATION

The literature referred to above concerns natives under colonial domination. It is true that culture contact under colonial control is quite different from that occasioned by migration: one is involuntary, whereas the other is more or less voluntary; also one involves acculturation of 'native' residents while the other involves acculturation of 'guests' into the host culture. Nonetheless, the theoretical standpoints, as delineated above, are generalizable, I believe, to the situation of immigrants insofar as the immigrants and their offspring carry a status stigma as being a minority or as inferior and are placed under pressure for emulating the dominant host culture. Under this assumption I shall apply those theories to the Japanese in Hawaii. It is my ultimate goal to generate an alternative hypothesis integrating the linear and non-linear models.

As far as Issei (first-generation) immigrants and their Nisei (second-generation) children in Hawaii are concerned, point (3) of the non-linear model, namely, social contingency, attains full significance in that the Japanese individual is trained morally as well as psychologically to be sensitized to the place he occupies in a social setting, to perform faithfully whatever role is assigned to him, and to respond to the expectations and evaluations of others. From this it seems to follow that the Japanese immigrant is equipped with native norms which maximize his readiness for acculturation to the extent that he interacts with members of the host society.

This certainly implies to the likelihood of: (1) biculturality and (2) selectivity on the part of Japanese Americans. To borrow McFee's phrase, the Japanese American can represent a 150-percent man. It is not only that to be Japanese and American at the same time is possible or that one has bicultural options of belavior. It is implied that the more Japanese one is, the more ready for acculturation. Given the immigrant's situation, it may even be expected that the socially sensitizing norms of Japanese culture are mobilized more systematically and intensely than would be the case with the Japanese in a familiar situation. Here one finds the native culture itself compelling the immigrant toward acculturation. Indeed, Issei Japanese, particularly those Issei who have decided on Hawaii as a permanent home, seem to try hard to be accepted in the American society or at least not to look obtrusively alien. They are only outdone in this respect by Nisei who as American citizens are naturally more committed to an American Identity. That compulsion for acculturation is built in the native (Japanese) culture is shown by the fact that successful Americanization of Nisei is taken as an 'ethnic' pride of 'Japanese' Americans. The hypothetical formula here is 'If pro-Japanese, then pro-American,' which is quite opposite from what nationalistic Americans in the 1920's believed; 'If pro-Japanese, then anti-American.

So far there seems to be no problem. The problem emerges when we take into consideration what happens to the Japanese once he is caught up on the main stream of Americanization. The Japanese culture, initially facilitative of acculturation, now appears obsolete, useless, or even un-American to the person who has once internalized American culture in some depth. The reason is obvious. Unlike Japanese culture, American culture is socially insensitive and non-accommodative; Instead, it capitalizes upon the individual's initiative, creativity, and self-determination. While Japanese culture is instrumental to the individual's Americanization, thanks to its emphasis on the virtue of social accommodation, American culture does not reinforce Japanese values but rather, with its individualistic focus, repels them.

The Japanese effort for Americanization itself, when looked at from the standpoint of individualistic philosophy, appears un-American. Reinforcement is thus not reciprocal but only unilateral.

I have argued that the more Japanese-oriented, the more responsive to the pressures of Americanization. The reverse is not true, however. Americanization does not necessarily reinforce Japanese values but rather tends to repress them. In the first instance the non-linear model is validated, but in the second the linear model is more applicable. Once Americanization takes place, acculturation becomes a more or less irreversible, linear process. This process involves: (1) replacement of Japanese culture, (2) conflict between the two cultures, and (3) total embracement by the individual of American culture regardless of social situation.

Combination of these two opposite processes involved in the acculturation of Japanese Americans is likely to generate ambivalence toward both American and Japanese cultures. Ambivalance is further complicated by the fact that the individual's 'sincere' effort for Americanization may not be necessairly appreciated or rewarded by members of the host society. This kind of asymmetric intercultural relationship may result in severe psychological conflict since Japanese culture has infused the individual with a sensitivity to social feedback.

The hypothesis implied in the foregoing is twofold. First the native culture (Japanese) facilitates acculturation (Americanization). Second, the reverse is not true; that is. Americanization does not reinforce Japanese culture, instead it involves an irreversible movement away from the native culture, and hence ambivalence and dilemma on the part of the acculturating individual.

EMPIRICAL ILLUSTRATIONS

I shall now turn to my empirical observations focusing on the Japanese language-school education in order to substantiate the two-fold hypothesis stated above.

Japanese language schools in Hawaii, since 1893 when the first school was created on the Big Island, continued to grow until 1939 when they had reached a total of 194 schools with an enrollment of more than 38, 000 students (Hawaii Nipponjin Iminshi 1964: 249). After Japan's attack on Pearl Harbor, the Japanese schools were closed, and many school principals were interned. Although the schools were reopened after Worid War II, the change brought about with the war was so drastic that they have never recovered their pre-war strength. The number of students has been declining every year, and as of today (1970), enrollment is estimated at 10,000.

Almost all Nisei informants I came across stated that they had had no choice in the pre-war era but to attend Japanese schools as well as public schools; and that every Japanese child in the informant's neighborhood also had attended a language school. How effective the teaching at language schools has been is difficult to determine. Moreover, there was a deliberate effort on the part of the language schools not to interfere with the requirements of public schools. They would hold students only for one hour per day after public school. As public-school requirements increased, many students dropped out of Japanese schools before completing the twelfth school year. Nevertheless, Japanese schools undoubtedly exerted some influence on most Nisei, whether positive or negative. It can be further assumed that the Japanese-language schools served as a major channel, along with families, for systematic transmission, perpetuation, and reinforcement of Japanese culture. The Japanese language was taught in reading, writing, and speaking but often in association with moral lessons; most major schools offered moral education as a special subject called *shūshin* using a separate textbook.

Information for this paper was drawn from three sources. First, the textbooks in moral education; second, interviews with school principals; and, third, interviews with Nisei who are former students of Japanese language schools.

ANALYSIS OF TEXTBOOKS

The textbooks initially used in language schools were the same as in Japan; inspected and approved by the Japanese Ministry of Education. Revision took place first in 1916, and then in 1937, in order to make them better fitted for students with American citizenship. The following analysis draws upon the 1937 edition of *shushin* textbooks (*Shūshinsho*). Five books were selected out of a total often available for the first to tenth grades. These five books include 61 stories or instructions meant for moral exhortation. Most of the stories (56 out of 61) refer to historical facts, especially those concerning notable personages. Actors who appear in the stories are mostly Japanese, although nine non-Japanese personages (Lincoln, Garfield, Hoover, Edison, Carnegie, etc.) are also included.

SOCIAL SENSITIZATION

The moral values alluded to by these stories are primarily socially oriented. They can be categorized as follows in the order of frequency, with some overlaps between categories (frequency shown for each category): Kindness (benevolence, generosity, tender care for the helpless) – 24; Devotion (loyalty, filial piety, selfless dedication) – 20; Sacrifice (including suicide) – 12; Trustworthiness (keeping one's word, the sense of responsibility, being dependable or conscientious) – 9; Cooperation (mutual help for a collective goal, solidarity, harmony, togetherness – 5);Tolerance (forgiveness for the err or wrong doing of others) – 5; Love (parent's or teacher's love) – 5; Repayment for benefit received (*on-gaeshi*) – 4; Compliance (obedience, respect for elders) – 2; Public morality (kotoku) – 2;Trustfulness (faith in the goodness of others) – 1; Politeness – 1.

These virtues are socially oriented In the sense that they are directed toward a person or group with whom ego interacts directly or indirectly.They are social also in deeper sense: these virtues are alluded to not as an immutable, God-given set of moral standards but as natural results of compassion or empathy for others. Particularly, the first three virtues – kindness, devotion, and sacrifice – are motivationally based upon the mechanism of vicarious experience of the pain and pleasure of others. Ego's action is determined by the needs and desires of others rather than ego's own, which are vicariously experienced or anticipated by ego.

About two-thirds of the textbook stories (42 out of 61) explicitly refer to moral compensation – rewards for moral action and punishments for immoral action. Actors are finally rewarded for their moral conduct: 27 cases involve goal attainment (in typical success stories); 10 cases are rewarded materially or physically (such as rescued from near death); but as many as 34 cases involve 'social' reward. Social reward takes such forms as gratitude expressed by the beneficiary (14), praise expressed by spectators (16), communitywide or nation-wide (and sometimes world-wide) reputation (17), status promotion (4), becoming a moral model for emulation by others (2), repentance expressed by the sinful in response to the moral actor's benevolence (2), and repayment by the beneficiary (*ongaeshi*)(3).

The relationship between socially sensitized moral action and social compensation can be understood in two ways. First, moral action may be considered as a sort of social investment which will be returned to the investor with a profit. Simply put, if you are good to others, they in turn will reward you with such social values as gratitude, praise, etc. To the extent that such social reward is valuable, there will be inclinations to show kindness, devotion, etc.

The second implication is that once a benefit is received there is an obligation to repay it. This is the basic logic of on morality, on being a diffuse mixture of benefit bestowed and debt incurred (Lebra 1969, 1971). Underlying one's motivation for moral action is one's awareness of being in debt to others, together with a compulsion for repaying the debt. The textbooks under consideration thus stress how indebted the readers are to their parents, teachers, and many others. How to repay a debt is shown by stories on the virtue of *ongaeshi* (return of *on*).

Socially sensitizing moral values, backed up by social compensation in these two senses, are likely to propel the individual to get socially involved, to become 'engaged' in social relationships. Readiness for social engagement is certainly an important factor, I believe, in expediting acculturation.

GENERALIZATION

Social sensitization alone, however, does not necessarily guarantee adjustment to an alien culture. If social environment remains confined, then social sensitization may operate against acculturation. The textbooks do include instructions with regard to immediate social groups and relations such as parent-child, or sibling relationships, or immediate neighborhood. However, a larger number of stories are oriented to non-immediate relations. Nine cases are kin-oriented, 15 to particular, but non-kin 'others,' and 29 are oriented to 'generalized others,' either strangers or general communities – local and national.

Generalization of 'others' is also shown in the way social compensation materializes. Reward for good conduct comes not only from the beneficiary, the receiver of good conduct, but from a general audience. While 21 cases refer to reciprocal compensation by the beneficiary, 23 cases find the agent of compensation in the third party, either an individual spectator or general public, who is not involved in benefit-exchange.

To keep the generalized others in mind, instead of getting involved in immediate social relationships, requires some character strength for the individual actor. The textbooks thus emphasize, along with social values, personally oriented values. The following is a list of such values shown again in the order of frequency: Perserverance (endurance, firmness) – 26; Industriousness (hard work, diligence, studiousness) – 22; Rationality (thoughtfulness, good reasoning, inventiveness) -13; Discipline (inhibition from capriciousness, punctuality, observance of rules, tidiness) – 11; Bravery – 6; Ambitiousness – 6; Honesty – 3; Frugality – 2.

The overwhelming emphasis upon perserverance and Industriousness is particularly relevant to generalization of social values. Moral lessons involved here are: that even when the individual is determined to do good he is not free of all sorts of predicaments and suffering; that he must overcome these difficulties through endurance (*gaman or shinbō*) and with firm resolution to carry out his initial will; that nothing will come to fruition unless he studies or works hard and persistently.

These moral attributes of the individual person are necessary for generalizing social compensation in a time dimension. Instead of expecting an immediate reward, one is supposed to look for an ultimate reward only after long perserverance and diligence. As social investment is thus made on a long-run basis, so should the social debt be carried and repaid on a more or less permanent basis. Given the difficulty of communication and the lack of consensus in intercultural contact, as in Hawaii, such a long-range perspective may be considered essential.

It may be concluded here that social sensitization coupled with such generalization, as emphasized in the Japanese language-school textbooks, should operate for Nisei students in favor of acculturation. As far as moral instructions expressed in the textbooks are concerned, the Japanese language-school education may be said to conform to the non-linear model in that being Japanese is perfectly compatible with being American, or that being Japanese helps one become American.

The use, interpretation, and absorption of these textbooks is best illustrated by observation of the instructors and students of these language schools.

INSTRUCTOR'S VIEWS

Interviews were conducted with three school principals, all male, one being Japan-born and the others Hawaii-born *Kibei* (*Nisei* who were reared in Japan, and later returned to the U.S.). All of them taught before the war, at least for a while, and are teaching at the present.

Asked about their educational philosophy, they all stressed the importance of moral education and the significant role of Japanese language schools in this area, particularly in pre-war Hawaii. The moral values they taught are certainly of Japanese origin but at the same time applicable, they argued, to citizens of any country. Compatibility or even indistinguishability between Japanese and American values was stressed. How was loyalty taught, then? By the time these informants started to teach – in the 1920's and 1930's – there was no loyalty problem, no ambiguity as to which country should be served.

The purpose of the Japanese language school was definitely to make good American citizens out of Nisei children. This did not mean renunciation of loyalty to Japan: it meant that loyalty to Japan was easily transferable to any country one belongs to. One of the principals reasoned this by saying, 'We taught them to be loyal to *kimi*. But *kimi* meant the emperor only for Japanese, and President for Americans.' Another principal recalled how he had been emotionally moved when he saw school children of different ethnic backgrounds voluntarily standing at attention while the American flag was being raised. Convinced that a good Japanese must be a good American, the other principal stressed the Japanese virtue of *ongaeshi* (repayment for received benefit) to explain loyalty. The Japanese know, he said, there are four kinds of *on* (benefit) – *on* from parents, on from teachers, *on* from all beings, and *on* from the country. It is this last on that Nisei owe to America and must repay by being loyal.

The extreme expression of combination between Japanese morality and loyalty to America was found in the 100th Battalion and the 442nd Regiment Combat Team composed of Nisei volunteers during World War II. In response to the question, 'In what ways have Japanese language schools contributed to Hawaii and American society in general,' my informants invariably mentioned this and attributed the Nisei loyalty and bravery thus demonstrated to their Japanese education. In addition to this, they mentioned the Nisei's contribution to the war, for example, as interpreters, with their knowledge of Japanese learned at language schools.

Another important contribution the informants all claimed the language schools had made was keeping children morally upright and disciplined. The distinctly low rate of crime and delinquency among Nisei, compared with other ethnic groups, was repeatedly mentioned as a strong indication of the effectiveness of moral education given by pre-war Japanese language schools.

So far I have delineated the instructors' views of language schools as perfectly compatible with or even necessary for Americanization of Japanese. However, the same instructors are now facing the 'deplorable' result of successful acculturation of Japanese Americans. They are encountering fewer and fewer local Japanese who are aware of the importance of Japanese-language education. Nisei parents do not speak Japanese to their Sansei children, complained my Informants, they do not push their children to attend a Japanese school because they 'suffered' too much as language school students. Today, everything is determined by egoistic interest and money. Look at the fantastic rise, the informants went on, in the rate of crime and delinquency of local Japanese. 'Japanese are now like all other Americans, Koreans, Hawaiians, Whites, Blacks, etc. They are just as bad as any other ethnic group. Even in classrooms. Sansei and Yonsei students are so dreadfully undisciplined. All this is a result of Americanization.' By losing Japanese qualities, it was contended, Japanese are becoming undesirable Americans. By forcing Americanization on its people, America is losing its resources. 'If a war broke out now,' one of the principals predicted, 'there would be no Japanese who would fight for America as bravely as the 442nd did.'

The school teachers' frustration comes partly from their financial difficulty as a result of diminishing enrollment. One of the informants, as the foremost leader in Hawaii Kyōiku Kai (Japanese Educational Association in Hawaii), is planning to request government subsidies from both the United States and Japan. He feels both governments should be more appreciative of the contributions Japanese language schools have made and are capable of making in the future. 'A subsidy for Japanese schools would be, for example, a much more effective measure for delinquency problems than any other measures introduced by the government.'

To outsiders it seems that acculturation has crossed a point of no-return so that efforts of the school teachers to restore the pre-war type of discipline does not look very realistic. The principals themselves are aware of the futility of their efforts. One said, 'I feel as if I am trying all by myself to stop the main current of the ocean.' This sense of futility was also expressed by another in terms of resentment against America, amusement at the Soviet Union surpassing America in science, and the revitalized conviction that Japan, as a superior nation, should lead the world.

Here two cultures collide and the clash seems all the more painful because of the acculturation facilitating aspect of Japanese culture. A most dramatic meeting of the two models – linear and non-linear – was seen during World War II. Local Japanese attained the unprecedented ethnic glory through their heroic commitment to the American cause; their ethnic pride reached a peak paradoxically when the whole Japanese community was suddenly 'de-Japanized' and the authority of Issei was downgraded to a nonentity. As Ushijima (1969) writes, Hawaii's Japanese experienced victory in World War II in contrast to the Japanese in Japan to whom the war is associated with nothing but defeat. Although Japanese language school teachers take credit for the loyalty of the 442nd, we know that this loyalty was demonstrated and recognized when the language schools were all closed and discredited.

RECOLLECTIONS OF FORMER STUDENTS

If the foregoing argument is valid, it should be further reflected in the recalled experiences of former students of Japanese language schools. I selected a group of Nisei who have 'made it' professionally. Ten University of Hawaii faculty members of professorial rank were interviewed and asked to recall and evaluate their experiences at Japanese language schools which they had attended from three to 12 years.

I wanted to see how the language-school education would be recalled and evaluated by those Nisei who have succeeded in American society, who therefore can be said to have succeeded in acculturation. The following analysis is based upon the responses to some of the open-ended questions.

As would be expected, the responses turned out to vary widely, some being extremely positive and some negative in evaluating the Japanese language education. Some underscored what the principals said about the contribution of the language schools but others invalidated these statements. Some recalled their experiences at Japanese schools vividly, while the memory of others was quite hazy; some showed emotional attachment to their school days and teachers, while others sounded indifferent or even hostile; some stressed the effectiveness of the language-school education in either a positive or a negative direction, and others doubted that it had left any stamp on them.

What complicates these variations is that no one viewed the language-school system exclusively positively or exclusively negatively. The respondents who had an overall favorable opinion had some reservations; while negative evaluators had to admit there were some good things. Such complexity can be understood in the light of the afore-stated hypothesis on acculturation: Japanese values as a reinforcer for Americanization, and American values as repellent of Japanese values. I shall analyze these complicated responses as efforts to minimize ambivalence or conflict and to maximize integration of the two contradictory images of Japanese culture. The following patterns of recalling language-school experiences have emerged:

LANGUAGE AS A SKILL

The questions relevant here were 'What did you gain from your language-school education?'; 'What are the most Important moral lessons that you learned at the Japanese language school?'; 'Do you think that Japanese language schools have contributed anything to Hawaii and American society In general?'. Positive evaluation of language schools was expressed in a selective manner rather than in their entirety. The first important selective point was language vs. moral education. Most respondents found a positive value in having learned the Japanese language. Even those who either disapproved or did not think much of language schools felt glad they had acquired the language that other Americans do not usually have available to them. Here the language school is seen in the light of value-free, purely technical, linguistic training which provides the learner with an additional repertoire for adaptation. The advantage of knowing Japanese was emphasized particularly by specialists in the social sciences and the humanities. We should note here that the language-learning aspect, compared with the moral education aspect, was a minor point in the view of the school principals.

PERSONAL MORALITY

Those who did not think the language school had been well-equipped with language-teaching ability tended to appreciate its moral education but not in totality. A systematic selection was made of personal, rather than social, moral values as what has been learned intensively and gainfully. Most frequently mentioned were perseverance, endurance, discipline, diligence. These virtues were considered by some informants as complementary to what one learned at public schools since the latter did not teach these things. One informant appreciated the sheer drill the school imposed on students – reading, writing, memorizing, speaking, regularly followed by exams. (This was, however, what was most strongly rebelled against by some other informants.) Pressure for hard work under encouraged competition was recalled with strong approval by another informant.

The personal virtues taught there were considered not only complementary to the American educational system, but also identical with middleclass Protestant American values. Mention was made in this connection of the ethic of work, success-orientation, emphasis upon the value of education, honesty, promptness, frugality, etc.

The curious point here is that personal virtues overshadow social virtues, and very few informants referred to those socially sensitizing moral values which were discussed before. The few who did mention social virtues such as filial piety or respect for elders did not advocate them without qualifications. Singling out personal morality as the main emphasis of *shūshin* may be interpreted as a way of integrating Japanese values and the Individual-focused American values.

ACTIVITY-FOCUS

The language-school training was recalled or appreciated often with reference to physical activities engaged in, as divested of meanings underlying them. 'Discipline by doing – meticulous writing, reading, etc. – was the most valuable training,' said an informant, who at the same time dismissed the *shūshin* teaching by moral precepts as 'worthless.' A couple of other informants had pleasant recollections of school songs they had sung, school plays they had participated in as actors. But they admitted that the meanings behind these had been completely lost. Activity-focus was thus a way of resisting the conceptualization of what was taught which might have put the student in culture conflict.

DENIAL OF LOYALTY CONFLICT

In response to the question, 'Did you experience loyalty conflict as a student of both school systems, American and Japanese?', everyone, with only one exception, said 'No' without hesitation. Loyalty had seldom been discussed in class or had never been brought up in terms of conflict. The lack of loyalty conflict was analyzed by informants in three different ways. First, the possibility of being loyal to both Japan and America had never been questioned – it was taken for granted. Second, loyalty never had become a serious issue because America was the only really existing country in the eyes of the students while all stories about Japan, including those about emperors, were taken only as 'stories,' never seriously. Here emphasis was on the harmlessness or ineffectiveness of Japanese language schools as a counterforce against American identity. To substantiate this view, one informant quoted aloud a passage from the Imperial Rescript with an unmistakable expression of hilarity and disrespect. Third, conflict was said to be lacking because loyalty had been exclusively and consistently to the United States, never to Japan. 'I don't know about other schools, but my teachers never mentioned loyalty to Japan, and there was no question about loyalty to America.'

With these variations, the overall impression was that loyalty conflict had not been brought into awareness. Asked why they had thought they had to be loyal to their country, many said, 'Because we are American citizens,' and one said, 'Well, good Japanese are loyal to Japan. Good Japanese Americans must be loyal to America, right?'

PRAGMATIC REINTERPRETATION OF SOCIAL VIRTUES

Some of the social virtues were accepted with rational or pragmatic qualifications. The concept of *on*, for example, of which a few informants claimed to have no comprehension, was accepted within a rational framework stripped of all irrational, sentimental elements. One informant reduced the concept to a rational exchange of benefits similar to an economic market which has no room for sentimentality. He owed *on* to his mother simply because she had worked so hard for her children, not because she was his mother. 'We Nisei are pragmatic.'

Pragmatic relativism was applied to other virtues as well, such as respect for elders. An informant stressed the universal validity of respect for elders not because of their age but because of their experience whereby they can guide the younger.

Such pragmatic reasoning seems to do away with the vicarious experience exhibited for others as the motivational basis for virtuous action, and to conform to self-oriented American norms.

COUNTER-EVALUATION

Counter-evaluation refers to positive evaluation of what was irrelevant or opposed to the intention of the school. One informant, with an overall negative attitude toward language schools, conceded to the fact that the school had kept him off the streets. If he had had more free time, he might have ended as a delinquent. (This kind of baby-sitting function seems to be most prevalent in post-war language schools and is much resented by the school principals.)

Another version of counter-evaluation is more revealing of the acculturation situation. Three informants said that they had hated and rebelled against the kind of drill they had to go through. But they now appreciated it; because without hatred of drill they would not have become as interested in public school lessons as they did. The language school offered 'something that you bounced off against.'

CONCLUSION

I have attempted to present a case to demonstrate the structural dilemma built in acculturation processes. Theoretically, special attention was paid to integration of the two models of acculturation. Analysis was made of the content of moral education textbooks used by Japanese language schools, expressed attitudes and opinions of school principals, and the statements by Nisei informants in various professional fields. The latter two revealed their experiences of dissonance and efforts to overcome it, as well as a wide discrepancy between the two groups of informants. In conclusion I shall underline the acculturation dilemma by referring to the self-image of Nisei. I asked my Nisei informants to characterize Japanese Americans. The highest consensus was found in their readiness for Americanization and in their behavioral affinity with Caucasian Americans as manifested in achievement orientation, studiousness, Puritanism, etc. One informant went further to reject the idea that there is anything distinct about Japanese Americans: 'We are almost 100 percent American.' Another described Japanese Americans, jokingly, as 'banana – yellow outside, white inside.' This characteristic was generally approved of, but at the same time was referred to in a tone of self contempt. One Nisei explicitly criticized this characteristic of Japanese Americans, particularly of Nisei, as an evidence of typically Japanese docility and conformity. The 'whiteness' of Japanese Americans is understood here as an outcome of slavish emulation of white-American culture rather than as a coincidence of two cultures. This dilemma was well-expressed by another informant when he referred to the guilt complex of Nisei which makes them simultaneously reject and support 'Haolified'[2] Japanese. 'They are against those Japanese who speak good English, saying "Are you trying to be a Haole?" Next moment, however, they vote for Sparky Matsunaga and Patsy Mink [Congressional Representatives from Hawaii], probably the two most eloquent English speakers.'

REFERENCES

Berreman, Gerald D. 1964. Aleut Reference Group Alienation, Mobility, and Acculturation. *American Anthropologist* 66: 231–250.

Caudill, William 1952 Japanese American Personality and Acculturation. *Genetic Psychology Monographs.* 45: 3–102.

Embree, John F. 1941. *Acculturation among the Japanese of Kona.* American Anthropological Association, Memoirs, No. 59. Menasha, Wisconsin.

Hawaii Kyolkukai. ed. 1937. *Hawaii Nihongo Kyo¯ikushi* (The history of Japanese language education in Hawaii) Honolulu: Hawaii Kyoikukai.

— 1964. Hawaii nipponjim iminshi (A history of Japanese Immigrants in Hawaii) Published by the United Japanese Society of Hawaii, Honolulu.

Kitano, Harry H. L. 1969. *Japanese Americans: The Evolution of a Subculture.* Englewood Cliffs, New Jersey: Prentice-Hall.

Lebra, Takie S. 1969. Reciprocity and the asymmetric principle: An analytical reappraisal of the Japanese concept of 'on.' *Psychologia* 12: 129–138.

— 1970. Religious conversion as a breakthrough for transculturation: A Japanese sect in Hawaii. *Journal for the Scientific Study of Religion.* 9: 181–196.

— 1971. Intergenerational continuity and discontinuity in moral values among Japanese. Paper presented at the Conference on Culture and Mental Health in Asia and the Pacific. Social Science Research Institute, University of Hawaii, and East-West Center, March 15–19.

Mayer, Philip 1962. Migrancy and the Study of Africans in Towns. *American Anthropologist.* 64: 576–592.

McFee, Malcolm 1968. The 150% Man, a Product of Blackfeet Acculturation. *American Anthropolologist.* 70, 6: 1096–1103.

O'Brien, Denise, and Anton Ploeg 1964. Acculturation Movements among the

Western Dani. *American Anthropologist.* 66, 4, Part 2: 281–292. (Special Publication)

Spicer, Edward H., Edward P., Dozier, and George C. Barker 1958. Social Structure and the Acculturation Process. *American Anthropologist.* 60: 433–455.

Ushijima, Hidehiko 1969. Hawaii no Nikkeijin, (Japanese in Hawaii). Tokyo: Sanseido.

NOTES

1. Part of this paper was read at the 67th Annual Meeting of the American Anthropological Association. November 20, 1970, San Diego. This research was conducted under the support given by the National Institute of Mental Health (Grant MH09243), and Social Science Research Institute, University of Hawaii; this assistance is gratefully acknowledged.
2. This word is derived from 'Haole,' the Hawaiian rendition for 'Caucasian,' and used to epitomize with derogatory implications those who follow the Caucasian-American style of life.

▸ First published in William P. Lebra (ed.), *Transcultural Research in Mental Health*, Honolulu: University of Hawaii Press, 1972

❹ Religious Conversion and Elimination of the Sick Role: A Japanese Sect in Hawaii

It seems safe to assume that every society has its definition of illness as a social role. The sick person as a role occupant can claim certain rights, such as the right to be exempted from work and other normal obligations and to be treated with 'compassion, support, and help' (Parsons, 1964, 113). Precisely because illness is a social role, the contents of privilege vested in illness are likely to vary from one social system to another such that they are fitted into a particular system as a whole, of which the sick role is a part. When a new social system emerges, a new definition is likely to be given of the sick role. An emerging religious sect is most likely to carry its own definition of health and illness, as well as death, as an essential component of its culture. If healing takes place as a sectarian performance, it can be understood, I assume, in the light of the sectarian definition of the sick role.

I would like to explore possible relations between religious commitment and healing phenomena, with special attention to the redefined sick role. Religious commitment here specifically refers to conversion to a new sect which involves intense interaction between the candidate and proselytizer for conversion, exclusive membership in the sect, sustained participation in the sect's collective action, and rigorous conformity to the sectarian norms.

The sect studied is formally called Tenshō Kōtai Jingu Kyō, more commonly known as the Dancing Religion because of the outdoor collective dance, a part of its regular ritual which is most visible to the outside public. Here I shall abbreviate it as Tenshō. Tenshō emerged in postwar Japan under the leadership of a middle-aged farmer's wife, Sayo Kitamura, who came to be addressed as Ōgamisama, great deity. In 1952, the first overseas division of the sect was established in Hawaii, and its membership is roughly estimated to have reached 500 as of 1965. The following analysis is based on a year-long field research (Lebra, 1967) on Tenshō converts in Hawaii. The data were collected through interviews with fifty-five Honolulu members over thirty years old and through observation of collective activities at local branch meetings. Most interviewees had had direct contact with Ōgamisama, the self-appointed messiah, at one phase of conversion or another, which was made possible by her occasional visits to Hawaii or by the follower's pilgrimage to the sect's headquarters in Japan. Being either *issei* (Japan-born immigrants) or *nisei* (*issei*'s American-born children) including *kibei* (American-born returnees from Japan after growing up there), the informants all understood Japanese with varying degrees of literacy and bilinguality. As for class background, they were found distinctly lower in education and occupation than members of a Buddhist church in Honolulu. Among various reported evidences of salvation, healing was mentioned most frequently. Sixty percent of the informants who had been ill or whose family members had been ill or both, (N = 40) declared that complete healing had taken place due to conversion; 20 percent claimed definite improvement. Post-conversion experience of healing was reported even more frequently in both interviews and weekly congregations. Whether one should accept such information as reliable or reject it as a wishful distortion, or whether conversion did not bring the opposite outcome (aggravation of illness or death) as well, does not affect our analysis. Our interpretation of the sectarian redefinition of the sick role should account for both the reported successful curing and unreported aggravation of illness.

As in many other religions, Tenshō ideology identifies illness as a sign of supernatural potency. Therefore, a brief review of Tenshō concepts of the supernatural is necessary. In my informants' vocabulary a variety of supernatural agents associated with illness were found. The supernatural being may be suprahuman, human, or infrahuman (e.g. dog spirit); it may be emitted from a dead person (a dead spirit) or a living person (a live spirit); and it may be familiar or strange to the person being possessed by it. It may be benevolent, malevolent, or neutral, and thus sickness may be taken as a sign of the disciplinarian intent of a fatherly supernatural, as an attack by a hostile spirit which is jealous or holding a grudge or as a gesture of a dead person's spirit trying to call attention and solicit help from the living person.

The central supernatural figure in Tenshō is the Kami, specifically identified as Tenshō Kōtai Jin (the heaven-illuminating, great-ruling deity), who is claimed to have descended into Sayo Kitamura's abdomen and transformed her from a simple farmer into a third messiah after Buddha and Christ. Tenshō Kōtai Jin has partial identity with the Shinto Sun-Goddess, Amaterasu – a point which cannot be overlooked in understanding the conversion of the people of Japanese ancestry, particularly of *issei* and *kibei*. This supreme Kami causes sickness to give divine tests. However, sickness is usually associated more with lesser spirits, or both the Kami and lesser supernatural agents are believed to be jointly responsible for sickness.

A word about a semi-supernatural agent called *innen*. *Innen* is understood as a Karma chain, fate or bondage that is transmitted from one individual to another through consanguineal links in most cases but not always. *Innen* is the most frequently mentioned symbol to explain sickness, although, here again, *innen* may join the spirit of one or another dead person in causing illness.

Given the above cognitive orientation toward sickness, it follows that the sick role must be redefined. The following analysis focuses upon the evaluative change of the sick role. Evaluation of the sick role refers to judgment of sick-role occupancy in terms of good or bad. It falls into two categories. One is evaluative judgment by a collectively shared and sanctioned standard involving moral principles; the other refers to judgment by the evaluator's own emotional acceptability. The former is objective; the latter, subjective. These two standards of judgment are identified here as legitimacy and desirability.

CHANGE IN LEGITIMACY

In Japan, where the individual is rigidly bound by role obligation as a member of a group, illness appears as a primary opportunity for release from obligation. Excessive legitimacy of the sick role seems to be necessitated to compensate for excessive demands for role conformity in daily life. This is shown by the overtolerance of the Japanese for the public figure who fails to fulfill his public responsibility because of illness as well as by the false pretense of being sick which the Japanese frequently resort to when they want to resign from a job. This tendency may be explained not only by the social function of sickness as suggested here but by the deep layer of personality system. The studies conducted by De Vos (1960) and De Vos and Wagatsuma (1959) delineated the Japanese conception of illness in connection with guilt. Illness is viewed as a sign of moral masochism which characterizes the behavior of Japanese women, particularly of the mother. The mother's illness as the physical expression of her self-sacrifice and self-blame for others' faults, the authors contended, induces guilt in the child, and the latter may also find in his own illness the desired expiation of his guilt. It may be said that the moral tone surrounding illness is so generalized that the sick person feels or appears righteous, and the people around him are compelled to feel guilty. Conversion to Tenshō brought about a radical change in this orientation. Illness, as such, has lost claim to legitimacy. It is not that what was described above as Japanese disappeared completely but that it was channeled in another direction.

In Tenshō, illness is looked upon as a signal of neglect of one's duty; it reflects or arouses guilt and shame in the sick person. This view is internalized in two ways: either through the relation between ego and the identified supernatural that is believed to be causing the sickness, or through the relation between ego and Ōgamisama or fellow members or both.

Conversion reestablishes not only cognitive but also moral relation between the convert and the supernatural. Sickness is caused by a spirit, it is true, but the spirit's activation is partly contingent upon the sick person's action. The Kami, for example, gives more tests to those who neglect the duty to Him than to those who are faithful.[1] The convert suffers from muscular pain because, as Ōgamisama interprets, he is greatly indebted to a deceased kin. As long as the latter's spirit continues to visit him and cause pain, he will feel guilty for not repaying the debt. Even hostile spirits such as *jashin* (a false deity), *inugami* (a dog spirit), and *ikiryō* (a live spirit) are supposed to be activated, at least in part, in response to ego's disposition or behavior. '*Jashin* comes from *janen* (wicked intent) [of the possessed];' 'to be possessed [by a spirit] is just as shameful as to possess [someone].' If a person is attacked by *ikiryō*, he must reflect that he has done something which made the *ikiryō* originator jealous or caused him to hold a grudge. Such retributive significance is clearly associated with *innen* as well; here is involved the idea that a person receives a certain *innen* as a reward or punishment for what he did in his present or previous life.

Moral masochism of the mother and the child's guilt toward her are both effectively mobilized toward denial of the legitimacy of sickness. The convert is reminded to recall his deceased mother who suffered all her life for the sake of her drunken husband and unfilial son. His guilt sometimes reaches the point that he bursts into tears. The only way he can expiate his guilt is to save her spirit which is signified by his own recovery. Righteousness is associated with being healthy.

The convert's moral obligation to the supernatural is effectively supported and controlled by his social relation to Ōgamisama and fellow members. Obligation to the supernatural seems to overlap with obligation as a member of Tenshō sect, as Ōgamisama's disciple, and as a *dōshi* (comrade) to other members. To become sick and unable to attend regular meetings is taken as a consequence of violating the sectarian norms. Among the norms are: renunciation of external religious memberships, symbols, and paraphernalia; minimization of social affiliations; minimization of non-religious solution of problems such as medical treatment; and avoidance of worldly indulgence. These norms are difficult to follow. Particularly, renunciation of religious symbols such as ancestral altars, mortuary tablets, ashes and graveyards, and withdrawal from the family-inherited Buddhist and Shinto affiliation creates utmost conflict and, in some cases, results in family dissolution. Once the convert overcomes this conflict and becomes committed to the sectarian norms, he tends to dramatize his experience and to be intolerant of uncommitted fellow members whose sickness he sees as the Kami's punishment. It is interesting to note, in passing, that Tenshō emphasis upon guilt toward deceased kin and ancestors may be reinforced by the required destruction of their reminders such as tablets and altars.

To what extent sickness is associated with guilt depends upon internalization of sectarian norms. It is proposed here that the driving force for internalization of sectarian norms was provided by the deep sense of indebtedness to the proselytizers (Ōgamisama or members). The benefits ranged from tangible to interactional. Tangible benefits include provision of food, shelter, money, employment, professional services, and customers for traders. One informant was assigned a house by Ōgamisama's order which had belonged to her brother against the expressed wishes of her parents and siblings, not to mention the rule of patrilineal inheritance. Another claimed that Ōgamisama saved him from bankruptcy by giving advice on management of his business. Several informants benefited from the professional services of fellow members such as carpenters, painters, masseurs. By receiving such benefits, an initially uncommitted convert feels increasingly obligated to become a true Tenshō follower. Among other tangible benefits, the provision of marriage partners and children for adoption may be included. Locally, a number of new families emerged through Ōgamisama's matchmaking, in most cases between a local convert and a convert in Japan. The sense of indebtedness for tangible benefits is further strengthened by Ōgamisama's declaration that this religion demands no membership dues. This alleged pecuniary indifference on the part of the prophet seems an exceedingly important factor in generating the obligation of total compliance among the converts.

More important locally than tangible benefits are interactional benefits. The benefit here is derived from the behavioral capacity of the proselytizer, verbal and nonverbal, in public or private scenes, to initiate and maintain interaction. At the most physical level, it includes tactile interaction – patting or pressing parts of the candidate's body where a spirit is supposed to be located, such as shoulder, back, stomach; pulling the candidate by the hand to stand up; in exceptional cases, eating and sleeping with Ōgamisama. It is not coincidental that masseurs have been effective proselytizers, as numerous local cases indicate. At another level, interaction consists of expressive communication. This includes facial movements (Ōgamisama's radiant face, compassionate smile, frightening gaze, frown, tearful eyes), hand movements (pointing at a person, beckoning to him to come forward), head movements (nodding, shaking), and combined movements (bowing with folded palms in a prayer form, showing a smile of welcome for any candidate).

Verbal interaction is through either direct speech or correspondence. The benefactor may play an active role as a speaker or a passive role as an eager sympathetic listener. Most early converts have the treasured memories of what Ōgamisama said to them in their first encounter with her. The meaning of the verbalized content does not necessarily seem to count. Many did not understand Ōgamisama's particular dialect and yet felt as if struck by a thunderbolt. The effect of exposure to vocal stimulation from the whole congregation chanting the meaningless phrase is another example.

Another dimension of interaction may be added. While the interaction described above refers to Ōgamisama's or a member's action directly oriented toward the convert, this involves the introduction of a third party, individual or collective, into the interaction situation. First, a transmitter's role or a go-between role is played by the third person, as when Ōgamisama's favorable comment on a new convert is transmitted to the latter through a leader close to her. As the access to Ōgamisama decreases, reliance upon such a go-between increases in order to maintain interaction. In fact, this form of communication can be even more effective than a direct one in that the third person, with better knowledge of the potential or new convert, can adjust or modify the information to be transmitted. Second, in a public scene where the candidate is introduced to Ōgamisama in front of a large audience, the audience's responses can be utilized effectively to gratify the candidate. Ōgamisama fully used this social resource to flatter, approve, upset, or shame the candidate.

Tangible and interactional benefits presented by Ōgamisama or members, however trivial they may look, tend to have a tremendous impact in obligating a new convert and urging him to do whatever the Kami (that is, Ōgamisama) tells him. The way he comes to feel deeply obligated, for a seemingly negligible benefit, may reflect the degree of deprivation, material and social, which made him inordinately appreciative of the slightest favor offered. The scarcity value of the benefit, in other words, must have been high. This was confirmed by the fact that livelihood had been a serious problem for many converts and by the fact that still more converts had been lonely as a result of family disharmony, especially of marital friction or of family dissolution. Thus, they were hungry for human warmth. The process of becoming obligated may have been accelerated also by the Japanese cultural idiom surrounding the concept of *on*.[2] Simply by labeling whatever is received an *on*, the convert may feel compelled to generalize it into an unpayable debt and to attempt to repay it at any cost.

When these benefits are accompanied, as they often are, by at least temporary relief from illness, the beneficiary becomes convinced that Ōgamisama is his lifesaver or, as informants put it, *inochi-no-onjin*, the *on*-person to whom he owes his life. To repay the *on*, he must become a further committed follower, and to be healthy is a sign of such commitment. As Ōgamisama says, 'If you discipline yourself hard enough, you will enter the world where there is no need of doctors or drugs.' Where there is any degree of ambivalence on the part of the convert, he is more likely to dramatize and publicly announce his experience of salvation, letting the audience know how deeply he is indebted to Ōgamisama for his life. Once committed to this extent, the convert must maintain his state of salvation (being healthy), not only as a moral obligation to the benefactor but to save face vis-à-vis fellow members. Thus, a deeply committed convert shows embarrassment and apologizes to Ōgamisama in his testimony when he falls ill.

As a human being subject to illness, Ōgamisama plays two roles. She takes a typically 'exemplary' leadership role (Weber, 1963) by stressing that she has attained absolute salvation and by telling her followers to emulate her. She says, 'Come up where I am. How good I feel!' At the same time, she lets them know that she constantly suffers from all sorts of illness. It is here that moral masochism is fully displayed. And yet masochism does not lie so much in being sick as in ignoring sickness and working regularly like a healthy person. Ōgamisama takes pride in the fact that she has never had a single day off from the duty of preaching even when she has been seriously ill. This form of masochism is demanded of the members. One of the local pilgrims to the headquarters testified that, while there, she had been scolded by Ōgamisama for using sickness as a reason for not attending the daily disciplinary meeting. She was told that she was indulging herself. Seventy-nine years old, this informant could not get out of bed because of pain and stiffness throughout her body. After learning of Ōgamisama 's scoldings through a go-between, she made up her mind to attend the meeting and even participated in yard work to which all pilgrims were assigned.

It has been shown that the legitimacy of the sick role is denied to Tenshō members and that they are obligated, once ill, to recover as promptly as possible.

CHANGE IN DESIRABILITY

With regard to the Japanese attitude toward illness, Caudill (1962) singled out the characteristically gratifying aspect of the sick role. Specifically, he noted that in Japan sickness provides an important social occasion for the emotionally satisfying communication between the patient and the nursing person from which they are ordinarily inhibited. People in Japan, it was observed, like to go to bed with mild illnesses. Caudill related such expectation of communication through sickness to the Japanese tendency to live out emotions. Institutionalization of *tsukisoi* (subprofessional nurses attached to particular patients on a twenty-four-hour basis), also studied by Caudill (1961), shows that such expectation of the sick role is not confined to home care but extended to the hospital situation. The desirability of the sick role described here is shared by the patient and the nursing person, and thus we can say that the function of sickness is socially integrative as well as ego integrative. If sickness justifies the wish to depend upon and be indulged by the attending person, it also legitimizes the wish to be depended upon and indulged upon by the patient. It may be recalled, in this connection, that many pure love stories widely read in Japan involve a love partner who is sick and sometimes fatally so. The socially integrative function of sickness can be seen not only in the form of reciprocity and communication between the patient and the attendant. Sickness further gratifies the wish for physical gregariousness with a larger group of people since relatives, friends, and other concerned people gravitate toward the patient to do *mimai* (inquiry after a sick person).

The general desirability of the sick role described here is also eliminated through Tenshō conversion. As the illegitimate aspect of the sick role is internalized by Tenshō converts, so is the undesirable expectation of it. Elimination of desirability can be analyzed from two points of view: change in expectation of dependency and gregariousness and vested interest in exemplary well-being.

Through conversion, sickness ceases to be an occasion for gratification of the wish for dependency and solidary gregariousness. Since sickness is believed to be caused supernaturally, recovery is expected to follow the ritual effort (prayer) of the sick person himself. The individuals around him, on the other hand, are supposed to stay away from him lest they should catch and carry with them the spirit causing the illness. This is one reason why Tenshō members are discouraged from attending secular funerals as well as visiting hospitals. Contact with a sick person is to be avoided, particularly by vulnerable members. Coupled with the realization of the supernatural causation, the conceptualization of sickness as illegitimate reduces sympathy for the sick. Such a cold attitude facilitates severing oneself from old secular obligations to sick people outside the sect, thus contributing to the autonomy of the sect. When a member becomes sick, he tends to express discontent with such forced isolation, as some informants indicated. However, this isolation seems only to reinforce the patient's wish to get well, to go back to the regular meeting, and to be approved by fellow members; the temporarily frustrated wish for solidary gathering is gratified through restored health. Ōgamisama strongly disapproves the desire for dependency and indulgence and stresses discipline and self-help even with sick followers, as we have observed before.

Desire to be sick is further inhibited by the fact that the convert has made a social investment in his well-being. First, commitment to sectarian norms involves self-sacrifice on the part of the convert in his secular interest which is likely to amount to an overpayment for whatever debt he owes to the sect. Not only does he cut himself off from secular ties, but he also positively contributes to the sect in money or kind on a voluntary basis. One important means to secure the payoff is to expand the sect and to make its prophecy – final salvation of the Kami's children and damnation of the rest of mankind on the coming day of judgment – come true. The convert has a vested interest in the successful recruitment of new converts. To demonstrate how the proselytizer himself has been saved is a most effective and generally used technique for persuasion. As living evidence of the experienced miracle, he must manage his front, as Goffman (1959) would phrase it, as a revitalized, young, healthy-looking man. His face is more persuasive than words. It is all too understandable that Tenshō emphasizes the importance of the facial look as the window of the soul. Such 'face-work' (Goffman, 1955) is constantly required when potential converts are within one's family. It is also necessary for self-defense when one's conversion has created family conflict, since any symptom of sickness on the part of the convert will give a reason for the family members opposed to Tenshō to attack him.

Social investment in well-being has further implications. Payoff for sacrifice is partly derived from the status obtained by the convert within the members' community. Particularly for those who are frustrated with status aspirations in the outside world, it seems crucial to assume and maintain a leader's status in the local branch. Here again, leadership is mainly exemplary in that the leader himself must look saved. Physical vulnerability will cost him the exalted status as well as his face.

The desirability of the sick role, or rather its undesirability, has been discussed with reference to both emotional pleasurability and calculated interest. We can see how change in desirability and change in legitimacy reinforce each other until the point is reached where the sick role is eliminated. This may account not only for Tenshō members' willingness to get well and to exaggerate healing miracles but also for actual instances of cures. At the same time, elimination of the sick role may be responsible for aggravation of illness, including sudden death, whenever recovery would have required physical and psychological rest more than anything else. Aggravation and death did occur frequently, though they were not reported as such. When death occurs, the survivors explain it this way: the deceased person was completely cured before he died, when he was dying, or after he died. The evidence of such a cure is found in the following situations: Ogamisama's declaration such as, 'Don't worry, your husband has now attained Buddahood in heaven;' the corpse remaining soft and warm long after death occurred; the survivor's hallucination with the vision of the deceased appearing healthy; and the belief that all poisons were squeezed out of the body right before death occurred.

QUALIFICATIONS

The preceding analysis was carried on with the assumption that Tenshō converts in Hawaii have redefined the sick role from a typically Japanese image into a less Japanese image. A close examination of interview materials, however, justifies this assumption only in part.

It is unlikely that Japanese culture, as the point of departure for redefinition of the sick role in legitimacy and desirability, applies to Hawaii's members of Tenshō completely. First, both legitimacy and desirability of the sick role in Japan are structurally supported by the availability of the nursing personnel as well as by economic security within a household. The multi-generational family system, together with solidary ties with collateral kin, will guarantee an attendant to a sick member and transference of economic responsibility in case the major breadwinner gets sick. Such security for emergency may be further provided by the mutual aid network in rural communities. In Hawaii, as far as my informants are concerned, the nuclear family, including single-member households, was predominant and the mutual aid, systems, e.g. association of immigrants from the same provinces, were breaking down. Thus, the sickness of one member tends to be disastrous. The working wife may share economic responsibility but then is not available as a nurse. No wonder that many informants, especially male converts, expressed deep attachment to their mothers from whom they had been long separated and that Ōgamisama struck the responsive cord in their hearts when she reminded them of the unpayable debt to their mothers. No more surprising is the fact that Ōgamisama was identified as 'like my mother or grandmother' or 'someone even more missed.'

Second, probably conditioned by such structural change of the family system and also by social contact with other ethnic groups, Hawaii's Japanese seem to have internalized some of the American compulsion for independence and autonomy. The informants recalled their sickness having caused depression and even suicidal attempts because the physical incapacity and forced dependency were too painful to bear.

It is now necessary to modify our assumption as to legitimacy and desirability of the sick role. Hawaii's members of Tenshō may have internalized the Japanese expectation of the sick role but lacked a structural basis for realizing it, and they may have learned two types of value regarding dependency – Japanese and American. What Tenshō did was to get rid of frustrations arising from the discrepancy between expectation and gratification, and it expelled ambivalence stemming from bicultural learning by demoting the Japanese expectation pattern. With all these qualifications, it is still clear that Tenshō brought about a change in the sick role which encouraged its total elimination.

CONCLUSIONS

With the hope of delineating an explanatory variable for faith healing, I have analyzed redefinition of the sick role triggered by religious conversion. Two aspects of the sick role – legitimacy and desirability – were analyzed with reference to their change through sectarian commitment. It was noted that sickness lost its legitimacy by being identified as a sign of moral deficiency and lost its desirability because of the isolation forced upon the patient and because of the new investment in well-being. A number of problems were implied: the influence of religious commitment, in general, upon sickness; the Japanese background of the conversion phenomena in relation to sickness, because the sect studied was Japanese and its sampled members were of Japanese ancestry; and the variations in Hawaii's members of the sect who were specifically studied. Despite the complexity of issues involved, it may be concluded that redefinition of the sick role, learned through the particular sectarian conversion, amounted to its elimination and that this change may account, in part, for miraculous healing.

REFERENCES

Caudill, W. 1961. Around the clock patient care in Japanese psychiatric hospitals: the role of the *tsukisoi*. *American Sociological Review* 26: 204–14.

—— 1962. Patterns of emotion in modern Japan. In *Japanese culture: its development and characteristics*. R. J. Smith and R. K. Beardsley, eds. Chicago, Aldine.

De Vos, G. 1960. The relation of guilt toward parents to achievement and arranged marriage among the Japanese. *Psychiatry* 23: 287–301.

De Vos, G., and H. Wagatsuma. 1959. Psycho-cultural significance of concern over death and illness among rural Japanese. *International Journal of Social Psychiatry* 5: 5–19.

Goffman, E. 1955. On face-work. *Psychiatry* 18: 213–31.

—— 1959. *The presentation of self in everyday life*. Garden City, Doubleday.

Lebra, T. S. 1967. *An interpretation of religious conversion: A millenial movement among Japanese-Americans in Hawaii*. Ph.D. dissertation. University of Pittsburgh.

—— 1970. Logic of salvation: the case of a Japanese sect in Hawaii. *International Journal of Social Psychiatry* 16: 45–53.

Parsons, T. 1964. Some reflections on the problem of psychosomatic relationships in health and illness. In *Social structure and personality*. London, The Free Press.

Weber, M. 1963. *The sociology of religion*. Boston, Beacon Press.

NOTES

1. This view does not preclude the totally opposite view equally held by the converts that the Kami does not bother to test the hopeless but only tests his true children (Lebra, 1970).
2. *On* refers to a relation between a benefit-giver and a benefit-recipient, implying the former's generosity and the latter's debt.
3. This was partly necessitated by the migration. Many of the parent generation either never came to Hawaii or returned to Japan for good.

First published in *American Anthropologist*, Vol. 74, No. 3, June 1972

5 Reciprocity-Based Moral Sanctions and Messianic Salvation[1]

The twofold theoretical assumption is developed that accumulation of social debt or credit in reciprocal transaction generates moral sanctions; and that guilt and indignation, thus generated, comprise resources which can be mobilized under charismatic intervention to bring about a sense of salvation. Four types of manipulation of these sanctions are identified: reciprocation, reversal, neutralization, and moralization. Empirical illustration is drawn from a study of a messianic sect, of Japanese origin, in Hawaii.

After World War II the defeated and 'liberated' country of Japan became a breeding ground for new religions. Tensho-kotai-jingu-kyo (hereafter Tensho), commonly known as the Dancing Religion, was among the several hundred new sects which came into being at that time. Tensho achieved its unique conspicuousness thanks to its public display of collective, extemporaneous dancing as well as the strong character of its founder, Mrs. Sayo Kitamura. Mrs. Kitamura, a farmer's wife, believed that she was the manifestation of the third messiah after Buddha and Christ in response to a command from the 'Absolute God of Universe.' Later she was called Ogamisama (Great Goddess) by her followers and the Dancing Goddess by outsiders. (For the early stage of Tensho, see May 1954.)

After several years of success in the home country, the sect launched overseas missionary work. In 1952, as a result of Ogamisama's personal proselytization, the first foreign division of Tensho was established in Hawaii. By the time my research was conducted in 1964, the membership numbered about 500 followers (for a comprehensive report, see Lebra 1967). Through observations of local converts in Hawaii it became clear that most of them had experienced, at different stages of conversion, what they termed a 'miracle' in one form or another. Among various evidences of miracles, healing was the one most frequently mentioned. Eighty percent of the informants, who had been ill or whose family members had been ill at the time of conversion, claimed to have been completely cured or had made definite improvement. Furthermore, post-conversion instances of illness followed by 'miraculous' healing – announced in the weekly testimonial meeting of the congregation as well as intimated in interviews – were countless. Diseases and illnesses which were claimed to have been cured varied widely: cancer, tumor, paralysis, asthma, bronchitis, tuberculosis, bladder disorder, stomach ache, skin disease, muscle pain, sinus trouble, tremor, epileptic seizure, mental disorder, etc.

Whether, and in what way, religious faith is responsible for healing is a challenging question yet to be explored. What did come out clearly was that the converts had experienced some sense of relief – sudden or gradual – through or after conversion, which may have triggered the healing itself. Such a sense of relief, when experienced dramatically, was identified as 'salvation,' 'mystery,' or as a sense of levitation. This feeling was most vividly recalled in association with the informant's encounter with the messiah and the latter's utterances in public sermons or through private instructions. Direct personal contact with Ogamisama was made possible by her occasional visits to Hawaii or by the convert's pilgrimage to the sect's headquarters in Japan. Even those who had had no opportunity to see the 'living' Goddess obtained relief, sometimes in a 'mysterious' way, while listening to or reading a passage from her biography, or from one of her circulated pronouncements. Frequent mention was also made of Ogamisama's appearance in the dreams of the informant to give 'dream guidance,' which later proved to mark a turning point in the informant's career. Thus, Ogamisama can be described as a charismatic leader in every sense of the term.

From recollections of the converts it was further learned that, in large measure, these messages from this charismatic leader and the responses by her followers involved moral sanctions.

This paper attempts to offer one way of understanding the 'salvation' experienced through conversion to a messianic sect. The explanatory frame of reference presented here is charismatic leadership in manipulating moral sanctions. The paper consists of two parts: setting forth a theoretical assumption with its conceptual elaboration, and illustrating the assumption with empirical observations.

THE THEORETICAL ASSUMPTION

Reciprocity Model of Moral Sanctions

The theoretical assumption taken in this paper is twofold: that the norm of reciprocity generates moral sanctions; and that the moral sanctions, thus generated, are subject to charismatic intervention to induce a sense of relief.

Moral sanctions are conceived here neither in terms of ethics and theology nor psychoanalysis, but in the sociological scheme of reciprocity governing social relations. Reciprocity refers to the mutual expectation between two parties in transaction, Ego and Alter, that they maintain balance between give and take. The main emphasis is on the socially double contingency of expectations and the equivalence of exchanged values, as implied in 'sociological dualism' (Malinowski 1959) or 'symmetrical contract' (Foster 1961). From the individual actor's point of view, this leads to the formula that Ego renders a service to Alter only if Alter returns the same amount of service. If, conversely, Ego has received the benefit, he will carry it as a burden of debt until it is repaid.

This simple, ideal-typical model of reciprocity is far from being real, as amply demonstrated in our daily experiences as well as in literature.[2] In the first place, the originally symmetrical exchange may be generalized into an asymmetric relationship where one party holds an established privilege and the other party assumes unlimited obligations. Blau (1964), for example, gives an analysis of the process whereby symmetrical reciprocity inevitably comes to generate power. This may be because what is exchanged in reciprocity is not only of economic value but of such social, emotional value as would make it impossible to keep a neat record of debits and credits. Anthropologists, familiar with primitive economy, have stressed the noneconomic, non-material, subtle aspect of exchanged objects (Herskovits 1952; Lévi-Strauss 1957; Firth 1967). This seems to have led Sahlins (1965) to propose a whole 'spectrum' of reciprocities including the 'balanced' and 'generalized' reciprocities as sub-types. Polanyi (Dalton 1968) goes to another extreme by clearly distinguishing reciprocity from economic exchange.

In the second place, initial symmetry itself may be impossible to attain, given the social structure with differential distribution of power and status. 'The norm of reciprocity' for Gouldner (1959, 1960) implies an ideological challenge against the class structure of society where one party can exploit the other party. In his argument against sociological functionalists, he links the concept of reciprocity to the egalitarian ideal subscribing to the fair distribution of rights and duties. Apart from Gouldner's polemical standpoint, there is a more subtle reason to believe that social stratification makes the symmetrical model of reciprocity unworkable. The value of an exchanged object is measured not only in terms of its own price but of the status of its giver relative to its receiver. The same object may be more appreciated when given by a higher-status person than by a lower-status person. Apology as a social price for misbehavior may be more readily accepted when expressed by one's superior than by one's inferior. On the other hand, generosity may be taken for granted as a status attribute of a superior person.

In such a stratified system, one party tends to assume the status of a more or less unilateral creditor and the other that of a permanent debtor. The interesting question here would be: Which of the two, the superior or the inferior, becomes a creditor and which a debtor? If the system is accepted as legitimate, it would be the lower-status person who is considered to owe a more or less generalized debt by virtue of his status inferiority. Insofar as the debtor has internalized the norm of reciprocity, he would feel compelled to carry out his obligations toward a superior, as his 'benefactor,' in order to repay his debt. If, on the other hand, the stratified system is rejected as unfair, it is the superior party who should feel indebted. The lower, under-privileged party will be the creditor who has over-given and under-taken. The latter, to the extent that he has internalized the norm of reciprocity, will feel resentful of the exploiting debtor. Gouldner evidently conceives reciprocity in the light of the latter case. Psychologically, this duality may take the form of ambivalence in which Ego swings back and forth from one extreme position to the other *vis-à-vis* the same Alter.

The third point, interlinked with the second, is that Ego conceives of Alter not as a unique, whole person, but as a member of a social group or a representative of a social category to which he belongs. Alter, thus socially stereotyped, tends to be generalized into a collective whole; while the specific Alter is visualized in the light of general characteristics of the collectivity he represents; his particular behavior, in turn, will be judged as the behavior of the collectivity itself. Generalization of Alter in this sense also makes reciprocity difficult or impossible to maintain.

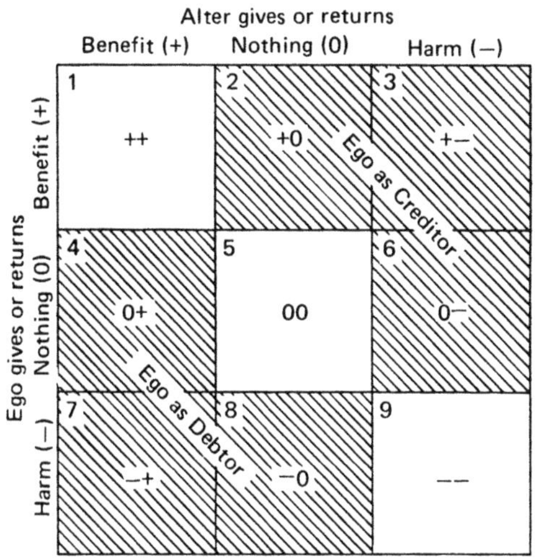

Figure 1. Reciprocity and asymmetry

Emergence of creditors and debtors out of the principle of reciprocity is schematized, as adapted from Wallace (1969: 33), in Figure 1.[3] Two parties in transaction are designated as Ego and Alter. Rows refer to what Ego gives (or returns) to Alter, and columns to what Alter gives (or returns) to Ego. Ego and Alter give and return benefit, nothing, or harm. By benefit I mean not only material gain but anything desirable socially and emotionally, such as love and esteem. Harm, likewise, refers not only to economic loss but to such things as hostility, ridicule, and lack of attention. Cell 1 represents the ideal state of reciprocity where Alter gives a benefit and Ego repays, or vice versa. Cell 9 refers to a hostile or conflict relationship in which Alter inflicts harm upon Ego and Ego retaliates, or vice versa. Both Cell 1 (++) and Cell 9 (– –) conform to the norm of reciprocity, one being 'positive reciprocity' and the other 'negative reciprocity.'[4]

All other cells, except the center, Cell 5, which indicates the absence of transaction, involve more or less asymmetric transactions as symbolized by unbalanced combinations of signs: +0, –0, and +–. In Cell 4 Ego has not repaid the benefit which Alter bestowed upon him; or Alter has done Ego a favor which the latter does not deserve. Cell 8 indicates that Ego has harmed Alter without provocation, or that Alter has shown no vindictiveness in spite of Ego having harmed him. In Cell 7 Ego has repaid his benefactor with harm instead of an act of gratitude, or Alter has benefitted Ego whereas Ego caused trouble for Alter. Exactly the opposite relationships are represented by the three cells at the upper right. With Ego and Alter reversed, exact correspondence obtains between Cell 2 and Cell 4, Cell 3 and Cell 7, and Cell 6 and Cell 8. The two corner cells, 3 and 7, represent the maximal asymmetry where Ego (or Alter) has received harm instead of a repayment for the benefit he granted.

The three cells at the upper right represent Ego as the creditor, whereas the three cells at the opposite end put Ego in the debtor's position.

This article proposes that debits and credits, thus defined, generate moral sanctions, if they have been irreversibly built up, among those actors who have internalized reciprocity as a standard of conduct. The creditor may find himself having suffered or sacrificed unduly or been overly generous. The debtor is likely to blame himself for having hurt someone unjustly or for his inability to repay his debt. Figure 2 is a condensed illustration of four types of moral sanction which are relevant to this article. Sanctions are either Ego-directed or Alter-directed, and either positive sanction (approval) or negative sanction (disapproval). Combining these variations with the creditor-debtor dichotomy, one can derive the eightfold table, including four empty cells. The creditor can afford to give positive sanction for himself, that is, to be self-righteous as in Cell 1, or is in a position to be punitive of Alter with indignation in Cell 7. The debtor, on the other hand, may sanction his benefactor positively with gratitude as in Cell 4, or blame himself for remaining indebted as in Cell 6. The debtor's self-disapproval is characterized as guilt. Note that my conceptualization of guilt is far apart from the long tradition of scientific literature on guilt which, with all its ramifications and lack of consensus, has been basically within a psychoanalytic and/or culture-personality frame of reference (Alexander 1928; Benedict 1946; Leighton and Kluckhohn 1947; Mead 1950; Jenkins 1950; Piers and Singer 1953; Spiro 1961).

The reason for half of the cells being empty is obvious: the creditor has no moral reason to blame himself (Cell 5) or to approve Alter (Cell 3); the debtor is in no position to approve himself (Cell 2) or to blame Alter (Cell 8).

Manipulation of Guilt and Indignation

Moral sanctions as defined above can be mobilized and manipulated as resources for charismatic persuasion. It is argued that not all, but only negative sanctions, are vulnerable to manipulation, since only those under the pressure of negative sanctions, either guilt or indignation, are anxious to change the situation. Guilt and indignation in their extreme forms are analo-

	Ego-directed		Alter-directed	
Ego's Status	Creditor	Debtor	Creditor	Debtor
Positive Sanction	1 (Self-approval) Self-rightousness	2	3	4 (Other-approval) Gratitude
Negative Sanction	5	6 (Self-disapproval) Guilt	7 (Other-disapproval) Indignation	8

Figure 2. Moral sanctions of debtors and creditors

gous to moral 'bankruptcy,' because the guilty person sees no hope of repaying his debt and the indignant person feels he has made a wrong investment which has turned out to be a disaster. The sense of relief induced by charismatic intervention may be said to correspond with salvation from such bankruptcy.

How are guilt and indignation manipulated? On the basis of the reciprocity matrix presented above, I have arrived at four types of manipulation symbolized by a variety of movements from one cell to another, as shown in Figure 3.

(1) Reciprocation: If the person is overburdened with guilt or indignation, that burden can be unloaded by restoring reciprocity, that is, moving his state toward Cell 1, which may be called positive reciprocation, or toward Cell 9, negative reciprocation. Ego unloads his guilt either by exposing himself as a culprit and accepting the disgrace of being punished in public (la) or by repenting and reforming himself into a trustworthy, self-sacrificing person (1b). If indignant, Ego releases that burden either by carrying out punishment of Alter (1c) or by having his investment paid off (1d). The four arrows may be identified as *self-punishment*, *self-reformation*, *retaliation*, and *pay-off*.

(2) Reversal: By reversal I mean promotion of a debtor to a creditor's status (2a), and demotion of a creditor to a debtor's status (2b). This does not mean that the guilty person becomes indignant or vice versa, but change of negative to positive sanction is involved. Through reversal, the debtor becomes a self-righteous creditor, and the creditor is made into a humble, grateful debtor. Indignation is replaced by gratitude, and guilt is transmuted into self-righteousness. The two arrows, then, may be designated as *self-righteousness inducement* and *gratitude inducement*.

(3) Neutralization: Neutralization refers to transference of the creditor or debtor into the central cell where there exist no reciprocal rights or obligations. This involves Ego's realization that, if guilty, he does not in fact owe any debt (3a) or that, if indignant, he has no reason to be angry (3b). Such cancellations of guilt and indignation, analogous to crossing-off of accounts, may be labeled *relaxation* and *resignation* respectively.

(4) Moralization: All these three types of manipulation are to release the accumulated moral tensions. A question may, then,

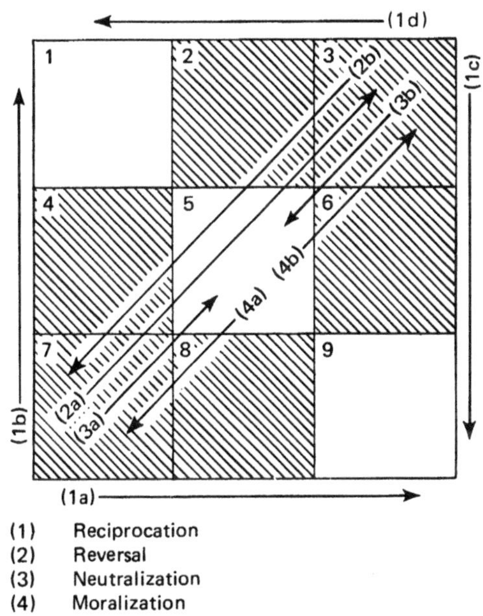

Figure 3. Manipulation of negative moral sanctions

be raised if guilt and indignation may not be released once and for all through one such manipulation or another so that no more moral burden will be left for further manipulation. This simply is not the case. New guilt and indignation can be generated and reproduced through charismatic persuasion, and this process is called moralization. Moralization refers to moves away from the center cell toward the debtor cells (4a) and toward the creditor cells (4b). One move implies inducement of guilt and gratitude whereas the other move points to generating new indignations and self-righteousness. Moralization, in other words, refers to accumulation of debits or credits on a new accountbook as a result of charismatic intervention. The terms *debt-accumulation* and *credit-accumulation* shall be given for the two directions of moralization.

The newly-generated moral burden offers itself as fresh resources for further reciprocation, reversal, or neutralization. Through the mechanism of moralization, the resources for manipulation will never be exhausted; this, in turn, means that an opportunity for undergoing a sense of relief will always be available.

Charismatic Intervention

The irreversibility of the debtor's status or the creditor's status suggests the mutually locked-up situation of a dyad where neither Ego nor Alter is able to restore reciprocity or become disentangled. Ego faces moral bankruptcy in this dyadic stalemate. Change can be introduced in such circumstances through effective intervention by a third party. Ego's accumulated guilt and indignation can be manipulated only at the hand of such a third person who is uninvolved in the dyadic stalemate. Here is the role played by a charismatic persuader. Charismatic persuasion is twofold: conceptual manipulation and social intervention.

(1) Conceptual Manipulation: The charismatic persuader, as an infallible source of information, is able to manipulate and change the listener's belief system simply by offering a new system of information. The listener's moral sanctions are manipulated through replacement by a new message of his old information concerning his debit or credit to certain Alters. Reciprocation, for example, refers to the charismatically-induced conviction that the debt or credit will be (or has been) unmistakably paid off. The listener is 'enlightened' to the 'truth,' and realizes that he has, until now, been blind. The point may be reached where reality and illusion are freely interchanged through the leader's arbitrary utterances.

Credibility of new messages as true, infallible, or of supernatural origin, is crucial here, and this boils down to the credibility of the information-provider as having a privileged access to the supernatural being. This 'social' aspect of information leads us to the second facet of charismatic persuasion.

(2) Social Intervention: Ego-Alter reciprocity, which has reached a stalemate, is intervened 'socially' by the charismatic leader playing a role *vis-à-vis* the dyad. Social intervention by a charismatic leader can be fully understood in view of the significance of the relative status of reciprocal partners in determining the value of exchanged objects. The same gift, material or

non-material, may be by far more deeply appreciated when coming from a God-like person than from an ordinary fellow-man.

It is suggested that charismatic alteration of the dyadic matrix can be achieved through one of three mechanisms: triadization, identification, and exclusion.

Triadization refers to the leader taking a third party's role in correcting and manipulating the reciprocal relationship of Ego and Alter. The leader acts as a judge, arbiter, prosecutor, or instigator. *Identification* refers to the disappearance of boundary between Ego and the persuader (Ego-identification) or between Alter and the persuader (Alter-identification) in Ego's eyes. Under the spell of the mechanism of Ego-identification, Ego shares the extraordinary power with the leader and acts toward Alter as if Ego were the leader. Conversely, Ego may perceive complete overlap, through the mechanism of Alter-identification, between a certain Alter and the leader and act toward the latter as if he, the leader, were the Alter. *Exclusion* involves total replacement of Alter by the leader, which causes Ego to act as if the Alter no longer existed. Reciprocity is built up between Ego and the leader to the exclusion of other Alters.

Social intervention by a charismatic persuader through such mechanisms can be achieved only if he has succeeded in obligating his listener to follow his instructions. Rearrangement of debits and credits between Ego and Alter can be made, in other words, through the persuader's own credit build-up. His persuasion will attain maximal effectiveness when he is regarded as the sole creditor to Ego.

EMPIRICAL ANALYSIS

Background

General background information will be given here of the case study which offers empirical illustrations for the conceptual schemes presented above.

(1) Delineation of 'Egos' and 'Alters': Information was obtained primarily from fifty-five Honolulu members of Tensho, including twenty-eight males, through interviews. The informants ranged in age from thirty to eighty, and consisted of *issei* (first generation immigrant Japanese), *nisei* (second generation Japanese – issei's children born and reared in America), and *kibei* (those Japanese who were born in America, reared in Japan and have returned to America). With varying degrees of literacy, all the informants understood spoken Japanese, while some were bilingual, mixing in pidgin English. Compared with members of the largest Japanese Buddhist church in Honolulu, Tensho members were found to be distinctly lower in educational background and occupational status. A large number of them were menial workers, including janitors, housemaids, and yardmen, or irregular, transient workers. These informants constitute 'Egos.'

Alters for these informants varied widely from specific to general, intimate to remote. At the specific, intimate extreme were members of a conjugal family among whom the husband was most frequently mentioned as a significant Alter. Among members of an extended family, parents – particularly the mother – stood out as the most important Alter; grandparents, siblings, and in-laws were also referred to. Indicative of the informants' family background were frequent references to divorced and remarried parents side by side with stepparents and half siblings. Allusion was made to the informant's (or the husband's) former wife or sweetheart. Many of these specific, intimate Alters had long been inaccessible to the informants by the time of interview because they were either dead or were living in Japan.

Less intimate Alters, beyond the kindred, were found among occupation-linked acquaintances (fellow-workers, employers), friends, neighbors, schoolmates, members of a religious group which they had belonged to previously. Whereas more female informants found significant Alters within the family, more male informants were concerned with those outside it. Alongside these specific Alters, the informants identified more generalized Alters either by class divisions or by ethnic and national boundaries. Members of the elite, dominant classes were conceived as a more or less unified Alter confronting Ego, which partially overlapped with ethnic grouping – especially the Caucasian group – in Hawaii. Nations like Japan and America were contraposed as Alters as much as they were identified with.

(2) Credibility of the Persuader: Ogamisama was believed by my informants to be the third messiah in whose abdomen God was enshrined and spoke through her mouth. Such belief in her supernatural quality was based on several kinds of 'evidence': her telepathic power demonstrated both in prediction and in retrodiction; many instances of miraculous healing credited to her; her extemporaneous sermons delivered with perfect fluency 'unlike those priests who just read sutras,' and so forth. The most important attribute of all, however, was the large following she could attract which included university-educated 'intellectuals' and celebrities. 'How could a grade-school educated country woman convince those guys, unless guided by God?'

Furthermore, charismatic intervention was by no means a unilateral action by the leader. Persuasion was completed, it seems, as a result of cooperative exchange and mutual supplementation of information between Ogamisama and the convert, although the former clearly took the initiative. It turned out that, in addition, she would make the most of the presence of the congregation as witnesses to her speech addressed to a specific convert. Charismatic influence seemed to flow out of the combination of the leader's performance and the overwhelmingly large audience surrounding Ego. The role of fellow-converts in supporting the leader's charisma was further demonstrated when the leader's remarks about a particular follower were transmitted by a fellow-member to the referee: this kind of indirect information sometimes proved to be more persuasive than direct information. Charismatic intervention to be analyzed below includes all this social complex supportive of charisma.

Analysis

(1) Reciprocation: The convert, apparently charged with guilt or indignation, released such moral tensions by restoring reciprocity under the persuasion of Ogamisama.

(la) Self-punishment: The guilty convert felt relieved when he was exposed by Ogamisama and castigated as a debtor in front of the congregation – his debt seemed repaid by accepting the punishment he felt he deserved. He was scolded for being *wagamama* (selfish), *kanshaku-mochi* (bad-tempered), *gojo* (stubborn), or *on-shirazu* (ungrateful). The Alters who had suffered from Ego's undesirable disposition were described, by contrast, as true-hearted, patient, kind, helpful, or selfless. An issei housemaid felt delighted and relieved with a dramatic sense of suddenness when Ogamisama scolded her for her lack of gratitude, 'because I wanted to be scolded and nobody scolded me.' What should have been said was 'nobody worth listening to scolded me.' Her husband was characterized as *otonashii* (meek), which had made her 'the ruler of the house.' Charismatic intervention with the husband-wife dyad was typically through triadization, particularly if both were present. Chances were that the wife was reproached while the husband was praised, unless the latter exhibited an asocial disposition or hostility toward Tensho. Sometimes, a remark by Ogamisama such as 'your husband is a nice man,' was enough to mobilize the wife's guilt and to make her confess and solicit forgiveness.

Many were reminded of their mothers to whom they owed an unrepayable debt.[6] The mother's creditor status in the Ego's eyes was overwhelming in that both the benefit received from her and the suffering caused her by Ego were extremely generalized and incalculable. Generalized benefit was expressed as having 'fondled' (*kawaigatte kureta*) or 'looked after' (*sewa ni natta*) Ego, whereas generalized suffering was indicated as having 'undergone hardship' (*kuro shita*) or 'worried' (*shinpai shita*) about Ego. An issei construction worker was convinced that Ogamisama had seen through his being an unfilial son when she mentioned his 'remarkable' mother. Although his mother had fondled him warmly and wanted to keep him with her, he ran away from home and came to Hawaii without telling her.

The mechanism for social intervention with the mother-child dyad could be described as triadization – the child always being judged as a guilty partner. However, since Ogamisama was a middle-aged woman, Alter-identification seemed a more important mechanism. She did remind the convert of his mother either with her warmth and compassion or with her apparent sacrifice and suffering for her followers. Such identification was made easier not only by her unsophisticated cultural background but by the fact that she had suffered as a mother, wife, and above all as a daughter-in-law,[7] before assuming the role of a messiah. Furthermore, many of the mothers were no longer accessible, and it is likely that local followers were ready to find a surrogate mother in Ogamisama.

Even when Ogamisama addressed herself to a general audience, the convert read into her sermon a severe punishment specially directed at himself. 'I knew Ogamisama meant me,' an issei janitress remarked, 'when she shouted, "you, good-for-nothing Hawaiian."' She then added that she enjoyed being scolded.

Reciprocation through self-punishment was carried out often only at a conceptual level when Ego happened to be sick or in some other sort of trouble. One explanation for an ordeal was that the spirit of someone deceased was causing the trouble. The spirit was associated either with a close kin who needed help from Ego, or with someone who had a reason to hold a grudge against Ego, such as the husband's former wife. Sickness or other suffering for Ego then could be taken as a self-punitive repayment for neglecting a kinsman or hurting someone.

(1b) Self-reformation: The guilty convert, along with self-punishment, was encouraged to expiate his guilt positively by doing a favor or making a sacrifice for those who had been victims of his selfishness. A selfish, domineering wife would become a self-sacrificing, obedient, patient companion; and a hot-tempered alcoholic father would be transformed into a considerate, sober, hard-working head of the house. It seems that the guilt-ridden convert had been willing to reform himself but had no opportunity to do so simply because his old self had been interlocked with the long-established expectations of a certain Alter. Encounter with Ogamisama seemed to provide a rare opportunity for the convert to transform himself overnight without embarrassment *vis-à-vis* those who knew well what he had been like. For instance, Ogamisama's order provided a good 'excuse' for self-transformation without having to admit his debt to his wife.

Becoming a Tensho member was considered as a step toward self-reformation. A kibei housewife stressed that she had joined Tensho not because she was ill or had any trouble but only because she wanted to become 'a good human being.'

Self-reformation of a wife or a husband, naturally, resulted in improved family solidarity, which in turn contributed to the good health of the family members. A nisei wife, scolded for being 'hysterical,' found herself a different person, which was impressive enough to induce her husband and children to join Tensho. Her change entailed the consolidation of the conjugal family (she had visited her mother constantly before), recovery of health for herself and children (they had been seeing a doctor regularly), and money saved with no medical bills to be paid.

(1c) Retaliation: It was revealed that my informants had been more preoccupied with indignation than guilt. Many women were indignant with their husbands, and this was typically the case when a nisei woman was married to an issei or a kibei man. Informants described their husbands as self-important 'as if he were an emperor,' as demanding absolute obedience from the wife, as bragging about their *samurai* ancestry, in a word, as 'typically Japanese males.' Not only was the husband incapable of supporting the family, leaving economic responsibility to the working wife, but he tried to save face through over-generosity toward his peers while ignoring his starving family. Besides, he did not know how to show tenderness or love toward his wife and children.

Less frequently, but equally intense, indignation was expressed against his wife, in-laws, siblings, and parents. A nisei woman had long been caring for her sick mother-in-law, but the latter 'did not show any gratitude, instead held a grudge against me.' A number of informants were resentful of their parents, especially of the father for neglecting the family, for being brutal toward the mother, or for 'abandoning' the children in Hawaii. Indignation was expressed against a stepmother and half-siblings for their unfair treatment of

Ego, and against Ego's own parents who had failed to provide Ego with the normal home which he deserved.

Retaliation was the most common way of releasing indignation. Ogamisama encouraged the convert to rebel especially if the target of this indignation was opposed to Tensho. Frustrated wives openly started to assert themselves against their 'godless' husbands; some left their husbands at Ogamisama's command. In one case the property was reallocated by Ogamisama's decision so that the informant's eldest brother, who had resisted joining Tensho, had to give away his inheritance right to the informant, the fourth daughter of the house. On conversion, another informant stopped sending a monthly allowance to her ungrateful in-laws.

The intervention mechanism here may be said to be triadization, Ogamisama being a prosecutor or instigator. Those wives who had suffered a miserable marital life were also likely to identify themselves with the messiah; and if so, Ego-identification was operating. Through this mechanism, they could share part of Ogamisama's charisma which equipped them with the courage to fight. Those converts who faced the choice between following Ogamisama and obeying their husbands found themselves under compulsive pressures to ignore their husbands 'because God demanded them to do so.' This suggests the operation of exclusion as an intervention mechanism.

Indignation was directed against generalized Alters as well. Those who identified themselves with Japan, had been convinced of Japan's victory in World War II, or had planned to go back to Japan, felt that they had been victims of the world situation. They were indignant with the non-Japanese in Hawaii, who had made fun of 'us Japanese as Jap, Jap.' They were angry with those Japanese, local or in Japan, who had forgotten their Japanese identity and belittled themselves to the level of gaijin, foreigners. Such ethnic resentment was cut across by class consciousness. Strong resentment was expressed against 'big shots,' greedy businessmen, corrupt politicians, arrogant scholars, hypocritical clergy who were exploiting the poor. 'If Ogamisama were a high-class person like the Empress, I could not have believed her.' Many converts did believe her every word precisely because she was a simple farmer's wife.

Indignation against generalized Alters or society itself seemed vindicated when the convert vicariously yelled at 'rotten' people in Hawaii through Ogamisama's aggressive public sermons. Not a few informants became convinced that Tensho was a true religion when they heard Ogamisama declare her intention to exterminate 'maggot-beggars' in Hawaii. 'Because in our business I know so many people who are like maggots,' said the nisei wife of an issei noodle-maker. The castigation of big men of the Establishment soothed a nisei mechanic since this was exactly what he had long wished to say. It was clearly the mechanism of identification, particularly Ego-identification, that was working here.

(1d) Pay off: While expressing vindictiveness against exploiters, converts realized through conversion that one's benevolence or sacrifice would never fail to be rewarded. Conviction of the infallibility of the reward system was brought about partly through sensitization to the slightest beneficial experience as God's special favor or reward. It was the millennial expectation, however, that was mainly responsible for faith in the ultimate pay off for one's past suffering.[8] The sect's millennial prophesy included the promise of salvation for the poor and true-hearted (*magokoromochi*) and damnation for the privileged. The sect's message confirmed the futuristic idea which a leading kibei member, a Japanese language-school teacher, had learned from a fellow internee during the war: that in the new century men of dedication will be rewarded with the *shōichii*, the top rank in the Japanese Imperial Court rank system. Convictions of a fair pay off reinforced the exhortation that one make as much sacrifice as possible at present; the converts were told to keep a savings account at the 'heavenly bank.'

The millennial pay off in the form of status reversal tended to combine with the new interpretation of the war and Japan's status. The last war had been intended by God to punish Japan so that she would rise from the bottom – this time as the true world leader. Another version was that Japan had won in the spiritual war and had lost only materially. Such a view of the war was eagerly accepted by those who had made a material as well as an emotional investment in Japan's victory and found themselves bankrupt. Their investment was, after all, paid off. This faith was concretely verified by Japan's remarkable recovery and re-emergence as a world power.

Another form of positive reciprocation for the indignant Ego was personal consolation through praise or sympathy by Ogamisama for Ego's sacrifice and endurance. The convert would never forget her remarks, such as: 'Oh, you, fellow, over there; you are a sincere person,' 'Woman, you have a nice face [implying a true heart],' 'You have sacrificed yourself too long.' An issei widow, a retired food-stand keeper whose son was a mentally disturbed delinquent, could not hold back her tears when Ogamisama said, 'You have gone through hardship (*kuro-shita*).' The widow's 'ghost-like' face was thereafter transformed into a normal one.

(2) Reversal: Reversal of guilt or indignation was attained primarily through conceptual manipulation.

(2a) Self-righteousness Inducement: Transformation of guilt into self-righteousness takes place when Ego feels his debt has been repaid over and beyond the balance of reciprocity. A nisei taxi driver apparently felt guilty about his mother who had been dead for more than thirty years. He was told by Ogamisama that his chest pains were caused by his mother's spirit which had not as yet been saved. By becoming a member and praying wholeheartedly, he found his pain gone, which was the signal of his mother's final salvation. 'Tears of joy kept pouring,' he said. Besides his mother, he 'saved' his father and brothers who had all been bedridden with tuberculosis. Although the father died, his complete recovery before death was attributed to the son's prayers. 'So I could carry out *oya-kōkō* (filial piety), though I did not spend a penny.' Thanks to the converts' membership in Tensho and the power of their prayers almost all deceased family members had been saved in a similar fashion. This was substantiated by the informant's own relief from illness, a vision of a deceased person who now looked healthy, a sensation of being lifted up or lightened, joined hands being pulled upward while praying, and so on.

Many instances of sickness, mental and physical, were attributed to disturbance by non-Japanese spirits. There was guilt expressed particularly toward native Hawaiians with reference to possession by Hawaiian ghosts. The Hawaiian ghost had kept appearing to a nisei woman because it was angry with her for trespassing on its territory by moving to her present house. It can be inferred from this that some converts had felt guilty for injuring the natives who would have been perfectly happy if left alone. Such guilt was transformed into self-righteousness when the trouble-causing spirits were saved; that is, when the difficulty disappeared as a result of the converts' faith and prayer. The frequency of upward motion of joined hands was a socially visible indicator of how many spirits were being saved by the convert.

(2b) Gratitude Inducement: If one assumed a savior's status, changing a debt into a credit, one tended conversely to reverse indignation (credit) into gratitude (debt). Many informants stressed that the most important teaching of Tensho was 'Change your grudge into gratitude.' A nisei mechanic who had held a grudge against his 'inhuman,' 'barbarous' parents now felt thankful to them since without such parents he would not have learned the meaning of hardship but would have been spoiled as were many of his nisei friends who did not endure such a harsh childhood. A nisei woman was now grateful to God for using her husband to give her *gyo* (disciplinary suffering). Often heard was the remark, 'If you think husband and wife are partners for *gyo*, then you can easily change your grudge into gratitude.' Such reversal was derived from the belief that one must go through one stage after another of *gyo* in order to enter God's kingdom. An easy life was considered as detrimental to faith itself. An informant thanked her deceased husband for his opposition to Tensho and his brutal treatment of her, because 'without such a husband I wouldn't have stuck with this religion so firmly.'

The ease with which reversal of guilt and indignation seemed to take place (and both types of reversal were often experienced by the same individuals) makes us wonder if the informants were not ambivalent in terms of guilt and indignation. Indeed, a number of informants made contradictory statements in evaluating their spouses and others, which clearly indicated a mixture of guilt and indignation toward the same Alter. An issei woman expressed her repentance for having been selfish, domineering, and harsh toward her late husband who, in spite of this, had been quiet, patient, and harmless. In another context, however, she revealed how impossible it had been to save money while her husband was alive because of his stupid generosity and vanity. Another issei woman, whose husband had died, declared that no one's death bothered her because 'people die when they have done something wrong against God's will.' She admitted, at the same time, that she had been relieved when Ogamisama announced that her husband had attained Buddhahood in heaven.

Given such ambivalence, guilt and indignation could be easily manipulated and reversed.

(3) Neutralization: Like reversal, neutralization was carried out conceptually by means of the full usage of a Buddhist term *innen*, roughly meaning Karma relation, fate, or predestination. Tensho teaching provided its followers

with a number of handy explanations for all kinds of experiences, good and bad, including sickness. In most cases it was the activation of one or another type of supernatural entity ranging from the supreme Kami (God) to *akurei* (evil spirits) to fox spirits that accounted for human events. *Innen* was an additional, yet apparently most convincing explanatory concept. Innen was to transmigrate in the manner of inheritance of the household property, most often along the consanguineal line, yet there was no fixed rule of transmission: one might inherit an *innen* not always from one's parent but from collateral kin, or from a remote ancestor who could not be identified. Furthermore it was also possible that *innen* could be passed between employer and employee or even between total strangers. All such arbitrariness contributed to putting *innen* affairs beyond the control of the individual.

(3a) Relaxation: It seems that once the convert realized the efficacy of *innen* in causing problems, he could become relieved from the tension of moral sanction. He would be relaxed from guilt if someone close to him, such as a spouse or a child, was understood to have fallen ill entirely as a result of the sick person's own *innen*. A husband's suicide was explained by Ogamisama as an *innen* which he had inherited from his former employer who also had committed suicide. The informant, the wife, although she expressed vindictiveness in another context by saying that her husband had died because God found his life useless for His purpose, seemed at the same time relaxed from guilt when she realized that she could not have interfered with his *innen*.

To maximize relaxation in this sense, Ogamisama sometimes first made the convert feel guilty about a misfortune and then attributed it to an *innen*. A nisei grandmother was scolded by Ogamisama for her disobedience when a grandchild died. In reply to the informant's letter of deep apology, Ogamisama then declared that the grandchild had been predestined by her *innen* for 3000 years to die so young.

(3b) Resignation: The convert charged with indignation would attain resignation when awakened to the efficacy of *innen* in bringing about fortunes and misfortunes. The incurably-ill convert became resigned, freed from resentment of healthier people around him, with the conviction that no one was responsible for his sickness. A nisei man, mentally ill, with a long past of physical sickness as well, was glad that he now had learned how to 'live with' his misfortune. A kibei man, who had made an irreversible investment in Japanese education, found himself out of place in this American society. In fact, he felt, everything had gone against his wishes all his life. Realizing that all his frustrating life experiences had been predestined for thousands of years, he now attained a feeling of indifference and freedom from regret.

Another concept used for neutralization was *muga* (egolessness). *Muga* meant the Buddhistic desireless state of mind, or renunciation of all kinds of preoccupation. Attainment of *muga* was believed to terminate all troubles, while strong *jiga* (ego) would produce predicament. Both the extra-punitive and intro-punitive states of mind, to the extent that they preoccupy the mind, would be far from *muga*. The teaching of *muga*, thus, seemed to promote cancellation of moral debt and credit. The extemporaneous dance, the publicly-displayed monthly ritual of the congregation, was supposed to lead one into a *muga* state, or to be an expression of that state. Worldly worries involving guilt or indignation would be taken as the evidence that one was still bound by *jiga*.

(4) Moralization:[9] In this last section I shall turn to the processes whereby guilt or indignation was generated and accumulated after conversion and because of conversion.

(4a) Debt Accumulation: First, every convert became deeply indebted to Ogamisama for the benefits she had bestowed on him. Evidence of these benefits were instances of action taken by her, such as: a little advice on business management, a warm mother-like gesture, a telepathic utterance in a public sermon or in a private consultation, praying for the convert's recovery, touching the affliction of a convert, etc. It was contended that these actions saved the lives of the converts. Informants stressed that they would not have been alive unless Ogamisama had saved them.

Not infrequently it turned out that the converts believed that they owed their lives or their health to Ogamisama because she had told them they would have been dead or fatally ill unless they had joined Tensho. Many believed that their *innen* of impending illness or premature death had been halted by the founder. A nisei woman was thankful that Ogamisama had added three years to her life expectancy.

Tensho imposed no membership dues, and this fact was emphasized as unique to this religion. Accustomed to other religions which demanded contributions, Tensho converts felt indebted once exposed to the messiah's 'free' sermon or free personal consultation. When this first exposure was accompanied by relief from illness, however temporary, the convert's debt grew to unrepayable proportions.

The most important way of repaying such a debt was to become a devoted member, conforming to all sectarian norms including the abandonment of old religious symbols such as ancestral tablets and ashes. Rigorous conformity turned out to be too difficult for many converts, and the failure to conform made them bound by guilt. Post-conversion troubles including illness were often accounted for by such a lack of sincerity on the part of the convert. Ogamisama could frighten a guilty and sick person so much by referring in her sermon to 'someone who is still keeping the nest of ghosts' (the household ancestral altar or shrine) that he could not withhold an immediate apology. Ogamisama herself sometimes fell ill and yet continued to preach. Such a self-sacrifice made her followers feel even more guilty; and to make matters worse, her illness was often attributed to the disobedience of her followers. This situation would remind the convert of the common dramatic theme of relationship between a self-sacrificing, benevolent mother and an unfilial, ungrateful child. This point has been alluded to with reference to the mechanism of Alter-identification.

Indebtedness and guilt toward Ogamisama thus internalized, the convert would begin to regard her as the sole Alter to be borne in mind. No matter who happened to do a favor for Ego, it was Ogamisama (or Tensho as a sect) who was credited and thanked for the benefits received. If his employer increased his wages, the convert-employee expressed gratitude to Ogamisama as the benefactor. Conversely, no matter who was actually injured by Ego, it was she who received the apology as if she had been the victim. An informant accidentally kicked his wife while trying on a new pair of pants and realized that Ogamisama was right in telling him of his habit of kicking things. He apologized to 'Ogamisama, not to my wife.' The mechanism of social intervention here was clearly exclusion.

So far I have referred only to the messiah, but the convert also held the sense of debt *vis-à-vis* fellow members as an extension of charisma, although to a much lesser degree, particularly those who had talked him into converting to this religion. The eager proselytizers would offer professional services such as massage and house painting at no cost or at a discount rate to the potential convert who, in turn, became obligated to commit himself.

(4b) Credit Accumulation: Moralization at the opposite pole, namely, creation of indignation or self-righteousness also resulted from conversion. To become a convert involved sacrifice: the convert was supposed to avoid indulgence, not to rely upon medicine too freely, not to accept gifts, and so on. Even though no dues were imposed, there was an unwritten law that members must donate as much money as possible as a token of their sincerity. While some members were compelled to separate from their spouses, others were required to marry, against their personal wishes, whomever Ogamisama was inclined to select as a marriage partner.

Such a sense of sacrifice should be appraised in the light of the moral dilemma that credit-accumulation within the sectarian community entailed debt-accumulation *vis-à-vis* the secular community. To demonstrate his faith and devotion, the convert had already done the worst thing to his dead kin and ancestors by throwing away their memorials such as the altar, tablets, etc. Besides, as a good Tensho member, he had cut himself off from old social obligations and ties. He was in the dilemma of feeling more guilty toward the external world, the more he tried to repay his debt to the sect and its spiritual leader. This dilemma was acutely felt where conversion entailed family tragedy. In my sample, there were four issei couples whose relationship ended with family dissolution mainly because of the wife's conversion. It is true that in all these cases there had been marital friction prior to conversion and that conversion only legitimized open retaliation by one spouse against the other. It is also highly probable, however, that the total result of this retaliation proved to be far beyond the expectations of the retaliating party.

Such irreversible commitment with sacrifice seemed to make the convert self-righteous and punitive whenever he saw some fellow members who were not living up to the standards imposed by Tensho. Internal struggle and mutual criticism were often observed, and I, as an observer, was encouraged by self-righteous converts to interview only a few 'real' members, and strongly forbidden to talk with the others.

Self-righteousness with a sense of superiority was also expressed toward the 'secular' world, since a multitude of spirits alive and dead in the world had been saved by Tensho. An issei janitress claimed that she had had a vision of a Caucasian man for whom she had worked as a maid, and had saved him with prayer. His unsaved spirit had been causing her to have headaches until then.

Tensho members seemed to take credit vicariously for Ogamisama's miraculous performances through the mechanism of Ego-identification. According to my informants, she had saved the spirits of many world-famous people, including Mahatma Gandhi. A former prime minister of Japan was said to owe his successful career to Ogamisama and, through her, to Tensho followers. If such benevolent deeds were not appreciated, but instead aroused hostility, self-righteousness would easily turn into indignation. An issei woman angrily told of her son who, despite the fact that he had recovered from a hopeless case of ulcers thanks to her faith, had long been opposed to this religion through his ignorance of what had really happened. While she claimed that it was she who had held the family together and that she owed that power to Tensho, the rest of her family were hostile to Tensho contending that all the trouble had started on her conversion.

Guilt and indignation, thus generated after conversion, offered revitalized resources for manipulation – for reciprocation, reversal, or neutralization. The point is that what may be called 'messianic salvation' is not something that occurs once and for all in the convert's life but that can be experienced repeatedly in varying degrees of intensity.

CONCLUSION

This paper has attempted to suggest a theoretical clue to understanding the experience of messianic 'salvation.' A link was sought between moral sanctions as resources for charismatic manipulation on the one hand and the internalized norm of reciprocity, on the other, as a basis for generating moral sanctions. It was hypothesized that the irreversibly unbalanced state of reciprocity gives rise to four types of moral sanctions: guilt, gratitude, indignation, and selfrighteousness. Vulnerable to charismatic persuasion are two negative sanctions: guilt as self-disapproval on the part of the debtor, and indignation as other-disapproval on the part of the creditor. Four directions of manipulation of guilt and indignation were identified: reciprocation, reversal, neutralization, and moralization. Through one of the first three, the guilty or indignant person is induced to mobilize and unload his moral burden, which corresponds, in my hypothesis, with the sense of salvation. The last type of manipulation – moralization – refers to the creation of new debits and credits which in turn will be subject to further manipulation, assuring the inexhaustibility of moral sanctions which can be mobilized.

Charismatic persuasion involves social intervention by a charismatic leader with the dyadic relationship between the debtor and creditor which has deteriorated into a stalemate. The mechanism of such social intervention is threefold: triadization, identification, and exclusion.

This general scheme was illustrated empirically with the information obtained from Japanese American members of a Japanese sect in Hawaii commonly known as the Dancing Religion who claimed to have experienced salvation, especially healing. Charismatic leadership was found here in the self-appointed 'messiah,' founder of the sect who has visited Hawaii occasionally and exerted a strong personal influence on her local followers.

Descriptions given were of how the converts' guilt and indignation had been mobilized, rechanneled, released, and revitalized through direct or indirect information exchanges between themselves and the messiah. It was noted that charismatic persuasiveness could reach the maximal point where the persuader, initially a third person intervening with a dyad of Ego and Alter, loomed in Ego's eyes as the sole Alter to the exclusion of all other Alters.

One may well wonder what general significance underlies the behavior of the converts studied here as an audience of a charismatic persuader. It might be argued that the extreme naivété exhibited by them reflects a characteristic of a culturally marginal, deprived immigrant group of non-European ancestry. I contend, however, on the theoretical basis presented above, that their behavior is of a quality which can be more or less generalized. First, since reciprocal rights and obligations tend to be generalized, social actors usually end up as debtors or creditors in various degrees of irreversibility and thus feel morally charged. Second, debits and credits being mutually non-exclusive, Ego is likely to hold both guilt and indignation toward the same Alter. These conditions tend to incapacitate the reciprocal partners to take care of themselves while placing a third person in an advantageous position to manipulate them. What was stated in this paper is expected to give a suggestion on the effectiveness of social persuasion in general, ranging from psychiatric persuasion to ideological brainwash.

REFERENCES

Alexander, F. 1928. Remarks about the Relations of Inferiority Feelings to Guilt Feelings. *International Journal of Psycho-Analysis* 19: 41–49.

Ausubel, D. P. 1955. Relationships Between Shame and Guilt in the Socialization Process. *Psychological Review* 62: 378–390.

Benedict, Ruth 1946. *The Chrysanthemum and the Sword: Patterns of Japanese Culture.* Boston: Houghton Mifflin.

Blau, P. M. 1964. *Exchange and Power in Social Life.* New York: Wiley.

Bohannan, P. 1966. *Social Anthropology.* New York: Holt, Rinehart & Winston.

Dalton, G., Ed. 1968. *Primitive, Archaic and Modern Economics. Essays of Karl Polanyi.* Garden City, New York: Doubleday.

De Vos, G. 1960. The Relation of Guilt Towards Parents to Achievement and Arranged Marriage Among the Japanese. *Psychiatry* 23: 298–301.

Firth, R. 1967. Themes in Economic Anthropology: A General Comment. In *Themes in Economic Anthropology.* R. Firth, Ed. London: Tavistock. pp. 1–28.

Foster, G. 1961. The Dyadic Contract. *American Anthropologist* 63: 1173–1192.

Gouldner, A. W. 1959. Reciprocity and Autonomy in Functional Theory. In *Symposium on Sociological Theory.* L. Gross, Ed. Evanston: Row Peterson. pp. 241–270.

—— 1960. The Norm of Reciprocity: A Preliminary Statement. *American Sociological Review* 25: 161–178.

Herskovits, M. J. 1952. *Economic Anthropology: A Study in Comparative Economics.* New York: Alfred A. Knopf.

Hsu, F. L. K. 1949. Suppression Versus Repression: A Limited Psychological Interpretation of Four Cultures. *Psychiatry* 12: 223–242.

Isenberg, A. 1949. Natural Pride and Natural Shame. *Philosophy and Phenomenological Research* 10: 1–24.
Jenkins, R. L. 1950. Guilt Feelings – Their Function and Dysfunction. In *Feelings and Emotions*: The Mooseheart Symposium in Cooperation with the University of Chicago. M. L. Reymert, Ed. New York: McGraw-Hill.
Kitsuse, I. J. 1962. A Method of Reform in Japanese Prisons. *Orient/West* 7: 11, 17: 22.
Lebra, T. S. 1967. *An Interpretation of Religious Conversion: A Millennial Movement Among Japanese-Americans in Hawaii.* Unpublished Ph.D. thesis, University of Pittsburgh.
—— 1969. Reciprocity and the Asymmetric Principle: An Analytical Reappraisal of the Japanese Concept of *On. Psychologia* 12: 129–138.
—— 1969–70. Logic of Salvation: The Case of a Japanese Sect in Hawaii. *International Journal of Social Psychiatry* 16: 45–53.
—— 1970. Religious Conversion as a Breakthrough in Transculturation: A Japanese Sect in Hawaii. *Journal for the Scientific Study of Religion* 9: 181–196.
—— 1971. The Social Mechanism of Guilt and Shame: The Japanese Case. *Anthropological Quarterly* 44: 241–255.
—— 1972. Religious Conversion and Elimination of the Sick Role. In *Transcultural Research in Mental Health.* W. P. Lebra, Ed. Honolulu: East-West Center Press.
Leighton, D., and C. Kluckhohn 1947. *Children of the People, the Navaho Individual and His Development.* Cambridge: Harvard University Press.
Lévi-Strauss, C. 1957. The Principle of Reciprocity. In *Sociological Theory.* L. A. Coser and B. Rosenberg, Eds. New York: MacMillan. pp. 74–84.
Malinowski, B. 1959. *Crime and Custom in Savage Society.* Paterson, N.J.: Littlefield.
Mauss, M. 1967. *The Gift: Forms and Functions of Exchange in Archaic Societies.* New York: Norton.
May, L. C. 1954. The Dancing Religion: A Japanese Messianic Sect. *Southwestern Journal of Anthropology* 10: 1, 19–137.
Mead, M. 1949. Social Change and Cultural Surrogates. In *Personality in Nature, Society and Culture.* C. Kuckhohn and H. A. Murray, Eds. New York: Alfred Knopf.
—— 1950. Some Anthropological Considerations Concerning Guilt. In *Feelings and Emotions.* M. L. Reymert, Ed. New York: McGraw-Hill.
Piers, G., and M. B. Singer 1953. *Shame and Guilt.* Springfield, Ill.: Charles C. Thomas.
Sahlins, M. D. 1965. On the Sociology of Primitive Exchange. In *The Relevance of Models for Social Anthropology.* M. Banton, Ed. New York: Praeger. pp. 139–236.
Spiro, M. E. 1961. Social Systems, Personality, and Functional Analysis. In *Studying Personality Cross-Culturally.* New York: Harper & Row.
Wallace, W. L., Ed. 1969. *Sociological Theory: An Introduction.* Chicago: Aldine.
Weber, M. 1963. *The Sociology of Religion.* Boston: Beacon Press.

NOTES

1. A shorter version of this paper was presented at the Joint Meeting American Psychiatric Association and the Australian and New Zealand College of Psychiatrists Reconvened in Hawaii, Honolulu, May 1970. Support was provided for writing this paper by NIMH Grant MH, 09243, which is gratefully acknowledged. I also wish to express my thanks to Drs. Burton Burton-Bradley, Robert Edgerton, Richard Jung, and Lew Langness for their comments on an earlier draft.
2. The complex aspect of reciprocity was analyzed by Lebra (1969) with reference to the Japanese concept of *on*.
3. The initial stimulus for this paper was generated by the basic reciprocity matrix developed by Wallace.

4. Note that my usage of 'negative reciprocity' is different from Sahlins (1965).
5. The relationship between reciprocity and guilt was explored by Lebra (1971).
6. For the Japanese guilt toward mother, see De Vos (1960).
7. In traditional, rural Japan the daughter-in-law became a virtual slave in her husband's household and was subject to the whims of her mother-in-law. The mother-in-law even had the option to 'send her back where she came from' if the conduct of her son's wife did not please her. In the case of Ogamisama (who was her husband's sixth 'bride') she was credited with being subjected to unbelievably harsh treatment and yet was successful in finally winning the respect and admiration of her husband's mother, later becoming heir to her mother-in-law's holdings.
8. This is part of the symbolic system of salvation which was dealt with elsewhere (Lebra 1969–70).
9. The data in this section largely overlap with the materials given in another paper (Lebra 1972), although interpreted in a different perspective.

First published in *The International Journal of Social Psychiatry*, Vol. 20, Nos. 3/4,1974

❻ The Interactional Perspective of Suffering and Curing in a Japanese Cult

An analysis is given of the behaviour of participants in a healing-oriented Japanese cult with the main focus on the causality of sufferings and therapeutic measures. As the frame of reference the author singles out the interactional perspective: the holistic view of the interrelationship between the actor and his social environment involving his keen awareness of social interdependence and sensitivity to social demands and approval. This perspective is described in terms of two postulates: (1) The repercussion postulate in which suffering is conceived as a repercussion of the undesirable output of ego's system, and (2) The dependency postulate which assumes the spirit causing the suffering to be totally dependent upon the human sufferer. The interactional perspective thus described is considered as an exaggerated expression of Japanese cultural values with their emphasis upon role sensitisation.

PROBLEM

This is a study of a contemporary Japanese cult which shall be fictively termed the 'Salvation Cult'. According to its publications, this cult was founded in 1929 under the leadership of a businessman-turned-religious-seeker who has been worshipped since by his followers as the most venerable teacher and savior. Under postwar conditions favourable for new religions to flourish, the Salvation Cult not only has survived the death of its founder in 1948, but has expanded itself rapidly into a claimed membership of more than 168,000 as of 1969 (*Shukyo Nenkan* 1970 edition).

The doctrinal ancestry of the cult is traced to En no Ozunu, known as the founder of the *Shugendo* Sect. Shugendo, or 'the way of mastering magico-religious power' (Earhart 1970: ix), is the earliest product of an amalgamation of indigenous mountain worship and imported Buddhism and Taoism. The Salvation Cult, while admitting its Buddhist identity together with its founder's affiliation with a Shugendo-based temple of Shingon Buddhism, stresses the ultimate sameness of all religions, native and alien. This accounts for both its refusal to be identified with any existing religion or sect and its non-discriminatory acceptance of all religions as legitimate. Thus, the cult is apparently non-exclusive; yet its Japan-centred orientation is undeniable. While Buddhas of Indian origin occupy an important place in the cult's pantheon, Kami, the deities of Shinto, which share the same altar, rank as high or even higher. The Shinto-inspired nationalism of the cult may be best illustrated by an annual 'disciplinary pilgrimage' to three 'sacred places' – Ise Shrine (of Amaterasu, the sun-goddess), Kashiwara Shrine (of the first Emperor Jimmu), and Senyu-Ji Temple (of the royal family).

Despite such ideological aspirations, because of the high frequency of reported experiences of illness and curing, the Salvation Cult can be characterised as a healing cult. Taking as a sample twenty-two serial essays on recalled 'experiences' written by members which appeared in the eleven issues (April 1970 to February 1971) of the cult's monthly organ, we found sixteen cases (72.7%) involving physical or mental disorders and disabilities which were allegedly alleviated due to the faith of the believer. My field observation in the summers of 1970 and 1971 also justifies characterising the cult as healing-oriented.

The cult is organised around two centres, administrative and spiritual. The administrative 'headquarters' is located in Tokyo and exercises control over more than 300 local branches (as of 1971), primarily through branch leaders and through 'instructors' regularly dispatched from the centre. The spiritual centre, the 'sanctuary,' is a shrine complex which has emerged at the site of the founder's birth in Saitama Prefecture. This is the most sacred place for members to visit as pilgrims or as spiritual trainees.

Most religious activities among the rank-and-file members take place in local branches where local leaders play crucial roles in face-to-face interaction. While their participation in the cult's activities is collective and thus organisationally regulated, as in periodic ceremonies or 'lecture-meetings,' the local branch is always open to irregular visitors (both registered and prospective members) for personal consultation and religious services.

This paper is based upon observations of two local branches, located in close proximity within a provincial city, each headed by an elderly woman. The membership of the two branches together is tentatively estimated as 200. Information was obtained through interviews with sixteen members including two males, and through observed interaction and communication, both in a ritual setting and in relaxed conversation, between the branch leader and irregular visitors coming for personal consultation and ritual services.

The theoretical frame of reference for analysing the healing cult thus described is 'the interactional perspective' as indicated in the title of this paper. By interactional perspective is meant the holistic view of the interrelationship between the actor and his social environment which involves the actor's keen awareness of social interdependence and sensitivity to social demands and approval. The importance of creating or restoring a desirable social environment, actually or symbolically, in religious therapy has been noted by some researchers. Fox (1960), for example, observed the therapeutic ritual among the Cochiti Pueblo Indians whereby the patient is adopted into matrilineal clans and thus gains new mothers; El-Islam (1967) saw in Arab rituals, such as the Sheikh-visiting and Zaar rituals, the therapeutically significant gratification of the need for submission to a master- or parent-figure. The Hutterite society, as reported by Eaton (1963), seems to place heavy emphasis upon social reintegration in treating mental patients, including encouragement to renew old acquaintances. In Malay spirit mediumship, Firth (1967) found the release of the desired communication, which would have been inhibited in daily interaction, between the patient and those surrounding him. More than two decades ago Gillin (1948) reported how the Guatemalan shamanistic curing involved the assumption of a temporarily created prestigious role by the patient.

Like these researchers, I would like to focus on 'social' therapy, but primarily from the standpoint of the subjects' cognition of suffering and curing in interactional terms. It is contended here that therapy in some cults – the Salvation Cult being among them – involves compulsive sensitisation of the suffering ego to mutual dependency and mutual influence between ego and alter(s) rather than just providing a passive role to be taken by ego. Such interaction, ego is made to realise, accounts for the maintenance, degeneration, or regeneration of the organic or mental states of ego or alter. Alleviation of suffering may result from overt action controlled by such awareness. The following is a brief summary of my interpretation of information obtained under the above-stated conditions.

1. The Repercussion Postulate

One way of making sense out of suffering, as taught by the cult leaders, is to attribute it to ego's own action or disposition which, after release into a social environment, returns to ego. Suffering, then, is conceived as nothing but a repercussion of the undesirable output of ego's system. This interpretation applies especially to those cases where suffering, including illness, is associated with social friction and estrangement such as between husband and wife, parent and child, employer and employee.

This repercussion postulate is derived from viewing social environment as an extremely sensitive receptor of whatever stimulus is emitted from ego, and, in consequence, as responding in exact reciprocity toward ego-rewarding or punitive. Such reciprocal retribution is mentioned often with reference to *urami*, grudge: ego receives *urami*, which may be the 'cause' of illness, in return for the initial *urami* with which ego has hurt alter.

Alter's sensitivity to ego's action is such that alter is often conceived, according to my informants, as a social mirror for ego's image. 'Other people are mirrors reflecting your face,' or 'everybody in the world is your teacher.' Both mean that ego can perceive his own sins and faults by watching others because their behaviour is the faithful reflection of ego's behaviour. (This sounds like an extreme version of Cooley's looking-glass theory. Many Japanese sects, including Seich-no-Ie and Soka-Gakkai, use this logic for indoctrination.) Alter, then, not only 'reciprocates' but 'replicates' ego, as the child replicates the parent.

Repercussion may take place either within a dyad as between husband and wife, or may cover more than a dyad so that ego's initial output circulates extensively – in both secular and supernatural worlds – before it returns. One culturally typical example involves a lineal triad – consisting of three generations – where ego suffers from the unfilial disposition or illness of his child as a repercussion of ego's own unfaithfulness to his parents.

If, unaware of such a repercussion of his own action, ego keeps accusing alter of causing trouble, our informants argue, the situation will cumulatively deteriorate, ending in tragedy for alter as well as for ego. There are two ways of terminating such a harmful repercussion or of reversing it into a favourable one. One way is ego's self-accusation, repentance, and apology to alter and deities for whatever suffering he, ego, is undergoing. The other, though not distinct from the first, is to purify or empty ego's system in such a way that nothing harmful will be emitted. The cult member is thus instructed to eradicate all spiritual pollutions from his system such as greed, grudge, envy, stubbornness, or in a word, *ga*, ego, itself. (Purification is facilitated by a special ritual in which the beginner sits for a long time under the leader's supervision, motionless, silent, eyes closed, hands folded at eye level, holding a charm between his palms.) Given these two measures for alleviating suffering, conversion to the Salvation Cult seems to require acceptance of a sponge-like selfimage which can absorb the enormous input of self-accusation and at the same time can be emptied or dried up in the process of ego-eradication.

2. The Dependency Postulate

The repercussion postulate seems to belong to the cult's doctrine more or less openly addressed to the public audience, and thus is offered to beginners – this is why many new converts are first 'scolded' by the leaders. We are now concerned with the interactional reconceptualisation recommended to those who have completed the earlier part of religious discipline, especially purification. If the first viewpoint is 'exoteric,' this second is 'esoteric.' To put it in a common language, the latter involves spirit possession. As far as the published instructions are concerned, spirit possession is not encouraged but only tolerated as an intermediary step toward ultimate enlightenment to the supernatural world. Local members, however, seem to consider the possession-inducing ritual as the most sacred, most gratifying, and unique aspect of this religion.

In this possession ritual, the leader, playing the role of an inducer of the supernatural into the secular world, invites a spirit to enter into a volunteer member who presents himself as the 'secular body,' the vessel, for the spirit in order to find out why he has been singled out as a victim of such suffering. The spirit's arrival is signaled by the sudden movement of the host's folded hands where a special charm is held.

The spirit, successfully invoked, identifies itself by speaking through the secular body. Observation of this ritual, together with reading some of the locally kept records of the spirits' utterances, has yielded the following information as to interaction between the spirit and its vessel.

The invited spirit is conceived to be dependent upon the vessel for its salvation. The spirit responsive to invitation is, most typically, one of those which are suffering, helpless, and solicitous of the help from living humans. Its predicament is primarily due to the *tsumi* (sin or ritual pollution) commited when it was still in this world such as homicide in warfare (in the case of a samurai), suicide, adultery, abortion, miscarriage, etc. (The reason these are considered *tsumi* is not only because they violate the sanctity of life, but because they involve pollution of the places of occurrence with blood or filth and thus infuriate the deities governing the places or elements. This means that one commits *tsumi* by being killed as well as by killing another.) Three other 'causes' of the spirit's suffering may be mentioned: being abandoned by the living and left *muen*, affinity-less, namely, in total isolation; dying a painful or frustrating death such as when one dies before one's life goal has been achieved, being possessed by another suffering spirit. These conditions are not mutually exclusive but may be all combined in a single spirit.

The suffering spirit tries to signal (*shiraseru*) to the human vessel, to appeal (*uttaeru*) for his sympathy, and to rely (*tayoru*) upon him for bringing relief. Such a dependency-wish on the part of the spirit turns out to have caused illness, injury, or other suffering in the vessel or his family. Sometimes, the spirit depends upon a part of the vessel's body, say, on an eye or a foot, which is evidenced by the vessel's eye disease or foot injury. Here is a remarkable demonstration of a sociologically intriguing case where a helpless, dependent alter, though only a symbolical alter, constrains and deprives ego through his dependency inasmuch as an infant controls its mother by means of its helplessness.

The spirit makes some discrimination in choosing a target of possession. Generally, it is said that only those who have special innen, an affinity or bond in the Buddhist sense, with the spirit are possessed. This accounts for the highest frequency of possession by ancestral spirits since the consanguineal link is considered to carry the strongest *innen*. Of sixty-five locally recorded possession cases, forty-seven (72%) turned out to be by the vessels' patrilineal ancestors or recently departed bilateral kinsmen. More specifically, the spirit seems to show preference for two types of humans as a target of possession: a person who shares the same attributes with the spirit as when the muen spirit possesses a lonely person; and a person who is helpful and religiously advanced as are many good members of the Salvation Cult. There are indications that a spirit tests one person after another until it finds the ideal person who is receptive to the spirit's signal and is prepared to devote himself to its salvation.

The spirit attains salvation by finding the proper place where it should belong and by setting down there once and for all. The places for belonging may be heaven, the house altar of the possessed person, the altar of the cult local branch, or as in most cases, the place where the ancestors of a family congregate. A suffering ancestral spirit seems most anxious to enjoy togetherness by joining the ancestral group (*senzo no nakama-iri*).

Such salvation of the spirit is attained by two kinds of help solicited from humans. One is kuyo, propitiatory religious service or mass presented to the frustrated spirit. This takes several forms: chanting sutras; offering the food – sometimes the spirit specifies what it wants to eat and where the offering should be placed; having a *kuyō-fuda* (a rectangular wooden board with the spirit's name on it) made to be placed and prayed to at the householud altar; *amacha-kuyō*, that is, pouring *amacha* (hydrangea tea associated with Buddhist folklore) repeatedly over the *kuyō-fuda* or any other spot where the spirit is believed to descend. (*Amacha* supposedly has a purifying effect and is drunk by members 'medicinally' so that either they or the possessing spirits or both get purified.)

The second kind of solicited help is *owabi*, apology, to be offered by the human helper on behalf of the sinful spirit to the deity who is punishing the spirit for its pre-mortem misconduct. While *kuyō* involves a dyad – the spirit to be propitiated and the human propitiator – and is oriented to direct indulgence of the spirit's wishes, *owabi* involves a triad – the sinful and suffering spirit, the human helper, and the punitive deity – where the human takes the vicarious role of being sinful. The spirit requests or commands – depending upon a relative status taken by the spirit – its host to make repeated visits to a shrine to present a sincere apology to the deity residing therein. Usually the spirit prescribes which shrine has to be visited for how many days consecutively (most often either multiples of seven or ten), and what must be taken as an offering. Most frequently visited are *ujigami*, shrines of tutelary deities belonging to respective wards of the city, which are the local basis of national Shinto. If the spirit's *tsumi* happens to be the pollution of water, apology is likely to be offered to a special water-protecting deity. *Owabi* is expressed in front of the shrine with words like: 'I apologize from the botton of my heart on behalf of (literally, 'as a substitute for') my ten-generation-old ancestor so-and-so for his *tsumi* in lacking respectfulness, faithfulness, and virtuousness. Please forgive me.' To reinforce the purpose of such a visit, the vicarious apologiser always carries with him a *wabijō*, a piece of paper with a brush-written statement of apology. Sincerity of repentance is often demonstrated by going through the monotonous action called *ohyakudo*, walking back and forth along the stone steps leading to the shrine a hundred times. (It is easy to see that physical exercise alone may contribute to good health.) Sometimes the spirit accompanies its vessel in a shrine-visit; and being helpless, allows all initiative to be taken by the latter. (The spirit's dependency is so complete that, even when *kuyō* is accepted, gratitude is expressed by the *kuyo*-giver on behalf of the spirit, the receiver.)

The two ways of saving the suffering spirit and thus of alleviating ego's illness – *kuyō* and *owabi* – remind us of the idealised role of the Japanese mother. The mother is expected to indulge the child's wishes and to be punished for all errors committed by the child through sacrificial role vicariism. Not only indulgence and role substitution but what was said with regard to repercussion also overlaps with the Japanese mother image. Can we speculate, then, that the Salvation Cult is among those religions which finds the main road to salvation in conceptually assuming a mother's role? One recorded case does indicate that the spirit of a young girl has appeared and begged its female vessel to become her mother.

As much as the mother is later rewarded by her grown-up filial child, the human helper can look forward to the day when the spirit, now saved, begins to repay him for his sacrifice. In the possession-inducing ritual after the prescribed *kuyō* and *owabi* are completed, the spirit expresses its indebtedness and gratitude to its vessel and promises to do its best, from now on, to improve his or his family's health, economic status, and so forth. It promises to 'repay for the *on* (benevolence) received.' Some spirits elevate themselves to *Kami* status and become guardian deities for their vessels.

Such final repayment makes 'symbolic interdependence' between ego and the supernatural alter complete.

CONCLUSION

Reconceptualisation of suffering and curing in a healing-oriented Japanese cult has been discussed from two points of view: repercussion and dependency. It seems that the repercussion postulate reorients ego towards his inner-self as the 'cause' of suffering while the dependency postulate arouses in ego a nurturance and empathetic role vicariism for a symbolic alter. These two are by no means mutually exclusive, but may be interlinked. The dependency of a supernatural alter provides an external reason for ego's suffering, which makes ego an innocent victim. Ego is to blame, however, in two senses: first, the continuation of suffering may be considered as the evidence of ego lacking sincerity in doing *kuyo* and *owabi* for the alter; secondly, as indicated before, a spirit prefers to possess a person who is similar to itself in some respects, which implies that an undesirable supernatural guest tends to visit a similarly undesirable human host, as when a spirit and its vessel share an offensively egocentric personality. Such interlinkage between dependency and repercussion seems to preclude the idea of the prime mover and to emphasize a continuous interchange within a whole socio-ecological system.

The interactional perspective as described in this paper is an exaggerated expression of dominant value orientations of Japanese culture with their emphasis upon social sensitisation (Lebra 1971). Japanese culture puts a high premium on the ability to play an expected role in a given social system rather than to be an independent actor; susceptibility to the wish of the other rather than one's own wish, coupled with the capacity for role substitution, comprises a major ingredient of this culture. The Salvation Cult, then, may be considered as one of those cults which mobilise and intensify underlying cultural values for therapeutic purposes.

REFERENCES

Earhart H. Byron, 1970. *A Religious Study of the Mount Haguro Sect of Shugendo.* Tokyo: Sophie University.

Eaton, Joseph, W., 1963. Folk Psychiatry. *New Society*, 48 (August): 9–11.

El-Islam. M. F., 1967. The Psychotherapeutic Basis of some Arab Rituals. *International Journal of Social Psychiatry*, 13: 265–268.

Firth. Raymond. 1967. Ritual and Drama in Malay Spirit Mednunahip. *Comparative Studies in Society and History*, 9: 190–207.

Fox, J. R., 1960. Therapeutic Rituals and Social Structure in Cochiti Pueblo. *Human Relations*, 13: 291–304.

Gillin, John, 1948. Magical Fright. *Psychiatry*, 11: 387–400.

Lebra Takie S., 1971. The Social Mechanism of Guilt and Shame: The Japanes Case. *Anthropological Quarterly*, 44: 241–255.

Messing. Simon D. 1958: Group Therapy and Social Status in the Zar Cult of Ethiopia. *American Anthropologist*, 60: 1120–1125.
Shūkyō Nenkan (Yearbook of Religion) 1970: Complied by Bunkachō, Japan.

NOTES

This was originally presented at the 30th annual meeting of the Society for Applied Anthropology, April 14–18, 1971, Miami Florida. I wish to acknowledge the assistance of the Social Science Research Initiute (NIMH Grant MH-09243). University of Hawaii, for this research.

First published in William P. Lebra (ed.), *Culture-Bound Syndromes, Ethnopsychiatry, and Alternative Therapies*, Honolulu: University of Hawaii Press, 1976

7 Taking the Role of Supernatural 'Other': Spirit Possession in a Japanese Healing Cult

THEORETICAL CONSIDERATIONS REGARDING SPIRIT POSSESSION

It is not uncommon to interpret the phenomenon of spirit possession not only in light of pathology but also in terms of sociological implications. Kiev (1961) noted that spirit possession among voodoo devotees in Haiti 'provides legitimized public roles for private repressed impulses and needs.' This view was seconded by Bourguignon (1965), who saw in this 'temporary substitution of other 'selves' the opportunity for acting out certain positively evaluated social roles.' *Saka* attacks, as observed by Harris in a Kenya tribe, allow women to demonstrate and execute their 'rights' vis-à-vis their husbands – 'the rights of dependents' (1957). The sociological implication of possession is evident from the use of such terms as 'legitimized,' 'roles,' and 'rights.'

Insofar as possession is viewed in terms of the supernatural 'role' taken by the possessed, we must recognize that the possessed has some degree of self-awareness of 'playing' that role. Without such awareness one would be incapable of assuming a role. This suggests the theory of self developed by G.H. Mead (1967) that the individual is not a self unless he is an object to himself. Such a reflexive self develops through one's taking the role of other individuals and responding to it. The role of other persons, thus vicariously assumed, becomes internalized and constitutes 'me' as distinct from 'I,' the subjective side of self. 'I' and 'me' together make up the whole self.

Mead's concept of self fits the phenomenon of spirit possession remarkably well. Indeed, Yap used it for his interpretation of the possession syndrome. He attributed possession to 'a disturbance in the balance of what Mead calls the 'I' and the 'me;' to 'the unusual predominance, temporarily, of one phase of the Self at the expense of the other; of a certain portion of the 'Me' at the expense of the 'I' (1960).

I shall take Yap's position as my point of departure. While Yap stressed the pathological imbalance of 'I' and 'me' in possession, I would like to delineate the sociological implication, as set forth in the first paragraph. Yap may be right in emphasizing the pathological aspect of possession, first because the role taken in possession is not that of social others, as Mead would expect, but that of the supernatural, and secondly because the 'me' (the role of the supernatural other) is externally acted out instead of being internalized as should be in Mead's self. However, we can look at the same phenomenon from the standpoint of the variety of roles that can be taken voluntarily by the possessed. We can further assume that taking the role of a supernatural other enables one to overcome, however temporarily, the role deprivation being suffered in the social world, which may trigger a change in the behavior system, including that of curing.

A role that is part of a social system can be taken and played only if other roles in the same system are complementarily played. The 'central role' to be played by Ego must be complemented by a 'counter-role' played by Alter. This requirement of 'complementarity' (Bateson, 1935, 1971; Watzlawick et al., 1967) is no less compelling in the assumption of a supernatural role, no matter how arbitrary that role may appear. The complementary role may be played by Ego himself or by other persons. The satisfactory performance of a supernatural role by the possessed requires Ego or other persons to accept the complementary role willingly. This means that the complementary role should be as desirable as the supernatural role. This is a major constraint on the repertoire of supernatural roles, and it precludes the randomness of possession behavior. In actuality, however, there seems to be no special problem since internalization of a role through socialization entails internalization of its complementary role; to learn how to play a dominant role, for instance, one must simultaneously learn how to play a submissive role.

I shall apply these assumptions to the possession behavior observed in a healing-oriented Japanese cult. The sociological interpretation of possession in the sense above, seems particularly relevant to the Japanese subject because Japanese culture sensitizes the individual to role gratification and role frustration as the primary source of his pleasure and pain. My objective in this paper is twofold: generally to validate the theoretical assumptions advanced above, and particularly to show how the selection of role types in 'Japanese' possession is culturally biased.

THE CULT, FIELD, AND DATA

The 'Salvation Cult' was established in 1929 and has continued to flourish since its founder's death in 1948, under the postwar freedom of religion in Japan. The membership of the cult as of 1969 is claimed to have reached more than 168,000 (Bunkachō, 1970). Doctrinally, the Salvation Cult traces its ancestry to Shugendō, the mystic mountain sect, which was the earliest attempt to amalgamate the indigenous Shinto with imported Buddhism and Taoism. This syncretism is at the heart of the Salvation Cult, which reveres all deities and spirits without discrimination, although it recognizes some loose, partial rank orders among them. The Shinto pantheon consisting of *kami* ('gods') is worshipped side by side with Buddhas of Hindu origin, and supernatural status is conferred on the ancestors and the departed as well. While 'qualified' members study abstract doctrines that were developed by the founder and his successors and that typically involve interpretations of Chinese characters, the rank and file are led to believe in the ubiquity of supernatural beings, including animal spirits.

The difference between leading members and rank and file is not limited to beliefs; the difference is also apparent in places for action. Important members operate primarily in the two centers of the cult. One is the 'spiritual' center, a shrine complex, which is the most sacred place for members to visit as pilgrims or as religious trainees; the other is the cult's 'headquarters' which administratively controls the whole organization. These centers not only take leadership in religious teaching but run 'health schools,' treating sick members 'medically' and prescribing 'natural foods,' which can be purchased at the cult's store. Ordinary members engage in cult activities most regularly in local branches controlled by local leaders. There were over 300 local branches as of 1971.

Fieldwork was conducted during the summers of 1970 and 1971, covering, intensively, two ward branches in a provincial city – let it be called Eastern City – and, more superficially, three other branches, located in central Japan. Activities at the two cult centers were also observed. This paper is based on information collected primarily in Eastern City.

The two ward branches together comprise roughly 200 members, although the number of regularly active members is much smaller. Each branch is headed by a woman in her seventies, one a widow, the other a divorcée. While in formal membership the sex ratio is about 2 to 1 in favor of female members, active members are overwhelmingly female, the ratio being approximately 5 to 1. (This gap between the formal and active membership owes partly to the Japanese inclination to register in the name of the head of the household.) In age the members were concentrated in the forties through the sixties.

Cult activites in local branches vary from regular, collective services to more private, informal ones. Collectively, periodic ceremonies are conducted at the branch leader's residence, involving a long, standardized ritual in front of an altar and a lecture by a teacher sent from the headquarters. Group visits to local shrines, cemeteries, and other supernaturally affected places are also regular activities. The branch is also always open to casual visitors (both registered and prospective members) for personal consultation and informal religious services. It is during such casual visits that interaction between a member and the leader is maximally intensified.

The information on which this analysis is based was obtained, first, from interviews with two male and fourteen female members conducted mostly in their homes, and secondly from direct observations of rituals and personal religious services at the branches. The latter were always followed by relaxed conversation and sharing of the food retrieved from the altar. These post-service social gatherings, immensely enjoyed by the participants, also provided valuable information. The sixteen informants ranged in age from thirty-eight to seventy-eight, a few of them having been members for more than thirty years. The following tabulation is a rough indicator of the socioeconomic status of the informants.

Occupation	*Number of Informants*
Storekeeper	5
Restaurant-entertainment business	3
Schoolteacher	2
Entertainer	1
Office worker	1
Candymaker	1
Hairdresser	1
Hotel maid	1
Fisherwoman	1
Total	**16**

In this list there are no special characteristics that would distinguish this group from other residents of Eastern City. Entertainer and hotel maid are not unusual occupations, since the city is a resort.

SITUATIONS AND BEHAVIOR PATTERNS OF POSSESSION

Possession takes place in different situations. The most 'sacred' possession is associated with a particular ritual, called 'Five Laws,' that is deliberately performed to induce supernatural visitation. The leader takes the role of *chūkaisha* ('mediator') between the visiting spirit and the human host. The host, presented as *bontai* ('temporal body') for the spirit to enter, is a member who is suffering from illness, family friction, or the like and who seeks a supernatural message that will explain this suffering. Note that the mediator and the host of the spirit are different persons, and that the receiver of the supernatural message is the same as the giver of the message. The *chūkaisha* and *bontai* sit side by side in front of the altar and go through a spirit-inviting ritual, invoking the names of deities and Buddhas and repeatedly bowing toward the altar. The spirit's arrival is signaled by the sudden rapid movement of the *bontai*'s folded hands, in which a special charm is held. Unless unusually resistant, the spirit identifies itself and conveys its message through the *bontai*'s mouth or hands (tracing letters on the floor) in response to requests and questions by the *chūkaisha*. The spirit is identified at least by sex and, if an ancestral spirit, by the number of generations it is separated from its descendant, the *bontai*. Beginners are said to be poor hosts 'because their souls are still polluted'; sometimes they are only able to cry or shake. It takes six months, I was told, for a convert to become qualified. During this time the convert is supposed to work at self-purification by means of a meditation ritual called 'Secret Law.' However, there are devices by which almost anyone can generate some information about the spirit and thus perform a supernatural role. The commonly observed resistance to verbalization is overcome by the ritually directed sign communication: the *bontai* indicates the sex of the spirit, for instance, by pointing to the left or right side of his own body; he indicates the number of ancestral generations by hitting his knee a certain number of times. Whenever the question-and-answer communication becomes deadlocked, the *chūkaisha* gives a binary choice of a yes or no answer. She will ask, 'Are you an ancestor? If you are an ancestor, please stretch your hands straight forward. Otherwise, raise your hands over your head.' After giving its message, the spirit is thanked and asked to return to where it belongs. The spirit that refuses to leave the *bontai* invites reproach from the *chūkaisha*. The whole possession performance is observed by any other members who happen to be present, unless the *bontai* demands privacy. I observed five instances of this possession ritual, one of which was performed especially for my benefit. In addition, one of the branches kept a written record of the possession ritual for a time, including sixty-five cases, which I was permitted to read.

While members consider such ritualized possession which tends to be a dramaturgical performance, the most important and legitimate form, a more spontaneous, unstructured possession also takes place. Some informants have experienced 'unexpected' possession during the purifying meditation or while chanting a sutra in front of the altar, praying at a local shrine, and the like. Some claimed that spirits had taken control of them while they were sleeping or talking to a neighbor. Spontaneous possession usually does not manifest itself vocally but through gestural simulation of the possessing spirit. If the spirit was a fox, the possessed might jump around like a fox. The snake spirit might be simulated by crawling and wriggling. Walking with a limp would show possession by the spirit of a person who was lame. These experiences were not observed directly but were described in interviews or at branch gatherings.

SUPERNATURAL ROLES

The supernatural visitors relate to the human host, the *bontai*, in a number of ways. Both my observations and the branch's record of possession rituals indicate that the visitor is most likely to be an ancestor or departed kin with a strong bias for patrilineality in the case of remote ancestors. Not only ascending generations but descending generations are recognized as supernatural: a living mother may be visited by her dead child or miscarried fetus.

If the spirit is of human origin but is not Ego's kin, it is likely to be the spirit of a person who committed suicide, was killed in warfare, or whose death was otherwise disastrous, in the place where Ego currently resides. A number of informants identified their residential lots as former battlefields where thousands of samurai were buried and whose spirits were disturbing the welfare of the current residents. These are called land-related spirits.

Different from these is the animal spirit. The spirit of a fox, for example, is recognized either as the deity who was worshipped by Ego's ancestors over many generations as the house protector, or as Ego's own guardian deity.

The other spirits mentioned are more or less miscellaneous, but I am tempted to group some of them into another class called sex-related spirits. Examples are the spirits of Ego's former fiancée, of a divorced husband, or of the raped maidservant of Ego's ancestor.

Now let us look at the supernatural roles that the *bontai* takes in possession through identification with one of these spirits.

The supplicant role. In an overwhelming number of possession cases the spirit is dependent and supplicant. The spirit which is most responsive to the ritual invitation turns out to be a sufferer from pain, floating around helplessly, and solicitous of human help for its salvation. The *bontai* discovers that it was this spirit that was causing trouble, most typically sickness, to himself or his family; that the spirit did so only to remind the *bontai* of its suffering and to appeal for sympathy.

The suffering of the spirit usually owes to some *tsumi* ('sin' or 'pollution') committed when it was alive in the world. Most often mentioned are *tsumi* of suicide, homicide, adultery, rape, abortion, and miscarriage. These are all considered *tsumi* because a moral standard was violated or because the sanctity of life was breached. They are *tsumi* also because they involve pollution with blood at the site where the action took place. Being killed or dying in a natural disaster is as sinful, in the polluting sense, as killing. Commission of such *tsumi* infuriates the deity governing or residing in that particular location, and the deity punishes the spirit by preventing its salvation. My informants frequently referred to 'strange deaths' (*henshi*) by hanging or drowning.

The suffering of the spirit is compounded by its isolation from other spirits; thus, most suffering spirits soliciting human help are also identified as *muen* ('lonely, affinity-less') spirits. A spirit is *muen* not only because of its *tsumi* but because it has been neglected or abandoned by human survivors. For this reason, too, the *muen* spirit must notify an appropriate living person of its loneliness by causing trouble. Salvation for the *muen* spirit means finding its proper place by joining a group of its own kind: an ancestral *muen* spirit is anxious to join its own group of ancestors; a *muen* fox spirit should have a shrine specially built for it or be placed in an existing shrine dedicated to the fox spirit.

The supplicant role of the suffering spirit must be complemented by a nurturant, indulgent role. The latter role is expected to be performed by the *bontai* after the possession. It is believed that the spirit is not indiscriminate in choosing the target of its possession. The spirit prefers a person who will be responsive, helpful, dependable, and experienced enough to solve its problem. Informants generally believe that blood ties are the strongest attraction for the spirit, and one male informant stressed that the spirit chooses its descendant in the direct line. The *bontai* promises to do his best to relieve the spirits suffering, to gratify and please the spirit.

The relationship between the supplicant spirit and the nurturant human is acted out in two ritual forms. One is *kuyō*, a propitiatory service offered to the spirit. An ancestral spirit, for instance, would ask the *bontai*, through the latter's mouth, to indulge it with *kuyō*. The *kuyō* takes several forms: the repeated incantation of sutras and prayers in front of a tablet that has the spirit's name on it; the repeated pouring of hydrangea tea, believed to be sacred and purifying, over the tablet or any other spot where the spirit resides; and the offering of food and drink that the spirit likes. The last form accentuates the maternal, nurturant role of the human feeder for the hungry, infantlike spirit. Indeed, the spirit quite often is a *muen* infant who solicits maternal help from the *bontai*, for example, by causing pain in the breast. Milk and baby food are then considered the most appropriate *kuyō* offering.

Sometimes the spirit, in response to the *chūkaisha*'s question, specifies what it wants to eat and where the food should be placed.

The other form of the nurturant role performed by the bontai for the sake of the spirit is *owabi* ('apology') made to redeem the spirit's *tsumi*. The *bontai* is asked by the spirit to present *owabi* on its behalf, since the spirit is incapable of doing so, in front of the shrine of the deity against whom the *tsumi* was committed. The spirit tells which shrine is to be visited, how many visits must be made (sometimes every day for thirty days), the kind of offering that should be taken, and so on. Usually *owabi* is presented at a local Shinto shrine, but if the *tsumi* had to do with water pollution, for example, the *bontai* will have to visit the shrine of a water deity. A standard statement of apology is given 'on behalf of such-and-such spirit.' Many informants told me that they had to go to shrines to present *owabi* before dawn every morning even in winter. Presentation of *owabi* includes a ritual endurance walk back and forth a hundred times in front of the shrine. This is supposedly to prove the sincerity of the one making the apology.

Owabi thus involves a substantial sacrifice made by the human helper for the sake of the sinful spirit. Informants agreed that without the completion of *owabi* the spirit is not permitted to receive *kuyō* and that *owabi* must precede everything else to save the spirit. Nurturance in the performance of *owabi* may involve role substitution: the human helper apologizes to the deity as a substitute for the sinful spirit. We are again reminded of a motherly role of the human complementary to an infantlike role of the spirit. Indeed, in one recorded case, the spirit of a suffering girl begged its young female *bontai* to search for her missing mother and, if the mother could not be found, for the *bontai* herself to become a surrogate mother.

The two mutually complementary roles, supplicant and nurturant, are taken sequentially by Ego – the succorant role during possession, and the nurturant role after possession. During possession, the nurturant role is being played by the *chūkaisha*, leader-mediator, in communicating with the spirit. The *chūkaisha*'s role thus involves temporary substitution for the *bontai*, who is busy playing the supernatural role. It is the *chūkaisha* who asks the spirit what it wants and promises to carry out *kuyō* and *owabi* so that the spirit will be perfectly satisfied; the spirit demands rice cake, miso-soup, and so forth, as if from the *chūkaisha*. Being fully aware of this role substitution, the spirit sometimes openly addresses itself to the *chūkaisha*, asking her to do something for it. In one of the ward branches the *chūkaisha*, the branch leader, is a grandmotherly woman whom the members indeed call Grandma as well as Teacher and Branch Head. She takes a nurturant, indulgent role vis-à-vis a member during possession. Even after possession, she helps the member offer *kuyō* and *owabi*, often accompanying the member to a shrine.

Whether the complementary role is performed by the *bontai* or the *chūkaisha*, it is evident that both the nurturant and supplicant roles are well cathected by my informants.

The reciprocal role. While the supernatural role is predominantly of the supplicant type, other role types are seen.

When the suffering of the spirit has been relieved through *kuyō* and *owabi* offered by the human helper, the spirit is obligated to return the favor. The spirit that appears in possession after the *bontai* has performed such services typically expresses gratitude and promises to repay the debt. Let this be called the reciprocal role. If the *bontai* is ill, a cure is promised; a bankrupt man can expect to recover his losses and prosper in business; a single girl is guaranteed to meet a good prospect for a husband.

Complementary to the reciprocally obligated role is the role of a benefactor – obviously a desirable role. Not only the *bontai* but also the *chūkaisha* and the audience at the possession ritual often receive the spirit's gratitude and promises of repayment since they have helped the *bontai*. General gratitude is expressed to 'every member' of the branch and to the cult as a whole.

A widow said that when she was possessed it was always by her deceased mother-in-law. One day the mother-in-law appeared to tell the daughter-in-law, 'You are troubled with your husband the spirit's son, so I shall take him with me.' Shortly after this, the informant found her good-for-nothing husband dead, which she seemed to take as a clear indication of her mother-in-law's gratitude.

The disciplinarian role. Some ancestors and personal guardian spirits scold the *bontai* harshly. Here the supernatural other assumes a dominant, disciplinarian role. In a commanding tone using a masculine style of speech, the spirit berates the *bontai*, expressing displeasure with his lack of discipline, sincerity, and devotion. Such a punitive role may be played not merely verbally but also physically: in one of the cases I observed, a woman possessed by an ancestor kept saying 'I am displeased,' shaking her head disapprovingly and striking her chest violently.

The complementary role taken by the *chūkaisha* during possession is dual. On one hand, she serves as an arbiter, trying to restore harmony between the spirit and the *bontai*. She tries to appease the spirit by assuring it that she will transmit its message to the *bontai* and oversee the latter's self-improvement. On the other hand, the *chūkaisha* occasionally slips into the complementary role to be played by the *bontai*, namely, an apologetic, self-accusatory, docile role. What takes place then is a temporary status reversal between leader and follower, the latter playing an authoritarian role and the former a submissive role. Status normalization follows as soon as possession is over, when the *chūkaisha*, now as the leader, reproves the *bontai* for displeasing the spirit. Comparing the two cult branches, the spirit's assumption of a disciplinarian role took place more often in one branch that is headed by a woman of a more disciplinarian character. (The other branch, headed by the indulgent 'grandmother,' shows a stronger inclination toward the supplicant role.)

Possession can thus gratify the wish to be both dominant and submissive. Also implied in this role is a disguised confession of guilt on the part of the *bontai* for neglecting his spiritual and social obligations. Finally, this role provides an opportunity for a member to demonstrate to others that he has a rigorous standard for religious devotion that keeps him discontented with what he is.

The retaliatory role. Similar to the disciplinarian role is the retaliatory role. The difference between the two is that, while the disciplinarian role is motivated by a benevolent intention, the retaliatory role is activated by a malevolent one. Malevolence is, in the vernacular of my informants, 'anger,' 'curse,' or, most commonly, 'grudge.'

Many instances of possession by animal spirits involved assumption of the retaliatory role. A fox spirit would be angry with the *bontai*'s ancestors for having abandoned it though they owed it so much for protecting their house. Usually these ancestors were samurai who moved from one battlefield to another, not taking the time to serve the house-protecting fox deity. Their worst offense was to destroy a shrine dedicated to the fox spirit. A woman discovered through possession the reason for her husband's neurosis: the fox spirit, angry at having been neglected by his ancestors, decided to punish the descendants of the house.

Spirits of human origin also play a retaliatory role. A divorcée informant was possessed by the spirit of a maid who had served one of her ancestors. The master apparently had raped the maid, said the informant, for she became pregnant and was discharged. In despair, the maid drowned herself in a well, cursing all the descendants of the family.

The retaliatory role calls forth its complementary role, that of the accused – not a desirable one. The difficulty is resolved by expanding the dyadic role system into a triad. The *bontai* does not take the role of the accused but of the innocent victim of the spirit's malevolence. The role of the accused is attributed to an ancestor of the *bontai* or of the *bontai*'s spouse. An ancestor angers a spirit, which takes revenge by punishing the wrongdoer's offspring. Such a triadic repercussion in punitive reciprocity is a common theme in the Japanese belief system: it reinforces the 'lineal' focus of self-identity, coupled with the Buddhist idea of karma.

In this triad, the *bontai* is able to identify with the spirit to form an alliance against the sinful ancestor, who has caused trouble for the spirit and the *bontai* alike. One might speculate that the aforementioned divorcée (who once was a *geisha*) perceived a parallel between the rapist ancestor and her former husband (or men in general) and between the raped maid and herself.

There are some exceptions to this rule of triadic interchange. The retaliatory spirit sometimes is against the *bontai*, as in possession by a former fiancée or a divorced husband who is still attached to the *bontai*. In such a case, however, the retaliatory role is softened into a more supplicant role, which elicits a nurturant response from the *bontai*.

The retaliatory role merges with the supplicant role whenever the spirit faces the problem of its own salvation. However malevolent it is, a suffering and *muen* spirit depends upon the very person it is cursing for its salvation, evoking a nurturant role in the *bontai*. A fox spirit will ask the *bontai* to restore its *kami* status by enshrining it, in addition to making *kuyō* offerings.

In triadic retaliation, the *bontai* performs two kinds of *owabi*. First, he assumes the role of the ancestor who was responsible for the spirit's malevolence and apologizes on his behalf to the angry spirit as well as to the deity of a local shrine; he then apologizes to the deity for the sin committed by the retaliatory spirit, the sin of holding a grudge.

The status-demonstrative role. The ancestral spirit tends to hold prestigious status, typically samurai status. A male informant was possessed many times by Taira Kiyomon, the first warrior-ruler of the country in the early twelfth century, who identified himself as an ancestor of the *bontai* eighteen generations removed. This motivated the *bontai* to study his genealogical background.

The *bontai* can elevate his status through being possessed by distinguished ancestors. In this case, the main complementary role is played by the audience, who may be impressed by the disclosure of such eminent ancestry. Many members do not question the credibility of such information and talk about it admiringly. Some individuals are singled out by leaders or fellow members as coming from a formerly distinguished house that has declined.

Ancestors of high status are uniformly sinful, since there is perfect correlation in the members' eyes between power and moral deficiency. Such ancestors killed people, exploited poor commoners to enrich their own coffers, engaged in political trickery, indulged in sexual promiscuity, even seducing a reluctant virgin, and the like.

The *tsumi* committed by a high-status ancestor is certain to activate a retaliatory drive in its victim. This means that the status-demonstrative role and the retaliatory role are mutually complementary and reinforcing. Such complementarity may be responsible for the intimacy observed between a woman once possessed by a victim of her ancestor and a man possessed by his distinguished and sinful ancestor.

The status-demonstrative role also becomes a supplicant role. The ancestor will ask the *bontai* to do *kuyō* and *owabi* for his sake and for the sake of the victims of his *tsumi*. Taira Kiyomori, in the case mentioned above, asked the *bontai*, the direct descendant of the Taira family, to apologize for his *tsumi* to the guardian deity of the family, and to save the spirits of those killed in warfare between Taira and Minamoto clans, the two most powerful warrior clans of the time.

There is a variant type of status-demonstrative role. An animal spirit occasionally appears in possession to signify its wish to receive *shugyō* (religious discipline) at the spiritual center of the cult. The *bontai* grants that wish of the spirit by sending the spirit to the center 'via' a local ward shrine, which means that the *bontai* goes to the shrine with offerings and 'sees the spirit off.' The *bontai* is accompanied by the leader and some fellow members as helpers and witnesses. After several weeks of *shugyō*, the spirit returns again via the local shrine, and the homecoming is marked by the ritual of 'receiving' the returning spirit. During the absence of the spirit, the *bontai* is supposed to undergo the same *shugyō*, as if he were accompanying the spirit. *Shugyō* involves the routine disciplines which a volunteer trainee would receive at the spiritual center, such as getting up early, keeping the house clean, performing religious services regularly, and avoiding meat.

It is believed that the spirit raises its status to that of *kami* after the completion of *shugyō*. The status elevation of the guardian spirit seems reflected in the status elevation of the *bontai*. Several months after joining the cult, many a member thus gets possessed by a guardian spirit who wants to undergo *shugyō* at the center.

Neither the role of *shugyō* candidate nor that of *shugyō* graduate can be played well unless fellow cult members play a complementary role. The *bontai* must be confident that fellow members would recognize his qualifications for playing such roles. In an observed case of possession, the *bontai* was informed that her guardian spirit wanted to go to the spiritual center. Instead of willingly accepting its wish, the *bontai* let the spirit decide to postpone the *shugyō* because it did not yet qualify. After possession, when the *chūkaisha* reprimanded her for not complying with the spirit's wish, the *bontai* confessed that there was criticism among fellow members about her being jealous of those who had already sent their spirits away for *shugyō*.

The informant role. Finally, the supernatural role can be identified as that of an informant. Unlike the roles above, to which the role players are attached as an end, the informant role is an instrumental one used to facilitate communication. A person is able to express himself more freely by taking a supernatural role than by representing himself. The informant role, in other words, allows its player to make a statement to others that would be too embarrassing or audacious to make outside that role.

First, the spirit possessing the *bontai* praises and thanks the *bontai* for his sincerity, devotion, and religious accomplishment. A whole list of ancestors may be named as having been saved by the *bontai*. The spirit sometimes describes in detail what the *bontai* has done for his own self-discipline and for the salvation of many spirits. A young girl had the spirit of her kin praise her and declare that everyone was talking about her favorably.

Along with such self-praise, the *bontai* can express disapproval and hostility toward others. The spirit of a male cousin criticized many relatives of the *bontai*, including the mother, grandmother, and aunt, clearly indicating the *bontai*'s displeasure with them. Criticism is directed against selfishness, greediness, stubbornness, lack of faith, resistance to the cult, and so forth. The spirit goes as far as to threaten that, if the person continues this behavior, misfortune would follow.

The *bontai*'s wish is sometimes expressed in the form of a command by the spirit. If the *bontai* wants to have a new house built for his family, the spirit commands the family to start construction on a certain date. That command was effective in one instance, despite strong resistance by the head of the household.

A credulous audience is a necessary complement to the informant role. The credulous person will be frightened if he is accused in this manner, even if the accused is skeptical, other credulous branch members may apply pressure to make him comply with the spirit's commands.

Reviewing the supernatural role types and their complementary roles, I am tempted to propose that many of the cult members, although they do not form a separate group in socioeconomic status, were (or are) deprived in the social roles available to them; and that through possession they are able to overcome such role deprivation, at least temporarily.

CONCLUSION

Spirit possession in a Japanese cult was analyzed from the sociological point of view of 'taking the role of supernatural other,' derived from Mead's concept of self. It was suggested that possession provides an opportunity to temporarily remedy role deprivation by assuming a supernatural role. Satisfactory performance of a supernatural role, the proposition goes, presupposes a complementary role. Field work in local branches of the cult revealed six types of supernatural role played by the possessed: suppliant, reciprocal, disciplinarian, retaliatory, status-demonstrative, and informant. These are paired, respectively, with the nurturant role, the role of recipient of gratitude, a submissive role, the role of a victim of retaliation, an admirer's role, and the role of a credulous listener. These complementary roles are played by the possessed person himself after possession, or by the leader-mediator, who converses with the spirit (the spirit host), and by fellow members, who constitute a congenial or supportive audience.

What stands out in this variety of role pairs is the supplicant-nurturant pair, which appeared with overwhelming frequency, either singly or in combination with other roles. It might be argued that this pair predominates because the majority of the cult members are women of middle age and older. I believe, however, that Japanese in general, regardless of age and sex, tend to find gratification in playing a supplicant or nurturant role, or, more likely, both. The main support for this position comes from Doi's (1971) theory of *amae* as a key to Japanese culture and personality. I deviate from Doi's point of view only in my stress upon role complementarity which requires both *amaeru* (to be dependent) and *amayakasu* (to indulge Alter's wish for dependency) to be desirable and satisfying.

The concluding hypothesis is that role gratification, temporarily facilitated through spirit possession, is likely to bring relief from illness.

Acknowledgement

I wish to acknowledge with gratitude the support of NIMH (Grant No. MH09243) in carrying out this research. The Social Science Research Institute, University of Hawaii, rendered technical assistance in the preparation of this paper.

REFERENCES

Bateson. G. 1971. The cybernetics of 'self': a theory of alcoholism. *Psychiatry* 34: 1–18.

—— 1935. Culture contact and schizmogenesis. *Man* 35: 178–83.

Bourguignon, E. 1965. The self, the behavioral environment and the theory of spirit possession. In *Context and meaning in cultural anthropology*. M. E. Spiro, ed. New York, Free Press of Glencoe.

Bunkachō [Japanese National Agency of Culture]. 1970. *Shukyō nenkan* [Religion yearbook]. [In Japanese].

Doi, T. 1971. *Amae no kōzō* (The structure of amae). Tokyo, Kobundo. [In Japanese].

Harris, G. 1957. Possession 'hysteria' in a Kenya tribe. *American Anthropologist* 59: 1046–66.

Kiev, A. 1961. Spirit possession in Haiti. *American Journal of Psychiatry* 118: 133–38.
Lebra, T. S. 1971. Social ecology of a healing cult. Paper presented at the thirtieth annual meeting of the Society for Applied Anthropology, April 14–18, Miami, Florida.
—— In press. The interactional perspective of suffering and curing in a Japanese cult. *The International Journal of Social Psychiatry*.
Mead, G.H. 1967. *Mind, self and society*. Chicago, University of Chicago Press, Phoenix books.
Watzlawick, P., J.H. Beavin, and D.D. Jackson. 1967. *Pragmatics of human communication: a study of interactional patterns, pathologies, and paradoxes*. New York, Norton.
Yap, P.M. 1960. The possession syndrome. *Journal of Mental Science* 106: 151–56.

NOTE

1. This cult was reported upon in previous papers (Lebra 1971, n.d.). While those and the present paper differ in focus, there is partial overlap in descriptive information.

▸ First published in William H. Newell (ed.), *Ancestor*, The Hague: Mouton Publishers, 1976

❽ Ancestral Influence on the Suffering of Descendants in a Japanese Cult

OBJECTIVE AND DATA

One of the anthropological preoccupations regarding ancestor worship has been to identify ancestral volition or disposition toward the living. Attempts have been made to ascertain whether ancestors in a tribe or in a society under study are benevolent, malevolent, ambivalent, indulgent, or punitive toward their descendants. A judgment on this matter appears significant or necessary primarily because it assumes the following kinds of relationship between the two generations.

First, ancestral will is responsible for an experience undergone by a descendant. If well disposed, forebears will benefit descendants and may 'never cause disasters to befall the coming generations,' as postulated by Hsu (1948: 241) regarding Chinese ancestors. If an ancestor is malignant, revengeful, envious, or punitive as is a Nayar ancestor (Gough 1958), then misfortune will be the inevitable outcome for the living. This logic can be reversed: if the living experience a misfortune, ancestral malignancy or wrath must be suspected.

Second, this causal relationship between ancestral volition and the experience by the living presupposes the power or authority held by ancestors over descendants. This has been extrapolated from the structural imbalance within this world between the power-holding generation (father, mother's brother) and the deprived succeeding generation (son, sister's son). The inevitable dilemma involved in intergenerational transmission of power may find its solution in ancestor worship as among Tallensi who believe ancestors 'retain final authority, chiefly by virtue of the pain and misfortune they inflict on their descendants from time to time' (Fortes 1960: 176).

Conversely, the same dilemma may result in repressed hostility, rather than 'worship,' toward ancestors; and this hostility may underlie a frequent attribution of illness to ancestral influence as among Okinawans (W. P. Lebra 1969). In either case, ancestral power or authority as the basis for efficacy of sanction seems unquestioned. Freedman (1966: 151) echoes this position when he sees Chinese ancestors in light of both their 'relative ineffectiveness' and 'general air of benevolence.' The implication is that Chinese ancestors are not punitive because their will is not bolstered by their power under the Chinese system of inheritance.

Third, ancestral influence is justified as a legitimate or at least natural response to the way the living are conducting themselves. A misfortune must be accepted as punishment for neglecting the welfare and wishes of an ancestor; whereas the proper attention to the needs of the ancestors will be rewarded by good fortune. Implied herein is the acknowledgment of guilt on the part of the suffering descendant. This projection of justice makes ancestral influence doubly contingent: upon the offspring's behavior as well as upon ancestral predisposition.

The main objective of this paper is to present another case of ancestor worship where the above rationale for experiences by the living generation does not apply in any significant degree. A misfortune or suffering endured by a descendant, when attributed to ancestral influence, does not necessarily stem from an ancestor's malevolence or wrath, or demonstrate an ancestor's power over the sufferer, or verify the latter's guilt. A benign, powerless ancestor may well cause trouble to an innocent descendant. What is the rationale behind this, then? I will attempt to answer this question.

The case introduced here is a Japanese cult which has been identified as the Salvation Cult in my previous papers (Lebra 1971, 1974, ip.). Founded in 1929, the Salvation Cult with its 'headquarters' in Tokyo commanded roughly 500 local branches scattered all over Japan, and claimed a membership of more than 170,000 as of 1970 (*Shūkyonenkan* 1971). The doctrine of the cult is highly eclectic, accepts Buddhism, Shintō, Taoism, Confucianism, and even Christianity, and grants a legitimate supernatural status to every conceivable deity or spirit, be it a Buddha, nature deity, animal spirit, village tutelary god (*ujigami*), or deceased human. (For more detailed descriptions of the cult see my previous papers.)

Fieldwork was conducted during the summers of 1970 and 1971 with a primary focus upon two branches in what I will call Eastern City, central Japan, whose combined membership was estimated at around 200. This paper is based upon information obtained through interviews with the two branch leaders and fourteen members. All but two members were female – this sex distribution roughly corresponds with that of those attending branch meetings regularly – their ages ranged from thirty-eight to seventy-eight, and their occupations (active or retired) varied widely and included storekeepers, cabaret operators, schoolteachers, a maid, and a fisherwoman. Further information was added through semiparticipant observation of rituals as well as casual conversation with attendants at branch meetings. 'Lecturers' invited from other branches or the headquarters were another source of information.

RELATIONSHIPS BETWEEN ANCESTORS AND SUFFERING DESCENDANTS

In the course of fieldwork, it became apparent that the cult members almost without exception have undergone a variety of suffering, particularly illness and family disharmony. Like many other 'new' cults, the Salvation Cult finds a ready explanation for suffering in supernatural influence or in a certain relationship between the sufferer and a spirit. The responsible spirit is identified either by the sufferer himself, by a leader or a fellow member, or cooperatively by both. While an informal talk often leads one to 'discover' the spirit, the cult offers its own ritual for spirit possession which induces the sufferer to be possessed by a specific spirit causing the trouble.

Among the spirits thus identified are ancestral spirits (*senzo no rei*). A *senzo* may be a remote ancestor, 'ten generations old,' or a recently departed parent or other kin. A remote ancestor is traced patrilineally in conformity with the Japanese ideal of succession pattern, while no such rule is applied to the recently deceased, a cognatic or collateral kin claiming a *senzo* status. A married woman finds a trouble-causing *senzo* among the dead members of either her natal house or her husband's house, more often among the former.

A consanguineally linked *senzo* makes no sex discrimination in selecting a descendant as a target of his influence, but in-laws do: a woman would find herself caught up by her departed mother-in-law, but not by her father-in-law. A *senzo* can be recruited from Ego's own generation (sister) and even from a succeeding generation (child).

The cult thus includes a variety of classes of dead people under the one term *senzo*, and this indiscriminatory attitude towards ancestors is by no means unique to this cult but widely shared by Japanese, as shown in past studies (Plath 1964; Smith 1966; Newell 1969; Kirby 1910). It may be partly due to this structural ambiguity of the ancestor category that the assumptions sketched above regarding ancestor worship, which are likely to have been derived from more rigidly structured systems of ancestor beliefs, turn out to be irrelevant.

Suffering by the living, if identified as related to ancestral influence, is attributed to the ancestor's own suffering. A suffering ancestor floats around this world because he is blocked from attaining a *hotoke* [Buddha] status and is thus unable to join the ancestral group (*senzo no nakamairi*). Such a lonely, homeless spirit is described as *muen* [affinityless]. Ancestral suffering accounts for a descendant's suffering under the assumption of one or more of the following relationships recognized between preceding generations and succeeding generations.

Inheritance

What stands out as the most basic premise is the belief that a descendant, by necessity rather than by choice, has inherited his identity from his ancestors to the extent that his experience or whole person is a near or exact replica of those of his ancestors. The same holds true with suffering.

Three levels of inheritance appear mixed together in the minds of the cult members: genetic-constitutional ('The blood running in my body is my *senzo*, therefore I must keep it clean'); jural (inheritance and succession of assets and liabilities attached to the *ie* [house] handed down over generations); and metaphysical (destiny, karma, reincarnation, or metempsychosis). All these ideas are put together under the folk-metaphysical term *innen*.

A retired schoolteacher looks back on her hardship-ridden career and says, 'All this is because many of my *senzo* have had hardships. I must cut this *innen* bond within my generation so that my *shison* [offspring] will not inherit it.' An informant's daughter almost died from excessive bleeding. It was found out later that her paternal great-grandfather had bled to death in the Russo-Japanese War. Another informant's daughter suddenly disappeared from home under the pressure of the *innen* inherited from her great-grandmother who had led a wandering life. A former cabaret owner had to suffer because of her promiscuous husband since she had inherited this *innen* from her mother-in-law who also had suffered from the same problem. The *innen* inheritance by the daughter-in-law from the mother-in-law in this case, of course, is anchored in the consanguineal *innen* bondage between father and son in sharing the same promiscuous disposition. A male informant specified the number of generations for completion of an *innen* cycle: 'You can judge someone's personality if you know his three-generation-old ancestor. You will reappear in your offspring three generations ahead.' The weight of *innen* varies according to the status, wealth, and power of ancestors: 'The wealthier the *senzo*, the heavier the *innen*.'

Reflection

The idea of *innen* inheritance is further extended into the esoteric belief that one's behavior or suffering is a mirror-reflection of an ancestor who is, at present, behaving or suffering in a similar way. Many instances of *innen* inheritance involve this reflection. The girl's bleeding is an indication that her great-grandfather still suffers from the same affliction. If one cries, it is because one's ancestor is crying. An informant came to realize why her adopted daughter (niece), being mistreated by the adoptive father (the informant's husband), cried so often: 'It was her real grandfather who was crying behind her; it was he who allowed her to be adopted.' A husband who is selfish and uncooperative is understood to be a reflection of his father acting through him.

This judgment does not result, as might well be suspected it would, in accusation of or hostility toward the ancestor behind the actor, not even in admitting that ancestors cause trouble for descendants. Instead, the idea of reflection, in the view of informants, can reverse the causal connection between an ancestor and a descendant. If a descendant's state reflects that of an ancestor, it is reflected back onto the ancestor's mirror. That is, Ego's suffering is equal to the suffering of his ancestor and vice versa. Furthermore, Ego's happiness will be reflected into happiness for the ancestor, and this feeling of joy will, in turn, come back to Ego. Thus Ego's suffering results in self-accusation for permitting an ancestor to remain unhappy.

Such bilateral reflection takes place not only between Ego and an ancestor but also between Ego and a descendant. A delinquent child is a reflection of an undisciplined parent, and in turn, such delinquency reflects back to cause the parent to suffer. A suffering mother then must apologize to both her ancestors and to her children. Masochism demonstrated here involves acknowledgment of guilt; and yet, bound by the 'logic' of mutual reflection, is far from recognition of a moral dichotomy between a guilty party and a punitive party.

Mutual reflection ends with a total fusion or identity between generations:

'My ancestors, I, and my descendants – we are one and the same.' 'Ancestors are myself, ancestors are descendants. *Innen* from ancestors is me.' 'Ancestor worship means self-worship.'

Vicarious Retribution

One major reason why an ancestor is deprived of *hotoke* status and continues to suffer is because he committed *tsumi* [sin] while in a fleshly form. The *tsumi* most frequently mentioned is *shikijō no tsumi* [sexual sin] which takes different forms. Extramarital indulgence and a number of remarriages are examples of such *tsumi* committed by male ancestors; whereas female ancestors are associated more with the *tsumi* of love suicide.

Among other *tsumi* are: homicide by *samurai* ancestors; abortion which left the fetus neglected in the state of *muen*; ruthless power manipulation and exploitation of the poor by ruling-class ancestors. Not all *tsumi* involve violation of a moral standard. A state or action of an ancestor which has anything to do with bloodletting is regarded as *tsumi*-ridden for the simple reason that blood is polluting and thus invites punishment from the god controlling the place, the natural element, or object that has been polluted. Menstruation, miscarriage, and being stabbed as well as stabbing someone all constitute *tsumi* commitment in this sense.

One more important ancestral *tsumi* must be mentioned. It is believed that most distinguished families – and most informants presented themselves as descendants of such families – used to have their respective guardian gods enshrined on their estates, well tended and worshiped. During the age of civil warfare, *samurai* ancestors, busy fighting and moving from one battlefield to another, either completely neglected the guardian gods or even destroyed their shrines. This constituted a serious *tsumi*.

It is one or more such *tsumi* committed by his ancestors that makes a descendant suffer. According to this interpretation, suffering is understood and accepted as a vicarious retribution by the sufferer on behalf of the sinful ancestor. A male informant, who claims direct descent from Taira, the first warrior ruling family in Japanese history, attributes his suffering as a husband and businessman to the unforgivable *tsumi* committed by his *senzo*. His first wife left him and his present marriage is also a frustrating one; meanwhile every business venture he has undertaken has been successful up to a point but has always ended in failure. All this was because his godless ancestors had committed *tsumi* of sex and money – by taking advantage of female retainers and robbing the poor of money.

A divorcee attributes her own marriage predicament and that of her relatives to the curse of an ancestor's maidservant who committed suicide after being impregnated and who was subsequently discharged by her master. 'She died, cursing all descendants of the Yoshii family.' A conclusive statement was given by another informant: 'Every time I face a difficulty, I convince myself that my ancestors have done wrong things.'

An instance of ancestral *tsumi* against the family guardian god, the fox spirit, resulted in the god's punishment of a descendant, an informant's husband, by making him mentally ill. The idea of vicarious retribution was put across by a leader of the cult when he said, 'If you loan money to somebody and worry about its return, both the loaner and the debtor will become unhappy. You ought to think that your ancestors did something that necessitated your loaning – that they were in debt.'

Vicarious retribution applies to Ego's descendants as well as to Ego's sin. One of the branch leaders revealed that she committed *tsumi* by disobeying her parents' wish to allow herself to be adopted by her childless brother as a daughter and successor to the *ie*. Realizing that her *tsumi* of *oyafukō* [unfaithfulness to parents] was punished through her daughter's illness, she knelt by her daughter's bed, bowing to the floor and tearfully begging her forgiveness.

Vicarious retribution ceases to be 'vicarious' once the boundary between ancestors and descendants is obliterated as stated in the preceding section.

Communication

Suffering is further interpreted as a means of communication between an ancestor and a descendant. Illness then should be taken as a message transmitted through the patient's body. Without receiving such a signal, one would remain uninformed, fail to rectify one's misconduct, and make more serious errors.

A mother once lingered on the verge of death from asthma, and this corresponded with the time of her son's death in the war. He 'notified his death,' it was understood later, through the pain undergone by his mother. This message signified that religious services and sacrifice should be rendered for the dead son to become a *hotoke*.

Communication sometimes involves a degree of elaboration of codes. Injury, for example, is a signal from someone who died an unnatural death or committed suicide; gynecological disorder is a message either from an ancestor who committed a sexual sin or from the spirit of a neglected infant; the problem of bed-wetting should be coded in relation to someone who drowned.

Gratitude is the proper response to receiving a message. The mother of two unfilial children became awakened to how rebellious she had been against her ancestors and how much displeasure she had caused them. 'I would have been blind to this if my children had not turned away from me.' In this case, ancestors used the children as a means of communication. She thanked the children for letting her know of her own rebelliousness. The more suffering, the more enlightenment.

As in the last case, the receiver of the message may happen to be too insensitive unless he 'sees' it through somebody else. An intelligent high school boy suddenly developed a school phobia, ran away from home, and ended up as a 'hippie' in a mountain hideaway. This incident was explained as his dead grandmother trying to inform her son and daughter-in-law of her homelessness. The latter would have been unreceptive to this message unless their intelligent, sensitive son were selected to act as a medium.

Ancestral communication is not always 'instructional' but occasionally 'instigative.' An ancestor who used to disappear from home instigated a descendant and father of the house to run away from home with stolen money. Even this kind of communication is accepted as beneficial by informants who interpret the family, not the victim, to be the true message receiver.

Reliance

All the above relationships are channelled into this final one, reliance of a suffering ancestor on a descendant for his salvation. A descendant's suffering is taken as a result of such reliance. The behavior of the ancestor is described as helpless, solicitous for help, hanging or mounting on, clinging, hugging, or attached to the person to be relied upon. Reliance may be localized as when a spirit hangs on the neck, leg, eye, breast, head, etc., which is realized through neck pains, leg injury, eye disease, breast cancer, mental illness. An infant tends to cling to a woman's breast or womb.

Being an activation of the *innen* bond, reliance tends to be upon a consanguineal kin or a member of the *ie* where the spirit once belonged. There appear to be varying degrees of legitimacy in the choice of the object-person for reliance. Reliance upon the eldest son and succeeding or incumbent head of the *ie* in the direct line is regarded as most legitimate but rarely practiced.

An informant took a neighbor to the branch church for a possession ritual to find out why her neighbor was forced to lead such a miserable life of illness and with an unfaithful husband. The informant's neighbor was possessed by her husband's grandmother who had drowned during a flood. The spirit held on to her and refused to let go because she loved the granddaughter-in-law more than any of her blood children or grandchildren. This meant that the woman looked 'like insane' and did not come back to consciousness for a long time. The informant, feeling responsible, tried to persuade the possessing spirit to release the neighbor. 'I told the spirit that relying upon your granddaughter-in-law makes no sense. "Rely on the direct main line, on the first son," I said.' The neighbor's house turned out to be a branch house established by a younger son.

Such structural constraint, as shown by the above example, is, however, often superseded by the spirit's preference for a certain personality type regardless of kinship and succession rule. In some cases it is the weakest, most vulnerable person, and in some other cases the person who resembles the spirit the most, that the spirit comes to rely upon. However, in an overwhelming number of instances it is the most reliable and helpful person who is selected by the spirit.

The ultimate objective of ancestral reliance is attainment of *hotoke* status which requires the spirit's contentment through sacrifice and attendance by the living. The *tsumi*-ridden spirit – and most suffering spirits are sinful – must make an apology to the angry god before it can enjoy the nurturant care given by the living. For that apology, too, the helpless spirit must rely upon the living. A descendant, thus relied upon, must visit a shrine to make a vicarious apology for the *tsumi* committed by an ancestor.

CONCLUSION

The above analysis of relationships between ancestors and suffering descendants, as observed in a Japanese cult, suggests the following. First, all the five relationships – inheritance, reflection, vicarious retribution, communication, and reliance – obscure the boundary between an ancestor and a descendant. What emerges here is a fusion or interlocking, instead of differentiation and confrontation, between two generations, between subject and object in ancestor worship. Anthropological assumptions, as delineated at the outset, such as ancestral volition, ancestral causation of misfortune, ancestral power and justice, seem derived from a clear demarcation line between ancestors and descendants. I am tempted to conclude that these assumptions do not apply meaningfully where one does not know or is indifferent to where an ancestor ends and a descendant begins. This may further relate to the difference between a culture which invests in social relationships and solidarity and a culture which cherishes individual autonomy.

Second, the consistent theme, appearing and reappearing in the Salvation Cult, is masochism and nurturance on the part of the sufferer. This may reflect a woman's role as a link between ancestors and descendants in a society where patrilineal ideology predominates and yet the woman looks after not only the children but the dead members of the household as well. The Salvation Cult, its members being predominantly women, may represent such a sexual bias more than other Japanese cults which are more male oriented.

Third, locked with the above two points is the structural ambiguity of the ancestor category as previously described. If *senzo* can include one's child as well as ascending generations, the mother's attitude toward a dead child may well be duplicated toward forebears. Indeed, it is the mother, selfless and reliable, who seems to offer a role model in the whole tenet of the cult. This may underlie both the lack of differentiation between ancestors and descendants, and the stress on masochism and nurturance.

REFERENCES

Crooke, William 1926. 'Ancestor worship and cult of the dead,' in *Encyclopaedia of religion and ethics*, volume one. Edited by James Hastings, 425–432. New York: Scribner's.

Dore, R. P. 1958. *City life in Japan: a study of a Tokyo ward.* Berkeley and Los Angeles: University of California Press.

Fortes, Meyer 1960. Pietas in ancestor worship. *Man: Journal of the Royal Anthropological Institute* 91(2):166–191.

Freedman, Maurice 1966. Chinese lineage and society; Fukien and Kwangtung. London: Athione; New York: Humanities Press.

Goody, Jack 1962. *Death, property and the ancestors.* Stanford: Stanford University Press.

Gough, E. K. 1958. Cults of the dead among the Nayar. *Journal of American Folklore* 71: 446–478.

Hozumi Nobushige 1912. *Ancestor worship and Japanese law* (second edition). Tokyo: Maruzen.
Hsu, Francis L. K. 1948. *Under the ancestors' shadow; Chinese culture and personality*. New York: Columbia University Press.
Kirby, R. J. 1910. Ancestral worship in Japan. *Transactions of the Asiatic Society of Japan* 38: 233–267.
Lebra, Takie Sugiyama 1971. 'Social ecology of a healing cult.' Paper presented at the 30th annual meeting of the Society for Applied Anthropology, April 1971, Miami, Florida.
—— 1974. The interactional perspective of suffering and curing in a Japanese cult. *The International Journal of Social Psychiatry* 20: 281–286.
—— i.p. 'Taking the role of supernatural 'other': spirit possession in a Japanese healing cult,' in *Culture-bound syndromes, ethnopsychia, try and alternate therapies*. Edited by W. P. Lebra. Honolulu: University of Hawaii Press.
Lebra, William P. 1969. *Ancestral beliefs and illness in Okinawa*. Reprinted from *Proceedings of the VIIIth International Congress of Anthropological and Ethnological Sciences 1968*, volume three: Ethnology and archaeology. Tokyo and Kyoto.
Newell, W. H. 1969. 'Some comparative features of Chinese and Japanese ancestor worship,' in *Poceedings of the VIIIth International Congress of Anthropological and Ethnological Sciences 1968*, volume three: *Ethnology and archaeology*, 300–301. Tokyo and Kyoto.
Plath, David W. 1964. Where the family of God is the family: the role of the dead in Japanese households. *American Anthropologist* 66(2): 300–317.
Shūkyonenkan 1971. *Shūkyonenkan* [Yearbook of religion], compiled by Bunkachō, Japan.
Smith, R. J. 1966. Ihai: mortuary tablets, the household and kin in Japanese ancestor worship. *Transactions of the Asiatic Society of Japan*, third series, 9: 83–102.
Yang, C. K. 1961. *Religion in Chinese society*. Berkeley and Los Angeles: University of California Press.
Wimberley, Howard 1969. Self-realization and the ancestors: an analysis of two Japanese ritual procedures for achieving domestic harmony. *Anthropological Quarterly* 42: 37–51.

NOTES

This research was funded by an NIMH grant (MH-09243) and assistance received from the Social Science Research Institute, University of Hawaii; this aid is gratefully acknowledged. Thanks are also due to Ms. Freda Hellinger for her editorial suggestions.

First published in Ellis S. Krauss, Thomas P. Rohlen and Patricia G. Stenhoff (eds), *Conflict in Japan*, Honolulu: University of Hawaii Press, 1984

9 Non-confrontational Strategies for Management of Interpersonal Conflicts

Understood as a process, conflict refers either to the phase at which conflict is generated and intensifies or to the phase at which conflict is reacted to and managed. These two phases may be labeled 'conflict genesis' and 'conflict management' respectively. It is not that genesis and management are always distinguishable or that one is necessarily followed by the other; the same phenomenon may be placed in the context of either genesis or management. The distinction is only for analytical purposes. Overlapping with these phases are such pairs of conflict states as latent and manifest, hidden and exposed, uncommunicated and communicated. This essay focuses on the management phase.

Depending on the phases of conflict as well as on whether conflict is ego-directed or alter-directed, different emotions accompany conflict experiences: ambivalence, frustration, anxiety, commitment, guilt, shame, embarrassment, anger, grudge, hatred, contempt, and the like. Underlying the two-phase conflict process and these emotions is the human personality, which has been captured by a variety of psychological models: the familiar 'frustration-aggression' model; the 'consistency' model as in Festinger's 'dissonance' and 'dissonance reduction';[1] and the 'relative deprivation' model in which the awareness of a gap between expectation and fulfillment is followed by an effort to fill the gap. Further, the conflict process, while it may be emotion-ridden as in these models, may be generated or managed strategically through a rational calculation of gains to be maximized and losses to be minimized. Thus the rational decision-making model is not precluded either.[2]

By conflict management I mean a reaction to a conflict situation without necessarily entailing a resolution. Management can involve procrastination, aggravation of conflict, or initiation of a new phase of conflict. The culturally available techniques for management at the interpersonal level (intergroup conflict is another matter) may be characterized as nonconfrontational. By confrontation I mean a direct challenge launched by A against B when A perceives B as the source of his conflict. It is not that Japanese never risk confrontations but that, as long as harmony, or the appearance of harmony, is to be maintained, nonconfrontational modes must be exhausted first. Probably this is a lesson which should have been kept in mind by the headman of Shinohata in Dore's account, when he learned that the village fire brigade had cut off the irrigation water in order to catch fish for a drinking party and had forgotten to readjust the dam to release the water. In response to the complaint made by the headman of the next village which was thus deprived of water for a short while, the Shinohata headman demanded a formal apology to be delivered by the fire brigade to the headman of the next village. This overreaction, or confrontational reproach, touched off a conflict escalation leading to the decision by the fire brigade, headed by the humiliated chief, to resign.[3] The modes of management discussed in the following sections are by no means unique to Japan only, but they may facilitate our understanding of the Japanese.

ANTICIPATORY MANAGEMENT

Anticipatory management means that conflict is managed in a preventive manner before it is generated. Anticipating his inability to reciprocate, party A may refuse to accept a favor. A resident of Henna Buraku refused to take a *koden*-gift from Kida with the explanation that he could not make a return gift. Pressed to accept it since no return was expected, the funeral host was adamant: 'But people around this area backbite against you if you don't make return gifts. I will accept your goodwill but please take the *koden* back. Accepting one, I would have to accept all others.'[4] Help may be withheld to prevent a conflict between self-interest and altruistic obligation. This concern led one of Dore's informants to avoid benefiting from his own mechanical expertise: 'Repair my own tractor? No. If you do that you end up 'clever poor.' All the neighbors start coming to ask you just to take a look at their machine. They think nothing of it. They're not particularly grateful. You lose a lot of time and you use up your spare parts.'[5] Similar anticipation prevents one of my informants from traveling abroad: 'Once my travel plan is found out by my neighbors, relatives, friends, they will all bring *senbetsu* [gifts for separation]. And, of course, they all will expect to receive souvenirs. I can't afford it. Isn't there any way of taking off without being noticed?'

Anticipatory management may require a painful, even masochistic, perseverance or effort, as when A anticipates an offer from B, his benefactor, that A wants to turn down. An informant, when he was a live-in apprentice with his uncle, knew he was going to receive a proposal from the aunt to settle down in the household as a *mukoyoshi* husband (one who adopts the wife's family name) to their only daughter. To avoid being trapped into this match, he tried to do everything that would alienate the aunt so she would give up the idea. His strategy was, as he put it, 'to make myself hated as much as possible.' He did so by working from dawn to midnight as hard as a man can work! Working hard is a good thing, but to do so beyond a point, my informant believes, brings hatred.

NEGATIVE COMMUNICATION

Once conflict is generated, the victim A may express his frustration or anger to B, the source, but only in a negative manner – that is, by not communicating it. Instead of confronting B, victim A avoids seeing or contacting him, thereby letting B know how upset he is or how strongly he disagrees with him. In a face-to-face conversation, A may indicate no by refusing to respond to B. In Henna Buraku, 'I did not answer' meant 'I objected,' and such a message of silence may be accompanied by feigned deafness.

As an expression of conflict emotions, silence may well be accompanied by some signaling behavior such as sulking. Even then silence could be an ineffective or even misleading means of communication: Japanese are so used to silence that they may see nothing wrong in it; silence could be taken as a sign of sincerity, *enryo* (social reserve), acquiescence, or even compliance, as when children are told not to talk back. Apparently the traumatic conflict that turned the whole community of Kurusu upside down, as observed by Smith, can be traced to this uncertainty inherent in communication through silence. It seems that at the meeting of the villagers the opposition to the project of allowing an outside company to build a chicken-processing factory was communicated by silence, which was in turn taken, deliberately or innocently, by supporters of the project as an expression of consent.[6] One of my informants, while abused by her mother-in-law and sister-in-law without being shielded by her husband, 'did not say a word.' This silence seems to have meant a curious mixture of 'unequivocal' compliance, endurance, grudge, and grievance.

SITUATIONAL CODE SWITCHING

Two parties in conflict may avoid each other but assume friendliness when certain situations call for it. In Takashima, Norbeck noted that persons in discord usually avoided one another but still exchanged greetings. Personal frictions were not permitted to interfere with *buraku* (hamlet) affairs. 'Foresworn enemies discuss with no trace of rancor the issues at hand during a *buraku* meeting ...'[7]

Likewise an estranged husband and wife, or a daughter-in-law and mother-in-law, argue freely or refuse to talk to each other when left alone but pretend to be harmonious when guests are present. For this reason, the party anxious to restore harmony tries to set up formal occasions necessitating an invitation of outsiders. Any two persons, kin or nonkin, who have not been on speaking terms may thus be able to talk to each other behind a formal mask appropriate in a ceremonial interaction. Providing such opportunities may be taken as one of the functions of ceremonies like death anniversaries.

An emergency such as illness or death is another important occasion for code switching. A family member's terminal sickness or death may become a rallying point for reconsolidation of the broken family or for readmission of an expelled member. The sick or dying person may or may not be a party to the conflict but stimulates guilt in all concerned, which in turn provides a leverage for code switching. Several life histories told to me involve a young son who, after severing himself from his family either by running away or being expelled by his father, is called back home when his father or mother falls ill. Even a fake illness may be used to soften hostility, as happened to one informant.

Implicit in code switching for formal occasions is a reversal from formal restrained interaction to informal and intimate interaction. Frustrations and anxieties may be freely talked out when A faces B in intimate conversation, probably over a drink, especially set aside from the usual formal routine in which A is inhibited from self-disclosure. Routine code switching of this sort seems at least partly responsible for the ability of male Japanese workers to maintain emotional balance.

TRIADIC MANAGEMENT

To avoid confrontation between A and B, Japanese often create a triad to manage the situation. Conflict between A and B may be communicated indirectly through the third party X who, as a go-between, represents A or B or both. The practice of arranged marriage can thus be interpreted in light of conflict management in case A's proposal is rejected by B. Mediated communication like this presupposes a supply of volunteers to mediate as well as a willingness to rely upon mediators. Japanese society satisfies both these conditions.

The third party X may take a more positive role as an arbiter for A and B in conflict. When conflict is in stalemate, X, who commands respect from both parties, may provide a breakthrough by presenting himself as the person on whose behalf A and B are advised to forgive each other. 'Save my face,' the arbiter would say, urging the conflicting parties to relent, with a tacit threat that he will take offense if his intervention is not heeded. In response, the parties may comply, even though they would rather remain adamant against each other, in order to avoid humiliating the arbiter.

The arbiter's role is fused into a surrogate role that X can play for A or B. When B offends A, arbiter X may offer a vicarious apology to A. This form of vicarious responsibility is institutionalized in Japan, as recently demonstrated by the public apology and resignation of the Tokyo Metropolitan Police chief taking responsibility for a rape and murder committed by a patrol policeman – a surprising consequence by American standards of official responsibility.[8]

The third party X may not mediate communications, but by his presence he may dramatize conflict and put pressure on A or B. When X is perceived as A's ally, A's accessibility to X will threaten B and thereby embolden A. Conflict between mother-in-law and daughter-in-law is often intensified by the presence of a sister-in-law. Likewise, the daughter-in-law visits or invites her natal family over in order to display *her* side of the alliance. A son or daughter-in-law neglectful of the aged parent or parent-in-law may also be sanctioned against, overtly or covertly, by a group of aged neighbors who congregate regularly to exchange information on their children and in-laws.

DISPLACEMENT

Displacement, a variant of triadic management, is manifested in diverse ways. In an attempt to convey his anger or disapproval to B, party A does so to X who is more vulnerable or whose retaliatory response A can better afford. A middle-aged contractor complains about his father-in-law, a retired contractor whose business he has inherited, for disagreeing with his modern way of living and doing business. 'But he never tells me directly; he scolds my employees instead. My son, too, has been harassed.' A mason recalls how his father, the master mason, rebuked him every time his apprentice employees went wrong with their jobs. The apprentices obviously understood this metacommunication and would console the son, saying, 'When you get scoldings, we know they are directed at us.' This informant believes one would be much better off if unrelated by kinship to a master.

Again, this kind of communication through displacement works only if the real receiver of the message is sensitive enough to catch it, as were the apprentice employees. Hypersensitivity, however, can be a cause of conflict. Many a grandmother complains of her daughter-in-law's harsh treatment of a grandchild, partly because, I found, she feels it was *atetsuke* or *tsuraate* (a covert slap in the face) against her, the grandmother and mother-in-law. The daughter-in-law, then, finds herself constrained from exercising her parental authority, while the mother-in-law indulges the grandchild even more, thus escalating the conflict.

The parent's over-expectation for a child's success, involving excessive investment in the child's education, may be understood as a form of displacement. The notorious *kyoiku-mama* (education mama) is more likely to be found among women who need compensations for unsatisfactory marriages and *kyoiku-papa* among men whose career ambitions have not been fruitful.

Displacement can be a rational strategy: For instance, when asking a neighbor to stop playing the piano at night, the speaker may say '*shujin-ga-nemurenai-to yuu mono-desu-kara* [since my husband says he can't sleep] rather than saying that she herself can't sleep.'[9] The request or protest is made in the name of another, which is less offensive to a Japanese listener. This strategy corresponds with what I call playing a delegate's role.[10] The speaker may even present herself as in *itabasami* (caught in the middle) between her husband and the neighbor.

Further, A may release all his or her frustration with B upon X when confident that X will not relay them to B, the source of frustration. In this case X as a sympathetic listener offers a dumping ground for A's *guchi* (personal laments). Women in particular regard one or two close friends who would listen to their *guchi* any time as indispensable to their lives. Usually two friends exchange their *guchi* whether it is about their husbands, mothers-in-law, daughters-in-law, or children. *Guchi* release is meant not for counseling but for catharsis or emotional exorcism.

The supernatural may also play the role of X in a displacement drama. Party A's conflict emotions toward B may be expressed either *to* a deity or ancestor (as when A fervently prays at the household shrine or talks to it in B's presence) or *through* one supernatural entity or another (as when one allows oneself or a shaman to speak up in the voice of a spirit). The cult called Gedatsukai, as I observed in 1970–1971, provides its members with an ingenious method of getting possessed and acting out their conflict emotions. The possession ritual permits a volunteer member, in the name of a possessing spirit, to articulate his or her feelings toward self or others in front of the altar as witnessed by other members: The spirit host is free to praise, boast, support, thank, plead, assail, castigate, or forgive himself or others. Conflict management here is twofold. On the one hand, the spirit host can play the kind of role he has been deprived of in the secular world and thereby overcome dissonance between expectations and fulfillment; on the other hand, the host can release feelings which ought to be concealed in mundane life. Spirit possession, in short, allows one to fulfill cultural expectations while at the same time transcending cultural inhibitions.[11] Witchcraft beliefs involving two victims – the person possessed and the person accused of possessing – manifest another form of supernatural displacement, as reported by Teigo Yoshida in this volume.

It is only natural that the individual comes to identify himself with his ancestors as he gets older. But even in ancestor worship among the elderly one can detect a strategic management of conflict through displacement. My informants are hesitant to articulate their expectations for being looked after by their offspring in fear of self-imposition as *meiwaku* (burden), but they are explicit in expecting the duty of ancestor worship to be transmitted from generation to generation. This can be interpreted as a circumlocution for the elderly parents, who are themselves destined soon to become ancestors, to convey their own expectation for dependency.[12]

SELF-AGGRESSION

Direct confrontation is also avoided through self-confrontation or self-aggression. What might be called 'remonstrative compliance' is an example. Party A expresses his grievance against B, his oppressor, by exaggerated compliance. A daughter protests the parental imposition of an arranged marriage by declaring that she will indeed marry the man, as did one informant. Party B's denigration of A with a derogatory label such as 'Fool!' may be retaliated by A's acceptance of that label: 'Yes, I really am a fool.' What appears to be compliance is supposed to be understood as a remonstration. Apology by a victim may well be meant as remonstrative compliance. Party A's self-aggression is intended to arouse B's guilt. This is a form of masochism involving what Reik terms 'rebellion through obedience.'[13]

Self-aggression may even go so far as self-destruction. Japan has witnessed incidences of suicide in connection with the recent disclosure of major scandals involving bribery such as the cases of Lockheed, Nissho-Iwai, and KDD (International Telecommunication Co.). This phenomenon was captured in the media as 'Suicide: The Japanese Way of Conducting a Scandal.'[14] The most controversial of all was the case of Shigesada Yasuda, an advisory staff member of the KDD president's office, who jumped in front of an oncoming train (6 February 1980). He had been under police investigation as a key figure implicated in KDD's bribery of government officials with embezzled foreign gifts. His suicide note indicated that he was going to die as a 'sacrifice' for his superiors. Self-destruction in this case is clearly a sign of resentment against the source of frustration.

This case was singled out as controversial because Japanese, in committing suicide, are expected to present themselves as conflict-torn, remorseful, or altruistic but not punitive of others. In fact all the other cases prior to that of Yasuda seem to have followed the expectation. Mitsuhiro Shimada, an executive of Nissho-Iwai, before leaping from a high-rise office building down to death (1 February 1979), wrote a suicide note addressing 'everybody of Nissho-Iwai': 'Men should maintain dignity. The company is eternal, and we should dedicate ourselves to its eternity. Each of us can work only for twenty to thirty years, but the company's life is everlasting. To protect the company's life we must be fearless like real men. For the suspected scandal which has denigrated the "image" of the company, I feel remorseful. I am taking my responsibility.'[15]

Yasuda and Shimada are thus in contrast as far as their suicide notes can reveal their motives. I speculate, however, that in a suicidal trauma an intropunitive or altruistic motive becomes confused with an extrapunitive or egoistic one. This confusion may be a clue to the confession of an informant that she had long vacillated between a wish to kill herself and a wish to kill her husband who had, she said, ruined her life. Similar confusion or ambivalence may underlie the suicide of the aged. Similarly, *shinju* (double suicide) may involve a mixture of contradictory motives as it usually includes killing a death partner as well as killing oneself; even in love suicide the male partner may first kill the female and then kill himself, unless the two choose a method of dying together such as drowning. A reported case of school avoidance is suggestive of this point: The mother, after exhausting all available means in vain to persuade her daughter to resume school attendance, became so desperate that she embraced her child, cried, and proposed that mother and daughter drown together.[16] The proposal of dying together obviously indicates a mixture of the mother's self-punishment and punishment of the child or a combination of love and hate.

What deserves attention is that self-destruction for Japanese is a 'tempting' answer to a wide range of conflicts whether intropunitive or extrapunitive, whether involving guilt, shame, or hostility, whether altruistic or egoistic. Death, or self-destruction in particular, was glorified in extreme terms by Yukio Mishima in his *On Hagakure: The Samurai Ethic and Modern Japan*, written three years before the author killed himself by disembowelment in front of stunned Self-Defense Force troops in 1970. Giving his interpretation of the text of *Hagakure*, Jocho Yamamoto's teaching for the samurai of Nabeshima-Han, Mishima writes:

> When Jocho says, 'I found that the way of the samurai is death,' he is expressing his Utopianism, his principles of freedom and happiness. That is why we are able to read *Hagakure* today as the tale of an ideal country.
>
> The occupation of the samurai is death. No matter how peaceful the age, death is the samurai's supreme motivation, and if a samurai should fear or shun death, in that instant he would cease to be a samurai.[18]

Mishima's own suicide is believed to have been meant to remonstrate with the Self-Defense Force for its lack of samurai spirit.

The general tolerance of suicide among Japanese is shown in a survey of high school students' attitudes: Only 30 percent disapproved of suicide, 28 percent did not think it bad, and 42 percent could not decide one way or the other.[19] Shimoyama, after proposing that a 'cultural' attribute may be captured intuitively by examining the syndromes of rare mental cases, suggests with some cautions that the 'death wish' (*kishi nenryo*) might be considered a Japanese characteristic.[20] He bases his argument on the case of a female patient under his psychotherapy who, deprived of close human relationships, had exhibited all signs of alienation, estrangement, hostility, and mistrust until a particular incident occurred. When she was hospitalized as a heavily bleeding victim of a traffic accident, the therapist (Shimoyama himself) offered his blood. Later on, when she learned of this act and discovered that the therapist had insisted on having as much of his blood taken as needed 'no matter what happened to himself,' she was stunned, could not stop sobbing, and refused to eat. 'That is how a death wish arose in her.'[21] Shimoyama says that a death wish like this is certainly not unique to the Japanese. What does make a cultural difference in his view is that this feeling can be intuitively understood and shared by normal Japanese, but not by Westerners.

Indeed, the idea of death seems to play a significant role in conflict management for Japanese. The imagined death (*shinda tsumori*) often provides a breakthrough for a person in despair. 'Imagine you are dead' is a common piece of advice for a victim of hopelessness to discover hope and gather the courage to make a fresh start.

The proclivities for self-aggression, including self-destruction, involve a tendency to react to certain conflict situations with self-accusation. Some of the Thematic Apperception Test (TAT) responses summarized and interpreted by De Vos indicate self-blame as a Japanese reaction, particularly among women, to a stressful situation.[22] For example: 'A husband comes home very late at night; the wife thinks it is for her lack of affection and tries hard; he finally reforms.'[23] Another example: 'An elderly brother did something wrong and is examined by the policeman; he will be taken to the police station, but will return home and reform. The younger sister also thinks that she was wrong herself.'[24] A result of sentence-completion tests confirms this assumption to an extent: In response to 'I could not do it because ...,' the Japanese displayed predominantly intropunitive feelings such as 'because I am not yet competent enough,' whereas the Italians tended to attribute the failure to other causes ('because I was too busy'; 'because I did not like to do it'); the American respondents stood between the Italians and theJapanese.[25]

Self-accusation thus can be translated as interiorization employed for the purpose of conflict management. The relative importance of inner sanction showed up in responses to a sentence-completion test I designed and administered cross-culturally. In response to 'After having done all sorts of bad things ...,' the majority of every sampled cultural group – Japanese, Korean, and Chinese – projected an external or objective form of punishment such as 'he was ruined' or 'he was finished' or 'I will be unable to be reincarnated.' But the Japanese sample did so least (66 percent), the Chinese most (86 percent), the Koreans in the middle (79 percent). This order is reversed in the responses indicating subjective retribution, which ranges from guilt to repentance, to confession, to resolution to reform: 'You feel uneasy at heart'; 'he will feel regretful and guilty'; 'he settled down to work seriously.' The Japanese had 23 percent in this category, while 14 percent of the Koreans and 10 percent of the Chinese responded this way. This finding is consistent with my analysis of responses to other sentence fragments; in that case the Japanese sample stood out in focusing on inner rewards for certain good deeds.[26]

Guilt, as a form of self-aggression, is interlocked with an allocentric worry that one may have hurt another person; shame, in contrast, is more egocentric. In my study, the response to 'If you do not know manners and etiquette ...' suggests the Japanese sensitivity to the feelings of others. The majority in all cultural groups responded either egocentrically ('you will be ashamed' or 'you will be called a barbarian') or with instructions that 'you had better learn them' or 'you should correct yourself to follow manners.' But more Japanese (33 percent) than Koreans (8 percent) or Chinese (6 percent) showed allocentric concerns: 'Your parents will be criticized' or 'you will cause discomfort in the people around you.'

Guilt is aroused especially when one feels that he has hurt his love object, hence the strong association discovered by De Vos in the TAT responses between the illness or death of parents, on the one hand, and the child's admission of guilt and repentance on the other.[27] This association provides, it seems, a psychological basis for the situational code switching discussed earlier; the death or serious illness of a family member enables people to restore family integration.

Guilt is a conflict emotion as well as a form of conflict management. To delineate the management phase of guilt more clearly we might well refer to instances of strategic 'guilt-consciousness raising' to alleviate stress or transform self-identity. Gedatsukai is only one of many cults which people join to alleviate illness, interpersonal friction, and other predicaments. Along with supernatural displacement as described previously, this cult, like others, inculcates self-blame and self-denial in its followers as means of offering leverage for alleviation of suffering. The followers are told to reorient their aggression inwardly with the understanding that their troubles actually originated in themselves, that the wrong one sees in another is only a reflection of one's own wrongdoing, that one's suffering is nothing but a noxious element that has made a return trip to its origin. Followers are thus advised to eradicate all spiritual pollution from their inner systems in order to attain an 'empty' selfhood.[28]

The Reiyukai cult reveals a similar emphasis upon self-blame as studied by Hardacre. A woman who was brought to a branch leader of this cult had made up her mind to divorce her delinquent husband, a man who had tormented her by his infidelity and gambling while depending on her supplementary income to support the family.[29] Instead of consoling the potential convert as expected, the leader blamed the whole trouble on her, the wife, rather than the husband because it was she who neglected the wifely duty of staying at home and, instead, managed a restaurant. 'Even if the husband is injured or chronically ill and the wife is forced to become the major breadwinner, it is recommended that she apologize to her husband for having usurped his role.'[30] Hardacre notes that there is sex asymmetry in that women, not men, are pressed to blame themselves. This is a crucial point in view of the fact that most of these cults appeal more to women than men. The seemingly absurd accusation encountered by this newcomer to Reiyukai apparently triggered her 'salvation.'

Naikan is a secular therapy which systematically builds up guilt in the client.[31] The client is supposed to reflect upon how much *on* (moral debt) he owes to some specific person, particularly his mother, how little he has returned to the benefactor, and above all how much worry and trouble he has caused her. He is guided to focus on *naibatsu* (inner punishment) and to discard *gaibatsu* (outer punishment). Egocentric indulgence and boasting are prohibited; sensitivity to the harm one has done to another is nurtured. By putting himself into another person's shoes (*aite no tachiba ni naru*), the client is to recode his experience in reverse: His self-pity as a victim of the other's hate, contempt, or negligence is to be converted into a deep appreciation of having been in fact loved by the same person; his grudge against the other is to be thus recoded into apology and gratitude; his boastfulness as a benefactor for the other is to be transformed into a remorseful humility after realizing that even though he has actually hurt the other person, that person has continued to love him and sacrifice for him.

It should be noted that self-aggression involved in a therapy like Naikan or religious conversion is achieved through triadic communication – through a leader or therapist who may have charismatic power of persuasion. It should be noted too, that the guilt thus intensified is released through confession or self-disclosure, which revitalizes the client and helps him to make a new resolution. As Yoshimoto, the Naikan founder and counselor, says, 'Before you jump, you must squat. As long as you remain standing, you cannot jump up.' Squatting obviously refers to the guilt-ridden posture, and jumping to revitalization.[32]

Whether in a cult, in Naikan therapy, or in other forms of moral or religious persuasion, an extrapunitive emotion – grudge, hatred, anger – is to be converted into self-improving energy. It is noteworthy in this light that energy for achievement often turns out to have derived from a vindictive commitment. What occurs to my mind immediately is a scene from a drama, *Chichi Kaeru* [Father's return], written by Kan Kikuchi. The 28-year-old eldest son refuses to accept his delinquent father who, after deserting the family twenty years ago, has returned home now old and poverty-stricken. He says:

> I don't know how you feel, Mother, because you are a woman, but as far as I am concerned, my father, if there is one, is my enemy. When we were still small and complained to you, Mother, about hunger and some such hardships, you used to say, 'All this is because of Father. Have a grudge against Father, if you wish.' If I have a father at all, it is he who has tormented us throughout since my childhood. I started to work as a waiter at the prefectural government when I was ten, and Mother earned money by pasting paper on match boxes. When Mother had no pasting job for a month, the

> whole family, four of us, skipped lunch. Have we forgotten all that? *I studied hard simply in order to avenge myself upon him, in order to look down upon the man who abandoned us.* I wanted to let him know you can attain manhood even if your father deserts you.[33]

In this drama the vindictive son has passed the difficult civil service examination and entered a respectable and secure career.

Another illustration of vindictive achievement in a real (as opposed to fictitious) world is a letter to a newspaper editor from a high school student with regard to the class discussion on why college entrance is desirable:

> My class consists entirely of those who did not make the prefectural high school. So they don't want to be defeated again by their former junior high school classmates who successfully entered the prefectural school. Also, because they failed in the entrance examination, their parents have been targets of malicious gossip among the neighbors, they said. They want to enter college, they argued, in order to triumph over the neighbors.[34]

ACCEPTANCE

As a final strategy for nonconfrontational management one should mention the acceptance of a conflict situation with equanimity. Instead of rejecting or correcting an undesirable state of affairs, the individual persuades himself or is advised by someone to accept it.

The idea of acceptance joins hands with fatalism or the belief in the karmic chain of predestination as phrased in such terms as *unmei*, *shukumei*, *sadame*, and *innen*. As pointed out by Minami, the common people of Japan have been socialized through 'popular culture,' represented by popular songs and Naniwabushi tales, to accept whatever hardships, tragedies, or absurdities they encounter as their *sadame* (destiny).[35] Once such fatalism is instilled in the masses, Minami continues, songs and tales with fatalistic themes are demanded and thus further reinforce fatalism. The fatalistic acceptance of misfortune leads to *akirame*: resignation. The person who is not ready for *akirame* is disapproved as *akirame ga warui*: resistant to *akirame*.[36]

The acceptance of *innen* should be added to supernatural displacement and guilt consciousness raising as conflict-management strategies shared by many religious cults in Japan. It is not that one's *innen* cannot be altered. Cults, in fact, offer ways of cutting one's *innen* bondage. The new freedom, however, cannot be obtained unless the *innen* is first recognized and accepted as such. *Innen* applies indiscriminately to every person, every occurrence, every experience. The cult of Gedatsukai, for example, applies the concept of *shikijo no innen* (*innen* of sexual emotion) to the victim of spouse abuse, divorce, premature widowhood, husband's promiscuity, prostitution, love suicide, rape, gynecological disorder, breast cancer, miscarriage, impotence, and many other misfortunes.

Fatalism facilitates the impersonalization of a highly emotional experience, which further reduces to an acceptance of 'nature' or the 'law of nature' as conceptualized in the symbols drawn from the Chinese cosmology: The inevitability of an event, for example, is judged in terms of the Chinese calendrical cycles, its spatial location or direction, and so forth. The subjective will, emotion, or reasoning, which accounts for conflicts, is to dissolve into nature. Hand in hand with such 'naturalism' is a reliance upon diviners (*uranai*) as revealed in the life histories I collected, for a resolution to a crisis.

Equanimity, associated with acceptance, is equated with a 'thought-less' or 'empty' state of mind. Traditional arts such as tea ceremony, calligraphy, and *shakyo* (brush-copying of sutras) are supposed to lead one to such a state. Some of my middle-aged and older informants are learning or practicing these arts to 'calm down' their upset hearts. In a way these activities offer occasions for escaping from a stressful life. Kabuki, Noh, and Bunraku seem to perform the same function for frustrated housewives, a Tokyo University-educated housewife admitted, because these traditional stage shows present a world which is totally separated from the real world.

Acceptance of things *arugamama* (as they are) is the main tenet of Morita therapy.[37] This makes sense, considering that it is a psychotherapy primarily for *shinkeishitsu* patients who are obsessed with normality and thus tend to find themselves in acute dissonance between what they perceive of themselves and what they 'ought' to be. Patients are urged to accept whatever bothers them, including their physical or mental problems, *arugamama*, instead of trying to control or correct them. A Morita therapist would tell a client to accept the hopelessness of his case, to 'obey' his symptom, to 'unite' with it, even to enact it. ('Try to blush' might be the advice for an erythrophobic patient who is morbidly afraid of blushing.) Rejection or repulsion is viewed as merely intensifying the symptom in a vicious circle. The principle of *arugamama* thus involves the liberation of mind from intellectual thinking, emotions, and volitions and its confrontation with 'facts.' In this sense, it is at the opposite pole from the escapism as mentioned above.

Acceptance of one's stress or conflict is facilitated by the realization that similar problems are shared by others. This feeling of 'co-suffering' or 'equality' is utilized by Morita therapists treating hospital patients. The patient with *taijin kyofusho* (anthropophobia: the fear of offending others by one's imagined bodily symptoms or abnormalities) is convinced that he is being eccentric, but he finds in the hospital what might be taken as a mirror reflecting himself – that is, other patients like himself. The feeling of equality thus acquired is an important step toward destroying the troublesome conviction. Moreover, by watching fellow patients he comes to realize that their symptoms are not as striking or unpleasant as they claim they are and that therefore his affliction, too, is a product of his subjective distortion of reality.[38]

CONCLUSION

Conflict management at the interpersonal level in Japan has been characterized here as nonconfrontational. We have analyzed several strategies in the preceding pages: anticipatory management, negative communication, situational code switching, triadic management, displacement, self-aggression, and conflict acceptance. Conflict management does not necessarily mean a resolution of conflict, though, but rather may intensify or systematically mobilize conflict emotions. The most salient strategy in this respect is guilt-consciousness raising for therapeutic – religious or secular – purposes. Thus the very same cultural values may both intensify conflict and be used for its management. The ultimate goal of self-transformation cuts across different strategies. Whether through religious conversion or secular therapies, whether through self-aggression or conflict acceptance, what is ultimately aimed at is an empty, egoless, joyful, and thus conflict-free self.

In conclusion I want to refer to a theoretical issue concerning contrastive models for studying Japan. When we focus on conflict, we seem to accept the conflict model and reject the harmony model as if the two were mutually exclusive. This is an oversimplified dichotomy that fails to capture reality. In fact, the logic of bipolarization may well be reversed: the more harmony-oriented, the more conflict-sensitive. If the Japanese place more value, as I believe they do, upon social interdependence, cooperation, solidarity, or harmony than, say, the Americans, they are more likely to interfere with one another's actions. The norm of harmony may be precisely what makes people more aware of conflicts with others, conflicts between their self-interest and obligations, and so forth. The unrestrained pursuit of one's own interest at the expense of another's goes against the norm of sociability. Concerned with his own interest, the individual will find the imperative of sociability and harmony oppressive. In other words, the cultural value of harmony may intensify, instead of mitigate, conflict. This effect is observed in a rural community – *mura* or *buraku* – where interdependence is an inescapable norm. In describing Shinohata, Dore observes: 'The "harmony of the village" has its cost. Underneath the placid landscape there are geological faults – a personal incompatibility, a clash of economic interest, a belief that one has been cheated – along with tensions built up which require occasional release.'[39]

That the maintenance of harmony itself can be responsible for intensifying conflict is further suggested by the following passage: 'Competition within a group which is in theory harmoniously united tends to become fiercer and more emotionally involved than in one where competition is accepted as normal. As such it leaves scars after the event in the resentful humiliation of the defeated.'[40] This passage was quoted by Smith in connection with a major conflict that occurred in Kurusu.[41] Elsewhere, in Niiike, researchers witnessed tensions and disputes over water control -- the very basis for village solidarity.[42] All these observations seem to point out that conflict is inherent in harmony[43] or at least interlocks with Benedict's views of the Japanese in terms of such bipolar adjectives as polite but insolent, rigid but innovative, submissive but not amenable to control, loyal but treacherous, disciplined but insubordinate, and so forth.[44] These bipolarities may make more sense if the 'buts' are replaced by 'therefores.'

In a social unit, like a *buraku*, characterized by its closure and tight network of cooperation, intense competitiveness, jealousy, and hatred may indeed predominate, though such conflict emotions usually may not surface. A resident of Henna Buraku, as reported by Kida, a participant observer, described the fellow villagers as always having their eyes wide open for every chance to 'tear up (*himmuki*) and win over one another ... Others' misfortunes are celebrated by cooking red-bean rice, and their good fortunes are cursed.'[45] That one should distrust insiders, contrary to general expectations, more than outsiders, was revealed by another resident: 'There is nothing to be feared about graveyards or the dead. They are dead and can do nothing. What is more frightening, you see, is a human being, alive and kicking. But mind you, it's not someone remote and unknown, but people who are around you and close to you.'[46] Kida was warned by another informant not to be put off his guard with the villagers however friendly they became because 'the mouth and belly are two different things.'[47] Obviously this kind of mistrust and hostility does not repudiate but rather validates Kida's claim that the *buraku* has its unity.[48]

What appears as a proof of unity may turn out to underscore the prevalence of disunity. In reference to the *tonarigumi* (an organized neighborhood unit), an informant, who had just moved into that area as a bride, says she was surprised to find that every *tonarigumi* meeting was religiously attended by all the ten women representing their respective households. The reason, she realized, was that one member's absence would encourage all the other members present to gossip about the absentee and her family. 'You show up just to avoid being spoken ill about.'

Implicit in this paradox is the fact that harmony is necessitated by the kind of interdependence that runs all the way from the positive extreme to the negative extreme. Positive interdependence or what Deutsch calls 'promotive interdependence' refers to the situation in which A can attain his goal only if B can.[49] Negative interdependence or Deutsch's 'contrient interdependence' refers to the opposite: A can attain his goal only if B cannot. In a *buraku* the former may be exemplified by its members' participation in collective enterprises – emergency aid, labor exchange, rituals, mutual entertainment, and the like – which benefit all the participants sooner or later if not all at once. What demands our attention is the fact that the same members of the community tied together in promotive interdependence are also constrained by contrient interdependence (A's win entails B's loss). Harmony in this circumstance requires one to refrain from outdoing others and to remain unobtrusive because 'a protruding stake will be pounded down.' The result is a reservoir of frustration and repressed hostility.

In short, I am suggesting that the two contrastive models – conflict and harmony – might be more profitably used in conjunction with one another than disjointly. This essay was written with the goal of discovering where and how conflict and harmony are dovetailed.

NOTES

This research was aided by the National Science Foundation (Grant BNS76-11301), the Japan Society for Promotion of Science, and the University of Hawaii Japan Studies Endowment, which is funded by a grant from the Japanese government. Research assistance and typing service by Linda Kimura were indispensable to the completion of this study. I wish to express my gratitude to all.

1. Leon Festinger, *A Theory of Cognitive Dissonance* (Stanford: Stanford University Press, 1957).
2. Markus and Tamer attempt to synthesize different models into a 'conflict model.' See Gregory B.

Markus and Raymond Tanter, 'A Conflict Model for Strategists and Managers,' *American Behavioral Scientist* 15 (6)(1972): 809–836.
3. Ronald P. Dore, *Shinohata: A Portrait of a Japanese Village* (New York: Pantheon Books, 1978), pp. 272–277.
4. Minoru Kida, *Nippon Buraku* [Japanese hamlet] (Tokyo: Iwanami, 1967), p. 5.
5. Dore, *Shinohata*, p. 268.
6. Robert J. Smith, *Kurusu: The Price of Progress in a Japanese Village*, 1951–1975 (Stanford: Stanford University Press, 1978), p. 232.
7. Edward Norbeck, *Takashima: A Japanese Fishing Community* (Salt Lake City: University of Utah Press, 1954), pp. 116–117.
8. *Japan Times*, reprinted in *Hawaii Hochi*. 16 January 1978.
9. Osamu Mizutani and Nobuko Mizutani, 'Nihongo Notes,' *Japan Times*, reprinted in *Hawaii Hochi*, 20 June 1979.
10. Takie Sugiyama Lebra, *Japanese Patterns of Behavior* (Honolulu: University of Hawaii Press, 1976), p. 123.
11. Takie Sugiyama Lebra, 'Taking the Role of the Supernatural "Other": Spirit Possession in a Japanese Healing Cult,' in W. P. Lebra, ed., *Culture-Bound Syndromes, Ethnopsychiatry, and Alternate Therapies* (Honolulu: University of Hawaii Press, 1976); Takie Sugiyama Lebra, 'Ancestral Influence on the Suffering of the Descendants in a Japanese Cult,' in W. H. Newell, ed., *Ancestors* (The Hague: Mouton, 1976).
12. Takie Sugiyama Lebra, 'The Dilemma and Strategies of Aging Among Contemporary Japanese Women,' *Ethnology*, 18 (1979): 337–353.
13. Cited in G. Piers and M. B. Singer, *Shame and Guilt* (Springfield, Ill.: Charles C. Thomas, 1953), p. 26.
14. *Japan Times*, reprinted in *Hawaii Hochi*, 3 March 1980.
15. *Hawaii Hochi*, 3 February 1979.
16. Shusaku Sato, *Toko Kyohiji* [Children in school refusal] (Tokyo: Kokudosha, 1968), p. 52.
17. Yukio Mishima, *On Hagakure: The Samurai Ethic and Modern Japan*, trans. Kathryn Sparling (Tokyo: Charles E. Tuttle, 1978), p. 8.
18. Mishima, *On Hagakure*, p. 27.
19. Eishi Katsumata, 'Jisatsusha no Shinrigakuteki Tokucho' [Psychological characteristics of the suicidal person] 'Jisatsugaku' [Science of suicide], in K. Ohara, ed., *Gendai no Esupuri Bessatsu* [Esprit of today: special issue] (1970).
20. Tokuji Shimoyama, 'Ningen Gaku Teki Shinri Ryoho ni Okeru Nihonteki Tokusei' [The Japanese characteristics of psychotherapy viewed from the standpoint of humanistic science], *Seishin Igaku* [Clinical psychiatry] 17 (13)(1975): 28–34.
21. Shimoyama, 'Japanese Characteristics of Psychotherapy,' p. 33.
22. George De Vos, 'The Relation of Guilt Toward Parents to Achievement and Arranged Marriage Among Japanese,' in T. S. Lebra and W. F. Lebra, eds., *Japanese Culture and Behavior: Selected Readings* (Honolulu: University of Hawaii Press, 1974).
23. Ibid., p. 128.
24. Ibid., p. 129.
25. Takao Sofue, 'Aspects of the Personality of Japanese, Americans, Italians and Eskimos: Comparisons Using the Sentence Completion Test,' *Journal of Psychological Anthropology* 2(1)(1979): 11–52.
26. Takie Sugiyama Lebra, 'Compensative Justice and Moral Investment Among Japanese, Chinese and Koreans,' *Journal of Nervous and Mental Disease* 157 (1973): 278–291.
27. De Vos, 'The Relation of Guilt.'
28. Takie Sugiyama Lebra, 'The Interactional Perspective of Suffering and Curing in a Japanese Cult,' *International Journal of Social Psychiatry*, 20 (1974): 281–286.
29. Helen Hardacre, 'Sex-Role Norms and Values in Reiyukai,' *Japanese Journal of Religious Studies* 6 (3)(1979): 445–460.
30. Ibid., p. 454.
31. Ishin Yoshimoto, *Naikan Yonjunen* [Forty years of Naikan] (Tokyo: Shunjusha, 1965); Nikichi Okumura, Koji Sato, and Haruo Yamamoto, eds., *Naikan Ryoho* [Naikan therapy] (Tokyo: Igaku Shoin, 1972); Takao Murase, 'Naikan Therapy,' in W. P. Lebra, ed., *Culture-Bound Syndromes, Ethnopsychiatry, and Alternate Therapies* (Honolulu: University of Hawaii Press, 1976); Lebra, *Japanese Patterns of Behavior*, pp. 201–214.
32. Ishin Yoshimoto, 'Naikan no Hoho to jissen' [The method and practice of Naikan], in N. Okumura, K. Sato, and H. Yamamoto, eds., *Naikan Ryoho* [Naikan therapy] (Tokyo: Igaku Shoin, 1972), p. 30.

33. Kan Kikuchi, *Chichi Kaeru; Tojuro no Koi* [Father's return; Tojuro's love] (Tokyo: Kadokawa Bunko, 1971), p. 16. (My emphasis and my translation.)
34. *Asahi* (Osaka edition), 9 October 1978.
35. Hiroshi Minami, *Nihonjin no Shinri* [Psychology of the Japanese] (Tokyo: Iwanami Shoten, 1953), p. 127.
36. Ibid., p. 138.
37. Akihisa Kondo, 'Morita Ryoho' [Morita therapy], *Seishin Igaku* [Clinical psychiatry] 8 (9)(1966): 707–715; Takehisa Kora, 'Morita Therapy,' *International Journal of Psychiatry* 1 (1965): 611–645; Shoma Morita, *Shinkeishitsu no Hontai to Ryoho* [The essential characteristics and therapy of Shinkeishitsu] (Tokyo: Hakuyosha, 1960); Takehisa Kora and Koji Sato, 'Morita Therapy – A Psychotherapy in the Way of Zen,' *Psychologia* 1(1958): 219–225; Lebra, *Japanese Patterns of Behavior*, pp. 215–231.
38. Hiroshi Iwai and Toru Abe, *Morita Ryoho no Riron to Jissai* [The theory and practice of Morita therapy) (Tokyo: Kongo Shuppan, 1975), pp. 121--122.
39. Dore, *Shinohata*, p. 266.
40. Ronald P. Dore, *Land Reform in Japan* (London: Oxford University Press, 1959), p. 343.
41. Robert J. Smith, *Kurusu: The Price of Progress in a Japanese Village, 1951–1975*, p. 237.
42. Richard K. Beardsley, John W. Hall, and Robert E. Ward, *Village Japan* (Chicago: University of Chicago Press, 1959), pp. 126, 136–138.
43. This view is in line with certain sociological theories of conflict. Simmel begins his analysis of conflict with the assumption that antagonism, aversion, repulsion, hostility, and dissociation are inherent in social order. The functionalist view of conflict, conveyed by Simmel, is seconded by Coser, who thinks violence contributes to a new social equilibrium. Similarly, Gluckman argues that the African 'rituals of rebellion' are to dramatize the existence of social order by displaying its opposite. See Georg Simmel, *Conflict and The Web of Group-Affiliations*, trans. Kurt H. Wolff and Reinhard Bendix (New York: Free Press, 1955); Lewis A. Coser, *Continuities in the Study of Social Conflict* (New York: Free Press, 1970), pp. 53–110; M. Gluckman, *Rituals of Rebellion in South-east Africa* (Manchester: Manchester University Press, 1954).
44. Ruth Benedict, *The Chrysanthemum and the Sword: Patterns of Japanese Culture* (Boston: Houghton Mifflin, 1946), pp. 1–3.
45. Kida, *Nippon Buraku*, p. 98.
46. Ibid., p. 99.
47. Ibid., p. 102.
48. Ibid., pp. 36–42.
49. Morton Deutsch, *The Resolution of Conflict* (New Haven: Yale University Press, 1973), p. 20.

First published in *Multilingua: Journal of Cross-Cultural and Interlanguage Communication*, Vols 6–4, 1987

⑩ The Cultural Significance of Silence in Japanese Communication*

Silence is a communicative act in all cultures. This paper discusses intended and perceived meanings of silence in Japanese communication and their cultural values. The author distinguishes and illustrates four dimensions of silence that are culturally salient and mutually contradictory: truthfulness, social discretion, embarrassment, and defiance. These dimensions may also be marked in other cultures in other ways.

It is well recognized that silence is a communicative act rather than a mere void in communicational space. If indirect or metaphorical speech is a way of 'saying one thing and meaning another', as Tannen (1985: 97) states, 'silence can be a matter of saying nothing and meaning something'. It is in this spirit that this paper was conceived.

Since I have made no comparative study on silence, the following discussion is based upon my personal observations and experiences in Japanese and American situations of social interaction. If cultures can be differentiated along the noise-silence continuum in a similar fashion to the fascinating comparison made by Maltz (1985) in worshiping styles between noisy Pentecostals and silent Quakers, there are many indications that Japanese culture tilts toward silence.

Compare, for example, American and Japanese soap operas on TV and just listen with closed eyes and you will immediately notice the difference in the amount of vocalization. Guided by Jourard's (1964) idea of the 'transparent' versus 'opaque' types of person, Barnlund (1975) compared Japanese with American college students in responses to questions regarding self-disclosure. In conversation, as well as in tactile communication, the Japanese were consistently found to disclose themselves less than Americans. Thus, the ratio of private self to public self, Barnlund contends, is larger for Japanese than for American communicants. It is my impression that Japanese silence stands out not only in comparison with Southern Europeans or New Yorkers but with East Asian neighbors like Koreans and Chinese as well.

Despite the prevalence of silence, the Japanese do not take silence for granted but instead cultivate it. Personalities are often described in terms of reticence or loquaciousness, and actions are characterized as taken 'in silence'. The cultural cultivation of silence, if I may digress a little, is best manifested in traditional music, in which silent intervals called *ma* are central while sounds play an auxiliary role in marking *ma*.[1] Similarly essential to

Japanese painting is the painter's awareness of the expressiveness of blank space, the spatial metaphor of silence, whether within or outside the picture frame. In theatrical dancing, kabuki performance, or even in film, too, freeze in motion may convey a peak of emotional intensity. In writing, which is verbal but nonvocal, Japanese writers pay special attention to silence, as noted by Saville-Troike (1985: 5-6), using the silence marker '……'. Writing itself may violate the cultural norm of silence. Miyoshi goes as far as to say:

> writing in Japanese is always something of an act of defiance. Silence not only invites and seduces all would-be speakers and writers, but is in fact a powerful compulsion throughout the whole society. To bring forth a written work to break this silence is thus often tantamount to the writer's sacrifice of himself, via defeat and exhaustion. (1974: xv)

The suicidal tendency of Japanese writers is thus imputed to such stress inherent in Japanese writing. This may be an exaggerated statement since writing is an important alternative, as will be shown later, for the vocally reticent Japanese, but it does illuminate the Japanese compulsion for silence.

It is in the light of such compulsive silence that we can better understand the function of *aizuchi*, back-channel signals generously supplied by the Japanese listener. The speaker in conversation will be unable to continue to speak unless supported and encouraged by the listener's *aizuchi* utterances signaling 'Go on, and then what?', which occur between words and phrases, many times within a sentence. The absence of *aizuchi* indicates the listener's hostility or distrust.[2] The English speaker, too, expects supportive signals like nodding from his listener, but the amount of vocal backchanneling by the Japanese listener seems by far to exceed the American counterpart. In intercultural communication, I notice that the English speaker is annoyed by the Japanese listener uttering *aizuchi* too often, too untimely, and too loudly.

CONTRASTIVE MEANINGS

If silence is a communicative act as stated at the outset, what do the Japanese try to convey through silence or what kind of meaning do they read in one another's silence? What cultural values and beliefs underlie their silent communication? What, in other words, does silence symbolize for the Japanese? I will show the polysemic value of silence involving its contrastive meanings. It may be hypothesized that the multiplicity, opposition, and, hence, ambiguity of the meanings of silence correlate with the prevalence of conversational silence. Instead of being exhaustive, the following analysis focuses on the four dimensions of silence which I regard as culturally salient and as mutually contradictory.

I am not arguing the uniqueness of Japanese communication style, but rather presenting the Japanese case in order to offer a possible contribution toward the understanding of human communication in general. It should be noted, however, that with my meager research experience outside Japan I am in no position either to assert the uniqueness of Japanese silence or to read universals into the Japanese case. The truth may lie somewhere between these two extremes. I suspect each of the four dimensions, taken apart, to find its parallel in some other cultures. The difference may be in the degree of prevalence or awareness, specific manifestations and elaborations, or the total complex of all the meanings put together.

Truthfulness

First, the Japanese view the person as sharply split into inner and outer parts, and believe that truth lies only in the inner realm as symbolically localized in the heart or belly. Components of the outer self, such as face, mouth, spoken words, are, in contrast, associated with disguise, distortion, deception, trickery, scheming; in short, cognitive and moral falsity. Truthfulness, sincerity, straightforwardness, or reliability are allied to reticence. Thus a man of few words is trusted more than a man of many words. Proverbs abound warning about the inner-outer duality of a speaker, calling for alertness to glib talkers, as in the following examples:

> *Kuchi ni mitsu ari, hara ni ken ari.*
> Honey in the mouth, a dagger in the belly.
> *Aho no hanashi gui.*
> A fool eats (believes) whatever is said.
> *Hanashi hanbun.*
> Believe only half of what you hear.
> *Bigen shin narazu.*
> Beautiful speech lacks sincerity.

Implicit in these cautions against spoken words, particularly smooth, eloquent speakers, is the image of a trustworthy person characterized as *kuchi gatai* (hard-mouthed). Even in the political arena oratory is not a necessary quality for leadership, and some prime ministers in the past have been known for their slow, clumsy speech style, as exemplified by Mr. Ohira, who was nicknamed the 'Ah-uh Premier'. Such leaders may be joked about but not discredited due to their poor speech. Silence could have a political appeal as in the case of Noboru Takeshita, the recently nominated successor to Prime Minister Nakasone, who is known as 'a man of silence and patience'.[3]

The truthfulness of silence is implied in the communicative value symbolically attached by the message seeker to the back of the unwitting message sender's body instead of the face.[4] There is a saying, 'The child grows up watching its father's back'. What has a decisive impact upon the child's development is not the father's face-to-face verbal instruction but his silent body motion while unaware of being watched. The expressiveness of the silent back appears in love songs as well as in the life histories of women I have interviewed.

Distrust of speech is further reinforced by the idea that it is associated with inactivity, that action can start only when speech stops. Thus talking is denigrated as an excuse for procrastinating in taking action, and decisive action is characterized as silent. Hence the proverbial admonition, '*Fugen jikko*' (Action before talking).

The equation of silence with truthfulness ultimately merges with the world view which, embedded in the Buddhism-Shinto context, recognizes no opposition, but rather idealizes a perfect union between subject and object, mind and existence, culture and nature. From this world view emerges the ideal of *mushin*, literally mindlessness, transcending all the boundaries and oppositions, dispensing with words and speech.

Social discretion

The above discussion has focused upon the generalized, and even ultimate, truth value – cognitive, moral, and esthetic – allied with silence. By contrast, this second point addresses a more mundane, concrete, situational, or superficial level of communication. Social discretion refers to silence considered necessary or desirable in order to gain social acceptance or to avoid social penalty. Silence here involves restraint from revealing the inner truth, whether cognitive, emotional, or moral, in consideration of propriety, sociability, deference, dignity, or whatever social value needs to be sustained in interaction with those people who count. Vocal hesitation may be thus understood as a sign of modesty, unobtrusiveness, politeness, empathy, acquiescence, avoidance of humiliation, and so forth. Such discretion may be exercised either because the silent addressor is affectively attached to the addressee involving love or respect, or because the addressor finds the silence strategy advantageous to his/her own social gain.

'Nonpropositional silences' (Saville-Troike 1985: 6) such as pauses between turns at talk are quite common in Japan and are indicative of polite avoidance of interruption. Like other culturally patterned modes of communication, this kind of polite pause may lead to a deadlock in intercultural communication. Fumiteru Nitta (1987) observed encounters in Waikiki between Japanese tourists and American Hare Krishna followers, the latter trying to extract 'donations' from the former. The Japanese, unalert, get trapped into passive silence and eventual compliance with the forceful demand made by the Hare Krishna devotees incessantly talking and flattering without giving the listeners a chance to interrupt. As long as someone speaks face-to-face, the Japanese listener feels compelled to pay attention, and therefore the tourists have no alternative, it seems, but to succumb in order to restore freedom.

The dual image of a person, inner and outer, remains intact, but the truth value of silence is reversed here in that silence conceals rather than reflects truth. Contrary to the first dimension where silence is truthful, it is the spoken word here that is dangerously truthful and may invite social disapproval, hostility, ostracism, or shame.

Again we find many proverbs and sayings exhorting reticence but with implications different from the above category, as shown by the following examples:

> *Iwanu ga hana.*
> Better to leave things unsaid.
> *Kuchi wa wazawai no mon.*
> The mouth is the gate of trouble (talking causes trouble).
> *Tori mo nakaneba utaremaji.*
> If the bird had not sung, it would not have been shot.

> *Mono ieba kuchibiru samushi aki no kaze.*
> If you talk, your lips will feel cold (it is safer not to talk).

These proverbs make no fuss about whether what is said or unsaid is true or false, but only call attention to the social advisability of silence.

Social discretion requires knowledge of what can and cannot be said to whom in what situation. Whether to keep quiet, or to speak up is relative to these variables. The same social discretion that calls for silent sociability in one situation demands vocal sociability in another. The normally socialized Japanese carries a verbal kit of highly conventional, innocuous, informationally empty expressions and clichés just to show congeniality. Thus silent Japanese prove profusely vocal in greeting, thanking, apologizing,[5] or self-denigrating, as well as in backchanneling. On proper occasions which Turner (1969) would call 'liminal', they become crudely boisterous as they are expected.

To reiterate the focal point of the argument: while the first dimension of silence attaches truthfulness to silence and falsity to the spoken word, the second dimension, social discretion, reverses the above correlation. This second dimension, therefore, explains why silence is sometimes associated even by the Japanese with inscrutability, concealment, sneakiness, disguise, and dangerousness, paradoxically, in the same fashion as speech is in the first dimension. This implies a degree of ambivalence on the part of the Japanese toward silence. Be that as it may, the two dimensions, while logically opposed, complement each other to sharpen the split of personhood into the inner and outer parts, or in the Japanese vernacular, *ura* and *omote*, or *uchi* and *soto*.[6] Both dimensions presuppose the existence of the gulf and the verbal-vocal manipulability of that gulf, and thereby together intensify the untrustworthiness of the spoken word because truth cannot be converted into speech or because truth should not be spoken. On the other hand, silence is not always accepted in trust as we have noted. The problematic aspect of silence will be taken up below in conjunction with compensatory channels.

Embarrassment

The above two dimensions are the most salient, but two more will be added. Discretional silence is usually addressed to the people who deserve the courtesy of protection from possibly harmful speech. Social discretion is necessary in the 'ritual domain', whereas one can be free from such constraint in the 'intimate domain'[7] as typically exemplified by a small group of intimate peers such as former schoolmates or coworkers. However, that does not mean that intimacy always goes with uninhibited chatting. Particularly to be noted is the conjugal relationship where intimacy prevails and yet the verbal expression of mutual emotions tends to be minimal.

I am not talking about the silence of the tired old couple with nothing to say to each other, such couples being abundant in Japan and elsewhere. I am referring to the husband and wife who are in love but too embarrassed to express their feelings in speech. Embarrassment extends to address terms, including personal names (until recently) for a spouse, so that husband and wife may end up termless in addressing one another. One explanation for conjugal embarrassment, given by my informants, is that husband and wife are *isshin dōtai* (in one mind and body). 'Isn't it embarrassing to express love for yourself?' It is for the same psychological reason that the Japanese husband and wife do not praise but rather denigrate each other in speaking to a third person as an expression of humility (Lebra 1984a).

The Japanese wife's maternal care for her supposedly helpless husband, at least during the earlier stage of marriage, may be understood as a nonverbal compensation for verbal inhibition in expressing tender emotions. Dressing and undressing the husband, for instance, is a substitute for saying 'I love you'. But, then, the husband only receives such care, he only 'hears', not 'speaks' love. It is understandable that more wives than husbands complain about the spouse's muteness. 'I want to know whether the dish I cook tastes good or not' is one example of the wives' complaints.

The above explanation does not tell the whole story about what underlies conjugal silence,[8] but it does shed light upon the other side of the second dimension. As ritual distance demands discretional silence, so does intimacy inhibit the verbal externalization of emotions. Just as the first two dimensions reinforce silence from the opposite directions, so do the second and third dimensions.

Defiance

The fourth dimension refers to the use of silence to express estrangement, hostility, or defiance. This is the logical inverse of the second dimension where silence is a means of creating or maintaining sociability, and from the third dimension where silence is a sign of embarrassment emanating from intimacy.

In order to say 'I disagree with you', 'I object', 'I am angry with you', or 'I hate you', one presents silence, usually accompanied by facial cues. When a Japanese says, 'I did not say a single word', defiant silence is often meant, as I have witnessed among my women informants in describing their postmarital hardship. Minoru Kida (1967), a sociologist researching in village communities, noted that the villagers meant 'objections' when they did not answer a question. Faking deafness may accompany such defiant silence.[9]

What is interesting about this dimension is the self-assertiveness of the silent speaker. Unlike social discretion and embarrassment in which silence involves hesitancy in self-expression, defiant silence is openly expressive and assertive of self. In a vocal culture, this would be the situation where verbal bullets are shot at the target ruthlessly. The noise contrast in TV soap operas mentioned earlier may have a great deal to do with the contrastive forms of asserting hostility: vocal battles amplifying to maximal decibels on one screen, and dead silence on the other screen.

It has been shown that silence is not only polysemic but symbolic of logically opposite meanings or emotions. This certainly generates confusion and misunderstanding for a cultural outsider, but for the native as well. The silent speaker, too, is likely to have mixed feelings or rationales. When a woman says she was silent throughout the period of her husband's extramarital indulgence, she can mean her feminine modesty, compliance, patience, resentment, unforgiveness, or defiance, and may mean all. A man's refusal to express tender feelings toward his wife may be explained not only as embarrassment, but as an expression of male dignity, or as his true, sincere love, which is beyond words. In the scene of collective decision-making, silence can be taken as polite acquiescence or disagreement.

To be sure, nonverbal cues and actions are mobilized to differentiate between the various meanings, but cultural tolerance for the ambiguity of messages, whether vocal or silent, must be present to allow for the prevalence of silence. In the Japanese case, such tolerance seems justified by the first dimension, truthfulness, of silence, which ultimately relegates the spoken word or word itself to the world of illusion.

SOCIAL HIERARCHY AND SILENCE

A word is in order here with regard to the distribution of silence behavior over social structure, specifically hierarchical relations between two or more persons in interaction. The hierarchy may be defined by age, gender, socioeconomic status, formal positions in a bureaucratic setting, etc. Asymmetry in ranking is certainly reflected in the asymmetric distribution of silence, and yet it is far from simple whether silence is skewed for the higher or lower ranking person. This is because silence is an inferior's obligation in one context and a superior's privilege in another, symbolic of a superior's dignity in one instance and of an inferior's humility in another.

When the family receives a formal guest, it is the husband who talks as head of the house while the wife remains silent or is relegated to the role of auxiliary speaker. This happened when I asked to interview wives: even though this was understood in advance, some wives could not help conceding the speaking right to their unsolicited husbands. The reverse also takes place. Some husbands regard speaking as a female role and let their wives speak even when a question is addressed to them, as happened in a TV interview with an old man where all the questions were answered by his wife while the 'interviewee' kept silent, smiling, and occasionally nodding his head. (In this particular case, the couple seemed to acknowledge that the wife as an all-round caretaker for the husband knew more about him than he did.) I know some men who, upon receiving a telephone call, unless it is from a business associate, immediately turn the receiver over to their wives. Verbal unresponsiveness is a male prerogative or a strategy for protecting male dignity. Conversely, verbal readiness is associated with the accommodative role of the woman; she may become a talking chief for the husband. Furthermore, talkativeness is characterized as a female liability, an indication of feminine (inferior) status and feminine (impulsive) character. Women complain about 'male reticence' (of their husbands and sometimes of their sons as well), but also do not approve of talkative, hence 'woman-like' men.

A similar difference can be observed in a bureaucratic setting. The boss, such as a division chief, may speak to a group of his subordinates while the latter listen in silence, or he may speak to outsiders on behalf of his subordinates. Again, however, he may rather exercise his status prerogative of silence while his deputy in 'wifely role' does the talking. A woman told me that in Japan the higher up you go, the more mute you become. She was complaining about her successful and silent son.

The relationship between hierarchy and silence is thus complicated: sometimes they correlate directly, and sometimes the correlation is inverse. But one thing is clear, and that is the asymmetric distribution of silence and speech instead of competitive, interruptive, or reciprocal interchange: one party speaks, the other is silent. Such asymmetry is observed typically in a college classroom or academic conference room.

Even in a less structured setting like group therapy where participants are all encouraged to speak spontaneously, Japanese participants tend to remain silent and look up to older participants or therapists to take the lead in speaking.[10] In anticipation of such a culturally imposed inhibition, the therapist in a group therapy session that I observed took an authoritarian role in ordering the patients to speak 'freely'. Many of the patients volunteered to express their emotions in compliance with the therapist and therefore addressed the therapist rather than one another. The therapist responded either with approval or disapproval.

To add another episode, I was struck with such asymmetry in conversation when I witnessed a group of Japanese tourists in Honolulu having dinner in a restaurant. About a dozen people, men and women, were talking with diners seated next to them. Soon, some voices became louder while the others settled into a listener's role, and eventually one man, obnoxiously loud, was yelling to the whole group as his audience. This was a good example of what Bateson (1958) calls 'complementary schismogenesis'.

COMPENSATORY COMMUNICATION CHANNELS

Even though silence is a communicative act, it is much too indirect, vague, polysemic, and confusing for satisfactory communication, unless communicants know one another very well and can do without verbal information about one another's thoughts and feelings. Cultural tolerance for vagueness notwithstanding, the Japanese are thus obliged to go through what is known as *hara-gei*, literally 'belly art', referring to indirect communication by means of subtle cues and intuition in understanding and letting others understand what has not been said. The abdominal metaphor is also found in such expressions as 'probing into one another's belly' (trying to find one another's true intention or feeling), 'having one's painless belly searched around' (being suspected despite one's innocence).

Still, with no directly verbal outlet, disturbing emotions such as rage, may build up until one's 'belly gets heated to a boiling point'. One may then find it necessary to 'cut open' one's belly (or heart), to talk frankly. This kind of surgical metaphor suggests the difficulty which the Japanese individual usually has in expressing his/her feelings directly to the target person, and the tendency, instead, of 'absorbing' such feelings into his/her belly. In avoidance of direct, face-to-face, dyadic communication, however, there are indirect channels to compensate for communicational barriers imposed by the silence code. Again, my approach is selective, not exhaustive.

Writing: Quasi-monologue

Since silence occurs in face-to-face interaction with another person(s), the frustrated silent 'speaker' may choose to break the silence through a sort of monologue which takes the form of writing. It is no coincidence that many Japanese keep or try to keep diaries – at least more than Americans to the best of my knowledge. In a type of psychotherapy called *Morita* therapy, which does not rely upon vocal communication between therapist and patient, the patient is required to keep a diary and the therapist writes his comment in the margin. Even if the writing is being addressed to someone, it may take the form of a monologue as in a diary.

Writing as a substitute for talking is also shown by the practice of loveletter writing, where an orally shy person may become emboldened, or a vocally inarticulate Romeo (or Juliet) may turn out surprisingly eloquent. This practice is still going on among sexually liberated young boys and girls even within the same classroom. Furthermore, from my teaching experience in both Japan and the United States, I found Japanese students more silent in class and more expressive and fluent in writing.

Triadic communication

Nevertheless, writing is a poor substitute after all. Much more common is verbal communication through a third person. If monologue is a monadic way of avoiding dyadic encounter, this is a triadic way of doing the same. Instead of talking directly to an addressee or of listening to an addressor, one speaks to a surrogate hearer or hears from a surrogate speaker.[11]

One form of triadic communication is *mediation* as in marriage negotiation through a go-between. Such mediation through a third person for consensus building may be a widespread practice across cultures. Not only in negotiation for a specific goal, but in routine communication a third person may be felt necessary as a mediator. Among my Japanese informants I found cases where the old husband and wife send messages to each other through their resident daughter-in-law, an outsider.

Another form of triadic communication is what might be called *displacement*. Here a third person is put into the role of a surrogate addressee instead of being a mediator. Displacement may be nothing more than cathartic as when the speaker confidentially dumps all grievances against an absent addressee upon the surrogate listener, only to empty his/her bursting belly. Cathartic displacement is quite common among the Japanese. Displacement could be an effective means of communication between the principals as well. A loving but reticent husband, unable to express his love, respect, and appreciation for his wife, may do so by baby-talking to his little child about 'Mom' when she is within hearing distance; a young mother may scold or even hit her child in front of her mother-in-law, which the latter may take as a retaliation against herself. The mother-in-law, in turn, may overly indulge the grandchild in order to punish her daughter-in-law. The smallest child often becomes an involuntary surrogate hearer – an interactional version of teknonymy. An informant grandmother told me, when her grandson was away on a trip with his parents, she realized that she and her husband had nothing to say to each other, leaving the whole house dead silent. This meant that the couple was in communication only if their two-year-old grandson was around as a surrogate hearer and speaker.

CONCLUSION

Silence in contrast to speech occurs in every culture, and there may be some universals in what silence means, and how it is compensated for. This paper is meant ultimately to contribute toward understanding such possible universals, but my immediate purpose was to present the Japanese variety. I selected some of the culturally salient dimensions of communicative silence, in disregard of extreme cases such as silence between total strangers who do not care about one another's inner thoughts or between the utmost intimates who understand one another without verbal exchange.

I speculate that the prevalence of silence among the Japanese has to do with their awareness of individuals being interdependent and interconnected, which inhibits vocal self-assertion. It is instructive to recall that even strong self-assertion in defiance can be expressed through silence. The question arises as to how their communicative behavior changes when the sense of separation strengthens, as is happening today. Will the Japanese become more talkative, less silent, to assert themselves? I cannot say yes or no. It is more likely, as far as my impression goes, that overt silence will continue or even intensify but its meanings change.

REFERENCES

Barnlund, Dean C. 1975. *Public and Private Self in Japan and the United States: Communicative Styles of Two Cultures.* Tokyo: The Simul Press.

Bateson, Gregory 1958. *Naven*, 2nd ed. Stanford: Stanford University Press.

Dan, Ikuma 1961. The influence of Japanese traditional music on the development of Western music in Japan. *Transactions of the Asiatic Society of Japan*, 3rd series, vol. 8, 201–217.

Doi, Takeo 1986. *The Anatomy of Self: The Individual versus Society.* Trans. by Mark A. Harbison. Tokyo: Kodansha International.

Jourard, Sidney 1964. *The Transparent Self.* Princeton: Van Nostrand.

Kida, Minoru 1967. *Nippon Buraku* [The Japanese Hamlet]. Tokyo: Iwanami Shoten.

Lebra, Takie Sugiyama 1976. *Japanese Patterns of Behavior.* Honolulu: University of Hawaii Press.

—— 1984a. *Japanese Women: Constraint and Fulfillment.* Honolulu: University of Hawaii Press.

—— 1984b. Nonconfrontational strategies for management of interpersonal conflicts. In Krauss, E.S., Rohlen, T.P., and Steinhoff P.G. (eds.), *Conflict in Japan.* Honolulu: University of Hawaii Press.

—— 1986. The Confucian gender role and personal fulfillment for Japanese women. In Slote, W.H. (ed.), *The Psycho-Cultural Dynamics of the Confucian Family: Past and Present.* Seoul, Korea: International Cultural Society of Korea.

Lehtonen, Jaakko and Kari Sajavaara 1985. The silent Finn. In Tannen, D. and Saville-Troike, M. (eds.), *Perspectives on Silence*. Norwood, NJ: Ablex.
Maltz, Daniel N. 1985. Joyful noise and reverent silence: the significance of noise in Pentecostal worship. In Tannen, D. and Savifle-Troike, Muriel (eds.), *Perspectives on Silence*. Norwood, NJ: Ablex.
Miller, Laura 1986. *Aizuchi*: Japanese listening behavior. Unpublished.
Miyoshi, Masao 1974. *Accomplices of Silence: The Modern Japanese Novel*. Berkeley: University of California Press.
Nitta, Fumiteru 1987. 'A flower for you': Patterns of interaction between Japanese tourists and Hare Krishna devotees in Honolulu. In Thomas, S. (ed.), *Culture and Communication: Methodology, Behavior, Artifacts, and Institutions*. Selected Proceedings from the Fifth International Conference on Culture and Communication, Temple University. Norwood, NJ: Ablex.
Saville-Troike, Muriel 1985. The place of silence in an integrated theory of communication. In Tannen, D. and Saville-Troike, M. (eds.), *Perspectives on Silence*. Norwood, NJ: Ablex.
Tannen, Deborah 1985. Silence: Anything but. In Tannen, D. and Saville-Troike, M. (eds.), *Perspectives on Silence*. Norwood, NJ: Ablex.
Turner, Victor W. 1969. *The Ritual Process: Structure and Anti-Structure*. Chicago: Aldine.

NOTES

Paper presented at the International Pragmatics Conference, Antwerp, August 17–22, 1987. I am indebted to Jack Bilmes and Fumiteru Nitta for their comments on an earlier version, and to Sachiko Ide for her editorial suggestions, while I alone remain responsible for any shortcomings in the paper.

1. According to Ikuma Dan (1961: 201), a well-known musician, '*Ma* is the term for the interval between sounds in Japanese music and is not to be confused with the rest in Western music. In Western music, the beat is all important and determines the rhythm, while the rest is subsidiary to the beat and merely emphasizes it. In Japanese music, however, it is the interval which determines the rhythm, while the beat is subsidiary and serves to enhance the interval.'
2. It is interesting that the Finns, who are known as a silent people, also expect the listener to send backchannel signals (Lehtonen and Sajavaara 1985: 195–196). On *aizuchi* I have benefited from Laura Miller's prepublication paper (1986).
3. This latest piece of information was brought to my attention by Sachiko Ide.
4. There is ambivalence toward the face and eyes in terms of their truth values. These elements of the outer region are often taken as 'windows' or 'mirrors' of the inner state. The mirror status, however, is not accorded to the mouth, lips, tongue, or words.
5. Even though the Finns and the Japanese share the silence-prone communication style, there seem to be fundamental differences. According to Lehtonen and Sajavaara (1985: 194), one of the Finnish conversational maxims is 'Try to avoid unnecessary small words like *thanks*, *excuse me*, and *sorry*'. These are precisely the words that are strongly encouraged for Japanese speakers since nobody will be hurt by them.
6. In his latest work, Doi (1986) analyzes this double-sidedness of the Japanese self, arguing its functional significance in maintaining the psychic balance of the individual.
7. In analyzing the situational variation of interaction patterns, I have used a threefold category of interactional domains: ritual, intimate, and anomic. The anomic domain involves interaction with a stranger who does not deserve courtesy (Lebra 1976). Neither the intimate nor the anomic situation is bound by the norm of discretional silence.
8. I argue that conjugal embarrassment results from a combination of two mutually opposite states of emotions. One is the feeling of intimacy to the extent of spousal fusion, and the other is that of sexual distance dictated by the traditional family ideology in which conjugal ties are subordinated to the father-to-son succession line (Lebra 1986). Sexual distance is best indicated by the arranged marriage, which, no longer mandatory of course, has still survived in different forms and functions. My argument here explains why the parent, mother in particular, is not so inhibited from verbal expression of love for the child despite the utmost intimacy between mother and child.

9. Lebra (1984b: 43) analyzes this aspect of silence as an example of 'negative communication' for conflict management.
10. I owe this insight to Yoshiko Ikeda, a psychiatrist who observed group therapy sessions in both Japan and the United States.
11. Different forms of triadic communication in avoidance of dyadic confrontation were discussed in Lebra (1984b).

First published in Roger T. Ames (ed.), *Self as a Person in Asian Theory and Practice*, New York: State University of New York Press, 1994.

11 *Migawari*: The Cultural Idiom of Self-Other Exchange in Japan

SELF-PERCEPTION AS SOCIALLY CONTEXTUALIZED

Many observers of Japanese, while they differ in specific emphases, concur that the Japanese self (or personhood) is socially defined, contextualized, or embedded. To the extent that the social construction of the self is a universal fact, it may be restated that the Japanese person not only acts in response to but also *perceives* his/herself as contingent upon a given social nexus. The result is the consciously socialized self. If viewed through the Western lens for perceiving the self as noncontingent, autonomous, or intrinsic, the Japanese self indeed appears situationally circumscribed or *on*/*giri*-bound (Benedict 1946); dependency prone (Doi 1971), rank conscious, and group-oriented (Nakane 1967); empathetic (Aida 1970), differentiated into *uchi* and *soto* or *omote* and *ura* as pointed out by Doi (1985) and many other authors, mindful of *sekentei* (Inoue 1977); indeterminate (Smith 1983); relativistic (Lebra 1976a); hanging 'between' persons (Kimura 1972; Hamaguchi 1977); uncertain, multiple, moving, or shifting (Minami 1983; Rosenberger 1989; Kondo 1990; Bachnik 1992). All these characterizations correspond to the linguistic absence of the fixed 'I' (or 'you') as well as the lexical variety of 'I' substitutes.

Given the current ethos of Western intellectuals against their own (or, more accurately, their colleagues') ethnocentrism, including self-critique among reflexive anthropologists, it is unnecessary to remind ourselves that the socially contingent self as described above should not be equated with emotional or cognitive immaturity just because such is typical of non-Western, particularly preliterate, tribes. Citing one recent work may suffice. On the basis of free-response test results on self-perception, Cousins (1989) refutes the notion that the socially situational self is incapable of thinking in abstract terms. Compared with American responses, Japanese self-perceptions, which were indeed found to be more sociocentric, surpass American counterparts in both concreteness and abstractness. This finding suggests that the boundaries of 'social contexts' are quite variable, contracting and expanding, immediate and remote, interpersonal and global, which in turn confirms the 'indeterminacy' of self.

The foregoing picture of the socially compact self has been repudiated by some authors as a 'stereotype' or 'group model' (Befu 1980). It is true that social contextuality, while characterizing the Japanese self as measured by the Western yardstick, does not exhaust it. In a paper (Lebra 1992a), I identified three levels of self as follows: the social or 'interactional' self is at the basic level, where Japanese find themselves most of the time; above this level is the 'inner' or reflexive self, which centers around the *kokoro* (heart/mind) and engages in monologue, with a leave of absence from dialogic involvement; at the highest level, there is the 'boundless' or chaotic self, where the boundary disappears between subject and object, self and other, or the inner and outer self, so that both the social and inner self are upgraded into an empty self. The point, however, is that the three levels are far from undercutting one another. The higher levels of self sustain the basic, social self not only by compensating, remedying, or counterbalancing the excess of the social self but reenergizing it when it is deemed deficient. Thus the Japanese emphasis upon *seishin* (spirit), singled out by Befu (1980) as a proof of Japanese individualism, is in fact mobilized in group training, as witnessed by Rohlen (1973). While critical of the group-model and in partial agreement with Befu, Moeran (1984) nevertheless concedes that the Japanese 'individuality' is immune to 'individualism' and instead can be allied with groupism via *seishin* and *kokoro*.

This paper pursues the socially contextualized, indeterminate, multiple self even further by focusing on identity exchange between self and other, where self assumes another person's identity or vice versa. The exchangeable or substitutable self is in striking contrast to the Western idiom of self as consistent, continuous, unique, intrinsic, or clearly bounded (see Shweder and Levine 1984; Marsella, De Vos, and Hsu 1985). By the Western standard, this extensibility of self to other might appear as a delusion. Needless to say, it has nothing to do with mental disorders, since it is only temporary, conscious, and even obligatory. I choose this topic because in my view it throws the social contextuality of the Japanese self into relief.

THE IDIOM OF IDENTITY SUBSTITUTION

I became keenly aware of this kind of identity exchange while doing fieldwork in the early 1970s on the cult called 'Gedatsu.' This particular cult has spirit possession as a main ritual, and it is not surprising that identity exchange between self and a supernatural entity takes place during possession. What aroused my curiosity was that members of the cult explained many instances of their behavior or experience outside possession as manifestations of identity substitution.

As I have reported elsewhere (1976a, 237–40; 1976b; 1986), my Gedatsu informants would visit shrines to apologize for sins committed not by themselves but by ancestors or other supernatural agents. Apologies were offered, in other words, by 'vicarious' sinners who were most likely to be victims of vicarious retribution such as illness. Identity exchange was articulated in the written and recited formula of apology: I am here, turned into so-and-so (*nari-kawatte*), to apologize for his (her) sin from the bottom of (my) heart. For X to 'become' Y in surrogacy (*kawaru*, *naru*, *narikawaru*) was a common idiom. Such identity exchange involved the human self and a variety of others, supernatural and human, dead and alive, known and unknown: My wife's illness is mine; I am just borrowing her body. You really can't tell whose illness it is. Surrogacy thus amounts to the mirror reflection, mutual replication, or fusion between self and other: My ancestors, I, and my descendants – we are one and the same; 'Ancestor worship means self-worship' (Lebra 1986, 362).

This extent of surrogacy is quite bizarre, even by Japanese standards. Nevertheless, through exposure to the cult's idiom of identity exchange in this extreme form, I became aware of how often ordinary, 'normal' Japanese speak in a similar language without raising anybody's eyebrows. Anecdotes are legion. When I paid air fare to a travel agent who took the trouble to come to my residence, he gave me a receipt, but not the ticket itself, assuring, 'Don't worry. I will become you, my honorable customer [*okyaku-sama ni nari kawatte*], to get your boarding card ready at the airport.' Indeed, he was there as promised.

In interviewing a woman in her sixties, I found her firmly dedicated to a Shinto sect without being a member of it. It turned out that her action had nothing to do with her own faith but was a surrogate devotion for the sake of her deceased mother, who had been a devout member. She missed her mother deeply and became a religious successor to her without, however, losing her own nonreligious identity. The latter example, as well as the Gedatsu example, shows that identity exchange can occur not only to serve expedience as in business transaction (e.g., the travel agent) but also to express a person's inner subjectivity, like faith or sincerity.

To add another anecdote: in a popular weekly television program, in 1989, I happened to see a famous twenty-two-year-old boxer who, after retiring from the ring because of injury, was training and coaching his followers. He said, 'When my trainee is in the ring, I am the one who is fighting the game. I become the boxer.' (By the way, the same athlete said, in answer to the question what had been sustaining him throughout, 'I thought of those people who have helped me, my parents, my mentors, and countless others. This is a very important point in winning the game. Those who don't think this way, those who think they have made it by themselves are sure to lose.' The socially loaded self thus emerged out of a boxer whom we would ordinarily expect to be dependent on nothing but his own body, skill, and will.)

Identity substitution may take a more subtle, less detectable form. One day when I was looking for a computerized library service in Japan, I asked for help from Professor A at X University, whom I happened to know. Professor A in turn asked his colleague, Professor B, about my request, whereupon Professor B designated Professor C at Y University as the most appropriate person to ask, because Y University was equipped with such computer services. B assured A that all I should do would be to tell C that B was the introducer. Understanding my apprehensiveness, Professor A wrote a letter of introduction addressed to C, mentioning B as the introducer. In order to get an appointment I called C, telling about this chain of introductions. C was too busy to help me in person, but introduced his colleague D. When I went to meet Professor D, he received me warmly, and bothered to guide me over to the library and introduce me to E, the computer specialist, and bowed to him with the request to help me. Mr. E was very kind and helpful. This was an unexpected and moving experience. I knew Professor A only, but each person at a chain link acted as if he knew A personally, or as if he were A himself and my friend because of the previous introducer. Sensitized to the prevalence of identity exchange at that time, I was tempted to see a series of that practice in this chain from A to E. A's kindness did not cool off in the course of serial substitutions but was rekindled and warm.

It may be that this sort of behavior, as an objective phenomenon, occurs in the West as well, but the subjective reasoning channeled by the culturally available idiom is likely to be quite different, different enough to suggest something noteworthy about the Japanese sense of self and other. I have been in a quandary over how to translate the Japanese expressions of identity exchange or surrogacy. Words like *delegate*, *proxy*, *representative*, *deputy*, or even *surrogate* – none of them convey the meaning of the Japanese *kawari* or *migawari* (the person, the act or state of substitution) to my satisfaction. The verb forms such as *naru*, *kawaru*, *narikawaru*, *mi ni naru*, which appear more frequently in conversation and were translated above as 'become' short of a more fitting alternative, seem even less translatable. This linguistic problem alone hints that a clue to the Japanese self underlies the idiom of *migawari*. As Doi (1985) says about *amae*, whether this term or its equivalent is available in a culture makes a difference in the way the universal emotions of dependency are released. Similarly I argue that the availability of the idiom of identity exchange for common usage does make a difference in the perception of self.

To continue on the linguistic discrepancy relevant to our discussion, another term should be mentioned as lacking an English equivalent, namely, *honnin*. There are many English terms for the person taking the surrogate role such as substitute, deputy, delegate, and other words listed above, but there is no English word for the person who is substituted for, delegated, and so on, that is, for the 'true' self-person. The Japanese *honnin* stands for such a non-substitutive, authentic self, used in implicit or explicit distinction from the surrogate (*kawari* or *dainin*). Let me illustrate this by another experience of mine. About to begin fieldwork in Tokyo, I called a ward office to ask what I should bring over for alien registration. The office clerk, after answering my question, reminded me, obviously as a matter of routine, that the *honnin* should show up. In this situation, he meant 'you yourself,' saying implicitly that a surrogate would not do.' *Honnin* is thus well marked in Japanese, more so than *dainin*, the latter usually being implied as a reference for *honnin*. This linguistic practice substantiates rather than weakens the above argument that *migawari* is quite common among Japanese, so common that the *honnin* marking is necessary.[1]

It may be further noted that, in the absence of the constant 'I,' the speaker may call him/herself, particularly in addressing a child, by the term likely to be used by the listener. Thus a schoolteacher calls himself '*sensei*' in speaking to his pupils, a father 'father' in speaking to his child, an adult man 'uncle' in speaking to an unfamiliar child, and so on (see Suzuki 1976 on terms for self and other). For a psycholinguistic moment the speaker may be said to 'become' the listener. The self-other reflexivity in this sense is doubled in honorific terms like *gozen*, *kakka*, and *heika*. These are for addressing or referring to someone much higher in status than the speaker and may be translated as 'my lord' or 'your (his) highness' or 'your-(his) majesty' (*heika*). Literally, these terms indicate the speaker's humble self present 'in front of' or 'down below' the venerable personage seated high above. Psycholinguistically, the speaker A addresses B by looking down upon himself from the height of B.

Substitution may be more institutionalized as in the practice of adoption. Japanese are known for their readiness to adopt a child or even an adult, as a child substitute, particularly when an heir is needed.

As my latest research on the aristocracy got under way, the *migawari* came into even sharper focus, since this class had been practicing it more frequently and in a more theatrical manner. It is as if it were symbolic of status. Below, I attempt to highlight a few salient features of *migawari*, drawing upon a variety of sources of information, including aristocratic informants.[2] The emperor as a key self or a key mirror of the Japanese self will also appear as a major actor on the *migawari*-stage in the following analysis. Three features of *migawari* are singled out as salient: protection, authentication, and implementation.

PROTECTION

First, the *migawari* is necessary when the *honnin* is physically or mentally disabled, sick, or too old, or young, helpless, or immobile to perform his/her role. There is nothing particularly Japanese about this. Substitution of the *honnin* in litigations by abundantly available lawyers is among the most common aspects of American life. The difference lies in the modes of such substitution. For Japanese, the *migawari* is supported by the culturally sanctioned dependency, the expected availability of nurturant substitutes, the representational capacity of fellow members of a group like a household, and the general acceptability of substitution as legitimate. This aspect of *migawari* involves protective nurturance.

Consider person A who wants or feels obligated to attend the funeral service for his friend B or B's kin, C. If A is too old, sick, or out of town, expectations are that substitutive attendance be made by A's wife, son, or other available kin, even though B is a stranger to the substitutive attendant. A hospitalized patient becomes a passive care receiver supported by a *migawari* taking an active role in communicating 'on the *honnin*'s behalf' with the doctor, nurse, and other hospital staff or in hosting well-wishing visitors. It is against this backdrop that the true diagnosis, if devastating like cancer, can be kept secret to the patient as *honnin* while disclosed to his caretaker as *dainin*. When I was hospitalized in this country, I became painfully aware of the difference: it was entirely my responsibility to let the hospital staff know how I was doing, to ring a bell if I needed emergency help, to ask for pain killer when I was in pain. It was a chilling revelation that the American health-care system assumes the patient as a nonsubstitutable *honnin*. When a Japanese child is studying day and night for entrance examinations, it may be his mother who commutes to a shrine every morning to offer a surrogate prayer for his success. It is as if Japanese gods are responsive to such surrogate worshippers.

In the imperial institution, a sick emperor like Taisho (1912–26) was substituted for by the Crown Prince (Hirohito, Taisho's son) as *sessho* (regent). Historically, the *sessho* office was politically abused by the Fujiwara clan from the ninth through the eleventh centuries. But such abuse was inevitable in view of the status of the *sessho* as nothing less than 'the substitute for the emperor,' which amounted to the emperor-*sessho* equation: 'the *sessho* is the emperor himself' (Ishii 1982,148–49).

AUTHENTICATION

When a 'true' inner state or feeling of the self is to be convincingly demonstrated, the *honnin*'s action alone may not be taken as sufficient. At issue here is 'sincerity,' held by Japanese as a key moral value. The receiver of a favor expresses gratitude, but his sincerity is to be authenticated by words of thanks from his family or fellow members of his group. The same holds true when a request is made, in that the requester's mentor or anybody that counts more than the requester *honnin* is expected to authenticate his sincerity by requesting the same on his behalf.

The function of the *migawari* for authentication is particularly important when a person commits a serious offense. He owes an apology to the victim, for whatever pain he has caused him, or to the public, for disrupting society (*seken o sawagasete*). Particularly if the offender is regarded as too young or low in his status to have his word taken seriously, the Japanese public expects the *honnin*'s apology to be backed up by a *migawari* apology from someone who is senior or superior to the offender, such as his father, mentor, or boss. A recent incident will illustrate the *migawari* for authentication.

The Self-Defense Forces submarine *Nadashio* collided with a sport-fishing boat in August 1988, resulting in the death of most of the boat's passengers. While the cause was under investigation and guilt was yet to be determined, the *Nadashio* captain called round some of the victims' families to apologize in tears. And something inevitable soon took place: the director of the Self-Defense Agency, Kawara, resigned. This incident was picked up in the popular 'Sunday Morning' show, where a social critic expressed his approval of the director's resignation as reactivating the *bushidō* (samurai chivalry) tradition of harakiri as well as the Japanese esthetics of *isagiyoshi* (gallantry). It looked for the time being (before the case was brought to the court) as if Kawara's resignation concluded the whole issue involved. An American participant in the show, however, said that Americans would not understand why Kawara had to resign, because he had no responsibility for the disaster. Only the person(s) in direct charge of the submarine operation, he argued, should be punished. For the Japanese, that was not enough. What mattered most, at least in the initial reactions of the Japanese public, was not the technical error but the alleviation of the stress through social management. The situation required that the sincerity of apology by those directly involved be authenticated by the self-punishment of an official whose status was high enough.

Another, more recent incident may be cited. In April 1989, a photographer of *Asahi Shinbun*, a major national newspaper, while taking pictures under water near Okinawa, inscribed two initials on the coral reef, apparently to leave this aquatic adventure recorded for good. This was exposed and severely criticized as a grave destruction of the marine environment; it led to the company's dismissal of the photographer and punitive action against a fellow-diver and several others deemed as responsible for this 'vandalism.' To conclude this incident, the president of *Asahi* resigned (*Japan Times* May 27, 1989).

It is in view of this overload of vicarious responsibility 'traditionally' assumed by superiors as a price of high status that the Recruit Scandal, exposed in 1988, appeared so offensive and, indeed, scandalous. Politicians, faction leaders in particular, alienated the Japanese public not so much because of their corrupt financial deals as because they blamed the corruption on their subordinates, such as managerial secretaries; their behavior was diametrically opposed to the rule of *migawari* for authentication.

There are cases where the *honnin* has no regrets about his conduct, as would be the case with radical students in the 1960s and 1970s. Many fathers came out to present themselves as *migawari* offenders, apologized, and resigned from their jobs, and some committed suicide. A typical statement made by a parent was '*Musuko ni kawatte owabi shimasu*' (I apologize as a substitute for my son). In this situation, the migawari apology is not for authentication but for a total replacement of the *honnin*'s identity.

IMPLEMENTATION

Status is an important determinant of who is to substitute for whom. In authentication, it is the superior who steps into a *migawari* role on behalf of the *honnin* holding a lower status, authenticity stemming from the substitute's status. But the correlations of high status to surrogate role, and low status to *honnin* role, do not always hold; they can be reversed when substitution serves other purposes. Note, too, that the status for authentication does not go upward indefinitely: it was the Defense-Force Agency director, not the prime minister, who resigned.

According to Linton (1936), status is coupled with role. Status as a cluster of rights or privileges to be claimed subsumes its role as a cluster of duties or responsibilities to be performed, the two constituting the passive and active side of the same coin. In actuality, however, they are often mismatched. It is possible that a given status is either too low or too high for its holder to perform a certain role incumbent on the status. A third feature of the *migawari* is for implementation to fill in the status-role gap when the status is too high or when it carries too much symbolically loaded weight, as happens to an eminent public figure.

Relevant here is what a sample of aristocratic informants had to say. The hereditary aristocracy has been out of existence since 1947, but since 1976 I have been in occasional contact with more than one hundred survivors or their descendants. In interviews, they were asked to recall their prewar life-style (see Lebra 1993 for comprehensive research results). The single most striking feature of their recalled life-styles was the omnipresence of servants to discharge almost all the responsibilities that the ordinary househead and housewife would have done by themselves. Domestic chores and child rearing in the residential section of the 'interior' were performed primarily by maid servants, while the male staff of the 'exterior' managed the household in relation to the outside or 'public.' Even poor members of the nobility, which numbered not a few, had several servants to buttress their aristocratic status. For the children, the personal maid servants were constantly available as surrogates for their mothers, which often, if not always, resulted in a closer bond with the former than the latter. While they spoke to the children with honorifics, they also 'became' disciplinarian parents or even *kyoiku-mama* (Lebra 1990). Fathers and husbands were often blind to the matter of the household treasury, which was under the jurisdiction of their surrogates: This accounted for the masters falling prey in the early postwar period to the former servants who took advantage of their masters' naivete. These stories demonstrate that the mundane household responsibilities, both internal and external, were beneath the status of the nobility and left to those of inferior status.

The main role in the household left to the aristocratic head and wife was ceremonial. Here, particularly among large, wealthy households of *daimyo* origin, some rituals were conducted by top servants. The managerial male servants were central actors in the ceremonial theater of marriage engagement, conducting the exchange of gifts for a son or daughter of the house. The wedding announcement was made in the name of the head manager. Periodical visits to temples, shrines, and mausolea to pay respect to the master's ancestors as well as to their caretakers (priests) were mentioned as the most important job of the head maid. This ritual action was called *godaihai* or *godaisan*, meaning 'surrogate worship.'

Even the sacred tradition of a household, which would appear embodied by the househead, was carried on by his surrogate. In some court-noble houses (*kuge*), styles of arts were transmitted, such as poetry, calligraphy, flower arrangement, incense art, court dressing, court music, and so on. Supposedly inherited from father to heir in secrecy, the art was not necessarily learned or practiced by the head of the house. Due to economic necessity combined with cultural revivalism, various house arts have been recently recaptured by the *kuge* descendants who now personally practice and teach them. 'In the seven-hundred-year history of this house,' said one of these descendants, 'I, the twenty-eight-generation head master, am the first to make a living out of this art through teaching it.' His predecessor, interested in perpetuating the art, nonetheless remained aloof from it, relegating the role of preserving and teaching it to a house retainer and commoner followers.

Interestingly, among the jobs taken up by the aristocrats were surrogate ones for the imperial house, including the role of surrogate parenthood for royal children. If the aristocratic househead recruited surrogate role-takers from among commoners to implement his status, so did the emperor from among aristocrats. Ritual roles were specially important. Imperial messengers called *chokushi* were, and still are, sent to various places, such as imperially sponsored shrines, as *migawari* for the emperor, that is, as the emperor himself, and they are to be treated as such. Except for major rites requiring the emperor's personal presence, chamberlains take turns every morning substituting for the emperor as the presiding priest for Shinto ceremony at the palace shrine. The chamberlain on duty purifies himself (*kessai*) by bathing, appears in full court-priest garment, and receives all the courtesy due to the emperor. 'He becomes the emperor.' It is in this sense that, according to a palace worker, the emperor goes to the palace shrine every day to pray and 'keeps all day long wishing peace for the whole nation.'

The imperial rituals conducted since Emperor Showa's death on January 7, 1989, gives further insight to this institutionalized surrogacy or the imperial self in connection with death pollution. I must digress a little to offer some detail on the background of imperial rituals. Upon Emperor Showa's death, the initial simple ceremony of imperial succession (*shokei*) was conducted for Crown Prince Akihito as the new emperor. Thereafter, all members of the royalty, including the new emperor, went into mourning, which would last for a year. Only after the passage of the mourning period, which coincided with the deceased emperor's maturity into the 'pure' status of a god and his spiritual relocation to the *koreiden* (one of the three palace subshrines that houses all the imperial ancestors), could the truly grand ceremony of enthronement (*sokui*) be held. The ceremony was scheduled in the fall, subsequent to the completion of the mourning cycle. This coordinated with the harvest of new rice, so the enthronement ceremony was combined with the *niinamesai* (the annual imperial rite for tasting new rice), which was thus specially designated *daijosai* (grand tasting rite). The reason for this double ceremony as well as the interval between the two rituals was because the mourning emperor was disqualified from presenting himself in the palace shrine, particularly the most sacred subshrine, called *kensho* (or *kashikodokoro*), which enshrines the Sun-Goddess, the primordial imperial ancestress. This is where the *daijosai* ceremony was held.

Is it because the new emperor was polluted? A Shinto scholar, hesitating to say yes, explained to me that the emperor in grief 'refrains' from attending the shrine, and he added that Shinto rites are *matsuri* (festivities), all for celebrations (*hare*), not for grief: Shinto gods welcome only those worshippers who are in a joyous mood. However explained, it is certain that the idea of pollution is essential to the shrine taboo, since shrine attendance requires body purification (*kessai*), abstinence from 'four-legged' animal meat, as well as being out of the menstrual period, in the case of a woman.

The death-polluted emperor was thus supposed to stay away from the 'pure' palace shrine as well as from the Shrine of Ise, where the 'original' symbol of the Sun-Goddess, *the* mirror, is enshrined. This means that he could not even send his close *migawari*, like a chamberlain, to the shrine as he usually would. And yet, the shrine could not be left unattended even one day.

The dilemma was resolved by the presence of another category of imperial attendants, ones not affected by death pollution. There are a number of palace-shrine priests called *shoten*, who assist the emperor (or his surrogates) and other members of the imperial family with conducting shrine rituals. It was the *shoten*, specifically the head *shoten* (*shoten-cho*), who stepped into the role of the 'pure' emperor while the imperial *honnin* was impure, and this began at the very moment of the previous emperor's death, immediately followed by the simple succession ritual.

Succession involves the transmission of three regalia: the jewel, sword, and the mirror. While the first two items (*kenji*) were handed over to the new emperor directly, the mirror, the symbol of the Sun-Goddess enshrined at *kensho*, was not. It was the head *shoten* who, substituting for the emperor (*tenno ni kawatte*), took over the *kensho* ritual of succession and read the *otsugebumi* (an oath to the imperial ancestress to be read by the emperor himself).

From this beginning until the expiration of the mourning period, the imperial postmortem rituals were bifurcated between the impure (in connection with the late emperor) and the pure (in association with the Sun Goddess and other Shinto deities). The latter domain was inhabited exclusively by the *shoten* priests taking over the 'pure' self of the emperor. It was the *shoten* who visited the Ise Shrine or conducted daily rituals at the palace shrine. In an informant's words, a *shoten* 'becomes the emperor.' The new emperor had not lost his pure self but while impure, he could not act out the pure phase of himself, relying instead upon the pure priests to assume his identity.

BEYOND THE SELF-OTHER OPPOSITION

The above discussion on the imperial self in rituals leads to our conclusion. Three points have emerged. First, the self-other exchangeability presupposes the double, multiple, or split self. I referred to the double self of the emperor, pure and impure. Complementarily, those retainers, secular and religious, who substitute for the emperor, also assume double selves – substitutive and nonsubstitutive (*honnin*). In this sense, the Japanese self may be said to be 'dividual,' instead of 'individual.'

First, since Japanese say that the *kami* (deity, supernatural entity, spirit) resides within the *kokoro* of each and every person, it may be conjectured that the dividuality of the human self relates to the dividuality of the supernatural. The Sun-Goddess, the sacred mirror, is housed at the Shrine of Ise, but we also have seen the *kensho*, which is the most sacred section of the palace shrine, enshrining her. The Sun-Goddess at the palace is said to be a *bunshin* (split deity) of the Sun-Goddess at Ise. After the imperial funeral, the center of the mourning ritual moved to the burial site, the mausoleum under construction, in rural, western Tokyo, where daily services were held by a group of lay ritualists (*saikan*) recruited for this purpose. But there was another center constructed within the palace, called '*gonden*,' the temporary shrine for the deceased emperor. The *saikan* thus took turns alternating between the two sites. The *gonden*, according to one of the *saikan*, enshrined a *wake-mitama* (split spirit) of the buried emperor. *Wake-mitama*, *bunshin*, and *bunrei* all refer to a split portion of the stem spirit or deity. Most local shrines all over Japan house *bunrei* invited over from major national shrines. Is it that the human self imitates the supernatural self in such divisibility without losing its identity, or vice versa?

Second, the *migawari* phenomenon has much to do with status hierarchy in ranks and age. As we have seen, substitution can occur upwardly and downwardly. In authentication, it is a higher-status holder who is expected to substitute, while implementation involves a lower-status holder as a substitute. In protection, the hierarchy can run in either direction. It is often the case, however, that protective substitution overlaps implementation. When a chamberlain, for example, substitutes for the emperor, we are not quite sure whether he is protecting the emperor or implementing his responsibility. Probably both. The same may be said to hold for the wife substituting for the husband. In a previous work (Lebra 1984) on women residents of a Japanese town, it was often found that the wife, as *the* home manager, substituted for her husband, the househead, in representing the house. She performed, for example, the role of officer for a neighborhood association in the name of the househead and formal officer. She seemed at once to be implementing his status and protecting him from the mundane chores of the neighborhood. It is interesting to note in this connection that Japanese gods are not only revered and worshipped but 'protected.'

The superior, including the emperor, who is substituted for by the inferior in implementation and protection, can be thus kept out of touch, 'elevated' (or shelved) to a pure symbol, or have his authority usurped. This situation can give rise to the vagueness of the locus of responsibility for action. While excessive responsibility of a superior is noted in authentication, the opposite (insufficiency in his sense of responsibility) can occur as a result of protective 'implementation.' The latter situation seems to underlie the refusal by the faction leaders implicated in the Recruit Scandal to admit their own guilt. This leads to the next point.

Third, that the nonsubstitutive self is well marked and recognized in the Japanese idiom as *honnin* implies its marginality in relation to the *dainin* that prevails in actual social life. In both protection and implementation, the higher person has a better chance to be a *honnin*, but is he really himself? Idiomatically he may be one: nobody talks about the emperor being a substitute for someone else except probably for high deities like the Sun Goddess. But psychologically he is far from being a *honnin* himself. To be remembered is the symbolic load of status: the higher the status, the more heavily guarded with symbolic meaning. In this sense the emperor may be said to be a pure symbol dissociated from his natural body.[3] As a symbolic being, his existence may allow no room to express his own self. Those of my aristocratic informants who were close to Emperor Showa in person pointed out that they had met nobody as 'pure' and 'selfless' as the emperor. To a lesser degree, aristocrats played a symbolically heavy role accompanied by the inhibited or nonself self. In other words, the elite, too, play(ed) a substitutive role on behalf of those below, inasmuch as a symbol stands for something else. It may be said that the *migawari* is a widespread cultural style adopted across classes.

NOTES

Research for this paper was undertaken while I was a recipient of grants from the Social Science Research Council, University of Hawaii (Fujio Matsuda Scholar), and Wenner-Gren Foundation. The support is gratefully acknowledged.

1. In connection with *honnin*, I should mention another interesting case of marking. In kinship terms, the Japanese speaker often qualifies the identity of his/her kin with 'real' (*jitsu*), such as *jippu* (real father), *jikkei* (real brother), *jisshi* (real child), in distinction from adoptive father or father-in-law. The kin category like 'father' includes both the natural and simulated type, or both *honnin* and *dainin*, and because of the high frequency of the latter type, the former is marked as real. See note 2.

2. Here it may be pointed out that I found a greater frequency of son adoption among aristocratic than commoner families, sometimes over three or more generations in a row, for the obvious reason that the hereditary aristocracy was more compelled to perpetuate the patriline (see Lebra 1989 for aristocratic adoption). Here a man, an incumbent househead adopted another man (who could be an adult or a daughter's husband) and 'became' his father and predecessor, while the adopted man 'became' a son and heir to his adoptive father. The ease with which such adoption was practiced is another indication, I believe, of readiness for identity exchange.

3. In discussing the British monarch, Hayden (1987) recognizes two bodies of the king or queen: 'body natural' and 'body politic,' one to be hidden within the private realm, the other to be on public display. This seems to suggest a feature shared by the two monarchies. But in the eyes of the Japanese public, the Japanese emperor, as exemplified by Emperor Shōwa, deemed much more hidden and inaccessible than his British counterpart. At the same time, the Japanese emperor seemed more constrained in being his natural self (Lebra 1992b).

BIBLIOGRAPHY

Aida Yuji. 1970. *Nihonjin no ishiki kozo.* Tokyo: Kodansha.

Bachnik, Jane. 1992. 'The Two "Faces" of Self and Society in Japan.' *Ethos* 20: 3–32.

Befu, Harumi. 1980. *The Group Model of Japanese Society and an Alternate Model.* Rice University Studies Series 66. Houston.

Benedict, Ruth. 1946. *The Chrysanthemum and the Sword: Patterns of Japanese Culture.* Boston: Houghton Muffin.

Cousins, Steven D. 1989. 'Culture and Self-Perception in Japan and the United States.' *Journal of Personality and Social Psychology* 56: 124–31.

Doi Takeo. 1971. *Amae no kozo.* Tokyo: Kobundo.

—— 1985. *Omote to ura.* Tokyo: Kobundo.

Hamaguchi Eshun. 1977. *Nihon rashisa no saihakken.* Tokyo: Nihon Keizai Shinbunsha.

Hayden, Ilse. 1987. *Symbol and Privilege: The Ritual Context of British Royalty.* Tuscon: University of Arizona Press.

Inoue, Tadashi. 1977. *Sekentei no kozo.* NHK Books. Tokyo: Nippon Hoso Shuppankai.

Ishii, Ryosuke. 1982. *Tenno: Tenno no seisei oyobi fushinsei no dento.* Tokyo: Yamakawa Shuppansha.

Kimura Bin. 1972. *Hito to hito to no aida.* Tokyo: Kobundo.

Kondo, Dorinne. 1990. *Crafting Selves: Work, Identity and the Politics in a Japanese Factory.* Chicago: University of Chicago Press.

Lebra, Takie Sugiyama. 1976a. *Japanese Patterns of Behavior.* Honolulu: University of Hawaii Press.

—— 1976b. 'Ancestral Influence on the Suffering of Descendants in a Japanese Cult.' In W. H. Newell, ed., *Ancestors.* The Hague: Mouton Publishers.

—— 1984. *Japanese Women: Constraint and Fulfillment.* Honolulu: University of Hawaii Press.

—— 1986. 'Self-reconstruction in Japanese Religious Psychotherapy.' In *Japanese*

Culture and Behavior: Selected Readings, ed. T. S. Lebra and William P. Lebra. Rev. ed. Honolulu: University of Hawaii Press.

—— 1989. 'Adoption among the Hereditary Elite of Japan: Status Preservation through Mobility.' *Ethnology* 28: 185–218.

—— 1990. 'Socialization of Aristocratic Children by Commoners: Recalled Experiences of the Hereditary Elite in Modern Japan.' *Cultural Anthropology* 5: 78–100.

—— 1992a. Self in Japanese Culture. In *Japanese Sense of Self*, ed. N. Rosenberger. Cambridge: Cambridge University Press.

—— 1992b. 'The Spatial Layout of Hierarchy: Residential Style of the Modern Japanese Nobility.' In *Japanese Social Organization*, ed. T. S. Lebra. Honolulu: University of Hawaii Press.

—— 1993. *Above the Clouds: Status Culture of the Modern Japanese Nobility*. Berkeley and Los Angeles: University of California Press.

Linton, Ralph. 1936. *The Study of Man: An Introduction*. New York: Appleton-Century.

Marsella, Anthony J., George De Vos, and Francis L. K. Hsu, eds. 1985. *Culture and Self: Asian and Western Perspectives*. New York: Tavistock Publications.

Moeran, Brian. 1984. Individual, Group, and Seishin: Japan's Internal Cultural Debate. *Man* 19: 252–66. Reprinted in *Japanese Culture and Behavior: Selected Readings*, ed. T. S. Lebra and W. P. Lebra. Rev. ed. Honolulu: University of Hawaii Press, 1986.

Minami Hiroshi. 1983. *Nihon teki jiga*. Tokyo: Iwanami Shoten.

Nakane Chie. 1967. *Tate shakai no ningen kankei*. Tokyo: Kodansha.

Rohlen, Thomas. 1973. 'Spiritual Education' in a Japanese Bank.' *American Anthropologist* 75: 1542–62. Reprinted in *Japanese Culture and Behavior: Selected Readings*, ed. T. S. Lebra and W. P. Lebra. Rev. ed. Honolulu: University of Hawaii Press, 1986.

Rosenberger, Nancy R. 1989. 'Dialectic Balance in the Polar Model of Self: The Japan Case.' *Ethos* 17: 88–113.

Shweder, Richard A., and Robert A. LeVine, eds. 1984. *Culture Theory: Essays on Mind, Self, and Emotion*. Cambridge: Cambridge University Press.

Smith, Robert J. 1983. *Japanese Society: Tradition, Self, and the Social Order*. Cambridge: Cambridge University Press.

Suzuki Takao. 1976. Language and Behavior in Japan: The Conceptualization of Personal Relations. *Japan Quarterly* 23: 255–66. Reprinted in *Japanese Culture and Behavior: Selected Readings*, ed. T. S. Lebra and W. P. Lebra. Rev. ed. Honolulu: University of Hawaii Press, 1986.

PART 2

GENDER

▸ First published in *The Japan Interpreter* 10, Nos 3–4: 284–289, 1976

⓬ Sex Equality for Japanese Women

Social change in postwar Japan has conspicuously affected the status of women. The new Constitution proclaimed sex equality, and legal reforms have gradually been implemented to emancipate women from their second-class citizenship. Moreover, change has gone beyond legal formalities; women have actually benefited doubly from Japan's accelerated economic growth over the last two decades. Industrialization has made possible an unprecedented degree of mechanization of housework, liberating women from heavy, full-time domestic responsibilities. Moreover, the insatiable demand for workers in industry has lured a large number of women into the labor market, providing them with an economic base for independence.[1]

The general trend is thus toward ever greater sexual equality, however tardy it may appear. Nevertheless, a clear consensus as to what equality really means in Japan has not yet emerged, and there is by no means unanimity with regard to whether equality is possible, or even desirable, from the standpoint of women's welfare. In the meantime, male dominance in most institutions remains basically unchallenged, and the Japanese women's liberation movement is the object of mockery rather than serious consideration, at least in the male-dominated press. In short, the contemporary trend toward sexual equality is complex and ridden with dilemmas in Japan, as it is elsewhere.

It is clear that the direction in which Japanese women are moving in relation to men is far from merely unilinear. My personal observations plus a cursory survey of available literature on the status of Japanese women, including government-sponsored statistical reports, popular magazines, and the publications of women's liberation groups seem to suggest a trilinear pattern. The three directions in which sexual equality seems to lead may be characterized as 'dimorphic,' 'bimorphic,' and 'amorphic.'

DIMORPHISM

Dimorphism refers to an extension and intensification of the traditional differentiation of roles, or division of labor, between the sexes. Men assume a full-time occupation outside the household while women occupy themselves full-time with domestic chores. This 'in-and-out' role differentiation has progressed alongside urbanization and family nucleation, and it is typically evident in urban, middle-class families composed of a 'salary man' husband, a housewife, and one or two small children. A survey shows that more than eighty percent of the women in Japan favor dimorphic role differentiation, while only ten percent oppose it.[2]

The dimorphic pattern is justified by the ideological claim that physical and mental differences between the sexes with regard both to capacities and disposition should be used advantageously rather than obliterated. Not necessarily an outright assertion of sex inequality, this rationale is rather an endorsement of role complementarity. Some social critics claim that such role differentiation actually promotes equality. Dimorphism, in which sex roles are not interchangeable, leads to complete mutual dependence between man and woman. The woman depends upon her husband for income, while the man depends upon his wife for domestic care. The sense of equality characteristic of this pattern thus derives from the interdependence itself, and the awareness of mutual indispensability, need for mutual trust and exchange of mutual appreciation, gratitude and guilt that it entails.

Consistent with role dimorphism is a cultural tendency to eulogize femininity and womanhood for sexual beauty, sensitivity, love, nurturance, and a unique form of intelligence. Femininity is not confined to wives and mothers, but is shared by geisha and bargirls as well as women of other professions. Robert Jay Lifton[3] fits Japanese women into three categories 'those who primarily nurture, those who provide sensual pleasure, and those who convey social wisdom' – labeled 'nurturer,' 'temptress' and 'knower,' respectively. Cutting across these three types is the psychic unity of women consisting in their 'close identification with organic life and its perpetuation.'[4] Making a cross-cultural generalization on this feminine quality, he suggests that women can play a crucial role as a bridge between biology and history. They can provide the human connection and sense of immortality required by a contemporary society ridden with anxiety over separation and extinction. An extension of Lifton's viewpoint, and yet a far cry from the stereotypic image of femininity, is the most recent conception of the contribution of women to society, as initiators and supporters of movements for consumer protection and ecological conservation, and opponents of industrial pollution.[5] This contribution stems from the household duty of watching out for the health of one's family. Here feminine qualities counteract the masculine drive for production and development.

Role dimorphism, supported by the supposed uniqueness of femininity, is reflected in the partition of prerogatives. The housewife dominates the domestic sphere while conceding outside realms to her husband. The more complete the dimorphic role differentiation, the more exclusive her control over domestic affairs. A survey showing that ninety-seven percent of urban *danchi* [housing development] housewives control the family budget, as against only sixty-six percent among rural housewives, is one indicator of this trend.[6] The husband entrusts his entire paycheck to his wife's management, accepts allowances from her, and is often ignorant of the amount of family savings.

The wife's dominance is less exclusive in the area of disciplining and educating the children, but even here she is far more influential than her husband. In fifty-six percent of the *danchi* households surveyed the primary educator and disciplinarian is the wife, whereas the husband takes those roles in only two percent. Husband-wife cooperation is claimed in forty-one percent.[7]

This domestic privilege probably explains why family life is considered an exception to the general rule of male dominance in Japan. In a survey designed to probe generational differences in appraisals of women's status relative to that of men, fifty pecent of the parental generation (and twenty-six percent of the youth sample) considered women's status to be higher in family life.[8]

Concomitant with the domestic prerogatives of the woman is the strong, often exclusive, tie between mother and child. The full-time housewife of a nuclear, urban middle-class family tends to find her main source of satisfaction in her child. This tendency represents an intensification of the traditional pattern of family solidarity where lineality takes precedence over the marital bond. The urban version of lineality, however, excludes the father and grandparents. The woman draws both her identity and pleasure from her child's dependence upon her. It was found that seventy percent of the women thirty to thirty-four years old found their *ikigai* [meaning in life] in children.[9] Like Chinese women in rural Taiwan, the urban middle-class Japanese woman forms around herself a 'uterine family.'[10]

Dimorphic egalitarianism, however, is a dead-end street, for a number of reasons. First, automation has simplified domestic work. Formerly highly skilled in the art of cooking rice, for example, the housewife has now been demoted to the unskilled level by the invention of automatic cookers. Furthermore, most laborious food-processing has been eliminated by packaged, 'instant' foods. Reduction of family size has further lightened the housewife's burden. These changes seem to make it increasingly difficult for a woman to claim significance for her role as fulltime housewife.

Reduction in the amount of housework might have resulted in more leisure that the housewife could enjoy and also use to develop proficiency in roles outside the home. Leisure has not increased, however. As of 1973, the housewife still spent seven and one-half hours per weekday on domestic work, no less than in 1960. Some predict that this will not change for years to come.[11] A possible explanation is that domestic work, by its very nature, is spread over an irreducible span of time in accordance with the circadian rhythms of family members. Also, unlike some occupational tasks, housework cannot be clearly differentiated from other kinds of work, or from play.

The second difficulty with dimorphism dovetails with the first. The male-dominated occupational sphere has been expanded and differentiated, requiring ever more highly skilled personnel. As a result, those in such occupations increasingly monopolize social status and prestige while domestic work loses its claim to respectability.[12] Women, as houseworkers, are thus compelled to acknowledge their diminished status and prestige, and to content themselves with prestige borrowed from their husbands or sons.

One effort to remove the stigma from domesticity and make dimorphism compatible with equality is reflected in demands that the economic value of housework be enhanced to the level of accepted male occupations. Given skyrocketing labor costs, the housewife's work, it argued, should be considered just as expensive as that of any worker. Some women's liberationists have even demanded that housewives receive wages. That movement seems destined to fail since the right to be a wage earner is obtained only at the expense of dimorphic prerogatives, such as control over the family pursestrings, a privilege which few housewives would forego.

Third, even within the household, where the wife is secure in her dominance and mother-child solidarity prevails, it is the father far more than the mother who is looked upon with esteem by the children. Mother-child intimacy may generate everlasting attachment, but the same relationship seems to prevent the development of respect. Indeed, the Japanese mother tends to indoctrinate her child to respect the father as the ultimate, albeit nominal, household authority.

Fourth, the woman whose identity is rooted in her maternal role must suffer anxiety as she ages and her children are 'weaned,' mentally as well as physically. As life expectancy figures increase, prolonging her probable post-parental lifespan, such difficulty intensifies. The anxiety of elderly mothers results in a compulsive need to be cared for by her children, thus reinforcing the traditional pattern of intergenerational dependence. Seventy to eighty percent of elderly Japanese live with their children and the percentage is higher among women.[14] Since it appears that inter-generational dependence is the inevitable outcome of sex-role dimorphism, the study of women's problems must take into account the entire life cycle. The elderly mother typically expects to be looked after by her eldest son. She must, therefore, rely upon her daughter-in-law for actual care. Confidence in her daugher-in-law largely depends upon an L-shaped chain of control involving the son as a link: mother controls son, and son controls wife. In order to secure her own position, the mother encourages her son to assert his authority as husband, ultimately contributing to the perpetuation of male dominance.

Dimorphism, then, ultimately reinforces the cultural tradition of sex inequality. From this standpoint, what have been referred to as the dimorphic prerogatives of women can be reconceptualized as compensation for status deprivation. Indeed, the controversial phenomenon of the *kyōiku mama* [education-obsessed mother] indicates more the woman's frustration with her lot in life than satisfaction with her maternal role.

BIMORPHISM

Bimorphism refers to a newer type of equality in which each sex performs both domestic and occupational roles. While retaining the distinction between role spheres, the woman invades the formerly male-dominated occupational world without, however, renouncing her domestic functions. This type is newer than dimorphism as a conscious route to equality, but has historical antecedents in the farming or fishing households of the subsistence economy of certain rural areas, and the sharing of economic responsibility in small family businesses. The historical pattern might be called 'symmorphic,' since the two roles, domestic and occupational, are relatively undifferentiated.

In recent years, a phenomenal number of women have entered the labor force. Women workers exceeded twenty million in 1970, representing forty percent of the entire labor force and fifty percent of the female population of fifteen years of age or above.[15] Not only the number, but the M-shaped age distribution of women workers is a recent departure: a high rate of participation prevails among women in their early twenties, the rate drops in the late twenties and thirties, and then rises again in the forties and fifties. Intrusion by women into male roles has gradually led to certain legal and institutional arrangements to make the two roles compatible, such as maternity leave, day-care centers and nursery schools.

Unlike the well-structured dimorphic type, bimorphism is ill-defined and protean. This lack of structural clarity makes bimorphism, which ideally should be symmetric, lean toward asymmetry. Asymmetric bimorphism can be conceptualized according to male as well as female viewpoints, each in terms both of individual inclinations and structural constraints. The bimorphic woman, who occupies dual roles, generally tends to feel that only her *domestic* role is fully legitimate, and that whenever the two roles conflict, priority should go to the domestic side. This subjective 'feeling' is structurally sustained and reinforced by the dominant ideology of the occupational world, which does not accept women as equal coworkers.

The dual constraint upon women takes several forms. The 'M-shaped' age distribution indicates that upon marriage or first pregnancy women prefer, and are expected, to quit their jobs and stay home as fulltime housewives until all their children are grown. Under the lifetime employment system this arrangement inevitably handicaps women. Also related is the irregular, auxiliary, and peripheral nature of women's jobs, the regular, primary jobs being more or less monopolized by men. In particular, many middle-aged women are part-time workers subject to insecurity and layoff during times of recession. Furthermore, in what might be called occupational dimorphism, women are assigned to 'feminine type' jobs. Thus they are excluded from the managerial and highly skilled professional spheres defined as 'masculine.' Anticipating occupational dimorphism, college women tend to major in 'feminine' fields, such as the humanities and home economics, rather than engineering or the social sciences, as pointed out by Sekiguchi Reiko.[16] It was further noted by Sekiguchi that, among women there is commonly a wider discrepancy than among men between their specialized fields in college and the types of job they can secure; schoolteaching and health-related jobs are dominant among women regardless of college training.

Asymmetric bimorphism among women is mirrored in males. In the ideal form of bimorphism, the male shares the domestic role as husband and father in addition to his occupational role. It might be assumed that the husband of a working woman takes half of the responsibility for housework. However, more than half the husbands sampled in a recent survey do not cooperate in housework at all, and refusal to cooperate is more prevalent in the urban sample.[17] The result is an extreme asymmetry in which the wife has moved toward bimorphism while the husband remains purely dimorphic. The resulting imbalance explains why working women must overwork, to the point of exhausion.

When the husband 'helps' the wife, his contribution is limited to certain kinds of activities acceptable to males, such as carpentry, looking after the children, taking a bath with the children, and making beds. He seldom, or never, does the cooking, dishwashing, grocery shopping or ironing. Domestic dimorphism is evident here as a mirror image of occupational dimorphism. By and large, there is little difference between the husband of a housewife and the husband of a working wife in the pattern and frequency of domestic cooperation.[18]

Even what is called 'my-homeism.' which seemed at one time to threaten the male's traditional loyalty to his employer and company and also to terminate his frequent long absences from home, in fact has not changed this basic structure. On the contrary, my-homeism has in some instances resulted in the enslavement of the entire household to the employer.[19]

The problem of asymmetry may be attributed partly to cultural lag shared by males and females alike. But it may also reflect a more basic dilemma inherent in bimorphism. If more symmetrical bimorphism is to be attained, extradomestic institutions must meet needs which until now have been taken care of at home, particularly childcare. Furthermore, special allowance must be made for the unique qualities of feminine physiology including menstruation, pregnancy, parturition, lactation, and menopause. The result is dramatization of sex differences while, if bimorphism is to succeed, sex differences should be deemphasized.

AMORPHISM

Asymmetric bimorphism is a combination of, or compromise between, dimorphism and pure bimorphism. Whether Japanese have reached an optimal level of compromise acceptable to both sexes, or whether they are moving toward more symmetrical bimorphism, remains to be seen. It may be that symmetrical bimorphism is the ultimate form of equality and that, until it is structurally guaranteed as a dominant culture pattern, there will be no true equality. Such an ideal, however, seems unattainable. Furthermore, this form of equality is often frustrated by the inherent variation among both men and women in capacity and disposition. It may be argued that equality should be based upon freedom of choice for both sexes to adopt any role that suits their abilities and wants. Here 'amorphic' refers to this third pattern.

Amorphism seeks, first, to expand and preserve the range of options available throughout the life cycle. Whatever narrows that range of choice must be avoided. Second, commitment to one possible pattern instead of another must result from individual decision rather than structural rules or mores. Third, a commitment once found to be mistaken should be considered reversible so that initial freedom of choice can be restored.

Amorphism stands in opposition to the prevalent idea that women should be wives and mothers, whereas both dimorphism and bimorphism take these roles for granted. Whether a woman finds her *ikigai* in marriage and motherhood or in something else is to be her own decision. At present, such an attitude would be revolutionary in Japanese female culture. Fourteen percent of a sample in one survey of single women indicated their firm intention to remain single.[20] But the overwhelming majority of women are bound by the idea of *tekireiki* [marriageable age] which generates a sense of urgency in a single woman over twenty-four and embarrassment in a 'leftover' woman of thirty or more. Whereas an unmarried woman is the object of derogatory gossip, an unmarried man arouses only nurturant sympathy.

A woman must face many other decisions throughout her life in order to preserve or restore role options. If marriage is chosen, the couple must agree which name – the husband's or wife's – is to be assumed as the family name. (This option is legally guaranteed but seldom activated.) Nor should they be bound by the traditional and still common idea that marriage is irreversible. Besides the freedom of divorce and remarriage, the woman and her husband must be able to decide on the desirability of parenthood. Free access to contraception, abortion, and foster parentage are essential. Once commitment is made to parenthood, the childcare roles should be assumed by whichever partner has the time or ability: husband, wife, or a day-care center if available.

Except for a handful of women who represent women's liberation movements, this amorphic point of view has neither been voiced nor practiced in its entirety. It is difficult therefore to make generalizations or predictions, but in my view this trend has clear implications for sex equality.

The maximization of role options and individual decision-making, free from conventional definitions, would ultimately lead to the random distribution of roles between men and women, and sex would become gradually less significant as a determining variable. In the first place, there would be greater variation among women in their roles, dispositions, and behavior patterns, *too* great to permit a stereotypic definition of 'femininity.' Such a trend would imply individuation rather than conformity to stereotypical roles.

Second, variation within the female population would overshadow differences between sexes, giving a general impression of uniformity across sexual boundaries. Similarity between the sexes is observable at a superficial level among teenagers and college students in their speech patterns, clothing, hair styles, and even the use of cosmetics and perfume. The popularity of singers of the 'unisex' type is another indication of the trend toward cross-sexual uniformity. Iwai Hiroaki found that in a list of twenty-eight dispositional attributes, high school girls identified 'gracefulness,' 'tender feeling,' 'home-orientation,' and 'obedience,' in that order, as desirable for women. Conversely, the same respondents chose 'toughness' and 'leadership' as desirable traits for men. This finding seems to demonstrate the persistence of a traditional dichotomy between masculine and feminine dispositions. He also shows, however, that all other attributes (seventy-nine percent), including initiative, and strength of will, were considered desirable for both sexes.[21] It remains to be seen whether the results of that survey are a sign of change toward random distribution of attributes between men and women.

Third, a random pattern of roles naturally involves the probability of change – or reversal of roles conventionally defined as feminine or masculine.

Ideally there should be a fifty-fifty chance for women to take over hitherto male-dominated spheres while men move into the female-dominated realm. In reversed dimorphism the man assumes domestic roles while his wife maintains a full-time occupation. Or, rather than a permanent role reversal, there may be role exchange or alternation between men and women according to situational necessity.

Role reversal is likely to be accompanied by status reversal so that a woman may be higher in status than a man in an occupational hierarchy or other institutional setting. What must be overcome first may be the woman's own resistance to having a female superior. Of course marriage with a younger, less educated man should be equally acceptable.

Reversal in role and status may be accompanied by reversal in behavior patterns. One of the slogans of the women's liberation movement was 'Change yourself from a woman embraced to a woman embracing.'

Fourth, the changes inherent in random role distribution do not extinguish male or female sexual desire, but rather support liberation of sex from convention and attainment of broader variation in erotic behavior. 'Free sex,' or pure eroticism, involves unrestrained non-marital sex, one-to-many, or many-to-many, partnerships, and the right to be an unwed mother, in contrast to monogamous sex. The same trend allows much greater variation in erotic behavior: rejection of dependence upon a male partner for intercourse, namely, the 'bisexual' or *rezu* (lesbian) movement: approval of masturbation; anal sexuality to replace vaginal sexuality, the latter being taken as a symbol of female submission to male egotism, and so on. This feminist version of eroticism is advocated by radical minorities within the liberation movement, such as contributors to the magazine called *Onna erosu*. One author in this magazine went so far as to recommend violation of the incest taboo.[22] Whether these radical liberationists really mean, let alone practice, what they preach is unknown, but the overwhelming impression is that they are utterly fed up with males. (It might be noted that many of these women libbers were once married to 'progressive' men whom they met in college during campus 'struggles' against academic representatives of the Establishment. This may explain their strong sense of despair regarding male participation in the movement.)

Amorphism, like bimorphism, requires structural support to implement individual decisions or to insure freedom of choice. Such support is twofold. On the one hand, role choice must be guaranteed through equal access to the same range of roles. On the other hand, some of the major domestic roles should be performed by public institutions. Particularly important are institutions to care for helpless members of the family, small children and the aged. Structural support is required by the young mother not only to choose between rearing her children by herself and relying upon a day-care center and nursery school, and to decide whether to look after her mother-in-law by herself or to put her in a nursing home, but also to enable an elderly woman to choose between reliance upon her children and entry into a home for the aged. As it stands now, use of such institutions is regarded as a necessary evil rather than a desirable option.

Once such structural support is relied upon, a dilemma similar to that of bimorphism, but even more evident and inescapable, must be faced. Structural support will be provided only if the individual foregoes some degree of freedom by conforming to the expectations of the general population. The majority of men and women bound by conventional dimorphism, or modified bimorphism, would resist the provision of a respectable occupational role for a lesbian or the establishment of tax-funded day-care centers for promiscuous unwed mothers. That is a dilemma to be resolved by amorphic liberationists.

CONCLUSION

Three directions taken by movements toward sex equality have been identified. In every direction lies dilemma, or paradox, attributable in part to social change but more so to structural rigidity and cultural conservatism. Women themselves seem to feel ambivalent: no single option appears totally satisfactory, but each in part seems to offer something irresistible. What she wants seems to be a mixture of them all with differing emphasis in accordance with personal idiosyncracies and situational variation. A dimorphic housewife, generally content, may sometimes wish for the challenge of a bimorphic experience and feel envious of the freedom enjoyed by the amorphic woman. Conversely, a woman who takes pride in her independence from domestic obligations and detachment from heterosexual entanglements may sometimes wish for a 'typically feminine' way of life, and perhaps even to bind herself to the role of wife and mother. In this sense, most women may be classified as 'ambimorphic.'

Ambimorphism seems to reflect a sharp awareness of the discrepancy between the woman's own wishes and her assumption of what is expected of her by others, particularly, by men. In a study of the feminine role concept, Inagaki Tomoko compared Japanese women with American women in terms of 'self-orientation' and 'other-orientation,' the latter being a more traditional, accommodative role type. Her data, drawn from a sample of college women, led to the conclusion that while American women want to be more 'other-oriented' and believe men to expect them to be so, Japanese women are more 'self-oriented' but assume that men do not want them to be.[23] It remains to be seen whether the Japanese woman estimates men's expectations accurately or if her sense of discrepancy between her own wishes and the expectations of men is exaggerated. But we can safely conclude that the dilemma between inclinations toward individuation and readiness for role complementarity, creates ambimorphism.

When we realize that every direction is blocked by dilemma, and that women themselves are ambimorphic, the unfathomable depth of the problem of status asymmetry between sexes begins to emerge. It also becomes clear that this problem is by no means unique to any one culture but is shared by all. The three directions proposed here, together with the dilemma inherent in each, seem to be present in American and other Western societies as well. Insofar as the universality of male dominance is an undeniable fact of the present day, the range of directions in which equalitarian ideology can be implemented, I believe, must be limited in all cultures. On the other hand, the culturally determined aspect of sex inequality, is also undeniable. Even Steven Goldberg, who asserts the 'inevitability of patriarchy' on the basis of hormonally-driven male aggressiveness, admits that some societies 'exaggerate' male aggressiveness and that Japan is one of those societies.[24]

NOTES

* This is a modified version of a paper read at the 27th annual meeting of the Association for Asian Studies, March 25, 1975, in San Francisco. I wish to thank Kazuko Tanaka, Esyun Hamaguchi, and Tomoko Inukai for allowing me access to Japanese published materials: thanks go as well to Emiko Ohnuki-Tierney and some anonymous members of the audience for their helpful comments on the original paper. Freda Hellinger, at the Social Sciences and Linguistics Institute, University of Hawaii, rendered editorial assistance. I also wish to acknowledge the support of the National Institute of Mental Health Grant MH09243.

1. For various aspects of change in the status of Japanese women, see Koyama Takashi, ed., *Gendai Nippon no josei*, [Women in Japan Today] (Kokudosha, 1962).
2. Fujin ni kansuru Shomondai Chōsa Kaigi, *Gendai Nippon josei no ishiki to kōdō* [Attitudes and Behavior of Contemporary Japanese Women] (Ministry of Finance Printing Office, 1974), p. 98.
3. Robert Jay Lifton, 'Woman as Knower: Some Psychohistorical Perspectives,' in R. J. Lifton, ed., *The Woman in America* (Boston: Beacon Press, 1967).
4. Ibid., p. 31.
5. See, for example, Matsui Yayori, 'Protest and the Japanese Woman,' *Japan Quarterly*, Vol. 22, No. 1 (1975), pp. 32–39.
6. Rōdōshō Fujin Shōnen Kyoku, *Fujin no chii ni kansuru jittai chōsa* [A Survey on the Status of Women], Fujin kankei chōsa shiryō, No. 61 (1972), p. 15.
7. Ibid.
8. Sōrifu Seishōnen Taisaku Honbu, *Seishōnen no sei ishiki* [Attitudes among Youth toward Sex] (Ministry of Finance Printing Office, 1971), p. 40.
9. *Gendai Nippon josei*, p. 137.
10. Margery Wolf, *Women and the Family in Rural Taiwan* (Stanford University Press, 1972).
11. NHK Hōsō Seron Chōsasho, *Zusetsu Nihonjin no seikatsu jikan* [A Graphic Presentation of Time Allocation in Everyday Life of Japanese] (Japan National Broadcasting Press, 1974), pp. 262-63.
12. For a convincing analysis of this double change, occupational and domestic, see Sekiguchi Reiko, 'Joshi kōtō kyōiku shūryōsha no shakaiteki ichi' [The Social Status of High School Graduates), *Shakaigaku hyōron*, Vol. 23, No. 4 (1973), pp. 83–100.
13. Kikuchi Misao, 'Kodomo no kachi ishiki chōsa' [Survey of Value Consciousness Among Children], *Kyōiku shinri*, Vol. 22 (1974), pp. 552–55.
14. *Gendai Nippon josei*, p. 138.
15. Women's and Minors' Bureau (Ministry of Labor), *The Status of Women in Japan* (1972), p. 9.
16. See Sekiguchi, note 12.
17. *Gendai Nippon josei*, p. 221.
18. Ibid., p. 225.
19. Tada Michitarō, 'The Glory and Misery of "My Home",' *The Japan Interpreter*, Vol. IX, No. 4 (1974), pp. 105–14.
20. *Gendal Nippon josei*, p. 36.
21. Iwai Hiroaki, 'Josei kōkōsei no shakai ishiki' [The Social Consciousness of High School Girls], *Taishō Daigaku kiyō*, No. 56 (1974), pp. 113-36.
22. Funamoto Emi, 'Shikijōteki ni, geijutsuteki ni – han kekkon no erosu' [Sensual and Artistic – Eros of Anti-Marriage], *Onna erosu*, Vol. 1 (1973), pp. 40–54.
23. Inagaki Tomoko, 'A Cross-Cultural Study of the Feminine Role Concept Between Japanese and American College Women,' *Psychologia*, Vol. 10 (1967), pp. 144–54.
24. Steven Goldberg, *The Inevitability of Patriarchy* (New York: Morrow, 1973).

First published in *Ethnology*, Vol. XVIII, No. 4, 1979: 337–353

13 The Dilemma and Strategies of Aging Among Contemporary Japanese Women

Two recent studies (Salamon 1974; Perry 1976) state that Japanese women are much more autonomous than recognized in the previous literature; and Salamon, in particular, reads an androcentric bias in the latter's general tendency to stereotype the Japanese woman as submerged in the household or in a mother-child symbiosis. This point warrants a careful examination. The claimed autonomy of the Japanese woman, however, turns out to be grounded in her dependency, if not upon her procreative family, upon her mother or close friends. Furthermore, the autonomy and nearly dictatorial power enjoyed by the housewife in relation to her husband, as elaborated by Perry, is in fact inseparable from her economic dependency upon her husband which permits her role monopoly as a 'full-time homemaker.'

Implicit to the foregoing observation is the assumption that autonomy .and dependency are not incompatible under certain circumstances. As one of such prerequisites I suggest the well-balanced reciprocity of dependency: to the extent that dependency is exchanged in reciprocal terms the two parties involved can remain autonomous, free from guilt, shame, or obligation of submission. Since the mutuality of such exchange is maximized between equals, interdependence among intimate age peers, as observed by Salamon, may be critical for autonomy maintenance.

AUTONOMY, RECIPROCAL DEPENDENCY, AND AGING

What concerns this paper and makes it difficult for me to accept the above studies in their entirety is the fact that the individual's state of autonomy and reciprocal dependency fluctuates along his or her life course. Obviously, a drastic change occurs as one enters into the aging phase. The above researchers did touch upon this phase, but did not integrate it into their theses probably because their samples were limited largely to women in the prime of life or younger. As aging progresses, a woman will become increasingly more dependent and less able to reciprocate, resulting in the loss of autonomy. While thus far she may have been dependent upon her mother or age peers, she is now compelled to be more dependent upon members of the younger generation, and in the Japanese case, preferably upon her children. Insofar as care for the aged remains within the female role sphere as part of her domestic chores, it is her daughter or daughter-in-law upon whom she must rely, and this reliance will eventually undermine the autonomy of the caretaking generation of women as well.

It might be argued that the dependency of an aged woman upon her children is part of a reciprocal chain. Indeed, she may feel fully entitled to the child-centered dependency as the final stage for restoring a balanced reciprocity. After all, she is asking for the same kind of service that she has supplied – the generalized human care involving body management and emotional support.

What characterizes this reciprocity is the long time-span encompassing the woman's whole life cycle coupled with that of her child. Unlike the short-cycled, contemporaneously on-going interchange which is likely to occur between age- or generation-peers, the long-cycled give-and-take operates only where the memory of debits and credits is well retained. It may be that intrapersonal or interpersonal memory must be supported by a 'cultural memory' in the form either of collectively shared ideology such as filial piety or ancestor worship, or of social structure such as the Japanese stem-family called *ie*. Under the patrilineal/patriolocal system where the senior woman is to be taken care of by her daughter-in-law, who is not personally indebted to her but only vicariously through the son/husband, cultural indoctrination of the moral obligation of long-cycled reciprocity would be all the more necessary. Focusing on the aging phase and looking downward to younger generations instead of looking upward, one may look away from an interpersonal and psychological toward a more cultural and structural perspective. The difference between the above cited studies and previous literature may be a difference in foci, perspectives, or levels of analysis.

CHANGE AND DILEMMA

Nonetheless, there have been cultural, structural, economic, and demographic changes which directly affect the life style and expectations of the aging Japanese, women in particular. First, the post-war abolition of the *ie* as a jural entity has undermined the structural support for the entitlement of the older generation to the younger generation's gratitude and long-cycled obligation to reciprocate. Second, post-war education, reversing the pre-war cultural ideology, has inculcated the young Japanese with the values of individual choice and right as well as inter-individual equality. Deprived of structural and ideological armament, the filial obligation to repay the aged parents is largely left to interpersonal memory and the affective bond of kinship. (Small wonder that the elderly woman today would rather have her own daughter than her daughter-in-law to depend upon in her old age.) Third, the above change has been further accelerated by the growth in economy and industrialization which lures young workers into large city-based corporations, and diminishes chances of filial succession to the family occupation as well as those of intergenerational coresidence. Geographical mobility, concommitant to industrialization, weakens the solidarity of residential neighborhood which might have functioned as a pressure, as it did in pre-war Japan, for the junior members of a household to fulfill their filial obligations.

Finally, the ever-increasing life expectancy, which places the Japanese among the longest living peoples in the world, compounds the problem of aging by protracting the period of aging as well as the pre-aging periods of a life. Women can expect to live for over 77 years (as of 1976), five more years than men, which gives them three decades of post-parental life.

All these changes, I assume, combine to make the old woman's expectation for filiocentric dependency increasingly obsolete, undesirable, or unsound. She is urged to reorient herself either to remain autonomous or to find other alternatives of dependency. At the same time, the prolonged life expectancy subsumes a greater likelihood of prolonged invalidism and senility calling for total dependency. The idea of nursing homes is an alternative being undertaken by a small segment of the aged population.[2] However, the majority of aging women – men can expect their wives to outlive and attend to them – appear to believe that they will need the kind of personal care which only a mother can provide and that the mother-for-child care can best be approximated by the child-for-patient care. This is the dilemma that is faced by contemporary Japanese women in the phase of aging. It is open to question whether this dilemma contributes to the continuing high rate of suicide among older Japanese despite the general improvement in living conditions, and specifically, to the fact that in 1973 Japanese women of 75 and over had the highest suicide rate in the world (World Health Statistics Annual 1973, cited in Koseisho, 1976: 116–117). It is obvious that the rosy picture of the Japanese elderly given by Palmore (1975) is a gross distortion of reality, as severely criticized by Kato (1977).

The following is an analysis of aging, in light of autonomy and dependency, as anticipated or experienced by a sample of Japanese women who were contacted in a small city, during my field work in 1976–77, and again in 1978. An attempt will be made to assess how the dilemma of aging is confronted, and what strategies are being explored to surmount it.

FILIOCENTRIC FULFILLMENT WITH MUTED EXPECTATIONS

Many of the women interviewed revealed their filiocentric preoccupations in terms of present or past fulfillment rather than expectations for the future. A son's devotion and the reliability of a daughter-in-law, as enjoyed by the mother, are among the favorite topics. Women with several children tend to find the greatest pleasure of life in the regularly repeated gatherings of all their children and grandchildren around them. A retrospective sense of fulfillment takes several forms: the satisfaction from having brought up the children properly, given them a college education and arranged good marriages for sons and daughters; the pleasure of having trained the daughter-in-law in etiquette and housework as one's successor; sympathy and gratitude expressed by the children for the mother's hardship; vicarious enjoyment of a son's promising career and of a granddaughter's success in the entrance examination to a national university.

The filiocentric fulfillment compensates for an unhappy marriage. A woman in her mid-fifties, recalling having once made up her mind to divorce her promiscuous husband, is glad to have stayed with him because with divorce she would have had to lose 'these nice kids' to her husband and in-laws. Now, her daughter, son-in-law (adopted)[4] and she form a close, viable team to run the family business and perform domestic chores; meanwhile her husband, reformed and harmless, has been 'promoted' to the honorable but obsolete status of a retired househead.

These observations indicate the norm of long-cycled reciprocity to be still at work, and yet the sense of fulfillment as the final phase of repayment does not seem translatable into an anticipation of repayment. While talkative about their child-centered contentment, the informants tend to be mute about their expectations from the children for their final phase of aging. Indeed, no informant takes her filiocentric dependency for granted. Every informant stressed that she would do anything to avoid being a burden to the children or standing in their way, and that it is totally up to the children whether they would live with her or not.[5] 'Children have their own ideas'; 'children will go the way that suits them. We as parents should not cause trouble for them.' Co-operation between the two generations should be voluntary on the part of the children rather than a matter of obligatory compliance. Pressed for an explanation, the informants tend to say, 'If you expect anything you are more liable to be disappointed; you had better expect nothing to avoid disappointment.'

Because expectations are muted, the question of the senile phase remains unarticulated. How are they going to manage this phase, I asked. My question was usually brushed off, evaded, or responded to with reluctance or irritation: 'I am determined not to think about it'; 'I won't know what to do until it really happens to me'; 'I hope I'll die *pokkuri* (abruptly).'[6] Expectations for filial dependency were expressed only timidly or indirectly: 'You find no warmth in the nursing home.[7] Only blood-related people can give love'; 'I don't think I'll be left alone dying in the wilderness. Somebody will take care of me'; 'My children are saying, "Don't worry".' The predominant attitude is twofold: avoidance of facing a denigrating, senile self-image, and transference of the decision-making responsibility from self to the children.

Paradoxically, in these remarks one detects an intensified version of filiocentricity, or a combination of the mother's desire to maximize the child's autonomy and her determination toward self-abnegation. The woman's acceptance of such an asymmetry in the distribution of rights and obligations may be explained by various factors that reinforce the post-war changes: the pre-war education which irreversibly inculcated her with the virtue of selflessness; the apprehension of incompatibility with or rejection by the younger, post-war generation; the horror of playing the same role as her own mother-in-law or as a 'mean' mother-in-law often depicted in television 'home drama' series in dominating and abusing the daughter-in-law. Many an informant identifies herself as the loser generation squeezed between the two demanding winner generations, and thus in her mind what Plath (1975) calls 'the last Confucian sandwich' extends to those born in the Taisho era (1912–1925) and even late Meiji (1868–1911), as well as the early part of the present Showa era (1926–).[8] Not without resentments, she nonetheless accepts and plays up this sandwiched status.

Many of the mothers' apprehensions are not groundless. Indeed, my sample includes those women whose children or in-laws have 'broken their hearts.' A carefully reared daughter with a college degree shocked her widowed mother by marrying an American, a shock from which the mother appeared unable to recover; an enormous educational investment by a *kyōiku*-mama (education-obsessed mother) in a son produced an elite university graduate without any motivations for work; a 73-year-old woman living alone in a large house, none of her four married sons volunteering to come back and live with her; the mother of two daughters not being on speaking terms with her elder daughter and adopted son-in-law since her husband's death, when her son-in-law demanded an immediate property inheritance – an appalling breach of cultural norms.

STRATEGIES TOWARD AUTONOMY

Aware of the need of dependency in the near or remote future, and leaving open the possibility or desirability of depending upon her children, each woman seems to be exploring other alternatives. If, as she claims, she really wants her children to be free, she realizes she, too, must be autonomous. The following strategies are identified.

Self-sufficiency

My informats, including those in their seventies, present themselves as desirous or capable of self-sufficiency in one way or another. First, economic self-sufficiency is stressed, rather than the old practice wherein the economic support of the old parents was a major part of filial piety. To maintain and build up economic autonomy, widows in their sixties continue to be the mainstay of the house enterprises inherited from their husbands: company presidency is held by elderly women, only a secondary position consigned to their sons who are in their prime. All the informants have one or another source of income of their own, including the widow's pension or the national government's welfare pension for the aged. For some, to be sure, the income is not sufficient for their livelihood, and yet the mere fact that they can spend some money freely in buying gifts to celebrate the school admission of their grandchildren seems to give them a singular sense of autonomy which their mothers did not enjoy. Money, rather than a child, as the ultimate source of security was emphasized by several informants. It was even pointed out that enough money has been saved for hospitalization or for hiring a professional caretaker in case one becomes bedridden. Here we find strivings to maximize economic self-sufficiency accompanied by reliance upon pecuniary nexus in avoidance of interpersonal reciprocity.

Second, inner self-sufficiency is sought through commitment of surplus energy, to self-oriented activity. Currently active working women tend to invest the energy freed from child care in intensified occupational commitment, which contributes to economic autonomy. For a grandmother pharmacist, 'Running the drugstore is my life.' Retired women and housewives, on the other hand, have taken up some regular activities to keep themselves busy. These are activities in pursuit of one or more hobbies or studies, which include classical and folk music and dance, Buddhist hymns, calligraphy and painting, composition of *haiku* and *waka* poems, tea ritual and flower arrangement, artificial flower design, leather-working, weaving, dyeing, wood or metal carving, plant growing, studies in current social problems such as consumer protection. Immersion in such studies for some women, no longer merely a pastime, has become *ikigai* (purpose of life) and strengthened their will to live. A 79-year-old housewife realizes to her surprise how strong her attachment to life is: 'I must study and understand the essence of human life as much as possible. I cannot die until then'; 'At night, when I am sleepless, I try to figure out the next step in weaving [which I am working on] to make it into this or that shape.'

Third, all the informants are invariably concerned with health as the most basic condition for physical self-sufficiency. Instructions on health care are pored over or listened to, and physical exercise is maintained. An 80-year-old woman, the oldest in the sample, gets up at 5:00 a.m. and jogs around the neighborhood. Special attention is paid to mental health. Activities are meant, I was told, primarily to keep one mentally alert so that one will not fall into 'ecstacy' (often quoted from the title of a best-seller novel by Ariyoshi (1972) depicting an old man struck with senile psychosis).

Continued Credit Accumulation

No longer confident of being a lifelong creditor, the old mother may continue to help her children in order to build up more credits or to keep herself in a short-cycled chain of reciprocity. This reciprocity usually takes the form of role co-ordination with the daughter-in-law either through a division of labor (e.g., one running a shop, the other being in charge of housework) or role alternations (the older wife prepares a Japanese meal one evening, the younger a 'French' dinner next evening). A 77-year-old widow works on her tangerine farms and undertakes all housework while her daughter-in-law goes out everyday to work as a caddy for a golf course in the vicinity. In the household with small children, the grandmother's babysitting responsibility tends to be essential. During interviews, more than one informant looked after their grandchildren whose undisciplined behavior constantly interrupted our conversation.

While one wants to age as 'a well-liked granny,' child-care is not necessarily a grandmother's choice. Particularly if she is engrossed in her 'studies' as her *ikigai*, the grandmother finds the babysitter role too demanding on her time. Pressured to look after a toddler while her daughter-in-law is doing kitchen work or helping her son with the house shop, the 56-year-old grandmother performs this role only reluctantly. She feels jealous of her friends who live alone, have lots of time to compose *haiku*, and are free to attend *haiku*-contest meetings held in Tokyo as well as locally. Even when she is alone in her own room with her door locked, all the grandchildren try to come in, thus disrupting her concentration on *haiku* work. As she admits, she accepts the babysitting obligation as a bargain binding the daughter-in-law to look after her in old age. Here it is not so much the mother's child-centered dedication as her selfish calculation that motivates her to help the daughter-in-law.

Dispersal of Interdependence: Intradomestic

Autonomy is further sought through dispersing partnerships of interdependence which may free elderly women from the filiocentric bond. Realignment involves not only a creation of new bonds but an intensification of existing networks and rekindling of long-forgotten ties.

Within the domestic realm, three directions are noted. One is an intensified identification with the *hotoke* (dead) enshrined in the household altar who are labeled 'ancestors,' as the term is understood loosely (Smith 1966, 1974; Plath 1964; Newell 1969; Lebra 1976). The husband's death tends to trigger such 'ancestral' commitment, and this may explain why more widows display this behavior than the still married women.

Ancestor 'worship' extends to a harsh, but now dead mother-in-law as well. An informant, while confiding the extraordinary hardships under an intolerant mother-in-law, says she can now appreciate the essential values which her mother-in-law tried to instill in her, regards herself as a reservoir of all the wisdom handed down from her predecessor, and believes its transmission to her successor (daughter-in-law) her duty.

Identification with household ancestors entails this-worldly obligations, particularly in the case of an old 'renowned' *ie*, which supposedly had been inherited from the ancestors by the last surviving member. A widow in her seventies refuses to leave her home and join her son and his family as she has been asked to do because she feels obligated to preserve the 'ancestral' house which 'has existed since the Tokugawa era.' The preservation of the house refers to the compulsive fulfillment of gift-giving obligations to all the houses into which its women have married over several generations. The informant does not even recognize the present-generation members of these houses and yet cannot afford, she claims, to disgrace the name of her honorable house by failing to deliver a cash gift on an occasion like a memorial rite. The bulk of her welfare pension, she says, is spent this way.

Devotion to ancestors is related to reciprocal payoff. A widow already enjoys such reward as the head of the main house which is highly regarded by many of its branch and sub-branch houses. As the most senior member of the whole *dozoku*, the Japanese version of lineage, she is offered a prominent seat whenever its members assemble. More commonly, ancestors are expected to benefit the worshippers with a graceful death by letting them die without the *netakiri* (bedridden) phase. The woman of 80, a devout member of the Reiyukai sect, says, 'I pray so that I will not become *netakiri*, that I can die *pokkuri*. I am sure the ancestors will help me.'

An elderly woman, through her devotion to ancestors, expects to join them some time; her worship of her dead spouse or mother-in-law merges with an anticipation to become an ancestor herself; her role as a custodian of the household altar is a step toward her self-enshrinement. Probably due to such belief, my informants are willing to talk about their wishes regarding their death and post-mortem care while resistant about pre-mortem care. A widow sounded as if she were looking forward to dying because 'your children remember only good things about you after you die,' a fact she learned after her husband's death.

Identification with and dependency upon ancestors, then, as a matter of course, comes to interlock with a filiocentric orientation in that ancestor worship is perpetuated by the children. Some women are happy that their daughters-in-law are already participating in this responsibility, and some admit that they venerate the ancestors because they themselves want to be venerated by their offspring.

Despite this overlap between reciprocal dependency with ancestors and that with descendants, indirect dependency upon the children through ancestor worship seems more protective of one's autonomy and dignity than the anticipation of direct dependency. The old woman's ancestor worship or her concern for post-mortem salvation may well be a metaphor to conceal her concern about the possible pre-mortem helplessness.

In pre-war Japan, the custodial care for the dead was inseparable from the transgenerational continuity of the *ie*. Many of my informants, however, are unsure of, or proclaim their indifference to, the perpetuation of *ie*. Confronted with virtual abandonment by a successor-son and daughter-in-law or with the imminent extinction of the *ie*, a woman tends to intensify her loyalty to the house ancestors as the 'last' caretaker for the dead. Lacking confidence in the cooperation of their offspring, or in order to avoid burdening the children, some women have tried to achieve post-mortem salvation through self-help. There is nothing to worry about, I was told, because tombs have been constructed, or because fees for 'eternal care' have been paid to priests. Two women received a three-day religious training course in Buddhist temples, at the conclusion of which they were presumably elevated, through a ritual simulating initiation into a nunnery, to the status of Buddha's disciple and granted a posthumous name. 'With this, I have no trouble departing this world,' said one of them, 'but what's going to happen to these people?' She pointed to the house altar.

The second direction for reorientation within the domestic sphere is a consolidation of the conjugal bond. Given the primacy of the filiocentric (or uterine) bond, the marital bond appears fragile, and the experience of conjugal love has been, as inferred from the life histories, less than usual (Lebra 1978). In some cases, the situation began to change when the children married' or left the parents for educational or occupational reasons. This 'empty-nest' crisis was sometimes overcome by a discovery of mutual congeniality between husband and wife. 'It takes long years,' observed an adopted husband in front of his wife, 'before husband and wife can become *isshin-dotai* (one mind, one body).' The wife responded to this comment by blushing and giggling. It appeared as if they were enjoying a delayed honeymoon in their sixties. Only after many years of co-living, I was told, spouses become confident of each other, with nothing to hide from each other. A widow muses on a good marital relationship: 'Husband and wife come to treat each other with tender care only after you reach fifty.' A retired kindergarten teacher has announced to her former colleagues that she is going to devote the rest of her life to her husband upon his retirement to expiate her guilt for wifely negligence during so many years of marriage. Marital intimacy was promoted for some couples through the husband's child-like dependency upon the wife and the latter's responsive nurturance, no longer inhibited by the presence of children and his parents (who are dead by now). A communication barrier, built up during long years of marriage, may be difficult to remove, as in the case of a housewife in her late seventies and her silent husband. The wife, even while sitting across from her husband at a table, concentrates on *haiku* composition, with no hope of intimate conversation. However, something unexpected occurred recently. She left the living room with the notebook where she had written her *haiku* open; she returned to discover a new *haiku* written down next to her. Her husband had, at long last, spoken to her in this fashion!

While identification with ancestors turns the lineal orientation vertically, the newly acquired intimacy between spouses replaces the lineal bond with the horizontal bond of affinity. The concept that genuine marital intimacy develops only after 30 or more years of cohabitation is nothing new, but it appears to assume a new meaning when husband and wife realize that they are going to live for a long time with no one but each other.

The conjugal bond has its limitation. The husband-wife dependency is less than reciprocal at this stage unless the husband remains active as a breadwinner. The retired, housebound husband tends to become a burden to look after without reciprocating the caretaker, the wife. Hence, middle-aged or older widows refuse to entertain the idea of remarrying, as they see no reason why they should 'wait upon another man all over again.' Likewise, a devotee to her enshrined husband unwittingly remarks, 'I have been living as if I were in paradise since my husband's death.'

The third alternative of intradomestic interdependence involves a grandmother-grandchild bond. It is not unreasonable for a woman expecting to live up to 80 or more to skip one generation and seek support from her grandchildren. Again, the grandmother's expectations are muted, but she would tell how her grandchildren have offered to care for her, and how they compete with one another in volunteering should she need their help. She sounds both pleased and amused, but such a prospect is becoming increasingly realistic. Two of the women in their seventies, living alone, have their grown grandchildren visit them more regularly than their children. The generational or age distance seems to facilitate a communication of interdependence without threatening each other's autonomy, although this hypothesis is yet to be substantiated. In in-law relationships, a grandmother-in-law, unlike a mother-in-law, may be looked upon as too old to dominate her granddaughter-in-law, and the latter, too young to intimidate the former. The greater congeniality generally observed between alternating generations than adjacent generations (Murdock 1949: 278) may be thus mobilized to secure caretakers for the aged with prolonged life expectancy. If the grandmother was a caretaker of the grandchild in his or her infancy, this role reversal will complete reciprocity.

Dispersal of Interdependence: Extradomestic

Social realignment for autonomy is further explored outside the household. Elderly women in general seem to be undergoing re-socialization primarily through interaction with their age-peers with increasing frequency, scope, and intensity. Hobbies and studies, pursued in order to attain self-sufficiency, are, for the most part, collective activities.

There exists a variety of recruitment fields for interaction and collective activities of age-peers, of which the most prevalent ones will be mentioned. First is the neighborhood, which in a broad sense encompasses many kinds of groups from small and informal to large and formal. The old notorious 'well-side' gossip group of neighbors has now found a more up-dated spot in a neighborhood supermarket where a couple of elderly women, while shopping, are often seen enjoying conversation, sometimes lasting over an hour. The house of a widow living alone is chosen by old neighbors as a favorite place for daily gathering and chatting. Conversation includes exchange of detailed information on the state of their health and that of mutual acquaintances. A, Tokyo-born, childless widow in her sixties, who used to do major shopping only in Tokyo has now decided to patronize neighborhood stores exclusively, because 'neighbors are most important in emergency.'

Planned group activities are engaged in by larger, formal units of the neighborhood community which, traceable to the pre-war period, are covertly linked to the city administration: *Fujinkai* (women's association), organized through such neighborhood networks and assisted by the local government, involves many of my informants as members. Another important association, also based upon neighborhood, is *rojinkai* (old people's association). The city residents tend to share the idea of life-cycle transition in membership in these associations: a woman in her thirties and early forties is still busy as a member of a PTA; around her mid-forties she 'graduates' and joins the *fujinkai*, and around 65, she switches to the *rojinkai*. Underlying the compulsion for avoidance of simultaneous membership in more than one is the traditional idea that one household sends only one member: by the time the woman reaches 65, her daughter-in-law is ready to join the *fujinkai* as a 'successor' to her which requires the older woman to move into the *rojinkai*.

Second, the relationship built up through school affiliation is maintained or, more typically, recharged when a woman reaches the post-parental stage. Most important in this educational network is the bond formed between classmates in grade school or high school. Generally, both men and women begin, in their forties, to show interest in alumni reunions and to attend them regularly. Women in particular form intimate groups consisting of several former classmates, and maintain friendships through telephone conversations and periodic meetings. Many of my informants stressed the importance of such classmate ties for sustaining their morale; when the group meets either in a member's house or at a hotel, they spend the whole night talking with nothing to conceal from one another. This phenomenon, again, is not new, but increased leisure and improved economic conditions allow the women to interact with one another more often and more freely.

PTA membership is another school-related basis of recruitment for collective activity. Women maintain or reactivate the bond of mothers of children in the same class. Mothers of kindergarten children in particular form the most intimate ties because of their daily contact with one another in the kindergarten playground and maintain these ties long after the children's maturation. Emotional ties exist among the mothers whose children became collectively involved in serious incidents: e.g., mothers of the high school students who were drowned during a school excursion, and of the university students who fought the Establishment and were brought to court trials. These exemplify age-peer solidarity as an extension of filiocentric preoccupation.

Third, occupational ties present another network. In particular, women who have had career occupations tend to attach the greatest importance to these. Occupational ties may be between co-workers, employer and employee, or professional and client. Retired kindergarten teachers, for example, who worked in the same place now get together to study leather handcrafts. Those feminine professions which involve intimate physical contact with clients generate everlasting bonds: intimacy between a midwife and her client is retained throughout their lives and is extended to the child delivered with her help.

Fourth, without a previously established network, a group may be formed or joined simply because there is a person who is able to take leadership or to teach some sort of speciality. Among the best-known leaders in the local community is a 93-year-old man, a former schoolteacher, who is followed by roughly 70 admirers, male and female, all elderly. This group is called 'The Health College,' with the leader as its 'president.' One of its semi-monthly meetings, attended by 40 members equally divided by sex, included: calisthenics (several attendants, physically frail, only watching), joint singing of the national anthem and the 'College Song,' reports on the health conditions of hospitalized members, the president's long lecture on health care with an exhortation of the vegetarian regimen (which commanded a surprising span of polite attention from the 'students'), a series of short-story presentations by a number of assigned members as a way of overcoming timidity, a leading member's lecture on *haiku* composition, the *senryu* (a humorous version of *haiku*) contest climaxing in the announcement of winners, mutual entertainment by a display of artistic skill in singing and dancing, and learning a new dance to a song dedicated to the national flag. After a six-hour long series of such activities, the meeting ended with a chorus of loud laughter. (This ritual stems from the president's conviction that laughter is a key to good health.) Leadership roles were assumed by males – male leadership was observed in every association where both sexes participated – but during periods of recreation and entertainment women dominated the scene. The semi-monthly meeting of this group and the monthly meeting of the *rojinkai* are the greatest sources of joy for the 80-year-old informant that make her lonely life livable. She can hardly wait for the next meeting, she said, and sometimes excitement keeps her from sleeping the night before the meeting.

Reciprocal dependency is intrinsic to such peer-group participation. Group members depend upon one another for the enjoyment of togetherness, exchange of sympathetic concern about one another, and the assurance that information regarding a member's ill health will be circulated immediately. A therapeutic function was already alluded to with regard to the interaction of classmates. Intimacy and emotional interdependency is further built up through group travels, a common feature of all kinds of groups, which provide opportunity for co-dining, co-bathing, and co-sleeping.

Persons with special skills or experiences find an eager audience or clientele in the group. An old retired midwife, equipped with some medical knowledge and tools, considers it her duty to give advice on health matters to members of the *rojinkai* to which she belongs, and to test their blood pressure regularly; 'experts' in dancing and singing entertain fellow members, and those skilled in weaving, calligraphy, flower-arrangement, etc., become instructors for their peers. Teaching Buddhist hymns in one of such groups is the true *ikigai* for an informant in her seventies. Needless to say, both parties benefit in that skills and service are exchanged for appreciation and admiration.

Sometimes, different age-groups exchange such benefits. The *fujinkai* organizes entertainment for *rojinkai* members annually on the Revere-the-Elderly-Day, by presenting old folk songs and dances on stage.

Involvement with age-peers in the extra-domestic setting is not devoid of ambivalence or constraint. A sense of domestic obligation toward the husband or children interferes with a total immersion in extra-domestic interaction and self-directed activities. The children and husband tease the *dezuki-basan* (outgoer-granny), usually with a touch of good-humored support. But the granny in her own mind seems pressured to justify her routine departure from the domestic sphere. At least she must be careful in her conduct not to join a 'well-side' gossip party disparaging the daughters-in-law, which would be fed back to her own daughter-in-law through the rumor network of young wives. Leaders of *fujinkai*, *rojinkai*, or other associations take pains to promote educational goals and to avoid reducing their activities to tea-drinking, chatting, and social entertainment. The mother-in-law/daughter-in-law conflict is taken up as a topic of seminar discussion under the guidance of a lecturer, preferably with representatives of the younger generation invited. The symbolic significance of 'educational' emphasis can be inferred from the names of many women's clubs with the designation of *Kyoshitsu* (classroom) as in 'Ceramics Kyoshitsu,' 'Folk-song Kyoshitsu,' 'Tennis Kyoshitsu.'

Participant-observation of a *fujinkai* group tour exposed me to how ambivalence and constraint are acted out by outgoer-grannies. The annual trip which lasts several days, with a daily long bus ride and hotel stop, does give a woman the opportunity to be physically free from domestic chores and to enjoy conversation and mutual entertainment with age-peers without inhibition – the absence of males indeed emancipates these female co-travellers from the codes of conduct pertaining to their routine life, and allows them to entertain one another with scatalogical jokes of extraordinary magnitude. But as soon as the bus stopped at a celebrated spot for sightseeing, all the bus riders rushed to souvenir shops to buy gifts for their families, especially for their grandchildren. Buying occurred at every bus stop so that at the end of the ride gift boxes were piled up to fill the bus. Even the most uninhibited joker was transformed into a straight, humorless housewife during the shopping intervals. This way the women appeared to alternate between the egocentric and extra-domestic enjoyment of license and identification with peers on the one hand, and domestic or filiocentric preoccupations on the other. Widows are more conscience-free than the married in extra-domestic affiliations and activities, but a 63-year-old widow confessed that every time she came home after 'playing' outside she felt guilty toward her enshrined husband. The general impression is that these women were trying to create or maintain a proper balance in the allocation of time and energy among different kinds of commitment and involvement, old and new, egocentric and altercentric. This attitude appears to convey their awareness that, however they may enjoy peer interaction, they will have to drop out and stay home sooner or later, as some of their friends have done already, when they cease to be ambulatory.

SUMMARY AND CONCLUSION

Autonomy and dependency are compatible insofar as the latter is based on well-balanced reciprocity. The dependency of aging parents upon their adult children rests upon a long-cycled chain of reciprocity involving two connected life cycles, parental and filial. The dilemma envisaged by the elderly women in contemporary Japan stems from the fact that the cultural, structural, economic, and demographic changes have attenuated the binding force of long-cycled reciprocity which would entitle the aged parents to the support and care of the filial generation. On the other hand, the elderly mother witnesses the obsolescence of filiocentric dependency and is more apprehensive than ever of prolonged invalidism and senility which requires personal body care, preferably by her daughter or daughter-in-law. Interviews with a sample of women who are anticipating or experiencing the aging phase have generated the following information with regard to their reactions to this dilemma and the strategies they resort to in order to overcome the dilemma.

Most of the women, while remaining primarily filiocentric as far as their expressions of fulfillment are concerned, are muted as to their expectations for dependency upon their children. They tend to stress their determination to avoid being a burden upon their children. One strategy by which the women strive to avoid filiocentric dependency is to maintain threefold self-sufficiency: economic, inner, and physical. Second, the claim to filial piety based upon long-cycled reciprocity is replaced by the mother's continued effort to build up credits by helping her children with the hope of binding the latter to repay. The third strategy is to disperse partnerships of reciprocal dependency, both intra-domestically and extra-domestically. Within the domestic sphere, woman rededicates herself to household ancestors primarily in exchange for her own attainment of ancestral status, which then may be interpreted as an euphemistic expression of filiocentric dependency. Consolidation of the conjugal bond is another alternative. The grandmother-grandchild tie, involving the latter as a caretaker for the former at the final phase of aging, is an increasingly realistic prospect. The extra-domestic dispersal of interdependence refers to intensification or reactivation of peer interaction based upon neighborhood, and educational or occupational affiliations, or new groupings.

It should be noted that the observed behavior of Japanese women in dealing with the dilemma of aging is far from consistent. We have seen the women bound by their filiocentric dependency drift away from it through either self-sufficiency or alternative social bonds. If there is any change in their behavior it is not so much a linear progression from an old to a new pattern as a vacillation between one set of expectations and another. The pendulum may swing between the filiocentric preoccupations and conjugal intimacy, dependency and autonomy, self-denial and self-assertion, intra-domestic immersion and extra-domestic engagement. Facing this uncertainty, the aging women in contemporary Japan are less likely to take their futures for granted but more alert to what is in store for them and more ready to bring the conventional values into question. A woman in her late seventies, seeing all her children totally engrossed in raising their own families, questions what woman lives for, although she has never doubted that woman's *ikigai* lies in caring for her family while a man's is in his occupational career. Uncertainty, while it is conducive to the constriction of the 'sandwiched' generation, may be turned into an awareness of choice: contemporary women may be more determined to secure and maximize options. Some women with substantial income, for example, have invested in additional housing so that they will have options to live alone in case they cannot get along with their daughters-in-law under the same roof. Greater self-awareness, alertness, choice, and planning – these may be what distinguish the aging women of this generation from those of previous generations.

BIBLIOGRAPHY

Ariyoshi, S. 1972. *Kokotsu no hito* (A Man in Ecstasy). Tokyo.

Kato, M. 1977. *Nippon no rojin mondai* (The Problem of the Aged Japanese). Kokoro to shakai (Mind and Society) 8: 113–127.

Koseisho (Ministry of Health and Welfare). 1976. Koseihakusho: fujin to shakai hosho (White Paper on Health and Welfare: Women and Social Security).

Lebra, T. S. 1976. Ancestral Influence on the Suffering of Descendants in a Japanese Cult. *Ancestors*, ed. W. W. Newell, pp. 219–230. The Hague.

—— 1978. Japanese Women and Marital Strain. *Ethos* 6: 22–41.

Murdock, G. P. 1949. *Social Structure*. New York.

Newell, W. H. 1969. Some Comparative Features of Chinese and Japanese Ancestor Worship. Proceedings of the VIIIth International Congress of Anthropological and Ethnological Sciences 1969, Vol. III: Ethnology and Archaeology, pp. 300-301. Tokyo and Kyoto.

Palmore, E. 1975. *The Honorable Elders*. Durham.

Perry, L. L. 1976. Mothers, Wives, and Daughters in Osaka: Autonomy, Alliance, and Professionalism. Ph.D. dissertation, University of Pittsburgh.

Plath, D. W. 1964. Where the Family of God is the Family: The Role of the Dead in Japanese Households. *American Anthropologist* 66: 300--317.

—— 1975. The Last Confucian Sandwich: Becoming Middle Aged. *Adult Episodes in Japan*, ed. D.W. Plath, pp. 51–63. Leiden.
Salamon, S. B. 1974. In the Intimate Arena: Japanese Women and their Families. Ph.D. dissertation, University of Illinois at Urbana-Champaign.
Smith, R. J. 1966. Ihai: Mortuary Tablets, The Household and Kin in Japanese Ancestor Worship. *Transactions of the Asiatic Society of Japan* 9: 83–102.
—— 1974. *Ancestor Worship in Contemporary Japan*. Stanford.

NOTES

1. This is a revised version of the paper originally presented at the 76th annual meetings of the American Anthropological Association in Houston, 1977. I wish to acknowledge the support of a National Science Foundation grant for the on-going research project from which this paper resulted. The Japan Society for the Promotion of Science also funded my research on women for which I am grateful. Manuscript typing was provided by the Social Science Research Institute, University of Hawaii.
2. As of 1975, Japan had 1,667 care homes, including both public and private institutions, accommodating 123,895 individuals – the figure amounting only to 1.36 per cent of those at 65 years of age or over. A 1972 survey indicated that 3.3 per cent of the old wanted admission to care homes (Koseisho 1976: 459).
3. The bulk of the data was collected during twelve months of field work in 1976–77 in a city of 70,000 on the east coast of central Japan, and supplementary information was gathered at the same site in five weeks during my 1978 field trip. This paper draws upon the life histories obtained through interviews with 35 women between 50 and 80 years of age (age refers to the final interview time for those who were contacted two or more times). All except two were healthy enough to do some work, domestic or nondomestic, with varying degrees of strenuousness. The two women, one with respiratory difficulty and high blood pressure and the other with hemiplegia triggered by an apoplectic stroke, had begun to avoid going out. The sample varies widely in socioeconomic status: the husbands' occupations range from highly skilled professionals (gynecologist, dentist) to businessmen to white collar employees to manual workers. The women, too, except a handful of full-time housewives, have been or are in the nondomestic working force, either with their own occupations or as family-team workers. Their occupations too, show a considerable variety, including midwifery, school teaching, pharmacy, insurance sales, cooking, maid service, 'hospitality' service (e.g., bar hostess, geisha), fish-processing, and farming. As for marital status, eighteen are married, sixteen widowed, and one divorced. All but four have from one to ten children (3.74 in average), and two of the childless women have adopted children. The majority (n = 29) have one or more married children.
4. In contemporary Japan, there is a greater tendency toward uxorilocal marriage without the husband being adopted by the wife's parents, but this case refers to the traditional pattern of son-in-law adoption which involves the groom assuming the bride's family name.
5. At the time of the interviews, 28 informants had their *atotori* (successor-child) – mostly eldest sons, some younger sons, and daughters – already married, and ten of the 28 (36 per cent) were not sharing the residence with them. The general pattern seems to be that intergenerational separation in residence is maintained until one parent, most likely the father, dies, whereupon the widow joins the children or the latter move into her house. A son, who is an employee of a prestigeous corporation and whose work site is beyond his control, has agreed to live with his parents upon his retirement. Co-residence may be postponed until the widow becomes incapacitated.
6. 'Pokkuri' has become a slogan-like symbol for the most desirable way of dying, and given rise to such terms as *pokkuri-shinko* (faith in abrupt death) and *pokkuri dera* (the temples which supposedly facilitate such death for their clients).
7. Such derogatory comments on institutional care are not always indicative of the informant's ignorance or cultural inertia. An increasing number of Japanese are becoming aware through exposure to their friends and relatives under such care as well as to the television reports from abroad that even the best-equipped institution does not produce well-contented elderly.
8. These era names, corresponding to the reigns of emperors, provide an important criterion for Japanese to determine their generational identity. Not a few informants identified themselves as 'Meiji-born,' 'Taisho-born,' or 'Showa one-digit born,' and distinguished themselves from those born in the previous or subsequent era. Sometimes a Taisho wife characterizes her husband as hopelessly old-fashioned or 'typically Meiji-born,' but then turns out to have been born in the first year of Taisho, only a few years behind her husband.

First published in *The Japan Newsletter*, Vol. 13, No. 1, 1980: 133–142

14 Autonomy through Interdependence: The Housewives Labor Bank

One of the goals proclaimed the world over in contemporary women's movements is the promotion of autonomy for women. Yet the meaning of autonomy is hardly self-evident. This paper begins with a proposed definition: autonomy, understood in its simple sense, is the opposite of dependency. Dependency negates autonomy in two ways: A lacks autonomy in proportion to A's dependence upon B; A lacks autonomy if B is dependent upon A. Woman may be considered less autonomous than man because she is not only more dependent upon others economically or otherwise but is more constrained by the dependency of others upon her. The latter aspect is often overlooked but easy to remember in association with a mother tied down to a helpless infant in constant need of her care.

Autonomy in this simple sense cannot be pursued too far, since its logical extreme is isolation, while people actually live in social interaction and mutual dependency. Autonomy must be defined further in relation to dependency to supplement the above definition. Dependency is not an irreducible term; some forms of dependency are more autonomous than others. I suggest three conditions for 'autonomous dependency.' First, there must be a variety of options for dependency. Options may refer to the content of help (the greater the variety of help available that one can depend upon, the more autonomous one can become); to the time and place (the more one can choose the time and place for receiving or rendering help, the more autonomous). Most importantly, options refer to the people to be involved in a dependency relationship. The greater the number of persons one can depend upon, the more autonomous one can be.

The second condition has to do with assurance that obtaining help does not damage the recipient's dignity or conscience. While there can be legal, public arrangements to entitle a person to dependency without making him/her ashamed or guilty, I want to call attention to a more personal strategy, namely, reciprocal dependency. Autonomy can be maintained if one is confident that dependency involves reciprocal exchange instead of unilateral giving and receiving. A's autonomy is based upon A's resources upon which B depends and which A can offer in exchange for B's resources. Third and finally, autonomy and dependency are compatible to the degree that the latter does not interfere with the predictability of one's life or routine. Total uncertainty lends to the loss of autonomy.

It follows that if woman is less autonomous than man it is because she has fewer options, is more unilaterally dependent, and more subjected to a haphazard way of life. Housewives are generally regarded as least autonomous. If this is because their options, reciprocity, and predictability are constrained by the confines of their households, the promotion of their autonomy requires them to escape their domestic boundaries. Liberationists would encourage them to reject their domestic role identity and to work outside for economic independence. Quite another solution is offered by a Japanese women's group, organized around the idea of a labor bank.

THE 'LABOR BANK'

The idea of a labor bank in its rudimentary form occurred to Mizushima Teruko, a housewife in Osaka, toward the end of World War II when survival was threatened by American air raids. She thought of pooling housewives' time and labor by communalizing the domestic work and responsibility which had so far been carried out in each household separately. For example, if five children are looked after by two housewives instead of by five respective mothers, Mizushima figured, the other three women could devote themselves to other tasks. This idea was put into practice by a group of housewives in her neighborhood, which in turn stimulated further elaboration of her 'theory.' It was not until 1973, when all her children had married and she felt her responsibility as a mother was completed, that the mutual-help organization was brought into formal existence with the name, 'Volunteer Labor Bank,' and provided with a charter. The basic idea is unchanged: the replacement of women's intradomestic responsibility by interdomestic cooperation. By 1978, the bank had grown to include roughly 2,600 members of all ages ranging from teenagers to women in their seventies, with an overrepresentation of housewives in their thirties and forties. The members are organized into over 160 local branches scattered throughout the country, and coordinated by the headquarters located on Mizushima's estate. In addition to serving as president of the bank, Mizushima has long been established as a social critic, writer, and public lecturer. Her resourcefulness is responsible for the basic structure of the bank, while its details have developed out of trial and error by members who were actually involved in its operation.

The Volunteer Labor Bank consists of two parts: volunteer work and labor exchange. This paper is concerned primarily with the latter part, and with its implications for women's autonomy. The data were obtained in the fall of 1978 through several contacts with Mizushima, interviews with seven members in Osaka and Kyoto, observation of monthly meetings at both central and local levels, and perusal of the bank's newsletters.

The Accounting System

What distinguishes the labor bank from the traditional mutual-aid system, still existing in rural areas of Japan and based upon neighborhood solidarity, is its rational accounting system. Labor is quantified by hours, one hour of ordinary labor counted as one 'point,' while especially heavy or skilled labor is weighted accordingly. Every member is issued the equivalent of a passbook on which the points of labor are recorded as 'deposit' or 'withdrawal.' If A helps B with three hours of ordinary labor, then B is supposed to put down 3 points in the deposit column of A's passbook, and A is to do the same in the withdrawal column of B's book. Technically, as long as there is a demand for labor, one can accumulate points. However, there tends to be an imbalance due to the oversupply of and low demand for labor. Moreover, points cannot be withdrawn unless they had already been deposited. To meet these problems, which are detrimental to active transaction, the bank allows cash payment for labor at a rate not below the current minimum wage. To expedite this double system of accounting – points and yen – the bank provides every member with two kinds of passbooks: one for labor, and the other, an ordinary postal passbook, to record cash transactions. The cash received is deposited in the postal passbook, annually converted into points, and entered into the labor passbook. Cash payment is a temporary measure to make sufficient labor currency available; there is a clear priority of points over yen. Every transfer of points and cash is monitored by the headquarters through monthly reports from branch leaders on local activities.

Generalized Exchange

The versatility of the accounting system is considerable. The conversion of labor into points induces 'generalized exchange' in contrast to 'restricted exchange.'[1] What A has offered B can be exchanged for what C, D, or anybody else can offer. Points are thus transferable to anyone whose labor is accessible. Usually labor is exchanged within a local branch and is arranged by the branch leader. Sometimes, however, help may be sought in a place far removed from the seeker's residence. Such transactions, involving different branches, are arranged by the headquarters. To expedite the transfer of points to a far-off place, the bank issues what is called 'gift cards' each of which counts as one point and is circulated from member to member. One can send a gift card either in payment for labor or as a gift entitling its receiver to one-hour of labor by a member. A member can send gift cards not only to another member but to her primary kin or to her teacher (reflecting the traditional view of the teacher as a benefactor to whom the student owes a lifelong debt). Through this mechanism a member can vicariously fulfill her obligation towards kin living at a distance through another member who will help the kin in exchange for the gift card, without visiting them herself.

Generalized exchange gives options for collective exchange as well: one person can help many persons at once as in babysitting for two or more children in one place and one person can receive help from many persons serially or simultaneously. The possibility of a many-to-one transaction enables a long-bedridden member or her kin, for instance, to receive daily care without overburdening one single member. Likewise, the same system permits a housewife to double or triple her domestic performance as needed during an emergency. A husband may be hospitalized with a disease calling for his wife's presence at his bedside around-the-clock, as actually happened to one of my informants (some hospitals demand such family nursing in order to supplement the hospital staff). Meanwhile her daughter may give birth and also need a mother's care (it is also common for a married daughter to depend upon her mother for nursing in the maternity hospital and after release from the hospital). The woman may stay with her husband, asking one member to help her daughter, another member to deliver meals to her at the hospital, and still another to check on the empty house occasionally. The system thus extends the range of options for interdependence.

Generalization is not unlimited, however. The system can operate only where members and branches exist, and this is why an increase in membership and geographical area is needed to realize the full potential of the system.

Life-Cycle Planning and Cross-Generational Interdependence

The degree of autonomy possessed by each individual fluctuates during one's lifetime. The fluctuations are more pronounced for women than for men. A man gains autonomy as he matures and retains it until his old age when autonomy declines. A woman loses her autonomy at the peak of her maturity due to her responsibility for childbearing and childrearing. There is also a parallel variation in the availability of time and energy from one life stage to another. For a woman, there is more time and energy than needed for her own survival during her premarital stage. Early motherhood requires that she not only use up her own but borrow additional time and energy from others. But from late motherhood through the post-parental stage a surplus of energy and time is restored, until finally energy goes down below the level of self-sufficiency in the course of aging.

The accounting system of the bank enables a young mother to plan out her life cycle to adjust to these fluctuations. She can deposit as many points as possible during her premarital stage in preparation for the next stage when she must withdraw the points. Again, the post-parental period can be devoted to the reaccumulation of points to be well prepared for aging. The labor bank thus suggests a solution to the current problems of longer life expectancy, increasing leisure, and aging.

The validity of such life-cycle planning presupposes a continuous turnover of generations. Furthermore, labor exchange must cross not only household boundaries but generational boundaries as well. Interdomestic exchange is thus coupled with intergenerational reciprocity. A young woman may help a mother with babysitting, or look after an aged woman; a middle-aged woman may render assistance to a young woman in childbirth or help an eighty-year-old. The cross-generational contact is a learning experience for both parties, including the anticipatory learning of how to age best. This is part of what Mizushima calls the 'interest' of the bank.

Revaluation of Domestic Labor

Any kind of labor is exchangeable only if it is in demand and free of restrictions by the established commercial standards and market system. The labor, demanded and supplied predominantly by housewives, tends to be of a domestic type but has proliferated to great variety, surprising even to the members themselves. It ranges from care for the helpless (infants, aged, sick, postpartum women) to custodial care for pets and watering plants; from cooking and feeding to bathing and body-cleaning, from laundry and house-cleaning to yard weeding; from house-sitting to housemoving, checking with carpenters and serving tea for them on behalf of a member who has hired them, and receiving guests as a surrogate hostess; from grocery shopping and running errands to taking a child to and from a kindergarten. Car owners can offer transportation, while the owner of a large house provides room and board for a travelling member. Even this list is far less than exhaustive.

The exchange of domestic labor between unrelated households leads to a reassessment and revaluation of the work of a housewife. Revaluation is reinforced by the conversion of labor into points, and housewifely work ceases to appear insignificant and unskilled. The implication is fourfold. First, the housewife realizes that, far from being fed by her husband, she is contributing more than enough labor to feed herself. Revaluation of housework thus induces a sense of autonomy to replace that of dependency. Second, while domestic work within one's household is nothing but routinized drudgery, working for another household amounts to a 'performance' to be appreciated by an audience. Successful performance generates not only satisfaction but self-confidence regarding one's 'uncovered' competence. Third, every performance is a challenge toward learning. When she lacks the confidence or skill to do a certain job, the performer prepares herself by collecting information on it. Making errors motivates her to improve in anticipation of a second performance, and new skills may be eventually mastered. Further, interdomestic help exposes the housewife to a variety of housekeeping styles and brings into question her own habitual style, which she has so far taken for granted. Finally, as the excellence of performance is measured in part by its efficiency, housework, which is usually regarded as endless, is now finite and scheduled. Since each member reserves certain days and hours in her weekly schedule for responding to labor demand, she must time her routine within her own household as well. Efficiency and planning thus become part of domestic work. All these factors help to professionalize housework. In fact there is a tendency emerging among the members to recognize themselves as 'specialists' in certain kinds of domestic work, such as 'care for bedridden old people' or 'house cleaning.'[2]

The bank's central policy, as explained by Mizushima, encourages such revaluation by declaring that domestic labor is harder to obtain than any other form of labor. A member is free to offer labor and skills other than direct domestic help. Most often this involves teaching some skill, be it cooking, sewing, doll-making, metal carving, piano playing, or English. Such work, though professional in a conventional sense, is secondary in value to domestic help, since people are generally less willing to do the latter than the former. In order to protect a member's right to receive the same kind of domestic help that she has rendered, the labor passbook records her work if it falls under any of the five domestic labor categories – postpartum care, nursing the sick, care for the old, babysitting, and housework in general.

This high evaluation of domestic labor has the potential to shake up the dominant, androcentric value hierarchy. The housewife's work may not bring in money, but it is concerned directly with human life. Why should the male's work to produce 'things' be regarded more highly than the female's work to create, develop, and maintain human life, health, and safety? While basically conservative in contrast to the liberationist movement, the Labor Bank contains a revolutionary potential to reverse the established value priorities.[3]

Role Reversal in Empathy

Role performance involves 'taking the role of the other' (Mead 1934), a principle stressed by the Labor Bank members as well as by the leaders. The helper is advised to put herself in the shoes of the help-receiver, that is, to be helpful without spoiling the receiver's privacy, dignity, or autonomy. Likewise, the receiver is supposed to accept help in a way that puts the helper at ease. Empathetic role reversal is the key to both roles.

Help-acceptance is not as easy as it might appear. The imbalance of supply and demand of labor is partially attributable to the general preference for self-help in the domestic sphere. The acceptance of domestic help entails an exposure of the backstage of the private domain to an outsider. This is naturally resisted by anybody whose identity rests on what Goffman calls 'front maintenance' (1959). Membership in the bank involves training in lowering the resistance of the help-receiver to such exposure. Dependency training in this sense is consistent, rather than contradictory, with the maintenance of autonomy. Obviously, receptivity to necessary help is a sign of maturity while rigid resistance makes one more helpless. This is particularly apparent in relation to the problem of an aged person who resists physical care from anyone outside of his/her family. The bank encourages its members to solicit help, even when they can help themselves, partly to train them in the 'skill' of accepting help from 'anybody' in preparation for old age.

The more involved in the Labor Bank, the more receptive of help one can afford to be for two reasons. First, receiving help does not arouse guilt or shame in the person who has accumulated sufficient points to withdraw. Second, there develops intimacy and trust among members through regular contact and labor exchange, which shields the help-receiver from embarrassment.

What is important is a sense of balance. By taking the role of the helper vicariously, the help-receiver is expected to realize that she should leave everything to the helper and accept help without resistance, but at the same time should be considerate enough to minimize the helper's work, trouble, and inconvenience. Rearrangement of kitchen utensils to improve their visibility and accessibility to an outsider is an instance of such consideration.

One should render and accept help, but should refrain from overdoing either. The necessary sense of balance is learned through role reversal not only in imagination but in practice among Labor Bank members. The more help one gives, the more capable one becomes of receiving help, and vice versa.

Human Insurance

The banking system, however rational it may be, does not run by itself but must be harnessed and kept in operation by human decisions and energy. The bank does not force its members to deposit or withdraw points. It is entirely up to each member whether or not she should offer labor in response to a request. How can one be sure, then, that the deposited points can be withdrawn in full value? This question focuses our attention upon the bank's claim that the whole system is ultimately based on human investment, or what I would call human insurance. A member's emergency call for help will bring immediate response by many members only if she is known as a helpful, cooperative, and trusted member. What is exchanged is not merely labor but human dedication, warmth, and gratitude. What is deposited is not only points but one's reputation as a dependable member and friend.

My informants agree that the best thing that has occurred to them since joining the bank is the friendship that has been built up among fellow-members. Within this group, I was told, are the friends whom one can absolutely trust and confide in without fear that one's privacy will be violated. Mizushima calls the members' friendship another portion of the 'interest' of the banking system, and proposes that the system adopt two kinds of currency with the same initial 'L' – Labor and Love.

In addition to the labor exchange itself, there are two other kinds of activity conducive to the accumulation of friendship or human insurance. One is volunteer work, imposed upon every member as a membership duty, for a minimum of two hours each month. Independent of the bank, volunteer work is unilaterally dedicated to people outside the system, primarily to old people in nursing homes, children in orphanages, and the physically and mentally handicapped. It is often arranged and organized by branches and conducted collectively by branch members. The other is the monthly meeting at the branch as well as the headquarters level where discussions are held on a selected topic such as 'How to be a professional mother.' Regular contact among members through volunteer work and meetings is crucial to the accumulation of a fund of trust.

Human insurance is self-regulating in that those who join the bank for selfish motives will soon want to quit while those who are likely to contribute to the fund of human insurance will remain. The informants are proud of fellow-members as 'incredibly good people,' and stress that a member's family recognizes the merit of her fellow-members and friends, which in turn results in upgrading her own position in the family.

SUMMARY AND CONCLUSION

The operation of the Volunteer Bank relates, in my view, to the three aspects of autonomy as set forth at the outset of this paper. First, the range of options for dependency is widened as the housewife moves from the intradomestic into the interdomestic realm of interdependence. The bank's accounting system permits generalized exchange of labor. The device of gift cards serves to connect two persons, geographically separated, into a reciprocal partnership. The possibility of one-to-many dependency and doubling or tripling the effect of housewifely performance further expands options. As the age range of members increases, options include cross-generational interdependence.

Second, the whole system is based on reciprocal exchange rather than unilateral dependency. Through involvement in the 'labor market' created by the bank, the housewife realizes the scarcity value of domestic labor and the significance of her contribution to her household, and discovers her own resources and capabilities to be exchangeable. 'Performance' for a household other than one's own leads towards professionalism in domestic skills. The accounting system enables her to 'save' labor, that is to say, to 'pay in advance' while she is able, to avoid going into debt. No less important is the likelihood that reciprocity will induce empathetic role reversal, which in turn serves to cultivate a sense of balance between a readiness for offering and accepting help.

Third, the housewife whose life is generally unpredictable because she must respond to family needs is now in a less vulnerable position to plan and schedule her life. Life-cycle planning is possible. Shorter cycles such as those of weekly and daily routine also can be timetabled. The membership obligation to leave open a fixed period of time for labor exchange, volunteer work, and meeting attendance requires planning for the remaining time as well. The desirability of efficiency in 'performance' reinforces planning. Furthermore, the assurance that help is regularly available may free a housewife to devote that much time to herself, whether in studying or pursuing a hobby. The resulting freedom from the constraints of routine implies that the bank generates a degree of autonomy in the simple sense as well.

A word is in order regarding the autonomy of working women, 'working' in the conventional sense. In Mizushima's view, the distinction between the housewife and the working woman is obsolete in that the former, as a result of mechanization of housework and increased life expectancy, can and should do more than take care of her own household, while the latter is entitled to fulfillment of the feminine role of wife and mother. A woman would be able to pursue a dual career – occupational and domestic – if she comes into interdependence with housewives (as well as with other working women at different life stages). As long as she remains isolated, this is impossible. The bank thus offers support for a woman who wants to attain autonomy through an occupation as well.

One may wonder how an alliance between working women and housewives could work; the former obviously stands to gain, but what does a housewife gain in exchange for her labor? How can the balance of debits and credits be maintained? The working woman can devote her post-retirement time surplus to repay, but the question still remains unanswered. One informant responded, 'If we help a professional woman continue her career, and she contributes to upgrading women's status, we, too, will eventually share the benefit.' Another informant, who had to give up the alternative of achieving autonomy through a career occupation, wants to fulfill her wish vicariously by helping construct social conditions which would enable her daughter and women of the next generation to pursue that alternative. These responses indicate the breadth of the meaning of 'exchange.'

NOTES

* Part of this paper was presented at the Tenth International Congress of Anthropological and Ethnological Sciences, New Delhi, 10–21 December 1978. The author wishes to express her gratitude to Mrs. Teruko Mizushima and her number-one assistant and co-leader, Mrs. Yoshiko Moriwaki, for facilitating the research on the Volunteer Labor Bank, and to members of the bank for accepting her role as an interviewer and observer. This report is part of an ongoing research project focused on the life cycle and adult socialization of Japanese women. The awards from National Science Foundation (Grant BNS 76-11301) and the Japan Society for the Promotion of Science are deeply appreciated. The author also acknowledges the hospitality of the Faculty of Human Sciences, Osaka University, my host institution. Manuscript typing was provided by the Social Science Research Institute, University of Hawaii.

1. My usage of 'generalized' here is closer to that of Levi-Strauss (1969) than that of Sahlins (1965).

2. This suggests that interdomestic exchange of domestic labor may be regarded as one possible step to bridge the gap which seems to lie between the formal, public, political sphere dominated by men on the one hand, and the informal, private, domestic sphere occupied by women. See Rosaldo 1974; Tiffany 1978.

3. The value reversal in this direction may be considered an extension of the line of argument that Ortner (1974) develops by paralleling the female-male contrast with the nature-culture contrast.

First published in *Ethnology*, Vol. XX, No. 4, October 1981: 291–306

15 Japanese Women in Male-dominant Careers: Cultural Barriers and Accommodations for Sex-role Transcendence[1]

Japan is among those societies whose cultural ideology supports male dominance and a sharp sexual division of labor in the professional world. Japanese culture thus poses a barrier to women's career opportunities and generates strain for professionally committed women. This is amply documented by various studies of Japanese professional women (Okada, Okifuji, and Hagiwara 1967; Sekiguchi 1973; Dilatush 1976; Osako 1978). However, there are indications that part of that same androcentric tradition spills over into the female world to propel some women into career professions. It is this assumed double function of the culture with respect to women's professionalism that the present study intends to explore. Specifically, the paper describes how some salient aspects of Japanese culture can both constrain and enhance the career opportunity and commitment of Japanese women.

Career refers to an occupation involving: full-time commitment instead of transient or part-time engagement; long-range training, development and accumulation in expertise; reliance on the job as the major source of livelihood rather than its enjoyment as a hobby; and, despite the last point, identification with it over and beyond economic necessity. This definition is general enough to include both elite and non-elite professions, and does not discriminate between male occupations and female occupations, although such distinctions will become necessary as we go along.

The Japanese media display an exaggerated reaction to a series of appointments of the 'first women' to conspicuous public positions: ambassador, academic research institute director, train stationmaster, company executive, and the like. These appointments may suggest that a sex role revolution is under way, but they also attest to the long history of the male monopoly of elite professions. As of 1975, for example, women held only a modicum of upper positions in the national civil service (only one member of the 1,145 top-grade civil servants, only 0.4 per cent of the second grade and 0.7 per cent of the third grade, etc., in the eight grade system, were women); they comprised only 2.5 per cent of the lawyers, judges and prosecutors; 1.8 per cent of the engineers; 5.1 per cent of the research scientists; 15.6 per cent of college faculty; 0.9 per cent of the civil servants in administrative positions; and 1.6 per cent of the elementary school principals (Fujin mondai kikaku suishin honbu 1977).

The primary sample of women used in this study consists of ten currently active 'career women' who were contacted in 1978 in Tokyo, Yokohama, Osaka, and Kyoto. These women vary widely in their respective professions – higher education, law, government, business, and journalism; six are employed by national institutions, one by a private institution, and three are self-employed; ages range from 64 (about to retire) to 32 (still waiting for a full-fledged career appointment). Some are of national stature, while others are known only locally or within particular fields of specialization. These women were selected under consultation with my Japanese colleagues in various fields whose knowledge and judgment I trusted. The accidental nature and limited size of the sample are, I believe, somewhat compensated by its variation.

Over the years I have also interviewed many other women – professional and non-professional, elite and non-elite, urban and rural – to gather their life histories.[2] Some of these women will be used as a secondary sample to supplement the primary one. Personal names (pseudonyms) are given to the primary sample women only. Ages are listed as of the time of the interviews, between 1976 and 1978.

SOCIALIZATION FOR DOMESTIC SUCCESSION

The first dimension considered is the domestic culture and family socialization that motivates a daughter toward a career. The traditional family system, centering around the *ie*, the stem-family household, first can be characterized genealogically, in terms of its transgenerational perpetuity under the rule of male primogeniture. Second, the *ie*, functionally defined, is a corporate body of coresidents, each performing his or her role to maintain it or promote its status. Combining these two, there emerges a domestic entity which transcends individual members of the family, as described by Befu (1962), Nakane (1967), Nakano (1968), Pelzel (1970), and many others.

As the name and status of the *ie* is carried on by a son or son-substitute (adopted son or daughter's husband), the genealogical norm supports male superiority and male dominance. Sons are more likely than daughters to receive a higher education either to succeed to the house occupation or to enhance the house status by assuming a promising new career. A 49-year-old informant, after telling me how she was financially unable to go on to a girls' high school because of her father's death, went on to say that when her younger brother reached high school age the family moved to a city where a reputable prefectural boys' high school was available – an extremely costly decision imposing sacrifices upon the whole family. While a poor family may pool its limited resources exclusively for the career preparation of its male successor, a wealthy or 'honorable' family tends to keep its daughters from taking up certain career jobs so as not to blemish its *ie* status, particularly those occupations which involve heterosexual contact. Thus an informant,

58, when she applied to a nurse-training school, took the risk of being expelled from the *ie* by her proud father, a descendant of a feudal-lord retainer residing in a castle. 'Nursing did not match our *kafū* (domestic life style).'

In this case, the family finally relented, but in another case a formal expulsion did take place. Born to an aristocratic family which had supplied Imperial court ministers for centuries, the informant, 46, became obsessed with the idea of becoming a movie actress. She proceeded to launch her career without even finishing the Peeresses' High School. This 'rebellion' resulted in her legal expulsion from the *ie* by her enraged grandfather, a descendant of an Imperial prince. She remained 'adopted' on paper by another family until the postwar democratization deprived her natal family of its aristocratic title.

While the genealogical principle thus works against a woman's career, the *ie*, when viewed as a functional unit, allows its male bias to be adulterated by the norm of economy, or by the exigency of labor-skill availability. If the genealogical view is sex-sensitive, the functional view can be sex-blind. A retired male school principal said that in his day most eldest sons of farmers had become school teachers, which made me wonder if they had not been successors to the house occupation of farming. 'Yes, they had. But that means their wives worked on the farms.' Eldest sons were nominal, and their wives were virtual successors.

Likewise, a house occupation is often taken over by a widow after her husband dies, even when the business is of a masculine type, such as a lumber business or plumbing. In such cases she is accepted by her male 'peers' as one of the boys. Such sex blindness is nothing unusual since the business belongs to the *ie*, not to a husband or a father personally. Any member of the *ie* is a potential representative of it, or a substitute for another member, regardless of sex.

It is against this cultural background that a daughter can be looked upon as either successor to the father's occupation or status, or as a potential, but substitute achiever[3] of the status aspired to by a male representative of the household. In the family which has no son, or no promising son, a career may be imposed upon a daughter, as happened to some of my informants. The elder of two daughters preferred to do feminine things like sewing, but her father practically dragged her into a career as a pharmacist. Thus, it is understandable that daughters who stay in the house and bring in *mukoyōshi* (adopted husband) to marry are more likely to have professional careers (Lebra 1978: 35). The daughter plays a male role as a successor and career professional, while her *mukayōshi* husband is seen as a genealogical successor.[4]

It may be argued that the *ie*, deprived of its legal identity in the postwar reform, is no longer a viable unit and that fewer and fewer Japanese are concerned with *ie* succession. However, what might be called a 'succession syndrome,' in a generalized sense, still determines the life courses of many Japanese, especially among the status-achievers. Shizuko Fukuda, 46, in a family of only two daughters, from the very beginning of her life was expected to go to a medical school as a successor to her physician grandfather who was a surrogate father, the parents being divorced. She somehow knew her talent lay elsewhere, but could not resist the pressures from her grandfather. Though she studied diligently, she ultimately proved unfit for a medical career. This woman ended up as a free-lance journalist, public lecturer, and organizer of adult education programs, whereas her sister assumed the successor status.

Involved in this succession syndrome is a father-daughter alignment. Education at a top-ranking university directly linked to an elite career was taken for granted by a majority of the primary sample women because their fathers supported that idea, and because the fathers themselves often were university graduates and served as career models. For Kyoko Aoi, there was a father-daughter conspiracy – while the mother was away – for the daughter to choose a particular college which was the only channel available then to women aspiring to become lawyers. The mother cried, convinced that such a move would cost her daughter the precious credentials thus far earned for the bridal market as a graduate of an elite girls' high school. It was the father who advised and encouraged Kyoko, every time she was tempted to drift away, to persist in the goal of a legal career. She became one of the first female lawyers and judges in Japanese history. Naoko Chitose overcame her mother's persistent objections by adhering to the conviction imparted by her deceased father that she was different from other girls. She passed the examination for the University of Tokyo (Todai hereafter), and upon graduation entered the national government as an upper-rank civil servant. Utako Higuchi, another Todai entrant, attributes her career aspirations partly to her father, also a Todai graduate, who 'may have wanted one of his two daughters to follow his steps.'[5]

Some of the above cases refer to the mother's resistance to the daughter's career commitment, suggesting that the mother plays a conservative role in transmitting the conventional feminine culture to the daughter and that this chain of transmission needs to be countered by a male mentor to produce a career-oriented daughter. This does not imply that the mother never encourages her daughter to take up a career. Her father having died in her infancy, Reiko Egawa was raised by her mother who inspired her with a spirit of 'freedom and independence.' The mother constantly imbued Reiko with an ambitious, idiosyncratic image of her (Reiko's) maternal grandfather who had been one of the intellectual pioneers in Hokkaido settlement and had risen to an imperial university presidency. 'My mother used to repeat to me what my grandfather had said all the time, "I would go (wherever I should) even if I have to confront ten million people against me".' Reiko also entered Todai, which paved the way for her entry into a government corporation. Orie Date and Wakako Ishii depict their mothers as 'the queen who reigned over household matters' and as 'a matriarch' respectively, both guiding their children's education single-handedly.

All these mothers were college educated, had some professional experience, and strongly advised their daughters against being resigned to a housewifely role. Again, a succession syndrome is discernible, this time from mother to daughter. In fact, Wakako reveals a successor identity by saying, 'I am from a matriarchical lineage – my mother was powerful and so were mother's mother and father's mother.' The fathers concurred, and in no case did the father oppose his daughter's career, while some mothers did object.

The succession syndrome as a factor motivating a woman for a career presupposes a high or professional status or a model career achieved by a parent. That is, the status to which she strives to succeed must be worthwhile. Furthermore, a cosmopolitan outlook was typical of the career women's natal families. Many of the families moved from place to place as the fathers were transferred as part of their career requirement; the daughters thus recall their families as different from those of the local residents and thus free from local mores.

The succession syndrome extends beyond the domestic unit and pervades every institution in Japan in one form or another. It is in the non-domestic sphere that women are excluded from, and therefore disinterested in, successor status. Yoko Jinbo, 32, recalls her undergraduate thesis adviser being frustrated about teaching at a women's university. This male professor had been teaching there for ten years without finding one student who would carry on his academic legacy. If it were a men's university, even if it were a third-rate one, there would be some successors and he would thereby feel 'linked' to the next generation. Yoko felt sorry for the teacher and thought someone must succeed him. Without claiming to be a successor, she went on to do graduate work in sociology, his specialty, at a national university, and thus began an academic career.

It is precisely because of the preclusion of women from successor status in the public sphere that career-oriented women need an extra strong push from their families. The family advantages of the professional women described above may be interpreted as a necessary compensation to offset public disadvantages. As long as the latter exist, women's career opportunities will be determined by their ascribed status more than those of men.[6]

THE EXAMINATION RITE OF TRANSITION

In Japan, competition for career achievement is institutionalized in a series of examinations, the fierceness of which is expressed by the terms 'examination hell,' or 'examination war.' Career candidates are sifted, first through entrance examinations for academic institutions which are roughly rank-ordered according to the career statuses of their graduates. The rank of the university to which one is admitted counts most for one's career, but this in turn tends to be determined by the rank of the high school one is able to enter. Not only universities but high schools, middle schools, and even elementary schools thus are geared into this rank system. Most pre-career Japanese are exposed to a series of competitive examinations from their childhood on. Such competition knows no limit, hence the proliferation of private extracurricular schools, generally known as *juku*,[7] which train students to take entrance examinations. A large proportion of school children attend *juku* classes after regular school hours. The intensity of the competition may be inferred from the fact that *juku* themselves are rank-ordered so that one must pass an examination to enter a high ranking *juku* and study hard to avoid flunking out.

Career success thus depends largely upon educational investment, and sex differences in career expectations are reflected in the level of such investments. Coeducational public schools aside, single-sex private schools exemplify a clear sex difference. The very top high schools, nationally known for the large number of their graduates who successfully enter Todai, are all for boys. Boys spend more time at *juku* than girls, and more boys assume the *rōnin* (unenrolled in any school, analogous to 'masterless samurai') status for one or more years. The *rōnin* concentrate on studying for examinations in order to enter the most desirable university instead of accepting the second best.[8] Girls are thus handicapped in the amount of their educational investment.

Examinations are applied universally and equally to boys and girls. Once the examination hurdle is surmounted, the public recognizes the individual's ability, independent of sex. Kiefer (1974) proposed an analogy between the Japanese examination system and typical initiation rites, obviously with male candidates in mind. I am adding a female counterpart as a more drastic case of transition: it appears as though a girl, by passing a challenging examination, goes through a life transition to remove her sex stigma whereas a boy attains manhoood by doing the same. The more 'infernal' the competition, the more completely she sheds her femininity. It was when she was admitted to Todai that Higuchi made up her mind to have a career.

Most career candidates undergo another major examination – at the time of graduation, for a professional degree or license, and for employment. This marks another transition in finalizing the public's recognition and the candidate's own commitment. Examination-based transitions, whether at university entrance or graduation, are particularly crucial for a female career since a woman must take more risks than a man in pursuing a career. She needs to overcome a greater ambivalence and inhibition before becoming unequivocally committed to a career. The above cited pharmacist admits that she had remained disinterested in her career prospect until she passed the licensing examination. Similarly, Kyoko Aoi was not quite committed to her career until she emerged as one of the first three women who passed the national law examination.

The examinations for career entry, especially those given by public institutions, are sex blind, and success in such examinations may even insure an equal rate of promotion for women as well as men, as will be referred to in the next section. One informant, a winner in a civil service examination and now occupying one of the highest positions ever held by a woman, advises women to choose a civil service career where, in her view, sex discrimination is absent: 'All you have to do is pass the examinations, and from then on there will be no male-female distinction.'

BUREAUCRATIC RIGIDITY

The above quotation, however, falls short of a faithful reflection of reality. A career candidate faces the rigid structure of a bureaucracy which has never opened its doors to women. Egawa, having specialized in economics at Todai, passed the civil service examination and applied to the Ministry of Treasury, where there is a preponderance of Todai graduates.[9] She received an evasive answer alluding to her sex, which was discouraging enough for her to give up. She then tried the Ministry of Health and Welfare, hoping that her sex would not be a barrier to welfare administration, but was told she would be acceptable for a middle-level position (corresponding with a junior college education) but not for an upper-level position.[10] A third choice was the Ministry of Education, which she knew housed officials who had planned and implemented the postwar coeducational system. One of these officials admitted that he was certainly responsible for initiating coeducation but had never anticipated a woman applicant for an administrative position at the Education Ministry. Finally, the candidate conceded to accept a less desirable alternative – a position at a public corporation which had never hired a woman at the upper level.

Similar bureaucratic rejections were met by Chitose, the only woman graduate from the law school of Todai who passed the civil service examination that year. To her disbelief, 'The Health and Welfare Ministry, for example, would not hire a woman except for janitorial work.' As of 1954, there was no upper-level woman in the entire government except in the Bureau of Women and Minors, the Ministry of Labor. Chitose accepted the offer from another ministry as the only alternative available.

A decade later, when Higuchi applied for a government job, a considerable change must have taken place in some ministries since she encountered no such bureaucratic allergy to women. However, academic positions, particularly those at national universities, still remain decidedly male dominated. Higuchi entertained the idea of an academic career but saw no hope of being accepted into the academic bureaucracy. Universities use the *kōzasei* system in which a discipline has one position for each rank – one full professor-chairman, and one assistant professor. Jinbo, a doctoral candidate, was fortunate enough to be invited as a tenured assistant under her professor's patronage, even though her duties to help the professor, assistant professor, and graduate students leave little time for her own research. Having been an assistant for five years, she feels pressed to find an instructor's position somewhere but knows most universities rule out women for faculty appointments.

The courts of justice, which had been occupied exclusively by 'male members of the Japanese Empire,' were opened up for women in postwar Japan, but acceptance was less than enthusiastic. Every time a woman was to be promoted to a new level of judgeship, there was resistance. Women were believed to be suitable to family courts only, considered unfit for criminal cases, and ruled out as presiding judges or court directors. A breakthrough came in 1971 when Aoi was appointed family court director. Her appointment was followed by a series of women given higher judiciary positions for the first time.

The bureaucratic protection of male dominance notwithstanding, it is also true to a certain extent that the sex-blind rules control men and women alike within the bureaucracy. 'It is hard to get in, but once in, you are equal to men' is an often heard remark. Such universalism is implicit in rule-consciousness which in turn correlates with bureaucratic rigidity and male preponderance. Paradoxically, it was at the courts of justice, a citadel of conservatism, that Aoi saw her male superiors and colleagues adhere to the principle of sex equality proclaimed in the postwar constitution. 'In the courts, I have benefited from being a woman judge, have never felt discriminated against. These judges are basically conservative, and many of them are autocratic toward their wives. But in a professional role they faithfully follow the constitutional spirit of sex equality. So I felt judges are trustworthy in this respect.'

The seniority rule tends to cross sex boundaries in a rigid bureaucracy such as the civil service: technically a woman can expect to be promoted to the same rank at the same time as any male colleague who has entered service with her. Such colleagues are clearly identified as *dōki* (the same year colleague) and grouped together by their year of entry (such as 'the 1960 group'). This seniority-based egalitarianism is in effect only up to a certain level of the hierarchy, generally up to the lowest managerial position or its equivalent. Because of the prevailing expectation for equal promotion, our informants did not hesitate to submit complaints to the top management when their *dōki* male colleagues were promoted ahead of them to managerial positions like *kachō* (section chief). Higuchi, an assistant to the *kachō*, who belongs to a younger generation, anticipates no sex barrier to the *kachō* status: 'Everyone becomes a *kachō*.' After that, only some are further promoted to the ranks of bureau chief, and ultimately to that of vice minister. 'But selection is considerably based upon objective criterion.'

Bureaucratic universalism further implies the precedence of bureaucratic rank over sex rank. The top management's presumption that no woman should hold a managerial position because no male is willing to serve a female boss has proved groundless. While she was the head of the corporation's local branch, Egawa became convinced that in Japan, although there are many obstacles for a woman to become an organizational leader, she will have no trouble once she becomes one. 'Probably because Japanese males are organization men,' she explained. I observed an unwitting demonstration of the above claim while interviewing Chitose, director of a government research center, supervising ten researchers, all male university graduates. The interview was occasionally interrupted by her subordinates stepping into her office for consultation or authorization. Their speech was polite and formal and their posture was low (some squatted to coordinate with the director's sitting position), while Chitose, relaxed, expressed her views and decisions in a nonpolite, informal style of speech. The Japanese usage of rank terms like *shochō* (director) or *kachō* for address facilitates a sex-blind hierarchy.

A Japanese-American comparison in this respect was given by Higuchi who had been to the United States, first as a high school student, and later sent by her ministry to study at an east coast university and thereafter as a researcher at an international organization in Washington, D.C.: 'In Japan rank distinction is clear and surpasses sex differences. Suppose I enter a male superior's office, I have to speak standing. When the superior comes into my room, I also stand up to respond. In getting into an elevator, too, I will let my superior in first. In the United States, I could not help standing up when my superior came in, and I realized he was ill at ease ... Conversely, I expect my subordinate to stand up and let me go in and out of elevators before him.' Indeed, she is not aware of her sex while in the office, she says.

It might be postulated that in Japan the hierarchical orientation insulates men and women from their sexual identities, whereas in the United States sex identity is inseparable from each individual, male or female, precisely due to its equalitarianism and individualism which does away with structural insulators. Higuchi, while favoring the free atmosphere of American offices, admits to the advantage of the Japanese office derived from its bureaucratic primacy.

In addition to the bureaucratic rules and rank distinction, the communal solidarity of a work group also tends to protect women from discrimination. Discrimination is more likely to originate outside the bureaucratic wall. Orie Date, 52, staff producer and chief director at a major television network, does not feel her sex is detrimental to her work and position, 'because what counts after all is your ability.' It is outsiders like the audience who are bluntly prejudiced against women. When there was a telephone call from a television viewer protesting about the program of which Date was in charge, she tried to answer. The caller stopped her by saying, 'Why! You woman! Let me talk to someone responsible,' and refused to accept her self-identification as officially responsible. This caller happened to be a minority-status person who would take being handled by a woman as a sign of discrimination against him. Similar sex discrimination by outsiders was experienced by other informants.

From the above it follows that a self-employed woman, without bureaucratic protection, is more exposed to arbitrary discrimination and prejudice. Mie Baba, president of a confectionary manufacturing and wholesale company, has been a victim of the prejudice of men in the same business. The first and only woman entrepreneur in this trade in the entire city, she witnessed her male peers constantly 'pulling her legs down' (to prevent her success). She heard that one such male rival had declared that if she succeeded he would walk on his head all around the city – a Japanese phrase declaring disbelief. Baba attributes her success to such harassments since 'the more trampled down, the more determined I became to fight back.' Wakako Ishii, self-employed as the president of a research corporation which sells information, also has been subjected to overwhelming prejudice on the part of her potential clients, particularly those who are in typically male professions and organizations. Government officials are among the worst. Here one can see sex prejudice crossing over the bureaucratic wall both inward and outward: a woman official is exposed to male outsiders' prejudice, and a female outsider like Ishii meets male officials' prejudice.

PATRONAGE

My informants concur in stressing the importance of an informal social network as a stepping stone toward success and in recognizing the female disadvantage in this respect. The typical social network supportive of one's career tends to have a vertical relationship involving guidance or patronage.

Such a relationship is often dyadic, such as *oyabun-kobun* (boss-henchman), *sensei-deshi* (teacher-disciple), or *senpai-kohai* (senior-junior), though equals like former classmates also form alliances. A patron-client bond may emerge between a chief and his subordinate within a ministry, a professor and his student in a seminar, an older and younger graduate from the same university, a senior and junior member of the same department of a company, and the like. Patronage, as a basic component of a clique, exists side by side with the formal structure of a bureaucracy. It supplements or interferes with the latter's function, and thereby plays a large part in determining the individual's career prospect. We have noted that the seniority rule guarantees equal promotion only up to a certain level. Beyond that level, patronage is likely to replace the bureaucratic rule, as described by Craig (1975: 11–12) with regard to a long-ranged process of clique formation in a ministry:

> When a new class of university graduates enters a ministry, they do not join a clique immediately. Rather, they spend ten years or so in one or another post learning the work of the ministry. During this period they establish working relationships with their seniors. Seniors want able juniors. By the time a junior becomes a section chief, he will probably have established particular good relationships with one or two senior officials. When the senior official becomes a bureau chief or vice-minister, he may recommend those juniors who are close to him for key positions. And after the senior official has retired, if he should enter the Diet or the Cabinet, or join a government commission, these relationships may become even more important.

Women are disadvantaged because patronage does not cross sex boundaries. For example, Rohlen (1974: 123) notes that the *senpai-kohai* relationship at a bank is clearly sex segregated. Women could form such a bond among themselves, but the career advantage to be derived from such a bond is decidely limited since most desirable positions are monopolized by male patrons.

A woman is precluded from a higher position not only because she cannot have a male patron but also because she is considered unfit to be a patron for male followers. When all her *dōki* colleagues were promoted to *kachō* status, Chitose confronted the chief secretary of the ministry with a demand for the same promotion: He said, 'If you become *kachō*, your subordinates will suffer pitiably. Let's take my own experience. I am most grateful to my superior for his speedy rise, thanks to his ability, in the hierarchy. From rank to rank he moved up quickly and became vice minister [the apex of the civil service hierarchy]. With his power, he pulled me up. You are not possibly hoping to become a vice minister, are you?' If the *kachō* is going to be stuck at a rank not much higher, he said, the subordinates will not be rewarded for their loyal service. They would be happier to work under a promising boss, he said.

Even such sex-discriminatory patronage turns out to have benefited some women at certain points in their careers. When the bureaucracy is off limits to a woman applicant simply because there is no precedent, its doors may be slightly opened by the arbitrary decision of a powerful top administrator at his own personal risk. I was often told that whether a woman could get into a ministry or not depends entirely upon what kind of men the ministry happens to have at the top. Being a risky investment as a career employee, a woman needs a special 'guarantor' responsible for whatever will happen to her. Women are more likely to be admitted or promoted to an unprecedented position when and where an influential man, in or behind the bureaucracy, happens to be self-confident, courageous, and sympathetic with women. In developing their professional expertise, a number of informants also mentioned specific male mentors as indispensable to their careers.[12]

Academic patronage spills over sex lines more freely. A woman who graduates from a first-rate coeducational university may be able to elicit support from her academic ties (with professors and alumni holding key positions in society at large). A Todai graduate is advantaged by her easy access to her *senpai*, *dōki*, and *kōhai* in government, industry, or wherever. A free-lance career may have to rely even more heavily upon academic patronage. In launching a career as a self-employed journalist after quitting a high school teaching job, Shizuko Fukuda took the initiative to test her talent and to get recognized: she kept writing letters to the editors until her letters began to be rejected because of their too professional quality; she won a contest for drawing newspaper illustrations, etc. However, she was also a beneficiary from her academic ties built up at her high school as well as university thanks to the elite status of both institutions. A high school classmate of hers, working at a radio station, invited her to one of his regular programs, providing her with a chance to publicize her essays. More importantly, her career as an organizer – be it a founder of adult education classes or of an international cultural exchange program – drew support from her alumni, professors, and distinguished members of the PTAs.

Tomoe Goto, unlike most others, regards her career as an unusually 'smooth' one. To begin with, she was free from the trauma of entrance examinations because of her enrollment in an 'escalator' school system for girls. That school includes all levels, from kindergarten up through university, and carries its own graduates from one level to the next without much competition. An honor student, she was allowed to stay on as an assistant after graduation from the system's university, while studying for a doctorate in biology. Several years later, she received her degree and was promoted to an instructorship, then to an assistant professorship, and at 40 she made full professor. No doubt Goto owes her academic career to her ability and strenuous work, but in addition she has benefited from academic patronage. Her professor and advisor recognized her ability, provided supportive guidance, and even took her to the United States with him to do graduate work. It is apparent that the professor-student bond has sustained Goto throughout. Furthermore, she found her career within her alma mater, probably without competing with male outsiders, simply because Japanese universities tend to protect their own graduates by hiring them for a substantial portion of their faculty positions (Shimbori 1965). Goto benefited from academic patronage more fully than Jinbo whose alma mater is a coeducational – and hence male-oriented – national university.

I should add another dimension of linkage between patronage and careers.

Baba, a war widow, was left with her mother, son, and nine more children, kin and non-kin. It was her responsibility to feed this large 'family.' Obtaining sugar, red beans, flour and the like at the black market she started a confectionary business, without intending to make a career out of it. When the crisis was over and economic improvement had begun to make the customers' palatal taste more discriminatory, she thought it was time for an untrained candy-maker like her to quit. By then, however, she had about 40 employees. 'What are they going to do if I quit? I thought about an employer's responsibility, and decided to make it into my lifetime work.' Then she turned herself, and her employees, into professional confectioners, holding classes given by invited specialists. More than 30 years since the beginning, she is now president of a reputable confectionary company in command of 230 employees and three dozen shops. Here the pressure to assume the responsibility of patronage opened up a career for a woman. Given a woman's nurturance, there seems to be no incongruence between womanhood and the patron's role.

ASYMMETRY IN SPHERE SEGREGATION

Japanese mores prescribe that the occupational/public sphere be clearly separated from the domestic/private sphere, except in the case of self-employment. This rule of sphere segregation is asymmetric in that the occupational demand can be fulfilled at the expense of the autonomy of the domestic sphere whereas the reverse is strictly forbidden. The domestic obligations of an employee are not supposed to interfere with his occupational obligations, or more positively, the domestic life should accommodate itself to occupational needs. These mores are detrimental to a woman's career assumption or continuance if she chooses to marry and become a mother. The career-oriented woman thus may remain unmarried (the primary sample includes one 'never married' woman, and one divorcee and one widow who have never remarried), but most career women tend to have both spheres and therefore must face conflicts. Sphere segregation is so taken for granted that a woman's marriage or childbearing is generally interpreted as an end of a short-lived career. When she gave birth to her first and only child, Egawa was subject to her superior's constant preaching: 'Woman's happiness lies in homemaking.'

Romantic involvement within a work place upsets the rule of sphere segregation, but some of my informants did fall in love and marry their colleagues or superiors. Chitose became intimate with a man working in the same office. Although they planned to marry, they were cautious not to reveal their intimacy so as not to disrupt the work atmosphere. When Chitose received an order transferring her to a prefectural government far north of Tokyo, she and her fiance confessed their marriage plans to their *kacho*, who was astonished and bewildered at this unprecedented incident. He said he was going to discuss their future with his superiors. The final decision was to confirm the order of transfer, forcing a separation and marriage postponement on the couple. Later on, Chitose was told that the transfer decision had been meant to give a 'cooling off' period to the 'hot-headed' couple, with an expectation for their breakup. They did marry and have been assigned to totally separate departments to insure sphere segregation.

Segregation sometimes is needed to protect the husband's male ego. One of the informants married a *dōki* colleague, which resulted in subjecting the husband to 'nasty' teasing by his superiors. They asked, for example, which of the two would cook meals, and speculated that the wife, being more able, would be promoted to *kachō* before the husband. The husband was too 'small minded' to ignore such humiliation and began to press his wife to resign. The marriage ended in divorce.

Under the rule of asymmetric segregation, the husband may be expected to devote himself entirely to occupational work, leaving no time and energy for his domestic role. It is not uncommon, therefore, that even the husband of a career woman takes no part in housework. Jinbo gives full credit to her husband for her career commitment, but admits: 'I made one miscalculation. My husband believes it's only natural that women work outside the home. I, therefore, took it for granted that he would participate in housework, but it turned out he also believes housework naturally belongs to women; he has never doubted that, he says.' The helpful fellow researcher who pushes his wife to stick with her academic career thus proved a typical Japanese husband who would not fold up his own bedding, would call upon her to bring his underclothing after a bath instead of getting it ready in advance by himself, and would not turn the television dial by himself. The wife is overwhelmed with the double workload and role strain.[13]

Such a husband is exceptional in my primary sample. The majority of husbands, who are also career professionals, do share housework and some turn out to be better than the wives in cooking, child-caretaking, or home management in general. Nonetheless, the public image of a helpful husband is not necessarily what the husband wants for himself, while the wife is inclined to boast of his domesticity. The husband of a government official, also an official, does housework more than the wife expected – preparing breakfast, bathing the child, house cleaning, trash collection, grocery shopping, dish washing, etc. But he warns her not to reveal this to anybody, particularly to his colleagues. Not that he is afraid of appearing henpecked, but that domesticity can be taken as a sign of a lack of dedication to occupational work. Again, the asymmetric rule of sphere segregation is evident.

It is difficult to extract anything beneficial to career women from the rule of sphere segregation, but a few points may be made. The primacy of the occupation over the domestic need holds for women and men alike, and thus frees the professional women from compulsions for dual-role perfectionism. Whether a woman is compelled toward dual-role perfectionism or not depends upon the kind of career she has. In the Eastern City sample I found women with non-elite professions such as hairdresser, cook, and the like, displaying compulsive domesticity. This was all the more true if the husband's occupational identity was not clear and the wife appeared to be the main breadwinner (Lebra 1978: 32–33).[14]

Social life for the professional woman may be primarily with her professional colleagues or clients, male and female, often at the expense of conjugal togetherness. This does not necessarily offend her husband, who is also bound by the segregation rule. Occupational duties may impose a long-term separation between spouses, as in the case of Goto, whose husband, also a biologist, holds a job in a place too far to commute from home, or of Aoi whose administrative responsibility requires her residence in government housing apart from her husband and son. Such domestic sacrifice is accepted by my informants (and their husbands) as a normal price for a woman to have a full career.

The severity of the segregation rule is mitigated by a special social arrangement. The professional woman, expected to be too busy to bother with domestic chores, is almost always helped by another woman who takes the role of substitute housewife. Both Egawa and Goto could concentrate on their work thanks to their mothers who volunteered to be in charge of house chores and childrearing. For the latter, this arrangement matched her uxorilocal marriage with the *mukoyoshi* husband. Fukuda, too, had her mother baby-sit for her children while she was teaching, and Higuchi, a new mother, is planning to live with her parents and her sister's family so that domestic labor will be shared. One's own mother is the most desirable, but not always available, as a helper. So the other informants have been helped by other kin, such as sister, mother-in-law, or sister-in-law, in coresidence. From my sample it can be inferred that professional women are more likely than non-working women to live with or near members of an extended family. The mother or other kin accommodates her residence to the person who needs her help most, the professional woman, under the rule of sphere segregation, and the latter accepts it as something natural. Without a kinswoman around, a live-in helper is hired.

Both parents having been dead by the time of her marriage, Date put her newborn child in a 'baby home' which provides custodial care for infants around the clock. Only on weekends she 'visited' with her baby. Ten months later, the child was taken back home to be placed under the care of a hired resident babysitter. This was repeated for the second child. Many of her female colleagues have done the same, she says, as there was no other alternative. 'I had no intention of rearing my children by myself.' The children now grown, Date no longer has a helper, and she describes this situation as 'I have my wife no more.' This remark, though meant to be a joke, reminded me of the African 'female husband' (Krige 1974; O'Brien 1977; Oboler 1980). The career woman in Japan indeed may represent a Japanese version of the female husband in the limited sense that she is entitled to the basic prerogative of the Japanese husband – another woman's domestic and nurturant service.

The primary sample women are of the opinion that in order to claim equality, they should compete with men in the open market and that their performance should be evaluated by sex-blind criteria, even though this could mean that women must work three times as hard as men. This view is sharply opposed, according to my informants, to the one held by another group of feminists represented by union leaders and the Bureau of Women and Minors. The latter position, recognizing women's handicaps, advocates protective legislation for women and counts women's domestic labor as equally valuable as any other labor. This group challenges the premise of sphere segregation whereas the other accepts it as a price of equality.

ROLE AMBIGUITY

The above mentioned dispute touches upon the basic issue of sex equality – the question of whether sex equality should be achieved on a 'competitive' or a 'complementary' basis; whether the same rights and duties should be shared by men and women alike or, as Spiro (1979) argues in reference to the kibbutz, equality should be considered compatible with sex-role specialization.

Thus far I have concentrated on those areas where the male-biased values and norms of career professions 'spill over' or are extended to the life sphere of some women, enabling the latter to pursue male-like careers. In the above terms, the competitive or shared aspects of equality have been explored. In this final section, I will look into the complementary or sex-specialized aspects of women's careers. Career women, handicapped as outsiders in the world of men, find some compensatory opportunities or advantages in the ambiguity of an outsider's role.

First and foremost, my career women converted their career frustrations into creative energy. Egawa, having been exposed to the prejudice of male colleagues and superiors (e.g., disapproval of the assignment of important tasks to her as inappropriate to her sex), lost self-confidence and thought of going to the United States in search of a breakthrough. Under a Fulbright grant she studied industrial and labor relations at an eastern university and travelled in the United States. This American exposure opened her perspective and was to influence her career after she returned to her job in Japan. Her employer remained resistant to putting her into the main promotion track for administrative positions and placed her in a research section – peripheral to the bureaucratic structure. She finally gave up hope of moving up within the corporation, and decided to re-educate the Japanese people, particularly employers and managers. Without renouncing her employee status, Egawa started to write books, made frequent appearances in the mass media, and gave public lectures, primarily to promote the utilization of women's capabilities and resources. In line with 'Student Power' or 'Black Power' which was in vogue in America then, she took the lead in spreading the word 'Woman Power,' and convening a woman-power meeting, the novel program of which attracted the mass media: She feels she has thus contributed substantially to a 'social revolution.' Meanwhile she has attained national fame as a public educator, which her employer does not mind because her fame serves as an advertisement. In other words, she created a new role for herself and converted her peripheral status within the corporation into a central one outside it. If she were a man, this would have been impossible, she says.

While men can afford to rely upon the operation of the bureaucratic system for their career maturation, women as outsiders must be alert to any opportunity as it presents itself. This is particularly true with self-employed career women. Ishii had been involved in creating commercially feasible information (useful for city planning, construction projects, advertisement, etc.) as an employee or member of various research teams. She now heads her own research corporation with several women employees. For her, opportunities for information production are ubiquitous only if one is perceptive enough to see linkages between various things which most people ignore. Inexhaustible curiosity, sensitivity, and imagination seem to be the main capital; there is no predetermined course for navigation.

Creativity may well be released through cross-cultural exposure. Significantly, six out of the ten women have been in the United States.

The role of a researcher is often imposed upon women to push them out of the main promotion track, as happened to Egawa. Chitose, kept out of the *kachō* position,[15] ended up as a research center director. Both women protested, but then decided to 'convert misfortune into a blessing.' According to my informants, the main promotion track requires one to be a generalist with a variety of experiences with no expertise developed in a single field. For such a person the bureaucratic status is all he carries with him, whereas a specialist with research experience will be called upon even after his retirement. This is an important consideration in view of the Japanese system of early retirement – informants in their forties are contemplating retirement soon. The retiree usually takes a post-retirement job for which a specialized expertise may be important.

There are other compensatory benefits inherent in the role ambiguity. Women may have easy access to men at the top of a bureaucracy because they are less constrained by 'proper channels,' whereas their male colleagues are not permitted to bypass their own superiors. This freedom allowed Egawa to participate in top-level decision-making in the government – a privilege beyond the grasp of her male peers. Easy access may be because women do not threaten men or are not taken seriously by men, as surmised by Ishii. 'Men are not on guard against women and so tend to divulge the information we look for more readily than they would with men.' She tells her employees to take advantage of that. 'Be a telephone beauty,' she tells them, so that they can get appointments for interviews without much difficulty.

CONCLUSION

Women's career opportunities and commitments are explained by a set of Japanese cultural values and norms which are clearly biased for 'career men': socialization for domestic succession, examination rites of transition, bureaucratic rigidity, patronage, and asymmetry in sphere segregation. This set refers to those values which cross over sex boundaries and thus can be shared by women. A last item, role ambiguity, involves sex specialization in which a woman finds sex-specific opportunities or advantages by virtue of her outsider status in the professional world of men: one refers to symmetric or generalized 'equality,' and the other to complementary or compensatory 'equity.'

This analysis is more open-ended than conclusive, which reflects uncertainty on my part as to the optimum strategy for a woman's career in Japan.

Two conflicting messages are implied. On the one hand, the findings suggest that a woman could be a beneficiary in the male-dominant value system of professionalism. This seemingly conservative message is congruent with the historical necessity that a new system of sex-blind professionalism, to take root, first must be grafted to the old stock. Moreover, at this time of transition, it may be desirable for a small number of talented and fortunate women to compete with men within the male-biased rules of the game, however unfair, in order to remove once and for all the tenacious proclivities for equating elite professions with males. Also, we have seen cases of cross-sexual alliance (e.g., daughter-father, man-for-woman patronage) as crucial to a woman's career development and commitment. The paper thus has explored the maximal limits to which the male-centered values serve career women as well.

On the other hand, it goes without saying that the above message is not unconditional but 'framed' within a higher-order message which basically denies it, involving a 'double bind' (Bateson 1972). First of all, the male-centered value system benefits only a handful of women, leaving the rest behind. This limitation becomes narrower as one proceeds from 'succession' to 'examination,' to 'bureaucracy,' and to 'patronage,' with the 'asymmetric sphere segregation' being the least supportive of women. Only those women who are lucky enough to have another woman's domestic help, for example, can afford full careers. Second, benefiting from the existing system or going along with the male-biased rules of the game may ultimately reinforce male dominance in the professional realm.

Finally, even the most successful and luckiest career women turn out not to be free from the conflict between their career commitment and other commitments, most importantly the commitment to motherhood.[16] Despite a baby-sitter's services being available, my informants recognize that their motherhood means a loss of time and freedom, a reduction in the amount of reading and studying, and an inability to concentrate on a research topic without interruption. If a woman leaves the childrearing responsibility totally to her mother, she still faces the problems of the child being spoiled by the granny, or the conflict between her mother and husband over the educational guidance of the child. She also has guilt feelings for having neglected the child's education when she realizes that the child's academic mediocrity will adversely affect any career prospects determined by the examination system.[17] While no informant regrets having had a career, many do express ambivalence as to what they could have done if they had chosen another course of life. These issues and problems seem to call for a fundamental change in the professional culture while no simple solution can be expected.

BIBLIOGRAPHY

Bateson, G. 1972. *Steps to an Ecology of Mind.* New York.
Befu, H. 1962. *Corporate Emphasis and Patterns of Descent in the Japanese Family.*

Japanese Culture: Its Development and Characteristics, eds. R.J. Smith & R.K. Beardsley, pp. 34–41. Chicago.
Craig, A. M. 1975. Functional and Dysfunctional Aspects of Government Bureaucracy. *Modern Japanese Organizations and Decision-Making*, ed. E. F. Vogel, pp. 3–32. Berkeley.
Dilatush, L. 1976. *Women in the Professions. Women in Changing Japan*, eds. J. Lebra, .J. Paulson, and E. Powers, pp. 191–208. Boulder.
Epstein, C. F. 1970. *Women's Place*. Berkeley.
Fujin Mondai Kikaku Suishin Honbu (Headquarters for the Planning and Promoting of Policies Relating to Women). 1977. *Fujin no Seisaku Kettei Sanka o Sokushin Suru Tokubetsu Katsudo no Suishin ni Tsuite* (On Special Actions to Promote Women's Participation in Policy Making). Japan.
Hennig, M., and A. Jardim. 1977. *The Managerial Woman*. Garden City.
Johnson, F. A., and C. L. Johnson. 1976. Role Strain in High-Commitment Career Women. *Journal of the American Academy of Psychoanalysis* 4: 13–36.
Johnson, C. L, and F. A. Johnson. 1977. Attitudes Toward Parenting in Dual-Career Families. *American Journal of Psychiatry* 134: 391–395.
Kanter, R. M. 1977. Some Effects of Proportions on Group Life: Skewed Sex Ratios and Responses to Token Women. *American Journal of Sociology* 82: 965–990.
Kiefer, C. W. 1974. The Psychological Interdependence of Family, School, and Bureaucracy in Japan. *Japanese Culture and Behavior: Selected Readings*, eds. T. S. Lebra and W. P. Lebra, pp. 342–356. Honolulu.
Krige, E. J. 1974. Woman-Marriage, with Special Reference to the Lovedu – Its Significance for the Definition of Marriage. *Africa* 44: 11–36.
Lebra. T. S. 1976. *Japanese Patterns of Behavior*. Honolulu.
—— 1978. Japanese Women and Marital Strain. *Ethos* 6: 22–41.
—— 1979a. The Dilemma and Strategies of Aging among Contemporary Japanese Women. *Ethnology* 18: 337–353.
—— 1979b. *Togoteki Josei Kenkyu o Mezashite* (Toward an Integrative Study of Women). Minzokugaku Kenkyu (Japanese Journal of Ethnology) 44: 105–132.
Mainichi Shinbun Shakaibu. 1977. *Ranjuku Jidai* (The Uncontrolled Proliferation of Juku). Tokyo.
Nakane, C. 1967. *Kinship and Economic Organization in Rural Japan*. London.
Nakano, T. 1968. *Ie to Dozokudan no Riron* (The Theory of the Ie and Dozoku Groups). Tokyo.
Oboler, R. S. 1980. Is the Female Husband a Man? Woman/Woman Marriage Among the Nandi of Kenya. *Ethnology* 19: 69–88.
O'Brien, D. 1977. Female Husbands in Southern Bantu Societies. *Sexual Stratification: A Cross-Cultural View*, ed. A. Schlegel, pp. 109–126. New York.
Okada, M., N. Okifuji, and Y. Hagiwara. 1967. *Senmonshoku no Joseitachi: Genjo to so no Ishiki* (The Present State and Consciousness of Professional Women). Tokyo.
Osako, M. M. 1978. Dilemmas of Japanese Professional Women. *Social Problems* 26: 15–25.
Peizel, J. C. 1970. Japanese Kinship: A Comparison. Family and Kinship in Chinese Society, ed. M. Freedman, pp. 227–248. Stanford.
Rapoport, R., and R. N. Rapoport. 1976. *Dual Career Families Re-examined*. London
Rohlen, T. P. 1974. *For Harmony and Strength: Japanese White-Collar Organization in Anthropological Perspective*. Berkeley.
—— 1980. The Juku Phenomenon: An Exploratory Essay. *Journal of Japanese Studies* 6: 207–242.
Sekiguchi, R. W. 1973. Joshi Koto Kyoiku Shuryo-sha no Shakai-teki ichi: Sono

Shokugyo ni tsuite Nippon to Nishi-Doitsu to no Hikaku Kenkyu (Social Locations of Female College Graduates in Japan and West Germany: A Comparative Study on Occupational Distributions). *Shakaigaku Hyoron* 23: 83–100.
Shimbori, M. 1965. *Nippon no Daigaku Kyoju Shijo* (Academic Market in Japan). Tokyo.
Spiro, M. E. 1979. *Gender and Culture: Kibbutz Women Revisited.* Durham.
Suenari, M. 1972. First Child Inheritance in Japan. *Ethnology* 11: 122–126.

NOTES

1. This is a result of research funded by the National Science Foundation and Japan Society for the Promotion of Science, which I wish to acknowledge with gratitude. Among many who helped me in the field I should mention Tomoko Inukai, Sachiko Ide, and Takemitsu Hemmi. Special gratitude goes to all the women who, despite their busy schedules, kindly accepted my interview requests. Thomas Rohlen and Keith Brown made helpful comments on the original draft. For editorial suggestions and typing service I owe thanks to Freda Hellinger and Linda Kimura.
2. Particularly central are the life histories of 57 women interviewed in a provincial tourist town (Eastern City) of central Japan, which was the site of my fieldwork for two periods between 1976 and 1978. The objective was to trace the processes of life-long socialization of Japanese women with particular attention to clashes and reinforcements between the individual's inner experience and the social structure. Compared with the primary sample women, these women have led more provincial and professionally limited, or only housewifely, lives (Lebra 1978, 1979a for more details).
3. The culturally conditioned readiness for role substitution among Japanese was noted in Lebra (1976: 87–89, 198, 251).
4. This acceptance of a daughter as a virtual successor may be historically rooted in the custom of sex-neutral primogeniture which prevailed prior to the Meiji era (1868-1912) and survived well into the post-Meiji period among the commoners. Suenari (1972), on the basis of house register records, claims that 'first-child inheritance' involving 50-50 chances of *ane-katoku* (headship assumed by the first-born daughter) was a 'norm' rather than a special arrangement for economic necessity. This proposition was confirmed by my older informants from rural areas.
5. The father-daughter bond was also recalled by American 'managerial women' as a determinant for their masculine career (Hennig and Jardim 1977).
6. In a British sample of 'dual-career families' Rapoport and Rapoport (1976: 42) noted that women 'tended to come from higher social class backgrounds than their husbands.'
7. The word *juku* is used here in a generalized and simplified sense. There are non-academic, extracurricular classes or schools, e.g., those for calligraphy or abacus lessons, also called *juku*; and there are examinations oriented schools having other names. See Rohlen (1980) and Mainichi Shinbun Shakaibu (1977) for further information on *juku.*
8. A sample of 'future autobiographies' I elicited from high school students of Eastern City, in which they projected their future lives, indicates that male students are most obsessed with university entrance examinations as the first major hurdle in their careers, whereas female students choose modest two-year colleges which will accept them as they are.
9. The career entry from Todai into the Ministry of Finance has been considered the utmost 'elite course.'
10. There are three levels of civil service employment: upper, middle, and lower. Four-year university graduates are expected to start their careers at the upper level.
11. The plight of 'token women' in large, male-dominant, American corporations, which Kanter (1977) attributes to their minority status, might be compounded by this problem of individual identity inseparable from one's sex.
12. An American sample of career women taken by Hennig and Jardim (1977) also recognized the important role played by their male bosses as their mentors and even likened them to their fathers.
13. Overload and role strain of career women are not unique to Japan. See Johnson and Johnson (1976).
14. Under American egalitarianism, even elite professional women may well be more driven by dual-role perfectionism, as suggested by Epstein (1970).
15. The rank hierarchy of the central office is different from that of a local office: it is not difficult for a woman to attain a *kachō* or higher position in a local office where she has been transferred, but upon

returning to the central office she is 'demoted' to a lower rank or a *kachō* 'equivalent' (a device to maintain the appearance of seniority-based egalitarianism), according to its own standard of hierarchy. My informants have been *kachō* or higher locally.

16. The mother-child bonding may be regarded as a compelling reason why the problems of women should be studied in terms of a 'triad' rather than a male-female 'dyad' (Lebra 1979b: 117–118).

17. Johnson and Johnson (1977) demonstrate that wives in American dual-career families feel the greatest strain in their maternal role, accompanied by a strong sense of guilt toward their children.

First published in Shumpei Kumon and Henry Rosovsky (eds), *The Political Economy of Japan, Vol. 3: Cultural and Social Dynamics*, Stanford: Stanford University Press, 1992

16 Gender and Culture in the Japanese Political Economy: Self-portrayals of Prominent Businesswomen

Gender is an issue that warrants special attention in considering the political economy. It is a generally shared preconception that the two institutional domains, public and domestic, belong to men and women, respectively. But a gender-focused inquiry into the political economy, a main sector of the public domain, will show how the two domains in fact so interpenetrate each other as to challenge the male-female domainal opposition. In Japan's political economy, women's minority status is more firmly established than in the postindustrial West. However, there is a fundamental difference between women and other minorities. Women not only constitute half the total population but are partners with men in sexual attraction and the interdependence created by conjugal and familial bonding within the domestic domain. This difference does not necessarily give women an edge in redressing their inferior status and may contribute to its persistence and complexity.

This essay consists of two parts. The first takes a broad view of the position of women in the Japanese labor market, which is further contextualized against two general considerations: (1) models of gender ideology supporting and challenging gender asymmetry, and (2) the age-linked life schedule underlying the gender issue. This part, which draws largely upon secondary sources of information, provides a frame or context for the second part, in which the primary data are presented.

The second part depicts twelve prominent businesswomen as they recalled and portrayed their careers and experiences in interviews. These women are company presidents engaging in what is broadly understood as 'entrepreneurial' endeavors. It is cross-culturally recognized that to establish one's own business is 'a viable strategy' for women squeezed out of the organized labor market.[1] Entrepreneurship as a route to beat the system is thus likely to attract women who aspire to careers. At the same time, one can easily imagine the difficulties and obstacles that confront such women, precisely because of their organizational independence, in surviving in the competitive and male-dominated world of business. How they seized opportunities and how they encountered and managed obstacles illustrates the general discussion of the first part. The two parts are thus interdependent, the first at once contextualizing and being amplified by the second. While the first part offers an outward macro view of where women stand in relation to men, the second part takes an inward turn to look into the subjective microcosms of the individual women by listening to their narratives. Throughout, Japanese culture explicitly or implicitly serves as a sorter of information in diverse contexts.

THE LABOR MARKET, IDEOLOGY, AND LIFE SCHEDULE

Gender in Economic Dualism

In his pioneering study of the Japanese employment system, James Abegglen points out that the rigidity inherent in 'lifetime commitment' is ameliorated by two buffer mechanisms.[2] One is the categorical distinction between insiders to the permanent system – namely, permanent or regular employees – and outsiders – that is, temporary or supplementary workers. The other is the system of subcontracting, in which the contracting 'parent' firm can displace its own burden upon the subcontracting 'child' companies attached to it. This mechanism involves a relationship between large and medium-to-small enterprises. The two buffers, which do not necessarily overlap, together constitute the 'economic dualism' of Japan, although granted there is some variation in what is meant by dualism.[3] Duality here involves status hierarchy between employees or companies, subordination of one party to the other, and possible exploitation of one by the other. Asymmetry is thus an essential characteristic of this dualism.

Whether this widely accepted view is valid or not may be open to question. Hugh Patrick and Thomas Rohlen, for example, noting the increasing viability and diversification of small family enterprises over the past two decades, observe that *economic dualism* 'has become an outmoded phrase.'[4] Rodney Clark proposes the use of *industrial gradation* to replace *dualism* in view of 'continuous variation' in size among firms.[5] Even the intrafirm dualism of tenured versus untenured workers, which seems much sharper than dualism in firm size, is no longer entirely certain, in that the lifetime employment system itself is threatening to break down, as is constantly reported in the media.

It is likely that the real economy reflects multiplicity or complexity rather than duality. I suggest, however, that when applied to gender, duality continues to be a striking feature. The above buffers find their gendered counterparts. Can we not say, for example, that women are to men what temporary workers are to permanent employees, and what small-scale subcontractors are to large-scale contracting firms?

This parallel is not merely a matter of analogy but involves actual overlaps. First of all, a large portion of employed women are in fact temporary, untenured, supplementary, peripheral workers outside the permanent employment system, which is quite literally 'manned.' Interlocked with the normative domestic career pattern, the woman employee's temporariness is typically demonstrated by her mandatory or voluntary 'retirement' upon marriage or first pregnancy, full-time engagement in housewifery and motherhood until her youngest child enters school, and reentry into employment as a middle-aged part-timer. The overall distribution of women employees by age thus forms a skewed M-curve, the first peak being sharp and the second peak more gradual. As of 1985, the 20–24 age bracket (i.e., premarital or pre-parental stage) formed the left peak of the M with 67 per cent employed, the 30–34 bracket hit the bottom per cent, and the curve began to rise again from age 35 on, reaching the right peak with 46 per cent employed at age 40 to 44.[6]

By international comparison, Japan stands out in the sharpness of its M-curve.[7] The term *pāto* (part-time) in the vernacular refers largely to the untenured, peripheral status of second-peak employees, who are not necessarily distinct from full-timers in terms of work hours. In 1983, 10.5 per cent of all employed workers were part-timers, and two-thirds of them were women.[8] The two peaks are totally discontinuous, in the sense that the second-peak workers do not return to their previous job but must find new jobs. And yet this two-stage employment career pattern, particularly second-stage employment, is attracting more and more women, reflecting the reality and anticipation of prolonging the postparental life stage further and further. From a woman's point of view, employment is largely an in-and-out matter, as indicated by a survey finding the percentages of women both entering and leaving employment to be twice those for men.[9]

Women are a significant half of the dual economy, not only as temporary workers but as workers in small-scale, family-based, and often subcontracting enterprises.[10] Women are concentrated in small factories, sales, and service industries, including 'minuscule units of fewer than five workers.'[11] In addition to being part-time and regular corporate employees working away from home, they manage their own businesses, join the work forces of family-owned enterprises, and do *naishoku* (piecework done at home, thus dispensing with the employers' need to provide a workplace).[12] Yoko Sato warns that as much as half of the census category of 'self-employed' women may actually include *naishoku* workers, 60 per cent of them engaging in tiny-scale subcontracting in manufacturing industries.[13] Traditionally notable in agriculture, women's presence is now more important in sales and other service industries. Women come to head their family businesses as successors to their late husbands, and also when the male heads choose to work elsewhere as wage earners, leaving farming, family-owned retail shops, or other family businesses to their wives.

It is safe to assume, then, that women's labor is largely localized in the lower half of the asymmetric dual economy. In this sense, as pointed out by Frank Upham, women are no different from other 'undesirables,' such as *burakumin*, Koreans, and the handicapped.[14] Further reinforcing this point is the gender-specific repertoire of jobs and businesses. Professional women specialize in areas associated with housewifely responsibilities and their extension, such as the health professions (nursing, pharmacology, pediatrics, nutritional science, etc.), teaching and caring for small children (as nursery and gradeschool teachers), and instruction in bridal arts such as flower arranging, the tea ceremony, and the like. Businesswomen, too, who start their own enterprises tend to stay within the traditionally or properly female repertoire, as exemplified by beauty shops, coffee shops, restaurants, bars, kimono shops, dress shops, and sales catering to women customers (e.g., cosmetics). This gender bias is confirmed by Barbara Ito's sample of 'entrepreneurial' women engaging in a variety of businesses.[15]

The gender-specific repertoire is reflected in employment as well. In 1981, 83 per cent of all employers admitted that their firms have certain jobs in which no women are placed.[16] Most striking is the absence of women from managerial positions. Among the total of about 1,400 companies listed on the Tokyo Stock Exchange, as of 1979, women constituted only 0.1 per cent of roughly 300,000 managerial/policy-making personnel (*kachō* or equivalent and above), and even in service industries, where women supposedly predominate, they hold only 0.5 per cent of these leading positions.[17]

Young women employees of large companies, those at the first peak of the M-curve, theoretically with 'permanent' status, are typically represented by the so-called 'office lady' (OL), who may or may not have a college education, working as 'a prelude' to marriage.[18] Lacking any prospect of promotion, the OL symbolizes the auxiliary, insignificant nature of work – simple, tedious, clerical – without authority or much responsibility, performed only to assist male bosses. Internationally notorious is her housewifely or servile role as an office waitress serving tea and cleaning ashtrays. The teapourers' rebellion that took place in the early 1960s at a division of the Kyoto City Office was unsuccessful, failing even to attract the attention of the union leadership as a legitimate labor issue, and the women resumed tea-pouring.[19] In the late 1970s, a company studied by James McLendon was training new women employees in such 'women's work' as serving tea to male colleagues and guests and keeping the office area clean, as well as in talking politely to customers and male staff.[20] At parties such as *bōnenkai* (year-end celebrations), McLendon observed women workers waiting on men, because 'no man should have to pour his own drink or serve himself rice.'[21] Women seem to accept this role as a matter of temporary obligation until they relinquish their tenured-employee status and retire at 25 or so to attain their real goal in life, marriage.

In short, gendered duality in work status is thus indicated by women's concentration in small-scale enterprises; the part-time status of middle-aged women; the short-term employment pattern in contrast to that of men in the same age range, who benefit from the seniority rule;[22] gender-segregated job categories; inaccessibility of managerial positions; the insignificant, auxiliary nature of the tasks assigned to women; and so on. This qualitative inferiority of women's status is manifested in a quantitative discrepancy in wages. Women's average monthly pay amounts to roughly half of men's, and this discrepancy has not improved over the years. If we take men's monthly average pay as 100, women's pay peaked at 56 in 1976, but then dropped to 52.8 in 1982.[23]

Despite gender barriers, the number of working women has been growing. A 1982 survey by the Prime Minister's Office showed 49 per cent of women aged 15 or older to be working, a continuing trend that accounts for the termination in 1984 of an extremely popular TV drama series addressed to the daytime audience, that is, housewives.[24]

Full-time housewives, the category paralleling that of full-time urban male salaried employees, are a recent phenomenon associated with the high-growth period of the 1960s and the unprecedented affluence and enlargement of the 'middle class.' (In pre-affluent Japan, except among the well-off classes, families could not afford specialized housewifery: women worked as co-breadwinners side by side with their husbands or in-laws. This corresponded with that stage of social and economic evolution where work and family life were not as sharply bifurcated as at the later, fully industrialized stage.) It is customary to distinguish housewives from working women as if the former were nonworkers. Indeed, the media image of the housewife is that of a leisurely, privileged woman with *sanshone hirune tsuki* (three free meals and a nap per day), devoting herself to aerobics and pursuit of her own hobby or pleasure. Accepting this image, some housewives appear embarrassed or apologetic about themselves, but a majority would be resentful and able to demonstrate that housewifery is full-time work, in fact more than eight hours a day.

Housework in Japan is more than just such chores as preparing meals, house cleaning, laundry, shopping, bookkeeping, or 'home management' as a whole. The Japanese housewife is expected to be perpetually available to her children, husband, and aged parents or parents-in-law. Every morning, she prepares her children for school and re-energizes her husband for another day of overtime at his firm. Her presence at home is taken for granted during the absence of the daily commuters at school and workplace. Her mothering resumes when they get home; now her task is to provide relaxation therapy for the tired returnees. 'If the wife is tired and unable to give the husband the soothing he desires, he will be annoyed and suggest that she cut down on outside activities,' observes Anne Imamura. 'Conserving her energies for the primary tasks of running the home, mothering, and comforting is the wife's major duty.'[25] Even women interested in outside activities such as consumer movements feel 'that a housewife must never participate in anything until she has taken care of her home and family,' according to Imamura; one civic activist, she reports, never attended evening meetings because 'it is not right that her husband should eat alone.'[26]

It may be that this perfectionist image of a housewife is not so much actually lived up to as put forward to counter the popularized image of the idle housewife. It is indeed true that with the proliferation of ready-to-eat food products and automation of housework, the housewife today has more free time than before, particularly if she is left alone without a small child or elderly parent to look after around the clock. But it is not the kind of time she can control or schedule at her will. One of my informants, a doctoral candidate at the University of Tokyo who had to quit to become a full-time housewife, described housewifery as a role of 'waiting' (*taiki*) for calls that could occur at any time, unpredictably. 'It does not matter how much time the housewife has. The time is for waiting, not for planning.'

The housewife's presence at home and care giving are part of a package in the employer's investment in her husband. The employer expects the employee to be well taken care of by his understanding, nurturant wife, so that he is ready to resume his work each morning with refreshed energy and single-minded dedication. The worst thing from the employer's point of view would be the wife's interference with her husband's work career and schedule. School is even more demanding. Mothering a schoolchild includes performing all kinds of tasks assigned by schoolteachers to parents, ranging from participation in frequent PTA meetings and activities, to supervising homework, to making a standardized cloth container for stationery or sewing the classroom cleaning dust cloth that each child must take to school. The school expects the mother to be ready, full-time, for educational collaboration, often competing with her husband and his employer for her time and energy. Even more pressing is the mother's responsibility for her child's performance in examinations, accounting for the common association between the housewife and *kyōiku-mama* (mother obsessed with her child's educational success).

With her total and exclusive involvement in a wide range of chores and tasks as a wife, mother, and homemaker, the housewife may develop domestic expertise, become adept in managing human relations, and acquire mastery, confidence, and autonomy within her realm. She may become a 'professional housewife.'[27] When she decides to work outside the domestic sphere, however, she realizes herself to be dreadfully unskilled, hence unable to find a job better than part-time kitchen work. On the other hand, the market for domestic expertise is wide open, and 'housekeeping' is a professionalized job taken by supposedly unskilled 'former' housewives.

Although full-time housewives are declining in number, I have discussed them at length partly in order to dispel the prevailing perception of a dichotomy between working women and housewives and partly to underscore the symbiosis of home, school, and workplace. Furthermore, few women workers, whether full-time or part-time, professional or unskilled, in the home or outside it, are completely free of their housewifely identity, whether as a matter of desire, obligation, ambivalence, guilt, or frustration. It is this identity that keeps women workers crowded into the lower half of the dual economy. One may well go as far as to say that the full-time housewife is one of the purest manifestations of gendered dualism in the Japanese economy.

Gender Ideology: Functional Complementarity or Egalitarian Justice

One way of explaining or legitimizing gendered dualism derives from the functional model. It may be argued that a woman's participation in the lower half of the dual economy is functional to the goal of a social unit, be it the woman herself as an individual, her family, the company employing her or her husband, or the national economy at large.

It is apparent that hiring a middle-aged woman as a part-timer is functional to her employer in terms of flexibility and low cost. A 1983 survey showed that, among nine reasons (which are not exclusive of one another) for choosing female part-timers, the undemanding nature of the work was indicated by 63 per cent of the responding employers, the lower cost of labor by 29 per cent, adjustability of labor supply to the amount of production or sales by 20 per cent, and seasonality of business by 18 per cent.[28] All these reasons imply labor-cost reduction and/or flexibility in hiring and firing.

Conversely, the woman, too, may find a part-time arrangement flexibly adjustable to her own and family needs and suited to her double life as a housewife and employee. 'Many women favor part-time work in spite of its limitations because the hours, although sometimes nearly as long as those worked by regular employees, are more flexible, allowing women with family commitments to schedule working hours accordingly,' says Ito.[29] If that is the case, part-time employment is solidly based upon functional complementarity between employer and employee. The growing number of part-timers among married women and mothers may attest to such functional complementarity between the two parties.

Similar complementarity may hold between a young woman employee who, despite her full-time, permanent status, accepts her work as a bridal apprenticeship or a premarital experiment, on the one hand, and her employer or boss, on the other, who wants to keep his regular female staff youthful. For the employer, women's early retirement kills two birds with one stone: it raises male workers' morale and cuts the financial burden that would accumulate with seniority if a full-time woman employee chose to stay on along with her male colleagues. Related to youthfulness and killing still another bird, is the functional consideration of beauty. McLendon notes that the company's hiring committee paid special attention to looks because a woman employee's attractiveness would contribute to creating positive rapport between the company and clients and because these women were prospective brides for male workers.[30] And, for Japanese, feminine beauty is inseparable from youth.

There are indications that the M-curve pattern is functional not only from the employer's point of view. Over half (56 per cent) of a surveyed sample of women were found to prefer a two-stage work career, with an interval of home life as wife and mother, whereas only 16 per cent favored a continuous work career. The same survey revealed that 50 per cent preferred that their second-stage work be part-time.[31] The familiar M-curve seems to have stabilized.

In the case of participation in family business, there is a functional unity between the woman's domestic role and her work role, between the woman herself and the family as a whole. The home-site job, including low-paid *naishoku*, is preferred by those women who want to supplement family income without sacrificing their domestic responsibility. As subcontractors, these women in turn fit the needs and interests of small, local contractors that cannot afford workplaces, facilities, or job security. Even entrepreneurial women, as observed by Ito in Niihama, find their business activities well integrated with their family roles and identities as wives and mothers.[32]

Finally, role division between housewife and salaried husband in urban, middle-class Japan may be viewed as a culmination of functional complementarity at two levels: (1) functional interdependence between the wife as a full-time care giver and homemaker and the husband as a full-time or overtime employee and economic supporter of the family; and (2) reciprocity between the family that refuels the worker husband daily and the company that rewards the workaholic husband with job security, promotion, and pay raises. Thanks to such role division, the wife can also devote herself to bringing up her children, the next generation of workers and housewives.

Extending our perspective to the societal level, one may argue that women's contribution is indispensable to the strength of Japan's national economy precisely because they occupy the lower half of the dual economy. It is not surprising, then, that Japan's economic success offers one of the rationales for excluding women from the upper half of the dual structure. The growth of GNP owes, the argument goes, to men's total devotion to work, which in turn is made possible by women's support at home.[33]

In the functionalist argument, gender segregation in career tracks has nothing to do with gender discrimination, but is a natural way of self-fulfillment for both men and women. This kind of polemic reached a peak when a provocative article attacking the Equal Employment Opportunity Law (EEOL) appeared in a popular journal. That the author, Michiko Hasegawa, was a woman with a career apparently contributed to the sensational ripples it caused. In Hasegawa's view, the EEOL degrades the housewife as a non-worker, whereas she is in fact a fullfledged worker, performing daily absolutely necessary chores; 'being' at home alone, while 'doing' nothing, is an essential part of her work. The introduction of the EEOL, Hasegawa believes, will end up demoralizing housewives and replacing mutual appreciation and cooperation based upon the division of labor with competitiveness and animosity among invidious status-seekers. Hasegawa extends the functional model to the 'ecosystem' of indigenous culture, which she predicts will be destroyed by this law of alien origin, externally enforced because of Japan's submission to international, 'colonial' pressures.[34]

As best exemplified by the Hasegawa article, the functional explanation of the gendered dualism thus derives from and in turn reinforces conservative ideology. It is not at all certain, however, whether the gendered dual economy is in fact functioning well, serving the needs and goals of each social unit concerned. Do women really opt for employment in smallscale subcontracting firms? Do they want to work in their family business or do piecework at home rather than go out to work? If working outside the home, do they find their part-time status really suited to their personal goals? Is it functional to the young woman and her employer for her to quit her 'permanent' job at age 25? In fact, many men and women alike deplore this early retirement phenomenon as a 'waste' of human resources and investment, and in turn use it as a justification for gender discrimination in the hiring practice.

Gendered dualism as such can be challenged in terms of its dysfunctional implications and consequences. Women may be only submitting to, not choosing, what is available to them. Far from it helping them attain their goals in life, they may find the prevailing asymmetry frustrating; part-time status may be taken as degrading rather than fulfilling. The survey of women's attitudes toward work cited above, while indicating the relatively prevalent desire for an M-shaped life-course, also shows that preference for a continuous career nearly doubled between 1972 and 1984 (from 11.5 per cent to

20.1 per cent), and that the perceived desirability of quitting upon marriage or first childbirth dropped from 30.9 per cent to 21.7 per cent over the same period.[35] Two opposite conclusions can thus be drawn from the same kind of information.[36]

Contrary to Hasegawa's view of her, the housewife may be one of a frustrated, unfulfilled, demoralized crowd of women who are no longer content with the endless cycle of domestic drudgery and care giving. The 'professional housewife' is more ideal than real. In reality, the housewife frequently finds herself under stress and may face serious crises in her life: perhaps her husband does not reciprocate her nurturant care giving, but instead becomes a mere 'boarder' of the house; perhaps he has to live away from home because he has been transferred to a distant branch office (*tanshin funin*); perhaps his career has reached a ceiling below what she expected; or, worst of all, perhaps he has started womanizing. Economically helpless, unable to risk divorce, she reintensifies her commitment to the future of her child. There are reasons to believe that the *kyōiku-mama* is symptomatic as much of the mother's neurotic obsession as of her devotion to her child. Still, there is no guarantee that her child will grow up into a successful, filial adult as expected. Furthermore, the Japanese housewife is likely to outlive her role as mother, inasmuch as her life expectancy is steadily lengthening.[37] According to latest reports, Japanese women can on average expect to live for 81.4 years and men for 75.6 years.[38] Widowhood and divorce make the functional-interdependence thesis bankrupt.

Asked if they agreed with the idea that the husband should go to work and the wife remain at home, 71 per cent of women respondents indicated unconditional or conditional agreement in 1982, 12 per cent fewer than a decade before.[39] The increase in the number of part-timers who are married women may be a sign of housewives attempting to escape these dilemmas and to capture a sense of autonomy, although such women tend to justify their action in terms of supplementing family income rather than of their own fulfillment.

What emerges is the stressful, demoralizing, pathological, wasteful, dysfunctional aspect of gendered duality. If there is anything functional about it, the functionality is one-sided, not complementary. The male employer may believe in the functional advantage of gender division between regular and temporary employees, but his opinion may be rejected as a 'topdown' view, not shared by those at the bottom looking upward.[40]

This asymmetrical functionality brings us to the idea of justice based on egalitarian ideology as another model for understanding gender dualism in the economy. This is a feminist point of view. In today's Japan, as elsewhere, the gender issue swings between the functionalist ideology and feminist ideology, the former seeing functional disaster in the latter, the latter finding an embodiment of injustice in the former. Self-proclaimed feminists are not the only ones trying to reform the gender asymmetry. The national government itself, not immune to domestic and international waves of feminism, is taking steps to rectify inequality and discrimination, and some progress has been made in the public sector. In 1975, out of 6,938 top-level administrative positions in the national government, 20 were occupied by women. Eight years later the number had increased to 47 out of 8,334, rising from 0.3 per cent to 0.6 per cent.[41] Feminists may groan over this persistence of overwhelming male dominance, but these figures can also be taken as an initial sign of change, at however slow a pace. The last male sanctuaries in the civil service, such as the defense force and police, have been opened up to women. In 1986, despite strong opposition by many Hasegawas, the Equal Employment Opportunity Law went into effect. A survey of about 7,200 private employers conducted ten months later by the Ministry of Labor indicates some movement toward equalization, especially among large-scale companies.[42] Once egalitarianism is embraced, functionalism comes to be seen as a mask for injustice and exploitation.

Controversy over these two ideologies goes on between men and women, the young and old, the privileged and underprivileged, the better-educated and less-educated, and so on. Nevertheless, the two models of gender ideology are not as far apart as claimed by the most vocal advocates of each. Nor is there consensus within each camp. In the feminist camp there is debate over the meaning of equality when applied to gender. If there is no way of denying sexual differences and complementarity between male and female or of 'ungenderizing' society completely, the question is how this fact is to be made compatible with gender equality. One feminist, for example, might demand total abolition of the existing law protecting women workers in order to bring about true equality, while another might advocate expansion of services and facilities such as child-care centers at work sites for working women. The revision of the Labor Standards Law, necessitated by the EEOL, is a product of compromise between such oppositions: retaining and expanding the mandate of maternity protection on the one hand, and removing and relaxing all other protection requirements. The question continues to pop up, 'Isn't the law overprotective of working mothers at the expense of all other women, let alone all men?' The rationale for maternity protection is protection not only of the mother's health but of the next generation to be born and reared.[43] It is interesting that the strong mother-child bonding sanctioned in Japanese culture can be ideologically mobilized in opposite directions: to keep mothers homebound as full-time childcare providers, and to support mothers working outside the home without sacrificing their mothering role and time.

If multiple meanings of egalitarian justice generate controversy, the functional model has its own share of complexity. What is often overlooked about women's status is the fact that women are not always losers and men winners in the functional division of labor. The gender asymmetry inherent in the functional model can produce a reversed hierarchy, in that role division actually gives the housewife the exclusive privilege of dominating the household. Under extreme role opposition, domestic matriarchy goes in tandem with public patriarchy,[44] the essence of functional complementarity. Further, as a housewife or peripheral employee, the woman may be a winner in the 'lifelong' run, as suggested, if not proved, by her longevity being greater than men's by six years. Men pay the price of male status in shorter, more stressful lives, and it is said that there are many men envious of women.[45] In the labor market, too, women's monopoly of pink-collar jobs (e.g., nursing, nursery teaching) is well justified in the functionalist perspective. Some men and women may see a reciprocal balance in this relationship, whereas others may find it an intolerable or unhealthy imbalance, whether in favor of men or women.

For Japanese, in my view, the two ideologies are linked by what I call the role complex, a system of meanings, values, and rules centering around the concept of role. I propose the role complex as essential to building and maintaining Japanese self-identity. A person 'out of role' is in an identity crisis. The role emphasis becomes easily allied with the functional ideology that justifies women's role as distinct from men's, since a role is recognized as such only in differentiation from other roles, and gender is a readily identifiable variable to dichotomize roles. The pervasive idea that each person has a role to play underlies the conservative stance in gender issues.

But this is only one facet of the role complex. Role also entails the value of performance and thus involves a work ethos. This is why the leisurely way of life symbolized, fairly or unfairly, by a housewife watching noontime soap operas or attending 'culture center' classes is belittled by both feminists and their opponents. Life as an uninterrupted work career is an ideal for men and women alike, as long as the work is within role bounds.[46] Furthermore, within the role complex one finds excellence in performance as a key standard of evaluation. Women can transcend their gender handicaps by excelling men in actual performance. There are reasons to believe that the small number of women who have established themselves in the top echelon of the national hierarchy have done so through their performance and competence, outdoing their male peers. Further, the role complex dictates that gender identity be superseded by the role the person has successfully obtained. True, gender for a woman is detrimental to entry into a male-dominated organization and to promotion to an administrative position, but once she gets in, she finds it easy to control her male subordinates because her positional role overshadows her gender.[47] In addition, the role complex allows one to take a surrogate role on behalf of another, as when a woman becomes a surrogate head of the family business when her husband is not available for one reason or another.

It is likely that the two models coexist within the same individual, the same mind, in varying proportions. Consequently, I believe most people, both male and female, in Japan as in other societies, are ambivalent toward gender issues. Emotionally charged opposition to feminism, expressed by a male executive or an older woman, is most likely to be an overreaction to awareness of the unstemmable liberationist tide. Conversely, the less hope an active feminist has of realizing her ideal, the more radicalized she may become. In both cases, there is an ambivalence, I think, in what is openly espoused. Otherwise, it would be difficult to understand the action taken by the well-known leader of the 'pink-helmeted' feminist group. The group had been organized to demand legalization of oral contraceptives and attracted media attention by its idiosyncratic tactics in assaulting male complacency. The leader, after losing a Diet election, made a sudden turnabout to withdraw into home life, to the dismay of her admirers. It is my assumption that most middle-of-the-road Japanese handle their ambivalence by distinguishing *honne* (spontaneous, personal feeling) from *tatemae* (socially acceptable belief or opinion) and alternating between these two sides of their selves. What is needed is a third model that mixes or supersedes the models presented here, something like 'neofunctionalism,' 'neofeminism,' or 'complementary egalitarianism.'

Age and the Life Schedule

The M-curve that has frequently appeared in the foregoing has foreshadowed the significance of age in determining a woman's engagement in and disengagement from the labor market. Typically, a young woman at 20, upon graduation from junior college, finds regular, full-time employment at a company, works as an OL, quits working and marries at 24 or 25, bears and rears about two children, and reenters employment in her late thirties or early forties to work as a part-timer until her fifties, assuming she is not laid off earlier. This pattern is a manifestation of the overall age norm and age-linked life schedule, which is standardized culturally and embedded in the social structure.

Japanese, compared with Americans, tend to be keenly aware of and curious about one another's age. Age is a major topic in greetings and conversation, particularly among older people, but young people for their part are strongly conscious of slight age differences, even of less than a year. Cultural reinforcers abound: terms of address indicative of the addressee's age or relative age difference between addressor and addressee (e.g., elder sister/brother, uncle/aunt, grandpa/grandma, for addressing a stranger as well as actual kin), including the *senpai* (senior member of a group such as a school, an alumni club, a company) designation by a *kōhai* (junior member); speech levels differentiated by the relative age gap between speaker and listener; age-marking ceremonies throughout life, notably, the later-life celebrations beginning with the 60th year of age. In a broad sense, Japan is an age-graded society.

The prevalence of age awareness hinges upon the different life schedules and commitments for men and women in the following ways. First, age enters the seniority system but only insofar as one stays on in a single work organization continuously. Age is thus articulated with seniority increments in status and wages for men, but not for women, whose work careers are typically discontinuous in both time and space. In other words, gender discrepancies in benefits are wider among older than among younger cohorts. Managerial positions are held by older men as a matter of age-seniority articulation, while they are hardly accessible to women of the same cohort, partly because of age-seniority disengagement.

Second, age has bearing on the view of life as a standardized sequence of stages and transitions that inhibits dropping out of a stage, skipping a stage, or reversing the normal sequence. The completion of school education must precede taking a regular job, which in turn should, for men, precede marriage. Dropping out of school, marrying, working, and returning to school – a fairly normal sequence for Americans – would be for Japanese a deviation that spelled a hopeless future. To begin with, school reentry would be even more difficult than job reentry for an overage ex-student. The low rate of school dropouts may have much to do with this irreversibility of lifestage sequence.

Implied here is Mary Brinton's 'condensed timing,' in contrast to 'diffused timing,' over the life cycle for investment in 'human capital.' Diffused timing, characteristic of the contemporary United States, entails 'multiple decision points,' spread over the life cycle, at which to enter or reenter educational institutions and work organizations for human-capital development. Underlying this flexibility is a culturally sanctioned variation in life sequences. Condensed timing, which is institutionalized in Japan, involves structural rigidity with a few key points, strong age barriers, a fiercely competitive examination system, primacy of internal over external labor markets, and so forth.[48] Condensed timing and irreversible sequencing are two sides of the same coin.

In a given sequence, one stage becomes preparation for the next life-transition test, toward an ultimate life goal. For men, the goal is to succeed in entering the most desirable job market and move upward into administrative rank: one's prospects for attaining the goal are directly conditioned by the rank of one's alma mater. For women, both education and employment are preparatory to marriage, which is clearly demonstrated by the choice of a junior college with only mild competition and two years of attendance. As observed by McLendon, marriage is 'the only appropriate life career for women,'[49] and postgraduation employment is undertaken to meet a marriage mate in the workplace, which is encouraged by the employer as well. The company office is 'a way station' one is expected to leave in about four years, and this is when the condensed timing scheme is pressed upon women relentlessly in full force.

'Marriageability' peaks at 25, after which a woman is said to become like a post-Christmas Christmas cake, which cannot be sold. Still single at 30, a woman employee is no longer at a way station but in a 'blind alley' with no prospect for a career job or felicitous marriage.[50] Marriage pressures during the few peak years of marriageability may be the female counterpart to the pressures put on boys for the few years before university entrance examinations. Each test must be passed as a necessary step toward womanhood or manhood. The sharp drop in the M curve is an inevitable result for women of the condensed and irreversible marriage schedule.

Third, age awareness goes with the importance of age-linked social relations. It is well known that individual Japanese careers are the product of joint endeavors by a group of collaborators. (David Plath's term *convoy* and Brinton's *sponsor* come closest to what I have in mind.[51]) The collaborative team is age-linked in two contrasting ways: cross-age and same-age.

Cross-age collaboration is familiar from many works on Japan. Chie Nakane's notion of 'vertical society'[52] sums up age hierarchy as a basis for the strongest bonding and patronage, such as between *senpai* and *kōhai*, *oyabun* (fatherlike boss or leader) and *kobun* (childlike subordinate or follower), *sensei* (mentor or teacher) and *deshi* (disciple or pupil). An individual begins to develop a career as a *kōhai*, *kobun*, or *deshi*, and, as he attains senior status, recycles his experience into the career development of juniors as their *senpai*, *oyabun*, or *sensei*. This vertical arrangement of collaboration affects the placement of a junior person in the job market as well as his promotion, which becomes competitive above a certain level of the bureaucratic hierarchy, replacing the seniority-based promotion automatically granted up to that level. The seniority system of a bureaucracy is interlocked with this vertical joint venture. Women are decidedly disadvantaged in this system, because such alliances are usually within the same sex and there are still too few female seniors, except in gender-segregated job markets, as potential patrons.[53]

Women's role in cross-age collaboration belongs elsewhere. As Brinton has noted, Japan is striking in its 'intergenerational' sponsorship, and this is terminologically symbolized by *oyabun/kobun*.[54] Brinton pays special attention to the educational system, where intergenerational sponsorship looms large, involving parents and teachers around a child, and culminates in a series of 'sponsored contests' in examinations. It is here that a woman becomes a major sponsor as a contestant's mother. After the first goal of marriage is achieved, it is motherhood that occupies a woman's time, energy, and mind.

The M-curve seems to indicate that a woman finds time for outside work when her youngest child enters school, but many mothers I listened to stressed and confirmed that infant care was nothing compared with the educational problems of a school-going child, a son in particular. Whether or not the woman regarded herself as a *kyōiku-mama*, and some did, she took her children's educational success as her heaviest responsibility.

It may be that with her last child's entry into school, a woman finds more free time in a physical sense, but becomes mentally busier. She has to expend more psychic energy, if less physical effort, and this mental preoccupation continues, throughout the child's school career and climaxes at examination time. If so, a part-time job with a flexible schedule and monotonous work content, requiring little concentration, may be the best such a mother can afford.

Maternal identity does not come to an end upon the child's successful performance in examinations, but is lifelong. The child's marriage is particularly high on the mother's list of responsibilities, and a 30-year-old unmarried daughter would be the most painful source of guilt and shame for her. Intergenerational sponsorship thus reinforces condensed timing.

The *kyōiku-mama* commitment can be explained in terms of cultural psychology: it is an identity interchange in which the mother experiences her child's success or failure as her own. Often coupled with this, the *kyōiku-mama* syndrome may also, as noted earlier, be a way to shift one's focus of attention from conjugal frustrations and estrangement to something else. Brinton's hypothesis of intergenerational exchange offers a more rational, less emotive explanation, viewing parental sponsorship of a child's career development as an investment in exchange for security to be provided to the sponsor in her old age by the sponsored.[55]

Few mothers I have met articulate perceptions of this sort of reciprocal payoff, and many explicitly deny such expectations, stressing their lifelong economic security, guaranteed by one type of pension or another. Still, non-monetary payoffs are not ruled out. Emotional support and sympathetic nursing care for aged parents on their sickbeds (and deathbeds, too), which no money can buy, are what they want and what 'only your own child can provide.' Since nursing care falls into the women's job category, 'your own child' means your daughter or daughter-in-law. The daughter is directly in debt, but the daughter-in-law is a vicarious debtor, expected to repay the obligation on behalf of her husband.[56] In either case, this is yet another aspect of cross-generational collaboration that keeps women at home and thereby barred from the organized sector of the job market.

The joint career venture is not confined to cross-age pairs. Even though Japan is better known for the prevalence of junior-senior solidarity, age peers also play a significant collaborative role. This is not surprising in view of the 14 preschool and school years up to high school in which children's social life is concentrated in classrooms and playgrounds with age peers. Peers, if placed outside an arena of rivalry, are indispensable helpers. In the work career, the same-year starters, called *dōki*, are also age peers because of the standard practice of hiring only new graduates at the same time of the year. Generally, *dōki* workers are placed in different sections so that rivalry is minimized and senior-junior solidarity is encouraged. The result is the formation of informal networks among *dōki* peers across sections; the importance of such networks for one's career is augmented with moves up the bureaucratic ladder. Here, too, reciprocal exchange takes place, although in much shorter cycles than in the case of intergenerational exchange. This is a story of men, and male solidarity is among the strongest barriers to women trying to share the job market.

Peer solidarity among women, which also arises among *dōki* entrants into the work force, is less articulated with their careers, for the good reason that for them the workplace is not a final destination but only a way station. As observed by McLendon, possible jealousy over marriage prospects in the company keeps women co-workers apart from one another. Paradoxically, a more stringent rule of seniority prevails among women than among men, bringing junior women under the strict supervision of senior women to compensate for the structural looseness of relationships among women.[57]

Classmate intimacy is carried over into the woman's post-graduation stage of life, as is the case with men. This tie is weakened through marriage and then selectively revived when women become 'maternal peers' sharing the same interest and concerns about their children. In a provincial town, it was found that classmate ties survive and are strengthened among those women whose children are in the same school year and enrolled in the same school.[58] This relationship is double-edged in that, while strongly tied together as best friends, they compete with one another in their children's school performance. Again we are reminded that, for women, even age-peer solidarity is contingent upon mother-child bonding. Whether this relationship is really one of peers is questionable because it contains two sets of peers coupled inter-generationally.

Analyzing the development of gender personality, Nancy Chodorow suggests that 'daughters are likely to participate in an intergenerational world with their mother, and often with their aunts and grandmother, whereas boys are on their own or participate in a single-generation world of age mates.'[59] My analysis of the Japanese case goes against Chodorow's generalization as far as men are concerned; Japanese men are deeply involved in both intergenerational and peer solidarity. Chodorow's proposition holds truer of Japanese women, in that for them intergenerational (mother-child) bonding has primacy over peer solidarity. Furthermore, age-linked solidarity, whether between junior and senior or between peers, is articulated in jobs for men, while for women it is either unrelated to a job or feeds back to maintain separate life-courses for the two sexes, as when a mother devotes herself to her son's education and her daughter's marriage.

CAREER RECOLLECTIONS AND SELF-PORTRAYALS OF TWELVE BUSINESSWOMEN

As mentioned earlier, women have been running their own businesses, incorporated or not, without necessarily contradicting their gender role. And yet numerically, the number of women in business is only a small fraction of the number of men. In 1982 there were over 500,000 Japanese companies with capital of a million or more yen, of which about 17,500 were headed by women. The percentage of women presidents was 2.4 per cent in 1980 and 3.7 per cent in 1984.[60] These figures include those women who have assumed presidencies as part of their domestic responsibility, as successors to husbands who died, fell ill, or opted to work elsewhere for wages. Women have also established their own enterprises, sometimes joined by their husbands or other family members, as exemplified by Ito's sample.[61] But these tend to be in 'female' businesses.

I chose to study a special category of businesswomen who do not fit the traditional type, and who instead received publicity in the news media precisely because of their novelty. These women have either entered male-dominated businesses or launched new enterprises whose character is not yet well known and thus may be regarded as neutral in gender. I assumed these women would personify a confluence of different ideologies and values, of tradition and a new era, of gender dualism and androgyny. The businesswoman operating within Japanese society must accommodate herself to the male-dominated business culture, but at the same time she is likely to identify herself as a leader of women partly because of the publicity she receives as such. She may champion feminism as expected by fellow women, but as an employer she may be more concerned with the functional efficiency of her employees than with justice. Is she more bound by the traditional dictum or more inclined to present a novel self? Where does she stand against the M-curve pattern and age-linked life schedule? It was hoped that the self-portrayals of these businesswomen would serve as a window to the present and future interrelationships between culture, gender, and political economy in Japan.

Table 1. Profiles of Twelve Businesswomen

Subject	Age	Education	Marital status now (then)	Child(ren)	Years of presidency	Staff size
A	75+	C	M(M)	+	15+	100+
B	75–	H	W(M)	+	35+	40+
C	70–	H	D(D)	+	35+	90+
D	65–	H	D(D)	+	25+	15–[b]
E	60+	C	M(M)	+	5–[a]	20+[b]
F	55+	H	S	–	20–[a]	180+
G	50+	JC	M(M)	+	10–	20+
H	50–	U	M(M)	+	10–	15+[b]
I	50–	U	M(M)	+	15–	5+
J	45+	JH	R(D)	0	5+	5+[b]
K	45+	U	D(M)	+	15+	25–
L	40–	U	S	–	10–	5–[b]

Note: The alphabetically coded subject women are ordered by age. Symbols for education: H = high school; C = prewar women's college; U = postwar university; JH = junior high school; JC = junior college. Symbols for marital status: M = married; S = single; D = divorced; W = widowed; R = remarried. Symbols in parentheses refer to the marital status at the time when the business was launched. In the column 'Child(ren)' a plus sign means 'has child(ren),' zero means 'childless,' and a dash means 'not applicable.'

The numbers for the three columns are given by intervals. For age and presidential tenure, five-year intervals are taken, and the closest numbers are given with plus or minus signs. Age 50+, for example, means 50–52 years old, and 50– means 49–48; likewise, 35+ for years of presidency means 35–37 years, and 10– refers to 9–8. For the number of regular employees also, the interval of 5 is adopted: 20+ means 20–22 employees, and 15– refers to 14–13.

[a] Cases where the women had years of entrepreneurial experience prior to undertaking the present business. The number refers only to the present business.

[b] Cases where temporary or part-time workers are hired in addition to the regular staff counted here.

After consulting several people familiar with Japanese businesswomen, I contacted 20 company presidents in Tokyo in the special category described above and subsequently interviewed the 12 who responded favorably to my request to do so.[62] The interviewees varied widely in age (ranging from 39 to 75), marital status, education, the kinds of enterprises they had launched, and the number of years they had been president of their companies. (See Table 1 for a synopsis of background information.) All the companies belonged to the category of *chūshō-kigyō* (medium and smaller enterprises), and they had from 4 to 180 regular employees. The employees of six of the companies were exclusively or predominantly male, the employees of three were exclusively or predominantly female, and the employees of three were relatively balanced between the genders. All the sample companies but one were in service industries; the nature of their businesses is detailed below.

Two summer months in 1985 were spent in interviewing the women presidents and other data gathering. All the interviews took place in company offices, except for one woman, who preferred to meet me in her apartment. Some of the women could spare me no more than an hour, but others were more generous than I had asked, meeting with me for up to four hours, for example. I asked open-ended, suggestive, but not explicitly directive, questions about how they had become involved in their business careers and their experience as businesswomen. I tried to get each informant to tell me about herself spontaneously because I wanted to see what each of them would stress.

Communication was possible to the extent that my informants and I tapped the same fund of cultural information, the collective store of symbolically mediated and embodied meanings, values, and rules, to create rapport and understand one another. This fund also guided each of these women, I assume, in recalling and organizing her experience through self-reflection and in presenting herself in conversation with me. In this sense, the interviews were to capture the 'culturally reconstructed reality,' rather than the phenomenal reality, of the interviewees' careers, loaded with meanings, values, and rules that define, explain, and regulate action and experience.

At the same time, it must be acknowledged that culture, while a collective reservoir of meanings, values, and rules that potentially generates patterned responses from interviewees, also manifests itself only through situationally variable discourses where individual concerns and biases, of both interviewee and interviewer, enter. Furthermore, culture not only constrains the individual in organizing her experience and regulating her action and self-presentation, but also serves her personal ends as symbolic resources to tap, manipulate, and modify in the course of communication.

My professional burden of keeping my informants anonymous is doubled by their conspicuousness to the media, particularly in the area of business. Finding out that financial conditions were a sensitive matter, for example, I stopped asking about them, which left me dependent upon voluntary sharing of information. In the following analysis, only scattered segments of autobiographical narratives appear in context, but lengthy accounts are also given of individual cases when they illustrate an argument. When necessary, individual informants are identified by the letters A to L (see Table 1).

Entrepreneurial Launching and Commitment

All the women had had experience as employees or had been self-employed before undertaking their present businesses. I shall first characterize how they launched their present businesses and became committed. As each informant appears, the kind of enterprise she has launched will be also revealed. Let me begin with some cases.

Mrs. A, a housewife, belonged to a local Christian church, and when an American chaplain sent by the Occupation authorities preached there, she volunteered to interpret for him. She was a graduate of a women's college well known for its English teaching. Her performance was witnessed by a government official, which led to her accepting a government job created in connection with the resumption of Japan's overseas trade. It never occurred to Mrs. A, who was content to be a housewife, that this temporary job would open up a sequence of opportunities and finally lead to her collaborating with American businessmen in establishing an international enterprise. The business specializes in (nongovernmental) inspections of the quality of industrial products to expedite international trade. In the beginning, its clients were almost all Japanese, and orders were for miscellaneous products. But the business has expanded, and it now receives orders from as many as 40 countries. Many clients are foreign governments seeking to import Japanese products. Exporters also use this inspection system to certify their products. The reputation of the company is such that the emblem of its certification is required by many importers around the world. The products to be inspected have also become large-scale, such as an entire oil plant in a Middle Eastern country, and some inspections take as much as two years to complete.

Although she was a co-founder and vice president of the company, Mrs. A, the only woman on the five-member staff, had to turn her hand to everything originally, including looking after a room heater, making tea, typing, interpreting, and sales. Then, to her great surprise, she was nominated to the presidency of the company to succeed the original American president. The company started as a branch of a firm in the United States, but with her assumption of presidency, it became a Japanese company, while the stockholders remain 100 per cent American. Under her presidency, the company has acquired over 100 employees, most of whom are internationally oriented engineers.[63] Success is apparent from the dazzling presidential office in a modern high-rise building at the business center of downtown Tokyo. Annual sales total one billion yen, actually a modest amount in view of the grand-scale contracts involved.

At the outset, the business was a hand-to-mouth operation, and Mrs. A did not think it would survive long or suspect it would expand so far. She took the job as a temporary one and continued to see it as such until she realized she had been with the company for decades. She is still spellbound by the unanticipated careers of both the company and herself.

In this tale, we are struck by the emphasis Mrs. A puts on *circumstantial forces* that moved her into a career track without her awareness. A subjectively set goal and the determination to pursue it are not part of the launching story. Instead, Mrs. A paints herself as a person who accepted whatever opportunities came by, and she marvels at what has in retrospect emerged as a business career. This style of self-presentation characterizes a majority of the autobiographies in their early phases and reaches an extreme with Mrs. I, who heads a company that produces and imports films and has other film-related business. As a child, Mrs. I loved to live in the world of fantasy created by movies, and upon graduation from university, she found a job at a small film-importing/producing company. She was perfectly happy to be an employee blessed with a variety of challenging experiences, relocating from the business department to the production department. But 'every time a new assignment was given, I was placed in a milieu that nurtured and shaped me' toward a business career. 'Step by step, I was pushed by natural forces into one opportunity after another. I yielded passively without resistance.' Mrs. I cited her 'fate' as responsible for her entrepreneurial engagement.

Both Mrs. A and Mrs. I portray themselves as receptors, not explorers, of chance and fate, pushed by circumstances, not by their own wishes or determination. Quite different in outlook from either, and not matching the stereotype of Japanese womanhood, Mrs. K nonetheless joins them in denying initial self-motivation. A successful free-lance journalist and writer, Mrs. K would not have gotten involved with a business career if her husband had not started a sort of stationery store dealing in paper products. Against her wishes, she was 'forced' into taking over the entire business to rescue it from near bankruptcy. She transformed the business into her own, based on her novel idea that paper is a means of communication, as exemplified by greeting cards of the Hallmark type, an idea that was yet to hit the market. Her fame as a journalist carried over into the new business, and her name became attached to the products like a quality brand. Mrs. K has succeeded in bringing the business to solvency.

These three cases all play down self as the central agent in launching a new career, consistent with the generally accepted notion of Japanese personhood. No mention was made by any of the three women of a need for achievement, self-fulfillment, or independence. In contrast, American women entrepreneurs have been found to perceive 'achievement' and 'independence' as the strongest motivations for starting their own companies.[64] Striving for success, assertiveness, goal-orientation, and high energy are also part of the American entrepreneurial profile. American researchers have developed such motivational assumptions into checklists against which a woman may examine her own personality to see if she 'fits' an entrepreneurial career.[65] Similar conclusions have been reached on the basis of a sample of British women entrepreneurs: more than half (ranging from 59 per cent to 76 per cent) find their motives in autonomy, achievement, or dissatisfaction with other alternatives.[66] From the Anglo-American point of view, the above sample of Japanese women might not be regarded as entrepreneurs. But I suggest that the two contrasting findings reflect the cultural biases with which career launching is interpreted and communicated, both sides probably exaggerating culturally sanctioned rationales.

The Japanese style of autobiographical presentation sketched above is generally consistent with my previous findings about professional women. Similarly, too, for ordinary women, in their recollections, marriage tends to lack bridal choice and decision, even in the case of 'love marriages.'[67] What surprises me is that launching an enterprise, which would seem to call for great commitment, is also recalled and presented in such a self-suppressing style. The inconspicuous status accorded to self may characterize both female and male Japanese autobiographies as a matter of cultural style, but the same principle is likely to be more rigidly applicable to women, who need extra justification for launching an unfeminine career to protect themselves from looking selfish.

This does not mean that these women remained uncommitted. As suggested by the above episodes, each woman became the fully committed leader of her company, taking overtime for granted, putting her entire fund of resources into the enterprise, and striving hard for success. Even Mrs. K, who is not sure of the fit between her personality and business career, shows a compulsion to succeed and admits she is having fun running her business. It may be that the woman president, once she sees herself in that role, takes it seriously and exhibits an entrepreneurial drive for achievement and success.

Emphasizing the role of circumstances in the recollection of the launching phase in fact highlights subsequent performance and success. I might further postulate that a Japanese woman, trained in role compliance, does not have to be intrinsically motivated to assume a new role such as that of a businesswoman, since an inner fit is likely to develop subsequent to role assumption.[68] Such role commitment, apart from the initial lack of motivation, confirms what was said about the role complex of Japanese culture. It seems that once placed (or caught?) in the role of business leader, the woman's dormant potential awakens and is harnessed toward the realization of her individual self through a business career. Rather than always contradicting it, role assumption can thus trigger individuality.

If strongly motivated at the very beginning, the autobiographer tends to stress *social mission*, instead of self-interest, as the incentive for entrepreneurial engagement. After starting her work career as an 'office lady,' Miss F subsequently ran a small, one-woman retail dry-goods store, which yielded substantial profit. She then wanted to do something with the money to contribute to society. In collaboration with a senior man, Miss F established a company specializing in computerized information services. Among the services are designing, processing, and storing psychological tests beneficial to society, such as those for safe driving (because she was concerned with the increasing rate of traffic accidents) and for normal child development (because she was worried that young mothers today do not know how to rear children). In the first few years, the business was a continuous loss, surviving only by sacrifice of the president's personal savings and real estate, a condition one could not have tolerated unless driven by something more than self-interest.

Again, the altruistic emphasis is nothing peculiar to businesswomen, but is familiar from the biographies of male business leaders, and male-led companies play up societal, national missions as their mottoes. A nonconformist woman may be under heavier pressure to legitimize her action in altruistic terms, probably to assuage her guilt or to compensate for her 'selfish' appearance. Mrs. A, too, expresses satisfaction at knowing that her business has contributed to Japan's post-war success as an exporter.

In the case of Mrs. B, the altruistic theme reflects an unresolved conflict between gender role and business career. She was a housewife until the end of the war, when her husband, a military officer, was arrested and imprisoned as a war criminal. Mrs. B first took a job and then opened a publishing company specializing in labor relations. It was a Christian mission, she explained, that motivated her to set up such a company. Through this business, the former housewife sought to restore harmony and love between labor and management, which were in confrontation with each other in the post-war era. Mrs. B is successful in running the company, which publishes and sponsors lectures and seminars, and she now heads a 40-member staff. At the same time, she insisted while talking to me that a woman's proper place is the home. Yet she could not explain why she continued to work even after it was no longer necessary for her to earn a living. It is quite likely that being trapped in this dilemma intensifies her Christian altruism. (It might be noted that three out of the twelve businesswomen I interviewed are Christian. This over-representation in the non-native faith may be suggestive of the cosmopolitan outlook in business, as shown below, characterizing the majority of the sample women.)

A third type of launching tale involves *gender barriers in employment*, which fits the more universal pattern in which starting a business is taken to be the only viable alternative for women blocked out of an employed career. Three cases stand out.

Miss L, a university graduate who had worked as a skilled employee for five years, saw no future in remaining with the company, since she was unable to share the prospect of promotion with her male colleagues. She sounded out friends for other employment, only to be encouraged, instead, to go independent. Even though she could not imagine herself running a company, she opened an office in a one-room apartment with a mere 100,000 yen in capital to launch a technical translation business, utilizing her previous experience. (Japanese manufacturers require technical translation of their service manuals and related documents illustrating their products into the language of importers.) Illustrating her success, her present modern office is located in one of the most expensive hillside areas of Tokyo. In addition to her in-office staff, she employs about 15 free-lance technical translators virtually on a regular basis.

Gender barriers are often imputed to the psychological complex of the male ego. As an employee, Mrs. E could not help reminding her boss of the errors and shortcomings in his decisions, which embarrassed, offended, and infuriated him. She realized she was more fitted to lead others than to be a follower and thus launched a successful multi-business career. The latest addition, which has made her famous and is of concern to this essay, was to build and run a hotel-like care home for the elderly, comparable to an American luxury nursing home. While our interview was going on in the lobby, a number of old, frail, but apparently wealthy men and women were sitting around and chatting with visitors. The president, who was often distracted from the interview by her staff asking for her instructions, was undoubtedly a central figure in the whole setup.

Psychological confrontation between a male boss and a female subordinate also drove Mrs. G to start her own business in the travel industry. As a young junior-college graduate, she first took what she thought was a temporary job at a local travel agency, and then worked in larger companies. When her expertise came to be recognized, Mrs. G was promoted to a managerial position but found herself still subjected to the prejudice of male colleagues. 'This is something inevitable in Japanese culture,' she exclaimed. 'The most stupid male is said to be equal to the brightest female.' Her male colleagues – she was the only female manager – would replace her travel projects with their own or steal credit for a job she had accomplished. 'A protruding stake is pounded down, indeed!' Another company invited Mrs. G to become its vice president, an extraordinary move in the male-dominated travel industry, but after bringing her in, the president, a newcomer in the field, behaved as if he would rather do without her, 'probably because he was irked that people knew my name better than his.' His masculine pride could not stand this humiliation. Mrs. G accordingly decided that 'in order to work fully among men, you must be independent' and opened her own travel agency in a condominium.

In all these cases, gender inequality in employment practices in combination with circumstantial inducement compelled women to embark on entrepreneurial careers as the only avenue to get ahead. In other words, the presence of women entrepreneurs is not necessarily an index of women's liberation, but can be a sign precisely of discrimination. It is only natural that resentment was part of the entrepreneurial motivation for these and other women. Mrs. G is most articulate in expressing her indignation about the gender dualism prevailing in the labor market.

As we have proceeded from circumstantial involvement to social mission to gender barriers, assertion of the woman's self in entrepreneurial launching has come to the fore. The fourth and last type refers to the extreme pole of *self-assertion*.

Mrs. H, a law school graduate, found herself a frustrated housewife and irritable *kyōiku-mama*, and above all became impatient with her economic dependence upon her husband, saying to herself, 'There is no money whatsoever that I am truly free to spend on my personal needs.' Her stress peaked when her husband was diagnosed – actually misdiagnosed as was disclosed later – with cancer. With no hope of finding employment better than dishwashing, a typical middle-aged part-timer's job, Mrs. H set an entrepreneurial goal. Gender barriers in employment thus entered her decision.

Mrs. H tested herself by starting out with a short-lived coffee shop. In the meantime, while shopping around for a residential condominium (the Japanese housewife is responsible, often solely, for making decisions on such purchases), she noticed a big gap in information between salesmen and customers: the male sales staff were insensitive to the needs of female customers, who are *the* managers and buyers of their homes, while the latter were too intimidated to express their thoughts. As an expert housewife, Mrs. H became convinced that she could do a better job selling condos by providing the kind of information wanted by fellow housewives. She began to plan her career in real estate and took examinations to acquire the necessary licenses and desirable credentials. Gender and age barriers continued to block opportunities for Mrs. H, then in her late thirties, in the male-dominated real estate business, until she persuaded a man to accept her on a tentative basis as a temporary member of a previously all-male sales staff. Her employer accepted her proposal to sign a contract to sell condominiums, and this was the beginning of her independence and her successful career as president of a company specializing in housing sales and housing consultation, meeting the demands of both 'users' and developers/contractors. She took over the company started by her husband and changed it into a new business, as in the case of Mrs. K, but in her case she was eager to do so. With an impressive record of accomplishments, Mrs. H now leads 16 regular staff members and about 180 part-timers, all women. Mrs. H is exceptional in stressing the need for 'independence' as the primary goal, not just a means, of her launching her enterprise.

Although very different from Mrs. H in age, education, and many other aspects of her background, Mrs. C belongs in the same category. Her self-assertive launching of a business of her own deserves to be looked at in some detail. She had been deserted by her husband and was supporting her daughter and herself by buying silk and rayon from producers in a provincial city, having the material worked into embroidered souvenirs in another city, and wholesaling these to stores in resort towns. While on a business trip shortly after the Occupation began, she happened to hear from a fellow passenger on a train that American servicemen were interested in buying souvenirs, and she lost no time in locating the main post exchange catering to U.S. military personnel and their families in Tokyo's Ginza.

'Two MP's were standing in front of the PX building,' she recalls. 'In those days, we women were told to run away from Americans, but why should I? I did not know what to do, just stood there for an hour, and then went home. On my way home, I said to myself, "I was not begging for things but for work." So I went back the next day and found a Japanese employee. I explained why I was there, and this man welcomed me, saying the store had been looking for someone just like me! It was sheer chance or luck that an amateur like me got in so easily.'

She was trusted at once, and the PX contracted to supply confiscated silk for her to have made into embroidered goods such as handkerchiefs and scarves. Being an amateur, she had to learn the technical details from the embroiderers, as well as how much profit she should charge. 'I did try hard [*doryoku*], and worked seriously [*majime*].' She commuted all on her own between the PX and the manufacturers, carrying on her back a bundle of material and goods wrapped in a *furoshiki* (wrapping cloth symbolic in this context of a person trying to survive under the socially and economically formidable conditions then prevailing). Seeing this one day, a U.S. serviceman offered her a car ride. 'All my effort was rewarded,' she says. From this beginning, the business went on to produce a wide range of things, including slips and gowns. She now had to learn something about dressmaking herself, and she got a graduate of a dressmaking school to accompany her to lessons from a professional designer.

In the meantime, she was turning a good profit, primarily from leftover pieces of the material supplied by the PX. 'To be honest with you, I had great fun making so much money,' she says. Her own family joined her in the business (*kazoku-gurumi*), and by the time the Occupation forces left, she had succeeded in building up her credibility (*shin'yō*) and establishing her *jiban* (solid support base). Turning to the domestic market, she opened her own store selling baby clothing and consequently expanded her business to emerge as one of the first few successful women entrepreneurs in postwar Japan. Now she has several factories working for her as subcontractors, with about 800 workers sewing dresses designed by her full-time staff, and sells her products through prominent national department store chains.

Mrs. C tells this success story with no false modesty or hesitancy. She credits her success to her foresight, fearlessness and hard work. She believes her career had its roots in her childhood, explaining, 'I was a shrew or tomboy.' In talking to me, Mrs. C showed little feminine inhibition in her speech or demeanor. She said she was no different from a man and repeatedly stressed that there is no 'male' or 'female' in the world of business. For her, transcendence of gender meant a woman becoming manlike, however, which suggests that in her mind self-assertiveness is intrinsic to masculinity. 'People say I am like a man,' she told me proudly. 'They say I talk crisply like a man.'

For both Mrs. H and Mrs. C, economic necessity was the primary initial concern. The one sought to achieve financial independence, the other simply to survive. They are both sure that making a profit is the goal of business, and they show no sign of self-effacement or altruism. Underlying this attitude, which is more or less free from cultural and gender constraints, both had good reason to want to go beyond their domestic, wifely identities. Mrs. H got married while she was a university junior and jumped into full-time housewifery without any qualms about wasting her legal training. After years of compulsive homemaking, she came to realize that there was no sense of accomplishment to be gained from the endless cycle of housework – 'making and unmaking' – or from the hobbies and studies she had tried. Overcommitment to the domestic role thus seems to have turned into unambivalent alienation from it. Mrs. C had to shed her domestic identity for quite another reason. Her husband left her to live with another woman and without her knowledge removed her name and that of their daughter from the house register by forging the family seal.[69] She quietly waited until after the war, when she sued him for damages and won. The bitter divorce engineered by her husband's betrayal and deception may have contributed to Mrs. C's surmounting her gender identity and ambivalence about self-assertiveness. She is different in this respect from all the other divorced women in this survey, for whom divorce was their own choice. It is interesting to note that marriage was a love match for both Mrs. C and Mrs. H. The latter's marriage in particular was a rebellious one, not blessed by her family, and her compulsive domesticity prior to launching into business may have been a way of justifying her rebellion.

Niches and Resources

Whatever the initial incentives, every entrepreneur, regardless of gender, must find or cut out a niche that matches her resources and expertise. How does womanhood function as a sorter in locating niches? In this section I attempt to identify the niches that my informants found or created and the resources they mobilized to adjust to those niches.

Of the twelve women, all but two found their niches in one aspect or another of *communication service*, centered around information to be searched out, produced, stored, organized, translated, printed, transmitted, or distributed. Included here, as we know from the above accounts, are technical inspection to certify the quality of industrial products for importers and exporters; publication and sponsoring of seminars; computerized data processing and storage; translation of Japanese engineering manuals into foreign languages; and film production and importation. The travel agency run by Mrs. C may well be understood as a communication service too, as may Mrs.

J's marketing research business, in which she and her staff use 'group interviews' to elicit the needs and demands of potential consumers. The advertising company headed by Mrs. D is also a communications industry par excellence. The most articulate about this feature of business is Mrs. K, whose business is in the production and sales of what she calls 'communication goods' such as greeting cards.

I was told that companies under female management tend to assume *katakana* names, usually derived from foreign words or at least giving that impression. Indeed, eight companies in my sample have *katakana* names,[70] and one of their presidents volunteered to elaborate on the meaning of her company's name for my benefit. Six of the eight are actually connected either directly or indirectly with foreign countries, as clients, suppliers, or, in the case of international travel, as hosts. In other words, the communication services typically involve *intercultural mediation* between Japan and foreign companies or governments – American, European, Middle Eastern, Chinese, Southeast Asian. It is no coincidence that half of my sample informants were trained in foreign languages, either in school or elsewhere. Foreign languages give women the most powerful resource to compete in the male world, said Miss L, since 'no man can do anything about women's language ability.' The best proof is Mrs. A, who really does not know the technical aspects of her business and manages her company mainly through her ease in communicating and negotiating with foreign clients. 'In my business I have never felt handicapped by being female,' she says. 'Quite the contrary, as the only woman in the [otherwise] entirely male group, I have been treated especially well. It may be because a foreign language is used frequently in talking with our customers.'

By mobilizing their linguistic or other communicative skills, these women found their niches in areas bridging cultural borders. Mrs. A again represents an extreme: she heads a company not only dependent upon foreign clients but inherited from an American predecessor and owned entirely by American shareholders. She credits the ease with which she has been able to manage the company without being handicapped by her gender to this unusual background. Further, the original models of this and some of the other businesses, such as marketing research and greeting cards, came from abroad.

A communications business becomes possible when communication gaps or 'crevices' are perceived. The most alert to such crevices was Mrs. H, who found her niche in filling communication gaps between housing consumers and housing developers in the domestic market. She calls hers an *interstitial industry* (*sukima sangyō*). Most of the other women's information businesses are also interstitial and meant to fill gaps between vendor and customer, worker and manager, producer and audience, visitor and host, well-wisher and receiver (through greeting cards). In such businesses, as one of the presidents emphasized, feminine sensitivity is an advantage.

Femininity as a resource is best utilized by the luxury nursing home run by Mrs. E. Assisted by the all-female staff and part-timers, the president herself looks after the residents, providing care for the incapacitated. This is a woman's business, she declares, because no elderly person, male or female, would want to be touched by men, and no man would like to touch the bodies of the aged, male or female.

At first thought, there seems to be nothing in common between communication industries and the nursing business. However, both involve human communication, after all, either with words or by touching. I speculate that one of women's primary niches is in human communication and human relations, where they can be resourceful.

The 'female advantage' is recognized by a whole range of women, from a conservative functionalist to an egalitarian feminist, in a sense broader than that proposed by George Murdock and Caterina Provost.[71] Mrs. E represents the functionalist view of the male-female division of role territory and makes a successful business out of this division. Others espouse the feminine contribution in opposition to such stereotypes of gender dualism. 'Both male dominance and male-female dichotomy are out of date,' Mrs. K says. 'The economy, like everything else, is destined to change, and, in the future, feminine, sensitivity ought to be learned and shared by men.' Mrs. K, who has predicted an upcoming era of women in a book she wrote, is the most eloquent advocate of this feminist ideology. 'From now on it is the female perspective that will open up new fields of business, because the male perspective has already been exhausted.' The female perspective is symbolized as 'soft(ware)' in contrast to male 'hard(ware),' or as 'heart' as opposed to 'thing.'

Heart versus thing and soft versus hard may be oversimplified polarities, but this calls attention to a single case in my sample that deals with 'things.' Mrs. C, as mentioned earlier, designs, manufactures, and sells dresses and appears uniquely masculine in speech and comportment. She characterizes herself as no different from men while at work, not like a woman whose speech is ridden with long-winded honorifics. She makes no apology about making a profit being the most important purpose of business, since 'business is not charity work.' She stresses that a company president, whether male or female, must always monitor how the business is going, above all by keeping track of 'numbers.' The measure for success or failure seems unambiguous: 'how many pieces have been sold, how many are in stock, and how many returned.' In no other case is the measure that clear and simple. Instead, the majority of my informants emphasized the importance of nonpecuniary profit such as trust and reputation, as will be touched upon later.

Styles of Management

This section is divided into external and internal management. Again, some of the remarks below are relevant more to Japanese culture, shared by men as well, and others more to gender, characterizing the female management style.

External management. External management refers to strategies for perceiving, evaluating, and handling the world outside the company, or people other than the company's own personnel. Included here are markets, clients, patrons, suppliers, banks, retailing outlets, business associations, the business community (*gyōkai*), rivals, and the general public. What is most emphasized by all is the benefit of *human relations* to business. A number of informants referred to human relations or networks as capital to draw upon or as profit gained through transactions. Particularly important are relations with corporate clients, but also mentioned were mentors, patrons, former employers, former bosses, and benefactors. These are predominantly male.

Starting from scratch, as most of my informants did, the first customer is all-important; if satisfied with one's work, he or she will in turn introduce a second and third customer, and thus snowballing takes effect. Mrs. I, the film importer and producer, describes her career as a cumulative expansion of her client network through introductions and word of mouth. She attaches importance to every kind of social gathering, and attends several, including a Buddhist class. Even Mrs. E, who is not shy about her native talent, ascribes her success to long, multiple chains of introductions. 'Nothing could have started without introductions,' she says.

Lacking organized sponsorship, these women built networks of sponsors by their personal sociability. It seems that men are willing personally to sponsor independent businesswomen, whereas within the organized job market they keep job-linked sponsorship to their own sex. This is in contrast to the organized resistance of financial institutions to women entrepreneurs encountered by some of my informants at the earliest stages of their enterprises. Banks have little trust in women, assuming their businesses to be no more than feminine pastimes. Only after a new business succeeds in creating its own market, as in the case of Mrs. K, do banks begin to rethink their male-centered loan policies.

Among my informants there is a tendency for human relationships, once formed, to last a long time. Social credit based upon *relational duration* is idiomatically expressed as 'not the kind of people you got acquainted with only yesterday' (*kinō ya kyō no tsukiai ja nai*). Mrs. D, an advertising agent, has been receiving orders from a Mitsubishi company for 30 years. A regular, stable relationship with fixed clients is typical of my sample companies. 'I deal with ten companies regularly, which is all I can handle,' says Miss L. To ensure relational durability, one must socialize and chat with clients or participate in their social club reunions. In the publishing business, durability may be secured by long-term subscribers. Mrs. B singlehandedly recruited such members through personal solicitation.

The longer the relationship lasts, the more advantage accrues to it, since the person in the client company with whom one has been in personal contact will have risen up the organizational ladder. Older informants in particular refer to 'old friends' who now, as executives of big companies, can do favors, and more substantial favors than before, more easily.

More efforts are made to retain and rekindle the customer network by those who are in established male industries, and thus are exposed to fierce competition with male rivals, than by those who are freer from competition because of the novel character of the industry. Among the former are advertising and travel agents. In the travel business, client relations are inevitably short, but Mrs. C tries to overcome this problem by her style of customer management. She goes out of her way to intensify interaction through pre-tour orientation classes, post-tour reunions, and follow-up correspondence, including sending birthday cards according to the computer-retrievable information on the clients' vital statistics. The trip itself involves elaborate interaction between the travel agency staff and travelers, resulting in the latter's complete dependence upon the former throughout. The customer's travel plan is perfected in advance, with an hour-by-hour schedule and instructional information on sites to be visited, all printed in diary form, and around-the-clock service is provided during the trip. All this reminds me of the 'around-the-body care' provided by a nurturant wife to her baby-like husband in the house.[72] The payoff has been customers returning to Mrs. C repeatedly over the years and bringing her the latest news on planned conferences or similar events requiring travel, whereupon she starts a travel plan before other agents catch on. Mrs. C's customer management exemplifies an extension of service above and beyond the bounds of a business transaction.

In order to create new relations and to maintain old ones, the president must be acceptable as a person, since her personal approach is crucial in a small-scale business. Her attractiveness as a woman counts, as I can infer from the good looks of all twelve informants. More culturally relevant is personally presenting a *low profile.* No informant is consistently self-assertive; even someone like Mrs. C, who is atypically self-assertive and masculine, referred to herself as an 'amateur.' A low profile was typical of the majority.

Humility and self-denigration are imbedded in the culture of reciprocal obligation (rather than reciprocal right) as represented by *on* (a moral sense of being in debt, which calls for acts of repayment). The history of a business that started with nothing whatsoever is a history of running into many benefactors whose help was indispensable for surviving and getting ahead in the ruthless world of business. A sense of debt and gratitude leads to humility and self-abnegation. Many of my informants look back on their lives in the light of this cultural formula of self-abnegation and gratitude in connection with their debts. The extreme is Mrs. D, who literally started from scratch, not only as a woman but as a post-war repatriate from China and a divorcée. She landed at an advertising company as an employee, which led her into contact with 'many' clients who recognized her talent and encouraged her to start her own advertising business. These people offered to sponsor her switching from her employer and taught her how to manage the business. Soon she found herself flooded with orders. Now she runs a company with 14 male employees. Looking back, Mrs. D cites a long list of men, including a former prime minister, whom she calls *onjin* (benefactor) or *onshi* (mentor). Her published autobiography is a record of meeting such benefactors, who have enabled her to launch a career in the advertising business and to achieve a series of successful transactions. Crediting others for her success, Mrs. D denigrates herself and her company with extraordinary humility, calling herself a 'fool' and trivializing her company down to 'mere snot.' If she speaks in that way to an outsider like me, who can be of no benefit to her business, she is likely to belittle herself with even greater hyperbole when speaking to business associates or clients. Humility is often associated with femininity, and some women extend it to female helplessness, especially in business. The helpless woman who 'did not know right from left,' who was 'about to fall apart,' evidently stimulated gallantry in the men who were around, even in potential rivals. In this context, too, the female advantage was stressed: thanks to her gender, the woman was able to present herself as helpless and to solicit help and advice from men.

In other words, women, while more constrained than men by the cultural norm of self-denigration, can also turn it to their advantage by using it as a strategy, particularly in transactions with men. My informants were cautious not to hurt the pride of the men they came across and decided that feminine humility and helplessness was the best strategy to boost it. 'If a woman tries to do business on an equal footing with men, pretty soon she will be crushed under a hail of kicks and blows. So, I try not to stand in their way, not to be obtrusive. Yes, that's the way I behave. Otherwise I would be ostracized ... After all, this is a male society,' Mrs. D says. Even Mrs. H, who betrayed no sign of self-abnegation, admitted that a woman, when she offers advice or a suggestion, must appear as if she were soliciting the other's opinion. Otherwise, 'he would lose face, being instructed by a mere woman.' Under these circumstances, the cultural value of humility is cynically manipulated in one's *omote* (externally presented) behavior, consciously differentiated from one's *ura* (hidden) thinking and feeling. Whether as a source of inhibition or as an object of manipulation, and probably as both, the theme of self-effacement appears central to women's business management, as well as in their launching stories.

The low profile further involves a defensive and passive, instead of aggressive, management style. Avoidance of aggressive strategies was mentioned by many, and this was often attributed psychologically and physiologically to their gender in contrast to male aggression. It was frankly admitted that the male physique and belligerence cannot be matched by women. Miss L, though the youngest, always anticipates the limits of her energy, she says. Mrs. J, a marketing researcher, is convinced that men are better fighters: 'They are different in their bone structure. They are accustomed to fighting, born to fight, love games and warfare. I love games too, but need to take breaks to rest.' The above finding, however, suggests that behind the physiological explanation lies the cultural preconception of aggression as incompatible with womanhood.

The *defensive strategy* means avoidance not only of getting involved in fierce competition but of taking risk, which counters our image of the 'entrepreneur.' Risk is avoided because, according to my informants, a woman, unlike a man, cannot afford a single mistake, since she will be unable to bounce back physically or socially, and because a woman president is too concerned with the security of her employees and their families to take risk. Consequently, the woman manager, I was told, instead of having herself recognized through quick, dramatic tactics, resorts to a more inconspicuous, slow tactic of waiting passively for her name to spread by word of mouth.

The aggressive management supposedly typical of men is exemplified by *settai gaikō*, extravagant dinner entertainments for clients, attended by geisha. The reason my informants preclude this familiar strategy from their repertory seems, however, to have little to do with male-female differences in aggressiveness. At a geisha party, there is a conspicuous role division between women and men: women are entertainers and waitresses, men are guests, entertained and waited upon. A woman president would be even more out of place amid this sexually charged dichotomizing than a wife would be.[73] To participate there comfortably, she would have to tailor her presence into the role either of a male client or of a female entertainer. That my informants stay away from such parties is understandable. One exception is Mrs. D, ironically the most self-denigrating woman of all, and her *settai* performance takes an extremely feminine form. Being a tee-totaler and having learned to play a *shamisen* as a hobby, Mrs. D escapes coerced drinking by contributing a musical performance! Temporarily, she becomes a geisha.

Mrs. D is a good example of those who play distinctly female roles in managing external relations. One of her extra-business services is to act as a matchmaker for the sons and daughters of her clients and associates. She explains that this is 'a small repayment' for the great favors she has received in business. 'I cut down on sleep to work hard at something that has nothing to do with my business. Sometimes I think I'm stupid, but then I decide that this is a proper way to repay my debts, and that if I didn't do. this, I would be unable to reach a nice place after death,' she says. But although she cites moral obligation and religious sentiment as her motives in providing this extra-business service, it is easy to suppose that it pays off in business since, as she tells me, many renowned families in business and government have been among her marriage clients.

Avoidance of outward aggression is accompanied by a stress on inward discipline or sincerity as a clue to recognition and success. 'Nothing is impossible,' says Mrs. A from her personal experience, 'if one tries hard enough with sincerity.' Many informants share the optimistic conviction that one's sincerity in doing one's best will win over the toughest adversary. Sincerity is at the heart of the Japanese ideal self shared by both women and men, and yet it is often discussed as an inner strength compensating for outer weakness, such as the lack of aggressiveness presumed to be characteristic of women.

Internal management. Turning to internal management styles, we see the woman as an employer and boss, which is naturally quite different from our image of a woman as a job hunter, frustrated employee, or contract negotiator subject to male dominance and prejudice. Let us consider the criteria used by the informants for employee recruitment and reward. All the informants agree that ability is the most important consideration in hiring, and record of performance most important in determining pay increases and promotion, but not all of them adhere exclusively to *ability/performance*, several conceding to the seniority rule to some extent. The concession is explained either positively as an encouragement of company-wide organizational identification and solidarity or negatively as acquiescence in the prevalent convention of Japan or as humane obligation. But all subscribe to the principle of ability and performance as a matter of *honne* or *tatemae*, and a majority practice it.

The primacy of economic considerations implied in this aspect of internal management may reflect the size of the enterprises more than anything else.

Like most *chūshō-kigyō* (medium-to-small-size enterprises), including both female- and male-headed companies, the sample companies hire experienced/skilled workers when need arises, instead of hiring inexperienced college graduates at the standard hiring time. They simply cannot afford to train new employees. They can only employ 'troops ready to fight' (*soku senryoku*). For the same reason, many rely on part-timers and external pools of skilled labor, including free-lancers employed on a contractual basis, thus minimizing regular internal staff. (It should be noted, however, that such contractual arrangements tend to be regular, fixed, and stable. Miss L hires the same external translators to work at home and consistently pairs each translator with a particular client to take advantage of his/her familiarity with the company's products and styles.)

Decisions on wages, bonuses, and promotion are made single-handedly by the presidents, a clear indication that none of the companies has a union and that the owner-president has the financial basis for such autocracy.

Internal management further involves *gender issues*. All of my informants believe in gender equality, but only in the sense that competence and contribution are what count, regardless of gender. They are strongly opposed to legal protection for women in hiring practices. The newly introduced Equal Employment Opportunity Law (EEOL) referred to earlier was blasted by one informant as 'disastrous to the Japanese economy.' Another remarked, 'All right! If you want equality, let it be equal in everything. Don't be ridiculous, demanding privileges and equality at once. Don't be spoiled.' She dismissed the new law as relevant only to public institutions.

'Spoiled' is my translation of being in a state of *amae*. This word was frequently used by several informants to characterize women employees. 'What infuriates me most is a woman's *amae*,' said one, a radical egalitarian who believes that there should be no division of labor by gender and that men should be free to be house husbands. Her severity in criticizing female employees comes precisely from her conviction of the need for equality. Less severe informants predicted with sympathy that the EEOL would be harder on women than on men. It was also felt that female workers were being overpaid, doing injustice to much more deserving male workers. My informants thus enunciate nonprotectionist egalitarianism, which joins with economic realism from the point of view of an employer. They are open and guilt-free in demanding this version of equality because they are aware of themselves as models ('I tell my women workers to "look at me as a good example"') whose achievements have resulted entirely from personal competence, performance, and effort.

As sex-neutral criteria, competence and performance, coupled with the immediate needs of the company, seem to end up revealing rather than burying gender differences and gender-bound assets or liabilities. This is reflected in the gender distribution of employees for the sample companies: six companies are exclusively or predominantly male, three are exclusively or predominantly female, and three have relatively balanced gender distributions. Nine out of the twelve are extremely skewed in favor of one sex, and the male bias is twice the female bias. Such sex-biased distributions were justified by my informants in terms of role fitness (*tekisei*). Further, the allocation of positions and tasks is equally skewed. One company employs 180 people, only 3 of whom are female; they are high-school graduates hired to serve tea and do simple clerical work – typical OLs.

Another company, with more than a dozen male staff members, recently dismissed its only female employee. 'The OL has been replaced by OA [office automation],' said its president, meaning that 'from now on men must do everything, including tea serving and toilet cleaning.' When I visited her office for a second interview, a young man brought me a cup of tea. The discharged OL, the worst ever hired, 'would not bother to pick up litter' lying around in the office, and when the president picked it up, the girl 'did not even apologize.' Earlier, the president had had better luck with women employees, but 'they all quit to marry, and I myself arranged marriages for them.' And 'girls do not hesitate to move to any company that offers a penny more.' The informant went as far as to say that she would welcome a woman determined to stay and aggressive enough to 'hijack' the company.

Except for companies that are exclusively or predominantly female, administrative positions are nearly monopolized by men. Several presidents expressed their wish to hire more women and to promote more women and regretted that they could not afford to. One company makes no sex discrimination in its hiring policy and, in advertising job vacancies, does not indicate sex preference. Yet its employees are predominantly male, because 'no woman has applied for an engineering job.'

Although they impose rather severe standards in terms of ability, the women presidents resemble other Japanese managers in likening a company to a family. Idiomatic expressions like 'eating together from the same rice cooker' were used by more than one informant. This particular expression, by the way, is not always figurative: in some cases workers do stay overnight at the office to meet a deadline and cook and eat there, as in the case of the film-producing company. Sharing the same cooker is always the case with Mrs. E, who runs the care-home hotel. She referred to herself and her employees as being 'ready to die together [*shinaba morotomo*].'

Family-like management was identified as the Japanese style of management being learned by foreigners. 'In my company, too,' said Mrs. A, 'I have a couple of foreign visitors studying the Japanese style of management. They are so eager to learn things Japanese and are becoming more Japanese than the Japanese.'

The family image makes the woman president symbolic of *maternal nurturance*. This is best represented by Mrs. A, the oldest of the twelve, who sees a parallel between being the president of a company and the mother of a family. She feels she has been raising the company the same way she raised her children. Her maternal concern for her employees is evident in the pride she takes in being the first to detect signs of illness in them and advise them to rest or, 'as a surrogate parent, take them to the company hospital. It is necessary to ensure that employees stick with you not only during a boom but in a slump as well,' she observes. Such relationships can be built up only with a motherly approach.

Mrs. A handled a labor dispute in motherly fashion and managed the union toward voluntary disbandment. As she recalls, the company, then under U.S. management, faced the threat of strike, but the American president refused to meet the union leaders, as the latter demanded, without being accompanied by a lawyer. Mrs. A, then vice president, volunteered to substitute for him and met with a union leader by herself. Her sympathetic attempt at persuasion was successful, and the union gave up on striking and gradually dissolved itself. 'In the family, the children, when grown up, begin to disagree with their parents. So do the employees. Conflict would only be aggravated if handled in a stiff confrontation.'

For Mrs. A, mothering goes with sincerity in managing company crises. She was not afraid to meet with a union leader all by herself 'because nobody would beat up someone who holds no hostility,' she explains. 'Facing him with whole-hearted sincerity [*seishin seii butsukaru*] was a breakthrough.'

Naturally, older informants accept and play the role of mother more readily than younger women. (Two older women fed me during their interviews with their own cooking.) The feeling of maternal love for employees was expressed as *kawaii* (cute, lovable). Even young presidents admit they are expected to be maternal whether they like it or not. Female employees in particular, I was told, want the assurance of maternal support to heal the emotional injuries they suffer in the workplace from time to time.

Maternal nurturance is said to have nothing to do with the gender of the manager. In Japan, both male and female presidents are expected to assume a maternal, not paternal, role, according to my informants. If so, the label *paternalism*, commonly used to characterize Japanese management, should be replaced by *maternalism*. Both sexes thus seem to share what Hayao Kawai calls the 'maternal principle.'[75]

Paradoxically, Mrs. H, the former frustrated, compulsive housewife and mother, is again exceptional in that she does not see any sign of 'maternal instinct' in herself. Maternal care for employees, in her opinion, is nothing but meddling. 'I think the employer's interest is different from the employee's,' she says.

All the informants, including Mrs. H, try to 'teach' their subordinates the 'know-how' of their business. For a relatively larger enterprise like that of Mrs. C, staff education includes management. Mrs. C wants to promote a woman to departmental chief, a position now monopolized by male staff, but not until the female managerial candidate learns to delegate some tasks to her subordinates instead of trying to do everything herself.[76] Again, our entrepreneurial women seem to follow the Japanese convention that expects a superior (*jōshi*) to assume a parental role to 'bring up' his/her subordinates (*buka o sodateru*). In this respect, far from handicapping it, their gender facilitates a leadership role.

Sexual involvement between a female employer and a male employee, not uncommon in the United States, did not appear in my informants' conversations, except that two older women alluded to mild forms of erotic fantasy. One referred to a company dinner party where, because of her sex, her presence aroused excitement among the male staff in a way that a male president's would not have done. The other woman mentioned some men on the staff wanting to have affairs with her. Both women, however, appeared to take such fantasies as amusing and to handle them with motherly indulgence. I am tempted to speculate that maternal nurturance is a culturally available defense against sexual vulnerability on the part of both employer and employee. By taking a maternal role for herself and placing male subordinates into a filial position, the woman president can symbolically structure an otherwise unstructured, unpredictable sexual relationship. There are indications that maternal symbolism is a way of transcending sexuality and the gender issue itself. Mrs. C, whose demeanor is most masculine, is also maternal toward her subordinates and is confident that she can tell them anything she wants in order to discipline them 'as long as you love them [*aijo ga areba*].' Needless to say, the 'love' here is maternal, nothing sexual.

Internal management further involves the problem of *authority*. The president's authority derives from her exclusive power to hire and fire personnel and to determine wages and promotion; her privileged access to clients, banks, and senior leaders in the business world (this explains why human relations are cherished as property); and, in most cases, her ownership of capital. In addition, the novelty and scarcity of female presidents tempts the media to feature them in such a way that their individual personalities overshadow the organizational aspects of a company. Moreover, some of my informants are the authors of autobiographical or business-related books, which adds to the impression of an autocracy.

A closer look reveals another aspect of presidential authority held by a woman. Maternal nurturance often comes close to indulgence and leniency at the expense of managerial authority. Some female presidents find it difficult to assert their authority and to exercise leadership vis-à-vis male employees. The general strategy seems to be to not interfere with technical work. Responding to my question about what it was like to work under a woman president, a staff member of Mrs. B's publishing company said that, under Mrs. B, the staff are free to exercise their own creativity and to enjoy a sense of full participation. Mrs. B, on the other hand, confesses that she cannot assert her authority and is unable to give orders. As a result, she tends to perform tasks that should be delegated to the staff, including janitorial work. In the same vein, Mrs. G feels unable to demand that her employees put up with hardship unless she burdens herself with greater hardship. 'There is absolutely no intention on my part to let them work hard and to exploit them. This, I think, is the weakness or strength of a woman entrepreneur who has lived in Japanese society.' She wishes to free herself from this culturally ingrained gender bind.

Both age and education make a difference in assuming authority, but the latter seems more important: an old high-school graduate has more difficulty than a young college graduate in managing college-graduated men. Men are more difficult to handle than women. Egalitarian ideology is another variable interfering with the authoritative role. Mrs. K, well-educated and confident of the business as her own creation, found herself unable to refer to her employees, in speaking to an outsider, without the honorific *san* as demanded by Japanese speech convention, to express humility about her own employees. It took a long time before she began to use the *yobisute* (unhonorific) form. Underlying this is her general guilt associated with the hierarchy. She felt guilty, for example, about receiving a higher salary than her subordinates. Mrs. K attributes all this to her liberal, egalitarian ideology, which her friends claim disqualifies her as a top executive. From my observations, I think this egalitarian attitude is more characteristic of female than male leaders.

Maternal leniency is one way of managing the authority problem, as suggested by the self-portrayal of Mrs. D, who transmutes authority into joking relations. 'You dumb fool [*bakatare*]!' or 'drop dead!' she yells at her male staff. 'Nobody takes me seriously, everybody makes a fool of me [*nameru*],' she added, again jokingly, in telling me this. The word *nameru* implies a total lack of respect and even a reversed hierarchy between employer and employee, but she really meant *amaeru*, as revealed by my questioning. This blurring of *amaeru* into *nameru* reveals that the desire for maternal indulgence may contain an element of disdain. Evidently, the staff enjoy this state of affairs. This can be inferred from the staff's reaction when Mrs. D had fallen ill, could not hope for a quick recovery, and invited in an acting male president with the intention of having him replace her eventually as formally titled president. The new administration 'terrified' the staff, resulting in their joint resignation. Mrs. D had to return.

What has been said in this section seems to contradict my earlier remark about the authoritative role, once assumed, overshadowing the gender of its player. I had in mind the women in large bureaucratic organizations, typically government officials. Apparently, these women are protected from gender stigma by the rigid bureaucratic structure. Lacking an organizational wall of protection, our businesswomen may be more exposed to the uninhibited prejudice or forcefulness of men.

Managerial success depends upon the caliber of the second in command. Unless the staff is exclusively female, the vice president is usually male, and this reversed gender hierarchy may give rise to psychological tensions. Miss F, for example, is teamed with an older man who is more experienced than she is in the business. It was this male vice president who received me first and took me into an inner room where the president was waiting. They sat side by side in front of me, which made me ill at ease, unsure of whom to address my questions to. As I feared, the vice president kept talking, as if he were a Samoan 'talking chief.' Finally, running out of patience, the president interrupted to ask me if I was getting the kind of information I was looking for. This gave me an opportunity to emphasize my purpose of studying women presidents, which forced him into silence. The president, a smart woman, is well aware that she is heavily dependent on him to run her high-technology enterprise and generously acknowledges her debt to him in speaking to interviewers and writing for magazines. Talking to me, she credited their successful teamwork, devoid of the conflicts likely to occur under such a reversed hierarchy (the president is not only a woman but much younger than the male vice president), to the vice president's good character. Nevertheless, she appeared silently to resent his over-playing of the leadership role. This was my conjecture based on her behavior in reaction to the vice president's lengthy exposition: she betrayed irritation and impatience by yawning, looking outside, or leaning backward.

The situation looked like a functionally complementary but uneasy duocephaly. Interestingly, the vice president characterized his role as that of a wife, but this does not mean that his role is secondary, any more than a housewife is secondary as a household manager. The vice president meant that his role was formally secondary but operationally primary. In another analogy, he likened the president to the central actor on stage and said that when she succeeds in capturing the attention and admiration of the audience, he flatters himself that he has performed his role well. Quite clearly he considers himself the producer of the play. Another figure of speech he used places the president at the center of an unfolded fan, surrounded by her staff, and equates himself with the rivet of the fan. The generous use of such metaphors is indicative of the difficulties involved in duocephaly.

Duocephaly is part of the cultural idiom of Japanese politics, and the separation and complementarity between a symbolic, center-stage authority figure and an actual, backstage power wielder has been all too familiar throughout Japanese political history. Nor is the female-male duocephaly alien to Japanese tradition. What makes the above case different from the traditional model is the lack of a hereditary status that would unequivocally legitimize the woman's (e.g., the empress's) symbolic but supreme authority.

In two other cases what seemed to have been a duocephaly in retrospect resulted in the 'righthand man' attempting to take over the enterprise. The president of one of the two companies decided that having two company heads was unhealthy. Instead of reclaiming unicephalous authority for herself, Mrs. B withdrew into the role of a helper to the vice president. 'A typical woman,' she called herself. She was actually trying to practice within her company what she believed a woman should be doing, that is, provide *naijo* (backstage assistance), which means wifely support without implying wifely dominance. Here the wifely role is reversed from the previous case – an exemplar of the multiple, mutually contradictory meanings of culture-loaded terms like *wifeliness*. Giving up her presidential authority, Mrs. B refrained even from talking to her employees 'for fear of interfering with the authority of the vice president,' who was virtually the top executive. The employees, too, 'would not dare to step into the president's office lest the vice president punish them.' The vice president apparently took advantage of the president's trust to rally his faction in an attempt to oust her and 'hijack' the company. Fortunately for the president, this attempted coup d'état met resistance internally and wound up with the exit of the usurper and his underlings. They tried, said the president, to set up their own company, stealing her ideas and projects, but failed. She became convinced through this incident that her business owed its success to her reputation and the social capital she has accumulated over the years.

The other case is not so poignant, but also involved an attempted 'hijacking' by the vice president. As the president observes: 'For a man it must be very difficult to be second to woman.' The only way for a male vice president to sustain his ego under a female president was to reduce her to an ornament for outward display while he took over the real power internally. 'That gives a man an excuse for working under a woman without losing his male pride,' she explained. To leave the internal affairs to such a vice president was truly a mistake, she admitted.

It is obvious from the foregoing that the conventional gender hierarchy interferes with the authority of a woman president. The temptation, then, would be to hire women only, and some informants do so because women are easier to manage. Nonetheless, the gender distribution of employees in these twelve firms indicates a bias for men over women. This asymmetry is mainly because of the companies' needs for certain skills, such as engineering, supplied by men only. Nevertheless, that is not the whole rationale. I was told over and again that, despite the hierarchical problems, men are less troublesome.

If intersexual relationships are problematical, so are those between members of the same sex. Women employees are regarded by women employers as more emotional and irrational, more *amae*-prone, less businesslike. The employer must refrain from using harsh words in criticizing a woman for fear of 'rain' (tears), while she has no such worry in scolding male employees.[77] Mrs. J, the president of an all-female company, confirmed this stereotype and illustrated it with the case of another company she knew. In that company, also exclusively female-staffed, the women support themselves by regularly praising one another.

Involved here is the problem of gender-related sensitivity. Obviously, women are just as sensitive as men, but the two sexes seem different in type of sensitivity. Male sensitivity seems focused on the ego or face to be sustained in the hierarchical order, whereas female sensitivity lies in unstructured interpersonal relationships. To borrow Victor Turner's typology, men's sensitivity may be more 'structural' and women's more 'liminal.'[78] Another problem with women that was mentioned by several of the presidents supports this hypothetical contrast. A woman employee tends to admire and like her employer (in fact she may have applied for a job because she is a fan of the president), orients her work to the president's approval, is overly concerned with what the president thinks of her, and wants a dyadic intimacy with the president. 'She is always looking up to me'; 'women try to relate themselves directly to me, unable to see the organization as a whole.' Thus, the presidents tend to be overloaded by the personal expectations of women employees, which are bound to be disappointed.

Domestic management. Finally, what concerns businesswomen much more than businessmen is the domestic realm. The following is an attempt to shed light on how a woman's entrepreneurial career tangles with her domestic career. The main issue here is how a woman can start and maintain a double career, an issue that brings to light the age-linked life schedule and condensed timing.

It is significant that of the twelve women, four were divorced either before or soon after they launched their enterprises; only one remarried, which she did much later. My sample also includes two women who have remained single. Half of the sample thus do not fit the stereotype of woman as wife and mother.[79] Husbandlessness impels a woman toward a nondomestic career for two different reasons: the need to make her own living and the freedom to pursue her own career. The former applied, at least initially, to the two precareer divorcees with children to support. The latter motive, the desire for freedom, is most clearly embodied by Mrs. K. When she became fully committed to managing her business, she found herself running out of time and energy to maintain a smiling face as a good wife. She stunned her husband by proposing divorce. The woman who remarried – the only such case so far – does not live with her second husband: hers is a weekend commuter marriage. One of the single women said she has no desire to marry at the expense of the freedom she is enjoying now.

All this confirms my general view that a husband inhibits a woman's aspiration for or commitment to a nondomestic career, whether because of the economic security he provides or the domestic burden he imposes. The only exception to this pattern is Mrs. J, whose first husband, upon seeing her launch into business, lost his own motivation to work and began to indulge in gambling and womanizing. She divorced him and thereafter worked harder to start a new life. Domestic conflict triggered by the wife's launching of an enterprise may thus involve the husband slipping out of his spousal role, but this is atypical, since the average Japanese husband considers it his *ikigai* (life purpose) to be the sole economic pillar of the household (*daikoku-bashira*) in support of his wife and children (*saishi o yashinau*). Not being tied to a husband makes a woman free to build up cross-gender alliances and networks in business. Indeed, extensive and enduring networks were highlighted more in the autobiographies of the divorced, single, and widowed.

If we are to generalize that a nondomestic career tends to be incompatible with full-fledged marriage, then we must explain why other women have had double careers. Five of the six women in this category have had a career mutation, so to speak. Around mid-life, after having been full-time wives and mothers for years, they embarked on their entrepreneurial careers for the reasons discussed above. Invariably, they are proud of having spent enough time in rearing their children, and some are critical of today's young women who neglect their home duties and simply want to go out. 'So, I tell young women to marry in their twenties, raise children, and thereafter be independent,' says Mrs. B, a 61-year-old woman who has been in business since age 35. She terminated full-time wife/motherhood and began a business career when the younger of her two sons became a first grader. Another woman, Mrs. I, at 48, recalled quitting her job when she was in the last trimester of pregnancy and enjoying full-time motherhood before returning to work and eventually starting her own business in a related field. This case confirms the generally shared desire for the M-curve career pattern. All these cases of late launching or career interruption suggest that marriage is inseparably tied with childrearing. All the late starters mentioned their children, not their husbands, as the reason for their mid-life careers. It is the flexibility of an entrepreneurial career that has enabled our informants to alternate two careers, domestic and extradomestic, in avoidance of role congestion.

Late starting and interruption are strategies to minimize the pressures of condensed timing by spreading the career role and domestic role over the life cycle. But this is not a solution for a divorcée with small children to support, as was the case with Mrs. C and Mrs. D. Likewise, the above option was not available to a woman who chose to start young and pursue a continuous career while married and having children, as with Mrs. C. It was the woman's natal kin who rescued her from the condensed schedule. Most important is the contribution of her female kin as surrogate home manager and mother. Mrs. C could not have had a continuous, full-time business career if her mother and sister had not looked after her daughter. 'When my daughter needed intimate love, my mother, sister, and brother were there to keep her company,' she says. 'I haven't worried a bit about my family. You can't work this way while running a home.' Her sister substituted for her at PTA meetings at her daughter's school, which she has never visited. Having been thus assisted early in her career by her mother and sister, Mrs. C is still a free businesswoman. Now she leaves all domestic responsibility to her married daughter, a skilled cook.

A similar course was followed by Mrs. D, another divorced woman with a daughter. '[My mother] stayed with me throughout for the sake of my daughter, even though she had three sons [with one of whom she should have lived according to the old Japanese norm]. My daughter grew up entirely under her care.' When the daughter was going to marry, Mrs. D learned later, the parents of her husband-to-be were convinced by a detective's investigation that their future daughter-in-law was acceptable because she had been brought up by her grandmother, an admirable woman. Now the married daughter keeps house for her mother.

Mrs. G, the only married woman whose career began early and has been continuous, also benefited from her mother's presence. Upon giving birth, Mrs. G brought her mother, then separated from her father, to her house. 'My mother look entire responsibility for caring for all the children, and for me and my husband. It was as if she had had so many children.'

These cases confirm my earlier finding that many of the career women in elite professions had their mothers as surrogate or at least supplementary homemakers and child-rearers, allowing them to devote all their time and energy to their careers.[80] Probably, this is where culture enters to a large extent, as best illustrated by the American situation.

Among middle-class Americans, according to Katherine Newman, the autonomy of the nuclear family is so sacred that it is understood that a woman, upon marriage, will be cared for by her husband, precluding her continued dependence upon her parents. Symbolically, one cannot be both a daughter and wife at once. This creates a serious problem for a divorced woman. If she is young enough to have active parents, she may be able to retrieve her daughter identity and receive help from them, as frequently occurs in the contemporary United States. Yet the retrieval cannot be complete. As a once-married adult, the daughter maintains her autonomy, and support from her parents tends to be limited to financial or material aid. The incongruity in this situation seems somewhat mitigated by the presence of grandchildren. As Newman points out, grandparents may 'exercise a culturally defined role as giftgivers to grandchildren without offending their daughters' sense of autonomy.'[81]

By contrast in the Japanese case, the woman's supporting relative lives with her and assumes overall responsibility for home management as well as childrearing. The cultural resource underlying this accommodation is a role complex expediting role surrogacy, in addition to the legacy of the extended family system.

The contrast may be an exaggeration.[82] Both the American ideal of nuclear-family autonomy and the Japanese extended family may well be dismissed as myths. Indeed, the former is becoming outmoded by the dramatic increase in single-parent families in the United States, whereas the latter is being replaced by the nuclear family as a normative pattern in Japan. Nevertheless, the American cult of each generation's independence embedded in the nuclear family scheme is likely to live on, causing an American divorcée to feel more hesitant about 'dumping' her children upon her parents, or guilty if she does. Her Japanese counterpart, on the other hand, backed up by recapture of the old culture of intergenerational co-residence, may have much less resistance to throwing herself and her children into total dependence upon her kin. The difference is even greater, I think, when the working woman is still married, as in the case of Mrs. C, and the whole family, including the husband, comes under the care of her natal kin. It is more difficult to imagine an American family living in such arrangement.

Dependence is reciprocal. The businesswomen thus helped by their kinswomen as surrogate housewives in turn financially support them. In this sense, the full-time businesswoman replicates the role of the husband as a breadwinner interdependent with the wife as a homemaker, and thus establishes her career within the framework of functional complementarity. The only difference here is that the reciprocal exchange takes place between women, usually mother and daughter, rather than between husband and wife or man and woman. One might detect a duplication of injustice perpetrated against the surrogate housewife subjected to female chores. However, the asymmetry inherent in such division of labor may be reversed when the debtor has retired from her career by her looking after her aged, perhaps bedridden, mother, just as the latter had cared for her grandchildren.

The above pattern involving businesswomen's natal kin, particularly mothers, as surrogate housewives is predominant. But the woman's in-laws, her mother-in-law first and later her daughter-in-law, are not totally resistant to such collaboration. When a supporting kinswoman was unavailable, as in the case of Mrs. K, a live-in baby-sitter was hired. Childrearing and homemaking is an around-the-clock job, so as the nuclear family becomes the dominant pattern, making relatives unavailable as surrogate mothers, working women have no alternative but to rely upon extrafamilial surrogates like day-care centers.

What is truly new is the husband's cooperation. The husbands of the younger informants do assist in housework or at least acquiesce in their wives' neglect or absence. When Mrs. I's business is at a peak season, she stays at her office for several days and nights, and the telephone is the only way for the couple to communicate. Mrs. H claims to have gradually succeeded in reeducating her husband, so that he has begun to do what he never did before, such as washing rice, making *miso* soup, and doing laundry.

The point here is that no 'independent' businesswoman is truly independent, any more than an independent businessman. While enjoying the flexibility of being self-employed, both businessmen and women are assisted, supported, or 'sponsored' by domestic collaborators, kin or non-kin. Freedom and equality are bought, in other words, by engaging in functional complementarity in a broad sense.

If a woman wants both a marital and an occupational career, she must manage her husband's mental and physical well-being, especially to protect his ego. Older women who were also late starters tend in particular to display their respect for their husbands. One informant called attention during her interview to the fact that she had never sacrificed her family for her career, that it was inconceivable for her to burden her husband with house chores. Her husband is a retired professor, studying at home.

Mrs. B, a widow, remains a firm believer, as described earlier, in the sexual division of labor, with the husband as the provider and the wife staying home and rearing children. Her emphasis upon Christian missions as her motive for staying in business may be compensation for the discrepancy between what she does and what she preaches.

In both cases, the traditional male-female distinction is played up. Whether this outlook comes from the women's convictions or has emerged as a necessary strategy to protect the male egos of their husbands is not certain. In an earlier study, I found that some professional women, more than housewives, exhibited compulsive domesticity, if only in talking.[83] Mrs. E presents a special case of rhetoric in traditional terms to legitimize the apparently incongruous relationship between herself and her husband. There is not much evidence of spousal respect on her part. In fact, she commented that her husband stays home and does nothing all day long, while she herself works as the top manager of the care-home hotel from morning till midnight without resting. Nevertheless, her husband is far from having fallen from the exalted status of a Japanese male: she describes him as a typical lord, *tonosama*, sitting still as a symbol of authority, leaving the real job of exercising it to his vassals. Mrs. E puts herself within the pre-Tokugawa feudal tradition of Japan, where, she claims, the lady, not the lord, actually governed the domain. (It may be noted here that the rhetoric of duocephaly is mobilized to justify as well as to disclaim female power under a gender-reversed hierarchy.) Before the Tokugawa period, 'the wife was president, so to speak, and the husband was more like a vice president. It was the lady who had real ability. Men were busy fighting on battlefields, leaving the government and financial management to their wives … Japanese women were smart indeed.' In historical discussion, Mrs. E jumped back to the prehistoric age when matriarchy supposedly existed (obviously she was parroting the widely accepted belief that ancient Japan was a matriarchy).

Mrs. E thus devoted her limited interview time to Japan's history, which first disappointed me but then led me to conclude that she was trying to justify the status reversal in her marriage by projecting herself into the role of the first lady of a domain. Moreover, it turned out that her husband was indeed descended from a domain lord (daimyo). Here, invoking an age-old 'tradition' characterized as 'matriarchal' legitimized the woman's new role as an entrepreneur and provider.

Finally, my informants would like their sons to succeed them in the business as much as male presidents would. Of the five owner-presidents with sons, two already have their university-educated sons on the staff and hope the sons will eventually take over the presidency. Two others are still too young to think about their successors, and the last one, Mrs. E, has nominated her son's wife as successor because her business requires a female leader. Those who have only daughters rule out the idea of filial succession, but Mrs. C hopes her son-in-law will take over the company soon so that she can retire.

In no case is a daughter a successor-nominee. This suggests that the woman president reverts to the cultural rule of patrilineality despite herself, that she feels her married daughter irretrievably lost to another 'house,' headed by her husband (a daughter-in-law is different in this regard). Daughters, when discussed, appear as domestic managers and assistants, which the mothers find essential to their pursuit of business careers. Whether or not this is a sign that the career-woman mother tends to be a counter-model for her daughter is unclear. But my limited sample suggests that gender dichotomy is intergenerationally more reinforced than superseded.

It is not that succession by a son or son-in-law is a smooth one. Mrs. B could not hold out her son to her staff as her successor and even discriminated against him in the company. '"You, mama, would listen to the vice president only, not to me," my son used to say. We Japanese tend to belittle our own kin. I am typically Japanese.' She was actually a typical Japanese woman in being inhibited about openly asserting her son's privilege as heir to her career. On the other hand, a son may be overly self-assertive and more interested in innovating or totally changing than perpetuating the company his mother founded, if only to prove his autonomy. Educated at an American university, Mrs. C's son is not particularly interested in the travel industry but wants to start a new business, something like an international information service. Although on the payroll of his mother's company, he engages in business transactions with small firms in the United States and Japan, supplying information on each other's business practices. While he was discussing his ambitious dream of 'expanding the horizon of informational antennae' far beyond the travel business, his mother, somewhat worried, interrupted to say that such business is compatible with the travel industry. The son wishes to make a lot of money and to renovate the office with plush furniture in accordance with the American idea of a 'corporate image' so that workers will be proud of working there. The mother warns him against 'a phony image.' She does so gently and indulgently, far from challenging her son. In both cases it is clear that the mothers are proud of and reliant on their sons.

Even though the business is established by a woman, it becomes a family business, as observed by Ito in regard to her sample of women entrepreneurs, when it is joined by a male member of her family. In none of my cases did the husband join his wife's business (whereas in two cases, the wife took over her husband's company and transformed it). Sons are another matter, and, although mother-to-son succession is not unproblematical, as seen above, the intergenerational link (including mother-in-law and son-in-law or daughter-in-law) may be more crucial to stabilize a woman's enterprise as a family business. To what extent such intergenerational stabilization *must* join hands with a perpetuation of the gender dichotomy remains to be further studied.

CONCLUSION

The oral autobiographies of these twelve businesswomen confirm, reinforce, replicate, or otherwise reflect the gendered dual economy in many different ways. All the companies led by these women are small, and most are family-owned. At one phase or another of their careers, all the women were victimized by institutional gender barriers and disadvantages. We have seen how career-minded women found themselves discriminated against prior to launching their own enterprises. Some mentioned the difficulty, by virtue of their gender, of getting bank loans at the initial stage of their enterprises. At a sociopsychological level, there were pressures for women entrepreneurs to present themselves in low profile in transactions with businessmen. Authority is another issue stemming from gender inequality. We have seen cases where the woman president was unable to assert or exercise her authority over her staff in a straightforward manner, extreme cases where a duocephalous structure emerged and 'hijacking' of the company was attempted by a 'right-hand man,' and so on.

Gender handicaps such as the above are likely to be magnified by cultural inhibitions in self-presentation. Women, more than men, must be on guard against 'sticking out' and appearing selfish (*wagamama*), and therefore may be compelled to suppress their 'selves' in shaping, reconstructing, and presenting their careers. It is quite conceivable that this kind of cultural program steered many women to stress circumstantial pressures or altruistic missions in their stories. In Japan 'individuality' is cherished but 'individualism,' even today, is not.[85] Dovetailed with self-inhibition is the role complex that allows self-expression within role bounds. Small wonder that initially unmotivated women soon became firmly committed to their entrepreneurial roles and began to actualize their selves through their business careers.

However extraordinary they are, the women entrepreneurs have thus not been immune from the dominant structure of gender stratification; they too have had to submit to gender-bound status inferiority. Nonetheless, their self-portrayals reveal much more than a picture of women as victims. Female inferiority was strategically manipulated and even played up in order to boost male egos, arouse gallantry in helping 'helpless' women, or bring transactions with male clients to success. Feminine self-abnegation was a key, paradoxically, to transcending gender barriers, in that it expedited the ability of women to establish and expand cross-gender alliances and networks as solid support bases for their business careers. An extreme example was found in the woman who, in the tea-house entertainment of male clients, used her musical talent to simulate the geisha role, which only a woman can play. Most of my informants have thus put into practice the adage 'Convert a misfortune into a blessing' (*Wazawai o tenjite fuku to nasu*), which I have frequently heard women leaders quote in Japan.

The conversion of the misfortune of female gender into a fortune takes a more positive form when women's superiority, rather than their inferiority, is brought into play. As newcomers in the male-dominated business world, the women had somehow to acquire a competitive edge against male rivals in existing trades or to carve out new niches for themselves. The majority of the women sampled came from an emerging group of women leaders who chose the latter alternative. Feminine sensitivity in human communication was captured as the greatest resource to be harnessed for communication enterprises. Women's linguistic facility in particular was singled out as a weapon in winning in international communications businesses. A former housewife harnessed her experiential understanding of other housewives' feelings and desires into a successful enterprise communicating between housing producers and consumers. We have also heard the feminist view that 'from now on it will be the female perspective that opens up new fields of business, because the male perspective has already been exhausted.'

The claimed female superiority can take a conservative overtone as well. As a management style, older presidents in particular stressed maternal nurturance. To be recalled is the woman who equated the president with a mother and the company with her child and claimed that her maternal approach had won over disgruntled male-led labor.

Gender does not always come to the fore as a political issue or as a matter of status inequity, but often is taken for granted or hidden behind the functional premise. This is especially true where the domestic career interlocks with the business career. Married women either started their business careers late or interrupted their careers in order to fulfill their domestic responsibilities or to enjoy a feminine identity as wife and mother. The M-curve life schedule as a way of mitigating the problem of time compression was largely taken for granted. One woman even embraced the idea that a woman's place is the home, an idea irreconcilable in her own mind with her entrepreneurial career.

The touchy problem of the husband's ego was handled in one case by a strong reassertion of the division of labor by gender. A more uneasy case called forth a justification of the woman's role as a president and sole breadwinner in terms of the Japanese tradition of functional dyarchy: the 'matriarchy' was supposedly intrinsic to the feudal system in that the domain lord was a symbol of authority and his wife executed it. The husband's role in a woman's business career may well be inferred from the fact that half of the total sample were divorced, single, or widowed. As for the future prospects of the enterprise, the owner-presidents tended to expect their sons (and sons-in-law) to succeed to the business, while no daughter was considered for intergenerational succession. This looks like a reversion to traditional male headship.

In no case was the problem of time compression solved by the businesswoman alone, particularly when she had small children. It was necessary to mobilize her mother or another kinswoman as a domestic helper or surrogate housewife/child-caretaker. Upon a generational turnover, a daughter or daughter-in-law might take over domestic responsibility. Without such a surrogate, I was told, it would have been impossible to carry on a full-time business career. This seems to mean that functional complementarity was lifted from the gender opposition only to be reimposed upon two women, one specializing in a career, the other taking a housewifely role. The career woman, then, might be likened to a man assisted by his wife, except that she is more likely than he is to reciprocate later by looking after the former domestic collaborator. The autobiographies of businesswomen illustrate the fact that a career is the product of interdependence and teamwork even for an 'independent' businesswoman or businessman.

Functional considerations cut across the domestic and public domains. As presidents of small enterprises, most of our businesswomen keep costs down by resorting to part-timers, temporary workers, and subcontractors. If both men and women are hired, a female president is no different from a male president in hiring more men in regular, technically higher-level, and managerial capacities, and more women as 'office ladies' or for irregular employment. Except for the cases of all-female enterprises, there seems to be no way of superseding the gender dichotomy prevailing in the labor market.

Furthermore, the enterprises studied are largely complementary to, not competitive with, large-scale, male-led businesses. They either fill gaps in the latter or perform functions better served by women. The majority of those in the communications-service industry are directly or indirectly involved in international trade or contacts and thus contribute in varying degrees to export-oriented, male-dominated industries, and ultimately to the national economy of Japan.

How about the egalitarian ideology? There is something paradoxical in my informants' attitude toward the political issue of gender. All the women are openly egalitarian, but not necessarily feminist or liberationist. Their egalitarianism is based foremost on the gender-blind principle of ability and performance, which results in a paradox: the more egalitarian, the more severely critical one tends to be of female employees for being spoiled, emotionally problematical, professionally uncommitted, and so on. Furthermore, none of the employers can afford to relinquish the idea of role-fitness, which provides the rationale for an imbalanced gender distribution of employees. Keenly aware of their role as new women leaders, they wish to promote women's status, but admit they cannot embrace the Equal Employment Opportunity Law unconditionally. This dilemma is understandable because they are not ideologues but business practitioners, not leaders in the sexual revolution but caught up in the day-to-day operation of surviving and winning in competitive money-making projects.

It would be wrong, however, to say that these women are only reinforcing or replicating gender dualism. They have, after all, demonstrated that an entrepreneurial career is a viable alternative to surmounting gender barriers in the labor market. Their insistence on gender-blind equality is a natural result of their having made it in the predominantly male world through their personal ability and perseverance. The media publicity given their innovative businesses and extraordinary careers is most likely to impress the audience with women's creative capabilities and to induce young women to follow them as successful models. Our women found mentors, supporters, and 'benefactors' only among men but as the number of women leaders increases, younger-generation women will be able to find female *senpai*.

The careers of the twelve women thus suggest prospects for a new generation of career-minded women. The organized labor market may open up for women, partly under the influence of the EEOL, but entrepreneurial opportunities look more promising, given the widely recognized viability of small enterprises in today's fluctuating technoeconomic environment, and the likelihood that a woman's personal strength, creativity, and sensitivity are best put to direct use by her own enterprise. The United States is witnessing an upsurge of female entrepreneurs, and it is possible that Japanese women will follow suit in the foreseeable future.

One of the industries receptive to women's talent and free from gender discrimination may be international communication, and this point was stressed and demonstrated by those informants who deal directly with foreigners. I believe women entrepreneurs will in future come to play an increasingly greater role in Japan's internationalization.

Another area of advance, I suggest, has to do with the life schedule. It is clear that the most common obstacle to women's careers is the burden of playing two roles, domestic and extradomestic, simultaneously. Men's participation in domestic chores, which is essential to equalization, does not seem likely to take place soon on any large scale. There seems to be no immediate solution, and to some extent this problem may persist indefinitely. But women's entrepreneurial vitality might well be channeled into enterprises that contribute to lightening the load of career-minded women. As the availability of kinswomen as surrogate homemakers dwindles, businesswomen can help other women by taking over domestic burdens and developing them into enterprises finely tuned to the needs of clients. Along with public institutions, there already exist private businesses, often run by women, catering to the needs of children and the elderly, such as laundry, house-cleaning, and meal-providing services, day-care centers, and so on. Much need is felt for improving this service industry in quantity, quality, and repertoire, and this is the area where I believe women's creative sensitivity can best be stimulated and harnessed.

Ideally, both men and women should be recruited to work in such settings, but realistically more women will be interested for the time being. The domestic industry serves, moreover, not only to help career women but to take care of the opposite side of the time-compression equation – namely, postparental women with time on their hands. This is not meant to reinstitute the M-curve and encourage middle-aged women to reenter the labor market as unskilled, low-paid part-timers. Women entrepreneurs may recognize these women's skills in caring for children, the elderly, the handicapped, and the sick, and in doing other domestic tasks, precisely when such skills are getting scarce, although in increasing demand. Promoting housewifely skill, efficiency, and experience to professional status and organizing it into a new repertoire may give domestic work new prestige.

This may perhaps sound like a dream, but it can confidently be predicted that the future will see the introduction of a flex-time system and/or employment at home to restructure the current rigid system. Women then will have more options to pursue careers, whether as entrepreneurs or employees, as full-time businesswomen or temporary workers. Women entrepreneurs may be expected to hasten this change.

NOTES

Earlier drafts of this essay were read and commented on by Hugh Patrick, Henry Rosovsky, Shumpei Kumon, and James Roberson, among many others. Their helpful suggestions, which convince me of the value of collaborative work, were partly incorporated into the final version, but needless to say, responsibility for any remaining errors rests with me. Fieldwork was conducted while I was a Japan Foundation research fellow, and I was the recipient of grants from the Social Science Research Council and the University of Hawaii Japan Studies Endowment Fund and of a Universitiy of Hawaii Fujio Matsuda Scholar award while I was writing the essay. I am grateful to all these individuals and institutions.

1. Stanley Cromie and John Hayes, 'Toward a Typology of Female Entrepreneurs,' *Sociological Review*, Vol. 36 (1988), p. 93.
2. James C. Abegglen, *The Japanese Factory: Aspects of Its Social Organization* (Glencoe, Ill.: Free Press, 1958), pp. 22–23.
3. For Robert E. Cole, the dual structure refers to the size of enterprise, and the duality of job security is inherent in the size duality. See Cole, *Japanese Blue Collar: The Changing Tradition* (Berkeley: University of California Press, 1971), pp. 37–40. To the two kinds of dualism, Hugh Patrick (in a personal comment) adds a third: 'competitive sectors' versus 'protected sectors.'
4. Hugh T. Patrick and Thomas P. Rohlen, 'Small-Scale Family Enterprises,' in Kozo Yamamura and Yasukichi Yasuba, eds., *The Political Economy of Japan*, Vol. I, *The Domestic Transformation* (Stanford: Stanford University Press, 1987), p. 354.
5. Rodney Clark, *The Japanese Company* (New Haven: Yale University Press, 1979), pp. 64–73.
6. Rōdōshō Fujinkyoku, ed., *Fujin rōdō no jitsujō* (Tokyo: ōkurashō Insatsu kyoku, 1987), table 20.
7. Kazuo Koike, 'Workers in Small Firms and Women in Industry,' in Taishiro Shirai, ed., *Contemporary Industrial Relations in Japan* (Madison: University of Wisconsin Press, 1983).
8. Sōrifu, *Fujin no genjō to shisaku: kokunai kōdo keikaku dai 4 kai hōkokusho* (Tokyo: Gyosei, 1985), p. 80.
9. Rōdōsho Fujinkyoku, ed., *Fujin rōdō no jitsujō*, table 41.
10. When all working women are grouped into the categories of employed, self-employed, and family workers, the number of employed women turns out to have been steadily rising, and by 1983 they constituted up to 66 per cent of all women workers. The reverse trend is observable among family workers, and the self-employed constitute the lowest proportion, with little change over time. See Sōrifu, *Fujin no genjō to shisaku*, pp. 70–71. But it should be noted that 'the employed' include all sizes of enterprises as employers.
11. Patrick and Rohlen, 'Small-Scale Family Enterprises,' p. 340.
12. Women are more likely to become permanent employees in small family enterprises than in large corporations but then, as Ito points out, their promotion has a ceiling below the managerial level because management tends to be monopolized by the owner family. See Barbara Darlington Ito, 'Entrepreneurial Women in Urban Japan: The Role of Personal Networks' (Ph.D. diss., University of Iowa, 1983), p. 130.
13. Yōko Satō, 'Hataraku josei wa dō kawattaka,' in Hiroko Hara and Meiko Sugiyama, eds., *Hataraku onnatachi no jidai* (Tokyo: Nippon Hōsō Shuppan Kyōkai, 1985), pp. 26-27.
14. Frank K. Upham, *Law and Social Change in Postwar Japan* (Cambridge, Mass.: Harvard University Press, 1987), p. 129.

15. Barbara Ito, 'Entrepreneurial Women in Urban Japan.' Doctoral dissertation, University of Iowa (1983). We might add that, although a woman's own business is likely to be thus gender-bound, her participation in a family business her husband established or inherited is not hampered by her gender. As a part of her domestic role, she is able and expected to participate in, become a mainstay of, and exercise leadership in even a typically male business such as a lumber mill. See Takie Sugiyama Lebra, *Japanese Women: Constraint and Fulfillment* (Honolulu: University of Hawaii Press, 1984), pp. 222–23.
16. Sōrifu, *Fujin no genjō to shisaku*, p. 9.
17. See Naikaku Sōridaijin Kanbō Shingishitsu, *Fujin no seisaku kettei sanka o sokushin suru tokubetsu katsudō kankei shiryō* (Tokyo, 1985), p. 31, and Patricia G. Steinhoff and Kazuko Tanaka, 'Women Managers in Japan,' *International Studies of Management and Organization*, Vol. 16, No. 3–4 (1987), pp. 108–32. This extreme asymmetry in the distribution of managerial positions pervades the public sector, national and local, as well. A nurse employed by the municipal government of a provincial city complained to me that all the employees of the public health section were women in nursing or other health-care professions, except the section chief (*kachō*), whose sole contribution was 'being male.'
18. Clark, *Japanese Company*, p. 194.
19. Susan J. Pharr, 'Status Conflict: The Rebellion of the Tea Pourers,' in Ellis S. Krauss, Thomas P. Rohlen, and Patricia G. Steinhoff, eds., *Conflict in Japan* (Honolulu: University of Hawaii Press, 1984).
20. James McLendon, 'The Office: Way Station or Blind Alley?' in David W. Plath, ed., *Work and Lifecourse in Japan* (Albany: State University of New York Press, 1983), p. 166.
21. Ibid., p. 168.
22. See Koike, 'Workers in Small Firms and Women in Industry.'
23. Yasuko Muramatsu, 'Kibokan kakusa: danjo kan no chingin kakusa o umidasu haikei,' in Hara and Sugiyama, eds., *Hataraku onnatachi no jidai*, p. 110.
24. Meiko Sugiyama, 'Nippon ni okeru hataraku hahaoya no jittai,' in Sumiko lwao and Meiko Sugiyama, eds., *Hataraku hahaoya no jidai* (Tokyo: Nippon Hōsō Shuppan Kyōkai, 1984), p. 2.
25. Anne E. Imamura, *Urban Japanese Housewives: At Home and in the Community* (Honolulu: University of Hawaii Press, 1987), p. 19.
26. Ibid., pp. 125, 134.
27. Suzanne H. Vogel, 'Professional Housewife: The Career of Urban Middle Class Japanese Women,' *Japan Interpreter*, Vol. 12, No. 1 (1978), pp. 16–43.
28. Rōdōshō Fujinkyoku, ed., *Fujin rōdō no jitsujō*, p. 35.
29. Ito, 'Entreprenuerial Women in Urban Japan,' p. 129.
30. McLendon, 'The Office,' p. 164.
31. Fujin Mondai Kikaku Suishin Yūshikisha Kaigi, *Fujii: mondai kikaku suishin yūshikisha kaigi iken* (Tokyo, 1987), pp. 76–77.
32. Ito, 'Entrepreneurial Women in Urban Japan.'
33. Hiroko Hara, 'Danjo no betsu o koeta tayosei o zentei ni,' introduction to Hara and Sugiyama, eds., *Hataraku onnatachi no jidai*, p. 12.
34. Michiko Hasegawa, '"Danjo koyō byōdōhō" wa bunka no seitaikei o hakai suru,' *Chūō Koron*, May 1984, pp. 79–87.
35. Fujin Mondai Kikaku Suishin Yūshikisha Kaigi, *Fujin mondaikikaku suishin yūshikisha kaigi iken*, p. 75.
36. For a refutation of the M-curve stereotype, see Karen C. Holden, 'Changing Employment Patterns of Women,' in Plath, ed., *Work and Lifecourse in Japan.*
37. The housewife's stress, in connection with Confucian ideology, is discussed in Takie Sugiyama Lebra, 'The Confucian Gender Role and Personal Fulfillment for Japanese Women,' in Walter H. Slote, ed., *The Psycho-Cultural Dynamics of the Confucian Family: Past and Present* (Seoul: International Cultural Society of Korea, 1986).
38. *Hawaii Hochi* (daily), July 11, 1988.
39. Sōrifu, *Fujin no genjō to shisaku*, p. 13.
40. What comes to mind here is the rejection of Louis Dumont's contention (*Homno Hierarchicus: The Caste System and Its Implications*, rev. ed. [Chicago: University of Chicago Press, 1980]) that the Indian caste ideology centering on the pure-impure opposition is commonly shared across castes. Critics have attacked this as a Brahmanic view, contradicted by the Untouchables' bottom-up perspective. See Joan Mencher, 'The Caste System Upside Down, or the Not-so Mysterious East,' *Current Anthropology*, Vol. 15 (1974), pp. 469–93; and Gerald D. Berreman, 'The Brahmanical View of Caste,' in his *Caste and Other Inequities: Essays on Inequality* (Meer, India: Folklore Institute, 1979).
41. Naikaku Sōridaijin Kanbō Shingishitsu, *Fujin no seisaku kettei sanka o sokushin suru tokubetsu katsudō kankei shiryo*, p. 5.

42. Rōdōshō Fujinkyoku, ed., *Fujin rōdō no jitsujō*.
43. Ryōko Akamatsu, *Danjo koyō kikai kintō-hō oyobi kaisei rōdō kijun-hō* (Tokyo: Nippon Rōdō Kyōkai, 1985).
44. Lebra, *Japanese Women*.
45. Shumpei Kumon, personal comment.
46. Nowadays, Japanese are learning how to enjoy leisure, necessitating an overhaul of workaholism. But whether Japanese are traditionally workaholic is questioned by Sepp Linhart, 'From Industrial to Post-industrial Society: Changes in Japanese Leisure-Related Values and Behavior,' *Journal of Japanese Studies*, Vol. 14, No. 2 (Summer 1988), pp. 271–307.
47. Takie Sugiyama Lebra, 'Japanese Women in Male Dominant Careers: Cultural Barriers and Accommodations for Sex-Role Transcendence,' *Ethnology*, Vol. 20 (1981), pp. 291–306.
48. Mary C. Brinton, 'The Social-Institutional Bases of Gender Stratification: Japan as an Illustrative Case,' *American Journal of Sociology*, Vol. 94 (1988), pp. 300–334.
49. McLendon, 'The Office,' p. 160.
50. Ibid.
51. See David W. Plath, *Long Engagements: Maturity in Modern Japan* (Stanford: Stanford University Press, 1980), and Brinton, 'Social-Institutional Bases of Gender Stratification.'
52. Chie Nakane, *Tate shakai no ningen kankei* (Tokyo: Kodansha, 1967).
53. Lebra, Japanese Women, pp. 243–44.
54. Brinton, 'Social-Institutional Bases of Gender Stratification.'
55. Ibid.
56. Takie Sugiyama Lebra, 'The Dilemma and Strategies of Aging Among Contemporary Japanese Women,' *Ethnology*, Vol. 18 (1979), pp. 337-53. The male counterpart of junior-senior exchange is the patron-benefactor being reciprocated by his protégé with loyalty. The latter, as he reaches his career prime, commands resources with which to patronize his patron, who has now passed his peak. The retired senior is likely to be helped by the junior to find a second job.
57. McLendon, 'The Office,' p. 169.
58. Lebra, *Japanese Women*.
59. Nancy Chodorow, 'Family Structure and Feminine Personality,' in M. Z. Rosaldo and L. Lamphere, eds., *Woman, Culture and Society* (Stanford: Stanford University Press, 1974), p. 57.
60. *Shūkan Daiamondo*, Feb. 19, 1983, Feb. 18, 1984, and Feb. 23, 1985.
61. Ito, 'Entrepreneurial Women in Urban Japan.'
62. For locating informants I owe thanks to Sadako Kuga, Fusako Baba, Michiko Kanda, Takako Hirano, and the staff of the Tokyo Chamber of Commerce and Industry. The views they shared with me of prominent businesswomen were also helpful.
63. In this sense, Mrs. A is not an entrepreneur in the strict sense, while all the other women are.
64. Eleanor Brantley Schwartz, 'Entrepreneurship: A New Frontier,' *Journal of Contemporary Business*, Vol. 5 (1976), pp. 47–76.
65. See Robert D. Hisrich and Candida G. Brush, 'The Woman Entrepreneur: Management Skills and Business Problems,' *Journal of Small Business Management*, Vol. 22 (1984), pp. 30–37; *The Woman Entrepreneur: Starting, Financing and Managing a Successful New Business* (Lexington, Mass.: D. C. Heath, 1985); and Sandra Winston, *The Entrepreneurial Woman* (New York: Newsweek Books, 1979).
66. Cromie and Hayes, 'Toward a Typology of Female Entrepreneurs,' p. 100.
67. See Lebra, *Japanese Women*, pp. 96–97, 230–32; and 'Japanese Women in Male Dominant Careers.'
68. This point echoes the comparative study of the attitudes of Japanese and American children toward schoolwork by Hiroshi Azuma and his colleagues, 'Receptive Diligence and Teachability: A Cross-Cultural Discussion of Motivation in Education' (Paper presented at the International Congress of Psychology, Acapulco, 1984). It was found that to carry out a task, American children must be intrinsically interested in the task, whereas Japanese children can be diligent in performing the task without being interested in it.
69. The house register (*koseki*) is a family legal document filed at a local government office, based on the family's legal place of residence. Family members are identified by name, kinship status, and reason for entry into the register (e.g., birth, marriage, adoption). To have one's name on a *koseki* amounts to legitimization of one's existence as a Japanese citizen. Divorce means the removal of a spouse from the *koseki*. Under the prewar civil code, the *koseki* was a legal expression of the 'house' (*ie*) that transcended and controlled its individual constituents. The postwar civil code, which does not recognize the *ie* as a legal unit, has outmoded the concept of *koseki*, and yet the latter, still in existence in a simplified and contradictory version, continues to bind all Japanese.
70. *Katakana* is a Japanese syllabic writing system, distinguished from the more commonly used syl-

labary, *hiragana*, and from Chinese characters. The katakana syllabary is used to transcribe special categories of referents, foreign words being a major such category.

71. George P. Murdock and Caterina Provost, 'Factors in the Division of Labor by Sex: A Cross-Cultural Analysis,' *Ethnology*, Vol. 12 (1973), pp. 203-25.

72. Lebra, *Japanese Women*.

73. Liza Crihfield Dalby, *Geisha* (Berkeley: University of California Press, 1983), describes how geisha and wives live in two disjointed role realms.

74. The Equal Employment Opportunity Law (Danjo koyō kikai kintō hō) was passed in May 1985, the culmination of many years of painstaking study and planning by leaders in and out of the government, and came into effect in April 1986. Estimates of the changes in employment practices likely to be brought about by this law inevitably vary, partly depending upon whether the estimator is an employer or employee. Revolutionary change is anticipated in some quarters (recall Hasegawa's argument), but many observers find a basically conservative feature in the law. What is pointed up, above all, is the wording in which the employer is supposed to 'strive' to ensure equal opportunity in recruiting, hiring, allocating, and promoting workers. It is argued that this terminology, phrased as 'the duty to strive' (*doryoku gimu*), strips the equality stipulation of its coercive power. The choice of the term *kintō*, instead of *byōdō*, for the title of the law, also seems, in my view, to soften its egalitarian content, even though this may not have been intended by the formulators. See Akamatsu, *Danjo kōyo kikai kintō-hō oyobi kaisei rōdō kijun-hō*, for the interpretation of a government representative who was deeply involved in the formulation of the law, and Masahiro Kuwabara, *Danjo koyō byōdō no un'yō kijun: Kanada, Amerika, to Nippon no kintō-hō ni terashite* (Tokyo: Sōgō Rōdō Kenkyūjo, 1980) for an outsider's view in comparison with the Canadian and U.S. laws.

75. Hayao Kawai, 'Violence in the Home: Conflict Between Two Principles Maternal and Paternal,' in Takie S. Lebra and William P. Lebra, eds., *Japanese Culture and Behavior: Selected Readings*, rev. ed. (Honolulu: University of Hawaii Press, 1986).

76. This difficulty in delegating responsibility to subordinates has also been noted with respect to American women managers. See Margaret Hennig and Anne Jardim, *The Managerial Woman* (Garden City, N.Y.: Anchor/Doubleday, 1977).

77. Rohlen has also noted that the emotional vulnerability of women workers poses a problem for managers. See Thomas P. Rohlen, *For Harmony amid Strength: Japanese White-Collar Organization in Anthropological Perspective* (Berkeley: University of California Press, 1974), p. 103.

78. Victor W. Turner, *The Ritual Process: Structure and Anti-Structure* (Chicago: Aldine, 1969).

79. Marriage tends to be postponed in proportion to the increasing number of women receiving higher education and being employed after graduation, which accounts for the decline in the marriage rate over the past decade. The proportion of single women decreases as age goes up: 78 per cent of women at age 20–24; 24 per cent at 25-29; 9 per cent at 30–34. The divorce rate has gone up from 1.07 per 1,000 of the population in 1975 to 1.51 in 1983. See Sōrifu, *Fujin no genjō to shisaku*, pp. 116–17. Nevertheless, marrying at 23 to 25 remains the norm for the majority of women.

80. Lebra, 'Japanese Women in Male Dominant Careers.'

81. Katherine S. Newman, 'Symbolic Dialects and Generations of Women: Variation in the Meaning of Post-Divorce Downward Mobility,' *American Ethnologist*, Vol. 13 (1986), p. 240.

82. Glenda Roberts, personal comment.

83. Takie Sugiyama Lebra, 'Japanese Women and Marital Strain,' *Ethos*, Vol. 6 (1978), pp. 22–41.

84. Ito, 'Entrepreneurial Women in Urban Japan,' p. 280.

85. Brian Moeran, 'Individual, Group and *Seishin*: Japan's Internal Cultural Debate,' in Lebra and Lebra, eds., *Japanese Culture and Behavior*.

First published in W.H. Slote and G.A. De Vos (eds), *Confucianism and the Family*, Albany: State University of New York Press, 1998

17 Confucian Gender Role and Personal Fulfillment for Japanese Women

The Japanese version of Confucianism, or more correctly of Neo-Confucianism – which was developed, systematized, and institutionalized during the Tokugawa era (1603-1867), and subjected to sociopolitical change thereafter – managed in one form or another to survive the revolutionary Westernization of the subsequent 'modern' period. Today Confucianism is dismissed and sometimes ridiculed as hopelessly antiquated, destined to soon vanish from the memory of the oldest generation. Whether this dismissal is warranted or not is open to question, and the use of the past tense in the following discussion should not be taken necessarily as exclusive of the present situation.

The primary human relation from the Confucian point of view is that of parent and child, most significantly, father and son, tied by filial piety. Let the parent-child relation, therefore, be called the Confucian bond. This chapter,[1] however, takes up another, secondary relation, the relation of man and woman as it is interlocked with the Confucian bond. Specifically, I will focus on women and attempt to recapture their way of life bound to what I regard as the Confucian gender ideology, as far as one can infer from oral autobiographies given in interviews. Life histories have been collected over the years since 1976 (Lebra 1984) and include materials on women from different classes – lower class, middle class, through the upper-class prewar aristocracy – both rural and urban.[2] For the present purpose, the sample of informants used will be drawn more from the prewar generation than from younger individuals. This includes the generation of the 'Confucian sandwich' (Plath 1975). The oldest informant, now deceased, was born in 1888, and the oldest age at an interview was 91. Some attention will be paid to class differences insofar as particular statements apply more to one class than to another.

My principal objective is to delve into the psychological problems faced by women that arise from the constraint of Confucian norms, their strategies in coping with them, and possible ways of attaining personal fulfillment. I could well reverse this objective by asking how they failed to cope with problems or to achieve fulfillment. It will be shown, however, that success and failure are complementary to and thus informative of each other. Equally informative of a Confucian type of fulfillment are non-Confucian alternatives, which I shall therefore touch upon at the end.

WOMANHOOD AND THE *IE* IN CONFUCIAN STRUCTURE

The main characteristic of the Confucian gender ideology in my view is its *structural* emphasis on the roles and statuses of men and women as an integral part of the overall social order, which in turn is embedded in the law of the universe. Man and woman are supposed to relate to each other through the complementary rights and obligations attached to their structurally assigned roles and statuses. The relations are to be structurally mediated rather than direct and immediate, and thereby protected from the impulses and whims of individuals. This structural bias may reflect the Tokugawa regime's political use of Confucianism to maximize the stability and predictability of human relations after centuries of civil warfare.

Confucian *structure* may be thus placed at the opposite pole from *personhood,* or to put it another way, personhood in Confucianism characteristically involves discipline or role discipline, not the entirety of a person including his or her emotions and impulses. Structure in this sense comes close to what Turner (1969) meant by the same term although for him it was merely a heuristic point of departure to elaborate on its opposite, *liminality.*

Confucian structuralism in this sense seems particularly important in governing gender relations. To my mind the following principles are involved for gender roles and womanhood: dichotomy in role spheres, gender hierarchy, and sexual distance.

Dichotomy in Role Spheres

Women's foremost role should be that of *good wife and wise mother,* and her role sphere should be domestic, 'inside,' and backstage, clearly set apart from the male sphere, which is public, 'outside,' and on stage. If a woman participates in the male sphere, she is obliged to do so only as a surrogate for her husband, son, or other male kin, or invisibly from the backstage. The Confucian woman, then, is a prime example of 'the Other' devoid of subjectivity (de Beauvoir 1972). Through this dichotomy, woman and man are expected to enjoy harmony as yin and yang based upon role interdependence.

Man is placed above woman, just as the heaven is above the earth, and the head above the body. This status asymmetry involving female inferiority, subordination, and vulnerability ties in with jural patricentricity in property ownership, household headship, and succession. Japanese Confucianism assimilated the Chinese idioms of such gender hierarchy as 'the seven rationales for divorcing the wife' (including jealousy and loquaciousness), and woman's 'three obediences' (first to her father, then to her husband when married, and last to her son when widowed). These were understood not necessarily literally but at least symbolically to impress male superiority and dominance.

Sexual Distance

Confucianism separates man and woman at a young age, as young as seven. The rule of segregation ought to be adhered to until marriage, which necessitates matchmaking for marriage by a third person(s) who defines the expected 'roles' of husband and wife for the candidates in advance. Even after marriage open intimacy is prohibited, since marriage means the incorporation of the incoming spouse into the receiving household, more than a dyadic union of man and woman as sexual partners. Filial piety to parents and parents-in-law precedes spousal compatibility. To compensate for the sexual distance of the married couple, the husband, but not the wife, has the prerogative of extramarital sexual access and concubinage.

Underlying the above gender ideology is the integrity of the *ie,* household, which was a basic jural unit in the prewar civil code. At this point we should remind ourselves that Japanese Confucianism became closely interlocked with the institution of *ie so* that one was inconceivable without the other. The concept of *ie* has been overworked in Japanese anthropology and sociology, leaving us little to explore. However, for the purpose of the present chapter, I would like to point out two attributes of *ie*: spatial and temporal. First, the *ie* refers to a spatial unit – physical, social, and symbolic – to which all the co-residents 'belong.' A person not only belongs to and stays in an *ie*, but may 'depart' from one *ie* and 'enter' another *ie.* This spatial image of *ie,* while the *ie* itself is no longer recognized as a legal unit, is retained even now in the form of the *koseki* or house register. The *koseki is* an official, cumulative record of a household cycle regarding the 'entries' and 'departures' of family members through birth, death, marriage, adoption, and divorce. Unlike the American birth certificate or marriage license, which is carried by an individual, this is a collective documentary unit to which all the members of the family 'belong.' Under the postwar civil code, each new couple is entitled to a newly 'created' *koseki* of its own, instead of entering the preexisting parental *koseki,* a change that reflects the legally sanctioned nuclear-family ideal. But at the same time, the couple is, in legal terminology, to 'enter' their new *koseki.*

Second, interlaced with this spatial dimension of the *ie is* its temporal one. The *ie* exists not only here and now but is an entity durable over generations (Peizel 1970). Viewed this way, the *ie* includes not only the living generation but ancestors who are dead and descendants yet to be born. Genealogy is a sacred symbol of *ie* continuity; and ancestor worship is an essential rite. Equally important is succession, and this is where the Japanese system differs from its Chinese and Korean counterparts. Succession is strictly unigenitural usually in favor of the eldest son but not excluding the options of succession by a younger son, daughter, brother, other kin, or non-kin.

The family with daughters but no sons would expect one of the daughters, usually the eldest, to stay as heiress or '*ie*-daughter' and to marry an adopted husband who 'enters' her *ie*. Historically, male primogeniture was a relatively recent outcome among commoners of the Meiji Restoration that assimilated features of the upper-class succession rule. Gender-blind primogeniture had been a more widespread pattern (Suenari 1972). Ironically, the 'successful' birth control of present-day Japan, causing male successors to be in short supply, seems to be contributing to a reversion to the option of succession by a daughter along with uxorilocal residence.

The imperative of succession required a marriage arranger to take precautions not to match two successors, heir and heiress. For the same reason and bound by the belief in female inferiority, a woman's worth was reduced to that of a 'womb-loaner' to nurture a male seed. A wife's status, therefore, remained precarious until she proved fertile.

The spatial and temporal dimensions together placed the *ie* above and beyond individual members of a family, even beyond kinship itself. An individual was insignificant or irrelevant apart from his/her membership in the *ie* and his/her contribution to the perpetuation and enhancement of the *ie*. It was this transcendental status of the *ie* that characterized Japanese family ideology. As for the class variable, upper classes were (and are) more likely than lower classes to carry the full weight of *ie* as a transcendental ideational entity.

In the modern era from Meiji through Taisho (1868–1926) there were heroic movements to emancipate women from the structural constraint of the *ie* and Confucianism. But they were eventually swallowed by the aggressive nationalism of Showa (post-1926) centered around the emperor. Women were reeducated into being good wives and wise mothers not only for their own families but for the country (Hirota 1982; Igeta 1982; Nagahara 1982). Prewar women thus embodied a patriotic version of Confucian womanhood.

How was this structural constraint taken, accepted, or rejected by women? And how could they achieve their personal fulfillment under the circumstances? By fulfillment I mean the emotionally charged attainment of one's long-range goals or expectations. A sense of fulfillment may be double-focused. On the one hand, fulfillment may be self-focused, involving one's achievement, accomplishment, mastery, autonomy, self-respect, and the like. On the other, it may be relation-focused in that fulfillment is derived from the awareness of interdependence, support, solidarity, intimacy, love, and so forth. These two foci, granted that they may well become indistinguishable, should be kept in mind in the following analysis as a frame of reference.

THE STRUCTURED LIFE COURSE AND EMOTIONAL LOADS

Listening to the life histories of Japanese and American women, I was struck by a cultural difference in recalling what agents steered their life courses. American women tended to recall and understand their past as a sequence of their own decisions and commitments, locating themselves at the center of each experience and relegating other people to the periphery or oblivion. Frustrating to me was the paucity of information on the society surrounding the individual. The whole life history was presented as more or less self-programmed. This does not mean that the American autobiography had held a clear notion of her life goal and adhered to it throughout. On the contrary, her life course impressed me as surprisingly precarious and hazardous, interrupted by indecision, bewilderment, drifting, and procrastination. This kind of randomness I regard as a proof (or price?) rather than a disproof of self-direction.

By contrast, a Japanese woman would typically underscore the absence of options and portray her life course as steered, sometimes forcibly, by someone else or by a surrounding group. This characteristic is best illustrated by the way in which a young woman faced her major life transition, marriage. Since premarital social segregation ruled out a woman's direct encounter with prospective mates, arranged marriage was a general rule. Even when a man and woman happened to meet without an introducer and fell in love, the proper thing for them was to call on or wait for a mediator to take action. To illustrate: when her male colleague confessed his love, a schoolteacher told him to desist, but recontact her through a proper channel.

The *miai* (an arranged meeting for introduction of the two prospective spouses) took place as a matter of course in most cases of arranged marriage. That the personal choice and emotions of a bridal candidate were not salient would be best demonstrated occasionally by the marriage of strangers that was *not* preceded by a *miai*. Some highly respectable families seemed to scorn it as too fashionable and kept their daughters blind to the appearance of their future husbands until the very day of their wedding. A woman, thus married, rationalized this by saying that she knew marriage had nothing to do with a woman's choice. (In such cases, the bridegroom also was blind, but there is evidence that grooms had opportunities to glimpse their future brides in a sort of socially contrived one-way mirror or at least to look at their pictures.) Such cases were the exception rather than the norm, but it was more common among upper-class women for whom status-matching of the two *ie* was the major consideration. Among the latter, I also found a few cases of child betrothal, another indication of total disregard of the principal's will and choice.

Marriage proposals were accepted for reasons that were extraneous to the candidate's emotions toward her husband-to-be as a person. Among the often mentioned reasons were: a debt of loyalty to the matchmaker (parent, brother,[3] uncle, other kin, employer, boss, etc.) or trust in his/her judgment; fear of offending the proposing family by rejection; the urgency of the woman to marry somebody because of her age or because her younger siblings were lining up awaiting their turn; the wish to prove her femininity (or desirability?); acceptability of the occupational status of the husband-to-be or his family. A remarkable example illustrating extraneous motives was that of a local leader of the National Defence Women's Association, a divorcee, inflamed with wartime patriotism, she agreed to remarry a widower fifteen years her senior because his daughter had just become a war widow.

It is clear that the bridal candidate's personal likes and dislikes were irrelevant to spouse selection. Arrangements were already going on, informants recalled, without any prior consulting with the candidate, so that they often found themselves already 'given' away to another *ie* when first learning about what was going on. Whether this was what really happened in each instance may be questioned, but the point is that my autobiographers tended to stress the absence of any concern with personal feelings or active suppression of their subjective preferences and choices by others responsible for decisions at this most critical time of life. Interestingly, even a successful 'love marriage' was in some instances described as a product of the uninvited interference by some third person or vague 'surrounding' that had 'trapped' the woman into a match.

With her life course seemingly programmed in advance, the Japanese woman did not have much time for random distraction. Usually, after school graduation, she would be trained in domestic skills or bridal arts[4] in anticipation of becoming 'a good wife and wise mother,' prepared to receive and accept a marriage proposal. On the surface, this might look like the life course of a *role robot*. Indeed, there were women who did not question the authority of their parents or other senior persons to determine their destinies, who fitted their given roles without feeling any discrepancy between their obligations and personhood, 'I thought that's the way things are;' 'I never thought I was not free.' We find this kind of perfect match between culture and personality more in upper- than lower-class women.

But true role robots were exceptional or perhaps nonexistent. Even those who sounded like robots would betray, in an in-depth interview, an inner self which was not entirely encased by role propriety. One informant as an heiress to an *ie* was prepared to accept 'anybody' who would be kind enough to move in as an adopted husband, and did marry such a 'proper man' It turned out, however, that there was another man whom she could not wipe out of her mind though she knew they could not marry since he, too, was to succeed as heir. At age 77, this woman was still obsessed with this unconsummated romance, unable to stop talking about it. No such intensity of feeling was to be detected about her actual husband who had died the previous year after fifty years of peaceful marriage.

Emotional loads thus seem to accumulate through the structured life course, which is quite understandable within our common-sense knowledge of human nature. In addition, it should be remembered that the tradition of Japanese culture has extolled pure emotions and sensitive feelings located in the 'heart' of the individual and immune to structural control. This heart-focus is traceable back to the prehistoric, and certainly pre-Confucian oral tradition as articulated in the *Kojiki* and *Nihongi* (Pelzel 1974). Romantic love, particularly illicit love, as an expression of pure or true heart has long been an essential ingredient of literary tradition. Motoori Norinaga (1730-1801), the most notable leader of the nationalist school that arose in reaction to the resurgence of Confucianism, found the truly *Japanese* spirit in poetic sentiment, pure emotions, heart, romantic feeling, or even illicit love, which would be revealed only if unencumbered by Confucian rigidity or any other alien influence (Yoshikawa 1969). If Japanese Confucianism is of a masculine nature (as exemplified by samurai warriors), Japanese nativism, as espoused by Motoori, comes to embrace femininity as its central quality.

While having internalized Confucian ideology sometimes to the point of performing as a role robot, women could not remain unaffected by the tradition of heart-centered romanticism, and their internal discontent seemed to seek surface from time to time.

Most women complied, resigning themselves to parental decisions, but some remained resentful, resisted, or even overtly rebelled, only to relent later. It is no wonder, then, that the narratives of Japanese women were highlighted with dramatic episodes of conflict between the inner self and external role demands. (Again, class differences should be noted: such dramatization is more characteristic of lower- or middle-class women than of upper-class autobiographers.) Not infrequently the narratives were given in tears. Paradoxical as it may sound, the structured life course binding Japanese women seems more conflict-ridden, dramatic, and eventful than that of the self-directed life course described by American women.

Unless one was an heiress within one's family, a sense of marital transition was sharpened by a woman's departure from her own *ie* and entry into an unfamiliar household. After this transition, internal conflict reached a peak. Most of my Confucian-trained informants, knowing that their primary obligations were to their in-laws, tried to do their best to become accepted, especially by mothers-in-law. The latter, however, were found voracious in making demands upon new brides. The jealous mother-in-law continued to mother her son, and subtly or unsubtly interfered with the growth of intimacy between the newlyweds. The continuing triad of mother-son-daughter-in-law was stressful enough, but what made it more insufferable occasionally was a further alliance of a mother-in-law and a sister-in-law.[5]

More serious in the long run than in-law problems was the husband-wife discord. The intensity of in-law stress would lessen if the husband were firm in support of his wife, but it was more likely that rules of conjugal distance mixed with the husband's filial guilt and unresolved attachment toward his mother kept the couple apart. In-law conflict contributed to marital estrangement as the husband began to stay away from home to avoid getting caught in the middle.

With or without an in-law in co-residence, the most common complaint of wives was about the emotional reticence of their husbands. The well-known silence of the Japanese husband may be attributed to an over-commitment to his occupational career, leaving no energy left for conjugal conversation, and this is certainly true with 'company men' of today, whether they are Confucian or not. Compounded with this was the traditional denigration of talkativeness. Especially embarrassing for a man was to express loving emotions to his wife. So, 'in our entire married life, my husband has spoken not a single tender word to me.' The wife would deeply appreciate a word of acknowledgment from her husband for whatever she did, but he would say nothing, no comment on the flavor of a dish she had cooked. An informant gave a detailed account of how a little gift delivered to someone in return for a small favor she had received was enthusiastically accepted and profusely thanked for. 'I have never been so happy,' she exclaimed, 'in my fifty-five years of marriage.' Her husband was a perfect provider preoccupied with his profession, making no fuss about his wife's home management, but was not inclined at all to engage in any conversation with her.

It may be unfair to attribute all this uncommunicativeness of the husband to Confucianism. More responsible may be Japaneseness, and in fact the wives labeled their mute husbands 'a typical Japanese male.' It is safe, however, to assume that the Confucian gender ideology – dichotomy, hierarchy, and distance – significantly contributed to the husband's aloofness or reluctance to express conjugal love. It may be also unjustifiable to blame conjugal coolness on the husband alone. As De Vos (1974, 128) observes, 'on the deepest level probably many Japanese wives do not 'give' themselves completely to their husbands because the marriage has been forced on them.' What cannot be denied is that emotional overloads are inherent in many a highly structured marriage.

Not that there was no affection. An initially loveless cohabitation, some informants confessed, gradually grew into a conjugal attachment of sorts, as expected of an arranged marriage. Nevertheless this attachment did not necessarily lead to emotional consummation, as revealed by several informants whose marital life was peaceful but lacked the excitement of sexual love: 'I want to know what love is like'; 'Ending a life without knowing love at all [as in my case] is truly abnormal, isn't it?'

Most painful in a conjugal life, informants concurred, was the husband's infidelity. The husband, emotionally as deprived as the wife, would frequently find an outlet in an extramarital liaison, and this was unbearable enough to drive his wife to contemplate or attempt suicide.[6] Just like alcoholic addiction, womanizing for some husbands was an 'incurable disease,' repeated over and over after promises of reform. Even at her husband's deathbed, such a wife might remain resentful and punitive.

Still, divorce did not seem a viable alternative for a number of reasons. Women had to leave children behind with the 'househead' to whom they belonged. Even when custody would be obtained, there would be worries about the future social plight of fatherless children. The honor of the wife's natal family could be besmirched. There was even fear of starvation, so complete could the ostracism of a divorcee be. The only strategy available was 'endurance,' a practice cultivated since childhood as a feminine virtue. Under the circumstances, endurance might even take the form of aggressive masochism, as inferred from such expressions as 'I persevered quietly, gritting my teeth inwardly.' As a defensive strategy, the wife might become totally detached from her unfaithful spouse, cease to be jealous, and go as far as to encourage his *affaire d'amour*.

A woman, if inordinately frustrated with her husband for his marital profligacy, inadequacy as a provider, uncommunicativeness, or any other reason, might try, as did some of my informants, to regain her autonomy by stripping herself of feminine identity and presenting herself as 'more like a man.' No self-denigration was involved in this sexually reversed self-image since the same women were firm believers in male superiority.

In addition to these self-focused strategies, relational strategies were called for to sustain emotional equilibrium. Most likely, a woman retained or revived her bond with natal kin, with her mother in particular as long as she lived. Such ties between mother and married daughter are being prolonged and intensified today in the urban middle class (Perry 1976) and more openly displayed. (And this daughter-mother alliance is to reproduce the in-law conflict, conflict between this team and the daughter/sister-in-law.) The prewar-generation woman, bound by her obligatory sense of exclusively belonging to her husband's *ie*, maintained her natal bonds in a more clandestine manner. Her elder brother, too, might provide her psychological support or present himself as a buffer between his kid sister and her husband or in-laws.

More indispensable for the woman's mental health was, of course, the presence of her child. As the aloofness of the Japanese husband is culturally typical, so is the Japanese mother's devotion. Unlike husband-wife intimacy, mother-child bonding is culturally sanctioned and revered. The wife's attachment to her child may be a compensatory reaction to her conjugal frustrations, but it, in turn, is likely to escalate marital estrangement. It is as if the emotional energy unexpended upon a spouse must be released upon a child or, conversely, energy being overspent on a child diminishes spousal love. This 'principle of equivalence' of psychic energy (Jung, cited in Maddi 1972, 80) or what Nadel (1951, 316) calls the law of 'uneven levels of mental energy' does not always hold true for the wife-husband-child triad (note, for example, the popular saying that the child cements a marriage). But as far as I could observe, and not surprisingly, there seemed to be a correlation between the woman's intensity or compulsion in her child care, and her frustrations with or indifference to her husband. A self-reflective informant admitted that her over-involvement as a mother of two children was a selfish compensation for her discontent as a wife.

The mother-child intimacy involved the prolonged breast-feeding, co-sleeping, and co-bathing, and, as observed by Caudill and Weinstein (1974), communication through physical contact more than verbal exchange. The mother tended to feel her child to be a part of herself (*bunshin*) and typically to develop a sense of double-identity in which the child's identity was fused into her own. When the child grew into school age, the mother's devotion intensified as a helper for the child's academic success. Even though the label *kyōiku-mama* is attached to contemporary mothers who thoughtlessly would drive their children for educational achievements in response to the postwar democratization in educational opportunities, I find among my Confucian-generation informants quite a few who labeled themselves 'incipient *kyōiku-mama*.' One of them sat in her son's class, much to the teacher's embarrassment, so that she would be able to tutor him with homework. (In those days there was no *juku*, the commercially run facility to supplement regular school training, which, today, is proliferating primarily to train examination candidates.) It is evident that these women enjoyed an incomparably stronger sense of vicarious achievement through their children's school performance than through their husbands' career success. It is equally clear that the woman ultimately reinforced the Confucian bond at the expense of the conjugal bond. To be noted here is the primacy of the mother-child (not necessarily limited to mother-son) bond over father-son bond. The patricentricity of Confucian ideology seems to be psychologically channeled into matricentricity. Moreover it is not filial but maternal piety that generates the matricentric version of Confucian bond.

FULFILLMENT IN RETROSPECT

The life history does not end here, but continues further to disclose something else. I came to realize that a typical informant would divide her life history into two parts so that her experience of frustrations, hardship, and endurance as described so far should pertain to the earlier half only. When her recollection reached into her prime or where she stood now, her perspective was turned around. She now became aware that her earlier suffering was necessary for later gratifications and fulfillment. Probably this retrospective turnabout may account for the possible exaggeration by some autobiographers of stress and conflict they had gone through earlier.

The middle-aged housewife would witness her once domineering, incorrigible mother-in-law, if she was still alive, no longer standing in her way but, instead, transformed into a dependent child calling her 'Mom,' and 'obeying' her; if senile, she would recognize and trust nobody but her daughter-in-law, her blood daughter and former ally having faded out of her memory; if dead, she would reemerge as a deified benefactor and mentor who had trained her so well. Nursing the long-living in-law was a burden, but the middle-aged daughter-in-law would take this opportunity to present herself as a role model for the younger generation, *her* daughter-in-law in particular.

Nor did conjugal perseverance prove totally futile. As the children achieved their independence, the wife realized the need of rebuilding her conjugal solidarity. By this time the husband who had been womanizing, gambling, drinking, violent, or otherwise abusive, was likely reformed. Having been obsessed with his occupational career, the husband now would see its ceiling, and turn around to redeem his guilt as a neglectful spouse. The woman who had thought of divorce many times was now glad that she had persevered. Even where marriage was broken irreparably and the wife welcomed widowhood, marital endurance meant something positive. It appeared as if many years of co-suffering in marriage were taken, in retrospect, as a form of accomplishment, and commiseration as a form of togetherness. (One is often told that marriage is not for pleasure or joy but to share suffering and perseverance.)

Something else is possible for a middle-aged couple. The wife, with years of experience as a mother, may come to settle into a maternal role in relation to her husband. My informants did not hesitate to liken their husbands to their eldest, and most unruly sons, and to characterize the behavior of their husbands in terms of childlike *amae*. *Amae* seemed to offer a culturally acceptable style for expressing conjugal love without threatening male dignity. In fact, *amae* in the Japanese context could be an expression of both love and male dominance.[7] It seems that the strained conjugal relationship could regain an optimal state of congeniality by converting wife and husband into mother and son, the blocked communication channel being reopened by a free flow of *amae* emotions. In other words, the woman in her prime could be a mother for all, for her aged in-laws and husband as well as her real children.[8]

However successful in the strategy of such role conversion, the wife would not take her husband for more than a substitute child. The most important source of gratification and fulfillment for a woman at a later as well as an earlier stage was her real children. The woman's fulfillment was intertwined with her son's passage of a competitive college entrance examination, his promising career in a large corporation, and with her daughter's marriage to, say, an electronic engineer. With no planned parenthood, she had many children, all of whom she was proud of having brought into full adulthood, allowing each to establish his/her *ie*. Her pride might extend to the school performance of her grandchildren. All these were achievements of none other than the mother herself, just as a child's underachievement broke the mother's heart as her own failure. It was she who had made such investments in the children's future with her own labor.

If these were the mother's self-focused accomplishment, however vicarious, she was fulfilled relationally also. Her grown-up children would not forget her hardship, sacrifice, and perseverance, which were for their sake; they would feel thankful and willing to repay her in filial piety. The mother might overhear her eldest son and successor telling his wife to be nice to the old lady 'because she had suffered so.' She would refuse to anticipate the day when she had to come under the care of her children, above all, her daughter-in-law, but most of my informants were comfortably sure that their children would be available if and when necessary.

The interviewer came to realize that the term *filial piety* was being used with two totally different meanings. An informant would look smug when talking about her adult children's *oyakoko,* but resentful when discussing her husband's *oyakōkō*. The latter is a sort of euphemism for the husband's lack of consideration for the wife. The woman was a beneficiary of one *oyakoko,* and victim of the other *oyakōkō*.

The earlier suffering would thus be reevaluated as a prologue to a later fulfillment, the earlier endurance as a worthy investment which was to yield profits. Having undergone this kind of lifelong investment and payoff, older women emphasized the importance of having a hard life while young.

The Confucian gender ideology and the transcendental status of the *ie*, which had been overwhelming sources of stress and deprivation for a bride, would begin to show a brighter side some decades later as she acquired domestic expertise. If a woman was role-bound, this constraint might generate a reward: role-obligations went hand in hand with role prerogatives. The homebound Japanese woman, while economically dependent upon her husband, was obliged *and* privileged to manage domestic affairs single-handedly. A woman engaging in real estate transactions without consulting her husband was not uncommon. Role monopoly or immunity of the Japanese housewife as a byproduct of the clear-cut role dichotomy amounted to the kind of power, mastery, and autonomy which her American sister would envy (see Vogel 1978 in this regard). The earlier struggle could now be reappraised as a necessary apprenticeship toward a matriarchical license, and the *ie* would become a sanctuary for its mistress. When her mother-in-law became incapacitated, an informant in her forties said to herself, 'Here comes my kingdom at long last!'

Furthermore, the woman master of the house, when aged, would feel closer to the ancestors of the house, not her own but her husband's, as she had been *the* caretaker for the household shrine, and would anticipate 'joining' them. Her final fulfillment would derive from the assurance that she was the key link between the forebears and descendants of the *ie*, not just loaning her womb but now handing down the *ie* tradition learned from her mother-in-law to her daughter-in-law. The Confucian life cycle thus came to complete itself.

ADJUSTMENT TO STRUCTURAL INSTABILITY

The foregoing is admittedly an oversimplified picture. Although most of my old informants described their life paths roughly in this manner, no one's life was in fact structured quite so neatly. First of all, the lifelong role investment is a risky business in that, like any other business, it is liable to bankruptcy. The husband may continue to play around without a sign of remorse against everybody's prediction, until he stops breathing. The risk is doubled and tripled if investment is made in one's children, in view of the unprecedented social and cultural changes taking place in present-day Japan. The heavily invested child may turn out to be a loser, a delinquent, or an ingrate. Popular 'home-drama' series on TV which used to depict a spiteful mother-in-law, now focus more on a heartless and greedy son and his wife who abandon his aged parents after swiping their savings. The life cycle of the older generation is unlikely to be repeated by younger generations. Hence the phenomenon of a sandwiched generation losing to both the ascending and descending generations. My informants, though not victims of this sort, told me about their neighbors and friends as such victims; they were keenly aware of media-carried signals and warnings about the breakdown or reversal of the generational hierarchy.

The structural or Confucian programming of a life course, thus becoming dubious, must be supplemented by something closer to self-direction. Role investment should be shorter-ranged or more self-focused; the need of perseverance must be weighed against its cost; divorce should count as a feasible alternative to the risk of enduring a miserable marriage too long; life should be regarded as reversible; a woman should have options to live outside the domestic confinement including options for singlehood. In other words, non-Confucian alternatives should be legitimized.

Indeed, Japanese women today are trying to redirect their lives toward a greater self-reliance. The steady increase of post-parental women employed as part-timers, in face of social critics' charges against working mothers as responsible for the delinquency, school violence, and mental disorders of contemporary children, would be inconceivable without taking into account the women's enjoyment of economic autonomy (even though they tend to justify their work in other terms). Further, an old woman's self-discipline to maintain good health hopefully until the very moment of sudden death indicates her concern for physical autonomy that does not need the nursing care of relatives. The housewife's involvement with studies and hobbies is a way of attaining emotional self-sufficiency. Interviews further revealed a special religious discipline which some women had undergone in order to achieve this-worldly Buddhahood, the purpose of which was to avoid relying upon their offspring for their postmortem salvation. They would not reject ancestor rites to be conducted for them by their descendants willingly, but not as a matter of burdensome obligation (Lebra 1979, 1984).

If the generational hierarchy is unstable or even reversed, intergenerational co-residence ceases to be an ideal for the older generation as well. Ambivalence to the idea of sharing residence with one's son and his wife is further compounded by the sharp rise in life expectancy, which protracts the period of two or three adult generations living under one roof. Some of my informants confessed that they would rather enjoy their 'privacy' than feel constrained in the presence of younger co-residents. The general tendency was either to postpone such joint residence until the mother became widowed or ill, or to resort to a new architectural design for the dwelling which would enable the two generations to live together while protecting each other's privacy.

Self-reliance, freedom, and privacy require a reallocation of time and energy to one's own work, study, play, ritual, and health care. The woman's workload as a caretaker for the family must be reduced accordingly. Not surprisingly, the Japanese mother, while she claims that her purpose of life lies in her children, still welcomes being relieved of maternal chores when her children have grown up. She may extend her maternal love to her grandchildren, but to repeat caretaking for them is contrary to her desire. Also at some point of life she would like to relinquish her wifely chores as an all-around caretaker for her husband as well, despite the maternal nurturance and childish dependency that may be curative of conjugal strain at a certain stage of the marriage. Widowhood often turns out, therefore, to be embarrassingly blissful even for a happily married wife, and remarriage is viewed as a foolish repetition of servitude.

If the Confucian life cycle is thus challenged, so is the Confucian gender ideology. Without bringing out the latest feminist movement in this connection, I should say a word on women's non-domestic careers, namely full-time, lifelong professional careers. Career women are not products of women's liberation in the 1970s but rooted in a longer history even in Japan. Change has taken place only in terms of the widened repertoire of such careers. Among my older informants there were career women, though none called themselves by that fancy name, for example, a kindergarten teacher, a hairdresser, a culinary specialist, a midwife, a pharmacist, and the like. Everyone of them was more eager to talk about their professional experience than anything else, and stressed her life would not have been so fulfilling without her profession. They assumed a double career, professional and domestic, which they admitted was difficult to adhere to, but in retrospect they found their life paths most satisfactory and would not trade them for any other alternative. (In some cases the double career involved two women, the career woman and her mother, the latter being in charge of domestic chores on behalf of her professional daughter. This arrangement could be made most naturally in uxorilocal marriage with an adopted husband, and probably this explains why uxorilocally married career women looked happiest and considered themselves luckiest.) The greatest pleasure seemed to derive from their performances for the benefit of the public clientele, appreciations expressed by the latter, and professional reputations thus built up. Ideologically conservative, these women's life reviews demonstrate that the most profound fulfillment for both men and women calls for an involvement in public roles.

CONCLUSION

Is Confucianism dead? Is there any Confucian legacy which is viable in contemporary Japan? I think Confucianism is dying if it is taken as a set of precepts governing particular human relations such as parent and child, husband and wife, and so on. The Confucian legacy continues to influence the Japanese way of life, I believe, as an abstract, generalized ideology applicable to a wide variety of human relations. A great majority of Japanese remain Confucian, I speculate, in the sense that they perceive a life course as a cycle with a beginning and an end. Aware of this trajectory of life, they believe life has to be built up from its very beginning in order to enjoy fulfillment toward its final stage. They seem to take it for granted that strenuous effort and hardship as well as deferment of gratification at the earlier life stage is a necessary investment for a later payoff, that there will be no reward without sacrifice, that there will be no success without trying. This long-range perspective of life seems even to be intensifying in view of the increasingly longer and greater expenditure of the child's energy and family resources for educational achievement.

Enmeshed with this life view is the suppression of self-interest as a motive for action, which may be also partially attributable to the Confucian legacy. The Japanese in general, while strongly concerned with themselves, shy away from outright selfishness or egoism. When in fact egoistically motivated, they are compelled to justify their action in altruistic terms since the pursuit of self-interest has not been culturally sanctioned. The content of altruism (altruism for whom, and in what way, for instance) has changed and probably become non-Confucian, but the suppression of self-interest is persisting as a cultural style of self-presentation or in the form of intolerance of some other person who has acted selfishly. For Japanese one's self is either what is to be intermingled in empathy with another's self or what is to be internally contained and disciplined.

The Confucian gender ideology, together with the *ie*, is becoming outmoded, but the above heritage of Confucianism cannot help affecting the woman's life as well. The longer the life stage of preparation and investment for later fulfillment extends, that is, the more the period of childhood is lengthened, the greater will be the portion of a woman's life to be taken up for motherhood. And motherhood is an embodiment of selflessness. The possible result is a strengthened bond of mother and child, as foreshadowed by the phenomenon of *mazakon*, mother complex, which young women today, after marrying by their own choice, are distressed to see in their well-educated, career-promising husbands. One might speculate whether this trend will delay the death of the Confucian gender ideology or exacerbate the emotional stress for young women that we have described as inherent in Confucianism.

NOTES

1. This paper was prepared while I was on sabbatical and a recipient of a Japan Studies Endowment Award, for which I wish to thank the University of Hawaii,
2. Fieldwork has been conducted four times since 1976 for different purposes under the support of the National Science Foundation, the Japan Society for the Promotion of Science, the Social Science Research Council, and the Japan Foundation. Their generosity is gratefully acknowledged.
3. In my sample, the elder brother's authority over younger sisters was striking, sometimes superseding the father's, particularly in the matter of spouse selection. The emotional ties between brother and sister were also noted.
4. The life interval between school graduation and marriage varied widely by classes: for upper- and middle-class daughters this was a time for learning bridal arts from house-calling tutors or at bridal schools; lower-class girls often became live-in maids with urban higher-class families, and while working, expected to learn good manners and domestic skills.
5. There was class difference in this regard in that the upper-class bride experienced much less hardship with her in-laws if she did at all. Many reasons are conceivable but to mention a few: because of the availability of servants, the bridal duty did not include labor; contact with parents-in-law was no more than ritual, with servants as communication mediators; mother-in-law's jealousy was weaker or nonexistent due to the emotional distance between mother and son (again it was a nurse-maid, not the mother, who actually reared the son). Furthermore, succession did not mean co-residence of two generations as automatically as in other classes: neolocal residence by a successor son and his wife was more common in the upper class.
6. Even the pre-Confucian elevation of heterosexual emotions, as cited above in association with Motoori Norinaga, seems sexually more asymmetric than might be expected. *The Tale of Genji*, for instance, which is often cited as a classical example of unhampered sexual emotionalism, reveals that free, multiple, illicit access to the opposite sex was enjoyed by men. Their wives and mistresses suffered tremendous agony, depressions, and, in some cases, psychogenic death imputed to a rival woman's witchcraft.
7. Salamon (1975) demonstrated that 'male chauvinism' could be combined with conjugal love through the cultural means of *amae*. The age group she was referring to was younger than mine, but her point nonetheless is instructive.
8. I think that in Japan mother and child are the 'dominant dyad' to borrow Hsu's (1971) phrase, in a generalized or figurative sense, covering a variety of relations including those between men. The boss and his subordinate in a modern company, for example, are more like mother and child than father and son in that the former is responsible for 'bringing up' the latter. It seems that trustful intimacy is best built up in the mother-child configuration irrespective of gender. In this sense, I propose Japanese 'paternalism' to be renamed 'maternalism.' And, of course, the other side of maternalism is filialism, if we may coin a word. Among Americans such intimacy seems to call for a sexual pair.

REFERENCES

Caudill, William and Helen Weinstein, (1974). 'Maternal Care and Infant Behavior in Japan and America.' In *Japanese Culture and Behavior: Selected Readings,* ed. T. S. Lebra and W. P. Lebra. Honolulu: University of Hawaii Press. Reprinted in the 1986 revised edition.

de Beauvoir, Simone. (1972). *The Second Sex.* London: Penguin.

De Vos, George. (1974). 'The relation of guilt toward parents to achievement and arranged marriage among the Japanese.' In *Japanese Culture and Behavior: Selected Readings* (See Caudill above for reference). Also reprinted in the 1986 revised edition.

Hirota, Masaki. (1982). 'Bunmei kaika to josei kaiho-ron' (Westernization and Women's Liberation). In *Nihon josei-shi* (The History of Japanese Women), vol. 4, ed. Josei Sogo Kenkyukai. Tokyo: University of Tokyo Press.

Hsu, Francis L. K. (1971). 'A Hypothesis on Kinship and Culture' In *Kinship and Culture,* ed. F L. K. Hsu. Chicago: Aldine.

Igeta, Ryoji. (1982). 'Meiji minpo to josei no kenri' (The Meiji Civil Code and Women's Rights). In *Nihon Josei-shi,* vol. 4. (See Hirota above for full reference.)

Lebra, Takie Sugiyama. (1979). 'The Dilemma and Strategies of Aging among Contemporary Japanese Women.' *Ethnology* 18: 337–53.

—— (1984). *Japanese Women: Constraint and Fulfillment.* Honolulu: University of Hawaii Press.

Maddi, Salvatore R. (1972). *Personality Theories: A Comparative Analysis* (rev. ed.). Homewood, IL: Dorsey Press.

Nadel, S. F. (1951). *The Foundations of Social Anthropology.* London: Cohen & West.

Nagahara, Kazuko. (1982). 'Ryosai kenbo-shugi kyoiku ni okeru ie to shokugyo' (The *Ie* and jobs in the Educational Policy in Favor of the Good Wife and Wise Mother). In *Nihon Josei-shi,* vol. 4. (See Hirota above for full reference.)

Peizel, John C. (1970). 'Japanese Kinship: A Comparison' In *Family and Kinship in Chinese Society,* ed. M. Freedman. Stanford, CA: Stanford University Press.

—— (1974). 'Human Nature in the Japanese Myths.' In *Japanese Culture and Behavior: Selected Readings.* (See Caudill above for full reference.) Reprinted in the 1986 revised edition.

Perry, Linda L. (1976). 'Mothers, Wives, and Daughters in Osaka: Autonomy, Alliance and Professionalism.' Ph.D. dissertation, University of Pittsburgh.

Plath, David W. (1975). 'The Last Confucian Sandwich: Becoming Middle Aged.' In *Adult Episodes in Japan,* ed. D.W Plath. Leiden: E. J. Brill.

Salamon, Sonya. (1975). '"Male Chauvinism" as a Manifestation of Love in Marriage.' In *Adult Episodes in Japan,* ed. D. W. Plath. Leiden: E. J. Brill. Also reprinted in *Japanese Culture and Behavior: Selected Readings* (rev. ed., 1986), ed. T. S. Lebra and W. P. Lebra. Honolulu: University of Hawaii Press.

Suenari, Michio. (1972). 'First Child Inheritance in Japan.' *Ethnology* 11: 122–26.

Turner, Victor W. (1969). *The Ritual Process: Structure and Anti-Structure.* Chicago: Aldine.

Vogel, Suzanne H. (1987). 'Professional Housewife: The Career of Urban Middle-Class Japanese Women' *The Japan Interpreter* 12: 16–43.

Yoshikawa, Kojiro. (1969). 'Motoori Norinaga no shiso' (Motoori Norinaga's Ideas). In *Motoori Norinaga Shu* (Collected Works of Motoori Norinaga), ed. K. Yoshikawa, Tokyo: Chikuma Shobo.

First published in CAS Research Papers Series No. 16, II, *Gender, Women and Motherhood*, 1999

18 Non-Western Reactions to Western Feminism: The Case of Japanese Career Women

INTRODUCTION

Every society is likely to carry its own legacy of gender culture. But today, it is Western feminism, though loosely understood, that has made and is making perhaps an irreversible impact on women's rights and movements world over. Japanese women and men are also getting increasingly sensitized to gender issues mainly under Western influence. They look to North America and Europe (especially Scandinavia) – let me call them together Euro-American or simply 'West' – for models to emulate or for standards whereby to measure their own progress or retardation. Behind all this is the international pressure coming from the United Nations resolutions for women from the mid-1970s.

One indication of this Western impact is the liberal use of English, or rather 'Jinglish' to describe gender-relevant phenomena (although, for that matter, this practice extends to all other fields as well in Japan). Just to mention a few: '*ūman ribu*' rather than the native equivalent, '*josei kaihō*' has been in the popular speech since the 1970s. Rape has appeared as '*reipu*' to replace the old '*gōkan*'; 'feminizumu,' 'kyaria ūman,' 'jendā' too are circulating along with many other such loan words.

Such anglicization, first, contributes to making gender awareness exotic and fashionable like most popular culture items, and to elevating familiar but tabooed subjects to public discourse. Second, it is to add new words for what have not been recognized in the Japanese dictionary. One such example is 'sexual harassment' which is called in a typically Japanese abbreviation 'sekuhara.'[1] This is no denying that there is strong undercurrent, as well, counteracting Western feminism whether from resentment, cultural inertia, or awareness of its limitation in universal application.

The bulk of this paper concerns the experiences of Japanese career women. These data, in relation to Western feminism, have emerged from years of fieldwork and interviews. Given various versions of feminism, I focus more or less on the demand for gender equality in economic, political, social, and domestic rights and duties. At the end, I contextualize this case study in a theoretical framework, especially in light of Western concerns with essentialism and constructivism and their implications for feminism.

SAMPLE WOMEN

I explore the lives of those women who have crossed gender barriers to enter the male sphere, and to climb the male dominant hierarchy, as recalled, constructed, and evaluated by themselves. Over the past two decades I have interviewed more than 40 such women who have achieved eminence as the first, only, highest-ranking, or otherwise pioneering women in their respective professions or workplaces (for earlier findings, see Lebra 1981; 1992). This includes 24 women interviewed in 1993, a few of them interviewed again in 1996, who constitute the main sample for this paper. Their careers were in civil service, business, academia, research, journalism, media, adult education, film making, politics, law, architecture, music composition, zoo administration, athletics.[2] At interview time, their ages ranged from mid-40s to early 70s, concentrating in the late 40s, 50s and 60s. Four women were divorced, one widowed, four single, the rest being married, seven including the four singles were childless.

By the time of the interviews, their careers had all reached fruition, gaining national recognition in terms of organizational ranks and leadership and/or records of individual productivity, creativity and performance in their respective professions. Their names appeared in national and sometimes foreign media, many were prolific authors, and several were subjects of biography written by admirers. They were recipients of prizes, including imperial decorations, governmental, corporate, or professional awards and commendations. In a one-page printed curriculum vitae which I was often given before each interview, I also found long lists of appointments to advisory councils or committees attached to the executive branch of the government. They were sought after as advisors and opinion-makers on public issues. My sample thus comes from a special category of women whose experiences and views cannot be extrapolated to Japanese women in general except in part. Still, I hope to suggest some differences between Japanese and Western concepts of women and gender.

TRANSNATIONAL EXPOSURES

For their career development, many of these women benefited from transnational experiences. Fifteen women out of 24 had overseas experiences and education in childhood, on a home-stay program, at a pre-career or early-career stage. All the returnees continued to be transnationally mobile by spending additional years abroad after their return. Four of the civil servants were sent abroad by their employer, the government, for further training at foreign universities or in international organizations. The United States was the host country for most of the post-war sojourners, with only a few European connections. The nine other women who did not belong to this category had mid-career overseas exposures.

Transnational experiences were the single most crucial factor for many of them to succeed in making a career, to carve out an unconventional career, to change a career course, to maintain a cosmopolitan outlook or to preserve career options. These women invariably cherished their Western experiences and credited them as among the most influential factors that determined their life courses thereafter.

Some women started their careers overseas, which gave them a head start in Japan's job market at multinational companies. A woman who returned to Japan with an American degree in communication and job experience at an American firm was hired at an American company's subsidiary in Japan, immediately to head a newly-created Public Relations Department, a field of speciality previously unknown to the Japanese.

Bicultural or multicultural expertise is not just a matter of skill but a conceptual resource. A returnee with an American MA, hired by a multinational company in Japan, was quickly promoted to managerial ranks. She succeeded because she could grasp Japan's market structure with its notoriously multi-layered distribution system through her bicultural lens. Another returnee started her own business in home building, borrowing the American cost-effective model as an inspiration to change outmoded techniques and labor relations in housing construction practices of Japan, which brought her national fame. These are just a few out of many examples.

FEMINIST CAREERS

Overseas experiences in the 1970s involved exposures to gender revolution, feminist movement, and women's studies, then flourishing in North America, as witnessed by our returnees. Some of them had their hearts deeply touched by contemporary Western feminism, which prompted refocusing their careers upon women's rights. Many of them carried a mission as pioneering women, as a role model or pathfinder for the coming generation of women. Some of them made careers out of feminism.

A national newspaper reporter, first assigned to the police department, gradually evolved into a more committed feminist eventually on a global scale. She viewed her life as marked by critical phases of history – Japanese and global – beginning with the post-WWII liberation, engaging in student activism, anti-nuclear and pacifist movements. While working as a reporter on women's lives, she came to learn the actual state of women's plight, which shocked her and drove her to cover instances of gendered injustice in her reportage. Earlier, her transnational perspective had been opened up when she traveled around the United States as one of the five foreign guests invited by the State Department. It was during this tour that she came upon Betty Friedan's *Feminine Mystique* (1964). The book struck her 'with a thunderbolt' and awakened her to what was taking place outside Japan, and the women's liberation movement sweeping in the United States became a favorite topic of her TV program in her new job as a broadcaster.

From 1975 on, she attended the UN-sponsored World Congresses for Women, and each time brought her reports to the national network. Quitting the media job, she now became an eminent national leader in promoting gender equality, in conjunction with the new government measures for women. When I met her, she had been director of a municipal center for women, and a member of the UN commission on women's status, representing Japan. At interview time, she was engaging in this commission's decision to eradicate sexual violence, and was personally concerned with human-rights issues, particularly Japan's guilt regarding comfort women. She was the most distinct example of making a career out of feminism in her latest career metamorphosis. As this case clearly shows, feminism was strongly tied to transnational influence. Another woman made a career out of women's right to divorce after she traveled to Sweden where she was inspired by women's way of life.

AMBIVALENCE AND COOLNESS TOWARD FEMINISM

Nevertheless, a large majority of my informants turned out to be ambivalent, cool, dismissive or critical of Western feminism or gender issues in general. Far from being traditionalist, they explained their anti- or non-feminist reactions by the claim that they had never questioned equality. The woman, who chose to be a prosecutor because she believed this was the most gender-blind profession, found herself too egalitarian to be concerned with gender. She had never considered herself responsible for elevating women's status, and was critical of American feminists, including Hillary Clinton, who seemed obsessed with women's issues. This prosecutor thought they were pathetically backward. Another informant, an internationally-known research scientist, made the point of herself having 'nothing to do with those who are active in Women's Studies.'

One of the civil servants presented herself as a marginal government employee appointed at the Prime Minister's Agency instead of a full-fledged ministry. This appointment entailed several temporary transfers to other agencies, one of which placed her in an office in charge of women's problems. This led to her opportunity of being sent abroad, twice, as part of her job to study women, first at a Canadian university and second at Harvard. She did research on American executive women. Her experiences with women, overseas as well as in Japan, culminated in her writing many books. Her marginal career route for a state bureaucrat thus turned out to be a blessing. She established a national and international reputation, not tied down to the bureaucracy, but rather as an expert on women's problems.

Still, this eminent career woman did not consider herself an 'authentic' feminist. The authentic feminist, by her definition, is someone who would oppose her position to that of men, someone who is critical and confrontational. Those women she met in North America were not radical feminists but successful women who were confident in making careers in the male-dominated world of business.

Another informant was adamant in claiming that she owed her successful career in business to her gender since she stood out as the only woman in a crowd of male peers. That a woman benefits from being anomalous, exceptional, novel and thus conspicuous was mentioned by several others as their own experience. When you are the only woman in a conference, participants will remember your name, said another civil servant, while male participants are too many to be so lucky. The woman's visibility also sensitized her male colleagues to female problems such as her need to go home earlier than others to look after her young child. This bureaucrat admitted that she had taken advantage of their generosity. Today, she continued, young women civil servants are having a hard time, because there are so many of them now that they don't stand out. They are 'buried' under the rule of strict 'equality,' which keeps them too busy to have their kids.

A woman's visibility and advantage in the male world may account for her concern with feminine appearance, as indicated by her dresses, accessories, cosmetics, and hairdo. Many of my informants looked carefully groomed particularly when I met them in office. A staunch feminist ironically adopted this feminine self-presentation as a career strategy as well who specially called my attention to this factor. A social critic, public educator, and prolific author, specializing on divorce, she came under severe attack from all sides when the rumor circulated that she was advocating women's right to divorce. On the first day of her venture into opening an adult-education class on divorce, she emerged as an instantaneous celebrity, and became a center of attention from reporters foraging for the latest news. When they saw her, they were surprised that she did not look like the fiendish feminist they had anticipated. Instead, my informant had 'a very soft voice' which countered the stereotypic image of a radical loud-mouth feminist and to her great advantage, she appeared harmless. She could thus disarm conservative men even while she was actually pronouncing a strong radical feminism. A marvelous instance of the word-appearance discrepancy![4] It was her external feminine appearance that sent a metamessage that wrapped up the lower-order verbal message of feminism.

This strategic concern also induced this feminist to be scrupulous in her dress style and grooming. She would spend more money than her means, I was told, on her expensive and colorful dresses and accessories – and from her appearance I could believe she was not exaggerating her investment. Moreover, she started to hold a seminar class in an 'event hall' of a beautiful modern building, located in a most fashionable district of Tokyo, a center where young people gathered for fun. The rationale was that she wanted to obliterate the fixed association between divorce and gloom and to create an image of cheery divorce. When she stood in front of scores of her students, followers and fans in a class, she looked more like a princess, a perfectly-groomed beauty, than a radical reformer.

DISCRIMINATION AND HARASSMENT

The question arises whether none of these women were victims of discrimination or harassment. Yes, many were. It was in creative professions such as architecture and music composition that the most flagrant discrimination was practiced. A graduate from the prestigious Tokyo National University of

Arts and Music with first-class license in architecture, a distinctly male profession, could not find an employment except as an assistant or clerk. Finally, she established herself as a self-employed architect when she found herself successful in attracting an increasing number of clients.

A music composer was most assertive about the prevalence of gender discrimination and prejudice, particularly in her field. A Julliard graduate, she claimed that music compositions was 'the most male-dominated profession,' or perhaps second only to that of conductor, and 'the last citadel for men to defend for life' even in the West.[5] Why didn't she go ahead with her composition work without bothering to seek support from such wretched men? A composition alone cannot make a job, she explained, because composed music has to be translated into public 'sound' to be orchestrated and appreciated by an audience. This conversion of personal creation into public performance and recording as well as marketing requires an institutional structure, and it is this structured medium that is staffed and controlled solely by men.

Discrimination could involve an offensive confrontation as in the case of an entrepreneur, a founder of a language school. Men, whose support she solicited, advised her against such a reckless adventure 'because the best a woman can do is what a monkey can.' These three cases represent women, lone and liminal, excluded from the solid male structure at their incipient career stage.[6]

Unlike unstructured careers like these, structured careers, typically those of civil service, are claimed to gender-blind. All the five civil servants in my sample confirmed that hiring is contingent only on passing the standard civil-service examinations, and that promotion is automatic, bound only by the seniority rule. Yet, this turns out to be an overstatement. Each ministry or agency is virtually an independent empire and can decide whether it will hire a number of women or no women at all this year. I was often told that this or that major ministry had closed its door to women applicants for more than ten years, while men were welcomed in open arms every year by every ministry and agency. In other words, at a transitional, liminal point of career – between graduating from university or passing an examination and getting a job – women lose structural support and must forage for a job by themselves. Even if a woman can enter the service, she will be quite limited in the choice of ministries. They enjoy equality only after they become restructured by employment.

In addition to these cases of exclusion, there were instances of sexual harassment. The only woman in a male crowd can draw men's excessive attention as nothing other than a female, and as an erotic object. I introduce one extraordinary case. A film director, when she started her long film-making career as an assistant director, was responsible for setting up everything necessary for the director to make a film. She had to assist the director, cameraman, lighting technician and all other specialists and workers in the film-making scene. At the same time, she had to 'look after' the staff's everyday life. When the team went out on location, she was overloaded with chores all day. She was a maternal caretaker, and maidservant for men – an exceedingly multiple, ill-defined, debased job.

At night her job turned into, in the eyes of male co-workers, sexual availability. The only woman, working side by side with many men, was vulnerable to their libidinal impulses. This shocked her greatly as she was in her twenties at the time. While making a film, the whole team often slept together in a workroom, making beds out of chairs and desks and rented *futon*. But this group-sleeping (*zakone*) in the same room was much safer than her sleeping alone in a separate room, as it happened at location sites where they slept in an inn. At night, after she withdrew into her own room, she would hear footsteps coming toward her *shôji*-doored room. She had to thwart a colleague's attempt to subdue her, and as this was repeated by one man after another, this future film director developed an extraordinary fear of men coming toward her. What finally rescued her from all this harassment was her marriage to a producer. 'Marriage made me happy most because it stopped men from bothering me.'

GENDER, AGE, SENIORITY AND RANKS

These instances of discrimination and harassment did not necessarily invoke feminist indignation because a man's advance was considered inevitable at that time, because the memories now appeared in the remote past, and because gender relations had changed over the years in Japan's latest history. As an informant contemplated, 'Once women were totally ignored because they were women, but now they are better off because they are women.' Such change reflects both Japan's strides over a couple of decades toward recognition of women's rights on the one hand (though quite tardy compared with the West's advancement), and my informant's career maturation on the other.

Career maturation further calls attention to the complexity of gender identity that accounts for a generally-shared coolness toward feminism. Gender rarely shows up singly but usually in combination with age and seniority, at least this is true in Japan. Putting it another way, gender becomes an issue more in young adulthood or at the beginning of a career when age and seniority have not yet contaminated it. I illustrate this generalization by a first year experience in civil service.

Civil servants are categorized into three levels, requiring three different examinations, and structured for three different career tracks. My informants were of the upper category, recognized as 'career' state bureaucrats, popularly labeled 'elite,' who take pride in shaping top-level decisions and policies of the state. The two other categories of civil servants, middle and lower, are 'non-career' employees who facilitate or support the upper category staff with technical, clerical, or menial services.[7] (For an exposé of between-category tensions and resentment, see Ito, 1998). My informants were referring to gender equality within their own upper category, not across the three.

In the office, a woman typically finds herself as the only female member of the upper category either because women were that scarce or because the personnel administration saw to it that if there were two women entrants, they would be assigned to different sections. There were many other women belonging to the lower categories in and around the office. This was the situation that my informant stumbled into at the very beginning of her career:

> There were many women of middle and lower categories. What were they doing? First, they would come to office 15 minutes earlier than others, clean the office, and then serve tea to all [even though these are not included in their job specification]. It became a big issue whether I should join these women. At first I thought I did not have to. But then I noticed older 'sisters' glaring at me, which was frightening. I felt ill at ease as if sitting on a thorny floor. So I decided to join and offered to help clean the office. This offer further engaged me to a rotationally scheduled regular duty (*tōban*). Today, this sort of thing is unthinkable. Twenty-five years ago, our level of consciousness was like that ... My superior, the section chief, did not know what to do, nor did he tell me not to do that. This state of affairs lasted one year, stopped by the section chief's announcement that Ms. X shall be freed from tea duty.

Tea service might sound trivial, but was symbolically significant of one's self-denigration and acceptance of gender inequality and gender-typed role, as well captured by Susan Pharr (1994).[8] It was a hot issue that involved all upper-ranking women in the government in the late 1960s. My informant questioned why she had to pour tea for the man who was a same-year entrant (*dōki*). It was a source of suffering for women. Now that equality had been more firmly established, but perhaps more importantly, because she was no longer an apprentice, she felt more comfortable and free to serve tea.[9]

This talk about tea service is symbolic of the complexity of gender issues as well. Firstly, it was not men but other women who put liminal pressures upon the upper-category woman to share their downgraded service work as a woman like themselves. She was an anomaly in the office that was dichotomized between upper-ranking male and lower-ranking female, with no allowance for a third category of upper-ranking women. Thus her status identity was uneasily split between the female rank and the male rank. This dissonance was resolved by downgrading the conspicuously anomalous woman to a typically female status. This suggests that gender issues are not always limited to the male-female dyad but may involve a female-female conflict to disorient the female-male opposition.

Secondly, and more importantly, she was 'promoted' into the full-fledged upper-ranking male group after a year, when she was no longer a fledgling. It was not just her gender but her being a neophyte that had kept her down. The lower-ranking women in the office were older and had been employed for many years. Their sense of seniority got in the way of recognizing the neophyte woman as outranking them (but note that they did not take this attitude toward neophyte men). It seems that one year of apprenticeship symbolically raised her to the fully upper-rank status in the eyes of women workers.

Gender discrimination was skewed at the entry level when gender inferiority was coupled with the freshman status, the lowest grade among all the upper-rank staff. In the course of increments in seniority and grade levels, a woman would shed her gender handicap. A long-ranged retrospective story of one's career is very likely to focus on career maturation in which gender is viewed increasingly in the light of time flow of age and seniority. Discrimination, exclusion and harassment, discussed in the previous section, were concentrated at the woman's initial stage or pre-career stage when she appeared more as a female.

MALE SPONSORS AND MENTORS

If gender is inseparable from age-seniority-based status and role, it is not surprising that many of my informants entered a collaborative relationship with men, particularly those outranking themselves. In the family, father encouraged the daughter to enter a top university and to pursue a career. At university, some women received crucial advice from their male professors as to their career directions, choice of jobs, and the like that did determine their futures.

School-based senior-junior (*sempai-kōhai*) ties continue to benefit women as well as men, particularly graduates from co-educational, prominent universities, by forming cross-gender support groups. An informant in civil service frequently referred to her Todai (University of Tokyo) background, as the basis of her self-confidence, which never wavered in face of career crises or harassment. She felt assured of support coming whenever she needed it, from the Todai senior graduates, who occupied upper positions of the same ministry. With this confidence, she could ignore any sign of discriminatory pressures from her male colleagues.

Further, many informants talked about training by male workmates as having been indispensable to the development of their future careers. A feminist informant came to learn how to be a journalist by being thrown into a group of 15 young male co-workers to draft news articles for various weekly magazines. It was a tough but rewarding on-the-job apprenticeship through participating in group discussions. So 'without paying tuition, I learned how to write articles, how to match an article with a proper title, how to stylize writing to fit a weekly magazine.' She had virtually been 'brought up' by these 'very kind guys,' to prepare herself to be a full-fledged and successful journalist, popular writer, and public educator.

Some women had a head start thanks to the administrative authority, embodied by a male chief, assuming sponsorship for them, thereby circumventing the traditional male-centered practice of hiring, job assignment, and seniority-based promotion. Such sponsorship was more pronounced in the private sector.

The newspaper reporter was first assigned to cover the police, and then the trial courts, which had been a strictly male territory. All these extraordinary assignments resulted from the single-handed decision of the editorial bureau chief in the head office, who believed that there should be no job differences between women and men if they were hired on an equal basis. Looking back, she appreciated her boss' progressive ideology and decision.

A returnee from the US launched into a business career. 'I was very fortunate,' she said, 'because my career started out with the company president's authoritative voice (*tsuru no hitokoe*).' It was he who noticed her potential for business administration. She was soon promoted to sales manager (section chief), the first and only female manager in the company among more than 40 sales managers. 'It was Mr. X who paved a career path for me.' She became devoted not only to her job but also to the president. His subsequent resignation to take a better job in the United States demoralized her about staying on in the company. She switched to one and then another transnational company, each of which backed her up through strong and personal executive sponsorship. It should be noted that in all the three companies, she had a non-Japanese boss.

A case from the liminal career type represents the overwhelming weight of a male executive in pushing and supporting a woman for jobs she did not have the slightest idea about how to do. The future film director, the only woman in the sample who had no more than high school education, after a film-related job assignment, was appointed assistant film director, and two years later, promoted to full-fledged director! Starting her career as a total amateur with no preparation, no knowledge or skill, she attained the very top of film profession in a remarkably short period. This was solely because an executive producer of the company took risks to push her up at each stage, prematurely. To prove worthy of his confidence, she emerged as an internationally-acclaimed documentary film director.

A male boss not only sponsored a female subordinate but became a mentor and trainer for her. The above-mentioned businesswoman was thoroughly trained by the Thai Chinese president of her third company, to master everything necessary to run the whole enterprise from marketing to budgetary to personnel matters. The president himself worked seven days a week, longer hours than anybody else, and demanded no less from every employee. From earlier experiences at two previous companies, she had become a sales expert well-known in the same business world, but now was facing many other aspects of a business enterprise that were entirely new to her. Financial details in particular were difficult to digest. The president was relentless in demanding that she master it all right away. 'I appointed you. If you failed', he said, 'it's going to be my shame!' His harsh yelling reduced her to tears countless times. He knew he had only one year before his anticipated return to his home country, to hammer all the necessary business expertise into her. Finally he said, 'I have taught you everything, it's all up to you how to implement it.' In recalling his mentoring, her voice was impassioned. To an outsider's ear, the whole 'training' could have bordered on abuse. At times, she could not help resenting him, but knowing he meant well, she devoted body and soul to meeting his high expectations. She felt very indebted and grateful. After all that hardship, she knew she had nothing to fear. She was able to deal with all matters and all persons in the company business.

Mentorship was a consistent theme in narratives of academic/research careers, particularly in natural science. The oldest woman in the sample launched her career as a research scientist when she met Dr. K who was to become 'a lifelong mentor and benefactor for me.' Upon college graduation, this budding scientist was employed at a research division of a national government agency to work and study under this master. It was Dr. K who guided her not only in the selection of research subjects and methods, but also in life philosophy in general and about the issue of male-female equality.

Toward the end of the World War II, the whole research staff under Dr. K had to evacuate in a group to a rural town and to live together in a local temple. Dr. K was with them thoroughout, constantly advising them to continue to study 'because the war will end soon.' Indeed the war ended soon, and Dr. K undertook to establish a full-fledged research institute out of the former research division. Under his tutelage my informant, initially a part-timer, rose to research-team head, 'an equivalent to assistant professor', and later to research-division chief. In the meantime, she worked on her doctoral dissertation on a topic suggested by Dr. K. Did he guide her dissertation research itself?

> Yes, of course, my *sensei* helped me throughout. Whenever I came to an impasse, he advised me to take this approach or that approach. My dissertation thus was a product of my constant consultation with my *sensei*.

For a dissertation to be considered for a degree, it was mandatory to have it first published in the most prestigious academic journal in her field. Again, it was Dr. K who eased the way for the journal's acceptance of her dissertation, through his own professor at Todai who was a review-committee supervisor. This resulted in Todai awarding her the first doctoral degree in science for women. This awardee was open about how much she owed Dr. K for all other accomplishments of hers, including her overseas appointments such as one at an American research institute, and to international conferences in and out of Japan where she played a central role. Her name often appeared in Western science journals. She was the first woman scientist to become a member of the Science Council of Japan, and this too she credited to Dr. K's endorsement.

The time came for her to reciprocate her 'lifelong benefactor and teacher' (*shôgai no onshi*), sadly, during the last months of his life with terminal cancer. She commuted to the hospital, spent all day there helping him continue on his manuscript and brought the notes home for word-processing at night, all in order to boost his morale to live on. She became tearful talking about Dr. K in his deathbed. This woman remained single. Her entire career thus centered on her master, marked by her heartfelt indebtedness and devotion to him. During the interview, I was struck by a double image of her: one as a distinguished scientist, the first female doctor of science from Todai, the first woman elected to the Science Council of Japan, the first in many other accomplishments; and the other as a female assistant dedicated to her male mentor and boss throughout her entire career.

Why did all these men exercise their structural authority to sponsor, promote, lead and train their women subordinates or followers? In the first place, most of these men turned out to be reform-minded, and it is likely that they envisioned the specially able women as facilitating a breakthrough to bring about the institutional and programmatic innovations they deemed necessary.

The businesswoman's first boss decided to promote her to sales manager after witnessing a contrast between her and male managers in their attitudes toward the drug company's important clients such as top-level physicians. The male managers were observed ingratiating themselves with these distinguished MDs, going out of their way to meet their personal needs. The president saw my informant being able to relate to these 'famous' doctors on a more equal footing, partly due to her American education.

Secondly, the male boss seems to have had a freer hand to treat a woman more personally than a man precisely because she was an unknown, liminal, marginal entity. In other words, he could favor or disfavor a woman subordinate at his discretion without arousing structurally-based resistance. It was the woman's marginality that allowed her male boss to bypass the bureaucratic strictures, to make an unprecedented decision to hire, promote, sponsor or mentor her without threatening the male-centered hierarchical organization.

Thirdly, because these women were entering careers unprecedented for women, they were more disposed to be receptive, malleable and compliant to their superiors. The film director repeated to me that the film career was not what she had planned and built up for herself, rather that she simply did whatever her sponsor told her to. This kind of malleability, in turn, must have motivated the sponsor and mentor all the more to invest in his female protégé.

The woman's liminal status, which we saw was detrimental to her career establishment in a structured setting, thus turned into a positively perceived resource. We cannot rule out sexual attraction entirely, but my informants were invariably adamant in denying that possibility when hinted at. Feminism did not stand in the way of accepting the men's support; quite the contrary, the male bosses were praised for their championship for the women's cause. I speculate that both the male boss and female subordinate were psychologically protected from sexual involvement by the gender-seniority mixture as described in the preceding section. At any rate, for the above reasons, the structurally-central male position and the female marginality seem to have made a complementary set.

Kanter (1977: 220), referring to the male sponsorship for female subordinates who achieved administrative positions in a male-dominant American corporation – Indusco – dismisses this type of male-female hierarchical alliance, saying that 'this strategy was made risky by shifting power alliances at the top,' and instead favors 'peer cooperation.'

The Japanese women appeared oblivious of 'shifting power alliances at the top' which would make sponsorship 'risky.' This may have to do with the relative stability of the superior subordinate relationship, which is reinforced by the cultural formula of 'indebtedness' not to be forgotten long after separation. Such stability may have made the mutual investment worthwhile. The research scientist who called her mentor 'the lifelong benefactor' best exemplifies this. Even the businesswoman who had three foreign bosses in succession remembered each of them with gratitude for their patronage and training.

And finally, these informants told me in a culturally-approved narrative style of self-presentation how much they owed their sponsors for their accomplishments. Perhaps in an American narrative style, one might present oneself more as a self-made career woman.

MALE AND FEMALE SUBORDINATES

Unless the work was solitary, career maturation entailed an increment of authority and power held by the woman over her subordinates, by her managerial effectiveness and the respect that her subordinates held for her. By interview time, all my informants in non-solitary careers were heading an entire organization or a unit thereof. In this section I look at my informants as chiefs in command of male and female subordinates, focusing on whether there is any gender difference. The best illustration is provided by one of the highest achievers.

A woman with an impeccable credential from the Todai Faculty of Law entered the Ministry of Labor, which was her choice but also was the only ministry that accepted women at the time. The ministry's exceptional open-door policy was because it housed the Bureau of Women and Minors (BWM) – later renamed with 'Minors' dropped. The BWM, which had been always headed by a woman since its inception, with a majority of women staff, was not her choice, but all other bureaus in the ministry were off limits to women at her entry time. In this unusual gender composition, this informant found a blessing of equality predominating in the office. For instance, the assistant section chief, her senior by 13 years, acted toward her like an intimate friend, doing things together with her. 'This was quite different from a male-dominant office where hierarchy predominates.'[10]

When she was transferred to a prefectural branch office of the ministry, she found herself in a decidedly male kingdom with a strictly vertical organization. 'Men are like monkeys on a monkey hill' with a strong sense of hierarchy, she said.[11] To make the matters worse for her, her appointment there was as a rank-and-file staff member for the purpose of apprenticeship, while she was the only national career bureaucrat therein. Probably perceived as a threat by the local male staff, she was abused, which she did not want to describe. Apparently this period hit the bottom of her career.

The differences were stark between the egalitarian head office with women of similar backgrounds including fellow Todai graduates (OGs: old girls), and this local branch office with its male-dominated hierarchical structure. Here was a distinct contrast between female and male, equality and hierarchy. Still she refused to be intimidated, and dared to announce she was not going to serve tea, period.

As she moved up the bureaucratic ladder, her gender or location of appointment ceased to matter. When she was again transferred to another local branch office, this time as its chief, things were totally different. 'Local men were nonplussed at their first woman boss, I heard, but they had to comply with the hierarchical order,' and they did so without fuss.

The above story, in my view, involves two career stages. On the one hand, when young, my informant benefited from the egalitarian subculture of the head office of the BWM because it was female dominated, and she suffered from the male-centered, gender-discriminatory hierarchy prevailing in the local office. At a later stage, she met no resistance from male subordinates precisely because she stood above them in a hierarchical structure that transcended her gender and anomaly. Her presence made sense to male subordinates in their own language – hierarchy. The male-biased hierarchy would work against a woman (or for that matter anybody) at her earlier, rankless stage of career, but would come to support her at her later stage when her career matured to command layers of subordinates.

When she was placed in a position to manage a group of male section chiefs who were only a little younger than she was, she found to her surprise that these men actually threw themselves into cutthroat competition with one another to prove their loyalty to her. To her amazement, the men competed even in fawning on her! If hierarchy is essential to a male subordinate's submission, it may be that similarly ranking colleagues would engage in fierce competition.

How did they compare with female subordinates? Generally, my informants found no gender difference in their preference for subordinates. But if there was any comment on differences between men and women, it was more in favor of male subordinates. Women tend to be more egalitarian among them, and this fact is likely to be appreciated favorably if one is at the lowest rank, but unfavorably when one assumes a managerial position. I was told that men were more willing to comply with their superiors as a matter of a formal rank order or bureaucratic rule, whereas women tend to bring more personal, emotional elements into the same-sexed hierarchical relationship. In my earlier study in 1992, I found among female company presidents more severe critics of female than male employees; there were twice as many companies that hired exclusively or predominantly male employees as there were companies that employed women only.

There is difference in compliance patterns. While male subordinates submit to the authority of a female boss as the mandate of hierarchical 'structure', female subordinates comply with their leader out of personal attachment, identification with her, adoration of her as a pioneer and model for them. This attitude of female subordinates seems to mirror an elite-career woman's sense of mission as a senior, model or pathfinder, to meet the expectations not only of her subordinates but of women in general. This is the point where Japanese women come closest to the Western type of gender essentialism whereby two hierarchically-ordered women see one another as belonging to the same general category of womanhood. The prominent career woman cannot fail or quit, I was often told, because her failure would not be just her own, but would eventually stigmatize women in general as professionally unfit and would hurt them in the job market. I read into this compulsive proclivity not only an ideological conviction of gender equality, but also the superior's sense of vertical or nurturant responsibility to her subordinates and juniors.

CONCLUSION: FEMINISM, ESSENTIALISM, AND CONSTRUCTIVISM

From the foregoing analysis of Japanese women's career narratives, what conclusions can we draw? I suggested that their resistance to feminism may have to do with the tendency of viewing gender in combination with other variables, particularly age, seniority and ranks. These variables are incremental over the career course toward status elevation and role enrichment, while gender, if taken apart, is more or less constant. It follows that being a woman traps a career neophyte to gender handicaps while career maturation helps one shed gender inferiority or reverse it into advantage through status-role increment in age, seniority, and ranks. This point of view leads to my following speculative conclusion.

Let's assume that 'authentic' feminism, as defined by an informant, is confrontational. An unequivocal acceptance of such feminism, I think, presupposes that womanhood is singled out as a distinct entity, bounded and uncontaminated, and that this calls for its counterpart – manhood. Only in the light of female-male opposition, womanhood can amount to a distinct entity. To quote Carol Mukhopadhyay (from her workshop speech, 1999), male and female are conceived as 'opposite sexes,' to begin with. Such female-male opposition entails a categorical generalization of each sex into an abstract gender 'quality' or 'attribute' such as womanhood, femininity, or femaleness, in opposition to manhood, masculinity, or maleness. The gender attribute in this sense of generalization is viewed as 'constant' over time, 'inherent' in and 'essential' to the 'nature' of women or men.

I am talking about a major target of attack by cultural anthropologists today, essentialism. I argue essentialism is a corollary of oppositionalism. Indeed, the European history of philosophy and ideas, from the Platonic realism through medieval theology down to the modern ages of Descartes, Kant, Hegel, and Marx, constitutes cycles of one kind of essentialism or another, based on one type of opposition or another. To strengthen one's own argument, it has to be opposed to another's and in this process both have to be generalized and essentialized in a sharp contrast.

This 'psycho-logic' of western culture accounts for its magnificent intellectual accomplishments, providing an engine for societal change as well. At the same time, in this oppositional, essentialized discourse, the vast amount of whatever was left out of the oppositional forces was probably destined to perish.

To characterize feminism in terms of oppositional essentialism might sound wrong, because today's feminism is strongly prone to de-essentialize gender and thus, to impute the apparent gender difference to cultural construction. Nevertheless, feminists, however constructivist, trying to de-essentailize gender, end up as super-essentialist because of their opposition of women to men, or of constructivism to essentialism.

Furthermore, constructivism, when applied to gender and feminism, serves to explain gendered injustice by de-naturalizing or de-essentializing it, that is, by exposing its culturally-constructed illusion. In doing so, feminist constructivism also reverts to essentialism in that, once the constructed gender inequality is exposed and destroyed, there should unfold the natural, unconstructed, and therefore essential equality or possibly gender neutrality. (I would rather ask, 'Why don't we use culture or construct a new cultural program to bring about gender equality?') Indeed the natural sexuality or sexual orientation is an important agenda in Western feminism.

The case of Japanese career women presents a contrast to oppositional gender-essentialism in that they tend to see gender as inseparable from other incremental, variable factors such as age, seniority and ranks. Yet their career maturation cannot be characterized in constructivist terms either. Instead, these women tend to pay more attention to or to be unconsciously oriented to connections and bridges between subject and object, I and you, self and other, woman and man, senior and junior, etc.

I think this is because Japanese in general tend to be sensitized to self-other relationality, interchange, and inter-reflexivity, more than to draw a boundary around self or other, more than to find an attribute inherent in subject and separate from object. Such emphasis on relationality or inter-reflexivity accounts for a resistance to abstracting or generalizing womanhood as a distinct category. This psycho-cultural tendency may lie behind a woman's trustful acceptance of hierarchical collaboration between man and woman.

I have focused on cultural difference, but this is not to say that Western feminism is doomed in Japan. As I said at the beginning, Japan is exposed to waves of feminism coming from the West, and Japanese look up to the Western model from fashion to political movement. The economic downturn that Japan is now facing may be conducive to a feminist vitalization as the male-led and male-staffed prosperity of the past three decades has come to end. Top-level career women, as sampled in this study, are likely to lead reform movement along a Japanese version of Western model, without opposing women to men but rather, by involving both sexes.

NOTES

1. At the point of this writing (April 1999), 'sekuhara' is on the national agenda, as all employers including university administrators are required to come up with guidelines to protect employees from it, while many are not sure of what sekuhara means. One of the latest bestseller books is *Sekuhara bôshi gaido-bukku* (A guide for prevention of sexual harassment). The sekuhara issue is part of the on-going amendments to the Equal Employment Opportunity Law, which had gone into effect in 1986 to conform to the 1981 UN-sponsored international treaty to eliminate all forms of discrimination against women.

2. 'The first' or 'only' woman is defined loosely, not strictly in a historical sense, but in reference to a certain stage of the woman's career, to a specific work organization ('first woman in X Division of Y Company), or to a certain rank (the only woman bureau chief in an entire ministry). The film director in my sample, for example, though probably best known currently, was neither the first nor the only woman. The appearance of the first woman director was in 1933. (For historical 'firsts,' see Nihon Keizai Shimbunsha 1998: 147–152). Given the speed of change, my 1993 field data may appear somewhat outdated in specific detail, but my purpose is to present an interpretation hopefully relevant over time, not to compete with the media on a marathon for the latest news.

3. This claim may be contrasted to Rosabeth Kanter's (1977) number theory. It is women's numerical 'rarity', she argues, not their femaleness, that gives rise to women's 'tokenism' and to whatever is wrongly attributed as a limitation intrinsic to femaleness. Rarity results in high visibility which, according to Kanter, ties the women down to negative, stressful, discriminatory, disadvantageous work conditions while enhancing men's awareness of being dominant and superior. A woman thus is

disadvantaged in the same way as any other minority member in a large majority group, like one black person in a large crowd of white people.
4. This reminds me of an article by Keiko Tanaka (1990) on the double messages she detected in advertisements in Japanese magazines addressing young women. She caught how traditional, domestic, stereotypic, 'chauvinist' images of femininity were reinforced in the opposite expressions such as 'intelligent,' 'individualistic,' 'feminist.'
5. The *New York Times* reports on a woman who broke the last gender barrier, after 'women composers, stage directors and designers had been admitted.' This may be a matter of a three-year gap between my interview and this report (4/9/96).
6. The convenient typology of 'liminal' vs 'structural,' borrowed from Victor Turner (1969), will reappear several times.
7. There is uncertainty in how to label these categories. In avoidance of stigmatizing the lower ranks, the labels were changed into first, second, and third to erase rank ordering. But my informants, who entered civil service before the label change, fluctuated in their designation of the three categories.
8. In corporations, tea-service, ash-tray cleaning and clerical or nonessential caretaker types of work are assigned to young women employees called OL (office ladies) who typically quit upon marriage or first pregnancy, as expected by employers and male colleagues (see Ogasawara [1998] for OLs' attempt to subvert the gender-bound status imbalance). The presence of an OL as a sort of surrogate wife may partially explain why a male employee does not mind working into late night in office.
9. According to a recent newspaper release (*Asahi* 9/3/98), requiring tea-service is added on the projected official list of harassments.
10. This confirms my earlier observation that wherever men join a group, there emerges a hierarchy (Lebra, 1984).
11. It is interesting that both male and female are likened to monkeys in this and another narrative, as putdowns of the opposite sex. But the reasons for denigration are quite different: the male monkey is hierarchy-obsessed and the female monkey is stupid.

REFERENCES

Ito, Terry 1998. *Okura Kanryō no Fukushū*, Tokyo: Asuka Shinsha.

Kanter, Rosabeth Moss 1977. *Men and Women of the Corporation*, New York: Basic Books.

Lebra, Takie Sugiyama 1981. 'Japanese Women in Male Dominant Careers: Cultural Barriers and Accommodations for Sex-Role Transcendence.' *Ethnology* 20: 291–306.

Lebra, Takie Sugiyama 1984. *Japanese Women: Constraint and Fulfillment*, Honolulu: University of Hawaii Press.

Lebra, Takie Sugiyama 1992. 'Gender and Culture in Japanese Political Economy: Self-Portrayals of Prominent Business Women' in *The Political Economy of Japan: Volume 3, Cultural and Social Dynamics*, ed. S. Kumon and H. Rosovsky. Stanford: Stanford University Press, pp. 364–419.

Nihon Keizai Shimbunsha ed. 1998. *Onna Tachi no Shizukana Kakumei*, Tokyo: Nihon Keizai Shimbunsha.

Ogasawara, Yūko 1998. *OL Tachi No 'Rejisutansu': Sarariiman to OL no Pawā Gēmu*, Tokyo: Chūōkōronsha.

Pharr, Susan J. 1984. 'Status Conflict: The Rebellion of the Tea Pourers,' in *Conflict in Japan*, ed. E. S. Krauss, T. P. Rohien, and P. G. Steinhoff. Honolulu: University of Hawaii Press, pp. 214–240.

Sōrifu ed. 1997. *Danjo Kkyōdō Sankaku no Genjō to Shisaku*, Tokyo: Okurasho Insatsukyoku.

Tanaka, Keiko 1990. 'Intelligent Elegance: Women in Japanese Advertising,' in *Unwrapping Japan: Society and Culture in Anthropological Perspective*, ed. E. Ben-An, B. Moeran and J. Valentine. Honolulu: University of Hawaii Press, pp. 78–96.

Turner, Victor 1969. *The Ritual Process; Structure and Anti-Structure*, Ithaca, NY: Cornell University Press.

PART 3

STATUS

First published in *Ethnology*, Vol. XXVIII, 1 No. 3, July 1989

19 Adoption Among the Hereditary Elite of Japan: Status Preservation through Mobility[1]

Adoption is one of those cultural phenomena so overwhelmingly diverse as to defy a universally feasible definition. Carroll (1970) lists many points where the American notion of adoption is contradicted by those of Oceanic peoples, and concludes that adoption as an analytical tool is useless. While looking at adoption in the light of 'transactions in kinship' and 'resource management,' Brady (1976) also demonstrates the variation and complexity of adoption. My purpose is not to reduce the existing confusion over the practicc of adoption but rather to contribute to it by presenting another variety from Japan. Furthermore, the case drawn from the Japanese nobility involves variation by status within Japanese society.

Although I am aware of the futility of attempting to generalize about adoption, I nonetheless begin with a universalistic statement. Adoption assumes two sets of kinship, one biological, real, or natural, the other simulated, analogous, or constructed. If one set is 'natural,' the other may be called 'cultural.' These two sets are not always mutually distinct or exclusive. It goes without saying that all kinship is a cultural construct, and even natural kinship becomes recognized and sanctioned as such only through cultural rules in defining it. Nevertheless, there are different orders of cultural construction, which may be translated as patterned symbolization where a symbol stands for something else. Natural kinship involves the first-order symbolization where S (symbol) stands for X (some fuzzy undefined reality), whereas adoption refers to the second-order symbolization where S2 stands for Sl, which in turn stands for X. One is a symbol of X, and the other is a symbol of a symbol of X. Without such a conceptual differentiation, there would be no such thing as adoption. I use the term, natural kinship, in distinction from adoptive kinship, in this sense of first-order or primary symbolization. Adoption, then, as further removed than natural kinship from natural reality, can be said to be more purely cultural and arbitrary and therefore is likely to take more diverse forms from one society to the next. Small wonder, then, that it is so difficult to come up with a universal definition. In this distinction of adoption from natural kinship lies the relevance of its study to cultural anthropology.

Among East Asian societies, Japan is known for its indiscriminate practice of adoption compared with China and Korea, for example, where more stringent rules and prohibitions are imposed. Even in the Tokugawa period (1603–1867), when law and order seems to have reached an unprecedented degree, a Confucian scholar, Dazai Shundai (1680-1747), deplored Japan's lawlessness, and singled out adoption as a major example of chaos. While exalting Confucian China and ancient Japan for their alleged adherence to the 'pure' family line, Dazai denounced his contemporaries for their 'barbarous' custom of promiscuous adoption (Kirby 1908). In the late nineteenth century, historian Shigeno An'eki (1887) discussed the 'evils' of adoption, along with those of imperial abdication. Despite these strongly worded critiques and governmental attempts to enjoin restrictions, Japanese apparently persisted in this 'barbarous' and 'evil' custom of unprincipled adoption. In fact, the new civil code, dated 1898, of Meiji Japan (1868–1912) relaxed some of the old restrictions, probably in part to come to terms with what was really going on. Unlike the afore-cited critics, Hozumi (1912: 164–165) gave a favorable interpretation of flexibility in adoption in connection with ancestor worship: 'From what I have stated, it may, I think, be laid down as a general rule that *adoption had its origin in Ancestor worship*; and the stronger the belief in that practice among the people, the wider is the scope allowed for adoption by the law' (emphasis in original). No matter which opinion is more defensible, it is clear that Japan stands out in the frequency and flexibility (or lawlessness) of adoption. I believe, therefore, that an examination of Japanese adoption is important from the Japanese studies perspective and as a possible key to the understanding of Japanese social organization.

While the above characteristic of Japanese adoption has been more or less true across all classes, there are indications that upper-class Japanese resorted more to adoption than did the lower classes. Both Dazai and Shigeno, cited above, were referring primarily to the samurai class and higher. On the basis of samurai family records gathered from four domains, Moore (1970: 618–619) reports a high rate of adoption and its increase during the Tokugawa period: 'The percentage rose from 26.1 percent in the seventeenth to 36.6 percent in the eighteenth and to 39.3 percent in the nineteenth century.' My research suggests that the upper-class produced a strikingly large number of adopters and adoptees. Even though my earlier research encountered instances of adoption among lower-class families, I realized that there are class differences in frequency as well as practice. As we shall see, there are good reasons why the upper-class had greater recourse to adoption. At the same time, one wonders how the practice of free adoption was reconcilable with the hereditary status of the elite which would call for a continuity in natural kinship. This challenge makes the study of adoption all the more important for understanding the culture of stratification and the elite. With this apparent incongruity in mind, this article characterizes adoption among the hereditary elite in terms of its functions and modes, and makes suggestions on the general question of the first-order vs. second-order symbolization of kinship. It is necessary to begin with a historical sketch.

A BRIEF HISTORY OF THE MODERN NOBILITY

The hereditary elite of modern Japan are the titled nobility, called *Kazoku*, which formally existed from 1884 to 1947. This group ranked below the imperial lineage, called *Kōzoku* (the royalty), headed by the emperor, and stood above the *Shizoku*, composed predominantly of former samurai vassals, and *Heimin*, commoners. The last, located at the bottom of the national pyramid of hereditary hierarchy, constituted the largest majority. While the boundary between Shizoku and Heimin was not too distinctive, the Kazoku was clearly marked off from all the lower strata. There was a clear demarcation line between the Kazoku and Kōzoku as well, but between the two groups there was crossover, both upward and downward, through marriage, adoption, and branching. Many Kazoku found careers in the imperial palace and the Ministry of the Imperial Household, which allowed personal contact with the emperor and Kōzoku. The Kazoku derived its honor and prestige, above all, from its social access to members of the royal lineage.

The Kazoku was established to replace the old aristocracy that had existed prior to the Meiji Restoration, on the one hand to provide a continuity, and on the other to revitalize and transform it with new blood. This double purpose is reflected in its composition. Initially, the Kazoku comprised three major categories of people: (1) the former court nobles, generally known as *kuge*, topped by five regent houses (*sekke*) – Konoe, Kujo, Ichijo, Nijo, and Takatsukasa – who had served the imperial court in Kyoto; (2) the former feudal domain lords, commonly called *daimyō*, who had owed loyalty to their overlord, *shōgun*, who, residing in Edo (Tokyo), capped the military government; (3) the meritorious people who rose from modest status, mostly of the low-ranking vassal status, due to their recognized contributions to the Restoration. Among marginal members were certain priestly houses and the *karō*, the chief administrators of feudal domains, second in command to the *daimyō*. In the course of time, the third category expanded to become the largest, including positions of high command in the modern navy and army, high government officials, financial magnates (*zaibatsu*), and professionals in various fields. In the 63 years of Kazoku existence, Kazoku ranks were awarded to 1,011 families, including those which have become extinct.

Kazoku were rank-ordered by five titles: the equivalents of duke, marquis, count, viscount, and baron. Again by a double criterion of pre-Restoration ancestral status and meritorious contributions to the Restoration and subsequent accomplishments, these titles were allocated with opportunities for promotion. In the following account, I may combine the Kazoku title with the prior status like 'a *kuge*-count.' The holders of the first two titles were privileged to be automatic members, while those of the other three to be mutually elected members, of the House of Peers, one arm of the bicameral system of the Imperial Parliament. Theoretically, only the male head of the house was a Kazoku, but his wife and dependent children were also entitled to Kazoku-status courtesy.

After WWII, with the new constitution enunciating universal equality and democratic principles, the hereditary hierarchy went out of existence, except for the emperor and his closest family. For many Kazoku and the rest of

Kōzoku, the legal abolition of their status was little more than a formal confirmation of what had already taken place through the war and postwar heavy property taxations. Nevertheless, it is too soon to predict that the former nobility will vanish totally. As long as the emperor exists, the hereditary distinction embodied by the former Kazoku seems to survive in the minds of ordinary Japanese, if not Kazoku themselves. There are signs of commercialized revival through televised popular historical drama series and local tourism where Kazoku ancestors play central roles.

Over the last ten years, I interviewed about 100 Kazoku survivors and their children to solicit their life histories. In the following analysis of adoption, I shall mix some segments of these biographies with data from written records and a questionnaire.

In order to understand the aristocratic practice of adoption, we must first locate it in the context of Japanese domestic organization (*ie*) which evolved in the upper-class through the medieval era and became a nationwide pattern in the Meiji period as formulated in the newly installed modern civil code pertaining to all classes.

IE AND ADOPTION

The *ie* as a key to Japanese social structure has been recognized by many scholars to mean more than just family and as not amenable to the framework of kinship or descent.[2] The argument centers around two interrelated features of the *ie*. First, it is a structural unit consisting of roles or positions, rather than a group of persons as implied in 'family.' Such structural elements as roles or positions are defined in reference to the *ie* as a corporate body with its own status, assets, career, and goal. It is in this light that the economic, political, and occupational profile is regarded as central in defining the *ie*, and that the constituent members are recognized as such by virtue of the functions they perform in contributing to the corporate status or goal. In this context, the *ie* is better translated as 'house' or 'household,' implying a group of co-residents, each occupying his/her place in it.

Given this structural feature of the *ie*, even though the headship is likely to be held by the father, 'it should be noted that his authority over the household members is validated by his *office* as the head of the household, not by his being the *father*: the authority of the head resides primarily in the office rather than the person' (Nakane 1967: 18, emphasis in original). Such positional emphasis also entails the primacy of role-fitness or competency over the kinship status of the position holder. Among many indications of this role-fitness requirement is the practice of retirement (*inkyo*) by an aged or incapacitated father from the office of headship so that a young, vigorous successor can take over. An outsider may be adopted not only by a son-less household but if he is considered better qualified than a natural son as an heir. A woman is accepted or rejected as a bride foremost on the basis of her physical and mental qualification as an additonal source of labor and then as a bearer of an heir. A house having a female occupation, such as a tea house or geisha house, is transmitted from mother to daughter in disregard of the 'normal' father-to-son link. Nakano (1968) amply demonstrates how the *ie* occupation takes precedence over the rule of descent and how in fact the descent rule is determined by the need of occupational continuity. Furthermore, insofar as the interest of *ie* as a whole supersedes that of an individual member, the redistribution of children through marriage or adoption may be captured as an opportunity to form politically beneficial alliances.

The second feature is the mandatory perpetuation of the *ie* entity through succession over generations. No one fails to mention this point as essential to the *ie*, and Pelzel (1970:229) in particular throws it into relief:

> [T]he Japanese term *ie* has traditionally meant both the household at a given point in time and a more durable entity, the 'house,' which exists over time and is composed of only one household in each generation – that household headed by the male who is the legal successor to the former household head. It is this succession of households down through the generations that is the basic and ideal meaning of the term *ie*; the extant household is merely the concrete but transient form of the latter. Assets, whether tangible or not, are always the assets of the *ie*, and a current household controls them for its time as a trustee. Organizational statuses in the contemporary household are subsumed in, and secondary to, similar statuses in the durable house.

Continuous succession thus subsumes or overrides other considerations, and it is in this context that the term stem-family is preferred as a translation of *ie*. Marriage and adoption can be then redefined as the means of producing or acquiring an heir to ensure succession.

The successional well-being of the *ie* for Japanese depends on the unity of the household as symbolized by one househead and one heir in avoidance of rivalry, fission, and resource dispersal. The unicephalous, unigenitural structure, involving a clear status distance between the heir and other children and the latter's departure from the *ie* upon marriage, is a core characteristic of the *ie*. This structure, while ensuring a smooth transmission of the *ie* over generations, keeps the family size relatively small (Smith 1972), with only one couple for each generation, and makes the *ie* outwardly look like a nuclear family. Thus Morioka (1967: 597) defines the *ie* as 'a vertically composite form of nuclear families, one from each generation.'

It is unigenitural succession that places Japan at the opposite pole from traditional China where the family is embedded in the patrilineage system. Nakane (1969) proposes two models of family structure, one being a large family based upon the collateral, fraternal or horizontal solidarity, the other a small-sized family structured along the successional line based on the lineal or vertical bond between the head and his heir. Japan represents an extreme of the latter, while China exemplifies the former. In this contrast lies an explanation for difference in adoption practices between the two societies. In China, adoption is not as much needed as in Japan because lineage continuity is guaranteed and security for old age is provided by collateral agnates when one has no successor. When adoption takes place, an adopted son should come from within the lineage in the descending generation (preferably a brother's son) for two reasons: because a candidate with this qualification is easily available therein, and because fellow-members of the lineage exert pressure for intralineage recruitment. Despite the prevalent rule of agnatic adoption, there are instances of outsider adoption (Watson 1975) involving buying an infant from a stranger family because of such advantages as the adopter's complete control of a poor outsider adoptee unlike a lineage-controlled agnatic adoptee. However, outsider adoption is accompanied by severe penalty such as the humiliating and costly initiation ceremony to which the adoptive father has to submit himself in order to secure approval signatures from lineage elders (Watson 1975). The Japanese focus on unigenitural succession makes adoption more necessary and less rule-bound, since herein exists no pool of insiders for adoption. An outsider is as acceptable as a close kinsman; a sister's son or daughter's son is just as adoptable as a brother's son; a brother can be adopted as a son; historically, the adoptee could be older than the adopter; the house with a daughter but no son can adopt a son-in-law; not just a single person but a married couple can be adopted; and so on.

Both features of the *ie*, structural or positional and durable or successional, stress the *ie* entity, be it the family name, house property, occupation, or status, as transcendental to individual persons and to the here and now. Involved here is a religious element of the *ie*, extending its membership to ancestors (Plath 1964) and to posterity. Further, by virtue of this transcendental nature, even an extinct *ie* is considered to carry on a latent existence, and can be restored in manifest form by a stranger (Befu 1962: 38)[3] through a sort of other-worldly adoption. Viewed by a critic like Shigeno (1887: 79), 'To attempt by any such means as adoption to raise up an already extinct house, is like attempting to set in motion the life-pulse which has ceased to beat.'

To further comprehend such free adoption, Kitaoji's (1971) bold argument is instructive. Pointing out the difficulty of grasping the Japanese *ie* in terms of descent rule or kinship terminology, he proposes 'positional succession' as an alternative tool for cleaning up the ethnological muddle over patrilineality and bilaterality. Central to positional succession, which to my mind combines the above two features of the *ie*, is a pair of key positions, househead and housewife. As the incumbents retire from these statuses, their successors (the heir and bride) step into the central positions. Here are three successive generations of paired positions filled by married couples who are also permanent members of the house: the retired couple, incumbent couple, and successor couple. Under the incest prohibition, each generation must recruit a successor-spouse from outside. If the house has a son, his wife must come from another house, and this mode of positional recruitment just happens to meet the patrilineal ideal. But when the house has a daughter but no son, she stays on and marries a man brought in from outside as an adopted heir and son-in-law, and this rule applies even when the house has a son who is not a fit heir. Kitaoji (1971) suggests that these two modes are structurally symetrical or identical, reasoning that in both cases one of the paired successors is adopted. In one, a successor to the position of housewife is adopted, as much as, in the second, a successor to the househead is adopted. Viewed in terms of positional succession, each generation is thus seen to adopt a successor. The case of adopting a married couple (*fūfu-yōshi*) then makes sense as a third mode within the same structural framework in that here successors to the househead and housewife are adopted simultaneously.

Kitaoji's proposition is further refined and developed by Bachnik (1983) from the standpoint of recruitment strategies for succession. She clarifies the order of preference of one strategy over another and suggests that all the strategies can be viewed 'in relation to one another as a gradual widening of the possibilities for accomplishing succession under conditions of increasing difficulty' (Bachnik 1983: 172). Recruiting a male heir from an out-group (son-in-law) and a female successor from the in-group (daughter) is less preferred than recruiting an outsider female successor (daughter-in-law) and an insider male successor (son). But these strategies are more desirable than recruiting outsiders for both positions; that is, adopting a couple already married (*fūfu-yōshi*). Nonetheless, all these alternatives fit the same rule of positional succession. Even the term *chōnan sōzoku* (succession by the eldest son), a favorite Japanese ethno-label to characterize their succession rule, should be understood as so polysemic as to cover 'the entire positional succession system' (Bachnik 1983: 176) including the least desirable alternative, *fūfu-yōshi*.[4]

All the cited literature on the *ie* refers to ordinary Japanese and emphasizes rural Japan. Nevertheless, I find the idea of positional succession exceedingly relevant to the urban upper-class households as represented by Kazoku. Certainly, as will be shown in the following section, the primary function of adoption among Kazoku was for positional succession as among commoners, but carried an additional flavor due to their status distinction as a major component of such succession. In some respects, Kazoku adoption took a purer form of positional succession, but in other respects it had to be reconciled with the fact that Kazoku status was hereditary. We shall later show another function of adoption which is more characteristic of this class and involves not just a second-order but a third-order symbolization.

ADOPTION FOR POSITIONAL SUCCESSION

When relating their pedigrees, my informants were certain about the number of generations that their family lines had continued. One would say unequivocally, 'I am the seventeenth generation head of the house,' or 'My brother is the 25th generation.' They took pride in having a long genealogy. Representatives of new Kazoku (the third category above) were, therefore, either embarrassed about their genealogical shallowness (two to four generations since the original awardee of a Kazoku title), saying, 'We are not true Kazoku,' or would lengthen their genealogies by tracing their founding ancestors farther back.

It should be noted that each generation is represented by a single incumbent of the house headship, despite Kitaoji's (1971) couple-succession model, and thus a genealogy consists of one straight line of succession to headship where the wives or consorts are either submerged in the chain of male heads or placed beside them without a lineal link. This is a formal expression of general patricentricity, which was more pronounced with the elite than among commoners partly due to the structural instability of the status of wife and mother under the historical legacy of polygyny. Even though a woman could hold a temporary headship when no man was available, as happened occasionally, the aristocratic title was given only to male heads. Thus the female head had to go through a special petition to regain the title when she secured an adopted male successor (son or husband).

In response to a mail questionnaire returned by 101 respondents (house-heads), 87 specified the number of generations that transpired since the original ancestor (see Table 1). As expected, there is variation in generational depth among the three major categories: *kuge*, *daimyō*, and the new, 'meritorious' Kazoku. The category 'Other' shows the greatest depth in generation because it includes priestly houses whose first ancestors were gods in the Age of Gods. These figures may be compared with the 125 generations of the imperial dynasty (following the death of Hirohito), counting from Emperor Jimmu, but more realistically 100 generations from Emperor Keitai (r. 507–531).

Table 1: Generational Depth by Ancestor Categories

	Responses	*Generations Av.*	*Range*
Kuge	19	27.0	2*–86
Daimyō	27	19.0	10–44
New Kazoku	33	7.9	2–34
Other	8	29.5	2–80

* Such genealogically shallow *kuge* houses are post-Meiji branches of main houses.

Logically incongruous but practically consistent with the importance of genealogical depth to validate the aristocratic status is the high frequency of adoption as unfolded through interviews. Few interviews went without revealing at least one instance of adoption involving either self or primary kin as a party to adoption, and in some cases it turned out that adoption had taken place over three generations in a row. A son of a *daimyō*-viscount, for example, was adopted by a *kuge*-count, the adoptive father himself had been an adoptee from another *kuge*-count house, and the former in turn has adopted a son from a *daimyō*-viscount. The informant, a middle-generation adoptee, said:

> In our circle there is no resistance to being adopted as there is in the world outside, since almost everybody here becomes adopted. My [natal] house has continued for over fourteen generations, but more than half the generations were taken by adopted sons.

It is impossible to obtain the precise figure for adoption frequency over generations. As a compromise measure, I gleaned quantifiable information from the two-volume genealogies, *Kazoku Kakei Taisei* (hereafter KKT), compiled by Kasumi Kaikan (the club organized for and by former Kazoku and their descendants), covering the most recent generations of headship for a total of 1,011 households (Kasumi Kaikan 1982–84). Selecting only those households which record ancestry minimally up to six generations back, including the present househead (the others are either genealogically shallow or did not bother to submit more complete records), I derived 485 such households. Table 2 shows the frequency of adoptions within this sample.

The table indicates 32 households as having had no adopted son over the last six generations, 89 households having had one adopted son, and so on. That as many as 32 households have continued in 'natural' father-to-son succession throughout does not match my interview data, and makes me suspect that adoptions are underreported or underrecorded. In one interview, I came upon an adopted son whose name appears without an adoption notation in the genealogy because he had been 'adopted as a natural son.'[5] Nevertheless, it is remarkable that 247 out of 485 households, 50.9 per cent have adopted three, four, five, or all six successor sons. Of all successors over six generations, totaling 2,910 men, there were 1,207 (41 per cent) adopted. Even though this figure underrepresents the actual frequency, it is quite substantial.

Table 2: Adoptions Frequency (Last Six Generations)

Frequency	*Number of Households*
0	32 (6.6%)
1	89 (18.4%)
2	117 (24.1%)
3	135 (27.8%)
4	84 (17.3%)
5	25 (5.2%)
6	3 (0.6%)
Total	485 (100%)

How often is one thing, who is adopted how is another important question that we will consider in more detail later. For now, let us see a few peculiar examples (taken from KKT) of genealogy by way of introductory illustration.

Cases 1 and 2 stretch from the late eighteenth century to the present. Each case is represented by a straight line on the right, as it appears in the official genealogy, and by a chart, on the left, more faithful to natural kinship, which is my translation from the straight line representation. The dotted line stands for adoption, the solid line for natural kinship. The curved line that appears to the left indicates the natural link between a man and his son given away for adoption. To show the significance of birth order, siblings are linked by an oblique line. The order of succession is indicated by alphabetical letters.

Case 1 is striking in its early history for the successive adoptions that took place over five generations within the first half of the nineteenth century. It thus exemplifies a short incumbency of each head (eight years on average) as well as the high frequency of adoption. Further, it may be noted that G was succeeded by his adoptive father F's younger brother H (thus theoretically going upward generationally) even though he had his own son J. But J succeeded the line two generations later, and was succeeded by his daughter's husband K (son-in-law adoption), and K's son L was succeeded by his younger brother M. Succession by a brother is conceptualized in accordance to the lineal succession model as in the right-side straight-line chart, which means that the successor brother was adopted as a son.

Case 2 also includes an instance of adoption while the adopter B had his own son D, who in turn succeeded the adopted son C. Further, E was succeeded by his sister H's husband F (brother-in-law adoption). After F's son held headship for a while, he was succeeded by his mother H (one of rare cases of succession by a woman) for an unknown reason, and after a

CASE 1

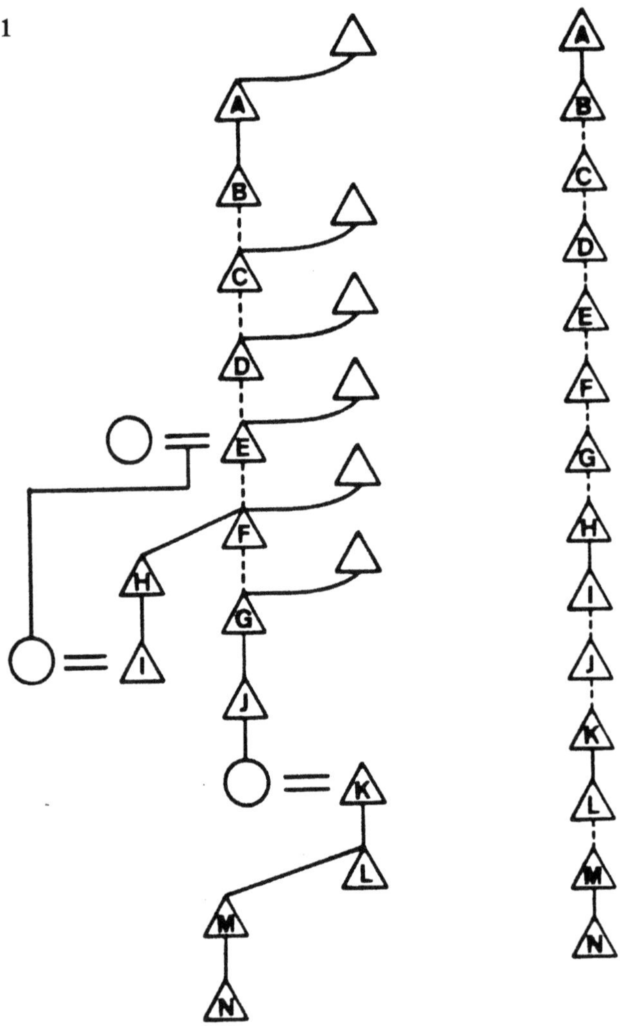

three-year incumbency, H was succeeded by her son I. The same man thus headed the house twice.[6] This peculiar example is indicative of the earlier practice of retirement (*inkyo*), which was prohibited by the Kazoku ordinance except under extenuating circumstances.

These examples confirm the argument that the *ie* defies a notion of descent rule. It may be assumed that the Kazoku had stronger reasons or compulsions for successional continuity and therefore adoption. It is possible that aristocratic families were less fertile or had higher mortality rates. My informants tended to assume this was the case and to attribute it to the feeble body (and mind) produced from close-kin marriage and overprotected childhood, and I suspect this is true to some extent (Lebra 1988). Almost in the same breath, informants also mentioned that their houses had been continued mostly by the children mothered by 'side consorts' or 'womb ladies' recruited from 'healthy' lower-status outsiders. Furthermore, there is ample evidence

CASE 2

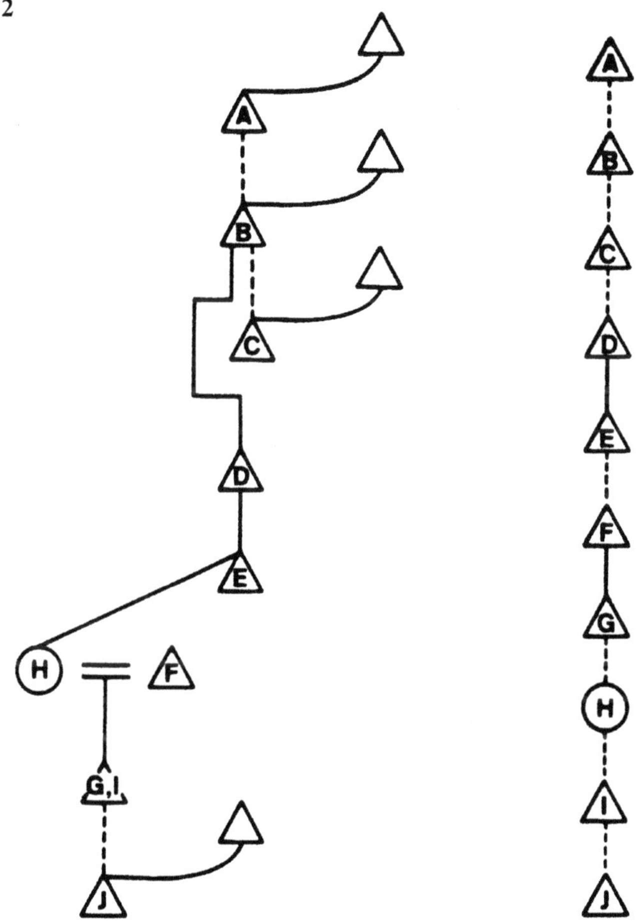

that sons were adopted by those houses which had natural, and long-living sons. Other reasons are therefore called for.

THE WEIGHT OF HERITAGE

The first and obvious reason lies in the weight of heritage to be carried on. Among elite and commoners alike, such things as the family name, the house estates and other assets,[7] and the authority of househead (*katoku*) had to be transmitted. Most Kazoku families transmitted not only their family names but part of personal names as well. For example, the successive heads of the Takahashi family may carry a character like Michi from generation to generation as part of their personal name, such as Michitoshi, Michiaki, Michinao, Michiyasu, and so on. Such name succession was only for sons, particularly successor sons. Adopted sons were expected to change their personal names as well as their family names.

What principally distinguishes Kazoku heritage from that of non-Kazoku was the hereditary title, the perpetuation of which was mandatory. The privileges and honors formally or informally vested in the title varied from symbolic to substantive, from social to economic to political:

> Imperial ranks of ancient origin accorded automatically at age 20 starting from the minor fifth rank (*jugoi*) and rising theoretically up to the minor first rank (*juichii*) hierarchically ordered ceremonial seats in the imperial palace (*kyūchū sekiji*); privileged access to the imperial 'benevolence' (*oboshimeshi*) – ritual, social, or economic (including gifts in cash or kind, and special cases of 'commensality' with the emperor); the right to wear specially styled and decorated court attires (*taireifuku* indicative of Kazoku titles and ranks; the Kazoku group as a legitimate pool of spousal candidates for members of the royal lineage from the emperor down; the right of each house to install the house law (*kaken*) binding on members of the house; the automatic or internally elected membership in the House of Peers; appointments to high offices in the Imperial House Ministry from its Minister down; the right (formerly duty) to designate certain items of property as 'hereditary' in order to keep them immune from possible loss through transactions like mortgaging; the right to send the children to Gakushuin free of tuition[8] (culled from Sakamaki 1987: 301–331).

In addition, Kazoku were treated with respect and courtesy by people in general. Moreover, the number of Kazoku being limited, status scarcity was another important factor to compel the title holder to secure a successor, whether his own or adopted son. In other words, a Kazoku had more to lose by failing to provide a successor, even though, in the subjective accounts of my informants, Kazoku assets tended to fade into liabilites. Compulsions to designate a successor were doubled by the rule laid down in the original Kazoku ordinance (which was relaxed in a later revision to be consistent with the civil code) that a successor be designated before the incumbent's death. This rule often forced a sonless Kazoku to adopt a successor prematurely and unnecessarily when the adopter later fathered his own son, a situation that set in motion a serial adoption in which the adopted successor in turn would have to adopt the original adopter's natural son. Premature adoption like this offers one explanation of why a son was adopted to succeed over one's own son.

If the title-holder died suddenly without an own or adopted son, as happened to an informant's grandfather, the death was not reported until the family secured an adopted successor. In this crisis, '*Anybody* could have been accepted as long as he was a male' (informant's emphasis). The widow, the informant's grandmother, scrounged around desperately until she found a third son of a *kuge*-count willing to become an adopted son-in-law. Offered to choose any one of the three daughters as his bride, he picked the informant's mother. It was not until the family completed the adoption procedure that the death of the last incumbent was announced. Both premature adoption and falsifying the death record amply demonstrate the importance attached to status succession: if interested in the perpetuation of the house alone, not that of the Kazoku status, one could have avoided these measures.

As far as Kazoku status was concerned, the weight of heritage was lifted after WWII when the hereditary aristocracy was dismantled. Does this mean the former Kazoku have lost interest in succession and adoption? No, they are still concerned with the continuation of their *ie* through successors, although not as sure of securing heirs as they used to be. A large majority of the respondents gave strongly positive answers to the question in the questionnaire, 'Do you think your house (*ie*) should be continued, even by adopting a son if necessary?'

Combining the first two categories of Table 3, 74 percent of the respondents gave more or less positive answers. This suggests that the weight of heritage is still being felt in connection with the genealogical depth and honor of the house, even though neither the Kazoku nor the *ie* exist as legal entities any more. In my view, this conservative attitude toward the *ie* is characteristic of many Japanese across class lines. Particularly, when one faces the parental death and becomes a househead, one seems to become sharply aware of the weight of the *ie* with its transcendental implications. There are indications, however, that the need to preserve the *ie* is more strongly felt with Kazoku houses. In the present generation many households are facing a scarcity of heirs and must allocate them in an optimal way. A daughter of an old, *daimyō*-count, age 55, agreed to give away her only son to her natal house as an adopted successor to his grandparental house. Her commoner husband supported the idea strongly because he thought her natal house, old and prestigeous, ought to be perpetuated, whereas his own house could be dispensed with.

Underlying this attitude is the cult of ancestors, as indicated by the questionnaire responses. Kazoku informants generally expressed their respectfulness and indebtedness toward their ancestors and emphasized their obligation to maintain the mortuary symbols (most importantly, tombs and tablets) and rituals (daily prayers and memorial rites). They would be overcome with guilt toward their ancestors, they said, if the house came to end during their generation.

The weight of Kazoku ancestors is more than a matter of inner feelings and

Table 3: Do you think your house should be continued, even by adopting a son if necessary?

Answers	*Respondents*	(percentage)
Positive	56	(63.6%)
'As long as Japan exists, it should be continued.' 'I don't want to bring to end in my generation the house status (*iegara*) that my ancestors endeavored hard to maintain.' 'Being a prominent house, it should be continued.' 'It is necesary to keep up the tomb for ancestors, and I am proud of my house status (*iegara*).' 'We have been living along an unbroken line of descent.' 'By all means I want to preserve the family line which has continued eighty generations.' 'I want to continue it forever.'		
Conditionally Positive	9	(10.2%)
'It is not necessary to adopt a son, but it would be nice to have someone maintain the ancestral tomb.' 'At present I have my son to continue it, but would let nature take its course thereafter.'		
Neutral	16	(18.2%)
'The future is uncertain.' 'It's up to the children.' 'I am not thinking about that particularly. I will leave things as they turn out' (*nariyuki ni makaseru*).		
Conditionally Negative	3	(3.4%)
''There will be no need of adoption in the future.' 'Nothing to say.'		
Negative	4	(4.5%)
'I don't think so.' 'I am only a new Kazoku, owing the title to my grandfather's merit. Since it is not a house worth continuing, I have no wish to.'		
Total Answers	88	(100%)

takes concrete and conspicuous form: tombstones are larger, more awesome, and less removable than ordinary ones; some ancestors are enshrined in magnificent mausolea or shrines open to the public. Furthermore, the religious establishments in charge of these mortuary heritages expect their Kazoku clients – whose ancestors were their patrons and masters – to adhere to their dedication to ancestors through them. The preservation of a prestigious house like a Kazoku through a line of successors is thus important to Buddhist and Shinto custodians of its ancestors as well. Some of my informants confessed that they were pressured by their priests to adopt successors. When quesionnaire respondents and interviewed informants mentioned the obligation to maintain ancestral tombs, they meant all these physical, symbolic, and social heritages.

Pressures for *ie* continuity came from another source: former castle towns. Some Kazoku of *daimyō* origin still have their vassals, more correctly, descendants of vassals (*kyūshin*) who served their ancestors, reside, or periodically assemble in their home provinces (*kunimoto*). They also pressure their latterday 'lord' to adopt an heir so that their own samurai roots are reassured. At a small social gathering of some 'top vassals' around their youthful bachelor lord to which I was invited, I asked what would happen if the lord had no son. The vassals looked stunned at the suggestion of such an outrageous possibility, and then assured me that there would definitely be an heir because they would take the responsibility to find a healthy, fertile bride for their master. The master, who listened passively, assured them with surprising seriousness that the choice of a bride would be up to them, not to himself.

It is clear that the weight of heritage thus entails both privileges and obligations, both volition and pressures. Positional succession and adoption to implement it were and, in a lesser degree, still are felt to be necessary in response to both. One heard remarks like, 'I personally don't care, but *kyūshin* in *kunimoto* are constantly pestering me to adopt someone.'

SUPPLY OF ADOPTEES

For the above reasons, adopted sons were in high demand. But what about the supply side? Given the *ie* structure, brothers were dichotomized between one successor and nonsuccessors. Concomitant to the distinction of Kazoku status that entailed the privileges mentioned was status distance between successor and nonsuccessors (usually between the eldest son and younger sons, as well as between son and daughter) which was greater than among the nonprivileged classes. Only the heir was addressed by positional terms like Junior Lord (*wakatonosama*, or *wakasama*) and referred to as an 'honorable heir' (*o-atotori*), while all other children were addressed and referred to by their personal names.[9] Status discrimination in the family (e.g., the eldest brother being served a meal alone by several servants in a separate room while all younger brothers were put together in one room) was recalled vividly and resentfully by the nonsuccessor brothers, whereas the successor brother tended to be oblivious of any favoritism. In one *daimyō* house, younger sons were treated, I was told, as 'vassals' (*kerai*) to their eldest brother, as if they were still living in the Tokugawa era. In a *kuge* house, too, where some house treasures including ancestors' writings had been handed down, it was the heir's exclusive right under the rule of *isshi sōden* (one-child succession) to look after them, keeping all others blind to the house tradition. No wonder that I heard scathing criticism and egalitarian ideology against the Kazoku institution more from nonsuccessor brothers than from successor sons.

While a daughter was expected to marry out, a nonsuccessor son had three life course alternatives as stated by my informants: (1) to set up his own house independently or, if allowed, a branch of his natal house; (2) to forego the right to become a househead by either remaining in his parental house as a *heyazumi* (room-occupant), a parasitic and potentially disruptive retainer, unmarried, and dependent on his lord brother, or to enter a Buddhist monastery to lead a celibate life; or (3) to be adopted by another house as its successor. The second alternative was hardly an option and I have knowledge of no example of *heyazumi*. I suspect it was drawn by informants from historical dramas to capitalize upon the deprived status of a younger son. As for priesthood, the Meiji Restoration terminated the rule of priestly celibacy. The first alternative differentiates independence and branching, the difference between which, however, is not always clear. Among Kazoku, the establishment of a branch house entailed the right or obligation to offer a son to the main house, or sometimes to receive a son from the main house, for successional adoption. By and large, however, the obligatory, subordinate status of a branch house in relation to its main house was a distinct characteristic of the *dōzoku* (quasi-lineage composed of a main house and branch houses) relationship in the Kazoku, as will be illustrated later. In other words, by branching, a younger brother would have had to prolong his subordination to his elder brother and head of the main house and forego autonomy for good. Branching could mean being awarded the title of baron or viscount under 'imperial benevolence' so as to join the Kazoku, but this was exceptional and limited to the highest-ranking (duke or marquis) or specially favored Kazoku. Independence, on the other hand, signified a downright demotion to commoner status.

The third alternative was favored by most as the only way for a nonsuccessor son to enjoy an autonomous lordship. As an adopted househead said, 'There was nothing you could do as a younger son. You could waste all your life as a *heyazumi*, or go independent, or enter the priesthood. Nothing else.' In other words, adoption was the best deal. Moore (1970) challenges the widely accepted notion that adoption was a major means available to a poor and bright boy for upward mobility by presenting contradictory data from samurai families of the Tokugawa period. He demonstrates that adoption took place most frequently within the same class, therefore without any mobility, and that, if there was mobility, it was more downward than upward. But, as the author admits, this argument is based on the relative ranks (as measured by stipends) of the adopting family and the adoptee's natal family, in disregard of the fact that adoption permitted a nonsuccessor to retain a samurai status instead of losing it entirely as he was otherwise destined to. Adoption, in other words, was not a means of status mobility but of status preservation. The same was true with the Kazoku.

So, nonsuccessor sons were availabe on the adoption market and were so understood by would-be adopters. An informant, a second son of a *daimyō*-marquis, received an adoption proposal from a new viscount Kazoku. When he turned it down, the proposal automatically went to his younger brother, who accepted it. Consequently, the informant ended up an independent commoner while his brothers all remained Kazoku and/or branched. Another informant, a younger son of a *kuge*-viscount, described how he, as a young man, was inundated with adoption proposals 'like rainfall' (a common metaphor for abundance usually used for marriage proposals), much more than marriage proposals. Indeed, the adoption market for sons was comparable to the marriage market for daughters, and both marriage and adoption are called *engumi* (tying two partners), the only difference being that the latter is marked as *yōshi-engumi*. The above informant declined all the proposals, but even after he was married as a commoner, proposals kept coming, asking him to bring his wife and children with him for *fūfu-yōshi*.

Rejection as exemplified by these two, however, was not common among my informants. Typically, the proposal receiver did not even question whether he should or should not be adopted, nor was he even choosey about adopters. When a small child was adopted, the adoptee's compliance did not come into question. A baron's youngest son was put into commoner fosterage upon birth as were many Kazoku children for a variety of reasons (Lebra 1988). One day, when he was three years old, a woman from another baron house appeared at the peasant foster house and took him away for adoption. Overnight, the little boy who had been running around like a peasant child, became a 'junior lord.' He had been moved around in infancy like a pawn from the house of his birth to the foster house and to the adoptive house. It was more common, however, to adopt an older child or adult whose judgment and compliance did count.

A 45-year old informant was in junior high school when his maternal grandfather, a duke, sounded him out for his willingness to be adopted. 'Grandfather asked me, "How about coming to my house?" and right away I said, "Okay, I will".' His immediate acceptance had childish reasons such as better food served at the adoptive house (an important consideration in the postwar, pre-affluence period) than by his poorer natal house, greater opportunities to watch sumo tournaments because the grandfather was a strong sumo fan, and the like. Not until much later did he become aware of the special status of the adoptive house. When he was taken by his adoptive father (grandfather) to the great shrine of the deified founding ancestor for a grand memorial rite, he realized what a formidable commitment he had made unknowingly. Eventually he became adjusted to his adopted status and began to find pleasure in playing ritual roles for cycles of ancestor rites, as his late predecessor did.

Unquestioning compliance or acquiescence with an adoption request was typical of adult adoptees as well. With daughters only, a baron house of priestly origin[10] adopted a son but this *engumi* ended in *rien* (severance of adoptive ties, the same word as divorce). Consequently, the eldest daughter, after having married out, was called back with her husband so that the latter, a professor of medicine, would take over the headship. The husband agreed and assumed the wife's natal family name. The wife labeled this adoption '*fūfu-yōshi*,' although it was in fact a variety of son-in-law adoption, *muko-yōshi*.

Although definitely incomplete, KKT provides some information on sons adopted out. The 201 households randomly selected[11] generated 196 codable households as a sample. Sons of three generations (or less in the case of genealogically shallow or unrecorded cases), going back from the latest generation born prior to 1945, were counted. Nonsuccessor sons totaled 553, and 156 of them (28.2 percent) were adopted out.

For more accurate information, let us focus on the highest ranking households, the five *sekke* (the top court nobles of Fujiwara ancestry which until the

Meiji Restoration had taken turns in assuming the highest position of the court, the imperial regent), and the main *shōgun* house in particular. Table 4 shows the frequency and percentages of adopted sons, both received and given, relative to all successors and all nonsuccessor sons respectively.

Table 4: Adopted Sons for Sekke and Shogun Houses

	Sekke	*Shogun*
All successors	45	9
Adopted successors	16 (35.6%)	5 (55.6%)
All nonsuccessor sons	72	21
Adopted-out sons	34 (47.2%)	16 (76.2%)

All the heads (successors) of the *sekke* houses and the *shōgun* house who appear in KKT total 45 and nine respectively, of whom sixteen and five heads (35.6 percent and 55.6 percent) are adopted sons. As for nonsuccessors, 34 out of 72 nonsuccessor sons, and sixteen out of 21 are given away for adoption (47.2 percent and 76.2 percent respectively). The data show remarkable percentages of adoptions both in and out, and the proportions of adopted-out sons are notably high, particularly in the *shōgun* house. It is no wonder that my informants believed all sons of the Tokugawa, other than successors, were adopted out. These given-away sons were all successors to headship of the adoptive houses with few exceptions. Table 4 suggests that sons of the top families were more subject to adoption than those of others and/or that adoptions in other families are underrecorded.

We have seen the advantages of being adopted, but the calculated interest alone would not be sufficient to explain such readiness of men to offer themselves for adoption, so different from Korean or Chinese men in this respect. More important was the fact that adoption, like marriage, was negotiated and arranged not only by the two families involved but often by many others who had voice over important family decisions, such as the kindred on both sides, top-level retainers of both houses, family counsellors, and sometimes the office within the Ministry of Imperial Household, *sōchitsuryō*, supervising the nobility and royalty. For Kazoku, adoption as well as marriage was thus a semi-public, semi-political matter beyond the individual's preference and choice, much more so than for commoners. One reason for this was that Kazoku were encouraged, although not enforced, to adopt one another's children in order to maintain the status boundary. Most informants were convinced, contrary to the stated rules, that the Kazoku was prohibited from marrying or adopting from outside the group.

My interview data suggest that individual members were socialized to be pliable enough to move from one prepared position to another as expected. 'Personal preference would have made no difference,' said an adopted informant, 'because there wasn't much variation in the Kazoku career any way. Everyone would end up as a member of the House of Peers, and the like.' So he would joke with his Gakushuin classmates who were also adopted, saying one's adoptive house could well have been another's (*torikawaru*). There was another reason for the ease of adopting and being adopted, which is detailed next.

The Positional Nature of Adoptive Relationship

As we have seen, adoption was primarily for positional succession. This meant a relative insignificance of personal rapport between parent and child in adoption. This calls attention to the 'family' which we have so far left out of the *ie*. In American practice, adoption is primarily between a childless couple and a child whose natural parent(s) is not available, capable, or willing as a nurturer, and enables both parties to satisfy their personal needs – one as parental, the other as filial. Concealing the identity of the child's natural parentage seems essential to developing an exclusive love and intimacy between the adoptive parties. Adoption in Oceania contrasts with the American pattern, as noted at the outset, but some researchers do find a simulation of natural parent and child relations. Goodenough (1970: 337), for instance, characterizing Trukese adoption, says, 'Adoption allows childless adults to validate their adult status by demonstrating their ability to play the role of nurturer, which is highly valued by Trukese.' Also, Hawaiian women manifest a strong need for babies, and for playing a nurturant maternal role (Howard et al. 1970: 48).

In Kazoku adoption, an affectionate parent-child relationship was not entirely lacking, particularly if adoption was by a close kin, as in the above-cited case of a grandfather adopting a grandson. Yet, by and large, nurturance and intimacy were secondary or irrelevant to the mandate of positional succession, and often were completely absent from the adoptive relationship.

First, adoption was not always accompanied by co-residence. The legal procedure for adoption may well have been completed when the adopted son was a small child or infant, but the child was likely to continue to live with his natural parents until he was a teenager or young adult. Further, when the adopted son finally left his natal house, it was also likely that spatial distance in residence between the adopter and adopted, even if in the same premises, was such as to do away with daily intimate contact. Residential separation, afforded by well-to-do Kazoku, was partly necessitated to minimize conflict between two groups of entourage, waiting upon the old couple and the adopted son respectively. In some cases such residential separation lasted until the adoptive parents passed away. Under these circumstances the adopter and adopted remained strangers to one another except as 'positional' parent and son or incumbent head and successor.

Such was the case, for example, with an informant's father, one of many sons of a *daimyō*-viscount, who was adopted into a *kuge*-viscount house in his teens. He moved to the adopter's Tokyo estate, but the adoptive parents were retired in another city, a two-hour train ride away. The boy was looked after by a retinue who accompanied him over from his natal house, without having much contact with his 'positional' parents. The result was that the successor to the *kuge* house learned little of its tradition and freely transplanted the *daimyō* culture of his natal house. His son, the present head of the house, having little memory of his grandparents, was reviving his *kuge* identity at the time of interview by studying the family background and having reunions with collateral kinsmen of his adoptive grandfather.

Distance was maintained between the adopter and adoptee, as exemplified by the above case and by others, because direct responsibility for child rearing was assumed more by servants than by the parents in the prewar period, when each household was staffed by several female and male servants. This was true with the natural as well as adoptive parent/child relationship (Lebra 1988). Nor was there a special need for a grown-up adoptee to look after his aged adopters for the same reason. Even economic interdependence was not all too necessary because the financial management too was largely undertaken by staff servants and trusted consultants. In other words, the daily chores and arduous work that could have brought the family close together physically or emotionally were carried out by people outside the family. Thus Kazoku adoption was more purely positional, involving little more than occupying a situs, compared with commoner adoption.

That adoption could have nothing to do with nurturance is further indicated by instances of adult adoption, best represented by son-in-law adoption (*muko-yōshi*) and couple adoption (*fūfu-yōshi*). An informant, a daughter of a *kuge*-count, was still unmarried in her late twenties when the house lost its only son and heir to the war. An adoptive marriage was arranged with a son of another *kuge* house, viscount, who was then at the prime of his life. But this type of adoption was common across classes. What is even more revealing of dissociation between adoption and the familial interaction is post-mortem adoption, which occasionally happened despite the general rule against it. An example involving a falsified death notice was previously given. Another case involved no such deception. A second son of a powerful *daimyō*-duke house was adopted into a count house of royal origin when he was nineteen years old. The previous head had died a year before while still unmarried, and the mother of the deceased, a royal princess desiring to perpetuate this branch house (demoted to Kazoku status) started by her nonsuccessor son, nominated the informant, her brother's son, from among three candidates. In other words, this was a case of post-mortem adoption by a cross-cousin, or a case of 'restoration' by a young man thus adopted. The informant, however, insisted that the house of count 'had continued to exist while nobody lived in it' and that 'with my entry the house regained its member.' The only connection here between the adopter and adoptee was an empty house. (But, of course, the empty house carried substantial property to make succession worthwhile).

To pursue the same point, mention may be made of instances of punitive adoption drawn from political history. Sometimes, political offence was punished by the government with a prohibition of house continuation through a biological son for the purpose of terminating the blood line, and this made adoption necessary as the only alternative strategy to avoid the extinction of the house. Matsudaira Yoshinaga (1828–90), the lord of Echizen in the late Tokugawa period, was a political activist in opposition to the major policies of the *shōgun* government. In penalty, he was not only forced into retirement but forbidden to have the lordship succeeded by one of his two sons. A successor, eight years younger than the predecessor, was adopted from a branch house. A similar punishment was enjoined on the Tokugawa *shōgunal* house by the Restoration government, involving the forced retirement of Tokugawa Yoshinobu, the last *shōgun*, and the denial of succession to any of his five sons. The headship was succeeded by an adopted son, Tokugawa Iesato, from a branch house. Punitive adoption such as these cases may be characterized as purely positional, devoid of interpersonal attachment between adopter and adoptee.

The high frequency of adoption and ready acceptance of adoption proposals among Kazoku may have been facilitated by the highly positional nature of adoption with less investment in interpersonal, exclusive bonding with the adoption partner.

THE RULELESS FLOW OF 'BLOOD'

At this juncture, we must return to the issue of kinship which has been so far neglected in the name of the *ie* defined as independent of kinship. It is important to reconsider kinship in view of the hereditary status of Kazoku. For my informants, kinship was conceptualized primarily in terms of 'blood' connections or flow. Sometimes, the blood was sharply opposed to adoption, the blood line (*chisuji*) to the *ie* line (*iesuji*), and so on. Sometimes, no such opposition was felt, and adoption and blood continuity were discussed in the same breath with no sense of contradiction.

Whether or not discrepancy was felt between the *ie* and blood, informants stressed or took for granted the value of blood and some discussed the 'legitimate,' 'true' blood line. A descendant of a *sekke* house was stunned when I carelessly asked his reactions to the ethnological generalization that Japanese easily find substitutes for blood relatives as successors. He strongly repudiated that notion, saying that his house had held a special position in the imperial court for no other reason than heredity. There would have been no justification for his house status, he argued, without the blood continuity with ancestors. In his house, he claimed, adoption had taken place only once in the long line of generations, and that adoptee was an imperial prince mothered by a daughter of the house, a consort to an emperor. The genealogical record does not validate his claim. Obviously, adoption had taken place without disturbing the sense of continuous blood flow. This raises the question of how the adoptee was related to the adoptive parent in kinship.

From my genealogical survey sample, the most recent adoption was taken from each household to see the relationship.

Table 5 shows that in the 194 codable instances of adoption, 30.4 percent of the adoptees are identifiable kin. More than half of these (16 percent) are full brothers, 6.7 percent constitute the adoption of a brother's son (the most preferred by Chinese), and so on. Although in a smaller number, daughter's son and sister's son, too, are accepted as well as patrilateral parallel cousins (father's brother's son) as one's son. 'All other kin' in Table 5 includes more collateral adoptions not only in descending generations (BrSoSo, FaBrSoSo), but also those in ascending generations (MoBr, FaFaBrSo). The nonkin adoptions (69.6 percent) includes *muko-yōshi* (DaHu) and three cases of husband adoption, which is similar to *muko-yōshi*. In husband adoption, apparently, a daughter was a temporary househead and when she married, the headship was taken over by her husband through adoption. Adoptees were certainly nonkin but in both son-in-law adoption and husband adoption the blood kept flowing through the daughter/wife. In other words, in 60.8 percent of all adoptions, blood continuity and adoption are consistent.

Table 5: Adopter-Adoptee Kin Relationships

Kinship	*Number of Cases*	*Per cent*
Kin	*59*	*30.4*
Br	31	16.0
BrSo	13	6.7
DaSo	4	2.1
SiSo	3	1.5
FaBrSo	3	1.5
All other kin	5	2.6
Non-Kin	*135*	*69.6*
DaHu (*muko-yōshi*)	56	28.9
Hu	3	1.5
Other	76	39.2
Total	*194*	*100.0*

Is the category of 'Other' (39.2 percent) that of complete outsiders? It includes relationships like step-kin, remote kin too distant to count as kin, but largely nonrelatives. Even here, however, blood connections are discernible in some cases, however 'thinned.'

Case 3 shows that A adopts B from outside but B in turn adopts A's son C, as would happen in premature adoption, mentioned earlier, and in other circumstances including cases of temporary adoption for entitlement, to be presented shortly. In Case 3, while the parties to adoption (A and B, B and C) are unrelated, A's blood line is restored by his son C. Case 4 is similar. Here C is A's brother's son rather than his own offspring. Case 5 represents serial adoption where two blood lines exchange sons in alternate generations. (Also included in 'Other' (Table 5) are several cases of *dōzoku* adoption discussed below).

There are many indications of attempts to make adoptions compatible with genetic preservation. In the effort, the rule of descent has to be ignored rather than adhered to, which leads to the paradoxical conclusion that rulelessness in adoption, as illustrated in Table 5, suggests the importance, not unimportance, attached to blood or natural kinship. The blood line, for all its fluidity, cannot be contained in the cultural box, but leaks in all directions. Looked at this way, the relatively high frequency of brother adoption makes much sense because a brother is the closest available male kin. Adopting a son-in-law, husband, cousin, uncle, or great-uncle is not as outrageous as it might appear to a Confucian. It is in view of the primacy of consanguinity in this loose sense that Brown's (1966) insistence on Japanese 'cognatic' descent as ideology is reappreciated.

To protect the house from a possible anemic outcome, many houses had branch houses organized into lineage-like *dōzoku*, primarily as suppliers of sons in case the main house ran out of its own. The Imperial House had four such satellite houses, called *shinnō-ke* (houses of imperial blood sons), during the Tokugawa period. The Tokugawa house, too, had three branches, and later added another three secondary branches. The *dōzoku* was characteristically centered on the main house to which branch houses were subordinated regardless of relative age seniority of *dōzoku* members.[12] The main house was entitled to adopt the eldest or even only son of a branch house and, in turn, to give its own excess sons to branches as their successors. The relationship between the adopter and adoptee might be distant in kinship but the *dōzoku*

CASE 3

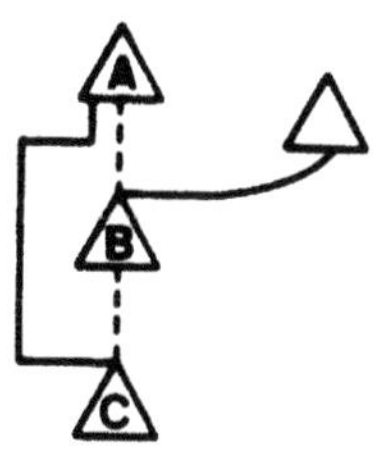

CASE 4

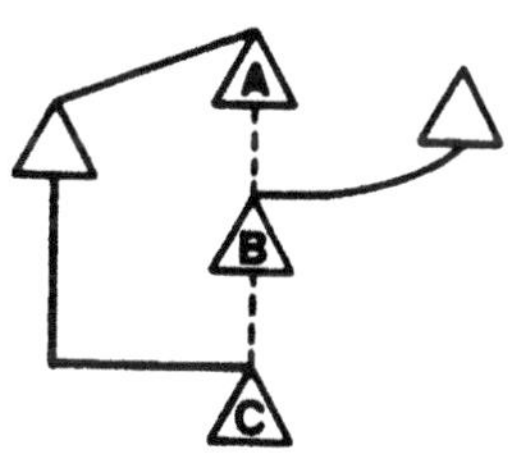

CASE 5

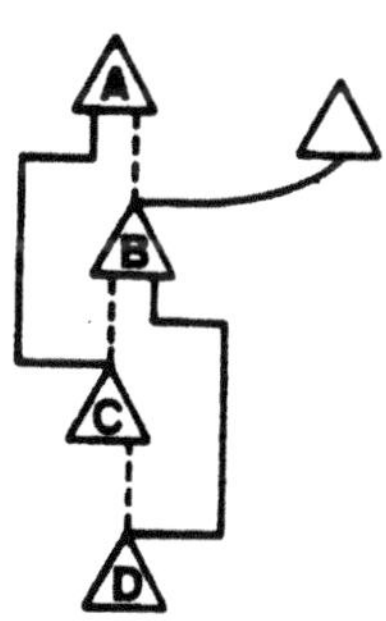

identity facilitated adoption without losing a sense of blood continuity. In the Kazoku, *dōzoku* formation was primarily for the preservation of what was regarded as a gene pool and therefore its size was kept small. (Large *dōzoku* such as those of the Mitsui and Shimazu were to carry other functions as well, particularly, political and economic collaboration.)

As expected, the *dōzoku*, basically *ie*-structured, was thus vulnerable to the split between the *ie* principle and the blood connection. Disputes flared up over the line orthodoxy, particularly when the blood was derived from a great ancestor. In one high-ranking *kuge* house, a nationally eminent ancestor A adopted a son B from his *dōzoku* before he fathered his own son late in life through a young concubine. Already committed to the adoption, the house had the blood son branch out. The main *ie* line, however, soon fell short of blood and the adopted successor's son, lacking a son, was about to adopt his brother. At this juncture, the blood grandson C of the initial ancestor, born in the branch house, claimed the rightful successor status to the main house because he was in the 'orthodox' blood line (*seitō no chisuji*). According to his relative, this succession dispute went to court and resulted in the blood grandson's victory.

In a more covert way, the orthodoxy of the main line was challenged by a branch house representative. Another distinguished ancestor left no son behind so that this main house was succeeded by descendants of his brother. In the meantime, some of the branch houses carried the blood of the great ancestor through his daughters. The head and his wife of one branch house were proud and somewhat resentful against the powerful main house. They declared that theirs and another branch were the only houses where the 'true' blood of Lord X ran. A member of another *dōzoku* group, and head of a branch house, did not consider his house separate from the main house because the second-generation head of the main house was an ancestor of his house, and the whole line was continued from his ancestor. For the informant it was not adoption. 'My ancestor actually *returned* to the original house,' he stressed. Historically, *dōzoku* were indeed ridden with conflict and fights over succession, and blood played an important role in justifying challenges against the *ie* structure. Nor is it surprising that, given the potentially disruptive forces of *dōzoku* members, the size of *dōzoku* tended to be kept to a minimum, unless a *dōzoku* group was essentially an economic unit as among commoners.

There were integrative efforts, however, to bridge the *ie* line and blood line when they came apart. The Matsudaira house, earlier mentioned, that underwent the punishment of blood discontinuation was succeeded by an adopted son, but his son was then married to a daughter of the original Matsudaira so that, in the words of a descendant, '*iesuji* and *chisuji* were converged into one line.'

Memories are blissfully short-lived. The split in one generation may be forgotten in the next. The adopted man may have brought his natal culture of *daimyō* into the *kuge* house he succeeded, as in a case mentioned earlier, but his son might identify himself with the culture of the adopting house, not his blood father's, and act as if he were a successor to a continuous *kuge* line.

Likewise, the head of a baron house, after talking about his adopted father who knew little about the predecessor and the house he succeeded, responded to my question regarding the continuation of the *ie*, 'Yes, I do want our line to be continued forever, because blood cannot be bought with money.' Obviously the 'naturalization' of the external blood into the natal blood of the *ie* occurred in the informant's mind. The adoptee may have resisted changing his personal name but, from his son on, the succession of the same character (*torina*) would resume. Paradoxically, such aligned naturalization was facilitated by the highly cultural representation of the blood by a single, rigid patriline of succession, as best symbolized by the *bansei ikkei*, a single unbroken line for all the emperors. Naturalization may occur within the adoptee's life time: 'Eventually, the adopted son will begin to look as if he were born there,' said the adopted head of a *kuge* house.

Finally, successional adoptions were from Kazoku ranks. The adopted son could be 'anybody,' informants agreed, but 'of course, he must be from a Kazoku.' This meant more than the substitutibility of status affinity for kinship. Since both marriage and adoption had been occurring largely within this status group, there had developed such kinship networks overlapping one another that everyone was able to find someone else connected with him/her. The mental picture of such group-wide networks was another factor, I think, contributing to the reconciliation of adoption and heredity.

METAPHORICAL ADOPTION FOR ENTITLEMENT

Quite another category of adoptions did not involve succession as the ultimate purpose or had nothing to do with succession. Adoption here was, above all, to bestow the adopter's house status upon the adoptee to entitle the latter to some office or role to be taken. This type of adoption was more common or more institutionalized prior to the Restoration, but deserves an analysis because its cultural overtone may elucidate the nature of more common adoption patterns.

Adoption of Outsiders

There was a temporary adoption of a brother or someone else as successor until a son, the ultimate successor, matured. The adoptee was entitled to an office, particularly in the court, since the 'hereditary' court offices were available only to the incumbents of and successors to househeadship. The stipend earned by the temporary successor apparently went to the house coffers. Adoption, in other words, was instrumental to maximizing the house revenue by always having two members of the house on the payroll of the court. This was one of the reasons why there were so many heads in succession within a relatively short period, and so many adoptions, particularly among the *kuge*.

While the above example involves succession, however temporary or instrumental, the other types of adoption for entitlement to be discussed had nothing to do with succession and included women as adoptees. To appreciate that the court was also a central place of employment for women, requires a brief historical introduction. The formal institution of *nyokan*, ladies-in-waiting, came into existence in the early eighth century as part of the court bureaucracy, and survived through the Meiji period. At the time of the Restoration, 300 women courtiers, high and low, moved from the Kyoto Palace 'down' to Tokyo, the new imperial capital (Kawahara 1987: 92). These women, the offices they held, and the quarters in the palace where they were waiting for calls was commonly referred to as *tsubone*. The secrecy[13] surrounding these ladies-in-waiting was due to their being a reservoir of hidden consorts for the emperor, recruited from validated virgins. In a simplified form the institution continued to occupy a part of the imperial palace through the modern period. Emperor Meiji, while officially married to Empress Shoken, a *sekke* daughter, was waited upon in his bedchamber by a host of *nyokan*, and fathered fifteen children (Kawahara 1987: 93), although only one son (to be Emperor Taisho) and four daughters survived. The traditional structure of this *nyokan* institution was abolished by Emperor Showa (Hirohito) with puritanical determination.

Traditionally, the *nyokan* were rank-ordered in a rigid hierarchy, and each of the offices was matched with the hereditary rank of its holder's natal house (Shimohashi and Hagura 1979). The *tenji* (also called *suke-no-tsubone*), the highest office, was held, for example, by daughters from *kuge* houses with 'special status' (*kakubetsu no o-iegara*). Under the Kazoku system, this house-status rule was relaxed, but the *tenji* were recruited primarily from count houses and a few designated viscount houses of *kuge* background.[14] When a daughter of an ordinary viscount was to become a *tenji*, she first had to be adopted into a proper count house as *yōjo* (adopted daughter, in distinction from *yōshi*, adopted son) to acquire status credentials (Shimohashi and Hagura 1979: 17).[15]

Adoption for entitlement to office was also resorted to when placing women in the royal or noble nunneries, another important area for noble women's career outside marriage. Before the Restoration, there were a host of Buddhist temples (*monzeki*) closely associated with the imperial house.[16] *Monzeki* temples, particularly nunneries, were run like miniature versions of the imperial court and headed by royal princesses who were waited upon by retinues of *kuge* daughters. Cynically viewed, these religious establishments were a terminal dumping ground for excess royal children who were thus bound to celibate life in exchange for economic security. The Restoration put an end to the *monzeki* institution, severed the imperial house from these temples, and recalled the priest princes to secular life as heads of the newly-established collateral houses of the imperial lineage (*miyake*). The break from the past was thus dramatic for the male-headed *monzeki* temples, but not so for nunneries in my view. The royal nunneries (*ama-monzeki*) persisted in their old identity in one way or another mainly because their clients and support groups wished them to maintain the temple status (*jikaku* or *teragara*). However, royal princesses were now barred from Buddhist priesthood,[17] and even high-ranking *kuge* daughters ran short to cap the remnants of these mini-palaces. Hence, adoption became necessary. The two priestesses I met in their respective nunneries were sisters who had originated in a modest baron house but had been adopted into its main house, a prominent *kuge* house with the title of marquis, before they were initiated into the *monzeki* nunneries. Many Kazoku informants, in response to my questions on *monzeki*, referred to the chief priestess of Zenkoji, a popular temple in Nagano, as adopted to the Ichijo, one of the *sekke.*

Basically the same type of adoption was used for status adjustment in the marriage market. Adoption served as a means to correct discrepancies in the ranks or reputations of the two houses involved in a proposed marriage. A daughter of a low-ranking house might gain status-fitness through adoption to marry a much higher ranking man. A daughter of a man whose disgraceful conduct (e.g., political radicalism, profligacy) smeared the house reputation to the point of jeopardizing the Kazoku status, would be able to dissociate herself from the source of ignominy by becoming a *yōjo* (adopted daughter) of another house. Matrimony could then take place. That adoption for such spousal entitlement was no secret is demonstrated by the fact that such adoptions were often engineered and arranged by the office of *sōchitsuryō.* According to an informant, her father was kept busy arranging marriages and daughter adoptions during his tenure as the director of the office.

The best known recent case of adoption for marital qualification is that of Princess Chichibu, the widow of Prince Chichibu, Emperor Hirohito's brother. Born a granddaughter of Matsudaira Katamori, a *daimyō* of Aizu, Matsudaira Setsuko was nevertheless a daughter of a nonsuccessor son of Katamori, namely, a non-Kazoku. When she was chosen and urged by the Empress Dowager, the mother of the imperial brothers, to be the bride of the emperor's brother, her family tried to decline the offer by calling attention to its commoner status. This excuse was ruled out, however, by the suggestion that Setsuko be adopted by her uncle, the head of the Matsudaira main house with the title of viscount. Rank discrepancy was thus removed and thereafter Princess Chichibu was to always appear on Kazoku records as a *yōjo* (or niece) of Matsudaira Morio, thus dissociated from her father (Ema 1983).

The very apex of the national pyramid historically involved such adoption, including some of the principal wives (*kōgo*, *chūgū*) of emperors. The Taira daughter, Tokuko, was adopted by Retired-Emperor Goshirakawa as his daughter so as to qualify as Chūgū to Emperor Takakura (Ponsonby Fane 1936: 145). Also among the wives (*midai*) of Tokugawa *shōgun* were *yōjo.* According to Tokugawa descendants, it was a rule that *shōgun* wives be daughters of either the *sekke* or the royal lineage, just as emperors' wives were, and if this rule was broken the bride had to be adopted into one of these houses to transcend their 'original' status. So, Tokugawa Yoshinobu's wife, a daughter of an ordinary *kuge*, became a *yōjo* of the Ichijo. The last of the three *midai* of the thirteenth *shōgun*, Tokugawa Iesada, known as Tenshoin, was born in a small branch house of the Shimazu. She was first adopted into the Shimazu main house, and, when nominated a *shōgun* wife or in anticipation of such nomination, was re-adopted into the Konoe house, a *sekke.*

If nonsuccessional adoption was indeed for entitlement, it was more likely for high-ranking houses to receive, and less likely to give, daughters for adoption than lower ranking ones. Table 6 shows the proportions of daughter adoptions by the *sekke* and *shōgun* as receivers and givers, relative to all the daughters, as they appear in the genealogies.

Table 6: Daughter Adoptions by *Sekke* and *Shōgun* Houses

	Sekke	*Shōgun*
All own daughters	122	31
Own daughters given	10 (8.2%)	0
Daughters received	21 (17.2%)	2 (6.5%)

For *sekke*, 8.2 percent of all daughters were given for adoption, while 17.2 percent were received. It is noteworthy that the Konoe, the highest of all the *sekke*, gave away only 5.9 per cent of all its own daughters (less than the average of all *sekke*) and received as many as 58.8 percent, by far surpassing all the collaterals. The desirability of being a Konoe *yojo* for status enhancement is beyond doubt. For the *shōgun* house, no daughter was adopted out, and 6.5 percent were adopted in, much lower than for the *sekke*. Does this mean that the *sekke* continued to be a source of greater prestige than the *shōgun* house or that the former were more receptive of *yojo* than the latter? The question will be explored elsewhere.

The term 'daughter-adoption' does not sound right for this kind of adoption. Since it was the woman who needed an adopter rather than the other way around, it was more like father-adoption. Indeed, Shimohashi (Shimohashi and Hagura 1979: 17), speaking about palace women, identifies adoption for *nyokan* appointments as *oya-tori* (parent-adoption).

All these cases of daughter-adoption for entitlement sound like empty, or metaphorical adoption where there was no real adoption but involved only a pretense. An adopted daughter may have lived in the adoptive house for a short while as a rite of transition and kept ritual contact subsequently, or the transition may have been only a matter of paperwork. In the case of Princess Chichibu, according to Ema (1983), Matsudaira Setsuko left her natal home the day before the nuptials and stayed with her uncle's family that night so that the next morning she could directly proceed from the viscount house to the imperial palace. (However, my informants said she moved to the main house months before.)

If adoption for succession represents a second-order symbolization, metaphorical adoption is, to my mind, a third-order symbolization. If the first is S_2 for S_1 for X, the second is S_3 for S_2 for S_1 for X. The third-order kinship, thus constructed, is further removed than the second-order kinship from natural, substantive, real kinship. We are looking at a distinctly and purely cultural phenomenon.

The initial question returns to us in a sharper form: How is it that such purely symbolic or fictional adoption was reconcilable with the hereditary status of the nobility? As far as successional adoption is concerned, we found a substantial degree of compatibility between adoption and heredity through the notion of blood flow. To my surprise, the same metaphor was expressed by an informant for explaining status-bestowing adoption. A viscount of *daimyō* origin, he said that several men in his genealogy became nominal or temporary successors: 'This way, the blood of my house entered their bodies, so they say.' He was half-joking, but I thought the use of the blood metaphor in this context is suggestive in that it transforms the rigid image of heredity into fluid substance. After all, blood is transfusable.

Adoption of Natural Children

The metaphorical blood transfusion is one idea, but a more fundamental, though not obvious, rationale seems to underlie the acceptability of empty adoption, which first occurred to me when I heard a daughter of *kuge* descent talk about her grandfather and father. Her grandfather did not marry her grandmother even though they had eight children, 'Probably because she was not from a respectable family.' Her father, one of the eight children born out of wedlock, was adopted by his natural father to become successor.

Here, we are no longer referring to two sets of kinship, but only one where adoptive kinship overlaps natural kinship. In one sense this involves first-order symbolization, but in another sense, third-order or even higher-order symbolization in that the natural son was adopted as if he were an outsider and became a full-fledged son as if he were truly adopted. Simply put, the adoption here was for legitimation, but its implications lead to the history of imperial parentage.

In the late Nara period it became a rule for an emperor to formally grant the title of *shinnō* (prince of the blood, *naishinnō* for daughters) to his children and siblings. The nomination procedure was called *shinnō senge*. From medieval times on, through the *shinnō senge*, the reigning emperor was allowed (or forced) to do two things: to nominate a person outside the above category as a *shinnō*, and conversely to select some of his natural children as *shinnō*; to the exclusion of others. *Shinnō senge*, in my view, amounted to adoption for entitlement, and as in the above adoption cases among the nobility, *shinnō senge* was often processed only after the child grew up (note that Emperor Meiji was designated Mutsuhito Shinnō at age nine). The crown prince, needless to say, had to be a *shinnō*, but royal children, including those outside the above category, who were to enter the priesthood also were granted the *shinnō* title to become *shinnō* priests or priestesses (Shimohashi and Hagura 1979: 30).

The first option was outsider adoption whereby the emperor's relative, but not his son, became a prince of the blood as if he were an imperial son. The second option involved a selective designation of an imperial son of the blood as a prince of the blood as if he were an outsider. At issue now is the latter. Apparently, imperial children remained nobodies until they received *shinnō senge* status, and the liminal status of the pre-*senge* children had much to do with the status of their mothers. Unless a child was mothered by the principal or highest wife of the emperor, such as *kogō*, *chūgū*, (and sometimes *nyōgo*), *shinnō senge* was not automatic. And yet, the emperor had sexual access to many other women among the *nyokan* and even lower attendants, and sometimes outside the palace. It was the latter women who, more often than the former, gave birth to imperial children, including heirs. This required the emperor to distinguish *shinnō* from other children through the adoption-like process of *shinnō senge*. The left-out children were considered children of the mother's natal house and were buried in its cemetery. The mother of a *shinnō*, particularly of the heir-apparent, may have been promoted to a rank high enough to claim official motherhood of the prince or, if too low in origin, remained hidden behind the public scene and known as *seibo* (bearer) in distinction from the formal mother and empress to whom the child belonged. This state of affairs explains another kind of imperial adoption; that is, the emperor raising his *seibo* to the status of Empress Dowager even though she had never been an empress. In my view, this is a case of mother-adoption to legitimize the natural mother into a culturally authorized 'imperial mother.'

The natural state of birth and procreation was thus messy, disorderly, uncertain, confusing, or entirely hidden. The history of the imperial bedchamber was duplicated on a smaller scale by the nobility, and the dual motherhood entered into the memory of Kazoku children as well. Several of my informants recalled their natural grandmothers having been *seibo* of their fathers or mothers, differentiated from their formal grandmothers, *obaba-sama*. The former were also referred to as *ohara-san* (womb lady), and addressed by their personal names without the minimal honorific, *san*, by their children and grandchildren, as if they were no higher than maids. Informants concurred that the surviving nobility, as well as imperial descendants, were almost all born of 'side consorts' (*sokushitsu*, *owaki*, *sobame*, etc).

If the natural origin was thus ambiguous, there should not be too much resistance to a creation of kinship through adoption. As we have noted, some forms of adoption like *shinnō senge* functioned to put the mess of natural procreation in order. In this respect it is extremely interesting to note that the Tokugawa Shogunate, overly concerned with the rigid maintenance of law and order, demanded imperial children mothered by *nyokan* to be adopted out into one of the four *shinnō* houses (Fushimi, Arisugawa, Kan'in, and Katsura) before being entitled to *shinnō senge*. As long as they remained within the palace, they were considered merely as natural products of their imperial father's illicit affairs, *otekake* (Shimohashi and Hagura 1979: 27). In other words, these children went through double-adoption, first to sever the natural tie, then to return to the original birth place, going out and coming in. The natural filiality became legitimized only after being denaturalized or culturalized.

The uncertainty of natural parentage could give rise to a double or triple sense of 'true' origin or reality itself. I speculate that it was this kind of ethno-epistemology based on multiple consciousness that made the empty, purely symbolic type of adoption acceptable since it was as real, if not more so, as natural parentage.

CONCLUSION

I have tried to make sense out of the promiscuous adoption practices of the Japanese hereditary elite. Positional succession, mandatory for the *ie*, necessitated free adoption, nonsuccessor sons were available as willing adoptees, and the positional nature of adoption did away with the interpersonally invested parent-child bonding. Further, adoption did not necessarily supersede blood ties but in most cases reinforced them. The blood metaphor, with all its 'fluidity,' facilitated tracing blood-related candidates in all directions in disregard of the culturally imposed descent rules. It seems that promiscuous adoption was what preserved the noble status for persons, houses, or the status system as a whole, that the fluidity of blood was what maintained the adherence to the 'orthodox' line of blood in its rigid form.

This paradox appears even more dramatized in another version of adoption, that for entitlement, which was practiced only infrequently and more in premodern times and yet culturally even more significant than adoption for succession. This involved more women than men. Contrary to successional adoption, that for entitlement was metaphorical or purely symbolical in that a person moved from her natal house to another house as if real adoption took place, but it was only to assume the status of the adoptive house and thereby to be entitled to a certain office or to an upward marriage. The fictional nature of such adoption ensured status mobility, and by doing so, stabilized and perpetuated the hereditary hierarchy. Metaphorical adoption for entitlement took a striking form when one's natural child was adopted as if the child were originally an outsider, as exemplified in the history of the imperial house. Adoption in this case was to bestow the adopter's house status upon a reclaimed child of his own to surmount the mismatched status of its natural mother. Again, adoption kept hereditary status mobile and fluid, which in turn facilitated its preservation.

Finally, we might conjecture that adoption practices described here exemplify a familiar theme of Japanese ethnography, namely, the split and reconciliation between reality and form, fact and principle, or *honne* (true feeling) and *tatemae* (formally enunciated principle).

NOTES

1. A portion of this paper was presented at the Center for Japanese Studies, University of California, Berkeley, November 15, 1988, as part of a monograph under preparation. For two periods of fieldwork, data analysis, and writing including this paper, I have been supported by the Joint Committee on Japanese Studies of the American Council of Learned Societies and the Social Science Research Council, the Japan Foundation, the University of Hawaii Japan Studies Endowment, University of Hawaii Fujio Matsuda Scholar award, and Wenner-Gren Foundation. I am indebted to Harumi Befu for his comments on an earlier draft, to Keith Brown for editorial facilitation and to Junko Yoshino who assisted me in coding data.

2. Despite the postwar civil code that removed the *ie* as a legal entity, and although Japanese thinking about the *ie* and family has changed, I refer to *ie* in the present tense because of the analytical, rather than descriptive, emphasis and because the old culture of *ie* still survives in one form or another, selectively if not in its entirety, as optional if not as mandatory.

3. Befu (1962) also cites Takeuchi with reference to 'the practice of *kaiyoshi* ("buyer-adoptive son"), in which a man on the verge of bankruptcy sells his entire property to a total stranger who is willing to take over the family occupation and adopt and continue its name.' It is interesting that buying in connection with adoption means two totally different arrangements for Chinese and Japanese.

4. Within the same system fits a case where a bride from outside marries an insider son (the ideal form of *chōnan sōzoku*) and is widowed young after giving birth to a child. She may be asked by her parents-in-law to stay and marry a newly recruited husband (adopted son-in-law). I (Lebra 1984) encountered cases of this variety in earlier fieldwork.

5. Adoption is usually called *yōshi* but in this particular case, the term *jisshi* was used. *Jisshi* means a

real, true, natural child, but also can refer to a special case of adoption where the adoptee is treated like a true child. So one hears a statement like 'A becomes B's *jisshi*.'

6. Such double-succession was not as deviant as it might appear. In the 125-generation-long imperial dynasty, there were two empresses who were enthroned twice under different names: Empress Kōgyoku (re. 642–45) and Saimei (655–661), and Empress Kōken (749–58) and Shōtoku (764–70). There is a technical term for this imperial practice-*chōso*, double accession.

7. The weight of estates as an explanation for succession varied extensively within the Kazoku group. At one extreme were big *daimyō* houses, as represented by the Maeda and Hosokawa, which, even after the Meiji Restoration reduced their wealth to fractions, still remained in possession of vast estates and wealth mainly due to the financial acumen of their vassals. Also there were *zaibatsu* houses such as the Mitsui and Sumitomo which were ennobled primarily due to their wealth and contributions. At the other extreme were impoverished Kazoku much worse off than well-to-do commoners, and these were stereotypically represented by the court nobles whose genealogical prominence was compromised by their legendary indigence.

8. The privilege of free tuition was terminated in 1924 (Kazoku Kaikan 1933: 93), but tuition loans were provided at the same time.

9. In some households, the eldest daughter was also held in special esteem as symbolized by a positional term, *o-hiisama* (little princess), attached to her but not necessarily to her younger sisters.

10. Among the Kazoku-title grantees were houses connected with satellite temples of the Kōfukuji in Nara, which came to be known as Nara-Kazoku. The rationale was that the chief priests of these temples had been supplied by the same *kuge* houses generation after generation, because celibacy precluded internal reproduction of successors. After the Restoration, when a temple was severed from its secular house and successor provider, the then priest was laicized and allowed to raise his family with a newly given family name. Under the Kazoku system these newly created houses were granted a baronage. The informant here was head of one of the two highest among these houses which had originated from *monzeki* temples. *Monzeki* will be explained later in the text. Also see Note 16.

11. Unfortunately, not perfectly random. Every fifth household on the list was selected only if the house included at least one adopted head. If not, the next on the list was picked.

12. The only exception I could see was with the *sekke* in that the five houses, while they carried a strong sense of kinship with common ancestry, were not organized into the main-house central hierarchy but were more or less equal. The Konoe was recognized as the *hittō*, the very top of the group, but never enjoyed the main-house status.

13. In the modern period these palace women were office holders in the Ministry of the Imperial Household, and yet none of them appeared on the staff list of the ministry until after the war (Kawahara 1987: 92).

14. Daughters of higher ranking houses such as those of marquises and dukes ranked too high to serve the court as ladies-in-waiting. Top-ranking *kuge* daughters were more likely to be reserved for full-fledged royal marriage. Empress Meiji was an Ichijō daughter, and Empress Taisho a Kujō daughter, following the long tradition of Fujiwara daughters offered for imperial matrimony. All this suggests vestiges of pre-Meiji court hierarchy in spite of the theoretical homogeneity of Kazoku as 'peers.'

15. The *shōgun* court also developed its own harem (*ōoku*, grand interior) which could recruit commoner women as *shōgun* consorts through adoption into samurai houses (Takayanagi 1965).

16. *Monzeki* also refers to the chief priests and priestesses, who were predominantly royal princes and princesses. While the royal status of *monzeki* temples was proudly claimed by informants, closer examination reveals that occupants of *monzeki* offices were not always royal children but included the children of high-ranking *kuge* and even *shōgun*. This calls attention to another category of *monzeki* categorized as *sekke monzeki*. My interview material, however, does not show a clear demarcation between the *miya* (royal) *monzeki* and *sekke monzeki*.

17. This policy change had to do with the suppression of Buddhism and the promotion of Shinto at this time of transition.

BIBLIOGRAPHY

Bachnik, J. M. 1983. Recruitment Strategies for Household Succession: Rethinking Japanese Household Organisation. *Man* 18: 160–182.

Befu, H. 1962. *Corporate Emphasis and Patterns of Descent in the Japanese Family. Japanese culture: Its Development and Characteristics*, eds. R. J. Smith and R. K. Beardsley, pp. 34–41. Chicago.

Brown, K. 1966. Dozoku and the Ideology of Descent in Rural Japan. *American Anthropologist* 68: 1129–1151.

Brady, I. (ed.) 1978. *Transactions in Kinship: Adoption and Fosterage in Oceania.* Honolulu.

Carroll, V. 1970. Introduction: What Does 'Adoption' Mean? *Adoption in Eastern Oceania*, ed. V. Carroll, pp. 3–17. Honolulu.

Ema, S. 1983. *Chichibu No Miya Hi Setsuko.* Tokyo.

Goodenough, R. G. 1970. Adoption on Romonum, Truk. *Adoption in Eastern Oceania*, ed. V. Carroll, pp. 314–340. Honolulu.

Howard, A., R. H. Heighton, Jr., C. E. Jordan, and R. G. Gallimore. 1970. The Traditional and Modern Adoption Patterns in Hawaii, ed. V. Carroll, pp. 21–51. Honolulu.

Hozumi, N. 1912. *Ancestor-Worship and Japanese Law.* Tokyo.

Kasumi Kaikan (Shoka Shiryo Chosa Iinkai) (ed.) 1982–4.

Kazoku Kakei Taisei, 2 vols. Tokyo.

Kawahara, T. 1987. Michikohi. Tokyo.

Kazoku Kaikan. 1933. Kazoku Yoran. Tokyo.

Kirby, R. J. 1908. An Essay by Dazai Jun. (Translated by R. J. Kirby) *Transactions of the Asiatic Society of Japan* 36: (part 1) 96–135.

Kitaoji, H. 1971. The Structure of the Japanese Family. *American Anthropologist* 73: 1036–1057.

Lebra, T. S. 1984. *Japanese Women: Constraint and Fulfillment.* Honolulu.

—— 1988. The Socialization of Aristocratic Children by Commoners: The Japanese Case. Paper presented at the 87th American Anthropological Association Annual Meeting, November 16–20, 1988, Phoenix, AZ.

Moore, R. A. 1970. Adoption and Samurai Mobility in Tokugawa Japan. *Journal of Asian Studies* 29: 617–632.

Morioka, K. 1967. Life Cycle Patterns in Japan, China, and the United States. *Journal of Marriage and the Family* 29: 595–606.

Nakane, C. 1967. *Kinship and Economic Organization in Rural Japan.* London.

—— 1969. Kazoku no Kozo: Shakai Jinruigaku-teki Bunseki. Tokyo.

Nakano, T. 1968. *Ie to Dozoku-dan No Riron.* Tokyo.

Pelael, J. C. 1970. *Japanese Kinship: A Comparison. Family and Kinship in Chinese Society*, ed. M. Freedman, pp. 227–248. Stanford.

Plath, D. W. 1964. Where the Family of God . . . is the Family: The Role of the Dead in Japanese Households. *American Anthropologist* 66: 300–317.

Ponsonby Fane, R. A. B. 1936. Kohi: Imperial Consorts in Japan. *Transactions and Proceedings of the Japan Society* 33: 111–168. London.

Sakamaki, Y. 1987. *Kazoku Seido no Kenkyū.* Tokyo.

Shigeno, A. 1887. The Evils of Abdication, Heirship, and Adoption. *Transactions of the Asiatic Society of Japan* 15: 72–82.

Shimohashi, Y., and K. Hagura. 1979. *Bakumatsu no Kyūtei.* Tokyo.

Smith, R. J. 1972. *Small Families, Small Households, and Residential Instability: Town and City in 'Pre-modern' Japan. Household and Family in Past Time*, ed. P. Laslett, pp. 429–471. Cambridge.
Takayanagi, K. 1965. *Edojō Ōoku no Seikatsu.* Tokyo.
Watson, J. L. 1975. Agnates and Outsiders: Adoption in a Chinese Village. *Man* 10: 293–306.

First published in *Cultural Anthropology* 5(1), February 1990.

20 The Socialization of Aristocratic Children by Commoners: Recalled Experiences of the Hereditary Elite in Modern Japan

In my previous research on Japanese women (Lebra 1984), I learned that, prior to the postwar educational liberation for ordinary women to go on to college, lower- and middle-class girls typically spent premarital years, upon graduation from grade school or high school, at households above their own classes as maids or 'etiquette apprentices.' For poor families, this was the only available and acceptable employment for a daughter if only to 'reduce a mouth to feed,' while better-off families considered it a rite of passage to transform an unfinished girl into a qualified bridal candidate. Matchmakers would count such cross-class apprenticeship as an important, sometimes mandatory, credential for a bride. This finding prompted me to turn to the upper-class Japanese, particularly, aristocrats, as the next research project with the hope of gaining a stereoscopic view of Japanese society. Indeed, I found commoners entering the interior of aristocratic lives and leaving an indelible mark there, in a way much more than as apprentices absorbing the upper-class culture. This article presents a portion of my current research on the Japanese elite, focusing on the part played by commoners in socializing the aristocratic children.

A HISTORICAL SKETCH OF THE MODERN JAPANESE NOBILITY

Aristocracy here refers to the modern nobility called the *Kazoku*, the 'flower lineage,' that formally existed from 1884 until 1947 when it was abolished under the postwar democratic constitution. The Kazoku as a status group stood right below the emperor and royal lineage group, and above the gentry (*shizoku*, largely coming from the samurai vassalage) that was fused into the lowest and largest class, commoners. The Kazoku membership was of diverse backgrounds, but comprised three major subgroups: the former court nobles called *kuge* who had served the imperial court in Kyoto; the feudal domain lords, commonly called *daimyo*, who had owed loyalty to the military government headed by their overlord, the *shogun*, residing in Edo, present Tokyo; and the meritorious nobles who rose, in most cases, from the modest status of the lower-ranking samurai vassals due to their performances contributive to the state. The Meiji Restoration of the imperial regime, at the dawn of modern Japan, marked the division between the first two groups as renovated old nobles and the last group as the newly ennobled. Under the Kazoku system, all these nobles of various origins were organized into a single group of 'peers' residentially concentrated in the 'high city' (Seidensticker 1983) of Tokyo. The generations of my informants were all of 'hereditary' elite in varying degrees of genealogical depth. The term Kazoku referred simultaneously to the status group as a whole, each family, and individual members.

In reflection of the 'absolutely sacred' sovereignty of the post-Restoration emperor, there was a clear demarcation line between the 'ruling' royal group (the main imperial house and its collateral houses) and the 'subject' nobility. And yet, there was mutual access and some mobility, upward (only for women) and downward (for both sexes), across the line by marriage, adoption, or branching. In many ways the royal family was a cultural model for noble families. For these reasons, my account below will touch upon the royalty where relevant. Like the Kazoku, the royal lineage group was also put out of existence in 1947, except the reigning emperor and his closest family.

The Kazoku group was rank-ordered by five nobility titles called *shaku*: *koshaku*, *koshaku*, *hakushaku*, *shishaku*, and *danshaku*. In order to avoid confusion over the homophones, I shall use English translations: duke (instead of the common translation, 'prince,' to be distinguished from the royal prince), marquis, count, viscount, and baron. The holders of the first two titles were privileged to be automatic members, while those of the other three to be mutually elected members, of the House of Peers, one arm of the bicameral parliamentary system. In total, there have been 1011 families, including those which have become extinct, that were awarded Kazoku titles in the 63 years from the inception to abolition of the Kazoku institution. Theoretically, only the male head of each house was a Kazoku, but his spouse and dependent children also were entitled to Kazoku-status courtesy. Most of Kazoku children were sent to Gakushuin, a school complex built primarily, though not exclusively, for them.

World War II and its aftermath devastated the Kazoku along with the rest of the nation, and uprooted them from their old life-style, the 1947 abolition of the Kazoku institution being little more than a formal enunciation, for most households, of what had actually taken place. I located and interviewed about one hundred surviving Kazoku or their descendants of various ranks and backgrounds. It is on the basis of fragments of their oral autobiographies constructed in response to my request and questions that this article was conceived. In view of the current climate of the epistemological self-criticism in anthropology, it may be noted that my reconstruction of the given narratives inevitably is a product of multilevel reflexivity and contextuality. This is not to mean that the following account is a fiction. More detailed discussion on this issue is to appear elsewhere.[1]

SOCIALIZATION: POSITIONAL AND PERSONAL

Socialization is to perform a double function: to train the child in assuming a series of roles and statuses on the one hand, and to meet and regulate the child's biological, emotional, and cognitive needs and potentials on the other. One refers to social structure to be reproduced through socialization whereas the other focuses on the person to be socialized. The two functions, structural and personal, must be combined but there is likely to be variation from society to society, from class to class, in the culturally pronounced primacy of one over the other as well as in the way the two are interlocked.

Pertinent to the above generalization is the binary typology of linguistic codes developed by Basil Bernstein and interpreted by Mary Douglas (1970: 42–45). In one of the types, called 'the restricted code,' the *social* function of speech is more dominant than is its *informational* function, so that utterances primarily 'express the social structure, embellish and reinforce it.' In the other type called 'the elaborate code,' conversely, not tied to particular contexts for speech acts, the two functions are reversed in priority and causation. Here it is speech that dominates and organizes social groups around it. In parallel with this typology is that of family system – positional versus personal – as a genesis of this polarity in codes. The 'positional family' where restricted codes are instilled draws upon 'ascribed role categories' in disciplining the child. The opposite type, the 'personal family,' correlating more with the elaborate code, prizes 'the autonomy and unique value of the individual,' and appeals to the child's sensitivity to the personal feelings of others and its own (Douglas 1970: 45–48).

All societies and all classes must fulfill both functions of socialization, both structure-centered and person-centered, or positional and personal, along with the two types of codes, albeit in varying distribution and combination depending upon classes, stages of social evolution, or the child's growth stages. When one side of the double function is overemphasized, the other neglected side is likely to erupt in demand of attention. This article addresses how this sort of conflict stemming from socialization imbalance is managed.

Applying the above typologies to Japan, it is safe to assume that the prewar aristocratic socialization was more structural or positional than was the commoner counterpart. Compared both with other classes and with the postwar situation of the survivors, the socialization that my informants underwent in the prewar period may be characterized as more positional or structural. In the family, a member stepped into a given role rather than made his role (Bernstein 1971:185). Individuals were in interaction more in accordance to the roles and statuses that they held in relation to one another, than as whole persons charged with personal needs and emotions. Status distance rather than intimacy, separateness rather than togetherness, predominated in most of the families. In this respect, the nobility was surpassed only by the royalty.

In speech, there are indications that might suggest an emphasis upon the elaborate codes in that the children tended, without being so trained by their parents, to master all possible speech patterns across class boundaries, that is, to develop ability freely to switch from one speech level to another in accordance with the status of the addressee. But this kind of elaboration was clearly framed by the restricted code prescribing the speech-level adjustment to each particular social context.

There were exceptions, of course, and some informants (paradoxically royal informants in particular) firmly and sometimes with resentment refuted this generalized picture as a stereotype. But such exceptional informants tended to add, 'My family was different from other Kazoku-san,' or it turned out that distance was so taken for granted as to feel natural. What complicates the matter is that Kazoku families on the average were much more Westernized than in other classes in certain aspects of their life-style as a result of overseas education or career, and frequent contact with foreign dignitaries as part of social life or official status, and so forth. Some families had the children kiss their parents, which was strikingly alien to the Japanese in those days. And yet this did not preclude the retention of the Japanese tradition of status culture as well symbolized by two houses built side by side in the same premises, one Japanese style, the other Western style. Furthermore, the Western influence was that of upper-class Westerners. Kissing was, it seems, more like a stylized ritual for daily greeting than expressive of love.

THE ARISTOCRATIC FAMILY AND SOCIALIZATION

Family socialization was centered on two major status incumbents: the head of the house and his nominated heir. Since these positions were taken by male members only and primogeniture was the rule, the children were clearly differentiated and rank-ordered by gender and birth order. A third son of a count recalled how his eldest brother was trained to be a lord while all the other children were treated indifferently, how the latter were not allowed to have a second bowl of rice before the heir-brother did. A special status term for address and reference, like 'highness,' 'junior lord,' was reserved only for the heir. Younger sons were disciplined to speak with honorifics to their eldest brother. This system placed all daughters as well beneath the successor son, regardless of birth order.

Such positional distinction of the heir was compounded by sex segregation. Particularly high-ranking families of daimyo origin literally practiced the Confucian tenet of sex segregation by removing the heir at age seven (actually six by the present system of counting) from the family quarters ('the interior' associated with women) of the residential estate, and putting him in the male quarters ('exterior,' namely, the office to manage the household financially and in external relations), as will be described again below in connection with servants. Some families sent their sons including non-heirs away from home. One of the segregated heirs, a former marquis said that he had no woman around except when nursed in sickbed, and had only male servants to look after him, until his graduation from university (there may be a good reason that he was a sickly boy).

Positional or structural socialization with an emphasis upon hierarchy and distance was further extended to parent-child interaction. Most informants of all backgrounds characterized their parents as having been distant, remote, and even 'cold.' In high-ranking, large households, children dined separately from their parents, but when co-dining took place, conviviality was not to be expected as recalled by a former viscount: 'Father was stern, and there was nothing jovial in the family at the dinner table. We were forbidden to talk. It was unpleasant. I wanted to talk and listen freely.' Merrymaking was disapproved of as an uncalled-for buffoonery (*warufuzake*). On a street he witnessed an enviable scene: a little boy mounted on his father's shoulders, something absolutely inconceivable for him and his father. A second son of a marquis repeated the same point: 'Today, children and parents joke with and embrace one another. When I was a child, I had nothing like that.' The child felt constrained not to initiate conversation, and, when speaking, to use honorifics. 'Parents were scary, and we were not able to show *amae* (desire for indulgence) to them.' Many informants referred to the parent-child contact as 'ritualistic,' or 'well-mannered as between strangers' (*tanin gyogi*). 'Twice a day we children went to see our parents for morning and bedtime greetings.' The parent-child distance was implemented as well as symbolized by spatial segregation in residential arrangements. The children's rooms were separated from the parental living rooms often with long hallways connecting them. It was common to have separate gates to the house for the parents and children.

The father as a distant figure is not surprising since he was the househead who singly embodied the house assets, including property, authority, nobility rank, prerogatives, and prestige, on which all the family depended. The positional emphasis in father-child relationship was more or less true with commoners although in a more compromised way, and even now the father's absence, if not father's authority, is a common feature of urban middle-class Japanese families. No more surprising is positional socialization with regard to gender and birth order, which was also shared in a milder form by other classes. What does strike as a class contrast was the mother's role.

Among commoners, especially middle-class families where there was a sharp division of labor by gender, it was physical closeness and emotional warmth that characterized the mother. The aforementioned double function of socialization was performed by the contrapuntal roles played by mother and father to generate a double image of parenthood as close and distant, warm and stern, supportive and disciplinarian, sympathetic and autocratic, or, in a word, personal and positional. The mother was autonomous enough to take a role complementary but counterbalancing to the father, and when necessary, to shield the child from the father's excess in authoritarian dominance. The child legally and positionally belonged to the father as the househead, but emotionally and personally to the mother. And the mother in turn belonged to the child more than to the father.

This somewhat idealized image of middle-class motherhood was far from reality for aristocratic children. The mother appeared in my informants' narratives as someone who was conspicuously absent when the child had bodily contact with a caretaker, be it during bathing, sleeping, changing diapers and clothing, sitting on laps, being held in arms, going to a bathroom, and so on. 'All my mother did,' claimed a daughter of a marquis, 'was bearing a child, and nothing more (*umi sute*). She would not have known whether her child was dead or alive unless so reported by someone.' This sounds like an exaggeration, but captures the general feelings held by many informants toward their mothers.

Since the war, this state of affairs has radically changed in a majority of cases so that the middle-class pattern has become predominant. Thus, the prewar-generation mother is experiencing the 'fun' of caring for her grandchildren, but at the same time tends to be critical of her postwar-generation daughter for being so irrationally attached and 'sticky' (*betabeta*) to her children. The daughter repudiates the senior critic by saying that it was easy for her, the mother, to be so aloof because she did not have to raise her children personally. This is not the whole story, however. Vestiges of old socialization survive to inhibit some men and women from feeling and acting like ordinary parents. A daughter of a viscount, who was determined to be different from her mother, found herself unable to 'hug' her child as she wished to. 'After all you cannot deny your blood,' she said. The man who wished to have had spontaneous and cheerful conversation with his children over dinner found a replica of his stern, silent father in himself. A disproportionate number of postwar mothers in their thirties and forties confessed that they felt cool toward their children and indifferent to the children's high or low performance at school as would obsess a typical middle-class mother. These examples are not meant to suggest that the way one was socialized determines how one socializes one's child, but they do confirm what was said about the older-generation parents.

Returning to the prewar times, we have noted that the mother's role was not as differentiated from the father's as among commoners, and that she remained positional like her husband. This was explained variously: mother, together with father, was too busy hosting VIPs or going out as an invited guest; father wanted her to remain elegant, intact from domestic chores; mother belonged to father, not to children. These explanations suggest that spousal obligations were stronger than mother-child bonding and that the wife joined the husband in living up to the house status.[2]

Another explanation, more readily given by almost all, referred to the ubiquitous presence of servants who were there to perform the maternal role for the children. Questions asked about mothers were often answered with reference to maid-servants as surrogate mothers, 'But we had maids to look after us.' Further, it was found that not only maids but other types of servants were involved in the socialization of Kazoku children. It is necessary, therefore, first to look into the variation of servants and their roles.

SERVANTS

There was a wide variation from one Kazoku household to another in the number and kinds of servants in reflection of the size of estates and wealth. The total number ranged from tens to several, one of the collateral royal families having about 50, and the exceptionally rich family Maeda commanding more than 130 servants (Kanazawa, Kawakita, and Yuasa 1968: 323). Generally, there were two major categories of servants. One was that of male staff in charge of managerial, financial, and secretarial tasks who occupied the area of the estate called the 'exterior' (*omote*) or office, and commuted there daily from houses provided by the master-employer around the periphery of the estate. Facing the outside world, their role was semipublic. The other was the category of female live-in servants who were in the 'interior' (*oku*) of residential quarters to attend the master and family in their private life. A wealthy family had such interior servants on one-to-one basis, at least one servant 'attached' to each and every member of the family, adult and child, in around-the-clock attendance. Such a maid-servant was called *otsuki* ('attached'). Because of this gender dichotomy of servants' quarters, the rule of sex segregation, as discussed above, marginalized sons at age seven or over, particularly the heir, and pushed them out of the interior into the exterior or totally away from home to be looked after by male servants (obviously the father and head could comfortably occupy the uppermost quarters of the interior, together with his wife, to be waited upon by female servants, without violating the segregatory rule). These servants were rank-ordered by seniority, each category headed by the head manager and head maid. There were other servants who were marginal to both the exterior and the interior, and yet were always present around the house: chauffeurs (earlier, *rikisha* men), gardeners, janitors, kitchen maids, and the like. When there were many servants, the hierarchy was so elaborate that a senior maid, for example, was waited upon by her own maid. Here one could see a miniaturized replica of a feudal society.

These servants were recruited largely from the classes of commoners, but as my informants stressed, the *otsuki* were high-school educated and from 'good' families. In the case of those Kazoku of daimyo origin whose power had not yet vanished from their former domains, high-ranking servants were brought over from among the families of former vassals, the *shizoku* class. In such cases, former vassals or their descendants fused into the category of servants.

Servants played multiple roles in socializing the Kazoku children, intentionally or unintentionally, directly or indirectly, which resulted in impressing the Kazoku children with a variety of often mutually inconsistent messages. In analyzing their socializing roles below, I will focus primarily on the *otsuki* as the most influential agents, and secondarily, bring other commoner personnel, both servants and nonservants, into discussion when called for contextually.

STATUS SUPPORT

Aristocracy would not exist unless there was a commoner class, and in the immediate environment of Kazoku children, servants represented the commoner class. The presence and collaboration of servants were indispensable in upholding and sustaining aristocracy as part of social order. Within the household, the lordly status of its head would not become a reality unless he had at least one servant who would call him 'Lord,' and the 'lady' or 'junior lord' would be nothing more than an empty status without servants addressing them with such terms and waiting upon them with proper deference. Aristocratic children were socialized to become aware of the hierarchy within the family, and at the same time to internalize the status of their family as a whole being distinct from that of their servants or commoners in general, through the servants' respectful speech and manners. Moreover, the children, like their parents, addressed their servants by their personal names without the minimal honorific *san*, and this fact was mentioned by an informant as an explanation of the widespread practice of changing a servant's name at the master's discretion when her name happened to be the same as that of a family member.[3]

Servants thus backed up the positional socialization of the aristocratic family. No wonder that the Kazoku household ceased to be aristocratic, not when it was legislated out of existence, but when it lost the last servant during or after the war. The converse was also true in that, as long as there was at least one servant, the family could retain marks of aristocratic life-style. This difference was observed when I visited various homes for an interview, some still had one or more 'loyal' servants to receive visitors at the entrance and to bring tea while most others had none.[4]

Servants also buttressed the Kazoku status in the minds of the children by mediating two persons, two classes, or two worlds that were supposed to be kept apart. The parent-child distance of the Kazoku family, described above, necessitated and in turn was maintained by servants mediating the two. The mother could send a message to her daughter through an *otsuki* maid. When an informant said, 'In my family it was mother who trained us in speech and manners,' it often turned out that the mother told the daughter's *otsuki* what to do.

The children, daughters more than sons, were secluded from the outside world, playing within the fenced estate only with the children of the male servants of the exterior who, unlike female servants, were married and raised their families. At school age, they commuted to Gakushuin by private carriages, *rikisha* or cars driven by their servant-drivers or chauffeurs, which protected them from direct exposure, as well as mediated them, to the street. Whether the family could or could not afford such private transportation (many families had their children walk and take trains and there were times when Gakushuin prohibited private transportation in order to train its students in austerity), the children were escorted by their respective *otsuki* maids. The chaperons waited until school was over in a room specially reserved for them at school, and accompanied their charges back home. In shopping, it was the chaperon who handled cash in transactions, keeping the real purchaser ignorant of or indifferent to pecuniary matters. Servants, as drivers or escorts, thus mediated the Kazoku children (and adults too) to the mundane reality of the external world, and thereby kept their status insulated and protected. They could play a mediating and, thereby, boundary-maintaining role because they were located on the margin of the boundaries, physically and functionally being inside the household, and at the same time being outside the status of the household.[5]

The servant was a status prop in still another sense. She represented and bolstered the status of the master family by her presence, appearance, and demeanor. It was not just the number but quality of servants that affected the reputation of the house. Even the children would feel their status pride enhanced in front of their schoolmates by being escorted by well-groomed, respectably dressed, and properly trained servants. Indeed, the servants, while waiting in the servants' room, watched one another and gossiped about one another's master households along these lines. There were good reasons that even impoverished Kazoku, frugal with food and other basic commodities, would spend money on the *otsuki* servants' dresses and hairdo beyond their means. Chaperonage and, for that matter, private transportation were not only protective of the child but symbolic of family status.

I have discussed three ways in which the servant buttressed the aristocratic status of the family and thus instilled the awareness of status distinction in the child: the observable status inferiority of the servant in interaction with family members, her role as a mediator and status protector, and her symbolic representation of the family status and reputation. The servant's support was by no means unilateral but reciprocated. The parents admonished the child to be kind and considerate to servants and subordinates, to act or not to act in a certain way toward or because of them. Several informants could not remember what their parents said to discipline them except about how to treat the servants. 'My parents were strict,' said a daughter of an enormously affluent marquis, 'in prohibiting us from behaving arrogantly toward the servants (and vassals) "because they are our treasures." I was not allowed to say, "Bring me tea," but "Will you please ..."' There were a variety of house rules to follow including punctuality mainly in consideration of the convenience of servants. A daughter of a duke recalled,

> Looking back, it was like being brought up in a dormitory. There were all kinds of rules, such as what time to take a bath ... We were not permitted to wait until bedtime. We were supposed to bathe by three or four o'clock P.M. so that the janitor could clean up the bathroom before going home for supper.

A viscount explained why he became unable to express his feelings in a straightforward manner: his parents advised the children to be sensitive to the feelings of the servants, not to say, for example, whether the meal was tasty or untasty, because discriminatory appraisals would have caused conflict among the servants, making one cook proud, and another miserable.

This mode of socialization focused on the servant seems to reverse what Bateson called 'ternary' exemplified by the 'parent-nurse-child' and distinguished from 'pure hierarchy' and 'triangle':

> Essentially, the function of the middle member is to instruct and discipline the third member in the forms of behavior which he should adopt in his contacts with the first. The nurse teaches the child how to behave toward its parents, just as the N.C.O. teaches and disciplines the private in how he should behave toward officers. [Bateson 1972:96]

The typical ternary, which is likely to have been derived from the European example of upper class, did occur among the Japanese aristocratic families as will be shown later, but my informants more vividly recalled the reversed ternary where they were taught by their parents how to behave toward and on behalf of their servants. In the reversed ternary, one might also expect the daughter to be trained by her parents to be polished in manners so that the servants watching her might emulate her as their model. This point was made by a student of the high society of Victorian England,[6] and, in Japan too, it would have been consistent with the conventional status name of the servant, 'etiquette apprentice.' Yet this kind of instruction was given only in two cases of my sample (a baron's and a viscount's family), while all the others (including these two cases) stressed considerateness and empathy for servants. In fact, the exemplary role and modeling role were more often reversed as will be seen below.

PARENTAL SURROGACY

More important in the informants' memories than the servants' role of status support was what they did directly and personally in rearing and looking after the children. While supporting positional socialization, servants performed what was left out of it, that is, personal or nonstructural socialization to gratify and control the child's biopsychological needs and development. In a word, a servant was a surrogate parent to fill the role left vacant by the real parent.

Intimacy

In the first place, mother-child bonding was transferred to the ties between a maid and her charge in terms of intimacy and interdependence. Surrogacy began upon birth. Some families hired nursemaids for various reasons: because mother had no lactation, because mother's milk was artificially stopped, because mother was supposed to stay free, young and beautiful, and so on. Even when the mother breastfed her baby, it was done more or less as a matter of necessity and the rest of caretaking was the responsibility of a servant. It was the *otsuki* hired right after the birth who was recalled with the fondest memories. 'I cannot remember myself ever left alone. Ume was always with me. She was there waiting when I woke up, she was there when I went to sleep.' In some households, each child had a meal alone, waited upon by his/her *otsuki*. It was the *otsuki*'s job to bathe the child while she herself was fully dressed, and the *otsuki* slept near the child. A recollection by a daughter of a duke depicted a striking intimacy:

> I have never sat on mother's lap. [But] I had an *otsuki* who, luckily, stayed with me throughout from my birth on until my marriage. She was a truly devoted servant. I played with her nipples and pretended to nurse – only pretended because she was not a wet-nurse. I feel her daughter and I are real sisters. Now it is her grandchildren's generation, and as if we were kin, we keep in touch ... Yes, she slept at the edge of my bed ... [Every morning] it took her an hour to fix her hair [in a Japanese style], which I could not stand because that kept me away from her. We were together wherever we went.

It was this maid who kept a 'developmental diary' for her, recording her weight, vocabulary, and the like. In the living room of her present tiny apartment, the former princess displays a picture of her now-deceased surrogate mother. As indicated in the above quote, such bonding was a product of a long duration of *otsuki* service for the same child. In most cases the maid quit to marry, but in some she remained single and dedicated her entire life, accompanying her mistress when the latter married.

The warmth and indulgence of the *otsuki* were recalled typically in contrast to the aloofness or formality of the real mother, attachment to the former in contrast to indifference to the latter, the former's leniency to the latter's dignity:[7]

> We were most scared of mother, but never cried for her when she went out. It was when the servants went home on holidays that we cried and screamed.

> If I were to choose [between mother and *otsuki*] I would have sided with my *otsuki*.

> When my mother died I did not cry, but when my *otsuki* passed away I did.

> In my house I was free to go and see my mother whenever I wanted, and my mother also could come into my room. But the *otsuki* was closer to me. I could sit on the laps of my mother or grandmother, but only in stranger-like etiquette (*tanin-gyogi*). Toward them we had to behave deferentially. With the *otsuki*, I was free to say whatever I wanted, free to fight. Parents were absolute.

The son and heir of a marquis, while his parents were always accessible, had an old maid from his birth on, who defended him when he was scolded by his father, talking back to him for being unreasonable. This sounds like a scene from an ordinary family where the mother protects a child from a harsh father. Another male informant recalled how unruly and rebellious he was as a child and how parental punishments were retaliated by mischiefs. It turned out that his disobedience was expressed against the maids, not his father, the very source of authority and discipline. Here we can see a displacement of aggression from the real target, the father, to a weaker object, the mother embodied by the maid.

As much as the ordinary mother-child bond can intensify to an unhealthy exclusivity and generate psychological conflict, intimacy between the child and maid could produce similar stress. Some *otsuki*, not many, as recalled by their former 'surrogate children,' came to identify themselves with the children so much as to lose their own identity. One result was sibling rivalry created and taken over by the maids. Where there was in fact no rivalry between the children, their *otsuki* competed with each other in favor of their respective children. An 88-year-old woman, a daughter of a count, recalled *otsuki* servants, each in support of her favorite child, fighting one another over such trivial matters as which child should or should not receive an apple or 'some such silly things.' The heir's *otsuki* was arrogant and aggressive as if she were privileged to be, which the others challenged. In one instance, two maids did not speak to each other for nearly one whole year.

In the above example the children were on-lookers, embarrassed or disgusted. But in another case a child was abused by a jealous mother surrogate in charge of the victim's sister. The informant, the youngest of three daughters but stronger than her immediately elder sister, always won over the latter in games, school athletic contests, school reports, and whatnot. She was also her grandmother's favorite. All this upset the *otsuki* of the elder sister, and compelled her to punish the younger sister by verbal and physical abuse. Didn't her own *otsuki* protect her from the assailant? The jealous maid was so mean to the informant's *otsuki* that no one would stay with her long enough to be protective, and this fact was picked up by the punitive *otsuki* as a proof of the victim's allegedly perverse character. The eldest sister, co-interviewed, turned out to be a victim of her own *otsuki* who was a former schoolteacher and acted like a contemporary 'education-mama.' 'I was constantly pressed to study, study, study every day. When I got a poor score in a Chinese-character writing test or something, she was mortified and vented her anger by scratching me. At times I bled. I did not know why I was abused so.' It never occurred to either sister to report what was going on to their parents. The parent-child distance in space and status did contribute to this information blockage but the victims also feared the inevitable retaliation by the maids. 'It is like you cannot take your grievance about your immediate boss, the section chief, directly up to the company president.' One of the sisters explained this deplorable situation as a 'hysterical' outburst of an unmarried woman trapped in a small isolated world.

Overall, servants may be said to have provided personal warmth, nurturance, and the feeling of kinship for the child, sometimes going to a pathological extreme of identification, in compensation for the relative distance and aloofness between members of the family, whether between parent and child, or siblings. It is paradoxical that there was a deeper intimacy between an aristocratic child and commoner maid than within the same-status family. While a commoner servant buttressed the status distinction of aristocracy, there was more equality in this sense across different statuses than within the same status. It might be wondered whether or not this is true across societies as inherent in the culture of elite. A member of the Kazoku, who had spent her childhood in London, wrote in her published autobiography (Sakai 1982:8) and confirmed in interviews to the effect that British servants and their upper-class masters never developed such intimacy even after three years of live-in service as did the Japanese counterparts.

Discipline

Servants could hamper the children and turn them into weaklings through their overprotective service and indulgence. A daughter of the late Konoe Fumimaro, a duke and prime minister, who headed *the* highest-ranking court-noble family, recalled what her father had said in response to a reporter: he was constantly waited upon by his servants, and when he washed his face it was a servant's job to wipe it. He had no chance to walk by himself and had to practice doing so before his entry into Gakushuin (Shukan Yomiuri Henshu-bu 1987: 268–269). A former viscount told me that he was so used to his in-house playmates who were children of the servants and looked up to him as their lord that he had a hard time at Gakushuin where students were equal. He had 'what people today call 'school phobia.'

Along with the possibility and actual occurrences of such pampering, Kazoku children were subjected to discipline as well. In discipline, parents played a greater role than in nurturant mothering as implied in the children's remarks about their parents as being 'scary,' 'frightening,' 'absolutely compelling,' 'always giving us orders.' But even here, servants played surrogate parenthood in disciplining the children 'directly' to convey the parents' instructions. Again it was not uncommon that informants associated their family training with their 'strict' or even 'frightening' servants more than their parents, and the higher the family rank, or the older the generation, the more so. A daughter of a viscount repeated what her maid used to say about her mother: 'She would say, "It's not me, but I am telling you as a substitute for your mother".' 'In her mother's days, the head servant was 'totally delegated' (*zenken*) the parental authority, and the children had no recourse to their parents except through their delegates. 'Mother used to say, "If you sit with your feet sticking out, your *otsuki* would step on them. If you scream, she would say, it's your fault".' A daughter of a top-ranking *kuge* stressed the severity of family discipline: she was not allowed, for instance, to use a floor cushion for herself or to wear a coat in the presence of her parents or grandmother until they gave her permission. Such injunction came from the head servant. Here is a good example of Bateson's ternary where a child was trained by a servant to behave deferentially toward its parents. There are indications, however, that the locus of ultimate authority was not always the parents.

A woman, marrying into a large household, could be subjected to the domineering head servant who had been there waiting upon her parents-in-law or husband and was in a position to teach the bride in the life-style of the family (*kafū*). A daughter of a prominent military house suffered under such a servant when she married into an equally prominent court-noble house: 'She was criticized,' said her sister sympathetically, 'in everything she did as "a warrior style."' In this case the stereotypically nasty image of a mother-in-law was embodied by nobody but the head servant. Here is another paradox, the paradox of status reversal between an aristocrat and commoner, master and servant. There was something that to me sounded like double communication going on. Many informants said that servants used polite language such as '*asobase*' to give orders. From what they said in answer to my question on this point, we can say that the 'order' was a higher message contextualizing the polite expression. They insisted that there could be a respectful command.

The above-cited examples suggest that discipline was focused on manners and demeanors, particularly for daughters. To add a few more examples: ladylike movement in the house ('Don't run in the hallways'), courtesy in receiving guests, the Ogasawara-style table manners ('Don't start with pickles'), selection of dresses appropriate to occasions, keeping the room tidy ('Don't leave your kimono lying around, but fold and put it away immediately after use'). These were instructed more often by servants than by mothers.

More important than the behavioral manners was the proper style of speech, particularly the use of *keigo* (honorifics), and it was here that the servant's role was even more crucial. It was because, I was told, your parents could not tell you to speak to them with honorifics nor could they use *keigo* in speaking to you, their child. The *otsuki* or head servant 'scolded' the child for using the 'bad' speech he/she picked up outside home, especially from Gakushuin classmates.[8] The children learned the *keigo* more 'naturally' and unconsciously by listening to their servants speaking to them, their parents and siblings, and guests. One of such learning chances came when a maid spoke on the phone in a high-pitched formal style to a representative of another noble or royal household. The servant's role in disciplining the child to this extent and in these modes calls attention to another paradox: the servant, especially maid-servant, supposedly entered the upper-class household to learn etiquette and other aspects of upper-class culture as an apprentice, but it was she who taught the master's child not only by instructing and 'scolding,' but by playing an exemplary model. The roles of trainer and trainee were reversed.

For school-age children, especially sons, discipline also involved character development such as austerity, self-reliance, and perseverance, and in this respect, we must extend our perspective to male servants. The staff of the exterior were quite authoritative and even punitive, as recalled by a woman regarding her father, a collateral royal prince. When her father was a Gakushuin student, many families were switching from carriages to automobiles. Discontented with the old-fashioned carriage kept by his family, he demanded, representing his siblings, that the manager replace it with a car. Instead of getting his demand met, he was ordered to sit in a formal style (a common mode of punishment) and to listen for half an hour to the manager's preaching on the virtue of frugality. Such authority of the managerial staff, I was told, stemmed from their exclusive power over budgetary decisions.

There were two directions of discipline regarding status. One was to reinforce the status distinction. The emphasis upon speech style, manners, and demeanors, for example, was primarily to bring up the children according to their aristocratic status. It was not just the status insiders but status outsiders such as servants and commoners in general who instilled and reinforced status identity in the children. The commoner apprentice expected her master, at least at one level of her consciousness (because I do not preclude status resentment at another level), to appear and conduct himself like a lord for the sake of her own self-esteem.[9] Indeed, in my earlier study, I did find out that former apprentices were more laudatory of truly upper-class-like families and looked down upon those who were basically no different from themselves in life-style.

This kind of status consciousness, incongruous with the simplistic version of the Marxist class consciousness, was particularly strong among those who regarded themselves as 'vassals,' for the good reason that their vassal-identity depended upon the presence of a lord. I met a latter-day 'vassal' residing in the castle town of the former domain who would wait upon his 'lord' every time he, the latter, came from Tokyo down there to re-enact the role of his lordly ancestors on ritual occasions. This lord was a third son, destined to lose the Kazoku status, and was raised as such, but in his forties he was suddenly called back to step into the heir's position due to the death of his eldest brother and soon thereafter into headship because of his father's death. He had to train himself into 'Junior Lord,' and then 'Lord' within less than a year. In such resocialization of the new lord, a heavy role was played by the self-appointed local vassal through correspondence and telephone conversation in an old-fashioned samurai style. In his direct contact with the lord in the town, as I witnessed, the vassal bowed and spoke to him in a stiff style as if he were acting in a samurai drama, much to the embarrassment of the lord. To me it was clear that the old vassal was dramatizing his status in order to give this upstart lord an intensive course on how to be a lord. The vassal confided to me that he could not stand the lord's Gakushuin classmates hanging around and freely touching him, with no respect. He wanted his lord to stay distant and aloof.

Status expectation of this type was not limited to servants and vassals who after all could partake of the master's prestige. Commoners outside also imposed status constraint upon members of the nobility and royalty, more so than did insiders in some circumstances, by virtue of their high expectations. I was told over and over again how Gakushuin children were made conscious of their status when they as a group were met by townspeople during their school excursion, and how Kazoku children became a center of attention during the war when they were evacuated to the countryside to avoid air raids. This was more true of the children who were individually thrown into village schools than those who stayed together in Gakushuin groups. A woman remembered one of her classmates who had been a tomboy at Gakushuin but returned from the rural site of evacuation totally transformed into an elegant lady. Village children obviously straightened her out.

Given such status-conformity imposed by outsiders and commoners, it is not surprising that the children felt relieved and relaxed only inside the Gakushuin campus. The crude, disrespectful speech used by Gakushuin students to each other is likely to have been an expression of such status-relief. Equally understandable is the strong, lifelong tie kept among Gakushuin classmates.[10]

Commoners, both inside and outside the Kazoku household, thus socialized its children (and adults) toward status conformity, even against the latter's natural inclinations. No wonder that few of my informants deplored the abolition of the Kazoku, that, instead, most of them felt 'liberated' from all the constraints attached to the Kazoku status. Women in particular would not trade the freedom, privacy, physical mobility, and anonymity thus gained for the status prominence, economic security, leisurely way of life, or convenience of having *otsuki* servants.

Status-conformity was one of the two directions taken in the discipline of Kazoku children. The other direction, opposite from the first, was toward breaking through the status boundary, and here sons more than daughters were involved. Some Kazoku fathers were concerned with their sons, as a result of being confined within a small society of elite, growing up unable to adjust to the wider society, and pushed them out of home to be raised by outsiders. Motives behind this practice varied, however: from tough-minded to tender-minded (for the son 'to be buffeted about in the rough storm of the outside world,' or to become sensitized to the hard life of commoners); from elitist to anti-elitist (to build up character and competency for leadership, or to prepare him to live like everybody else); to complete sex segregation, or to contact people in all walks of life. There are indications that some parents predicted an imminent revolution to destroy the whole status system and tried to prepare their children for a dire future.

At the intermediary level of education, boarding schools kept Kazoku sons away from home except on weekends and vacations. Gakushuin was a boarding school for a while, and so were some other private schools like Gyosei attended by upper-class sons. There were other facilities. Top-ranking daimyo families in particular carried on the tradition of training their sons with their age-mates under distinguished teachers in private all-male boarding houses specially built by the families for that purpose, while the sons were also attending Gakushuin as regular students. An informant talked about his family's boarding house to discipline his father, an adopted son, into a full-fledged heir under a great master, together with several bright boys, all brought over from the home province. They were taught things like swordsmanship and Chinese classics like the Analects of Confucius. The informant also was put into the same house when he was a third grader at Gakushuin to be trained similarly. A daughter of the shogunal family felt sorry that her late brother, in accordance to the family tradition, was removed from home at age seven to live in the family's boarding house (called *Gakuryo*) just as his father had gone through. He was waited upon by co-living male student-servants,[11] and taught by a tutor, while commuting to Gakushuin from there. He was allowed weekend home visits but had to return without staying overnight. His sister interpreted this family tradition, which by then had become anachronistic, as a way of having the heir achieve manhood, away from the feminine quarters of home.

These and other similar cases of boarding-house training were elitist oriented with the purpose of character development for a future lord, and the model came from the imperial private school (*Gogakumonjo*) for the crown prince. The protective nature of the environment was retained, servants were in attendance, and the boarding houses were located near or on the estate. Training here was in fact more purely status centered than home training was. There were instances, however, of out-of-home discipline totally deprived of protection.

Sons of a marquis of daimyo origin, as recalled by one of them, were sent to a tough national school, not Gakushuin which their father ruled out as too soft. And at the same time they were put under the custodial care of schoolteachers, 'probably in order to make us feel close to common people.' Being kept away from home so long, it was not until the time they got married and lived in their own houses that they tasted the convenience of having a private bath. From the teacher's house the informant used to go to a neighborhood public bathhouse, and the meals were so poor that even *natto* (fermented soybean dish) was considered a feast and served only occasionally. The recaller, at 78, did not appreciate this kind of over-discipline, and confessed he felt no warmth toward his parents.

This last case tapers into the category of 'fosterage' (*satokko* or *satogo*) mentioned by several informants. Since there was no uniform pattern in how and why fosterage took place among upper-class Japanese, I must digress a little. Fosterage was something 'natural,' I was told, and even automatic for every birth, from the royal family down the line. This statement is an exaggeration, of course, but it is common knowledge that the late Emperor Shōwa and his brother, the late Prince Chichibu, were raised by foster parents, the Kawamura. Royal daughters such as Emperor Meiji's daughters were also foster children of the Sasaki. The last shogun, Tokugawa Yoshinobu, had his children, all born of two concubines, reared by a number of foster families.

The child's health was of major concern here. It is said that the strikingly high mortality of royal children motivated Emperor Meiji to send his surviving children, and later his grandsons, to foster homes so that they would grow up strong and healthy away from the palace.[12] The foster families for royal children were of Kazoku status and treated them respectfully even though the emperor told the foster parents to deal with the children in exactly the same way as with their own children. The foster families for Kazoku children, however, were commoners and even peasants who, as revealed by informants' narratives, did not necessarily treat the children with respect. Here the child's health was also an important consideration as indicated by the fact that foster families were selected from among those having healthy women who had just given birth and afforded lots of 'natural milk.' The foster mother in this sense combined the role of a wet-nurse. Narratives unfolded more than the health reason, however.

Born the youngest of the 16 children ('from one single womb'!) of a baron, the informant was immediately taken away to a peasant family to be nursed by a new mother. But he stayed on with the foster family for some reasons. Was it because his parents wanted to bring him up tough so that he, a nonheir, could live in the stormy world outside? 'That reasoning would be only a face-saving excuse,' he exclaimed to deny my guess. He claimed, instead, that he had been unwanted and 'abandoned.' His foster parents used to tell him that his parents, having so many children, never bothered to show up to see him, and only dispatched a steward to deliver a small amount of fosterage fee (*satobuchi*) once a year. 'So they said, "This child is not wanted at all. But we farmers need as many boys as possible [as farm hands]" and they were about to take me as a *satonagare* (unretrieved foster child, much like *shichi-nagare*, a forfeited pawn).' But he was retrieved by an adoptive family, his own uncle and wife, when he was three years old. When the adoptive mother went to meet him, she could not tell him from the farmer's children, wearing straw sandals and sucking bamboo-shoot skin. Overnight, he became a junior lord of a Kazoku house commanding six servants (see Lebra 1989 on adoption).

This incredible story is not unique. There are indications that the *satonagare* recycling into the commoner class was, at least historically, not a totally unlikely fate of upper-class nonheir children, since keeping nonheir children would not only dissipate the family resources but might become a possible cause of family conflict (such as sibling rivalry). All the parents could hope for such children would be to marry or adopt them out. A descendant of a count of *kuge* origin read in an ancestor's diary that all the children, both sons and daughters, except the heir had been taken away into fosterage upon birth for unknown reasons. She suspected that the family had been too poor to feed excess children and that fosterage had been a recourse for 'mouth reduction' (*kuchi-berashi*). The daughters, mentioned in the diary, later returned at about ten just before they again moved away, this time, to live with the families of their future husbands. But what happened to sons? The children, born of different women away from the home residence and immediately sent to foster houses, were strangers to their father, and much later some of them returned and became formally recognized as his children. With this weak or nonexistent tie between father and nonheir sons, *satonagare* recycling is likely to have occurred. Apparently there was economic complementarity in that working-class foster parents wanted the children as laborers while noble parents could not afford the surplus children.

Discipline, the central topic of the present section, has not entered the cases of fosterage thus far described. But an extreme case of discipline is found in a grandson of a nationally eminent leader, and heir to a count. What he called his foster family sounded more like a bunch of bullies. Because of the astonishing tale that unfolded, I shall quote what he said at length with some editorial alteration:

> When I was eight, I was put into the custody of Satō Sensei, a teacher in Chinese studies, together with two other boys [one was a son of another Kazoku, the other of a rich businessman]. I was there from age 8 through 18.
>
> (Was that your father's idea?) Generally all the boys of our clan were sent out for fosterage. My father [to be adopted later] was fostered by a rice trader; one of my father's older brothers, who was also adopted [into a Kazoku house], was fostered by a stone mason, and another brother and heir was by a pawnshop keeper.
>
> [In the foster house] as if we were shop apprentices, each of us was given a box in which you kept your rice bowl, chopsticks, and other utensils. You used the box as your table as well. The box with each person's name on it was placed on a shelf, brought out at meal time. Utensils were washed by yourself after meal, put away into the box and back to the shelf.
>
> (How was such a foster house selected?) Every Kazoku house had several counsellors who looked over the candidates and reached consensus.
>
> (What was the purpose of such fosterage?) To learn etiquette(!), and not to become eccentric. Training was extremely Spartan. We were disciplined more severely than ordinary boys, to keep our rooms clean and orderly, to scrub the hallways, to clean up the toilets and yard. (Together with the children of the foster family?) Oh, no, they were warming themselves in *kotatsu* [a quilt-covered foot-warmer]. We were there for training, but among us trainees there was discrimination. My father never bothered to visit the *sensei* but only sent errands, while others had their parents come to pay respect. In winter, they were all sitting around the *kotatsu*, eating rice cracker, but when I went in they hid it. Very mean. But all that was for my discipline.

(Do you think it was a good experience?) Yes, to some extent. The character [of the foster parents] should have been better investigated. But thanks to that experience, I can endure any kind of hardship, and also understand how people in lower positions would feel. (Did you come to feel that the foster parents were like your real parents?) That would be impossible. But when in the army, the hardship I had as a foster child did help me a lot ... [As a foster child, however,] I was crying all the time. In winter, my hands were frostbitten and hurt as if pricked with needles.

Even on Sundays we were told to study and study. In the morning, on Sundays, after study, we cleaned the toilets and yard, with nothing else to do in the afternoon. So I would go out for a walk, and [at one time] I deliberately tore off the straps of my wooden footgear [to create a good excuse for returning late] and went to a movie. (Under such circumstances, you might develop hostility toward people around rather than kindness?) Yes, there was such feeling somewhat. When I did something wrong, the *sensei*'s wife ordered me to sit on the wooden hallway in a formal style for two or three hours. Yet I never apologized. She and I competed in the contest of stubbornness. When there was a fire in the neighborhood, I wished to go out to look but would not volunteer to apologize.

(Would you, then, feel warm toward your own parents?) I hesitate to say this, but toward father I had no warmth at all. Heaven might punish me for saying this, but even when he died I did not touch his finger. When asked to help cleanse his body with alcohol, I refused. No feeling of kinship at all. (Who was the most intimate with you in your life?) There was nobody. Spartan education seems to make your life miserable. I have no confidant.

It is hard to believe that this was told by a seventy-year old grandson of a famous lord, who as a child was addressed 'Junior Lord' by as many maids as 12 serving the family. With all the contradictions and dramatization, this account makes us wonder whether such 'discipline' was really meant to develop a character. He entered a business career after postwar repatriation but, as he admitted, has been a failure in whatever project he undertook. This narrative shows how some status outsiders, foster parents in this case, socialized Kazoku children to break through their status identity, not always in a positive direction but possibly toward a curtailment of character development.

CONCLUSION

We have seen a variety of essential roles played by servants and other commoners in socializing aristocratic children in prewar Japan, and filling the role vacancy left by their parents as a result of excessive emphasis upon positional socialization. The parental surrogacy of servants as well as other commoners like foster parents, providing intimacy and/or discipline, turned out to involve unexpected ramifications. Whether or not it produced 'good' results in the retrospective eyes of aristocratic autobiographers, it is certain that commoners significantly contributed to the shaping of their lives and characters. We have noted the paradoxes of the commoner-elite relationship that challenged the stereotypic image of hierarchy, involving the cross-class intimacy surpassing the within-family intimacy, commoner-elite status reversal, and role reversal between the 'etiquette apprentices' and their supposed models. There were indications that commoner servants were a repository of aristocratic culture.[13]

Commoners, as represented by servants, buttressed the status of aristocrats, and pressed them for status conformity even against the inclinations of status holders. Viewed in this light, the parent-child distance or the whole positional emphasis in family relationship could be reconstrued as a consequence of servants' expectations rather than as a cause of servant's parental surrogacy. Conversely, some parents had their sons trained tough by exposing them to commoners outside the home ground, as represented by foster parents, with or without success.

Thus, commoners were indispensable participants in sustaining and reproducing the status and subculture of aristocracy on the one hand, but on the other hand, they had many opportunities to influence the elite children with their own subculture. Servants, in particular, were a window through which aristocratic children could see the outside world. Without her parents' knowledge, a child learned 'the low-city Tokyo way of life,' for example, from her servant who came from that area; another picked up flippant popular songs as sung by her maid while giving a bath to her; another daughter, hearing the servants complaining aloud to one another in her presence about the master family's stinginess in redistributing the received gift foods to the servants, made up her mind to become a generous master. A granddaughter of a wealthy count was shocked to learn from her maids that there were families living on nothing but cucumbers and that one thousand yen, the amount of her grandfather's monthly allowance, would be enough for a whole family to live on for an entire year. She succeeded in smuggling in progressive magazines with the help of a male servant and became 'a little red.'

It may be concluded that, while the downward flow of elite culture is likely to occur generally, the socialization of aristocratic children in Japan suggests that the upward flow of commoner culture also took place with a possible consequence of modification of elite culture.

NOTES

Acknowledgments. A portion of this article was presented at the 87th annual meeting of the American Anthropological Association, Phoenix, Arizona, November 16-20, 1988. For the long-term research, including two lengthy periods of fieldwork, which is responsible for this article, I have been supported by grants from the American Council of Learned Societies and the Social Science Research Council, the Japan Foundation, University of Hawaii Japan Studies Endowment and Fujio Matsuda Scholar fund, and Wenner-Gren Foundation. I wish to express my gratitude to all.

1. In a monograph on the Japanese nobility in progress.

2. The implication is twofold. First, aristocratic families were more patriarchal than in other classes, as observed in a few studies of upper-class women in the West (Ostrander 1984; Rundquist 1987), in that women acknowledged the authority of their husbands (except in extremely hypogamous cases) more readily. This status asymmetry between husband and wife was strengthened in Japan by the patricentric rule of succession. Further, while commoner women would have regained more autonomy and power through motherhood, aristocratic motherhood did not contribute to diminishing status asymmetry. The other implication is that aristocrats were more Westernized as mentioned earlier. The primacy of spousal ties over parent-child bond was partly due to the influence

of Western culture. It is interesting that the Western idea of marital partnership became locked with the patricentricity of Confucian tradition to intensify gender asymmetry. It should be remembered again, however, that the influence of Western culture was primarily through upper-class or aristocratic Westerners.

3. This kind of depersonalization of servants could go to an extreme: in one household, for example, two *rikisha* pullers, regardless of who were hired, were made to adopt the names 'Crane' and 'Turtle,' respectively. The same sort of standardization is reported from Victorian England: 'Because these servants were seen as an extension of the household "aura," they were deliberately depersonalized, hidden under standardized liveries and often called standardized names, e.g. Thomas and Susan, whatever their real names might be' (Davidoff 1973: 88).

4. My questionnaire reveals that, as of 1985, only 14 respondents out of the total 98 had one or more 'helpers,' either live-in or commuting, while 84 had none. Even this figure is above the average, however.

5. The term 'insider-outsider' was suggested by George Marcus (personal communication).

6. The upper class in Victorian England was aware of servants as possible emulators. 'It was felt that in some way their own personal behaviour would stand as examples to the working class even in the minutiae of living. Thus card playing on Sundays should be banned as it set a bad example to the servants. And, when speaking of setting an example to the lower classes, most women really meant their servants who were the only representatives of another class they saw at close quarters and whose deferential response, outwardly at least, reinforced the seeming importance of formal propriety and individual gentility' (Davidoff 1973: 40).

7. Such contrasts are likely to have reflected invidious comparisons resulting in exaggerating the polar characteristics. It is beyond the scope of this article to delve into the epistemological precariousness of recalled 'facts,' as stated earlier.

8. Gakushuin, of all places, was (and still is) known for its students' subculture of speech with deliberate violation of rules of deference, distinct from the honorifics-ridden speech addressed to the family, teachers, or outside the circle of intimate classmates. From the information I gathered, this phenomenon may be interpreted as a combination of three attitudinal propensities held by upper-class children: to create equality and intimacy among close friends, to act out a small rebellion against the family-based hierarchy and enjoy status release, and to satisfy a reversed snobbery in opposition to conventional snobbery exhibited by pseudo-aristocrats. In a word, this may be understood as a linguistic 'liminality' (Turner 1969), and it was more dramatically practiced by boys than girls.

9. This may hold true elsewhere as well. One of my informants, while living in England to be trained in the life-style of British aristocracy, said he and his family had to dress formally at dinner table every evening because the British butler he hired would have refused to serve them otherwise.

10. This is a point involving misunderstanding between insiders and outsiders that still exists regarding the royalty. The high fence built between the royalty and commoners, the Imperial-House insiders and outsiders, is understood, according to a journalist informant familiar with the Imperial House affairs, by insider officials as necessary for privacy and temporary relief from status constraint, but by the outside public as an obstacle to the freedom of royal personages including their free access to the people. There seems to be an agreement that the emperor and his family should be freer, but the two means to that end are diametrically opposed.

11. The male counterpart to the *otsuki* service was performed by *kyuji* or, more commonly, *shosei* who were hired to serve school-age or older boys with daily chores and to escort them to school or wherever. Older than their charges, the *shosei* played the role of big brothers for the children. In exchange for their service, they were allowed to attend night school. For sons of poor families, becoming a *shosei* was almost the only alternative for getting higher education. One former *shosei*, now 64 years old, told me in an interview that he was still very grateful to 'Lord Shimazu' for five years of higher education at night school.

12. The high mortality of princes and princesses in the history of the imperial household is attributed to the genetic weakness resulting from close-kin marriage, and the unhealthy and dangerous conditions of the palace life involving royal nannies and ladies-in-waiting: jealousy involving possible murder, the nanny's lead-heavy cosmetics licked by the child, sleeping drugs given to put the child to sleep quickly, and so on (Kawahara 1983: 12).

13. Such relationship between the aristocratic family and commoner servants is reminiscent of the 'dyarchy' that has been a historically perpetual feature of Japan's political institution – the formal authority symbolized by one person or one institution (e.g., an emperor and court administration) and the actual power exerted by another person or another initially nonlegitimate institution (e.g., a regent, retired emperor, or shogun, and their respective institutions). The power-wielding person or institution in its surrogate capacity protected, sustained, and implemented the formal authority on

the one hand, and undercut, superseded, robbed it on the other. In a miniature version, a servant could or did do the same with his/her master family when opportunities presented themselves. The sudden impoverishment of many Kazoku households in the postwar aftermath was not merely due to heavy taxations. According to my informants it turned out that the managerial servants of many households (either the informant's own or his/her relatives' or friends') took advantage of their exclusive control over the household finance to appropriate the house property. This kind of problem may be inherent in the status hierarchy, whether of a political or a domestic unit, where positional constraint is excessive.

REFERENCES

Bateson, Gregory 1972. *Steps to an Ecology of Mind.* New York: Ballantine Books.

Bernstein, Basil 1971. *Class, Codes and Control. Volume I: Theoretical Studies Towards a Sociology of Language.* London: Routledge & Kegan Paul.

Davidoff, Leonore 1973. *The Best Circles: Women and Society in Victorian England.* Totowa, N.J.: Rowman and Littlefield.

Douglas, Mary 1970. *Natural Symbols: Explorations in Cosmology.* New York: Vintage Books.

Kanazawa Makoto, Kawakita Yotaro, and Yuasa Yasuo, eds. 1968. *Kazoku: Meiji hyakunen no sokumenshi.* Tokyo: Kodansha.

Kawahara Toshiaki 1983. *Tenno Hirohito no Showa-shi.* Tokyo: Bungei Shunju.

Lebra, Takie Sugiyama 1984. *Japanese Women: Constraint and Fulfillment.* Honolulu: University of Hawaii Press.

—— 1989. Adoption Among the Hereditary Elite of Japan: Status Preservation through Mobility. *Ethnology* 28: 185–218.

Ostrander, Susan A. 1984. *Women of the Upper Class.* Philadelphia: Temple University Press.

Rundquist, Angela 1987. Presentation at Court: A Corporation Female Ritual of Transition in Sweden 1850–1962. *Anthropology Today* 3(6): 2–6.

Sakai Miiko 1982. *Aru kazoku no showa-shi.* Tokyo: Shufu to Seikatsusha.

Seidensticker, Edward 1983. *Low City, High City: Tokyo from Edo to the Earthquake.* New York: Knopf.

Shukan Yomiuri Henshu-bū, ed. 1987. *Nippon no Meika.* Tokyo: Yomiuri Shinbunsha.

Turner, Victor 1969. *The Ritual Process: Structure and Anti-structure.* Ithaca: Cornell University Press.

First published in the *Journal of Japanese Studies*, 17:1, 1991

21 Resurrecting Ancestral Charisma: Aristocratic Descendants in Contemporary Japan

Japan today magnifies the familiar split image of itself, one half looking to the future with insatiable zest for change and novelty, the other half facing backward to the past to recapture tradition and continuity. Ironically but understandably, the unprecedented magnitude of economic prosperity and technological advancement that is enabling Japanese to rush to obtain the newest possible things is also funding and expediting a nostalgic journey in search of their roots and history.

The split is not between change and continuity but rather between two perspectives of change. After all, tradition is not something that exists 'out there' ready to be retrieved, but is a product of cultural construction and reconstruction, oftentimes to provide a rationale for some vested interest or even for a revolutionary change as in the case of the Meiji 'Restoration.' Bestor calls this type of propensity for tradition-creation 'traditionalism,' which is to be distinguished from tradition itself.[1] In this paper I analyze the 'resurrection' of ancestors as a form of traditionalism manifested in affluent Japan.

An NHK survey in 1984, which was generally meant to demonstrate a 'reversion' of Japanese to religious conservatism, showed a widespread sense of attachment to the dead and ancestors. For instance, 57 per cent of the survey sample were found to pray at the *butsudan* at least occasionally, and 28 per cent every day; 89 per cent visit cemeteries on days of major annual rites for the dead (*bon* and *higan*) at least occasionally, 69 per cent regularly; 59 per cent feel 'connected with ancestors in the depths of their hearts.'[2] Furthermore, in a recent study Reid found that '25 per cent of the Christian respondents to his questionnaire had *butsudan* and that these Christians were similar to non-Christian Japanese in conducting periodic ancestor rites, performing routine rituals in front of the altar, feeling connected with ancestors, and otherwise exhibiting ancestor-oriented behavior.'[3]

I assume that such resiliency in the ancestor-oriented faith and ritual has much to do with the fact that ancestors participate in constructing the identity of a descendant.[4] It seems that the ancestor-'other' and the descendant-'self' enter into one another through various psychosocial mechanisms: projection and introjection in psychoanalytical terms, reflexivity and symbolization in culturalist terms, 'taking the role of other' in interactionist jargon.

The ancestor-other participates in the construction of the living self in two contrastive but interrelated directions. On the one hand, ancestors are beyond a descendant's control as much as genes are and bind him/her to a certain ascribed identity. This belief tends to be allied, transcendentally, with the karmic chain of destiny. On the other hand, insofar as ancestors are nothing more than a symbolic creation, their images are subject to contemporary political and ideological trends[5] and technological manipulations as well as the personal needs of the descendant generation. Ancestors are as inventable as traditions are. In the latter perspective, ancestors may appear as resources at the disposal of a descendant to build up and sustain a desirable identity of his/her own. Particularly relevant to such manipulability is the general elusiveness of the categorical boundary of Japanese 'ancestors,' as demonstrated by Smith.[6]

I apply the above generalization to descendants of the Japanese aristocracy to show that the two-fold impact of ancestors is felt and expressed by this group of Japanese in a striking manner. Many call themselves 'fatalist' in that they find their lives and careers predetermined by their ancestral status, allowing them little freedom to pursue their personal choices. At the same time, aristocratic descendants (and those around them) find their ancestors a valuable source of self-esteem and symbolic capital to tap for new careers. Both views of ancestors coexist in the same individuals. Let me begin with a historical sketch of the Japanese aristocracy.

HISTORICAL BACKGROUND

By the Japanese aristocracy I mean the status group called Kazoku (capitalized to avoid confusion with the 'family' also pronounced as *kazoku*), the flowery lineage.[7] The term refers simultaneously to the status group as a whole, to each member family, and to individuals.

As a formal entity, the Kazoku existed for 63 years between 1884 and 1947. This group ranked below the royal lineage group capped by the emperor and above the rest of the population. The latter was further differentiated into the *shizoku*, the gentry composed predominantly of former samurai vassals, and *heimin*, commoners, who made up an overwhelming majority of the Japanese, including the former outcaste now known as new commoners. The Kazoku members were of diverse backgrounds and can be grouped into three major subcategories: the *kuge* who had served the imperial court in Kyoto; the daimyo who had owed loyalty to the military government headed by the shogun of Edo; and the meritorious nobles who rose, in most cases, from the modest status of lower-ranking samurai vassals due to their performances contributive to the state. The Meiji Restoration marked the division between the first two groups (Kuge-Kazoku and Daimyo-Kazoku) as old nobles on the one hand, and the last group as the newly ennobled (Shin-Kazoku or Kunkō-Kazoku) on the other. In addition to these, the Kazoku included more peripheral members such as priests of specially recognized shrines and temples and the chief administrator-vassals (*karō*) of powerful daimyo. Under the Kazoku system, all these men of diverse origins were organized into a single, European-styled group of peers residentially concentrated in Tokyo. In time, new Kazoku, recruited from a variety of professions and fields including *zaibatsu* families, came to outnumber old nobles.

The Kazoku group was rank-ordered by five nobility titles which might be translated as prince, marquis, count, viscount, and baron.[8] The holders of the first two titles were privileged to be automatic members of the House of Peers, one arm of the bicameral parliamentary system, while those of the other three were internally elected fellow members. In total, 1,011 families,[9] including those which have become extinct, were awarded Kazoku titles in the 63-year existence of the Kazoku institution. Formally, the Kazoku title was assumed only by the head of the house and inherited by his sole heir, which makes 'descendants' synonymous with 'successors.' In practice, the head's wife and dependent children were entitled as well to Kazoku-status courtesy (*reigū*).

The Second World War and its aftermath devastated the Kazoku along with the rest of the nation, uprooted them from their old life-style, and resulted for many households in their acceptance of the 1947 abolition of the Kazoku institution as a *fait accompli*. Through chains of introductions, I located more than 100 surviving Kazoku or their descendants of various ranks and backgrounds. The following account is based on fragments of their oral autobiographies constructed in response to my request and questions. Where appropriate, some of the observations made of their activities will be also added. I have worked on this project off and on since 1976, with two major fieldwork periods between 1982 and 1985, and most recently a short trip in 1989. The age given for an informant is the age at the time of first interview. In order to save space, I designate informants as 'Kazoku,' 'baron,' '*kuge*,' 'lord,' etc., not always modified as 'a descendant of ...' or 'a former ...'

THE 'REALITY' AND REVIVAL OF ANCESTRAL HERITAGE

While ancestors are symbolically constructed and could be so fashioned as to satisfy one's fantasy, there is class difference in the epistemological status of ancestral charisma. Many Kazoku ancestors were national figures: holders of the highest offices of the state, famous warlords, eminent civil leaders, and generals. 'Open any history book,' said the 66-year-old prince and head of a prominent court-noble house, without bothering to detail his ancestral background, 'you will find that my ancestors served emperors from generation to generation as imperial regents.'

This remark inadvertently reveals that the public status of prominent ancestors is based on the record accessible to the public. As part of the recorded collective memory, aristocratic ancestors are more culturally represented than commoner counterparts. The double-edged function of culture is self-evident in relation to the 'reality' it represents. Because Kazoku ancestors are more culturally constructed and represented, they appear more real while at the same time they are more liable to be mythologized.

The cultural representation of ancestors took multifarious forms in addition to historical accounts: genealogies; family treasures including letters, diaries, poems, scrolls of calligraphy and paintings, tea bowls, other art objects handed down from remote ancestors; awesome mausoleums, shrines, and ruins of castles. Many legacies have been lost, burned down, sold, or simply forgotten, but some have survived even against the wishes of a descendant who is now too impoverished to maintain the family legacy. Rows of extraordinarily huge tombstones representing generations of daimyo lords would be impossible to remove, as acknowledged by the wife of a daimyo descendant. The weight of an immovable gravestone is symbolic of the 'real' weight of ancestors that cannot be lifted from the backs of descendants. The existence and weight of ancestors thus have been real for Kazoku descendants both as a source of honor and as an unremovable burden.

Furthermore, in contemporary Japan, famous ancestors are far from being dead but are revived as popular subjects for televised dramas and best-seller historical novels, which are major sources of historical knowledge for today's Japanese. And by being thus publicized, they gain more fame. In a 1985 mailed questionnaire, I asked a sample of the heads of Kazoku households whether they had seen their ancestors appear in televised dramas or historical novels. Of the 101 who returned the questionnaire (one-fifth of the total recipients), 68 answered affirmatively, only 18 said no, 15 giving no answer. There are indications that the interest of Kazoku descendants in their ancestors has become kindled by such media exposure.

Some ancestors are more eminent than others, and there is a tendency to single out the 'first' ancestors (*shodai*) as the most important or the most memorable. This means that my informants generally had no trouble in identifying themselves or their husbands by the degrees of generational depth: 'I am the fourteenth-generation head of the house'; 'my husband is the twenty-seventh generation.' In the above questionnaire, 87 out of the 101 respondents specified the number of generations since their *shodai* ancestors: the average number of generations was 28.4 for *kuge* descendants, 19 for daimyo, and 7.9 for new Kazoku.[10] Further, the identities of ancestors in most cases are recognizable through genealogies, individual *ihai* (mortuary tablets), or tombstones. In the specificity as well as memory durability of ancestry, the hereditary elite thus stands out among the ordinary Japanese for whom ancestry tends to be short, collective, or impersonal except for the recently deceased.[11]

It is likely that, while the Kazoku as an institution no longer exists, Kazoku ancestors continue to affect the identities and careers of surviving successors, at least more so than commoner ancestors do. The following account shows that the ancestor-descendant interaction involving self-other appropriation among the hereditary elite goes far beyond the ordinary memorial rites practiced by the majority of Japanese. It will become clear that the ancestor-descendant interaction involves the identities of not just Kazoku but of those around them.

ANCESTOR-RESURRECTING CAREERS

In the prewar period, Kazoku were subjected to the supervisory authority of the Imperial Household Ministry in their choice of occupation. A military career was strongly endorsed, and membership in the House of Peers was taken for granted. Among other status-bound careers were the high-level foreign service, high offices in the Ministry of the Imperial Household, especially in personal attendance to the emperor and his family, and the priesthood at national shrines and temples.[12] Many fathers or fathers-in-law of my informants ended as career-less gentlemen or at best as dilettantes. The careers of my contemporary informants, while some were still destined to status-proper life courses, by and large reflect a greater freedom from ancestors, much more biased toward full-time 'occupations' in business and professions, most being 'salaried' employees. Ancestors enter their lives after retirement or only as a part-time side job while still engaged in a primary secular occupation. In some cases, a midlife conversion has taken place from an ordinary to an ancestral career, or a whole career is molded around ancestors.

Reorganizing the dead. One ancestor-career pattern is involvement in reorganizing symbols of the dead. Old Kazoku houses typically have many cemeteries distributed widely, particularly, in the case of daimyo, as a result of domain transfers, the mandatory double residence under the Tokugawa regime, or personal choices by lords or ladies in patronizing temples and priests. Some descendants are obsessed with imposing order upon this chaotic situation of the dead, and some successors dedicate their free time or post-retirement life to relocating their ancestors, possibly in a single, central cemetery. Given the number of ancestors involved, the size of each cemetery, and weight of each gravestone, as well as resistance on the part of the temples to which the cemeteries are attached, this alone is a full-time effort. In the course of reorganizing the cemeteries, tombstones are often collectivized under the name of 'House X's tomb for generations of ancestors,' at least for the most recent generations, so that 'all descendants from now on will enter underneath this same stone.'[13]

Other symbols are also involved. One of my businessman informants, a baron, upon the death of his widowed mother who had been the main caretaker of ancestors, became keenly aware of his responsibility as househead and began to study and identify his 'true ancestors.' At the time of my interview, he was, at age 64, preoccupied with ousting wrong ancestors (mostly matrilateral kin) from the *kakochō* (the recorded roster of the dead) and sending them back to their proper households. Each name removal calls for ritual intervention by a priest. Apparently, his occupation as a company president is secondary to this newly assumed ancestor career. Among various factors necessitating such reorganization of the dead I discern an internal urge on the part of the reorganizer to straighten and purify his own identity or to place himself on a single straight line of succession.

Investigating and documenting ancestor history. A number of informants were amateur 'historians' specializing in their ancestors, not just watching popular dramas but actively collecting and reading whatever is published on their ancestors or the history of the Japanese elite. In interviews, I was often given the titles, and sometimes gift copies, of such publications. Academic historians solicit their help for access to family records, and in some instances archaeologists dig in their ancestral mausoleums for burial remains in coordination with the efforts of descendants to reorganize or reconstruct the shrine complexes. These academic stimuli in turn motivate Kazoku survivors to study their ancestors in collaboration with the scholars, whose help is particularly needed in deciphering the old-style handwriting of ancestors.

One purpose of historical study is to discover or verify the extraordinary character, performance, or caliber of this or that ancestor. A historian and daughter of a *kuge* count has delved into the house archives and perused the diary kept by an ancestor of the Restoration period. She admires this particular forebear because he stayed on in Kyoto through the time of the mass exodus of *kuge* to follow Emperor Meiji to Tokyo. The ancestor's refusal to go along with the change of the times seems to mirror this descendant's own determination to stay in her natal Kyoto house and perpetuate its tradition.

Sometimes, more than collecting and deciphering relevant records is involved. A retired dean of a medical school and baron has turned a room into a historical and archival library, writes and lectures on ancestral history to groups of fellow-descendants of the Fujiwara lineage to which his (actually his wife's) house belongs, and repairs tattered scrolls for exhibition. With the amount of time, labor, and money poured into these activities, his, too, is a full-time commitment, his private clinical practice being only secondary.

Historical study is tied up with genealogical inquiries, since genealogy is among the most important records for the hereditary elite. The above questionnaire disclosed that 83 per cent of the respondents do (16 per cent do not) possess genealogies. The genealogical orthodoxy is measured first by generational depth. This is the reason that new Kazoku express embarrassment over their genealogical shallowness, saying 'We are not true Kazoku.' But even for them a historical study helps deepen it by extending it further and further back. Hence the average generational depth for new Kazoku is as much as 7.9 generations, as shown above, going back about four or more generations before their 'first' Kazoku-title grandees; there is an unwritten rule for a new Kazoku to start from the original awardee as his first ancestor. One of such new Kazoku descendants, while proud of having descended from a series of 'scholars' since the late Tokugawa period, nonetheless prefers to identify himself as 'the thirteenth generation' of the line founded by a warrior who was a petty lord of a branch castle 'at the time of Oda Nobunaga' (1534–82).

If a genealogy is not quite credible, greater effort is made to dig up archives to substantiate it. The archival research of a retired engineer and head of a baron house seems geared toward validating the claimed genealogy of his house which is embedded in mythological times. His house is that of a prominent national Shintō shrine of prehistoric origin, and as such it is called a house of *kokusō* (*kuni-no-miyatsuko*) like several other shrine houses including those of the Izumo Shrine (the Senge and Kitajima). All these houses, after the Restoration, lost the hereditary status of *kokusō* and in its stead received the rank of baron. The informant is the eightieth generation head from the first ancestor, a god who accompanied Ninigi, the grandson of Amaterasu, in descent from heaven to earth, followed Emperor Jimmu in his eastward expedition for conquest, and was assigned to rule a province. The survival of prehistoric ancestral shrines in the province is the best evidence, and yet, this eightieth descendant admits the difficulty of verifying the godly origin of his family, 'as difficult as the origin of the imperial house.' While making skeptical comments on the mythological tale, he nevertheless produced for me one document after another in an effort to substantiate his claim. In a second interview, he showed a neatly printed genealogy which went back to Ame-no-minakanushi 'preceding the origin of the imperial line.'

The above tale, closely linked to the national myth, suggests that what matters in this historical investigation is not genealogical depth alone but the place of ancestors in the national hierarchy of lineages (*uji*). Genealogical study is heavily oriented toward the most prestigious lineages, topped by the imperial, followed by the Fujiwara and the Genji, either in descent or at least in alliance or vassalage. The prestige of the above *kokusō* house derives not only from its long duration but, more importantly, from its primeval ancestors belonging to the group of heavenly gods (*amatsukami*), allied with imperial ancestors, landing from heaven to conquer the natives. Implied in this narrative is the invidious comparison between the informant's own and the Izumo shrine's *kokusō* house. 'They were natives, they were defeated ... We were with Emperor Jimmu and came down as occupation troops.' They were *kunitsukami* (earthly gods).[14]

For this informant it did not suffice to establish an ancestor's alliance with the imperial line during the mythological age, for he continued to discuss how his ancestors were repeatedly connected with the imperial family at later times through marriage or in descent. For example, Emperor Sujin married a daughter of his *kokusō* ancestor who then gave birth to Princess Toyosuki, the first chief priestess of Ise Shrine. Emperor Kogen's grandson fell in love with a daughter of another *kokusō* ancestor, which resulted in the birth of Takenouchi-no-sukune, the legendary figure of the early Yamato court. The informant took the trouble to verify each of these statements by pointing to a particular document, which impressed me with the intensity of his research commitment if not the plausibility of its outcome.

Preserving and displaying the heritage. The treasures that have been handed down are a major vehicle to connect ancestors and descendants. If a Kazoku household, having luckily escaped air raids, is still in possession of valuable treasures such as archival materials and notable art objects created or collected by ancestors, it must bear the heavy and costly job of maintaining them. Many of these, along with historical buildings or sites of Kazoku ancestors, such as castles, palaces, mausoleums, and shrines, have been designated 'important cultural properties' (*jūyō bunkazai*, abbreviated as *jūbun*) or 'historical sites' (*shiseki*) to be sponsored by the national or local governments and foundations. Although such treasures are now housed in museums or libraries accessible to the public, their original owners have not relinquished their custodial responsibility entirely. Portions of the owners' estates may be used as museums or libraries and the househeads may be appointed their directors.

The cultural properties of daimyo houses are attached to provincial castle towns as local historical landmarks. Under such circumstances, the original owners must be bilocal, going back and forth between their Tokyo residences and ancestral homes. One of my informants is a museum director commuting between the two places constantly, and while feeling overburdened, he is devoted to this mission as a grandson of the distinguished lord he particularly admires. A young lord of a northern province has begun his career in his 20s as a future director of the museum founded in the shrine complex and mausoleums of his ancestors, by moving, to his mother's surprise, to the castle town permanently and enrolling at a local university to obtain a degree in the museum profession.

The lordly duty to visit the castle town in response to frequent calls from the local office managing the domainal cultural properties interferes with a regular career. An employer may tolerate occasional absenteeism in exchange for the reputation an elite descendant's distinguished name brings to the firm, as was the case with a banking firm president employing one of such lords. But the same situation is likely to block the employee from getting promoted to an executive position, let alone the presidency, of a company: 'I was categorically ruled out of consideration for the presidency,' said the lord of a former southwestern province in his late 50s, 'because they knew I would eventually go back to the country to take charge' of the museum and the whole estate designated as *jūbun*.

There are cases where the residential house in use is designated as a cultural property. The latest example is an old *kuge* house in Kyoto. Its resident family, having thus lost control over its own house, cannot help feeling ambivalent about this decision, about being tied down to the inconvenient old-style housing instead of replacing it with a modern concrete building. However, they accept the fact that this arrangement is the only alternative to preserve the ancestral legacy, which after all supersedes all other considerations. The widowed mother of the family was actually delighted that the media-publicized nomination of her house as a *jūbun* had attracted royal attention resulting in visits by princes and princesses.

In another such house (of small-daimyo origin) in Kyushu, an old couple appeared completely tied down and as immobile as the *hina* dolls on display in the house-treasure museum. My interview revealed that their whole life has been to replicate the ancestral way of life, performing house rituals and arts such as *nō*, tea, and martial arts such as *yabusame* (ritual archery in which a rider on a galloping horse shoots at a target). Perhaps partly because of their age (the husband was 86, the wife 81), they looked like living ancestors themselves.

The preservation of ancestral heritage thus amounts to its display to the public. Some Kazoku shy away from the display role and are critical of those who are overly eager to 'show off.' Yet, many more are aware that their ancestral heritage could not be preserved and handed down to posterity without public access to it. Entrepreneurial lords have updated their museums with audiovisual equipment.

The effort of reorganizing cemeteries and other ancestor symbols, as described above, is likely to go hand in hand with redesigning them for public display. A baron, the head of a 'top-ranking' branch of a large daimyo house, now retired from a long career as an engineer, is devoted to his ancestors, deciphering archives and writing a family history. His ancestral mausoleum, occupying a part of the vast hill preserved entirely for the burial of the lineage headed by the main house, has been cleaned up, and sign boards have been put up, clearly for the benefit of curious tourists, showing a map and indicating the identity and biography of each ancestor buried.

Among the *kuge* there are houses that have handed down the art of court dressing (*kuge*-house arts are discussed further below). As interest in the ancient court life-style spreads and intensifies, such arts are not only studied and taught but displayed in the form of actual garments which were worn or received as imperial gifts by ancestors of the house. At one such exhibit in a busy shopping area of Tokyo, I joined a crowd of enchanted viewers, mostly women, gazing at many sets of multi-layered colorful court dresses, head gear, belts, and other accessories, on display. The court rank of the wearer was shown, according to the expert giving me a guided tour, by the color, material, form, and accoutrements of the dress. The guide punctuated almost every statement with, 'This was worn by the third-rank or above only.' Dress shows like this are probably one of the most effective ways of resurrecting noble ancestors in the minds of viewers.

A word should be added about the Kazoku autobiographies that have been coming out in recent years, signaling a new trend to reverse the political and ideological currency of the earlier postwar period when the degraded aristocracy felt forced into silence. Authors combine recollections of their personal experience with the ancestral histories they have studied for public readership. Women in particular are active in such authorial careers.[15]

Reenacting the roles of ancestors. Ancestors are thus reorganized, studied, documented, preserved, and displayed. They can be also replicated in live form. Affluent and reflective, Japanese now find themselves in search of their 'roots' and identities, receptive not only to historical dramatic series but to enticing tour programs, concocted by the ever-thriving travel industry, focused on historical sites and monuments. Improved transportation by land and air carries tourists much faster over greater distances. Equally receptive to such travel programs are provincial municipalities trying to attract spendthrift tourists, which leads to collaboration between local governments and industries to further revitalize local histories. Politicians zero in on the game of nostalgic dramatization to appeal to voters. Historical monuments are reconstructed, and famous scenes are visually displayed. More importantly, grand festivals, glossed as *ibento* (events), are organized as major tourist attractions featuring rulers of the feudal age, daimyo, and samurai vassals. Among the most popular are the *sennin gyōretsu* (thousand-people parade) in Nikko in honor of the transfer of the burial site of Tokugawa Ieyasu and by *hyakumangoku-matsuri* (million-*koku* festival) in Kanazawa to commemorate

Maeda Toshiie's accession to lordship of the province. Daimyo descendants, invited as guests of honor, thus watch their ancestors being resurrected in carnival-like shows.

In some prefectures, where remnants of the former domains still embody a focus of provincial solidarity, contemporary 'lords' are mobilized into more active roles. Let us look at a few examples. Lord A is from a province that, according to local residents, is 'strongly unified around the *tonosama* (lord).' Its castle town is also very active in developing a tourist center that focuses on the town's history. A huge budget was allocated to reconstruct the castle with accommodations for group tours, the restored samurai mansion attracts nearly a million visitors a year, and the 1868 Restoration war and the collective suicide of young soldiers are major themes of museum displays. The mayor's idea of a parade featuring the civil war has become a main annual event, with local high school students impersonating the suicidal soldiers. Politicians compete to be selected as top-ranking samurai to parade on horseback, but 'no one volunteers to be lord' in fear of the town gossip against such audacity. 'The lord must be the lord himself, they insist, and so I am pushed into this.' Lord A confesses that once he fell from the horse, and since then has been frightened of horse-riding. It is not easy for this retired salaryman to portray his grandfather, a true lord and the last one in his family.

In another prefecture, I observed a series of events centering around Lord B. They began with a memorial rite at the shrine located at a castle site now converted into a public park. Seated on one side of the main hall for worship were about 20 priests, and on the opposite side were about 30 lay participants including Lord B, his wife, and representatives of various associations such as the foundation run by 'vassals,' the shrine-support group, and the neighborhood organization (*chōnaikai*). A typical Shinto ritual was underway, involving the *norito* recitation, the elaborate offering by several priests of food to the gods, each lay attendant in turn lying prostrate and offering a sprig of a sacred tree in front of the magnificent altar, and the equally elaborate withdrawing of the food. Court music was played by three lay musicians. The sleepy monotony was broken twice by 'Woo-o!' uttered by one of the musicians to signal the appearance of gods, when the interior door of the altar was opened and when the invisible gods were transferred into the *mikoshi* (portable shrine). The gods were four ancestors of Lord B.

After the ritual, the stage was moved to a banquet room located at the rear of the shrine's main hall. The lord, still fully dressed in a black priestly robe, was seated on a stool at the upper center of the room and looked down upon everyone else, including his wife, sitting on the floor. One senior man in a dark suit after another entered and bowed deeply to the lord, who acknowledged each with a nod. Ten men, selected from the ritual participants, were invited here to join in a take-out-lunch ritual of commensality called *naorai*. There was not much conversation, and none spoke to the lord, which made me think that not only an inferior but a superior person is treated as if he did not exist. These elderly temporary 'vassals' seemed inhibited from talking to the lord in such a formal setting.

The lord left for a costume change, this time to be dressed in a brilliant combat outfit suitable for horse-riding. A loyal 'retainer' about his father's age was there to help him dress properly. Starting from the shrine ground, a long procession moved along the city's main streets, with children dressed up like pages, young men in samurai style, and several older men saddled on horseback impersonating high-ranking vassals and imperial envoys. A group of white-robed young men were carrying or guarding the *mikoshi*. The participants totalled about 200. At the midpoint of the procession was the lord mounted with dignity. Behind each horse were men picking up and dumping into a wagon the horse dung. It was drizzling, and the expensive costumes were getting spoiled. Still, the parade was conducted in high spirits, presenting an exciting pageant for local residents and tourists standing along the streets. When the procession returned to the shrine at the completion of the three-hour show, the city's fire brigade, waiting at the entrance, stood at attention and bowed to two objects: the *mikoshi* carrying the ancestor gods, and the live lord. Later, the lord told me that he could see the shopkeepers and pedestrians watching the parade bow to him in prayer fashion.

Various agents with their respective purposes and interests are interlocked in such projects: the tourist industry, local politics, the national or local government committed to the cultural preservation policy as seen above, and the Kazoku dedicated to their ancestors. To some extent these complement one another, but friction is inevitable. Some of my informants are upset with the excessive commercialization of the 'memorial rite,' which 'desecrates my ancestors.' The 'silly' things like candy being sold on the premises of the mausoleum infuriate a youthful lord who is seriously devoted to the *shodai* warrior ancestor buried there. Such staged self-presentations on parade described above seem to arouse a mixture of ambivalent feelings in older lords as well. No doubt, there is a sense of self-elevation as the focus of attention or even reverence, as acknowledged by Lord B, from the huge crowd. At the same time, a sense of humiliation for 'clowning' creeps in. While the whole affair is, theoretically, a serious matter involving the lord's obligation and dedication to his ancestors, one cannot help seeing a collusive play going on. By and large, older, experienced lords take the negative side (humiliation and playfulness) for granted, while younger, fresh lords holding positive expectations (elevation and seriousness) reveal stronger resistance to the preponderance of tourism.

There is another problem involved. Among the participants in the parade are a group of 'vassals,' self-claimed descendants of those who were loyal retainers of lords. Along with the publicity of spectacular daimyo parades, associations of vassals have been created or revived in many areas and their size is growing. A large association inevitably faces organizational problems such as the rank order which is important in determining the order of procession, seating, and incense-burning for memorial rites. Another serious issue is the genealogical veracity of vassalage. The vassal association of one province rose to over 300 in membership, which did not necessarily delight Lord C and core vassals. An inner circle was formed with a name different from that of the larger *Hanshikai* (vassals' club). Members of the inner circle call themselves '*jūshin*' (senior councillors) and gather around Lord C, who is as young as their sons, to help, advise, and 'discipline' him,[16] without being bothered by the rank-and-file vassals, contemporary city politicians, businessmen, or the tourist industry. In response to my interview request, Lord C 'summoned' four *jūshin*, who were apparently more than eager to comply. Sitting at a hotel-restaurant table, they took turns introducing themselves to me: Vassal W, at age 63, was a descendant of the very top retainer among those who killed themselves following the death of the first lord (in the early seventeenth century); Vassal X, age 51, was a descendant of another suicide following the second-generation lord's death; Vassal Y, age 64, was a descendant of 'the right-hand man' of the first lord credited as responsible for the latter's success; Vassal Z, age 52, was a progeny of a front-line fighter who was killed in the Restoration war.

Latter-day vassals and lords are co-actors in a drama to replicate and revitalize the esteemed status of their ancestors, and by so doing, support one another in the enhancement of their own identities. The surrogate ancestor role is played not only as a serious matter involving the player's identity and ancestor worship, but also as a jovial pastime. The same group gathered again the same evening for a drinking-dining party at a country-style bar-restaurant. Relaxation and conviviality, while *sake* cups were being exchanged and emptied in a small *tatami* room, threw the participants into a playful mood for acting out their ancestral roles. The vassals addressed Lord C as 'Your Highness,' called one another by their ancestors' ranks and personal names, and spoke in the old samurai style. Everyone looked happy, was having great fun, and declared that the lord would be helped to 're-establish the House' (*o-ie saikō*). Infectious euphoria prevailed. The lord, apparently feeling good and encouraged, remained more or less reticent with dignity, but smiling. It occurred to me that ancestors can be thus mobilized back to life to produce a therapeutic psychodrama.

Thus far I have concentrated on daimyo-Kazoku, but *kuge* too have opportunities to replay ancestral roles. Court-centered festivals that originated in the Heian period, for example, mobilize *kuge* descendants to take prominent parts. An informant, a son of a *kuge* count, has played an imperial envoy (*chokushi*) at the annual Aoi festival which features a long, spectacular parade of Heian courtiers in Kyoto. At the televised poetry party held in the imperial palace each New Year, several *kuge* descendants present themselves as reciters, as ancient courtiers used to do. Further, a group of *kuge* or honorary *kuge* Kazoku have formed a court-music (*gagaku*) club, practice instruments once a week at the palace music hall, assisted by professional court musicians, and perform on stage in court dress for palace ceremonies. After retirement from the Self-Defense Ground Forces, a *kuge* informant entered the imperial palace as a palace-shrine ritualist (*shōten*) to be close to the emperor as his ancestors had been. The head of a *sekke* (one of the five pre-Meiji imperial-regent families of Fujiwara ancestry), upon retirement from a long successful career as an electronic engineer with a doctoral degree, accepted the invitation to the position of *daigūji* (grand chief priest) of the Ise Shrine. This case is not exactly a re-enactment of his ancestors' role, the position being 'too low for a *sekke* head,' but rather a re-enactment of the long history of the intimate relationship between the *sekke* and the imperial house.

More important, however, is the revitalization of courtly arts that have been handed down in some *kuge* houses, such as incense art, tea ceremony, flower arrangement, court dressing, poetry, calligraphy, and court music. According to my informants, each *kuge* house developed and handed down its own style of art as a matter of course. There was no fixed name like *iemoto*, but for the sake of convenience, let me call such *kuge*-house art *ieryū*, *ie* being the perpetual 'house,' and *ryū* the style.

The *ieryū* as an *ie*-embedded tradition was far from a profession, was oriented toward court entertainment, and was not necessarily practiced by the househead but often relegated to retainers. 'All he had to do was to hold the headship,' said a contemporary *ieryū* master about his predecessor. It is said that the *ieryū* art has been transmitted to but one heir (*isshi sōden*) for each generation or kept strictly within the house never to be released outside (*otomeryū*). Many *ryū* became totally extinct after the post-Restoration abolition of the *kuge* status.

On the other hand, some *kuge* houses, after the Restoration or more commonly after World War Two, began to recapture their *ieryū* legacies and to make professions out of them. They now engage in what their ancestors never did: they hold classes to teach the arts, exhibit the results of training for publicity, and issue certificates, recruiting disciples and audiences from the former commoner class which now has affluence and leisure time and is receptive to the culture of the bygone elite. 'In the 700-year history of this house, I, the twenty-eighth generation headmaster, am the first to make a living out of this art.' To his amusement, a disciple once asked what his occupation was, 'as if teaching the art of flower arranging were my hobby!' The *ieryū* is thus evolving into an *iemoto*-like structure which developed among the warrior class and commoners, where the original creator and headmaster of the particular art plays a predominant role as the ultimate authority for orthodoxy, as implied by *moto*, meaning origin or stem. For the *ieryū* art of *kuge*, however, the identity of the original master is not always certain because no attempt was made to teach it to outsiders. A current master said that the style had 'evolved naturally,' as epitomized by *ryū* (flow) instead of *moto*. In the course of recent metamorphosis, the term *iemoto* has been adopted by these *kuge* houses as well.

After assuming the *iemoto*-master position, an informant studied and wrote in the *iemoto*-school magazine about the life of the *shodai* of the house who had served a retired emperor in the early Kamakura period. As the first career professional in the *ieryū*, the informant felt 'as if I returned to the *shodai*,[17] and assumed the same professional name (*gō*) as the *shodai* ancestor. His narrative, which is loaded with philosophical contemplations, informs readers that he lives in a world beyond here and now or in a timeless universe inhabited by successive ancestors and descendants. He is creating a tradition for his *iemoto* school. The best-known among the presently active and professionalized *kuge* arts are the incense art of the Sanjo-nishi, the flower-arranging art of the Sono, and the poetry of the Reizei.

Professionalized as they are, these *kuge*-art schools still retain features of their non-professional predecessors. The headmasters are proud to say that they are not motivated to build up *iemoto*-like networks for commercial gain. One of them had contemplated the meaning of *iemoto* and concluded that his responsibility was to transmit the art style to at least one person of the next generation who could be his own son. For him neither money-making nor network-building is relevant to his role; instead, 'my duty is to teach what I believe in.' In the teaching style, too, these *kuge-iemoto* present themselves more as co-participants instead of imposing themselves upon their pupils as authorities, as do other *iemoto*. Further, the arts are to be enjoyed as play rather than to be studied for spiritual, moralistic discipline as Zen-inspired *buke* (warrior-class) arts are said to be.

CONCLUSION

I have discussed how contemporary descendants of the Japanese aristocracy are resurrecting their ancestors on the assumption that the constructed images of their ancestors are essential ingredients of their selves. Only salient role repertoires are delineated: the roles of reorganizer, researcher, preserver/displayer, and reenactor. There is a difference among these roles in terms of distance between resurrected ancestors and resurrecting descendants. The first three seem to involve a greater distance in that the two parties are differentiated as object and subject of action. The distance shrinks in role-enactment where the actor 'becomes' an ancestor. In this sense, this last role category may be regarded as the most essential to the identity fusion between self and ancestor.

These roles, in most cases, occupy only a part of one's career, either after retirement from a regular occupation or as an avocation. Nevertheless, they amount to 'careers' in terms of the time, energy, and preoccupations committed to them. Involvement in the ancestor career ranges from 'obligatory' role play to 'living it up,' from collusive clowning to serious role-embracement. However variable from one individual to another, most of my Kazoku informants lead double careers – mundane and other worldly, contemporary and ancestral – in a more distinctive way than ordinary Japanese. A well-balanced view was expressed by the 'purely postwar' successor to a prominent daimyo house with the rank of prince, and active employee of a company. At the beginning he resisted the role of ancestor reenactor whether in memorial rites or at 'vassals' club' reunions but has now reached the point where he finds it a refreshing relief from the hectic daily life of a section chief working overtime. In fact he is inspired with the process whereby all participants make 'sincere efforts' to fit into the solemn form of ritual.

It might be thought that the above forms of ancestor resurrection concern only a tiny group of people living in isolation and out of touch. As a matter of fact, the people marginal or external to the Kazoku group participate in these activities as much or even more zealously than core members of the group. I found, for example, that portrayal of a daimyo ancestor was urged and encouraged by vassals. The degree of marginality may be further elaborated by an example. Among the four *jūshin* of Lord C described above, Vassal Z was included at the lord's discretion even though he was, according to another *jūshin*, too low in rank to be a senior vassal. 'His ancestor fought on the front line. Truly high-ranking retainers would stay behind, close to the lord.' When this was told to me confidentially, I remembered having witnessed all three vassals turn off whenever Vassal Z joined in discussion. However low Z's rank was, it was he, I noted, who was best informed of the history of the domain and lordly ancestors with exact dates; it was he who could detail the wealth of the domain, the stipends of major vassals, and the local history of the Restoration war. A barber by occupation, he had studied the domainal history in depth, as if he had assumed the role of domain scribe. It may be that the lord became dependent upon the historical expertise of this descendant of a lowly samurai. Further to be considered is the importance of the general townspeople and tourists in sustaining the pageantry or preserving 'cultural properties' as their audiences. The same is true with the *kuge-ieryū* professionalization made possible by the presence of receptive commoner students.

The expert guide for the tour of the court dress exhibit was not a descendant of the house that had maintained this dressing art. Apparently, it is outsiders more than house insiders who actually study and teach the art. The art of flower-arranging, too, had been practiced and maintained by retainers of the house until the present *iemoto* master took over the leadership as a professional.

Within the Kazoku group, too, I find marginal members among the most committed to ancestor-resurrection, such as adopted sons and wives who have entered the house from outside. To my knowledge, a daughter's husband as an adopted son-in-law is as deeply committed, if not more than the daughter herself, to the duty of resurrecting *her* ancestors. In the two cases that came to my attention, insider wives were found indifferent to or ignorant of house traditions. Conversely, I have seen outsider women married to insider heirs who were well versed in the details of New Year's rituals handed down in each house. It is their responsibility to resurrect their husbands' ancestors in perfect conformity to house rules. One of such women learned the rules from her father-in-law because he was an adopted son-in-law and his wife (the informant's mother-in-law) – insider – knew nothing about them.

Admittedly, this observation cannot be generalized too far. There are indeed instances of strong insider commitment, and there are marginals such as non-successor sons who are alienated, for good reasons, from the total system of Kazoku hierarchy. Yet, the above examples are suggestive of the aristocracy being deeply and extensively embedded in larger society, involving cross-class complicity. It may even be said that, by resurrecting ancestors, aristocratic descendants in contemporary Japan are participating in the production and consumption of popular culture.

Finally, it might be suspected that all these nostalgic orientations toward ancestors are parochial, destined to fade out in the course of Japan's internationalization. However, I found two men, both of the postwar generation, who became truly committed to the role of *iemoto* master only after traveling abroad. Earlier, one of them had doubts about his acceptance of the *iemoto* position – he was not even born into it but adopted from a branch house – in terms of whether it was worthy of his entire life, and he left Japan in search of a resolution to his inner conflict. During eight months of travel in Europe and exposure to different countries, he became convinced of the unique value of Japanese traditional culture and especially of his *ieryū* art. He returned a true believer.

The other young man was long unsure of what he wanted for his life except that he wanted to 'absorb anything new.' Eager to learn something different, he accepted an invitation from an American friend, traveled to California to live with the friend when campus unrest was at its peak, and made friends with Berkeley students. His travels extended to South Asia, the Middle East, and Europe, while he supported himself with a variety of odd jobs. India particularly intrigued him with its life-style enduring for millennia and 'liberated' him to accept the fact that he himself, despite all the new learning experiences, could not change basically but had to return to where he had come from. Back in Japan, when his mother fell ill, he was ready to take over the role of the *iemoto* master of tea as 'deputy *iemoto*.' His mother, originating from a *sekke*, had established the *iemoto* in 1970 by revitalizing the privately carried *ieryū* of her natal house. Her son was able to retrieve what he had learned in this art from his mother in his childhood. The informant does not like to dramatize his foreign experience as a turning point of his career but admitted that his American friend-host was surprised at his transformation. The friend also astonished the informant by his total conversion from a long-haired rebel against his own upper-class family into a respectable, well-groomed lawyer. The two saw themselves in one another.

These instances suggest that internationalization does not necessarily subvert atavism but rather can reactivate it. More generally, in a post-industrial society like Japan where people are subject and sensitized to the new information constantly produced and instantaneously circulated on a massive scale, it is all the more likely that a nostalgia for order and stability attributed to the centuries of ancestors is kindled. It does not matter that resurrection is an invention, and in fact no 'tradition' may be 'revivable' without an inventive alteration, to reiterate the introduction of this paper. What matters is the participant's faith in the fidelity of preserving and reproducing his ancestors and their symbols.

NOTES

This is an extension of a paper presented at the annual meeting of the Association for Asian Studies, Washington, DC, March 17–19, 1989. For my long-term research to write a monograph of which this paper is a part, I am indebted to several funding agencies: the Joint Committee on Japanese Studies of the American Council of Learned Societies and the Social Science Research Council, Japan Foundation, Wenner-Gren Foundation, and University of Hawaii (Fujio Matsuda Scholar and Japan Studies Endowment awards). I also owe thanks to Junko Yoshino for her assistance in data coding.

1. Theodore C. Bestor, *Neighborhood Tokyo* (Stanford: Stanford University Press, 1989). For general discussion, Eric Hobsbawm and Terence Ranger, eds., *The Invention of Tradition* (Cambridge: Cambridge University Press, 1983). For the tradition invented by Meiji Japan, Robert J. Smith,

Japanese Society: Tradition, Self and the Social Order (Cambridge: Cambridge University Press, 1983); Helen Hardacre, *Shinto and the State, 1868–1988* (Princeton: Princeton University Press. 1989).
2. NHK Yoron Chōsabu, ed., *Nihonjin no shūkyō ishiki* (Tokyo: NHK, 1984), pp. 6–11.
3. David Reid, 'Japanese Christians and the Ancestors,' *Japanese Journal of Religious Studies*, Vol. 16 (1989), pp. 259–83.
4. I have analyzed the identity interchange between ancestors and living descendants as it was observed among members of a cult called Gedatsukai. See Takie Sugiyama Lebra, 'Ancestral Influence on the Suffering of Descendants in a Japanese Cult,' in W. H. Newell, ed., *Ancestors* (Hague: Mouton, 1976), and 'Self-Reconstruction in Japanese Religious Psychotherapy,' in A. Marsella and G. White, eds., *Cultural Perceptions of Mental Health and Therapies* (Dordrecht, Holland: D. Reidel, 1982). Reprinted in Takie S. Lebra and William P. Lebra, eds., *Japanese Culture and Behavior: Selected Readings*, revised edition (Honolulu: University of Hawaii Press, 1986).
5. Sakurai Tokutaro, *Shūkyō to minzokugaku* (Tokyo: Iwasaki Bijutsusha, 1965), pp. 136–37.
6. Robert J. Smith, *Ancestor Worship in Contemporary Japan* (Stanford: Stanford University Press, 1974).
7. The etymology of Kazoku is not certain. One possibility is that it was derived from the same name referring to one lineage group of *kuge* nobles, Seiga (ga=ka). Kasumi Kaikan, ed., *Kazoku kaikan-shi* (Tokyo: Kasumi Kaikan, 1966), pp. 84–85. An anonymous reviewer suggested 'glorious lineage' as a better translation.
8. The Japanese terms are *kōshaku*, *kōshaku*, *hakushaku*, *shishaku*, and *danshaku*, abbreviated as *kō-kō-haku-shi-dan*. These are avoided here to preclude confusion of the first two homophonous terms. The first *kōshaku*, translated as prince, is to be distinguished from 'royal' prince.
9. The number is based upon the two-volume comprehensive genealogies of the Kazoku published by Kasumi Kaikan (the contemporary successor to Kazoku Kaikan, the Kazoku Club). *Kazoku kakei taisei* (Tokyo: Yoshikawa Kobunkan, Vol. 1, 1982, Vol. 2, 1984).
10. Such specificity in generational depth presupposes that each house has been perpetuated through a single straight line of househeads from father to son, that is, through succession by one son for each generation in preclusion of all other children who are destined to disappear from the house genealogy. This further means that adoption, which must take place when the incumbent head has no son of his own or if his son does not succeed him for one reason or another, has to simulate a father-son relationship no matter who the adoptee is. Hence, one's brother is adopted as one's son (resulting in a larger number of ancestral generations than the normal counting of 'generations') and so is one's daughter's husband. Adoption, which has been very frequent among the Kazoku population, is analyzed elsewhere: Takie Sugiyama Lebra, 'Adoption among the Hereditary Elite of Japan: Status Preservation through Mobility,' *Ethnology*, Vol. 28 (1989), pp. 185–218.
11. For these characteristics of commoner ancestors, see David W. Plath, 'Where the Family of God ... Is the Family: The Role of the Dead in Japanese Households,' *American Anthropologist*, Vol. 66 (1964). pp. 300–17; Robert J. Smith, '*Ihai*: Mortuary Tablets, the Household and Kin in Japanese Ancestor Worship,' *Transactions of the Asiatic Society of Japan*, 3rd. ser., Vol. 9, (1966), pp. 83–102.
12. Commoners, in turn, could join Kazoku ranks through eminence achieved in military and civil careers.
13. The collectivization of recent ancestors among the Kazoku reverses the commoners' practice. For commoners, remoter ancestors have lost their individual identities and are put together into one collective *ihai* and gravestone as 'all generations of ancestors,' while the recently deceased retain separate identities. See Plath, 'Where the Family of God'; Smith, '*Ihai*.'
14. This view is far from being shared by descendants of the Izumo *kokusō*, and even to outsiders the Izumo Shrine would appear as beyond challenge, as second only to the Ise Shrine of the imperial family in prestige. The 82nd head priest of the Izumo Shrine and successor to the *kokusō* house, Senge, writes:

> Thus, the Izumo *kokusō* has been succeeded by a single unbroken line [*ikkei*] of descendants of God Amenohohi since the Age of Gods and has kept its name *kokusō* of ancient origin to this day. I do not want to sound self-promoting, but it would not be an exaggeration to say that this *kokusōke* embodies the spirit of Japan's history, that it is of pedigree of rare distinction, the oldest of all old houses, second only to the imperial house, older than the five regent families of the Fujiwara lineage in origin. Amenohohi, the primordial ancestor of the Senge, is not an earthly god but a son of Amaterasu, the imperial progenitrix. Senge Takamune. *Izumo taisha* (Tokyo: Gakuseisha, 1968), p. 195.

15. To mention a few: Sakai Miiko, *Aru kazoku no Shōwa-shi* (Tokyo: Shufu To Seika tsusha, 1982); Tokugawa Motoko, *Tōi uta* (Tokyo: Kodansha, 1983); Torio Tae, *Watakushi no ashioto ga kikoeru* (Tokyo: Bungei Shunju. 1985).

16. For the role of socializing Kazoku children taken by servants and vassals, see Takie Sugiyama Lebra, 'The Socialization of Aristocratic Children by Commoners: Recalled Experiences of the Hereditary Elite in Modern Japan,' *Cultural Anthropology*, Vol. 5, (1990), pp. 78–100.
17. The New Year's food offering to gods and ceremonial meals are preserved by many Kazoku households as the last surviving ritual supposedly 'unique' to each house.

First published in Takie Sugiyama Lebra (ed.), *Japanese Social Organization*, Honolulu: University of Hawaii Press, 1992

22 The Spatial Layout of Hierarchy: Residential Style of the Modern Japanese Nobility

Social relations are ordered in and across space as well as time. Put in Giddens' (1984) terms, 'structuration' involves space-focused 'regionalization,' in conjunction with time-focused 'routinization.' The spatial representation of social hierarchy in particular, whether physical or symbolic, literal or metaphorical, is widely recognized and often taken for granted particularly in its vertical dimension, namely high and low, above and below, upstairs and downstairs, and so on. Barry Schwartz (1981) argues the universality of 'vertical opposition' as conceptualized in line with structuralism (without, however, presuming it to be inherent in the structure of the mind). I extend Schwartz's vertical dimension to other dimensions to show how the actual operation of a hierarchy can deviate from the linear vertical model. Suggestive in this light is Feinberg's (1988) proposition of two contrastive models of spatial hierarchy, derived from two Polynesian outliers, Anuta and Nukumanu. One is 'linear' and 'unambiguous,' while the other is 'circular' and 'relativistic' where high and low are reversible. This essay takes Schwartz and Feinberg as a point of departure to further elaborate the spatial design of status and hierarchy. In the concluding section, I suggest that the spatial analysis can generate a clue to what might be called 'dyarchy,' as it is applied to the hereditary elite of Japan including the emperorship.

The spatial focus makes much sense in dealing with the Japanese concepts of hierarchy since spatial references are a common alternative to personal names or pronouns for Japanese speakers in address as well as in reference. Avoiding direct use of a personal name, Japanese use spatial terminology to indicate respectful distance, and indeed, a spatial reference often amounts to an honorific. To mention a few out of countless examples of status-indicative spatial nomenclature: The literal equivalent for 'Your (or his) Excellency' is 'Lord Palace' (*tonosama*), the lordly status symbolized by the palace where the addressee resides as its master. A common term for identifying a royal prince or princess is *miya*[*sama*] (venerable house), *miya* also referring to a shrine for gods. The special honorific reserved exclusively for emperor and empress, the equivalent for His or Her Majesty, is *heika*, literally meaning 'below the stair,' an instance of reflexive twist in which the sacred personage is identified by the low position taken by an imaginary retainer speaking upward to the august one seated above the stair. The same reflexive logic holds for some other spatial terms like *denka*, *kakka*, and *gozen*, all meaning 'your (or his) highness'. Spatial terminology is not limited to 'respectable' persons: an ordinary man may he referred to by his relative or acquaintance in terms of the city or district of his residence, as, for example, 'Hiroshima is coming to stay with us.' Even widely used terms for 'you' and 'I' literally mean spatial directions, for example, *anata* or *sochira* (over there) for 'you' and *kochira* (over here) for 'I.' Such spatial nomenclature sounds natural to Japanese; most of their family names, after all, originated from the names of districts, locations, or landmarks.

Japan today is an egalitarian society as far as hereditary status is concerned, with no legally sanctioned ascribed elite except the imperial family. The following analysis will touch upon the imperial status, but most of the data come from a more anachronistic source, namely, the abolished nobility, whose life is only recalled and whose status is only ritually reenacted by those who have outlived their titles or by their descendants. The legally outmoded nobility, I claim nevertheless, is culturally contemporary (Lebra 1992), as much as the legally obsolescent *ie* (stem-family household) or the outcaste status is. For this reason, tense switch will become necessary from time to time. My analysis is centered on the 'domestic' space as it interlocks with the 'public' space.'

THE HISTORICAL BACKGROUND OF THE NOBILITY

By *the nobility* is meant the status group called *kazoku*, 'the flowery lineage,' the term applying at once to the group as a whole, each constituent family, and the head of the family to whom the title belonged, which definition allows the term to appear in singular or plural. As a legal entity the kazoku was formally established in 1884 and thrown out of existence in 1947 together with the royal lineage group, the *kōzoku* (except the emperor and his closest family), under the new constitution that replaced the 1889 Constitution of the Great Empire of Japan. The kazoku ranked immediately below the royal lineage group headed by the emperor and stood tall above the rest of the nation. The latter was further graded into gentry called *shizoku* (primarily of samurai-vassal origin) and commoners (*heimin*), and remnants of the outcaste variously renamed. For my present purpose, however, all three can be classified as nonelite or 'commoners.'

The kazoku was an institutional creation, felt necessary by leaders of Meiji Japan (1868–1912) after the old aristocracy was brought to an end through the Meiji Restoration. Originally and informally the kazoku consisted largely of two major categories of old aristocrats: (1) the former court nobles, generally known as *kuge*, who had attended the imperial court of the Kyoto Palace until the Restoration; (2) the former feudal domain lords, commonly called *daimyō*, who had centered at the Edo (Tokyo) Castle of the shogunal court and their respective provincial castles. Later, in 1884, when the kazoku was formally established, a new group of men joined the ranks, much to the dismay of the *kuge* and *daimyō*; the new group was elevated because of their recognized contributions and performances through and after the Meiji Restoration. These achievers came primarily from modest-ranking former samurai-vassals. Indicative of their respective origins, the three categories were named in popular vernacular as *kuge-kazoku*, *daimyō-kazoku*, and *kunkō-* or *shin-kazoku* (*kunkō* and *shin* mean 'meritorious' and 'new').

The above composition alone suggests two contrastive purposes involved in the creation of this modern aristocracy. On the one hand, the kazoku was to provide a symbolic continuity in hierarchy; it was thus meant to be conservative, propitiatory of the discontented old elite, particularly the daimyō, who had lost most of their former privileges, power, and wealth through the Meiji reform. On the other hand, this reorganization of aristocracy was to perform progressive functions as well. First, it allowed a continual assimilation of 'new blood' with fresh energy into the 'hereditary' elite to cope with the urgent tasks of modernizing the country. Second, the men of such diverse backgrounds were now integrated into a single 'peerage,' symbolic of a newly centralized national state under a single sovereign, the emperor. One of the kazoku privileges was that of membership – automatic or internally elected – in the House of Peers, one arm of the bicameral parliament established in 1889.

Kazoku were classified into five ranks, named after the five nobility ranks of ancient China but conceptually modeled on the European aristocracy. The five paralleled prince, marquis, count, viscount, and baron. These ranks were allocated, subject to promotion, according to pre-Restoration status, loyalist contributions to the cause of the Restoration, and subsequent performances in various fields of activities and professions. When the source of information is to be specified in the following account, the pre-Meiji status and nobility rank may be combined, such as 'a son of daimyō-viscount,'

The former kazoku continues to maintain its visible identity as a social club in the heart of Tokyo; from time to time it publishes records of itself as one of its major activities. The most comprehensive set of genealogies, published by the club (Kasumi-Kaikan 1982–1984), indicates there have been 1,011 kazoku families in total, including those that have become extinct or have lost kazoku titles for one reason or another since the inception of this institution. Initially about 500, the membership thus doubled, which means that the category of 'new' kazoku, a small minority at the beginning, eventually came to outnumber the kuge- and daimyō-kazoku.

The kazoku privileges and duties both centered upon the emperor. They had special access to the imperial household such as social or ritual contact as host or guest, durable intimacy stemming from having been playmates and classmates with princes or princesses, opportunities (or obligations) of marriage with members of the royalty including the emperor, high-level employment in the court, and so on. Theoretically the nobility titles were awarded out of 'the imperial benevolence,' and they were transmitted to successors with the imperial sanctions. In return, the kazoku as a group was expected to dedicate itself as a human bulwark (*hanpei*) for the imperial house (Lebra 1992 for detail).

I have been in contact with surviving members and descendants of the former kazoku intermittently since 1976. Uninterrupted fieldwork was conducted for five months in 1982, for ten months in 1984–1985, primarily in Tokyo, with occasional trips to other parts of Japan. Surviving members of kazoku, their descendants, and families were interviewed for their life histories. In addition to this retrospective, reconstructive set of information, direct observations were made of contemporary group activities and 'events' involving former kazoku or their successors as central figures. Further, I was able to contact (not exactly 'interview' in all cases) a limited number of royal princes and princesses. By the end of my last field trip (1989), I had met more than one hundred individuals. All my informants have outlived their own or their forebears' aristocratic titles, but modifiers like 'former' will not always be given in the following account.

THE SPATIAL HIERARCHY OF RESIDENCE

Kazoku households, even though they were a small group of 'peers,' were diverse, as is already clear from the above threefold categorization of kazoku composition. They varied in genealogical depth – from a kuge whose 'first' ancestor appears as a god in the Kojiki, the mytho-historical chronicle compiled in the early eighth century, down to an upstart of 'obscure' or 'lowly' origin. A more conspicuous variation existed in wealth; here the category ranged from a rich daimyō-kazoku[2] commanding hundreds of acres of real estate – enormous by the Japanese, if not by the European or American, standard – and several dozens of servants, down to a pauperized kuge who refrained from social activities because he/she could not afford proper accoutrements, whether attires, vehicles, or a quality retinue. Financial giants, who too were eventually ennobled, stood in contrast to modest salaried men. Further, the lifestyle differed extensively along the continuum from extreme Westernization ('We had our shoes on indoors') to adherence to 'the age-old Japanese style of life,' as represented by the residential architecture. In addition to intragroup variation, one must consider a tremendous change that took place within the sixty-three-year span of kazoku existence: 'My mother was still wearing *ohikizuri* [outer garment of kimono with train],' said an informant, 'like many other women. But such was stopped overnight by the Russo-Japanese War [1904–1905].' Besides that war, my informants identify two more major turning points: the great earthquake of the Kanto region (1923) and World War II.

All these variations and changes defy a generalization about spatial design. Nevertheless some patterns, admittedly always to be qualified by exceptions, do emerge, probably thanks to two factors: first, some more or less standardized culture of the elite was developed and learned at Gakushuin, a special school system catering to royal and kazoku children and other selected upper-class children; second, a high frequency of intermarriage and interadoption (Lebra 1989) within this status group contributed to a sense of shared kinship and cultural homogenization. Given the above diversity in life conditions, such standardization reflected shared mental constructs rather than uniformity of physical layout. The same vocabulary was uttered by informants with various backgrounds in reconstructing their residential architecture.

Residential Locations

First, I locate the kazoku residential space in a larger map. The Restoration government maneuvered the old aristocracy to settle permanently in Tokyo. Further, for any ambitious men who were later to rise to nobility ranks through merit, the new capital seemed the only place to provide opportunities. In other words, there were good reasons for the kazoku population to concentrate in Tokyo (although a few among the kuge stayed on in Kyoto).

Since this initial resettlement, there have been many residential relocations, as told by my informants, either by choice or by necessity. And the war, Tokyo air raids, evacuation, and postwar radical taxation upon properties ruined their residential grandeur, forcing most of them to forego their estates considerably or entirely and to live in cramped sections of their former servants' quarters or to disperse into rural areas.

Today, one might think that there would be no geographical pattern of residence that distinguishes the former kazoku. It was found out, however, that former kazoku still concentrate disproportionately in Tokyo. Of all the households whose addresses are known (N = 916 according to Kasumi-Kaikan 1982-1984), as many as 57 percent reside in prefectural Tokyo, whereas the percentage for the whole nation is only 11.9 percent (Jichishō Gyōseikyoku 1984). The second most settled prefecture is Kanagawa, adjacent to Tokyo, where many kazoku used to own resort villas along the coast of Sagami Bay; these became their permanent homes when their main estates in Tokyo were lost. Here, the percentage for the kazoku is 16.7 percent, compared with 6.5 percent for the nation. In sum, 73.7 percent of kazoku live in these two prefectures while the national representation is only 18.4 percent.

Prefectural Tokyo divides into the urban center situated in the eastern portion facing Tokyo Bay, and the vaster rural area stretching westward. Taking all the prefectural households as 100, we find 86 percent of kazoku households reside within the urban limits, while only 74 percent of the general population do so. More telling is the pattern of concentration within urban Tokyo, which breaks down into twenty-three wards (*ku*). We find 66.6 percent of the kazoku households residing in the twenty-three wards concentrated in five wards (Minato, Shibuya, Setagaya, Meguro, and Shinjuku) whereas only 24.3 percent of the general residents live in the same wards. Conversely, eight other wards (Katsushika, Sumida, Arakawa, Adachi, Kita, Kōtō, Edogawa, and Itabashi), have 2.6 percent of kazoku, 35.2 percent of the general residents. These figures confirm our impressions that there is a class cleavage in residential geography within the city limits between what are vaguely and misleadingly designated *yamanote* (hillside) and *shitamachi* (downtown).

The yamanote-shitamachi dichotomy is far from clear or consistent, partly because the boundary and internal division of urban Tokyo has changed extensively since the initial installation of the 15-ku system in 1878. Twenty more ku were added in 1932, and this total of 35 ku was reorganized into the present 23-ku system in 1947. (It should be noted that these changes were occasioned by the two events of Tokyo devastation: the 1923 earthquake and the 1945 air raids). The result is that there are many areas that cannot be characterized as either yamanote or shitamachi. Nevertheless, Japanese adhere to this dichotomy because these designations are strongly symbolic of class divisions more than denotative of geography. Seidensticker (1983), while limiting his analysis to the old 15 wards, calls the two regions 'high city' and 'low city,' combining physical altitude and social class. He takes us back to the historical origin of this division:

> When in the 17th century the Tokugawa regime set about building a seat for itself, it granted most of the solid hilly regions to the military aristocracy, and filled in the marshy mouths of the Sumida and Tone rivers, to the east of the castle. The flatlands that resulted became the abode of the merchants and craftsmen who purveyed to the voracious aristocracy and provided its labor. (1983, 8)

So there is a reason why the yamanote region is associated with the *buke yashiki* or *daimyō yashiki*, 'mansions of the ruling class.' The former kazoku, despite many relocations, continue, albeit in less density, to cluster in the choice areas of the 'high city.' That such geographical condensation must have been much more pronounced in prewar times can be inferred from the previous residences revealed in interviews. Most frequently mentioned were the two wards of the old city: Azabu and Akasaka, both presently part of Minato ward. These comprised the heart of old yamanote. *The Tale of Akasaka*, a popular essay by Kōbata (1984), for example, is primarily about the former elite.

Confinement

The above-sketched residential geography is the first sign of the spatial confinement in which the kazoku life was led. Confinement meant one's relative seclusion from the outside world, remaining in the 'high city,' in one's status group, in one's household. A daughter of a daimyō-marquis recalled that, while her 'unusually liberal parents' allowed her as a child to visit areas like Asakusa (a popular entertainment district of shitamachi, not to be confused with Akasaka) on occasions like local festivals if escorted by 'several maids,' they themselves would step into such a place 'under absolutely no circumstances.' To this day, some upper-class yamanote residents are strangers to the heart of shitamachi even though they are familiar with major American and European cities. So an author who only recently discovered the wonder of shitamachi confesses, 'Yes, Asakusa was more remote than New York' (Inukai 1989, 37).

In this seclusion the sexes were not equally confined; girls and women were more strictly bound by this rule of spatial confinement than boys and men; the boys in fact were allowed and sometimes encouraged to enter the social wilderness of the outside world. Older women informants particularly recalled their girlhood as secluded within the enclosure of the estate. Some were frustrated, but most accepted the seclusion as 'natural'; they did not become awakened to the 'freedom of mobility' until after their marriage to possibly 'liberal' husbands or after the war. The old *ohikizuri* (trained) garment epitomizes the woman's indoor life and immobility.

What stands out in kazoku life histories in sharp contrast to those of average Japanese is the insignificance or total absence of neighbors. This is pointed out as a characteristic of the yamanote lifestyle in general and was more pronounced among the upper class. There was almost no contact with neighbors beyond perfunctory greetings in accidental encounters in the residential vicinity until wartime, when everyone was forced into a neighborhood association and had to line up for rationed foods. Even children did not find their playmates among neighbor children. A fifty-five-year-old woman, daughter of a count, recalled that when she was a young girl she lived temporarily in an area where she heard the sound of neighbors for the first time in her life. Neighbor children came to invite her to join them in play, but she did not know how to respond. She was curious about them and enjoyed watching them, but she had no wish to participate in their play. That the lack of neighborly contact may have had something to do with the Gakushuin subculture was suggested by a daughter of a baron: she somehow lost the freedom of playing with neighbor children when she began to attend Gakushuin.

The only neighbors whose names and homes my informants remembered were fellow kazoku, Gakushuin classmates, high government officials, financial giants, and the like. All this is consistent with the previously stated geographical clustering of kazoku residences in selective areas. When there was contact with neighbors, the usual characteristics of neighborliness – such as mutual and easy visibility, unannounced visits, mutual help in emergencies and so on – were missing. 'There was no easy way of having *tsukiai* (interaction) with your neighbors. You couldn't just drop in, saying "Hi, here I am!"' Even between classmates it was impossible, I was told, to visit one another at home on the spur of the moment: parents on both sides had to be informed first, and then visiting was scheduled. An adult visitor was bound, not only by such an appointment rule, but by the dress code and gift-giving obligation. All this class-bound tsukiai was devoid of the 'natural,' informal, spontaneous sociability typical of shitamachi or rural neighborhoods. One of the old institutions essential to shitamachi neighborliness is the public bathhouse, where bathers enjoy 'naked' tsukiai. Yamanote also has public bathhouses, and many club houses built by ward governments for the elderly have bathing facilities in them. A ninety-one-year-old woman of kuge origin, married to a wealthy commoner, would shudder, said her daughter-in-law in response to my suggestion, at the idea of bathing together with neighbors.

No household being self-sufficient, seclusion was far from complete, and in fact there were constant interchanges between inside and outside the house but only in a way minimizing the free exposure of the family to the outer world. Routine domestic labor was supplied internally by a pool of servants, and specialized services such as hairdressing were provided by regularly hired professionals. Necessary goods like food and clothing were delivered by house-calling sales clerks (*goyōkiki*) of certain stores. Not a few informants recalled their curiosity about such salesmen, hairdressers, or gardeners as the only 'windows' to the outside.

Even when members of the kazoku family had to go out, exposure to the outside world was curtailed, first, by means of transportation. To commute to school, go shopping, or visit any other place, many of my informants walked, if the distance was short enough, or took public transportation, 'like everyone else.' If the train was divided by grades, they were likely to take a higher-class car. High-ranking and wealthy families used private transportation. Historically, the vehicles changed from early Meiji on (see Seidensticker 1983), and my informants talked about their family-owned vehicles shifting from horse carriages to *jinrikisha* (rickshaw) to automobiles. Today, car ownership is no longer a status symbol, but in pre-war Japan it was a special luxury.

It may sound strange, but private transportation was another factor inhibiting access to the outside world. The vehicles were driven by a privately employed driver who usually lived within or near the family compound and who thus served as a guard as well as a driver. The most adventurous mischief a girl could perpetrate was to steal a moment to get away from the watchful eyes of a servant driver. Under these conditions, it was difficult to meet people outside, even one's own kin. The wife of a count, seventy-six years old, recalled that, after marriage, she was not free to visit her mother, ironically because she had to be chauffeured around wherever she went. Apparently, she was bound by the idea that married women belonged exclusively to their husbands and in-laws and therefore could see their natal kin only surreptitiously. It was not until World War II, when she lost this private convenience and had to use trains, that she acquired freedom of mobility and contact.

Whether one walked or took private or public transportation, the most commonly practiced pattern was chaperonage. Servants escorted the children from home to school and back home, at least up to about the third grade but in some cases throughout high school, much to the embarrassment of their charges. In the case of a female servant, she waited sewing in an escorts' room (*tomo-machi beya*) of the school until the end of the school day. Daughters were not the only ones chaperoned; some families assigned male escorts to their young sons. Adults, too, were shepherded by servants. In shopping, it was the accompanying servant who discharged all the actual transactions with store clerks, leaving the master or mistress aloof from or ignorant about money. Even the newly-wed couple was escorted by an entourage on their honeymoon, said some of my older informants chuckling. After the last escort servant was lost, 'I still kept forgetting to carry a wallet.'

Kazoku women, and to a lesser extent, men, too, even when they stepped out of the house, were thus insulated from the outside world, precisely because the private transportation and chaperonage kept them from being left alone. Insulation and the lack of privacy were two sides of the same coin. Only through the war and postwar collapse of the old hierarchy did they gain unrestrained freedom for external self-exposure and privacy. It might be noted that insulation, while a constraint, was also a protection. The protective function was sometimes fulfilled to conceal 'embarrassments.' One of my informants had a mentally retarded brother who was protected from public exposure by being educated and cared for at a school built privately by the family.

The selectivity of destinations for commuting or traveling further inhibited exposure. A large majority of the children attended Gakushuin. Some parents chose other schools, but these were similarly exclusive, catering to the upper or upper-middle class, and therefore they also narrowly circumscribed classmate contact.

Traveling away from Tokyo meant staying at private resort villas or prominent hotels that accepted regular patrons only. Kazoku shopped at particular stores where the head managers would meet and attend the elite shoppers; occasional eating out meant going to special restaurants or hotels; and reputable theaters provided entertainment. Most often mentioned were the Mitsukoshi department store at Nihonbashi, the Imperial Hotel, Tokyo Clubhouse, Imperial Theater, Seiyōken (the first Western hotel, built in 1867 in Tsukiji – the initial district for settlement by foreigners[3] – which later opened a Western restaurant in Ueno) – places that are no longer elitist but used to appeal to the yamanote taste. The Peers' Clubhouse (Kazoku Kaikan) was another center of recreation of kazoku families. For hospitalization, St. Luke's (in Tsukiji) and imperially sponsored Red Cross hospitals were mentioned most.

The Domestic Space

The foregoing discussion on seclusion was concerned with boundaries between a kazoku person and the external world, external in a double sense to his/her household and to his/her status. Attention is now called inward to spatial boundaries within the residential premises. It will be shown that the above seclusion from the external sphere was reproduced within the domestic sphere.

One can imagine the magnitude of the previous estates of the kazoku from what have replaced them; school campuses, parks, golf courses, government buildings, foreign embassies, rental office buildings, hospitals, hotels, art galleries, sports arenas, wedding halls, new billionnaires' dwellings, condominia, and so on. The group of 'Prince Hotels,' owned by a parvenu family, the Tsutsumi, is indeed, in part, a replacement of estates of the imperial house, royal princes, and kazoku. According to one prince, his family had a lot of 30,000-*tsubo*, which roughly corresponds to 1 million square feet (1 tsubo equals 35.5 square feet). The prewar main premises of my kazoku informants ranged widely from one extreme of 100,000 tsubo to the other of less than 100 tsubo, but most stood between some thousands to several hundreds of tsubo. One of the largest main estates (commanding 38,000 tsubo) employed twenty-two gardeners. In addition, many of them had resort villas on the Shōnan seashores (e.g., Hayama, Zushi, Kamakura, Oiso) or highlands (Karuizawa, Nasu, etc.) as well as other real estate. The Maeda, the richest of all kazoku, owned, in addition to a 50,000-tsubo main residential estate (a large part of which comprises the present Komaba Park of Meguro ward), secondary estates (*bettei*) in Kamakura, Karuizawa, and Kanazawa (the castle town of its former province), ranches and forests in Hokkaido, and more lands in Kyoto and Korea (Sakai 1982, 120). Some of the new kazoku did very well, too, taking over old daimyō estates. Haru Reischauer (1986) writes

Table 1. Land areas in prewar and present ownership

Total area (tsubo)	*Prewar owners (N)*	*Present owners (N)*
100 or fewer	7	35
500 or fewer	16	32
1,000 or fewer	13	5
5,000 or fewer	21	6
10,000 or fewer	6	1
50,000 or fewer	7	1
100,000 or fewer	1	0
200,000 or fewer	1	0
600,000 or fewer	1	0
N. Total respondents	73	80

Note: 1 acre = 1,224 *tsubo*; 10,000 *tsubo* = 8.6 acres.

that Matsukata Masayoshi, her grandfather, who rose from a modest samurai to count and eventually to prince, owned, in addition to the residential house in Shiba ward, which had formerly belonged to Matsudaira Sadanobu, a famous daimyō, a twenty-two-acre lot (called Matsukata Hill) in Azabu ward (1986, 104–105), summer homes in Kamakura, and 4,000 acres of wasteland in Nasuno, which was developed into farms, pastures, forests, and the like (117–118).

In a questionnaire, I asked about prewar and present land ownership. Several respondents did not know the prewar ownership, and more respondents, now living in condominia or rental housing, wrote 'none' for present ownership. For a comparison, only those responses that indicated some forms of private landownership are tabulated. Table 1 compares the total areas of land owned, including nonresidential lands, during the two periods.

The seventy-three prewar owners held on average approximately 16,700 tsubo each. Some had very extensive holdings, including several estates and/or forests combined. The postwar reduction is phenomenal, the average of the present eighty owners being roughly seven hundred tsubo, 4.2 percent of the prewar figure. Since the sample excludes apartment or rental dwellers, the actual percentage is even lower.[4]

The imperial house surpassed all in the possession of estates. As of 1937, it controlled roughly 627 million tsubo (over one-half million acres), including the central Tokyo palace (637,170 tsubo; 520.5 acres), eleven secondary or detached palaces, and many forests, which were a main source of its 'private' revenue (Kodama 1978, 314–315).

The kazoku main dwelling in Tokyo consisted typically of two architecturally distinct parts – Japanese- and Western-styled – either as two separate houses (*nihonkan* and *yōkan*) or as two sections of a single house. While there were purely Japanese houses, some kazoku, including the Maeda, had an entirely Western house. This is one of the visible indications of how yamanote residents, upper class in particular, in contrast to the conservative, poorer shitamachi people, were influenced by the Meiji slogan of 'Civilization and Enlightenment' and lured into the Western way of life, which in turn sharpened their status distinction. And this is why many kazoku houses, after the war, were commandeered to serve as lodgings for high officers of the Occupation forces. It might be noted in this conjunction that the heart of 'high city' where kazoku residences congregated has been densely populated by foreign nationals and embassies.

The Three-Dimensional Boundaries

The spatial demarcation of residence was multidimensional, geographically, and symbolically marked. The boundaries were associated with the ranks, functions, or sex of the occupants. I detect three partially overlapping dimensions even though these do not completely match the mental map held by my informants. The first was the universally recognizable 'vertical opposition.' Some areas of the premises were conceptualized as low and marked off from high areas. The personnel of the pre-modern imperial court, for example, used to be dichotomized between *den-jōbito* (literally, 'people up on the palace floor,' namely, nobles who were allowed into the emperor's living quarters) and *jige* ('down on the ground,' i.e., non-noble retainers).

The kazoku family occupied the upper domain (*kami*), the servants the lower domain (*shimo*). These vertical terms referred both to the areas and their respective occupants – master family and servants. Within the family, the uppermost area was quarters for the head of the household (and his wife); it was some distance from the nursery, which was at the lower end of the upper domain; in some households the head of the household or the family as a whole was designated *o-kami* from the humble standpoint of a servant (shimo).[5] Servants, maid-servants in particular, who as a whole constituted the shimo domain, were further broken down into kami and shimo: upper maids (*kami-jochū*) attended the master family; lower maids had little contact with the master family; they (*shimo-jochū*) worked around the kitchen and/or waited upon the upper maids. The living room and bedrooms of the head and his wife thus constituted the uppermost area, the kitchen area the lowermost. Occupancy varied with time: involving shifts and bedtime. Kami-jochū, for example, belonged to two levels: while attending the master family they waited for calls in a room close to the uppermost quarters, and therefore they were designated *otsugi* (the adjacent room);[6] at bedtime, they would withdraw, except one on duty in some cases, into the maids' living quarters, which was another lower point of the domestic space.

The vertical opposition, universally recognizable, sounds simple, but it remains largely metaphorical. What is more important and what complicates the spatial analysis is the lateral opposition of *omote* and *oku*, which was interlocked with the vertical opposition of kami and shimo in an intricate fashion. Vertical metaphor in fact translated into the literally physical space spreading laterally. The boundary between omote and oku to which every informant drew attention in describing his/her residence turned out not to be so sharp and self-evident as it appeared in the informant's mental map. In the intricacy of this boundary lies, I argue, a clue to the Japanese conception of ascribed hierarchy.

Omote and oku may be translated as 'front' and 'interior' respectively. The front versus interior opposition appeared as a logical dichotomy to my informants for good reasons. First, the two sections were architecturally separated, situated either in two distinct parts of a single house, removed from each other and connected by a long hallway, or in two separate buildings. Further, the dichotomy between omote and oku was strongly associated with the sex of occupants of the respective spaces: the omote refers not only to the frontal space but also to male servants, and the oku to female servants of the interior. The omote versus oku opposition further corresponded to that of the 'public' versus the 'private' sector of the house. The omote staff managed the house in relation to the outside world, and thus the space was also called 'office'; the oku staff was in charge of the private life of the kazoku family.

The question is where the master family belonged in this lateral dimension, or how the vertical dimension of kami/shimo was related to the omote/oku dimension. It would make no sense to say that kami is to shimo what omote is to oku because the kami person, the lord of the house in particular, belonged to both oku and omote. Conversely, some of the lowest personnel seem to have belonged neither to omote nor to oku. The confusion is untangled when the omote/oku opposition is further broken down into two subdimensions. The opposite of the front is not the interior but the rear, and the opposite of the interior is the exterior, not the front. The two dimensions are thus restated as front/rear (*omote/ura*) and interior/exterior (*uchi/soto*). These two can then be neatly paralleled with the above/below (*kami/shimo*) dimension: there were rough alignments between above, front, and interior on the one hand, and below, rear, and exterior on the other.

Figure 1 implies that the uppermost person (the head of the house) belonged to the innermost and frontmost domains whereas the lowest person (janitor or kitchen maid) occupied the outermost or the rearmost areas.[7] Other residents intermediary in status, whether family or servants, would find themselves somewhere in between in variable permutations of the three dimensions. While assigned to one domain for usual occupancy, there were varying degrees of freedom or obligation to cross the boundary. An upper maid was in the interior, as mentioned above, in attendance to the master and family; hence she was called *oku-jochū*[8] (interior maids) or otsugi as well as kami-jochū; but she would retire at night to her living quarters closer to the exterior or rear, unless she slept by a child in her charge (Lebra 1990). An upper managerial male servant, usually occupying the exterior, would be privileged to enter the interior to discuss 'public' affairs with the master. Among the 'exterior' personnel, some were higher, closer to the front, with greater access to the interior, than others, like rickshaw pullers, who were closer to the rear pole.

While some personnel were free on occasion to cross the boundaries, rules of segregation were otherwise adhered to. Between the interior and exterior there were various degrees of sex segregation, more strict among high-ranking or traditional kazoku. During the night in particular, sex segregation was stringently enforced, as symbolized in some households by a special door, opening from one to the other region, which was locked at night from the interior side.

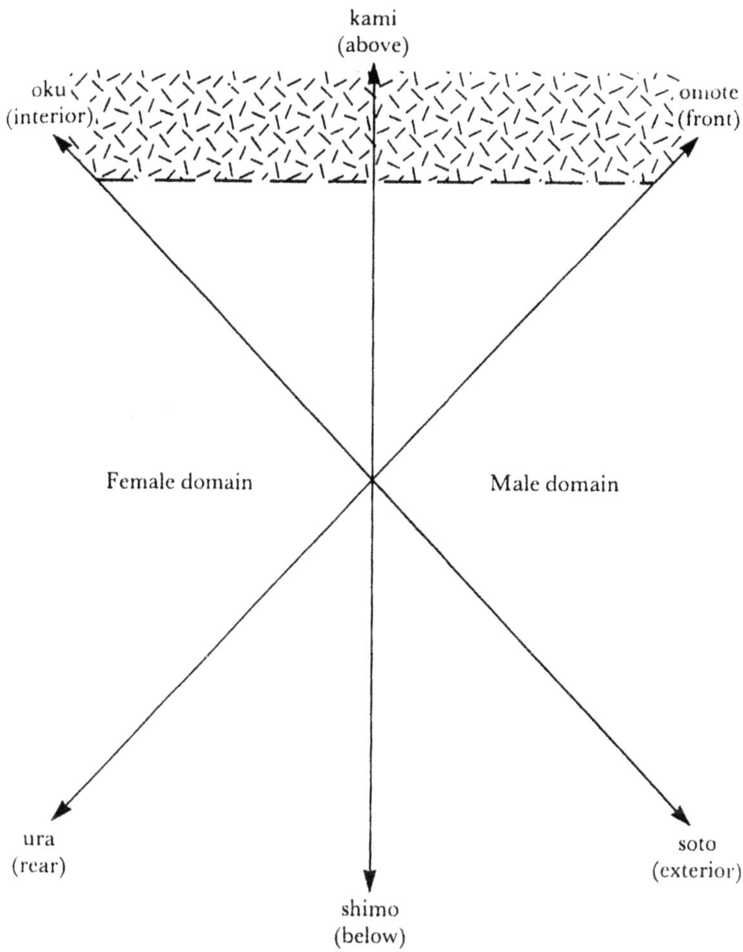

Figure 1. The tri-dimensional hierarchy of space

All boundaries for segregation give rise to marginals or anomalies. The interior versus exterior sex segregation produced an anomalous situation for male members of the family occupying the female domain, the interior. The head of the household, the foremost example of such anomaly, was exempted from the segregation code (indeed he was *the* innermost person) for a reason to be stated below, but sons were not. In some households, especially shogunal and high-ranking daimyō houses, sons at age seven (the supposedly marginal stage when a child was still totally dependent upon his parents and interior maids and yet began to assume sexual identity) were, according to the Confucian decree (*Danjo nana-sai ni shite seki o onajū sezu*), removed from the interior to the exterior to be waited upon by young male attendants called *shosei* (student-servant) or removed to all-male dorms away from home

(Lebra 1990). Complete removal of a son from the interior was rarely practiced, however. A son's marginality was well exemplified by a royal informant whose ordinary day was marked by crossing the boundary inward and outward: in the morning, the prince would wake up in his exterior bedroom, enter the interior to have breakfast with his family, go to Gakushuin, come home after school, study and play in the exterior, go back to the interior for dinner and stay there until bedtime, and sleep in the exterior.

Sex segregation was related to the difference in marital status between male and female servants. The male staff, except the shosei, were married and commuted to the office from their private residences ('tenements') provided by the master and situated on the periphery or in the vicinity of the premises. The female servants, unmarried, lived and slept within the interior to be available for calls around the clock.[9]

In conjunction with the interior-exterior sex segregation, there was a rule of vertical segregation within the interior. Lower areas, closer to the rear, were tabooed to higher persons (as higher, front areas were tabooed to lower). Women informants in particular recalled rooms they would not go near. Servants' quarters were avoided by the master family, especially the head and his wife. The wife, coming from another family, thus often knew nothing about the rooms and hallways reserved for the maids whereas the children, who were more free to move about, were more informed about the house design. This kind of spatial taboo was more rigid for the lowest section of the house, centered on the kitchen. A daughter of a wealthy baron recalled having been told not to walk by the kitchen. When she had to, she ran fast. There was no exchange of words between the lady of the house and lower servants. A daughter of a kuge-prince, married to a royal prince, did not know where the kitchen was and never talked with either the kitchen maids or the janitors. One day, she accidentally caught sight of a kitchen maid, who, too frightened either to bow or to run away, froze with her face turned away. No wonder that many informants could not give the exact number of house servants, 'because I don't know how many lower maids we had.'

The spatial taboo was reciprocated by the servants. They stayed away from the rooms occupied by the master except when they were in attendance. The head of the house seated in the uppermost/innermost room was spoken to by a servant kneeling outside the room behind the door.

Here, too, we come across anomalies such as old-time concubines, known as *oharasan* (uterine ladies) or, again in a spatial metaphor, as *sokushitsu* or *owaki* ('side room' ladies). When a concubine mothered the heir, her status was raised from that of an attendant, but not all the way up to the kami. She was residing elsewhere, but when she visited her 'master's' house, she had no room to occupy, 'neither in the otsugi nor okami section' and so was found 'standing around the hallway.' Her spatial marginality was sometimes translated into a seated position and posture, as recalled by a woman whose father-in-law, the head of a collateral royal house, was mothered by a uterine lady: 'Every one of us was seated in a chair, but this woman [when she visited us] alone sat on the floor and knelt, thanking. Members of the family all referred to her by her maiden name without *San*.' The uterine lady occupied the same space as the master family, but at the same time her body, posture, and speech were telling that she did not belong 'upstairs.'

Kitchen maids personified the lowest end in the vertical opposition, as well as the rearmost position in the front-rear opposition. At the same time, they were marginal to the interior-exterior boundary, and thus spatially uncertain. According to a shogunal descendant, they were 'loitering around the kitchen area as if there was no fixed place to belong to.'

The outdoor area of the premises was also subject to the segregation code. Some daughters were not even allowed to step out into the garden unless escorted by servants; playing within the grounds, most sons and daughters found playmates among the children of the exterior staff, but some of them were forbidden to have such contact. There were boundaries in the premises inside which kazoku children were confined, the area of the servants' tenements being especially tabooed (which taboo only tempted some daring children to break it).

The Front-Interior Double Occupancy

Thus far no question has been raised about the seemingly contradictory nature of the master's double occupancy of the frontmost and innermost regions. Hosting distinguished guests or being invited as one of such guests was among the most regular activities of the head of a kazoku house. Banquets and entertainments were held in the frontmost section of the house, namely, the reception hall built away from the interior, as well as in the landscaped garden (for a 'garden party'). In consideration of foreign dignitaries or the Westernized royals and peers to be invited, some households would use the Western-style section or house primarily for such receptions. Accompanied by his wife, the master was most conspicuously present in the frontal section when hosting an entertainment or ceremony. The personnel in both the exterior and interior were mobilized to prepare the master (and lady) to present himself in the front.

Symbolic of the front-rear hierarchy was the rank order of entrance gates and doors. The front gate, leading to the main entrance door, was reserved for the household head and his prominent guests; the lowest rear gate, which was behind the kitchen door, was for the lowest-ranking servants or outsiders like fish or produce venders. Others – such as lesser members of the family, lesser guests, sellers of more 'clean' goods such as candy and clothing – used one of the side or 'inner' gates, which ranked somewhere between these two extremes. The importance of the gate hierarchy to the sense of order can be inferred from the complaint of a woman quoted by her niece: 'It used to be that only my father-in-law and husband walked through the Grand Gate. But now everything is mixed up and confused.'[10]

The lateral hierarchy of front versus rear thus correlates with the vertical hierarchy of above versus below. The structure of 'above : below : front : rear' is also found in the models presented by Schwartz (1981) and Feinberg (1988) respectively. What does look problematical in the Japanese case is the addition of another lateral hierarchy: interior versus exterior. The lord of the house, while seated in the front and thus on display face-to-face with distinguished outsiders, was also the resident of the innermost region of his household, hidden from outside. Even within a front-staged reception room, the highest person was seated at the innermost center. In this connection one might recall that in a samurai movie the hierarchy is best dramatized by an extremely elongated hall where rows of vassals seated according to ranks prostrate themselves toward the lord, who is hardly visible, sitting at the farthest inner end.

For the hereditary elite, royal and noble alike, the double occupancy of the ceremonial front and the hidden interior was inevitable. First of all, the status of the hereditary elite was both public and private – public because of their symbolic eminence in the national hierarchy, private because their status was deeply rooted in the family, kinship, ancestry, 'blood.' In other words, the public status presented in the front domain was inseparable from the family life led in the innermost domain protected from the public view. In this connection, it is significant that guests were categorized differently, according to a daimyō-viscount, on the basis of the above duality of hereditary status: public guests – high officials, kazoku peers, royals, foreign ambassadors and ministers, and so on – were invited into the formal reception hall (front); private guests – kin of the master family – were privileged into the parlor of the interior for intimate contact. Visitors lower on both scales (public status and kinship proximity), those who were neither public enough nor private enough – such as low-ranking former vassals or tradesmen – were met and dealt with in the lower guest rooms attached to the exterior and hosted by the house staff, not the head of the household.

The front-interior separation is unavoidable or even necessary also as a matter of presentational strategy familiar to us through Goffman's writing in dramaturgical sociology. To play a ceremonial role on the front stage effectively requires the concealment from the audience of what goes on behind the stage. Writing about the British royalty, Hayden (1987) discusses the monarch's 'two bodies' – 'body natural' and 'body politic' – which should be kept apart. 'The Queen's body politic is relentlessly on display' while 'Her body natural is assiduously hidden by 'the impenetrable secrecy' of the Palace' (1987, 11). The natural body is manifested, to put it in Douglas' down-to-earth terms, by 'organic eruption' such as excretion, vomiting, spitting. The 'purity rule' is to keep nature from culture, organic from social (Douglas 1975, 213). One might add 'erotic eruption,' which could require multiple bedchambers within the interior, as in the case of polygyny[11] practiced by my informants' forebears. For Elias (1978), concealment of the natural body and its functions from the public self amounted to the 'civilizing process' marking modern European history.

The front-interior separation was all the more necessary for the eminently public elite, who played a central role on the front stage and therefore needed extra relaxation offstage. The natural body had to be protected as much as the public body, through the separation of the two bodies.

DYARCHY

What does all this add up to in terms of the overall hierarchy? Because of the omote-oku double occupancy, royalty or aristocrats necessarily depended upon the retinue to mediate between spheres. As a front-stage, ceremonial actor, the master had to be propped up and guided by the stage producers. As an occupant of the interior, he depended upon exterior personnel and outside counselors to manage his external affairs and relations. Furthermore, his positional interiority often even kept him from playing a front role, and this spatial dilemma stemming from double occupancy was resolved by the institutionalized surrogacy by kin or head servants. The 'surrogate worship' (*godaïhai*) at the ancestor shrines or temples was a major responsibility of the head maid in high-ranking kazoku households. In the imperial household, a chamberlain on duty does the same at the palace shrine every morning as the surrogate for the emperor, and imperial messengers (*chokushi*) are sent out from time to time in the same capacity of imperial surrogacy to the Ise shrine and other imperially sponsored shrines (*chokusaisha*) and temples away from the capital.

The lord master was thus more or less kept out of touch from or control of the 'real' space which lay 'down below,' 'outside,' or 'behind.' This was all the more true, the higher the position and therefore the more interiorized its holder was. It followed, then, that the 'authority' of the master – unless he was an unusually strong character determined to make decisions and exercise authority by himself, to be autonomous, and thus to deviate from the conventional norm of the ascribed elite – was destined to become ritualistic, symbolic, or empty. Actual decisions tended to be made, power to be exercised, budgets to be allocated, the stage to be 'produced,' by the high-ranking subordinates who were free to move between exterior and interior, front and rear, up and down. A typical lord would leave everything to his subordinates, telling them, as the cliche goes, 'Do it as you think best' (*yoki ni hakarae*). It was this situation that gave rise to a dyarchy with duocephaly – a symbolic head and a managerial or operational head.

Against the backdrop of dyarchy, it is understandable that informants held ambivalent feelings toward their former servants. On the one hand, the latter were recalled with warmth as having been helpful, caring, loyal, dependable, indispensable, more intimate than one's family, and so on. The prosperity of the house was generously credited to the loyalty and managerial acumen of the staff. The master-servant bond is still surviving, in some cases, into the descendant generations, even though their contemporary socioeconomic statuses may well have been reversed.

On the other hand, negative remarks were heard as frequently. The head maid was recalled as domineering, more oppressive to a bride than the worst example of mother-in-law, and the top manager was resented as laying an iron hand over budgetary matters, overruling the master's request. 'In those days, the lord could say nothing to his employee-subordinates,' said a daimyō-countess regarding her father-in-law. What went on backstage or outside the premises was kept secret until a household crisis erupted. Post-war bankruptcy was attributed, in addition to the extraordinary property taxes and the loss of status privileges, to the managerial servants who took advantage of the master's financial naïveté, and 'cheated' and 'robbed' him. These contrasting views of the former subordinates reflect two different roles played by one party of the dyarchy in relation to the other: supportive and complementary on the one hand, expropriative and usurpatory on the other.[12]

The dyarchy took a dramatic form with the imperial institution because the emperor represented the unparalleled charisma of the hereditary status. While required to be spatially split, the body is nevertheless 'indivisible' (Giddens 1984), needless to say, and it was in the indivisible body that the hereditary charisma resided. The general tendency would then be to isolate the charismatic body by pushing it further inward. In other words, interiority tended to encompass the other dimensions.[13]

Generally, then, the responsibilities involving decisions and executions that were vested in the status holder would have to be left to his subordinate surrogate. Spatially, if one was confined in the interior and front, the other dominated the exterior, rear, and, above all, intermediary areas. One embodied the status, the other implemented it; one authenticated the decision made and executed by the other. Historical examples of dyarchy are legion and at many levels, notably the emperor and his regent, a shogun and his regent, the imperial court and shogunal government, a *shoen* proprietor and local manager, a daimyō and his chief vassal, the emperor and *genrō*. One represented symbolic/cultural hegemony, the other politico-economic domination. We can extend this type of dyarchy to the aristocratically affiliated *iemoto*, schools of art. An iemoto was (and still is in some cases) topped by a court noble who does not practice the art as authenticator of professional licenses; classes are actually taught and led by the practicing iemoto master of the art (Lebra 1991).

The two parties were interdependent, complementary, or instrumental to one another, but the duplex arrangement also opened the way to a reversal of the hierarchical order to the point of virtual subversion or usurpation. Nevertheless, the formal structure of dyarchy was not destroyed, neither party supplanted the other to claim a *mono-archy* – a true monarchy. Again the imperial institution provides the best illustration. The imperial authority was expropriated, but not annihilated. The Tokugawa ruler could and did demonstrate the shogunal hegemony over the imperial court, and yet even at the peak of its power, he needed *shōgun senge*, the imperial authorization for shogunal investiture. The murder of an emperor did not mean that the murderer wanted to put an end to the 'sun dynasty' but to replace the victim by another member of the same family. Emperor Hirohito, supposedly targeted by ultramilitarists, would have been replaced by Prince Chichibu, his brother. The dyarchy contributed to the preservation of the 'symbolic capital' (Bourdieu 1977) carried by the imperial dynasty. The Japanese monarchy thus may be said to owe its place as the world's longest-lived dynasty to the *dy*archy itself, whereas a true *mon*archy would have been shortlived.

It was the purpose of this essay to throw light upon this historical legacy of dyarchy from the standpoint of the spatial demarcation of hereditary hierarchy. The hereditary elite was characterized as an embodiment of the 'public' eminence on the one hand and of the private identity embedded in kinship and ancestry on the other. This duality was represented by the spatial oppositions of residence such as interior-exterior and front-rear. The head of the house as the hereditary-status holder was to divide his indivisible body between the front-public and interior-private space, with a strain toward interiorization. It was concluded that the spatially constrained charisma of hereditary status contributed to the production and reproduction of the dyarchy. It might be speculated that the dyarchical legacy explains the cultural survival (or revival) of the hereditary status of the nobility and royalty, a status that is legally, politically, and economically empty.

NOTES

The long-term research that underlies this essay has been supported at various stages by the joint Committee on Japanese Studies of the American Council of Learned Societies and the Social Science Research Council, the Japan Foundation, the University of Hawaii Japan Studies Endowment, the University of Hawaii Fujio Matsuda Scholar award, and the Wenner-Gren Foundation. I wish to take this opportunity to express my heavy sense of indebtedness.

1. Robben (1989) analyzes the domestic space in a Brazilian fishing community. Employing Bourdieu's 'practice' theory, the author connects the domestic architecture with 'sea' and 'street,' the private with the public space. I find it a good demonstration of the productivity of domestic-space analysis.

2. Through the Restoration, the daimyō lost most but not all of their domainal wealth in terms of rice revenue. The retention of even a fraction showed the significance of the pre-Restoration estate, so that a bigger daimyō house was that much wealthier than a smaller one after the Restoration. Further, with the fraction that was later commuted into bonds and cash, some daimyō houses reemerged with enormous wealth through well-advised investment and financial management (mismanagement threw some others into bankruptcy). No longer a domainal lord, the former daimyō possessed such wealth as his 'private' property.

3. This is a good example of the discrepancy between the status symbolic meaning and the physical location of the yamanote-shitamachi division. Tsukiji is a definitely shitamachi district, but in early Meiji it emerged as a geographical forerunner of 'Civilization and Enlightenment' because it was selected for foreign settlement, to cater to the Westernized yamanote taste.

4. Even the prewar figures show how little land the Japanese aristocracy commanded, compared, for example, with their British counterpart who own(ed) tens of thousands of acres. One thousand acres (more than 1 million tsubo) would be 'not much' for a British baron (Perrott 1968, 34) but would be beyond a dream for most Japanese princes.

5. The term *okami* was used for the late Shōwa emperor privately by his entourage as well as by the empress. The same term was used for kazoku household heads according to several informants. (Likewise, *ue-sama* was also used for a top person like the shōgun, *ue* being identical to kami as *shita* to shimo). Kami also means gods. Resemblance between a god and a high-status personage can be also shown in the usage of *miya*, which means both a shrine and royal person. Such resemblance stems from spatial symbolism.

6. This is one meaning of *otsugi* given by several informants; another was suggested in vertical terms as 'second to or lower than the head maid.'

7. While a janitor's low position is understandable in view of the location of refuse collection at the rear end, outdoors, of the premises, why a kitchen maid was so low may not be as obvious. The kitchen was subdivided between the section, often with a lowered floor, closest to the rear door, where rice was cooked, and the more frontal section with an elevated floor, which was occupied by the male chef in command of assistant cooks engaging in 'professional' cooking. The kitchen maid(s) specialized in rice cooking and thus was called *meshitaki* (rice cooker); she may have also cleaned bathrooms. It is interesting that the upper-class households considered rice cooking unskilled, peripheral to the whole repertoire of culinary art, and thus to be relegated to the *hashitame*, lowly maids. Some aristocratic daughters were tutored in fanciful French or Chinese cookery, but they had no idea how to cook rice. For middle-to-lower-class women, rice cooking was a skilled job to be mastered as a required curriculum for bridal training. This class difference may reflect the differential weight of rice itself as a staple.

8. In a household where the hierarchy of maids was more elaborated, the term *oku-jochū* was reserved for the head maid, also known as *jijo-gashira* or *rōjo*, who supervised the whole female retinue and/or carried an exclusive right to wait upon the head of the house.
9. From this circumstance one can surmise the vulnerability of a maid to sexual 'harassment' by a male member of the family unless the segregation rule was imposed. The rule was less stringent among court nobles (*kuge*) than warriors (*buke*). A son of a prominent kuge kazoku, viewing the family history with a scholarly detachment, discussed how his ancestors typically had experienced sex in their adolescence with live-in maids-in-attendance, called *ie nyōbō*, long before their formal marriage with noblewomen. Pregnancy led to the discharge of the 'hand-laid' maid, and the child thus born out of wedlock was, according to this informant, dumped into certain Buddhist temples as a priest or nun. The informant thus disclosed the mundane side of prestigious royal or noble temples, commonly called *monzeki*.
10. The symbolic significance of entrances and doors was noted by a student of Victorian England's aristocracy as well. 'All business and trade inquiries went to the back door. The front door was opened by a servant correctly mannered and dressed to suit the status of the family … In larger houses, the Servants Hall was sometimes used to hold special categories who were halfway between back and front door status, e.g., the doctor, schoolmaster, important tradesmen or unimportant kin' (Davidoff 1973, 87).
11. 'Polygyny' is not quite an accurate term since there was clear status inequality between the principal wife and secondary consorts.
12. This argument has some implications for male-female relations. The imperial and aristocratic world was definitely male-centered, and yet women played important roles, as shown in this essay, for good reasons. We have seen how the master was placed in the innermost section of the residence, which was also a predominantly female domain. The male master depended upon female servants to take care of his corporeal needs. Some male servants, too, helped the master in similar capacities, but it was taken for granted that women were better equipped for domestic caretaking chores. (It might be further footnoted here that female service seems indispensable for gods' well-being also. Closest to the Amaterasu of the palace shrine, it turns out, are female ritualists, called *naishōten*, who, according to an informant, 'as caretakers' could enter the *nainaijin*, the holiest and innermost chamber, which was off limits even to the emperor.) The kazoku recollections suggest that the master's overall dependency made some higher-ranking maids, head maids in particular, quite powerful and domineering. Can we speculate, then, that all-around servility, as embodied by a female servant, or even a housewife in the commoner class, may lead to a reversal of hierarchy, in this limited sense, between male master and female servant or between husband and wife?
13. An analogy may be drawn from a Shintō god in that the interiorized, hidden emperor was like a god whose presence, forever invisible is symbolized by a shrine. Even when the god is brought out to make a tour around the community under his jurisdiction in an annual festival, he is transferred by a mystic rite from his residential shrine into a temporary portable shrine (*mikoshi*) with no moment of exposure. This kind of spatial confinement of a god is likely to have magical implications because invisibility is a genesis of supernatural potency, as argued by Luhrmann (1989). As if to ensure invisibility and thereby maximize magical efficacy, mystic Shintō rites are conducted in the dark, during the night or before dawn. Like a god confined in the hidden interior of a shrine, the emperor was in no position to use his potency, instead only to have it available to a magician who was outside the shrine, or, in a Japanese metaphor, by 'the carrier of the mikoshi,' who invoked to his advantage the name of the august one inside and invisible.

Not that emperors were voiceless like gods. The Shōwa emperor expressed his opinions for or against what went on outside the palace, oftentimes in his name, by means of *gokamon* (imperial questioning) (Titus 1974). He did so, however, only through his closest entourage (*sokkin*) like the lord keeper of the seal, genrō, and grand chamberlain. The sokkin not only represented the emperor but influenced his will and coached his conduct – and for this reason were targeted for assassination as *kunsoku no kan* (evil men of the imperial entourage) by the radical right wing of military officers, culminating in the February 26, 1936, coup. Even at the *gozen kaigi* (the nonconstitutional conferences, in the emperor's presence, of topmost state leaders to make important decisions to determine the state's destiny), the emperor was there to listen, not to speak, or only to authenticate, not to make, decisions by his presence. Frustrated, the Shōwa emperor attempted to speak up but was politely discouraged by the sokkin, or if he did speak against the sokkin's advice, he was gently overruled by the conferees.

As has been well documented (Kido 1966, 1223–1224; The Pacific War Research Society 1968, 34–35), the Shōwa emperor broke the tacit rule of silence to have his voice heard and heeded on August 10, 1945, at the gozen kaigi to decide whether Japan should accept or reject the Potsdam Proclamation. He could do so because Prime Minister Suzuki solicited His Majesty's opinion to break the tie in the vote.

REFERENCES

Bourdieu, Pierre. 1977. *Outline of a Theory of Practice*. Cambridge: Cambridge University Press.

Davidoff, Leonore. 1973. *The Best Circles: Women and Society in Victorian England*. Totowa, N.J.: Rowman and Littlefield.

Douglas, Mary. 1975. *Implicit Meanings: Essays in Anthropology*. London: Routledge & Kegan Paul.

Elias, Norbert. 1978. *The History of Manners*. Vol. 1: *The Civilizing Process*, translated by E. Jephcott. New York: Pantheon Books.

Feinberg, Richard. 1988. 'Socio-Spatial Symbolism and the Logic of Rank on Two Polynesian Outliers.' *Ethnology* 27: 291–310.

Giddens, Anthony. 1984. 'The Constitution of Society.' *Outline of the Theory of Structuration*, Cambridge: Polity Press.

Hayden, Ilse. 1987. *Symbol and Privilege: The Ritual Context of British Royalty*. Tucson: University of Arizona Press.

Inukai Tomoko. 1989. *Tomoko no nihon suteki sengen* (Tomoko's discovery of Japan's wonders). Tokyo: Jōhō Sentā Shuppankyoku.

Jichishō Gyōseikyoku (Administrative Bureau, Home Ministry), ed. 1984. *Zenkoku-jinkō: setaisū-hyō, jinkō dōtai-hyō*. (The national population: tables of households and demographic trends). Tokyo: Kokudo Chiri Kyōkai.

Kasumi-Kaikan, ed. 1982–1984. *Kazoku kakei taisei* (The complete compilation of kazoku genealogies). 2 vols. Tokyo: Yoshikawa Kōbunkan.

Kido Kōichi. 1966. *Kido Kōichi nikki* (The diary of Kido Kōichi). 2 vols. Tokyo: Tokyo Daigaku Shuppankai.

Kōbata Yoshiko. 1984. *Akasaka monogatari* (The tale of Akasaka). Tokyo: Aki Shobō.

Kodama, Kōta. 1978. *Tennō: Nihonshi shōhyakka 8* (The emperor: a short encyclopedia of Japanese history, no. 8). Tokyo: Kondō Shuppansha.

Lebra, Takie Sugiyama. 1989. 'Adoption among the Hereditary Elite of Japan: Status Preservation through Mobility.' *Ethnology* 28: 185–218,

—— 1990. 'The Socialization of Aristocratic Children by Commoners: Recalled Experiences of the Hereditary Elite in Modern Japan.' *Cultural Anthropology* 5: 78–100.

—— 1991. 'Resurrecting Ancestral Charisma: Aristocratic Descendants in Contemporary Japan', *Journal of Japanese Studies* 17: 59–78.

—— 1992. *Above the Clouds: Status Culture of the Modern Japanese Nobility*, Berkeley and Los Angeles: University of California Press.

Luhrmann, T. M. 1989. 'The Magic of Secrecy' (1986 Stirling Award Essay). *Ethos* 17: 131–165.

The Pacific War Research Society. Compiled 1968. *Japan's Longest Day*. Tokyo: Kodansha International.

Perrott, Roy. 1968. *The Aristocrats: A Portrait of Britain's Nobility and Their Way of Life Today*. London: Weidenfeid and Nicolson.

Reischauer, Haru Matsukata. 1986. *Samurai and Silk: A Japanese and American Heritage*. Cambridge: Harvard University Press.

Robben, Antonius C. G. M. 1989. 'Habits of the Home: Spatial Hegemony and the Structuration of House and Society in Brazil.' *American Anthropologist* 91: 570–588.

Sakai Miiko. 1982. *Aru kazoku no showa-shi* (The Shōwa history of a kazoku). Tokyo: Shufu to Seikatsu Sha.

Schwartz, Barry. 1981. *Vertical Classification: A Study in Structuralism and the Sociology of Knowledge*. Chicago: University of Chicago Press.

Seidensticker, Edward. 1983. *Low City, High City: Tokyo from Edo to the Earthquake.* New York: Alfred A. Knopf.

Titus, David A. 1974. *Palace and Politics in Prewar Japan.* New York: Columbia University Press. Translated into Japanese by Otani Kenshiro as *Nippon no tennō seji* (Tokyo: The Simul Press, 1979).

▸ First published in *Ethos* 23 (1): 79–102. Copyright © 1995, American Anthropological Association

23 Skipped and Postponed Adolescence of Aristocratic Women in Japan: Resurrecting the Culture/Nature Issue

This article attempts to interpret the narratives of life experiences given by former aristocratic women of Japan, with a focus on adolescence and marriage. We will see how the extraordinary status of their families was of central concern in controlling their life courses and interfering with their sexuality. I begin by outlining a theoretical frame that revives the issue of nature and culture. I locate adolescence, like other instances of human experience, between the two. To illustrate my argument, I borrow and reinterpret the controversy in Samoan studies triggered by Derek Freeman's confrontational challenge of Margaret Mead.

THE MEAD-FREEMAN CONTROVERSY

It is an anthropological convention to dichotomize nature and culture in such a way that nature is subordinate to culture. In this tradition, the psychobiological body, as a representative of nature, is understood as malleable enough to be regulated by cultural norms and shaped by cultural values, as empty until it is filled with cultural meanings, as fluid unless it is fixed by cultural signifiers. The nature/culture dichotomy, however, can take another direction of thinking because it dramatizes a fundamental conflict of human life: the conflict between cultural control, backed up by political suppression, and 'bodily dissent' (Lock 1993: 141), or between the malleable body and the resistant body. The likelihood of such conflict may explain why careful socialization is mandatory in order to inscribe cultural codes onto the potentially rebellious body and to culturalize the natural body to the possible extent that cultural rules become assimilated in the latter to be felt 'natural.' To relate this general viewpoint to adolescence, I resurrect the Mead-Freeman controversy.

In an attempt to falsify Mead's (1928) depiction of Samoans, Freeman (1983) brings to the fore two major characteristics of Samoan sexual proclivities. One is rigorous inhibition, contrary to Mead's version, manifested by the ideal of chastity, the cult of virginity, and the rule of segregation between sexes; the other is aggressive, forceful, violent sex, including rape, as a not-uncommon practice. These characteristics are highlighted by Freeman as diametrically opposed to Mead's emphasis upon the free, easy, and peaceful sexuality of Samoan youth that makes the transition of adolescence smooth and unproblematic. The two opposing tendencies – sexual restraint on the one hand and violent outbreak on the other – are linked together in Freeman's mind via the universalist schema of repression-frustration-aggression.[1] In turn, this schema presupposes that the 'nature' of the embodied human is not as malleable to culturally imposed ideals and rules as 'cultural determinists' claim. Represented by Mead and other Boasians, cultural determinists, Freeman argues, exclude biology from anthropological inquiry – the point he reinforces in his defense (1991) against his critics. He tries to restore biology to anthropology and to qualify culture by nature and relativism by universalism.

Freeman's version of Mead's Samoa is thus clear and simple, but my reading of Mead is quite different. Mead's portrait of Samoans, or, more correctly, of Samoan adolescent girls, is to me much more complicated, multifaceted, subtle, elusive, confusing, contradictory. In many places, Mead does indeed underscore the easy, stress-free, and nonviolent aspect of Samoan sexuality, which is attributed to the Samoan gratification of erotic impulses. Ironically, even though this is the very point that divides Mead and Freeman in terms of whether or not Samoans are repressed, the two portraits stem from the same universalist thesis regarding human nature. This thesis holds that repression leads to stress and aggression, whereas gratification results in peace and happiness. If Samoans suffer from repression/violence at all, Mead suspects, it is probably due to the effects of Christian missionary activity. Where Samoan native culture represents the gratification-ease-peace scenario, Western civilization stands at the opposite pole, namely, the repression-frustration-aggression syndrome. In nature/culture terms, Samoans appear more 'naturally' free while Mead's compatriots are more 'culturally' repressed.

On the other hand, this thesis is not pursued consistently, but contradicted in other parts of Mead's portrayal. Mead details how Samoans, far from being free and spontaneous, unquestioningly follow cultural rules in their daily and sexual lives. In fact, it is this culturally programmed routinization that enables Samoan youth to pass through this transitional stage of life without Sturm und Drang. By contrast, American society, heterogeneous and subject to fast-paced change, confronts individuals with choices between old and new ways of life, with cross-pressures from the parental generation and peers. Seen from this angle, the stress of American adolescence is not so much because of repression as because of this plethora of demands for individual choice and commitment. I even read in Mead that American adolescents go through emotional conflict and storm in reaction to the freedom, independence, or discontinuity from childhood bonds they suddenly confront at this life stage. Samoans are spared such conflict and left in peace, not because they are unrepressed, but because they are bound by a set of more or less homogeneous and stable mores that are taken for granted and, thus, 'natural.' This is why Samoan emotions, in Mead's view, appeared flat, lacking the depth, passion, stress, and neurotic obsession associated with the individually focused Western notion of emotion. Nature and culture are reversed here: while Samoans are culturally controlled, it is American youth who are lost in the wilderness of nature.

The nature/culture opposition, far from being clear-cut, involves the double notion of nature, as paradoxically shared by both Mead and Freeman, explicitly or implicitly. Both assume nature to be a self-regulating system with its own law that resists or lashes out at excessive control and interference by culture. With nature understood this way, culture stands as repressive. The term 'repression' alone presupposes the boundary of nature that tends to maintain itself even under repression. Repressibility, like malleability, never achieves 100 percent. On the other hand, nature is also identified as entropic, meaningless, or anomic. Culture, then, shapes up nature, creates a lawful universe out of chaos, directs energy flow, channels emotions, makes meaning out of absurdity, order out of anomie. It is in this latter relationship of nature and culture that every human phenomenon appears as a 'cultural construct.'

I believe that neither of these two themes can be ruled out: nature is both self-regulating and entropic; culture is both repressive and directive. What is necessary is to fill the gaps, or, rather, to examine interpenetrations between the two themes, between cultural repression and direction, nature's boundary and malleability, and between nature and culture. I attempt to throw light upon this subtle, problematic area through the following analysis of recalled experiences of Japanese aristocratic women. Because they represent the status distinction of the hereditary elite, culture is seen preeminently as 'status culture.'

THE JAPANESE ARISTOCRACY

The Japanese case is taken from my long-term research on the hereditary elite based primarily on autobiographical narratives released in interview by aristocrats and their descendants who outlived their no longer legally sanctioned titles (Lebra 1989, 1990, 1991, 1992, 1993).[2] This status group, called *kazoku* (the 'flowery family' group), was a product of modern restratification of the elite, which combined the previous aristocracy, composed largely of court nobles (*kuge*) and feudal domain lords (*daimyo*), with the new, meritorious elite of humbler origin. Centered around, though immediately below, the emperor and his family, and towering in prestige over the rest of the nation, the kazoku formally existed for 63 years, from 1884 to 1947. During this brief history of Japan's modern aristocracy, the kazoku title with one of five ranks – prince (nonroyal), marquis, count, viscount, and baron – was awarded to roughly one thousand families. The old elite, though embodying a traditional distinction, was thus rehabilitated into a modern aristocracy that was designed mainly by new government leaders who had studied European monarchies and aristocracies in the late 19th century, particularly the British, German, and French examples (Kasumi Kaikan 1966).

My earliest contact with survivors goes back to 1976, but intensive fieldwork began in 1982 and continued intermittently through 1990, covering more than 100 men and women. In the following discussion I include members of the imperial lineage, even though royalty and aristocracy were two distinct categories, unlike European counterparts, one the 'sovereign' group and the other 'subjects' no different from commoner Japanese in this regard. I take this strategy because the two groups were physically and socially close to each other, and the boundary was often crossed in marriage, adoption, or branching. I discuss the premarital and marital experiences of members of this elite as recalled and reflected upon mainly by women informants. This focus on women informants is partly because women had more to say and were more frank about this topic, but mainly because women's experiences fit this article's theme better. Although sharing the same status culture of kazoku to some extent, men differed from women in adolescent, sexual, and conjugal opportunities, constraints, and experiences, reflecting the even greater male supremacy among kazoku than commoners. In the following account, some remarks refer to both sexes without gender markers, but many are gender-qualified, referring to 'daughters,' 'wives,' or 'women.' Instances of gross polarity between men and women will be noted.

ELITE MARRIAGE

In the ideology of prewar Japan, marriage was not a matter of individual choice but a grave concern of a household, involving possible enhancement or degradation of its status and well-being. The household (*ie*), represented by the house head, was the basic legal unit that overrode the wishes and emotions of its individual members. Marriage was, foremost, to produce an heir to house headship and thus to continue a line of *ie* succession by one (preferably male) child per generation. Second, marriage was an opportunity to establish a desirable alliance in the interest of the *ie* with another *ie*. For the elite such as kazoku, such household-centered consideration at the expense of personal feelings of marital principals was all the more necessary, but, more significant, aristocratic marriage involved much more than the two households. Marriage for kazoku could have political, economic, and symbolic impacts upon larger groups and institutions, extending to large kin networks, the kazoku group as a whole, interest groups, political factions, former daimyo domains, government, and possibly the whole nation. Marriage was thus a distinctly public matter transcending individual or household interests. No wonder that an instance of marriage involved an array of persons who were brought together around the two principal households. They participated as counselors, petitioners, or surrogates in searching and investigating prospects, negotiating for agreements, making decisions, exchanging engagement gifts, and arranging, announcing, and conducting wedding ceremonies.

Throughout Japanese history, status marriage (and adoption[3] as well) took the form of political alliances among the ruling class. The best known is the Fujiwara, the highest clan in the court nobility. Beginning in the 800s, for centuries this clan held the office of imperial regency, allowing its leading men virtually to take over the imperial sovereignty by marrying their daughters to emperors or crown princes. During the medieval period, too, the shogunal and warrior class engaged in marriage politics. Daughters (and sons) were transferred and distributed as pawns in alliances between warlords and court nobility, shogun and emperor, as well as between fellow warriors. Between warring clans, women were transferred as hostages for peace settlements, to demonstrate allegiance, to change sides, or even as disguised spies. The most famous political marriage in the last phase of the Tokugawa rule (1600–1867) was between the 14th Tokugawa shogun, Iemochi, and Princess Kazuko, a sister of the reigning emperor Komei.

In the modern period (1868–present), with which this article is concerned, the brazenly political nature of marriage subsided although politics continued to be part of it. Observers outside the elite, in particular, tended to impute the political rise of certain men to the strategic exchange of children in marriage or adoption with the view to building up and using *keibatsu* (cliques based upon affinal networks). Yamaguchi's (1932) tale of kazoku is loaded with stories of such *seiryaku kekkon* (political marriage) and successful careers propelled by keibatsu.

My informants, as insiders, were more reluctant to detect political motives, and yet some referred to the 'political marriages,' used in multiple senses, of their grandparents or parents. Political motives were read in the marriage, for example, between the mutually hostile parties of the Meiji Restoration civil war (which ended the premodern feudal age). It was said to have been engineered to heal the wounds or to benefit both parties in the new era. Marriage between allies was also interpreted as political.

Striking and unquestionably political were those nationally marginal marriages that resulted from Japan's colonial expansion. To complete Japan's 1910 annexation of Korea, colonialists forcefully maneuvered to arrange a wedding between a Japanese royal princess and the Korean crown prince in 1919. Princess Masako Nashimoto, who did not know exactly what had been taking place, was shocked when she read the announcement of her engagement in a newspaper and saw pictures of the prince and herself side by side. Her parents had tried to decline, she wrote in her autobiography, but the Imperial Household Ministry persuaded them by saying that this marriage was desired by none other than His Majesty as a wedge to strengthen the Japan–Korea alliance and as an exemplar for people in general (Ri [Yi] 1973: 35–38). Her mother protested but was pressured into tearful compliance 'for the sake of the country' (Nashimoto 1975: 138–143). The same kind of crudely political, colonialist marriage was forced in 1937 upon a high kuge daughter, Hiro Saga, to a brother of the puppet emperor Pu-yi of Manchukuo (Aishinkakura 1984).

Along with political alliances as a main motive was status validation, because matrimony was not just instrumental to politics but symbolically demonstrative of the status of the families involved. Status validation was felt all the more necessary by genealogical parvenus. Back in the Tokugawa period, shogun looked up to the imperial court for wives, particularly among the top-ranking court nobles (Fujiwara daughters)[4] or imperial princesses to demonstrate its status as being equal to the imperial house – ironically, by submitting to the imperial model. In the modern kazoku system, aristocratization of new kazoku, including business barons, called for marrying not only daughters but sons upward into the old aristocracy for status validation, which, in turn, benefited the latter politically or economically.

STATUS ENDOGAMY

After the installation of the kazoku system, marriage, together with adoption, became an important vehicle to build up multiple networks of kinship that would contribute to creating a homogeneous 'peerage' out of a heterogeneous array of houses. This goal would be achieved only if a status boundary were erected to inhibit the matrimonial crossover between the kazoku and lower strata. There was no formal stipulation against unions of kazoku and non-kazoku, and such unions did occur more often than expected. Nevertheless, most of my informants were firmly convinced that they were strictly bound by the rule of status endogamy.

For a kazoku it was necessary to apply for a marriage approval to the Imperial Household Ministry, indicating the status of the spouse's family (Kazoku Kaikan 1933: 232–236), to 'receive the imperial authorization.' It was indeed very likely, as strongly argued by my informants, that the *sochitsuryo*, the agency set up within the ministry to supervise the aristocracy and royalty, made special investigations of cases of marriage with non-kazoku and exerted its authority formally or informally against any 'disgraceful' match that would 'spoil the honor of kazoku.' Anticipations of such pressures were inflated into statements such as 'It was *absolutely forbidden* to marry someone outside the kazoku, no matter how rich.' In a questionnaire I mailed to heads of former kazoku houses, a number of respondents referred to the severity of kazoku endogamy to which they had submitted or from which they had a hard time in deviating. One wrote, 'Mine was an arranged marriage. Since [my wife] was a commoner, it was terribly difficult, in those days, to explain the case. But because her family was as prominent as any kazoku, we were able to get approval.' This comment is surprising in view of the fact that the respondent's marriage occurred after the war, when the kazoku name became tarnished.

Status endogamy sometimes meant more than marriage within the kazoku in general. A daughter of a marquis, married to a count, grouped the five ranks into two classes – the upper three and lower two – between which she said there were few instances of marriage, with the implication that viscounts and barons were of no genuine nobility. Another woman, who married a commoner after the war, said, 'In the prewar period, it was inconceivable for us to marry anyone other than a military officer of daimyo origin,' such as her father. A grandson of a well-known domain lord and national hero, a viscount, had been reluctant to have his daughter marry the heir of a financial giant house (*zaïbatsu*) with a baronial title – this also happened in the postwar period. In a long discourse, he justified his final consent. Having been reared in a daimyo family, he told me, he had been trained to be concerned with nothing but affairs of state, and thus he became extremely distrustful of businessmen, who he felt were selfishly preoccupied with making profits. But the zaibatsu house in question, with its long history, was not like the postwar nouveau riche. Furthermore, he said, this mercantile house had adopted a man from a distinguished kuge house after all. Some other informants who were still concerned with status congruity explained their marriages with commoners in terms of either the kinship connections of their spouses with full-fledged kazoku or, more commonly, Gakushuin background. (Gakushuin is the multicampus school for royal and kazoku children, which admitted severely screened commoner children as well.)

In many such instances informants were overstating the mandatory nature of endogamy. Difficulty of adhering to strict endogamy, particularly for the higher ranks and royalty, was partly due to the limited supply of spousal candidates within a desirable category, rank, or age. Furthermore, not only did the smallness of the marriage market necessitate outside marriage, but sometimes outside marriage was more tempting for pragmatic reasons such as the advantage of a union between a prominent but destitute aristocrat and a wealthy commoner – not a rarity even before the war and a common practice after the war.[5]

Informants stressed the rigor of endogamous rule because they had been successfully indoctrinated in it by their parents, elders, and official authorities and had been frightened by occasional gossip about scandalous violators and the penalties enjoined on them, such as the name removal from the family register. Instances of gross mismatch did not result in easing up the rule of endogamy but rather revalidated it. Status match and status-proper behavior were often insisted upon by status aspirants who had climbed up into aristocracy through marriage. In her autobiography, Viscountess Tae Torio (1985) candidly discusses how she, a daughter of a wealthy commoner businessman and Gakushuin student, wanted to marry a kazoku, which she did. She suspects that her mother-in-law was disappointed with this match because she had a daughter of another viscount in mind and had informally arranged a marriage. The author reveals that the mother-in-law was from a rural landlord family with no title. Her grandmother-in-law allegedly was a dancing entertainer from a well-known geisha quarter in Kyoto. Three generations of wives were commoners. Still, the author observed her mother-in-law having become a perfect viscountess, with mastery of the special kazoku vocabulary that 'sounded like a foreign language' to the bride. It would thus appear that breeding could be erased or achieved and that the elite status and its marriage restriction could be reproduced and renewed by its aspiring marginal members.

REPRESSION?

By insisting on the inescapability of the rule of in-status marriage, informants were telling me why they *had to* marry their spouses and were sharply contrasting their own generation with their children's and other postwar generations in terms of marriage choices. It seems that they deeply internalized their extraordinary status and vulnerability to public visibility, resulting in extraordinary suppressions and inhibitions regarding spouse selection. For the prewar royalty in particular there was supposedly no way of rejecting a proposal made by the sochitsuryo and presented as imperially authorized. The following was a conversation with a 75-year-old former royal princess married to a count of kuge origin:

> Was your marriage arranged?
> Of course. Ours were all by chokkyo [imperial authorization]. Because it was the emperor who made the decision, likes and dislikes were out of the question …
> Was it decided by the sochitsuryo?
> Yes, by the office which looked after the kazoku [and royalty].
> Were you prepared for that kind of marriage?
> Of course I was.

Status constraints such as this, which categorically precluded personal choice, were described by many, royals and kazoku alike. A sense of patriotic duty inherent in the elite status was the motive of one young woman in accepting the proposal from a royal prince: because he was a military officer, she thought 'it would be the best way of dedicating myself to the state to marry him so that he could go to the war-front without worrying about his personal future.'

She had no thoughts about what a husband should be like. This marriage ended in divorce after the war.

The freedom of choice that some informants enjoyed was attributed to the Western influence on their parents: 'Because my father spent years in the West, first as a student and later as an ambassador, he was able to leave us free to accept or reject his choice of spouses.' Even in this case, selection of a prospective spouse for each child was the father's prerogative, and the freedom of rejection was not exercised because the father's choice was 'excellent.' A daughter whose parents both had lived in Europe for years and were 'completely' Westernized in their life style was nonetheless matched, without her being consulted, to a son of a branch house with a lower kazoku rank. In other words, parental exposure to the Western way of life did not guarantee children freedom in spouse selection, as Westernization meant a selective emulation of Western aristocracy with all its status norms and constraints.

That the individual's subjectivity, emotion, or choice was irrelevant in spouse selection can be best inferred from a number of narratives indicating that young girls were kept deaf and blind to marriage negotiations going on for them until they were final. Like the princess married to the Korean prince, a daimyo daughter was stunned at the newspaper announcement of her engagement before she was told. Another daughter of a kazoku prince was told by her mother one day, 'You are going, it seems, to marry Prince K., because his father visited us.' Obviously, the mother was not informed either. It was 'as if the whole matter concerned someone else, not me,' said the former princess. No wonder that some of the informants and questionnaire respondents did not know who had been involved in arranging and planning their marriages. This kind of blindness was shared, though to a lesser degree, by men as well.

Insignificance of subjective awareness on the part of marriage principals is further illustrated by proposals received in their pre- or early teens. A kuge daughter met her future husband in a formal introduction (*miai*) when she was a sixth grader. 'I didn't know what the miai meant, but only thought I was gaining a new cousin.' Another, older kuge informant generalized that kazoku children in those days 'had miai at about ten years of age.' Some girls dropped out of high school without protest to begin matrimonial preparations (boys were expected to go through university graduation). An extreme was a prenatal engagement, which had occurred in older generations: 'After my father was born, it was decided that if so-and-so family happened to give birth to a baby girl he would be engaged to her.' The decision was made by a large group of high-ranking and powerful former vassals and retainers, and the plan materialized. A variety of motives for premature arrangements is conceivable, including political ones. I suspect that the limited marriage market was another factor influencing some parents to secure suitable mates for their children as soon as possible.

What does all this amount to? It seems that kazoku children, daughters more than sons,[6] were decidedly repressed in their sexual impulses and emotions, as if they were expected to skip their adolescence except as a stage of preparation for a properly arranged marriage well anticipated by childhood engagement. Behind this repression was the threat of political coercion institutionally embodied by the Imperial Household Ministry, state power, and even the emperor himself. Such repressive status culture did produce a few rebels who dared to 'elope' with a personally chosen lover disapproved by the family or sochitsuryo; they thus took the risk of being disgraced in public and being formally expelled from the family register so that the family's kazoku status could be kept clean on record in the eyes of peers. Not surprisingly, a few instances of clandestine homosexual bonding for men and women were heard of in gossip and innuendoes.

For the large majority of young women and men, repressed adolescence did not mean conflict, storm, or aggression. Quite the contrary, third-party control in mate selection was accepted as a matter of course, as something 'natural.' I recall how many times in an interview a 91-year-old widow of kuge origin disappointed me by giving unexpected answers to my provocative questions. 'Didn't you want to be free?' I asked. 'No,' she said, 'I did not feel restrained at all. I thought such was the way things had to be [*sonna mon da to omotte*].' Lacking the feeling of being restrained, kazoku daughters largely seem to have shared the characteristics of Samoan girls as described by Mead. But unlike Mead's Samoan girls, who enjoyed sexual freedom, kazoku girls were repressed to the point of skipping adolescence as a free time of experimenting and preparing for adult sexuality. In this sense they were more like Freeman's Samoans, and yet their behavior invalidates Freeman's universalist proposition that excessive repression results in aggression and violence. This seeming contradiction calls for an explanation, which I think lies in the depth of status socialization to which kazoku children were subject. Only in retrospect did kazoku women realize their 'astonishing' or 'regrettable' malleability – a point to which we will return.

SOCIALIZATION IN AND FOR SECLUSION

Cultural construction of sexual emotions began much earlier than adolescence. Girls were socialized not to question status regulations over the sexual and marital matters they would face in the future, and this was done mainly through seclusion from the outside world – outside one's status group, outside one's residential area, outside one's house. A daughter of a daimyo marquis recalled that although her 'unusually liberal,' Westernized parents allowed her as a child to visit areas such as Asakusa (a popular entertainment district in downtown Tokyo) on occasions like local festivals if escorted by 'several maids,' they themselves would never step into such a place.[7] For older women informants in particular, girlhood was recalled as secluded within the enclosure of the estate. Some were frustrated and wished to be out on the street, but most accepted it as 'natural,' not being awakened to freedom of mobility until after their marriage or the war.

What stands out in kazoku life histories in sharp contrast to those of average Japanese is the insignificance or total absence of neighbors. The only neighbors whose names and premises my informants remembered were fellow kazoku, Gakushuin classmates, high government officials, financial giants, and the like. This reflects the geographical clustering of kazoku residences in selective areas of uptown Tokyo. When there was contact with neighbors, the characteristics of usual neighborliness such as the mutual and easy visibility, unannounced visit, and spontaneous, natural sociability were missing. The absence of neighbors meant that the children did not come under peer pressures from fellow neighbor children, which could have broken through the family-based status socialization.

As no household was self-sufficient, seclusion was far from complete, and in fact there were constant interchanges inside and outside the house, but these were only in a way that minimized the exposure of the family to the outer world. Routine domestic labor was supplied internally by a pool of servants, and specialized services such as hairdressing were provided by regularly and privately hired specialists. Necessary goods such as food and clothing were delivered by house-calling sales clerks of certain stores. Not a few informants recalled their curiosity about such sales clerks, hairdressers, or gardeners as the only 'windows' to the outside.

Exposure to the outside world was curtailed even when members of the kazoku family went out. High-ranking and wealthy families used private transportation as a matter of status mandate. Historically, the vehicles changed from early Meiji on, and my informants talked about their family-owned vehicles shifting from horse carriages to rickshaws to automobiles. Today, car ownership is no longer a status symbol, but in prewar Japan it was a special luxury. Strange as it may sound, private transportation was another way to inhibit access to the outside world. The vehicles were driven by the privately employed men who usually lived within their employer's residential compound and who thus served as watchful guards as well.

Whether one took private or public transportation or walked, the most commonly practiced pattern was chaperonage. Servants escorted the children from home to school and back home, at least up to about the third or fourth grade, but in some cases throughout high school, much to the embarrassment of their charges. Not only were the daughters chaperoned, but some families also assigned male escorts to their young sons. Adults were shepherded by servants as well. In shopping, it was the accompanying servant who discharged all the actual transactions with store clerks, leaving the master aloof from or ignorant about money. Even the newlywed couple was escorted in some cases by an entourage on their honeymoon. Having lost the last escort servant in the postwar period, one woman told me, 'I kept forgetting to carry my wallet.'

Kazoku women, and to a lesser extent men (children and adults alike), were thus insulated from the outside world, precisely because private transportation and chaperons kept them from being left alone. Insulation meant a lack of privacy. Young daughters in particular were thus innoculated against the wish for self-exposure to the outside world and for individual privacy.

'What further inhibited exposure was the selectivity of destinations for commuting or traveling. A large majority of the children attended Gakushuin. Some parents chose other schools, but these were similarly exclusive to the upper class and narrowly circumscribed classmate contact.[8] Traveling away from Tokyo meant staying at private resort villas or prominent hotels that accepted regular patrons only. Shopping was at particular stores where the head managers would meet and attend the elite shoppers; occasional eating out was at special restaurants or hotels; and entertainment was at reputable theaters or the kazoku club house.

Servants, as drivers or escorts, thus mediated the contact of kazoku children (and adults too) with the mundane reality of the external world and thereby played an essential role in the children's distance training. They were in a position to contribute to maintaining the status boundary because they were located on the margin of the boundary, being inside the household physically and functionally, and at the same time being outside the status of the household.

Educational seclusion at Gakushuin meant more than contact with status peers to reinforce socialization in status culture. It should be noted that commoner teachers inculcated their pupils with status identity, status pride, and status missions. Informants recalled how their prewar teachers repeatedly instructed them 'to stand above people,' 'to be a model for the whole nation,' and 'to serve as a protective fence for the imperial house.'

Personal likes and dislikes were not totally out of consideration, and fortunately, in some cases, personal love and choice went together with status mandate and parental approval. But if personal emotions contradicted the status propriety, they were overruled as irrelevant. Most of my informants went along this primacy of status imperative, as amply demonstrated above, because a rejection of the parental proposal had never occurred to them or because they accepted the conventional idea that love had nothing to do with marriage. Children of the elite appeared more conditioned than commoners to comply with the status-proper marriage proposal for several reasons: greater parental authority, the larger *ie* asset, the highly public, even statewide visibility of their marriage, supervision by the sochitsuryo, pressures from vassals and retainers, and physical and social seclusion from the outside world. All these conditions entered the socialization process to produce children malleable enough to accept repressive status culture as natural. The question of what happened to the repressed emotions, whether they found any channels to release them, remains.

LIBERATION AND EMOTIONAL BREAKOUT

The old way of life was suddenly changed during the last phase of World War II and the earliest postwar period. The Tokyo air raids in 1945 reduced to ashes the residential grandeur and elegant lifestyle of the aristocracy overnight, and many kazoku families had already begun to send back their servants to their natal homes for safety until none was left with them. No longer enveloped in the dignity of status culture, individual members of kazoku became subject to the natural conditions of existence. In addition, the postwar American-led revolutionary democratization reversed the prewar value hierarchy and converted the prewar pride of status into a sense of liability tinged with guilt and shame. It might be presumed that the sudden overhaul of the prewar status system threw the privileged class such as kazoku into fury, despair, or self-pity. For some kazoku, this was indeed a time of demoralization and defeat. But for many of my informants, particularly women, it turned out to be a period of awakening to new freedom and emancipation from the old status that, in retrospect, they associated more with oppressive liability than with gratuitous privilege.[9] Intense emotions were aroused, the so-far unquestioned compliance and conformity were challenged, and personal passions were kindled. Armed with the newly instituted ideology of liberty and equality, young went against old, children against parents, students against school authorities. No less vulnerable was the age-old patriarchy in which women had to tolerate their husbands' promiscuity when their own sexual indulgence had been absolutely forbidden or sensationally scandalized. The postwar breakout thus meant that women became more resistant to male dominance; in many instances wives left their husbands. In retrospect it appears as though until then the honor of kazoku status alone had been sustaining the facade of normal marriage in many families.

Still, the new freedom did not mean freedom from stress and conflict. On the contrary, it often generated tensions between past commitments and a new outlook and prompted a passionate search for a path to break away from the past. A daughter of a wealthy baron ran away to live with a man of her choice whom her parents unconditionally ruled out as their son-in-law. Having been confined to the status-bound and protected way of life, she was attracted to the rugged man from a poor family, to his vitality for survival like that of 'weeds.' As a result of this rebellious action she felt guilty for a long time until finally her parents relented and approved her marriage. The media continued to send out sensational news about high-ranking kazoku or royal wives who left their esteemed husbands and joined their commoner lovers. A woman, married to a royal prince, was convinced that divorce was absolutely impermissible because of their public visibility even after the war and considered suicide by stabbing herself with the dagger given by her family at the time of marriage.[10] In the end, her hospitalization for cancer treatment secured her a divorce by consent. Inspired with the American idea of women living their own lives, and expedited by her fluency in English, she worked at American government agencies and studied at a New York university. This daughter of a viscount and former princess remarried a commoner.

Another royally married woman was the plaintiff in the first court case of divorce among royalty and kazoku that had been brought to public attention. The case took years of struggling until the court finally ruled in favor of divorce, which, of course, was widely publicized by scandal-mongering weeklies. The scandal was intensified all the more by her dating another man. According to a recent revelation in a popular weekly magazine (Kawahara 1990), the prince, a major general, was more interested in a particular man who was under his command in the army than his wife, and yet he was adamant in maintaining the fiction of the practically nonexistent marriage. After the war he brought his homosexual partner into his house to live with him but still refused to let her go. The dispute landed in the court, and after ten years of battle the childless wife won a divorce and remarried.

Another case involved a daughter of a kazoku prince who was married to the heir of another kazoku prince. The princess left her husband to live with their house-calling physical therapist. This case suggests the possibility that physical distance between persons as maintained by aristocrats as part of the aristocratic life style made them all the more vulnerable to body contact occasioned by massage or other kinds of body care. I found several love affairs between kazoku men and nurses, including an adultery, which outraged kin and fellow kazoku.

Some kazoku women were natural links, because of their fluency in English and overall cosmopolitan savoir faire, between the occupation authorities and the occupied Japan. In the beginning, they were even mobilized by the Japanese government as social liaisons to lubricate communication between victors and defeated. Love affairs erupted, exciting the grapevine and magazines. This was how Viscountess Torio, for example, fell in love with an American colonel, Kades, presumably second only to General McArthur, Supreme Commander for the Allied Powers, to influence the earliest policy making of the Allied Occupation. Torio met Kades at a reception hosted by the Chief Cabinet Secretary of Japan for high-ranking officers from the Occupation's General Headquarters. She was one of the women speaking English and familiar with the Western way of life who had been asked by the secretary to join him as co-host to the foreign guests. As both Torio and Kades were married, this affair did not end in marriage. It was widely cited by resentful Japanese as a prime example of kazoku decadence in the postwar era. Nearly four decades later, in her seventies, Torio disclosed this extraordinary experience in her autobiography (1985).

Some informants inside and outside the aristocratic circle claim that sexual license among kazoku, kuge in particular, is not new but rather traditional, persisting since the ancient times. This claim is associated with classical Heian court tales such as *The Tale of Genji*, which focuses on the uninhibited sexual adventures among nobles and royals. Again, we have to consider gender difference. It seems that upper-class men, aristocratic or not, enjoyed sexual freedom with impunity while women were under more stringent control, even at the Heian court. Women would express their sexual emotions most strongly through jealousy, with spirit possession (*mono no ke*) as the ultimate ammunition, against rival women or unfaithful male partners (Bargen 1988). Lady Nijo, the sensational medieval author of *Towazugatari*, a documentary narrative of the author's own life, engaged in multiple, even simultaneous, affairs with retired emperors and nobles and appears wildly licentious by modern standards. I think even this extraordinary court lady was more an object of male lust and whims than a subject free to pursue her own passions. It is not until she renounced the this-worldly life of flesh to become a wandering nun that Lady Nijo gained personal autonomy and integrity. From the late medieval through the modern age, rigorous chastity became a norm for upper-class women, deviation from which was severely punished. In this respect there has been a greater divergence between men and women of the upper class than of lower classes.[11]

Instances of postwar emotional combustion confirm that these women had long been subjected to an extraordinarily intense repression. Some women took the risk of being disgraced in public in order to retrieve and relive their passed-over adolescence. It should be remembered, however, that such action would not have been taken had it not been for the physical and cultural turmoil caused by the war and the postwar value reversal and liberation. Some other women, for whom change came too late to start life over again, expressed their discontent by talking with admiration and envy about those kazoku women of notoriety who had lived their romantic passions, daring to destroy their reputation, under the prewar regime of oppression.

CONCLUSION

The case of Japanese aristocracy, as described in this article, calls for a rethinking of the Mead-Freeman controversy or, rather, Freeman's challenge to Mead in her absence. There is no doubt that aristocratic women were repressed because of their status, decidedly much more repressed than Samoans appeared to Freeman. Adolescence for kazoku girls, if recognized at all, was only for bridal preparation for the prearranged marriage, not for romantic love affairs or sexual experimentations. It even appears as though adolescence were nipped in the bud or entirely bypassed. Nevertheless, most of them were resigned to status constraint, instead of releasing their repressed energy into rebellious or aggressive acts, as a matter of nature or destiny to the extent that personal likes and dislikes were considered irrelevant to marriage. Many did not even feel constrained. In other words, culture was accepted as nature, or, more correctly, culture became assimilated into the natural body as a result of thoroughgoing socialization. It was not until the war destroyed the status quo and the postwar overhaul of the prewar hierarchy began to lift the repressive yoke of the past that these women, now awakened to having been unjustly oppressed, dared to counter their parents and husbands and to relive the emotions of their belated adolescence. This was when they perceived options. At this point they were more like Mead's American adolescents going through the stormy break from their parents and elders. Besides, even this rebellious outburst was not quite blind or irrational, but was steered by the new ideology of liberty, equality, and independence being sponsored and disseminated by the occupation-backed authorities. The imperial institution, the most sacred center holding together the national hierarchy, was coming under attack. Conflict was still inevitable since it was humanly impossible to relinquish the old values overnight and in entirety.

In sum, I challenge the commonly held thesis that repression leads to stress, conflict, and aggression. My study shows how far women's sexuality could be repressed through socialization without necessarily provoking conflict, resistance, or rebellion. Repression may contribute to stormy sexuality, but it is not sufficient to generate it. Repression converts into stress and aggression only if it is perceived as an unjustifiable oppression. Such a perception was made possible for these women when the old culture broke down, to be replaced by temporary chaos and a new set of values. Through this change, nature and culture that had been fused into one were suddenly separated so that the unnaturalness of repressed emotions was recognized. As stated at the outset, culture does not only repress natural forces, it also provides meaning and order for an otherwise meaningless, chaotic nature. It was the change of culture in the latter sense that separated the repressed nature from the repressive culture and redirected the repressed energy into conflict-ridden passions for romantic adventures. The romantic passions and rebellion that Westerners associate with adolescence came at a different time of life for this group of Japanese daughters and wives, permitted by the breakdown of social constraints and driven by Western ideals of romantic love and love-based marriage.

It should be clear, on the other hand, that my emphasis upon the cultural control of natural sexuality is not meant to annihilate the latter. Certainly, nature can be surprisingly malleable, and the degree of malleability itself is culturally determined. (In the culture in which love is considered a necessary prelude to marriage, the kind of emotional neutrality imposed upon premarital kazoku women would not have been tolerated.) Nonetheless, malleability is not reducible to emptiness, repressibility is not unlimited, and cultural construction does not dispense with natural foundation. Otherwise, it would be difficult to understand the romantic outbursts of the long-repressed women, as described in this article, to relive their skipped adolescence. In this regard I find the critique of extreme constructivism offered by Scheffler's (1991) refreshing and agreeable. Turning back to the Mead-Freeman controversy, it is regrettable that Freeman, being too eager in destroying Mead, missed a chance, as noted by Levy (1983), to make a positive contribution toward an integration of nature and culture.

It is then conceivable that excessive repressions, if not externally released, hurt the individual's physical or mental health internally even in the repression-tolerant circle of the Japanese aristocracy. Without solid evidence, I am tempted to link the sexual and conjugal frustrations and unhappiness to some (not many) cases of chronic illness, neurosis, and premature death that my informants mentioned regarding their older-generation kinswomen. Here, my position amounts to another challenge to the deconstructionist version of cultural constructivism, which reduces nature to cultural code, discourse, signifier, representation, text.

Finally, we are trapped, as both Mead and Freeman are, by the nature/culture dichotomy because it is conflated with the universalism-particularism dichotomy. Why is it that culture should be regarded as unique and variable while nature is to be looked upon as universally uniform? Lock provides an appropriate answer when she says, 'It cannot be assumed ... that dialectics exist between an infinity of cultures and a universal biology, but rather between cultures and local biologies, both of which are subject to transformation in evolutionary, historical, and life cycle time bytes, and to movement through space' (1993:146). This view fits the profiles of bodies and status culture as they emerged in the narratives of the Japanese aristocratic women regarding their adolescence, sexuality, and marriage.

NOTES

1. I am using the term 'repression' in a broad sense, not one confined to the psychoanalytic 'unconscious,' without categorically distinguishing it from similar words such as 'suppression' (Hsu 1949) or 'inhibition.'

2. For the long-term research from which this article is derived I received support from several funding sponsors: the Joint Committee on Japanese Studies of the American Council of Learned Societies and the Social Science Research council, the Japan Foundation, the Wenner Gren Foundation for Anthropological Research, and the University of Hawaii (the Presidential Scholar Award, and the Japan Studies Endowment Fund). Much of the data presented here overlaps portions of previous publications but is newly interpreted along the thesis set forth in this article.

3. Like marriage, adoption involved a transfer of a child, here a son, from one household that had excess sons to another that had no heir of its own. Adoption was often combined with marriage, in that being adopted meant becoming at once a son of the adopter and betrothed to the latter's daughter. For these reasons, marriage and adoption are considered together either as equivalent or inseparable, and they are both termed engumi (tying the knot).

4. Fujiwara women's unsurpassed matrimonial status as imperial consorts outlasted the Fujiwara political dominance through the medieval into modern age.

5. Kazoku-commoner marriage occurred for both sons and daughters if all the children are considered. But if only heirs are taken into account as title holders, men had more options to recruit commoners as their spouses than did those women who, as heiresses, invited men over as adopted husbands. Heiresses were more bound to marry within kazoku ranks because it was their husbands who, as heads of the households, would assume the kazoku title.

6. Men were as much constrained to marry properly selected women, but they had non-marital access, before and during marriage, to 'professional women,' notably geisha catering to elite clients, for temporary outlets. Many of my informants had grandfathers who had kept such women as concubines and fathered their children as a matter of unquestioned status-appropriate practice, thus leaving their wives all the more frustrated (Lebra 1992). Some men went bankrupt as playboys and thereby jeopardized their kazoku status.

7. In seclusion there was gender asymmetry again in that girls and women were more strictly bound by this rule of spatial confinement than boys and men, the boys in fact allowed and sometimes encouraged to enter the social wilderness of the outside world.

8. Again, some fathers chose to toughen up their sons (not daughters) by sending them to extremely competitive public or national schools.

9. Apparently, a similar reaction was felt, contrary to the generally held assumption, by another category of status losers at another historical time. We hear much about the samurai discontent over the annulment of the samurai status after the Meiji Restoration, which is said to have accounted for a host of losers' rebellions. However, another side of the story is revealed by Yamakawa (1992: 71): the

samurai, as exemplified by those of the Mito domain, actually welcomed, instead of deploring, their status loss. Being stripped of the samurai status meant being liberated from the extremely restrictive status fetters and gaining freedom to live like commoners.

10. A dagger given a daughter when about to marry symbolized her chastity in that it was to be used to protect her chastity from an assailant and, if necessary, to kill herself. Some kazoku women, including my informants, daimyo daughters, or wives in particular, kept such daggers symbolically.

11. For a similar observation in the American upper class, see Ostrander 1984. For sexual life among rural peasants in 1930s Japan, see Smith and Wiswell 1982.

REFERENCES CITED

Aishinkakura, Hiro. 1984. 'Ruten no ohi' no Showa-shi. Tokyo: Shufu to seikatsusha.

Bargen, Doris G. 1988. Spirit Possession in the Context of Dramatic Expressions of Gender Conflict: The Aoi Episode of the Genji monogatari. *Harvard Journal of Asiatic Studies* 48: 95–130.

Freeman, Derek. 1983. Margaret Mead and Samoa: The Making and Unmaking of an Anthropological Myth. Cambridge, MA: Harvard University Press.

—— 1991. On Franz Boas and the Samoan Researches of Margaret Mead. *Current Anthropology* 32(3): 322–328.

Hsu, Francis L. K. 1949. Suppression versus Repression: A Limited Psychological Interpretation of Four Cultures. *Psychiatry* 12: 223–242.

Kasumi Kaikan, ed. 1966. Kazoku kaikan-shi. Tokyo: Kashima Kenkyujo Shuppankai.

Kawahara, Toshiaki. 1990. Michiko kogo, No. 8. Moto kozoku e nojogen. Shukan-gendai December 8: 210–213.

Kazoku Kaikan, ed. 1933. Kazoku yoran (authored and published by Masahiro Iai on behalf of Kazoku Kaikan). Tokyo.

Lebra, Takie Sugiyama. 1989. Adoption among the Hereditary Elite of Japan: Status Preservation through Mobility. *Ethnology* 28: 185–218.

—— 1990. The Socialization of Aristocratic Children by Commoners: Recalled Experiences of the Hereditary Elite in Modern Japan. *Cultural Anthropology* 5: 78–100.

—— 1991. Resurrecting Ancestral Charisma: Aristocratic Descendants in Contemporary Japan. *The Journal of Japanese Studies* 17: 59–78.

—— 1992. The Spatial Layout of Hierarchy: Residential Style of the Modern Japanese Nobility. In *Japanese Social Organization*. T. S. Lebra, ed. Pp. 49–78. Honolulu: University of Hawaii Press.

—— 1993 *Above the Clouds: Status Culture of the Modern Japanese Aristocracy*. Berkeley: University of California Press.

Levy, Robert I. 1983. The Attack on Mead. *Science* 220: 829–832.

Lock, Margaret. 1993. Cultivating the Body: Anthropology and Epistemologies of Bodily Practice and Knowledge. *Annual Review of Anthropology* 22: 133–155.

Mead, Margaret. 1928. *Coming of Age in Samoa*. New York: Morrow.

Nashimoto, Itsuko. 1975. *Sandai no tenno to watakushi*. Tokyo: Kodansha.

Ostrander, Susan A. 1984. *Women of the Upper Class*. Philadelphia: Temple University Press.

Ri (Yi), Masako. 1973. *Sugita saigetsu*. Seoul: Publisher unidentified.

Scheffler, Harold W. 1991. Sexism and Naturalism in the Study of Kinship. *In* Gender at the Crossroads of Knowledge: Feminist Anthropology in the Postmodern Era. M. di Leonardo, ed. Berkeley: University of California Press.

Smith, Robert J., and Ella Lury Wiswell. 1982. *The Women of Suye Mura*. Chicago: University of Chicago Press.

Torio, Tae. 1985. *Watakushi no ashioto ga kikoeru.* Tokyo: Bungeishunju.
Yamaguchi, Aisen. 1932. *Yoko kara mita kazoku monogatari.* Tokyo: Isshinsha.
Yamakawa, Kikue. 1992. Women of the Mito Domain: Recollections of Samurai Family Life. Kate Wildman Nakai, trans. Tokyo: University of Tokyo Press.

First published in Wakita Haruko et al., *Gender and Japanese History*, Osaka: Osaka University Press, 1999

24 Fractionated Motherhood: Gender and the Elite Status in Japan

NATURE, CULTURE, FEMINISM, AND MOTHERHOOD

The family today appears to be on the verge of collapsing, as signaled by the alarming rates of divorce, single parenthood, unwed cohabitation, and gay and lesbian unions. This trend is not unwelcome to those feminists who believe that the family, as the last fortress of male dominance and female slavery, had better be demolished. Academic feminists in social, cultural, and political disciplines provide theoretical ammunition by emphasizing that, like gender, the family is a cultural construction having nothing to do with the natural, biological givens of life. They reject the functionalist idea, as theorized by Malinowski, that the family is an institution to fulfill universal human needs. Rather, they argue, the 'family' is in fact 'an ideological construct associated with the modern state' which necessitates a split between the public and private spheres, or between the market and home, with spatial, moral, and emotional boundaries between the spheres.[1] Feminism, in short, calls for an overhaul of the anthropological theory of kinship itself.[2]

The idea of cultural construction extends to motherhood. Drawing upon Gathorne-Hardy's study of the British nanny,[3] Boon refutes the thesis, attributed to Goodenough, of mother-child 'natural bonding,' on the ground that nannies replaced 'genetrices' to take the mothering role.[4] Inspired by Boon's argument on nannies as mother surrogates, Drummond goes still farther, defining motherhood as a semiotic phenomenon that is far from natural: 'The birth of a child is a dramatic intrusion by a noncultural being into the heart of the domestic sphere. A woman, in nurturing and protecting that being, establishes a perilous conjunction between opposites: a fully human adult becomes intimate with a nonhuman, even antihuman form.'[5] Denaturalization of motherhood is recaptured by Moore to strengthen a feminist argument.[6]

By and large, motherhood is denigrated or condemned in some feminist writings as the ultimate source of oppression and danger to women, although for diverse, often ambivalent reasons.[7] Motherhood, in this view, is nothing but men's appropriation of women's bodies to reproduce patriarchy and therefore should be totally relinquished by women.[8] The ideological denaturalization of motherhood has gained momentum from biotechnologies of reproduction, such as in-vitro fertilization, artificial insemination, delayed fertilization by freeze, sperm or egg donation, surrogate pregnancy and birthing, which amount to 'the deconstruction of motherhood.'[9]

To my mind, cultural constructionism, or rather deconstructionism, stems from the very Western opposition of culture and nature (or mind and body). This dichotomy attests to the indelible legacy of Cartesian rationalism, which continues to offer an epistemological guidepost for many cultural anthropologists, feminist and nonfeminist, structuralist and poststructuralist alike, despite their arguments to the contrary.

The same logic of dichotomy is reversible toward naturalization, or deculturalization, of the family as well. In fact, logically implicit to the above feminist rejection of the culturally constructed family is the desirability of restoring nature to life, humanity, sex, womanhood, motherhood, and family. It is no coincidence that, even as women are stepping out of the family, men are admonished to enter it as rehabilitated natural fathers. Naturalization of gender, as conceived in the feminist perspective, can mean putting men and women in one single category of humanity devoid of the idea of gender division. Conversely, it also brings into question the old male-centered premises entrenched in a rational, impersonal, external, independence-oriented, political, economic, technoscientific single-mindedness. Involved here is a positive reappreciation of the female-centered worldview, one embedded in relationality, attachment, intimacy, empathy, and caring, as shown by Gilligan.[10]

Gilligan's view sheds entirely new light on the structural gender theory advanced by Ortner, which correlates the male with culture and the female with nature,[11] and on Chodorow's theory of gender personality, which explains the development of masculinity versus femininity in terms of the boy's separation from his female caretaker (mother or mother surrogate) and the girl's continuing attachment to hers.[12] Nature, far from being denigrated, as by these authors, emerges above culture, and, by implication, women above men. Indeed, a recent feminist trend is to assert the natural basis of gender difference and to claim the biological superiority of women over men.[13] This deconstruction of the male-centered value hierarchy is allied with the ecological concern for the protection of the natural environment from its culturally engineered devastation. In the meantime, the natural, biological, precultural basis of sexuality, and of motherhood, is reconfirmed by other scholars without attaching either superiority or inferiority to women.[14]

ELITE STATUS AND MOTHERHOOD IN JAPAN

Inspired but confused by these debates current in Western academia, I propose to interject another viewpoint drawn from a non-Western case. Japan has gone through several phases of the feminist movement in its modern history, and now appears to be catching up with the newest wave of worldwide feminism, which got under way in the 1960s. What stands out in the Japanese history of feminism is the centrality and persistence of the motherhood issue, that is, whether maternalism is to be advocated as essential to women's rights or downgraded as detrimental to the feminist cause.[15]

Aside from feminism, students of Japan concur that motherhood has attained a prominent status in Japanese culture, shaping Japanese women's identity on the one hand and capturing the children's hearts on the other. This image of motherhood is not only reproduced by the media through popular family dramas; it was also largely confirmed by a sample of women in autobiographical discourses given me in interviews[16] as if they had been enculturated (or deceived?) into assimilating this image. Nevertheless, motherhood, like womanhood, is far from being unitary but is variable and multifarious and has changed historically, as historians have amply documented.[17] Class is another important variable in the definition of motherhood. What we visualize as a Japanese mother is likely to be an urban middle-class, full-time mother of modern Japan.

In this study, I focus on upper-class motherhood in the modern era prior to World War II, when Japan was still rigidly stratified. One reason is that, because this class has been ignored as an object of academic research, I feel it necessary to fill this void in our knowledge. Second, I have been working on the modern aristocracy for years, and want to take advantage of what I have learned.[18] While partly overlapping with the previous research results, the present paper throws new light on upper-class motherhood from a gender perspective.

When I refer to my aristocratic sample, it is to be understood as drawn from survivors and descendants of the *kazoku* (flowery families), the modern aristocracy recreated and restratified around the emperor in Meiji Japan. The *kazoku* as a group was composed of pre-Meiji aristocracy, primarily daimyo and *kuge* (court nobles) as well as new recruits ennobled on the basis of recognized merits. The *kazoku* institution formally existed for sixty-three years, from 1884 to 1947. During this period of modern history, the *kazoku* title (with one of five ranks: prince [nonroyal], marquis, count, viscount, and baron) was awarded to roughly one thousand households.

Topping the aristocracy was the royalty, which will also be included here because, despite a clear formal status barrier between the aristocracy and royalty, subject and sovereign (*kazoku* and *kōzoku*), in practice they often merged together. Further, I do not entirely confine my discussion to the hereditary elite but include cases of the nonhereditary, untitled class of wealth and/or power, again because the boundary between the two groups was somewhat elusive. I cast a large net to catch whatever I could, written as well as 'live' information. My theoretical approach is to appropriate and redesign the nature-culture dualism as it fits the subject at hand, eventually to deconstruct it.

The nature-culture contrast is significant for class differentiation. What distinguishes the elite lifestyle from that of the nonelite is the prominence in the former of culture over nature. Aristocratic behavior is to be controlled by cultural protocols of conduct, dignity, and honor, involving body management. The elite actor is supposed to be psychologically or socially inoculated against the outburst of natural drives, distanced from natural vagaries. Indeed, aristocratic activity is characterized by aloofness from the survival of one's organic existence, as exemplified by esthetic or ritual preoccupations rather than pursuit of utilitarian gain, leisurely play instead of strenuous work, dilettantism instead of professionalism. What is at stake is the elite status, which is defined, constructed, maintained, and displayed in cultural terms. It is status culture, in other words, that binds the aristocratic way of life.

Nevertheless, aristocrats, like any other people, are 'embodied' and must meet the needs, impulses, and constraints of their bodies. Because they are more bound by the imperative of status culture, there is a greater gap for them than for other classes between culture and nature, rule and existence, ceremonial dress and naked body. Writing about the British monarchy, Hayden captures the same point when she elaborates a segregation between the monarch's 'body politic' and 'body natural.'[19] I argue that the whole elite subculture addresses the need to fill and manage the nature-culture gap. While this subculture may have similarities across cultures, it may also manifest some cross-cultural variation; thus the Japanese way of managing the gap could be somewhat different from, say, the British way.[20]

This split holds for motherhood in a distinct and interesting fashion. The aristocratic mother is expected, above all, to represent her family status through a culturally appropriate repertoire of behaviors and appearances, while her natural self, left behind and hidden, is to be managed. The nature-culture split for a mother is doubled because motherhood is interlocked with the nature-culture split of the child as well. Below, I discuss the split and interrelationship between the cultural mother and the natural mother under two categories: lady-mother and nurturer-mother; symbolic mother and uterine mother. It will be shown that these two sets of paired motherhood were interrelated. Furthermore, the aristocracy is charged with the continuous supply of 'blood' to ensure the 'hereditary' lines of succession.

LADY-MOTHER AND NURTURER-MOTHER

Middle-class mothers are, ideally and often in practice as well, total nurturers and caretakers for their children, and children in turn feel physically close and emotionally attached to their mothers while distanced from their fathers.[21] In the lower classes, too, children are more or less attached to their mothers, who are overworked in and out of the home. This image of motherhood is far from that of aristocratic motherhood. The mother appeared in my informants' narratives as someone who was at a distance or absent when the child was under bodily care. 'All my mother did,' claimed a daughter of a marquis, 'was give birth, and nothing more [*umisute*]. She would not have known whether her child was dead or alive unless so reported by someone.' This statement was an exaggeration, but it captured the general feelings held by many children toward their mothers.

Since the war, this state of affairs has radically changed in a majority of cases, so that the middle-class pattern has become predominant. Thus, the prewar-generation mother was finding out what mothering is all about, only with her grandchildren. One such woman, a countess, said, 'I had no experience of rearing children until I had grandchildren. It was fun.' She was nevertheless critical of her postwar-generation, commoner daughter for being too closely attached and 'sticky' to her children. The daughter repudiated her senior critic by saying that it had been easy for her, the mother, to be so aloof because she did not have to raise her children with her own hands. This class-bound distance was not limited to older generations, however. A thirty-four-year-old mother, who was determined to be different from her mother, found herself unable to 'hug' her child as she wished to. 'After all, you cannot deny your blood,' she said. A disproportionate number of post-war mothers in their thirties and forties confessed that they felt cool toward their children and indifferent in their high or low performances at school, unlike a typical middle-class 'education-mama.' It looks as if even these mothers who do raise their children, to some extent, are recreating the mother-child distance characteristic of the previous generation.

In prewar times, the mother's role was not as differentiated from the father's as anion, commoners, and [tie mother embodied the family status as much is her husband did. Together with her husband, she was busy hosting VlPs or accepting invitations from them, and as such she was a status-symbolic lady more than a child-nurturing mother. She was supposed to be or look aloof from domestic chores and bodily child care, to stay elegant and clean – in other words, to be a cultural, not a natural, mother.

THE RESIDENT *OTSUKI* MAID

Natural motherhood was relegated primarily to surrogate mothers, maids in residence who were there to perform the maternal role for the children. Questions asked about mothers often prompted mentions of maidservants as surrogate mothers: 'But we had maids to look after us.' Surrogacy began upon birth. Some families hired wet nurses for various reasons – because the mother had no lactation: because the mother's milk was artificially stopped; because the mother was supposed to stay free, young, and beautiful; and so on. Even when the mother breast-fed her baby, which did in fact occur in quite a few cases, it was done more or less as a matter of necessity, with the rest of the care-taking left to a servant. There were various kinds of mother surrogates, but it was a personal maid, called *otsuki*, assigned to a child, usually on a one-to-one basis around the clock, who played the most decisive, indispensable, and responsible role in rearing, looking after, and socializing the child.

The result was predictable. Mother-child bonding was transferred to ties between an *otsuki* and her charge in terms of intimacy and interdependence. My informants' fondest memories were often of the *otsuki* hired either after or simultaneously with a wet nurse. Said a royal princess' daughter: 'I cannot remember myself ever left alone. Ume was always with me. She was there waiting when I woke up, she was there when I went to sleep.' In some households, each child had a meal alone in his or her room, waited upon by his or her *otsuki*. It was the *otsuki*'s job to bathe the child. Although she herself was fully dressed, and so the practice of co-bathing enjoyed by children of other classes was ruled out, in some cases the *otsuki* slept by the child's bed. A Tokugawa woman, a daughter of a prince, revealed an astonishing intimacy:

> I have never sat on mother's lap. [But] I had an *otsuki* who, luckily, stayed with me from my birth until my marriage. She was a truly devoted servant. I played with her nipples and pretended to nurse, only pretended because she was not a wet nurse. I feel her daughter and I are real sisters. Now it is her grandchildren's generation, and as if we were kin, we keep in touch … Yes, she slept at the edge of my bed. [Every morning] it took her an hour to fix her hair [in a Japanese style] which I could not stand because that kept me away from her. We were together wherever we went.

This maid kept a 'developmental diary' for her little mistress, recording her weight, vocabulary, and the like. In the living room of her present tiny apartment, the prince's daughter had a picture of her late surrogate mother on display. As indicated in the above quotation, such bonding was a product of a long duration of *otsuki* service for the same child. In most cases the maid quit to marry, but in some she remained single and offered her entire life, accompanying her mistress when the latter married out. In other words, she outdid an ordinary middle-class mother in dedicating her life to her surrogate child. Dedication was so complete that an *otsuki* was described by Nashimoto Itsuko, a Nabeshima daughter married to a royal prince, 'as if she were born just for my sake.'[22]

The warmth and indulgence of the *otsuki* was recalled typically in contrast to the aloofness or formality of the real mother, attachment to one in contrast to indifference to the other, the leniency of one in contrast to the authority of the other:

> We were most scared of mother, but never cried for her when she went out. It was when the servants went home on holidays that we cried and screamed.
>
> If I were to choose [between mother and *otsuki*] I would have sided with my *otsuki*.
>
> When my mother died I did not cry, but when my *otsuki* passed away I did.
>
> In my house I was free to go and see my mother whenever I wanted, and my mother also could come into my room. But the *otsuki* was closer to me. I could sit on the laps of my mother or grandmother, but only in stranger-like etiquette [*tanin-gyōgi*]. Toward them we had to behave deferentially. With the *otsuki*, I was free to say whatever I wanted, free to fight. Parents were absolute.

This type of contrast, granted that it could be an overstatement, is significant. The son and heir of a marquis, while his parents were always accessible, had an old maid from his birth on who defended him when his father scolded him, talking back to his father and her master for being unreasonable. This sounds like a scene from an ordinary family where the mother protects a child from a harsh father. Another male informant, a baron, recalled how unruly and rebellious he was as a child and how he retaliated against parental punishments with mischief. It turned out that his disobedience was expressed against the maids, not his father, the very source of authority and discipline. Here we can see a displacement of aggression from the real target, the father, to a weaker object, the mother as embodied by the *otsuki*.

We know that the middle-class mother-child bond can intensify to an unhealthy exclusivity and generate pathological conflict for the mother or child or both. A similar excessive bonding between the child and the *otsuki* did develop in a few cases. Some *otsuki*, as recalled by their former 'surrogate children,' came to identify themselves with the children so much that they lost their own identities. One result was a sort of sibling rivalry, not among the children themselves, but created and taken over by the maids as the *otsuki* competed with each other in favor of their respective children. An eighty-eight-year-old woman, a daughter of a count, recalled *otsuki*, each in support of her favorite child, fighting over which child should or should not receive an apple or 'some such silly thing.' The heir's *otsuki* was arrogant and aggressive, as if it were her privilege, which the others resented and challenged her. In one instance, two maids did not speak to each other for nearly an entire year.

The children were not always onlookers, amused, embarrassed, or even disgusted, but could become involved, despite themselves, in sibling rivalry taken over by the *otsuki*. In one case a child was abused by the jealous mother surrogate in charge of the victim's sister. The informant, the youngest of three daughters but stronger than her immediately elder sister, always won over the latter in games, school athletic contests, school reports, and whatnot. She was also her grandmother's favorite. All this success upset the sister's *otsuki*, who felt compelled to punish the younger sister with verbal and physical abuse. Asked if her own *otsuki* did not protect her from the assailant, the informant said that the jealous maid was so mean to her *otsuki* as well that no one would stay with her long enough to be protective. This fact was used by the jealous and punitive *otsuki* as proof of the victim's allegedly perverted character. The eldest sister, co-interviewed, turned out to be a victim of her own *otsuki*, who was a former schoolteacher and acted like a contemporary education-mama. 'I was constantly pressed to study, study, study every day. When I got a poor score in a Chinese-character test or something, she was mortified and vented her anger by scratching me. At times I bled. I did not know why I was abused so.' It never occurred to either sister to report to their parents what was going on. The parent-child distance in space and status did contribute to this information blockage, but the victims also feared inevitable retaliation by the maids. One of the sisters explained this deplorable situation as a 'hysterical' outburst of an unmarried woman trapped in a small isolated world.

In short, *otsuki* provided their charges with personal warmth, nurturance, indulgence, and feelings of kinship, sometimes to the point of pathological identification, and thus made up for the relative distance and aloofness within the family, whether between parent and child or between siblings. It is ironic that here was a deeper intimacy between an aristocratic child and commoner maid than between family members sharing the same family-status.

It is not that the mother played no part in child rearing. When she did get involved in mothering, however, it was more through verbal communication, ritual contact such as daily greeting, or indirect instruction via the servants. She participated more in disciplining her children than in looking after their physical and emotional needs. In other words, she could remain unsoiled, unlike the maid who fed, diapered, and bathed the child. Both categories of women engaged in transforming the child from a natural to a cultural being, but at different levels of a nature-to-culture continuum. The mother's role was more cultural, the surrogate's more natural. To apply Ortner's scheme, the aristocratic mother was to her surrogate (servant) what father is to mother and what male is to female.[23]

The Japanese aristocracy thus resembles the British counterpart in child-rearing patterns as described by Gathorne-Hardy (1972), and I can go along with Boon's (1974) claim that displacement of mothers by nannies amounts to a denaturalization of motherhood. But not without reservations. After all, it was the mother who gave birth to the child, and this distinctly natural connection was never forgotton by either party. If nature is identified with reproduction, the nature-culture split as discussed in this section must be reversed. It was the lady-mother who was a natural reproducer, and the nurturer-mother who was a cultural agent to socialize the child. My informants were always aware of the existence of their 'real' mothers, even if the latter were not as accessible as their *otsuki*, and even if the children were critical of their mothers for not being mother-like. This point, however, is further complicated by the second type of nature-culture split, to be discussed in the next section.

FOSTER MOTHERS

Before going into the next section, I should add another category of nurturer-mothers, that is, foster mothers. A surprising number of aristocratic children went through fosterage by commoners. Fosterage was something 'natural,' I was told, and even automatic for every birth, from the royal family down the line.

Though this remark is not literally true, it reveals the prevalence of this practice. It is common knowledge that the late Shōwa emperor and his brother, Chichibu, were raised by foster parents, the Kawamuras. The Meiji emperor's daughters were also fostered by other families. The last shogun, Tokugawa Yoshinobu, had his many children reared separately in foster homes.

Rationales given by my informants for this practice were variable and often contradictory, so much so that one wonders if the word 'fosterage' (*satokko*, *satogo*) was not a convenient umbrella term for a range of different purposes and practices. The child's health was of major concern. It is said that the strikingly high mortality rate of royal children in the history of the imperial household motivated the Meiji emperor to send his surviving children, and later his grandsons, to foster homes so that they would grow up strong and healthy away from the palace. This high mortality rate is partly attributed to the unhealthy and dangerous conditions of palace life: cutthroat jealousy among royal nannies and ladies-in-waiting; the wet nurse's lead-heavy cosmetics to cover the chest, licked by the child: sleeping drugs given to put the child to sleep quickly; and so on.[24]

Foster families for royal children were of *kazoku* status and treated their wards respectfully, even though the emperor told the foster parents to deal with his children exactly as they did their own. Foster families for *kazoku* children, however, were commoners and even poor peasants who, in informants' recollections, did not necessarily treat the children with respect. Here, too, the child's health was an important consideration, as indicated by the fact that foster families were selected based on the presence of healthy women who had just given birth and so afforded lots of natural milk.' Thus the foster mother also performed the role of wet nurse. Nevertheless, narratives revealed more than reasons of health for placing a *kazoku* child in fosterage.

One future baron, born the youngest of sixteen children 'from one single womb,' was immediately taken away to a peasant family to be nursed by a new mother. But he stayed on with the foster family for some reason. Was it because his parents wanted to bring him up strong so that he, a non-heir, could live in the wilderness of the world outside? 'That reasoning would be only a face-saving excuse,' he exclaimed to deny my guess. He claimed, instead, that he had been unwanted and 'abandoned.' His foster parents used to tell him that his parents, having so many children, never bothered to come see him and only dispatched a steward to deliver a small amount of fosterage fee (*satobuchi*) once a year. 'So they said, "This child is not wanted at all. But we farmers need as many boys as possible" [as farm hands], and they were about to take me as a *sato-nagare* [an unretrieved foster child, much like *shichi-nagare*, a forfeited pawn].' Unexpectedly, though, he was retrieved by an adoptive family, his own uncle and aunt, when he was three years old. When the adoptive mother came by rickshaw to meet him, he was wearing straw sandals and sucking bamboo-shoot skin; she could not distinguish him from the farmer's children. Overnight, he became a junior lord of a baron house commanding six servants.

This incredible story did not stand alone. There are indications that the recycling of *sato-nagare* children into the commoner class was, historically, not an unlikely fate for upper-class non-heir children, since keeping non-heirs would not only dissipate the family resources but might also cause family conflict. All the parents could hope for such children would be to marry or adopt them out. A descendant of a count of *kuge* origin read in an ancestor's diary that all the children, both sons and daughters, except the heir, had been sent away into fosterage at birth for reasons unknown. She suspected that the family had been too poor to feed excess children and that fosterage had been a recourse for 'mouth reduction' (*kuchi-berashi*). Here one finds what amounts to class reversal between feeder and the fed: working-class foster parents wanted the children as laborers while noble parents could not afford keeping the surplus children.

There was another reason to send the children to foster homes. As will be discussed in the next section, many children were born of concubines or even sub-concubine women such as geisha and housemaids. Fosterage was an established way of disposing of such children, either as a temporary measure, to allow the family to determine their parentage, or for abandonment, that is, *sato-nagare*. Foster homes thus served as halfway stations or permanent receptors of upper-class children whose status was uncertain or doomed to infamy.

Although a few informants recalled their foster-home experiences with bitterness, most held warm feelings toward their foster parents, especially mothers in whom they found 'real mothers.' Yanagiwara, a daughter of a former court noble (*kuge*), writes in her fictionalized autobiography how deeply attached she was to her foster parents; when her natal family tried to retrieve her she stubbornly resisted for a long time. Even after she was forcibly removed back to her natal home she tried to persuade her foster mother, who had accompanied her to ease the painful separation, to take her back 'home.' Years later, when she was to be coerced into an arranged marriage with an industrial tycoon, it was her foster home that she looked to as the last sanctuary for escape. Attachment was mutual. Her foster parents, too, were saddened at the separation. Yanagiwara thus gives another side of the *sato-nagare* story: foster parents, having developed an irreversible bond, found it difficult to let the child go. In short, foster mothers in many cases, like *otsuki*, were more closely tied to the children than their own mothers were.[25]

Another autobiography tells a similar story: Okura Yuji, a son of a financial giant, Baron Okura Kihachirō, was put into fosterage when he was about five years old – unlike Yanagiwara and the above-mentioned baron-to-be, who were sent away right upon birth. Contrary to everyone's expectations, he soon considered himself one of the 'natural' children of the foster parents, addressing them as 'Papa' and 'Mama' and reluctant to comply with his natal mother's occasional demand that he come and visit her.[26]

GENEALOGICAL MOTHERS AND UTERINE MOTHERS

The foregoing has assumed that the lady-mother was the biological genetrix. Indeed, most of my informants claimed to have been born of such mothers, and I have no reason to doubt them, except a few who were evasive about the status of their reproductive mothers. In addition, many mothers nursed their infants rather than hiring wet nurses, supporting the proposition that they were indeed their biological mothers.

When talking about their grandparents, however, many of my informants did not hesitate to say that their grandmothers were not ladies of the house (*seishitsu*) but concubines (*sokushitsu*), sometimes on both paternal and maternal sides. Indeed, it was claimed that 'all' aristocrats had concubinal ancestors. That this statement was no overstatement is demonstrated by Yanagiwara. Both of her parents, and almost all other kinsmen and kinswomen as well, turned out to be born of concubines. To her great dismay, the author, too, found that she had been born of a geisha-concubine, not of the wife of her father, whom she had long believed to be her reproductive mother. Okura, mentioned above, was also a concubine's son, it is a reasonable inference, therefore, to connect the prevalence of concubinage with that of fosterage.

Until the modern age, Japan had had a long history of concubinage or quasi-polygyny,[27] institutionalized particularly among the ruling class, as consummated by the imperial 'hinder palace' (*kōkyū*) and the shogunal grand interior (*ōoku*).[28] It was not until the 1870s that the concubinal institution began to be publicly challenged by opinion leaders as something repugnant. Along with prostitution, it became one of main targets for the earliest women's rights movement led by the Reform Society, which was founded in 1886 by women inspired by the Christian temperance movement in the United States.[29] Nor did the government stand still on this issue. The new criminal law proclaimed in 1882 terminated the legal recognition of concubines (though it did not prohibit concubinage outright), and since the late 1920s court rulings have moved toward binding the husband, like the wife, to the duty of fidelity, backed by accountability for damage compensation.[30]

As far as the law was concerned, the rule of monogamy was thus to replace concubinage. However, because concubinage was not terminated in practice, this change resulted in transforming it into a clandestine practice and in stigmatizing concubines as hidden women (*hikagemono*) and, to a lesser degree, their children as well. As a downgraded legacy from the past, concubinage thus remained covertly condoned and even encouraged, especially for upper-class men, the hereditary elite in particular. Note that monogamy was violated by the head of the state, the Meiji emperor who, no longer furnished with a hinder palace as previous emperors had been, continued to have sexual access (polycoity?) to office-holding ladies-in-waiting, all *kuge* daughters with the title of *tenji* or, *gontenji* (acting *tenji*). Besides his empress, Meiji had five such publicly recognized bedside ladies-in-waiting,[31] who gave birth to five princes and ten princesses altogether. Only one prince, the future Taishō emperor, and four princesses survived to adulthood, the rest having died at or shortly after birth. Behind the imperial concubinage was the Imperial Household Law, which stood above the state law to sanction this practice covertly. The imperial model was also followed by other men, members of the hereditary and nonhereditary elite who could afford it; this was where my informants' grandfathers came in.[32]

The rationale for concubinage, which persisted into the modern period, derived from what I call the succession ideology. The succession ideology had been internalized by the upper, ruling class for centuries but came to prevail nationwide across classes in terms of state law (the house-registry law, and the civil code) after the Meiji Restoration (1868). Underlying the succession ideology we find a mixture of two principles: one was the principle of patrilineal succession which was shared by East Asian neighbors, and the other was that of the *ie* (corporate household) succession which was more Japanese than East Asian. These two principles overlapped and reinforced one another to an extent, but also were mutually contradictory.

The patrilineal principle refers to the genealogical representation of continuity from a man to his son to his grandson. Underlying the patrilineal genealogy is the patrilineal biology that determines reproduction. It entails a sperm-centered ethnogenetics, in that the male partner was considered the sole contributor to genetic transmission and conception, the female being no more than a womb-loaner providing the soil for the male seed (*tane*) – a striking example indeed of the cultural distortion of nature. A sperm, the rationale went, depends for its fertility on the congeniality of the womb, and therefore it requires access to various wombs until its potency is proved. In a peculiar twist of this pseudogenetic approach, the child's sex was determined by the borrowed womb, which further rationalized the seed carrier's multiple mating until a male heir was born. The higher the status, the more pressure there was for the status holder to produce a male heir through multiple unions.

In this sperm-centered reproduction 'theory,' there was no essential difference between wife and other women: they were all 'borrowed wombs' (*karibara*). In fact, *hara* (belly, womb) is a trope for women in general, and the children mothered by different women, that is, half-siblings are called *hara-chigai* (of different *hara*). The idea of *karibara* from the borrower's point of view, in which the *hara* contributes to reproduction as a vessel for a sperm, not for an egg, has long survived the dissemination of scientific knowledge, as it has appeared in conversations across classes. It follows that the man, as a patrilineally loaded sperm carrier, is unique and irreplaceable, whereas there is no basic difference between two women – one womb loaner being interchangeable with another.

This patrilineal genetics justified that the children born of concubines (*sokushitsu*) ought to be no different from those of legitimate wives (*seishitsu*): they were equal in sharing the fathers 'blood.' Some of my informants strongly insisted on 'perfect' equality between half-siblings.

This, of course, was untrue, nor were concubines equal to legitimate wives. Women were symbolized by *hara*, as stated above, but there was difference between the *honbara* (the main womb) and *wakibara* (side womb). Such discrimination was inherent in the institution of marriage except where perfect polygyny was practiced.[33] The status difference between the two women was sharpened by the second principle of the succession ideology, that is, the *ie* principle. While there is a tendency in academic as well as popular discourse to equate the *ie* with the patrilineal principle, I argue the two are distinct in that the *ie* is a unified organizational entity, identified as a household which transcends lineality, whether patri or matri. Members of an *ie*, whether adult or child, male or female, together share its identity, its honor, its tangible and intangible assets. Until the end of the war, the *ie* was the basic unit of society where the individual was no more than a fraction and would become a whole person only by being united with the *ie*. The pre-war *ie*, as a legal entity, thus preponderated over its individual members.

The *ie* principle complemented the patrilineal principle when the latter was found impossible to follow. To put it another way, the *ie* principle justified a deviation from the patrilineal principle. In the absence of a son to succeed the *ie*, a daughter had an adopted husband (*mukoyōshi*, or just *yōshi*) who would become successor. Here, what was borrowed was not a female *hara*, but a male seed, the very origin of reproduction. The childless household would adopt a boy or girl and upon his/her maturation would invite a spouse to the adoptee. In this case, both the seed and womb were borrowed. The so-called *fūfu-yōshi*, adoption of a married couple, was to process this double borrowing all at once. These instances demonstrate the flexibility of the *ie* principle in recruiting successors and thus doing away with the rigid rule of patrilineality.

How did this double principle affect motherhood in the elite class? Status distinction between the *seishitsu* and *sokushitsu* always existed but it was more elusive in the pre-Meiji period when the patrilineal principle was more firmly established. A concubine, once she became a formally sanctioned *oharasan* (uterine lady), above all if she emerged as the birth mother (*seibo*) of an heir, was greatly elevated to a prestigious position, often becoming more powerful than the childless *seishitsu*. In some cases, informants' family records revealed that the uterine mother of an heir had been allowed to assume the surname of her shared 'husband.'

By and large, however, the recalled experiences of my *kazoku* informants indicate that the *oharasan* and even the *seibo* of an heir were generally kept in a servile status, if not totally hidden. This suggests a Meiji transformation. These women's children, though, were supposedly integrated into the father's household without a stigma. This change was particularly dramatic for the imperial house, which had long been loose in practicing the rule of bifurcation between the wife and concubinal consorts. Articles 3 and 4 of the 1889 Imperial House Law stipulated that in the imperial succession sons mothered by the legitimate wife (*chakushi*) should precede those mothered by concubines (*shoshi*), with the latter allowed onto the throne only if there was no *chakushi*. In my observation, what in fact happened among the royalty and *kazoku* was that concubines were further downgraded and hidden, while the children, *chakushi* and *shoshi* alike, were allowed legally, if not socially, to share the father's status equally – that is, the patrilineal principle survived to this extent.

A concubine's children thus had two mothers: genealogical and uterine, or cultural and natural. Status discrepancy between the two mothers was stamped upon the children's minds by terminology. The children respectfully called their cultural mother by a polite kin term such as *otāsama* or *otatasama* (lady mother), whereas their natural mother was often addressed by her personal name, with or without the minimal honorific suffix, *san*.[34] To drop *san* is known as *yobisute*, a rude form of address. According to those informants whose grandmothers were *oharasan*, 'they were no different from other maids,' or at best situated 'in between *okami* [members of the master family or their living quarters] and *otsugi* [maids or their waiting rooms].' When these women visited their former masters' houses after being widowed to pay their respect, they were described as 'hanging around somewhere in the hallway, neither in the *okami* nor in the *otsugi*.' None of these *kazoku* informants addressed these ladies with a kin term like 'grandmother,' but used their personal names instead. 'I called my grandmother "Shige" in *yobisute*, because my mother [the addressee's daughter] did so.' Such informality was taken as a matter of course, said these granddaughters. A woman saw the old uterine mother of her royal father-in-law who occasionally visited him: 'Every one of us was seated in a chair, but this woman alone knelt on the floor and thanked us. Members of the family all referred to her by her maiden name in *yobisute*.'

The dissociation of the children's status from that of their natural mothers was justified by the same idiom that justified concubinage: 'Because,' said a count, 'the children carry the blood, but the womb is a borrowed thing.' Such dissociation of genes and blood from the womb culminated in the imperial house as the ultimate model for all Japanese. The Meiji emperor, mothered by Nakayama Yoshiko, a *kuge* daughter and lady-in-waiting, was made into a genealogical son of his imperial father Kōmei's *nyōgo*,[35] Kujō Asako, who had never been an empress but was promoted to empress dowager (*kōtaigo*) when she was widowed. The Taishō emperor was even more completely disconnected from his uterine mother, Yanagiwara Naruko, another woman of *kuge* origin, aunt of the above quoted Yanagiwara Akiko, and became the Meiji empress's son more unequivocally. Correspondingly, and reflecting the decline of the concubinal, uterine mother's status in modern Japan, Yanagiwara, known as Nii-no-tsubone (lady-in-waiting with second court rank), appeared lower and more hidden than Nakayama. (It may be noted in this connection that monogamy came to be practiced by the Taishō emperor and was firmly established by the Shōwa emperor.)

Meanwhile, the sons of these ladies-in-waiting – Meiji and Taishō – reigned as sovereigns (because there were no *chakushi*). Even non-heir children shared their father's imperial status. One informant, at age eighty-three, recalled how she used to know two of Meiji's daughters through her grandmother, who waited on them as a virtual foster mother. She heard that the Meiji empress, Shōken, the genealogical (not biological) mother of the princesses, would remove her floor cushion (as a gesture of humility) to greet them when they visited the palace to see her. Embarrassed, the princesses protested that the empress should stay on the cushion because she was their *otatasana*. The 'wise' empress supposedly replied, 'I cannot. I came from a subject family (*shinka*) but Your Highnesses are His Majesty's children by birth.' By contrast, these same imperial princesses, according to the informant, treated their uterine mother, Sono Sachiko, another lady-in-waiting, like a servant and addressed her by her *genjina*,[36] Kogiku no suke, in *yobisute*.

Even among low-ranking, upstart *kazoku*, the child was trained to discriminate its genealogical mother from its uterine mother in hierarchical terms. Although Okura lived with his uterine mother in a mansion and called her 'Mother' (*kāsan*), she in turn addressed him as 'Little Master' (*botchan*) as if she were his maid. When he was in the presence of respectable half-siblings and other kin, he had to switch from 'Mother' to 'Oyū,' her personal name, in *yobisute*.

UNFULFILLED MOTHERS AND CHILDREN

The nature-culture split of motherhood thus took a double form: status-holding lady-mother versus nurturer-mother, represented by a nursemaid or foster mother; and genealogical versus uterine, or legitimate versus illegitimate mother. The two sets partly overlapped. By combining the two, we come up with a greater variety of mother types in terms of nature-culture distribution. The following simplified table shows three types of mothering: reproductive/uterine motherhood is at the nature pole, whereas status/genealogical motherhood is located at the culture pole. Between these two is nurturing/bodily mothering which combines the biological care and socialization of the 'natural' infant into a cultural being.

Type A is a total mother, representing the middle to lower classes, who represents motherhood today more or less across classes. Type B refers to the most common upper-class type as far as my informants' generation was concerned, in which the legitimate mother gave birth but left the caregiving role to an *otsuki* or foster mother (though in not a few cases the mother took part in the role of nurturing as well, particularly nursing). Type C is a surrogate mother, the *otsuki* or foster mother, who did caregiving only, to fill the missing role of type B. Types D and E refer to the concubinal mothers, the E type keeping and raising her child whereas the D type lost her child to the child's father's *ie* unless given away for fosterage. Some D- or E-type mothers, moreover, were later promoted to type B when this position was vacated by the death of its holder, Type F, as a counterpart to type E, was a purely cultural, symbolic mother who had no natural basis either in reproduction or in nurturing.

Variability of Mothering between Nature and Culture

	A	B	C	D	E	F
Reproductive/uterine mother	X	X		X	X	
Nurturing/body caretaker	X		X		X	
Status/genealogical mother	X	X				X

A = Ordinary middle-class total mother
B = General upper-class mother
C = Nursemaid, foster mother, wet nurse
D = Concubine removed from her child
E = Concubine raising her child
F = Purely symbolic, genealogical mother

Upper-class mothers tended to be divided between nature and culture, or between different points on a nature-culture continuum. In the meantime, the children were tossed from one mother to another, often with the pain of separation at each move, unless they were already molded into compliant role robots. Yanagiwara Akiko had four mothers: the uterine mother and geisha (type D) whom Akiko did not know until much later in her life; the legal mother (type F) whom she mistakenly took to be her reproductive mother; her caregiver-foster mother cum wet nurse (type C), to whom she became bonded as a 'real' mother; and an *otsuki* (also type C), who took over maternal care after she was forced back from her foster parents to her father's home, where she belonged genealogically. Later, she was adopted as a daughter by a branch of her natal house, which then added another (adoptive) mother (type F) to the above list. If several women joined around a single child serially or simultaneously through their fractionated roles or capacities, the child was split between double, triple mothers.

I learned that the aristocratic childhood was recalled with relative discontent because the mother had not been what a mother should be; consequently, daughters were determined to be different, to raise their children by themselves, that is, to do everything by themselves like type A. Just as the children were unhappy, so were fractionated women. Those women who were purely cultural mothers (type F) – whom my informants described as 'ornaments' (*okazari*) – must have been particularly frustrated. Their unfulfilled lives were discussed with pity by the grandchildren of concubines. Their frustrations in some cases resulted in physical or mental illness and premature death; in other cases they found release in circuitous forms of aggression. A daimyo-viscount's daughter witnessed her parents-in-law living practically separated while sharing the same dwelling. Her father-in-law, a royal prince and himself a concubine's son, kept a concubine of his own elsewhere (the wife in this particular case was not a type F, since she had her own children). When the prince was about to leave home to visit his concubine, the entire household from his wife down to the lowest ranking servant lined up at the main gate and bowed to see him off!

Conversely, the purely natural concubinal mother (types D and E), left without cultural sanction, was deprived of the basic human right to live openly as a public person and instead was confined to a clandestine, isolated, shameful, and servile existence. Her children shared shame and agony even when they were their father's legitimate, or even his only children. A woman confessed how she had been humiliated as a Gakushūin student by the gossip circulating among fellow students that she and her brother were mothered by a concubine. In this case, as far as the informant could remember, the children and their mother had always lived with their father and grandparents and were treated like ordinary family members. And yet she was aware of the existence of another woman living elsewhere, 'recuperating from some kind of neurosis.' In this unusual reversal of residential arrangement, which made her natural mother a type E instead of type D, the informant still had to differentiate the two mothers by nomenclature, attaching the respectful term for mother, 'Otāsama,' to the cultural mother and calling her natural mother merely 'Mama.'

The claim that there was no discrimination against the children mothered by concubines thus should be taken with a grain of salt. A grandson of a Meiji government leader, a count, told me that the huge estate was hierarchically divided into three residential parts: the top level was occupied by the informant's grandparents, the second level by his parents and their children, including the informant himself; and the bottom level by the grandfather's several concubines and their children. Despite this hierarchical order, the informant, the eldest son and heir mothered by the *seishitsu*, claimed there was no discrimination. If he were a concubine's son, he would have had another view. Even if there was no discrimination within the household, outsiders and schoolmates would gossip about the child's birth status. Mothered by a maid-turned-concubine, Okura was burdened with a strong inferiority complex, feeling surrounded by ridiculing eyes. Let us recall the Meiji emperor's daughters, whose two mothers were sharply bifurcated terminologically as a full-fledged imperial mother and a servant. Even in this circumstance, it is unlikely that the imperial daughters felt no hurt or guilt, if ashamed, at having to treat their natural mother as a servant, as if she had had nothing to do with them in birthing.

Two factors account for fractionated motherhood, natural or cultural, type D or type F. One was the rigid status culture in which the elite status precluded an embodiment of nature and culture in one person, thus requiring fractional or surrogate motherhood. The other, more important factor was status asymmetry by gender where, given the patrilineal and androcentric view of genetic transmission and of women as borrowed wombs, the man had easy access to women other than his wife, whereas for the woman, whether wife or concubine, fidelity was unquestioned. The male-centered ideology and gender hierarchy were more compelling for the elite than for commoners.

CONCLUDING REMARKS

This paper started with a feminist argument which sends a contradictory message. On the one hand it tries to deconstruct the naturalistic view of the family and motherhood, by revealing the culturally constructed features of these. On the other hand, this anti-naturalistic argument carries the hidden message, paradoxically, that the family and motherhood had better be left to natural tendencies. Here I discern a logical opposition of culture and nature in such a way that each is purified against other.

My study of Japanese motherhood in the historical elite, which was framed by the male-centered ideology and social structure, having nothing to do with feminism, has arrived at its own view of culture and nature. The nature-culture opposition is a useful concept for considering the upper-class mothers and their fractionated experiences in old Japan. I have found, however, that such fractionation gave rise to suffering and tragedy for women trapped in it. It appears that these women wished culture and nature to collapse into one. Women would have chosen to be total mothers, combining natural conditions and processes on the one hand, and cultural status and legitimacy on the other, rather than to be partial mothers, purely natural or purely cultural.

On the other hand, I share the feminist contention that total motherhood can be oppressive to women. The problem faced by women today is vastly different from that of women discussed in this paper. Today, women have a greater freedom to choose their life course, to optimize their opportunities. Middle-class women can choose, to a greater degree, to be total mothers (full-time mothers), or to be fractionated mothers by relying on professional, institutional or personally hired mother surrogates (nursery schools, daycare centers, baby-sitters). Or they can opt to stay childless, as an increasing number of Japanese women appear to be opting today not to give birth.

This latest trend is another strong reminder that the culture-nature opposition is far from sufficient for a characterization of motherhood. Nature accounts for the biological condition and emotional/spontaneous drives for motherhood, whereas culture regulates these in socially appropriate and legitimate directions and forms. Neither nature nor culture allows for individual subjectivity, volition, choice, in other words, agency. I think the culture-nature dichotomy should be expanded into a circle of triple action orientations as mutually interlinked: naturalization (spontanization), culturalization (regularization), and voluntarization (optimization). But this is a subject for another paper.

ACKNOWLEDGEMENT

This paper is an integration of two earlier articles, one appearing in English (Lebra 1993) and one in Japanese (Lebra 1995). I also acknowledge several grants which have supported the long-term research directly or indirectly related to this paper, especially the John Simon Guggenheim Foundation, the Social Science Research Council, and the Japan Foundation.

NOTES

1. Collier et al. 1982, p.25.
2. Collier and Yanagisako (eds.) 1987.
3. Gathorne-Hardy 1972.
4. Boon 1974.
5. Drummond 1978, p. 3l.
6. Moore 1988, pp. 26–28.
7. Chodorow and Contratto 1982.
8. Rich 1976; Allen 1983.
9. Stanworth 1987.
10. Gilligan 1982.
11. Ortner 1974.
12. Chodorow 1974.
13. Bando and Kunugi 1997.
14. Rossi 1985; Spiro 1979.
15. Joseishi Sōgō Kenkyūkai 1982; Kano 1989; Ehara 1990. Recently, this issue culminated in a series of heated debates, involving popular journalists and academics alike, over Agnes Chan, a singer and star, who took her infant son and babysitters with her to her studio to keep both her career and nursing motherhood intact; see Ehara 1990, pp.20–21.
16. Lebra 1984.
17. Joseishi Sōgō Kenkyūkai 1982; Wakita 1985; Bernstein 1991.
18. Lebra 1989, 1990, 1991, 1992, and 1993. A comprehensive ethnography appears in Lebra 1993.
19. Hayden 1987.
20. Norbert Elias gives a vivid picture of the historical moments of Europe when the medieval warriers transform their barbaric behavior into courtly gentility. Elias 1978, 1982.
21. A large portion of this section has appeared in a previous publication on socialization; see Lebra 1990. Here it is reinterpreted in the context of the nature-culture polarity of motherhood.
22. Nashimoto 1975, p. 62.
23. This dichotomy was repeated within the group of servants as well. In households with large retinues, high ranking, senior servants, male and female, did play the role of stern disciplinarian while relegating the more natural caretaking role to junior maids.
24. Kawahara 1983, p.12.
25. Yanagiwara 1928.

Okura 1985, pp. 36–37.

27. The Japanese case is not exactly polygyny if polygyny presupposes equality among all the women involved as defined by Murdock 1949, pp. 26–27. Status discrimination between the wife and other consorts among court nobles was recorded even in Heian literature (McCullough 1967, pp. 103–107), and the hierarchy seems to have been even more rigid among warriors. In fact, the idea of concubinage is contradictory to polygyny. Worldwide, Goody (1976) states, Eurasia was a practitioner of concubinage, whereas Africa was more genuinely polygynous. He thus distinguishes 'polycoity' (p. 42) for the former from polygyny for the latter.
28. Miller 1978; Nomura 1978; Asai 1985; Saiki 1946, pp. 450–452: Takayanagi 1965.
29. Mitsui 1963, pp. 27–29; Sievers 1983, pp. 87–113.
30. Tamura 1985, pp. 36–37.
31. Euphemistically called 'talking companion' (*otogi*); see Nashimoto 1975, p. 129.
32. This paper is concerned only with motherhood, but concubinage extended over and above the

procreative function. More common, in fact, was the practice of having a concubine as a total caretaker, nurse and maid for a man, often for an old, sick, or overworked man. Tokugawa Motoko, in her autobiography, writes about her grandfather's young concubine living with his wife and family, looking after him around the clock. The author, a granddaughter of this former daimyo of Ogaki domain and count by *kazoku* rank, comments in her autobiography that coresidential concubinage like this continued to be an accepted custom even in the Showa period; see Tokugawa 1983, pp. 103–106. Also see how Andō Terū (1927) waited upon the overworked Prime Minister Katsura Tarō as a geisha-concubine in a similar capacity.

33. See note 27.

34. Some of the *kuge* descendants attributed the use of honorific suffix, *sama,* to warrior class usage (*buke,* in contrast to *kuge,* the court nobles). For *kuge,* everyone was addressed or referred to with *san,* instead, they claimed. Even the *tennō* (emperor) was called *Tennō-san.* Insistence on this kind *sama-san* difference between *buke* and *kuge* seems to indicate the *kuge*'s pride vis-à-vis the *buke.* By today's standard, *san* is too ordinary to be respectful.

35. *Nyōgo* was one of the titles for imperial consorts that came into use during Emperor Kammu's reign (781–806). Initially, it ranked below the existing consort titles, but later rose so high as to be promotable to the status of empress, and eventually became an equivalent to 'empress.' The viscissitudes of the *nyōgo* status is one of many indications that the status of empress had long been fluid, not quite secured by the rule of bifurcation between wife and concubinal consorts. In this sense, the imperial household may have come closest to polygyny. See Fane 1936, pp. 111–158, for detail.

36. Ladies-in-waiting, generally called *tsubone* or *nyōgo,* supposedly assumed new names, probably to sever themselves from their natal families. Such names were called *genjina* because they originally, but not later on, were taken from the titles of the fifty-four volumes of *The Tale of Genji.* The *genjina* for Yanagiwara Naruko was Sawarabi no suke. The assumption of *genjina* came to be adopted by other kinds of women, especially those in the sex trade; see Nihon Fūzokushi Gakkai 1979, pp. 672–673.

REFERENCES

Allen, Jeffner. 'Motherhood: The Annihilation of Women.' In *Mothering: Essays in Feminist Theory,* ed. J. Trebilcot. Totowa, NJ: Rowman & Allanheld, 1983.

Andō Teru. *Okoi monogatari, Zoku Okoi monogatari.* Fukunaga Shoten, 1927.

Asai Torao. Nyokan tsūkai. Kodansha, 1985.

Bando Masako and Kunugi Yukiko, eds, *Seisa no kagaku* (The Science of Gender). Domesu Shuppan, 1997.

Bernstein, Gail Lee, ed. *Recreating Japanese Women,* 1600–1945. University of California Press, 1991.

Boon, James A. 'Anthropology and Nannies.' *Man* 9 (1974), pp. 137–140.

Chodorow, Nancy. 'Family Structure and Feminine Personality. In *Woman, Culture, and Society,* ed, M.Z. Rosaldo and L. Lamphere. Stanford University Press, 1974.

Chodorow, Nancy and Susan Contratto. 'The Fantasy of the Perfect Mother.' In *Rethinking the Family: Some Feminist Questions,* ed. B. Thorne and M. Yalom, New York & London: Longman.

Collier, Jane and Sylvia Yanagisako, eds. *Gender and Kinship: Essays toward a Unified Analysis.* Stanford University Press, 1987.

Collier, Jane, Michelle Z. Rosaldo, and Sylvia Yanagisako. 'Is There a Family? New Anthropological Views.' In *Rethinking the Family: Some Feminist Questions,* ed. B. Thorne and M. Yalom. New York & London: Longman, 1982.

Drummond, Lee. 'The Transatlantic Nanny: Notes on a Comparative Semiotics of the Family in English-speaking Socieites.' *American Ethnologist* 5 (1978), p. 31.

Ehara, Yumiko. 'Feminizumu no 70nendai to 80nendai' (Feminism in the 1970s and 1980s). In *Feminizumu ronsō: 70nendai kara 90nendai e* (The Feminist Debate: From the 1970s to the 1990s). Keisō Shobō, 1990.

Elias, Norbert. *The Civilizing Process, Vol. 1: The History of Manners,* and *Vol. 2: Power and Civility.* New York: Pantheon Books, 1978, 1982.

Gathorne-Hardy, Jonathan. *The Rise and Fall of the British Nanny.* London: Hodder and Stoughton, 1972.
Gilligan, Carol. *In a Different Voice: Psychological Theory and Women's Development.* Harvard University Press, 1982.
Goody, Jack. *Production and Reproduction: A Comparative Study of the Domestic Domain.* Cambridge University Press, 1976.
Hayden, Ilse. *Symbols and Privilege: The Ritual Context of British Royalty.* University of Arizona Press, 1987.
Joseishi Sōgō Kenkyūkai, eds. *Nihon joseishi* (History of Women in Japan). 5 vols. Tōkyō Daigaku Shuppankai, 1982.
Kan Masanao. *Fujin, josei, onna* (Lady, Woman, Female). Iwanami Shoten, 1989.
Kawahara Toshiaki. *Tennō Hirohito no Shōwashi* (History of the Shōwa Period, the Reign of Emperor Hirohito). Bungei Shunjū, 1993.
Lebra, Takie Sugiyama. Above the Clouds: *Status Culture of the Modern Japanese Nobility.* University of California Press, 1993.
——, 'Adoption among the Hereditary Elite of Japan: Status Preservation through Mobility.' *Ethnology* 28 (1989), pp. 185–218,
——, 'Bosei ni miru shizen to bunka no kyōkai: Kindai Nihon no kizokusō to boshi kankei' (The Boundaries of Nature and Culture as Seen in Motherhood: The Modern Japanese Elite and the Mother-Child Relationship). In *Jendō no Nihonshi,* vol. 2, ed. H. Wakita and S.B. Hanley. Tōkyō Daigaku Shuppankai, 1995.
——, 'Fractionated Motherhood: Status and Gender among the Japanese Elite.' *U.S.-Japan Women's Journal,* English Supplement 4 (1993), pp. 3–25.
——, *Japanese Women: Constraint and Fulfillment.* University of Hawaii Press, 1984.
——, 'Resurrecting the Ancestral Charisma: Aristocratic Descendants in Contemporary Japan.' *Journal of Japanese Studies* 17 (1991), pp. 59–78.
——, 'The Socialization of Aristocratic Children by Commoners: Recalled Experiences of the Hereditary Elite in Modern Japan. *Cultural Anthropology* 5 (1990), pp. 78–100.
——, 'The Spatial Layout of Hierarchy: Residential Style of the Modern Japanese Nobility. In *Japanese Social Organization,* ed. T.S. Lebra. University of Hawaii Press, 1992.
McCullough, William H. 'Japanese Marriage Institutions in the Heian Period.' *Harvard Journal of Asiatic Studies* 27 (1967), pp. 103–167.
Miller, Richard J. *Japan's First Bureaucracy: A Study of Eighth-Century Government.* Cornell University China-Japan Program, 1978.
Mitsui Reiko, ed. *Gendai fujin undōshi nenpyō* (Chronology of the Modern Women's Movement). San'ichi Shobō, 1963.
Moore, Henrietta L. *Feminism and Anthropology.* University of Minnesota Press, 1988.
Murdock, George Peter. *Social Structure.* New York: Macmillan, 1949.
Nashimoto, Itsuko. *Sandai no tennōto watakushi* (Three Emperors and I). Kodansha, 1975.
Nihon Fūzokushi Gakkai, eds. *Nihon fūzokushi jiten* (Dictionary of the History of ... in Japan). Kōbundō, 1979.
Nomura Tadao. *Kōkyū to nyokan* (The Palace and Female Officials). Kyōikusha, 1978.
Okura, Yūji. *Gyakkō kazoku: Chichi Okura Kihachirō to watakushi* (Spotlight on the Family: My Father, Okura Kihachirō, and Myself). Bungei Shunjō, 1985.
Ortner, Sherry B. 'Is Female to Male as Nature Is to Culture?' In *Woman, Culture, and Society,* ed. M.Z. Rosaldo and L. Lamphere. Stanford University Press, 1974.

Ponsonby Fane, R.AB. 'Kōhi: Imperial Consorts in Japan.' *Transactions and Proceedings of the Japan Society* 33 (1936), pp. 111–158.
Rich, Adrienne. *Of Woman Born: Motherhood as Experience and Institution.* New York: Norton, 1976.
Rossi, Alice S. 'Gender and Parenthood.' In *Gender and the Life Course,* ed. A Rossi. New York: Aldine, 1985.
Saiki Kazuma. 'Tokugawa shogun seibo narabi ni saishō-kō' (Thoughts on the Birth Mother of the Tokugawa Shogun). In *Rekishi to jinbutsu,* ed. Nihon Rekishi Gakkai, pp. 450–452.
Sievers, Sharon L. *Flowers in Salt: The Beginning of Feminist Consciousness in Modern Japan.* Stanford University Press, 1983.
Spiro, Melford E. *Gender and Culture: Kibbutz Women Revisited.* Duke University Press, 1979.
Stanworth, Michelle. 'Reproductive Technologies and the Deconstruction of Motherhood.' In *Reproductive Technologies: Gender, Motherhood and Medicine,* ed. M. Stanworth. Cambridge: Polity Press, 1987.
Takayanagi Kaneyoshi. *Edojō ōoku no seikatsu* (Life in the Grand Interior of Edo Castle). Yūzankaku, 1965.
Tamura Gorō, *Katei no saiban: Fūfu* (Family Trial: Husband and Wife), rev. ed. Nihon Hyōronsha, 1985.
Tokugawa Motoko. *Tōi uta* (Distant Song). Kodansha, 1983, pp. 103–106.
Wakita Haruko, ed. *Bosei o tou: Rekishiteki hensen* (Questioning Motherhood Historical Trends). 2 vols. Kyoto: Jinbun Shoin, 1985.
Yanagiwara Akiko. *Ibara no mi* (The Fruit of the Thorn-tree). Shinchōsha, 1928.

Bibliography

The following is a list of published books and articles by Takie Lebra, in the order of the oldest first, classified as A=Books; B=Articles; C=Book reviews. The year of publication appearing in bold type identifies those articles which are reproduced in this collection.

A. BOOKS

1974 Co-editor, *Japanese Culture and Behavior: Selected Readings.* First Edition. Honolulu: University of Hawaii Press.

1976 *Japanese Patterns of Behavior.* Honolulu: University of Hawaii Press.

1984 *Japanese Women: Constraint and Fulfillment.* Honolulu: University of Hawaii Press.

1986 Co-editor, *Japanese Culture and Behavior: Selected Readings,* Revised Edition. Honolulu: University of Hawaii Press.

1992 Editor, *Japanese Social Organization.* Honolulu: University of Hawaii Press.

1993 *Above the Clouds: Status Culture of the Modern Japanese Nobility.* (Berkeley Award from the Association of American University Presses).

2000 *Kindai nihon no jōryū kaikyū: Kazoku no esunogurafi.* Japanese Translation of *Above the Clouds,* 1993. Trans. Takeuchi, Y., Y. Kaifu, and Y. Inoue. Kyoto: Sekai Shisosha.

2004 *The Japanese Self in Cultural Logic.* Honolulu: University of Hawaii Press.

B. ARTICLES IN JOURNALS OR AS BOOK CHAPTERS.

Articles selected for the Global Oriental republication, are specially delineated in three categories: These are differentiated as 1 (Self), 2 (Gender), and 3 (Status). 1, 2, and 3, if emphasized (bold face), indicate that they have been selected for reproduction in this volume.

1969a Reciprocity and the Asymmetric Principle: An Analytical Reappraisal of the Japanese Concept of *On. Psychologia* 12: 129–138.

[1974 Reprinted in *Japanese Culture and Behavior: Selected Readings,* edited by T. S. Lebra and W. P. Lebra. Honolulu: University of Hawaii Press.]

1969–70 (1) The Logic of Salvation: The Case of a Japanese Sect in Hawaii. *International Journal of Social Psychiatry* 16: 45–53.

1970 Religious Conversion as a Breakthrough in Transculturation: A Japanese Sect in Hawaii. *Journal for the Scientific Study of Religion* 9: 181–196.

1971 (1) The Social Mechanism of Guilt and Shame: The Japanese Case. *Anthropological Quarterly* 44: 241–255.

1971 Shukyo-teki kaishin to bunka hen'yo. Japanese translation of the 1970 article. In *Kokusai shukyo nyuzu* (International News on Religion) 12, No. 4: 16–34.

1978. Reprinted in *Gendai no esupuri* (L'Esprit d'aujour d'hui) 136: 156–174.

1972a Millenarian Movements and Resocialization. *American Behavioral Scientist* 16: 195–217.

1976 Reprinted in *Social Movements and Social Change,* edited by R. H. Lauer. Carbondale: Southern Illinois University Press.

1972b (1) Religious Conversion and Elimination of the Sick Role: A Japanese Sect in Hawaii. In *Transcultural Research in Mental Health,* edited by William P. Lebra. Honolulu: University of Hawaii Press.

1977 Abridged version, reprinted In *Culture, Disease, and Healing,* edited by David Landy. New York: Macmillan Publishing Company.

1972c (1) Reciprocity-Based Moral Sanctions and Messianic Salvation. *American Anthropologist* 74: 391–407.

1972d Acculturation Dilemma: The Function of Japanese Moral Values for Americanization. *Council on Anthropology and Education Newsletters* 3, No. 1: 6–13.

1973a Compensative Justice and Moral Investment among Japanese, Chinese, and Koreans. *Journal of Nervous and Mental Disease* 157: 278–291.

1986 For a revised, and expanded version, see 1986, *Japanese Culture and Behavior: Selected Readings,* Revised edition, edited by T. S. Lebra and W. P. Lebra

1973b Shakai jinruigaku-teki ni mita nihonjin no kokoro to kodo (The Japanese mind and behavior in social anthropology perspective). *Kokoro to shakai* (Mind and society) 4: 35–46.

1974a Intergenerational Continuity and Discontinuity in Moral Values among Japanese. In *Youth, Socialization, and Mental Health,* edited by William P. Lebra. Honolulu: University of Hawaii Press.

1974 Reprinted in *Japanese Culture and Behavior: Selected Readings,* edited by T. S. Lebra and W. P. Lebra. Honolulu: University of Hawaii Press.

1974b (1) Interactional Perspective of Suffering and Curing in a Japanese Cult. *International Journal of Social Psychiatry* 20: 281–286.

1975a An Alternative Approach to Reciprocity. *American Anthropologist* 77: 550–585.

1975b Dogi kankaku no bunka-teki ruijisei, soisei (Cross-cultural similarities and differences in moral sensitivity). In *Rinsho shinrigaku no kiso* (Foundations of clinical social psychology), edited by Koichi Ogino, Hitoshi Aiba, and Hiroshi Minami. Tokyo: Seishin Shobo.

1976a (2) Sex Equality for Japanese Women. *The Japan Interpreter* 10, Nos. 3–4: 284–289.

1976b (1) Ancestral Influence on the Suffering of the Descendants in a Japanese Cult. In *Ancestors,* edited by William H. Newell. The Hague: Mouton Publishers.

1976c (1) Taking the Role of the Supernatural 'Other': Spirit Possession in a Japanese Healing Cult. In *Culture-Bound Syndromes, Ethnopsychiatry, and Alternate Therapies,* edited by William P. Lebra. Honolulu: University of Hawaii Press.

1978 (2) Japanese Women and Marital Strain. *Ethos* 6: 22–41.

1979a Togoteki josei kenkyu o mezashite (Toward an integrative study of women). *Minzokugaku Kenkyu* (Japanese Journal of Ethnology) 44:105–132.

1979b (2) The Dilemma and Strategies of Aging among Contemporary Japanese Women. *Ethnology* 18: 337–353.

1985 Abridged and edited version, reprinted in *Japan Today: Old Views, New Perspectives.* The College Women's Association of Japan.

1980 (2) Autonomy through Interdependence: The Housewives Labor Bank. *The Japan Interpreter* 13: 133–142.

1981a (2) Japanese Women in Male-dominant Careers: Cultural Barriers and Accommodations for Sex-role Transcendence. *Ethnology* 20: 291–306.

1981b The Designed Gemeinschaft: An Essay toward a Model for Understanding the Japanese Social Organization. *Proceedings from the First Nordic Symposium in Japanology,* Occasional Papers No. 3. East Asian Institute, University of Oslo, Oslo, Norway. pp. 35–45.

1982a Self-Reconstruction in Japanese Religious Psychotherapy. In *Cultural Conceptions of Mental Health and Therapy,* edited by Anthony J. Marsella and Geoffrey M. White. Dordrecht, Boston, and London: D. Reidel Publishing Company.

1982b Nippon no onna (Japanese women). In *Onna no bunka jinruigaku* (Cultural Anthropology of Women), edited by Tsuneo Ayabe. Tokyo: Kobundo.

1982c Hogai no ho to taiketsu kaihi-teki komyunikeeshon (Law behind law, and confrontation avoidance in communication). *Jurisuto* (Jurist), No. 762, March 15: 96–100. Tokyo: Yuhikaku.

1983a Shame and Guilt: A Psychocultural View of the Japanese Self. *Ethos* 11: 192–209.

1983b Three entries in *Encyclopedia of Japan:* 'Naikan,' 'Morita therapy,' and 'Bun.' Tokyo: Kodansha International.

1984a (1) Non-confrontational Strategies for Management of Interpersonal Conflicts. In *Conflict in Japan,* edited by Ellis S. Krauss, Thomas P. Rohlen, and Patricia G. Steinhoff. Honolulu: University of Hawaii Press.

1984b Josei kenkyu no ichishiten (Research on women). A revised and abridged version of the 1979a article. *Gendai no Esupuri* (L'esprit d'aujour d'hui), Special issue, Josei no jinruigaku (Anthropology of women), edited by Iwao Ushijima and Kazuko Matsuzawa. April, 23–55.

1985a Is Japan an *Ie* Society, and *Ie* Society a Civilization? (Symposium on Ie Society). *Journal of Japanese Studies* 11: 57–84.

1985b Josei o meguru shomondai: Onna no shugyo ni tsuite iken ga wakareru itsutsu no yoten (Women issues: Five sets of Contrastive views). In Hataraku onna-tachi no jidai (The era for working women), edited by Hiroko Hara and Meiko Sugiyama. Tokyo: Nippon Hoso Shuppan Kyokai (NHK Books).

1986a (2) The Confucian Gender Role and Personal Fulfillment for Japanese Women. In *The Psycho-Cultural Dynamics of the Confucian Family: Past and Present,* edited by Walter H. Slote. ICSK Forum Series No. 8. Seoul, Korea: International Cultural Society of Korea. pp.

1986b (2) Gendai kazoku ni okeru tsuma no sutoresu: Nichibei bunka hikaku no shitenkara (The wife's stress in the contemporary family: A Japan-America comparison). Keesu Kenkyu (Case studies) 207: 24–36.

1986c Co-authored. Introduction to: Japanese Culture and Behavior: Selected Readings, edited by Takie Sugiyama Lebra and William P. Lebra. Honolulu: University of Hawaii Press.

1986d Expanded version, reprinted in *Japanese Culture and Behavior: Selected Readings,*

1987 (1) The Cultural Significance of Silence in Japanese Communication. *Multilingua: Journal of Cross-Cultural and Interlanguage Communication* 6–4: 343–357.

1989 (3) Adoption among the Hereditary Elite of Japan: Status Preservation through Mobility. *Ethnology* 28: 185–218.

1990a Nippon no keizai shakai ni okeru gender to bunka – businesswomen no jigazo o baikai to shite. An abbreviated, Japanese version of the 1992a article above. NIRA Seisaku kenkyu 1990, Vol., No. 4, Gendai nihon no seiji keizai – Bunka to shakai keizai system. Pp. 38–45.

1990 (3) The Socialization of Aristocratic Children by Commoners: Recalled Experiences of the Hereditary Elite in Modern Japan. *Cultural Anthropology* 5:78–100.

1991 (3) Resurrecting Ancestral Charisma: Aristocratic Descendants in Contemporary Japan. *Journal of Japanese Studies* 17:59–78.

1992a (2) Gender and Culture Japanese Political Economy: Self-portrayals of Prominent Business Women. In *the Political Economy of Japan: Volume 3, Cultural and Social Dynamics,* edited by Shumpei Kumon and Henry Rosovsky. Stanford: Stanford University Press. pp. 364–419.

1992b Self in Japanese Culture. In *Japanese Sense of Self,* edited by Nancy Rosenberger. Cambridge: Cambridge University Press. pp. 105–120.

1992c (3) The Spatial Layout of Hierarchy: Residential Style of the Modern Japanese Nobility. In *Japanese Social Organization,* edited by Takie Sugiyama Lebra. Honolulu: University of Hawaii Press. pp. 49–78.

1996 Reprinted in *Setting Boundaries: The Anthropology of Spatial and Social Organization,* edited by Deborah Pellow. Westport, CT: Bergin and Garvey. pp. 137–160.

1992d Introduction to: Japanese Social Organization, edited by Takie Sugiyama Lebra. Honolulu: University of Hawaii Press. pp. 1–21.

1993a Culture, Self, and Communication in Japan and the United States. In *Communication in Japan and the United States,* ed. William B. Gudykunst. Albany: State University of New York Press. pp. 51–87.

1993b Fractionated Motherhood: Status and Gender among the Japanese Elite. *U.S.-Japan Women's Journal,* no. 4. 3–25.

1993c (2) Sex Equality for Japanese Women. In *Communication in Japan and the United States,* edited by W. B. Gudykunst. New York: State university of New York Press.

1994a Josei ni totte shinmitsuna kankei: nichibei no bunka-hikaku o toshite (Intimate relationships for women: A US-Japan comparison). U.S.-Japan Women's Journal 17: 3–28.

1994b Mother and Child in Japanese Socialization: A Japanese-U.S. Comparison. In *Cross-Cultural Roots of Minority Child Development,* ed. Patricia M. Greenfield and Rodney R. Cocking. Northvale, NJ: Lawrence Erlbaum Associates, Inc., Publishers. 259–274.

1994c (1) *Migawari*: The Cultural Idiom of Self-Other Exchange in Japan. In *Self as Person in Asian Theory and Practice,* ed. Roger T. Ames with Wimal Dissanayake and Thomas P. Kasulis. Albany: State University of New York Press.

1995a (3) Skipped and Postponed Adolescence of Aristocratic Women in Japan: Resurrecting the Culture/Nature Issue. Special Issue on Adolescence. Ethos 23 (1):78–101.

1995b Bosei ni miru shizen to bunka no kyokai: Kindai nihon no kizokuso to boshi kankei (Between nature and culture in motherhood: the modern Japanese aristocracy and mother-child relationship). In Gender no nihonshi (A Japanese history of gender), ed. Haruko Wakita. 2 vols. Tokyo: University of Tokyo Press. Vol.II, Pp.543–584.

1996 Nihon bunka no ronri to ningenkan (Cultural logic behind the Japanese view of personhood). In *Nihon bunka wa ishitsu ka* (Is Japanese culture peculiar?), ed. Eshun Hamaguchi. Tokyo: NHK Books. 35–39; 216–246.

1997a Self and Other in Esteemed Status: The Changing Culture of the Japanese Royalty from Showa to Heisei. *Journal of Japanese Studies* 23:257–289.

1997b Sozialstruktur und Ideologie des Blutes in Japan (Social structure and the blood ideology in Japan). *Minikomi: Informationen des Akademischen Arbeiskrei Japan,* Nr.3, September. 5–11.

1998 (2) Confucian Gender Role and Personal Fulfillment for Japanese Women, In *Confucianism and the Family,* ed. W. H. Slote and G. A. DeVos. Albany: State University of New York Press.

1999a (2) Non-Western Reactions to Western Feminism: The Case of Japanese Career Women. CAS Research Papers Series No. 16. Centre for Advance Studies, National University of Singapore. 1–35.

1999b (3) Fractionated Motherhood: Gender and the Elite Status in Japan (A combined revision of two previous articles: 1995b and 1993b). In *Gender and Japanese History: The Self and Expression/Work and Life,* ed. Wakita H, A. Bouchy, and Ueno C., Vol. 2. Osaka: Osaka University Press. 449–476.

2000 New Insight and Old Dilemma: A Cross-Cultural Comparison of Japan and the United States. Commentary on Rothbaum. Pott, Azuma, Miyake, & Weisz, 'The Development of Close Relationships in Japan and the United States: Paths of Symbiotic Harmony and Generative Tension.' Child Development 71(5):1147–1149.

C. BOOK REVIEWS

1974 George A. DeVos, *Socialization for Achievement: Essays on Cultural Psychology of the Japanese*. Berkeley and Los Angeles: University of California Press. 1973. *The Asian Student,* May 11.

1981a David Plath, *Long Engagements: Maturity in Modern Japan.* Stanford: Stanford University Press. 1980. *The Journal of Japanese Studies* 7: 442–447.

1981b Kenneth J. Gergen, Martin S. Greenberg, and Richard H. Willis, eds., *Social Exchange: Advances in Theory and Research.* New York: Plenum Press. 1980. *American Anthropologist* 83: 963–964.

1982a Winston Davis, *Dojo: Magic and Exorcism in Modern Japan.* Stanford: Stanford University Press. 1980. *American Ethnologist* 9: 618–619.

1982b Susan J. Pharr, *Political Women in Japan: The Searchg for a Place in Political Life*. Berkeley and Los Angeles: University of California Press. 1981. *Oral History Review* 1982: 176–178.

1983a Yoshiko Uchida, *Desert Exile*. Seattle: University of Washington Press. 1982. *Pacific Affairs* 56: 386–387.

1983b Ross Mouer and Yoshio Sugimoto, eds., *Japanese Society: Reappraisals and New Directions*. Social Analysis, Special issue, No. 5/6, December 1980. *Man: The Journal of Royal Anthropological Institute* 18: 422–423.

1983c Joy Hendry, *Marriage in Changing Japan*. New York: St. Martin's Press. 1981. *The Journal of Asian Studies* 42: 412–414.

1984a Esyun Hamaguchi, *Kanjin-shugi no shakai nippon* (Japan: A society of *kanjin* principle). Tokyo: Toyo Keizai Shinposha. 1982. *The Journal of Japanese Studies* 10: 462–468.

1984b Samuel Coleman, *Family Planning in Japanese Society: Traditional Birth Control in a Modern Urban Culture*. Princeton: Princeton University Press. 1983. *The Journal of Asian Studies* XLIII: 755–757.

1984c Robert J. Smith and Ella L. Wiswell, *The Women of Suye Mura*. Chicago: University of Chicago Press. 1982. *Signs: Journal of Women in Culture and Society* 9: 502–503.

1984d Michiko Y. Aoki and Margaret B. Dardess, eds., *As the Japanese See it: Past and Present*. Honolulu: University of Hawaii Press. 1981. *Ethnohistory* 31: 57–58.

1984–85 Liza Crihfield Dalby, *Geisha*. Berkeley, Los Angeles, and London: University of California Press. 1983. *Pacific Affairs* 57: 701–702.

1985a Emiko Ohnuki-Tierney, *Illness and Culture in Contemporary Japan: An Anthropological View*. Cambridge: Cambridge University Press. 1984. *The Johns Hopkins University Bulletin of the History of Medicine* 59: 439–440.

1985b David E. Apter and Nagayo Sawa, *Against the State: Politics and Social Protest in Japan*. Cambridge, MA: Harvard University Press. 1984. *Man: The Journal of the Royal Anthropological Institute* 20: 354–355.

1985c Baroness Shidzue Ishimoto, *Facing Two Ways: The Story of My Life*. Stanford: Stanford University Press. 1984. *Monumenta Nipponica* 40: 245–246.

1986–87 Rokuro Hidaka, *The Price of Affluence: Dilemmas of Contemporary Japan*. Tokyo, New York, and San Francisco: Kodansha International. 1984. *Pacific Affairs* 59 (Winter 1986–87): 696–697.

1987a Harold Steven, Hiroshi Azuma, and Kenji Hakuta, eds., *Child Development and Education in Japan*. New York: W. H. Freeman. 1986. *Science* 236 (Apr. 10):205–206.

1987b Joseisahi sogo kenkyu-kai (The Association for Comprehensive Research on Women's History), ed., Nihon joseishi. 5 volumes.

Tokyo: University of Tokyo Press. 1982. *The Journal of Japanese Studies* 13: 135–140.
1988a Sheila K. Johnson, *The Japanese through American Eyes*. Stanford: Stanford University Press. 1988. *Monumenta Nipponica* 43: 517–518.
1988b Anne E. Imamura, *Urban Japanese Housewives: At Home and in the Community*. Honolulu: University of Hawaii Press. 1987. *American Anthropologist* 90: 209–210.
1988c Takeo Doi, *The Anatomy of Self*. Tokyo: Kodansha International. 1986. *Chanoyu Quarterly: Tea and the Arts of Japan* 53: 68–70.
1990 David K. Reynolds, *Flowing Bridges, Quiet Waters: Japanese Psychotherapies, Morita and Naikan*. Albany: State University of New York Press. 1989. *Journal of Japanese Studies* 16: 477–481.
1991a Eyal Ben-Ari, Brian Moeran, and James Valentine, eds., *Unwrapping Japan: Society and Culture in Anthropological Perspective*. Honolulu: University of Hawaii Press. 1990. *American Anthropologist* 93: 1021–1022.
1991b Review Article. 'The Shamanic Portrayal of Korean Women and Society.' Laurel Kendall, *Shamans, Housewives, and Other Restless Spirits: Women in Korean Ritual Life*. Honolulu: University of Hawaii press. 1985. *Reviews in Anthropology* 16: 71–75.
1991–92 Susan Pharr, *Losing Face: Status Politics in Japan*. Berkeley, Los Angeles, and Oxford: University of California Press, 1990. *Pacific Affairs* 64: 582–53.
1992a Rubie S. Watson and Patricia Buckley Ebrey, eds., *Marriage and Inequality in Chinese Society*. Berkeley: University of California Press. 1991. *CWAS Newsletter* (Committee on women in Asian Studies). Vol. 11, No. 1, pp. 16–17.
1992b Yamakawa Kikue, *Women of the Mito Domain: Recollections of Samurai Family Life*. Trans. by Kate Wildman Nakai. Tokyo: University of Tokyo Press. 1992. *Chanoyu Quarterly*. No. 71: 73–75.
1993a Stephan S. Fugita, and David J. O'Brient. *Japanese American Ethnicity: The persistence of Community*. Seattle: University of Washington Press. 1991. *Pacific Affairs* 66 (1): 154–156.
1993b Sumiko Iwao, *The Japanese Woman: Traditional Image and Changing Reality*. New York: The Free Press, a Division of Macmillan. 1993. *Monumenta Nipponica* 48(2):281–282.
1993c Carl Goldberg, *Understanding Shame*. Northvale, NJ: Jason Aronson. 1991. *Journal of Nervous and Mental Disease* 181(6): 397–398.
1996 Eiko Ikegami, *The Taming of the Samurai: Honorific Individualism and the Making of Modern Japan*. Cambridge: Harvard University Press. 1995. *Harvard Journal of Asiatic Studies* 56(2): 535–540.
1998 Anne Imamura, ed. *Re-Imaging Japanese Women*. Berkeley:

University of California Press. 1996. *American Historical Review* 103(2): 571–572.

2000a Kenneth G. Henshall. *Dimensions of Japanese Society: Gender, Margins and Mainstream*. New York: St. Martin's Press. 1999. *The Journal of Asian Studies* 59(4): 1019–1020.

2000b Scott Schnell, *The Rousing Drum: Ritual Practice in a Japanese Community*. Honolulu: University of Hawaii Press. 1999. *American Ethnologist* 27(3): 769–771.

2000c Joy Hendry, *An Anthropologist in Japan: Glimpses of Life in the Field*. London: Routledge. 1999. *Journal of Japanese Studies* 26(2): 461–465.

2001 Long, Susan Orpett, ed., *Lives in Motion: composing Circles of Self and Community in Japan*. East Asia Program, Cornell University: Ithaca. 1999. *Monumenta Nipponica* 56: 131–134.

2001 J.S. Eades, Tom Gill, and Harumi Befu, eds., Globalization and Social Change in Contemporary Japan. 2000. *Japan Quarterly*.

Index of Names

General Index